HIGH COURT™
CASE SUMMARIES

Editor in Chief **Dana L. Blatt, J.D., Esq.**

Managing Editor **Marie H. Stedman**

Written By **Stephanie Ostrove, J.D., Esq.**
Anne Marie Jancola, J.D., Esq.
John M. Huberty, J.D., Esq.
Daniel R. Dinger, J.D., Esq.
Annette L. Anderson, J.D., Esq.
Jennifer Peters, J.D., Esq.
Alex Vinnitsky, J.D., Esq.
Glen Stohr, J.D., Esq.

Memory Graphics By **Norman Vance**

Cover Illustration and Page Design By **Terri Asher**

Keyed to Cribbet, Johnson, Findley and Smith's Casebook on Property, 8th Edition

Published By **WEST GROUP**
610 Opperman Drive
Eagan, MN
55123

A Message from Dana L. Blatt, J.D., Editor In Chief
High Court Case Summaries

As Editor in Chief of High Court Case Summaries, I am pleased to be associated with West and its tradition of providing the highest quality law student study aids such as Nutshells, Hornbooks, the Black Letter Series, and Sum and Substance products. I am also pleased that West, as the new publisher of High Court Case Summaries, will continue its tradition of providing students with the best quality student briefs available today. When you use these High Court Case Summaries, you will know that you have the advantage of using the best-written and most comprehensive student briefs available, with the most thorough analyses. Law students cannot afford to waste a minute of their time. That's why you need High Court Case Summaries. You'll find that with High Court you not only save time, but also have the competitive edge with our exclusive features such as memory graphics, "party lines," overview outlines, and case vocabulary. The following two pages will introduce you to the format of a High Court Brief.

Dana L. Blatt, J.D., Editor In Chief

FORMAT FOR A HIGH COURT BRIEF

THE HEADNOTE

Like a headline in a newspaper, the headnote provides you with a brief statement highlighting the importance of the case to the course.

"PARTY" LINE

A quick memory aid. For instantaneous recollection of the names of the parties and their relationship to each other.

MEMORY GRAPHIC

"A picture is worth a thousand words." Our professional cartoonists have created an entertaining "picture of the facts." To assist you in remembering what a particular case is about, simply glance at the picture.

INSTANT FACTS

Another great memory aid. A quick scan of a single sentence will instantly remind you of all of the facts of the case.

BLACK LETTER RULE

This section contains the single most important rule of the case (determined by reference to the chapter of the casebook where the case can be found). Read together with instant facts, you have a perfect mini brief.

CASE VOCABULARY

Every new or unusual legal, Latin or English word found in the original case is briefly defined in this section. This timesaver eliminates constant references to separate dictionaries.

PROCEDURAL BASIS

In a single sentence we summarize what happened, procedurally, to cause the case to be on appeal.

FACTS

"Just the facts ma'am..." Our facts are clearer and easier to understand than the original case. In fact, you can have a complete understanding of the original case without ever having to read it. Just read our brief.

ISSUE

Utilizing our I.R.A.C. format (Issue, Rule, Application, Conclusion), we put it all in focus by simply stating the single most important question of every case.

DECISION AND RATIONALE

We know you need to understand the rationale of every case to learn the law. In a clear, concise, and meticulous fashion we lay it all out for you. We do the work of separating what is important from what is not. Yet, we provide you with a thorough summary of every essential element of every case. Every concurrence and dissent is summarized as well.

ANALYSIS

We provide you with an extensive analysis of every single case. Here you will learn what you want to know about every case. What is the history or background of the litigation? What do authorities say about the opinion? How does it fit in with the course? How does each case compare with others in the casebook? Is it a majority or minority opinion? What is the importance of the case and why did the casebook author choose to include it as a major opinion in the casebook? What types of things will the professor be asking about the case? What will be said about the opinion in class? Will people criticize or applaud it? What would you want to say about the case if called upon in class to brief it? In other words, what are the "secret" essential things that one must know and understand about each case in order to do well in the course? We answer these and many other questions for you. Nobody else comes close to giving you the in-depth analysis that we give!

A Great All-Around Study Aid!

Henningsen v. Bloomfield Motors, Inc.

(Auto Purchaser) v. (Auto Dealer)
32 N.J. 358, 161 A.2d 69 (N.J. 1960)

M E M O R Y   G R A P H I C

Instant Facts
An automobile purchaser sued the dealer and manufacturer for breach of an implied warranty of merchantability, although the express contractual terms of the sale disclaimed all implied warranties.

Black Letter Rule
A contract of adhesion does not trump statutory implied warranties of merchantability.

Case Vocabulary

CAVEAT EMPTOR: Let the buyer beware.
CONTRACT OF ADHESION: A contract between parties of unequal bargaining position, where the buyer must "take it or leave it."
IMPLIED WARRANTY OF MERCHANTABILITY: A warranty that means that the thing sold must be reasonably fit for the general purpose for which it is manufactured and sold.

Procedural Basis: Certification to New Jersey Supreme Court of appeal of judgment awarding damages for breach of implied warranty.

Facts: Mr. Henningsen purchased a car from Bloomfield Motors Inc. (D), a retail dealer. The car had been manufactured by Chrysler Corporation (D). Mr. Henningsen gave the car to his wife for Christmas. Mrs. Henningsen (P) was badly injured a few days later when the steering gear failed and the car turned right into a wall. When he purchased the car, Mr. Henningsen signed a contract without reading the fine print. The fine print contained a "warranty" clause which disclaimed all implied warranties and which granted an express warranty for all defects within 90 days or 4000 miles, whichever came first. Mrs. Henningsen (P) sued Bloomfield (D) and Chrysler (D). The trial court dismissed her negligence counts but ruled for Mrs. Henningsen (P) based on the implied warranty of merchantability. Bloomfield (D) and Chrysler (D) appealed.

Issue: Does a contract of adhesion trump statutory implied warranties of merchantability?

Decision and Rationale: (Francis, J.) No. A contract of adhesion does not trump statutory implied warranties of merchantability. In order to ameliorate the harsh effects of the doctrine of caveat emptor, most states have imposed an implied warranty of merchantability on all sales transactions. This warranty simply means that the thing sold must be reasonably fit for the general purpose for which it is manufactured and sold. The warranty extends to all foreseeable users of the product, not merely those in privity of contract with the seller. In order to avoid the implied warranty obligations, many manufacturers, including Chrysler (D) and all other automobile manufacturers, include an express warranty provision which disclaims all statutory implied warranties. We must determine what effect to give this express warranty. Under traditional principles of freedom of contract, the law allows parties to contract away obligations. However, in the auto sales context, the fine-print disclaimer of implied warranties is a contract of adhesion. It is a standardized form contract, and the purchaser has no opportunity to bargain for different terms. He must "take it or leave it," and he cannot shop around to different dealers because all of them use the same standard contract. Because the purchaser and seller occupy grossly inequal bargaining positions, we feel that justice must trump the principle of freedom of contract. Chrysler's (D) attempted disclaimer of an implied warranty of merchantability is so inimical to the public good as to compel an adjudication of its invalidity. Affirmed.

Analysis:

This well-written opinion presents an excellent exegesis of several areas of law, ranging from products liability to various contract principles. The opinion notes several conflicting interests and principles which the court must weigh. First, the traditional principle of caveat emptor faces the modern doctrine of implied warranties of merchantability. The court has little difficulty in holding that modern commercial transactions require protection for purchasers. An implied warranty of merchantability is imposed in all auto sales transactions in order to protect the buyer. Second, the requirement of privity of contract is weighed against an implied warranty. The court notes that, in modern sales transactions, a warranty safeguards all consumers of a product, not merely those in direct contractual privity with the seller. Third, the principle of freedom of contract is weighed against this implied warranty. Freedom of contract is one of the fundamental tenets of the law. Parties should be free to contract for any provisions, and generally parties are bound by the terms of their contract. However, an important exception exists when a contract is one of adhesion. Contracts of adhesion typically involve terms in fine print, written by a powerful seller to limit liabilities or impose responsibilities upon an unsuspecting buyer. No bargaining occurs for these terms, and indeed the buyer is in no position to bargain. If the buyer attempts to change the terms of the contract, the seller simply will not complete the transaction. In order for a contract to be considered "adhesive" or "unconscionable," the buyer usually has nowhere else to go. As in the case at bar, all sellers of a particular type of goods may include similar terms in their adhesive contracts. Weighing all of these factors, a court may rule that the express contractual terms are invalid, notwithstanding the principle of freedom of contract. The arguments for and against this approach are easy to see. On one hand, a buyer should not be allowed to benefit from his failure to read the terms of a contract or to attempt to change some unwanted terms. On the other hand, social justice requires that the buyer be protected from an all-powerful seller, especially where the buyer has no other option but to accept the contract as written. All in all, public policy, and not traditional law, shapes this court's opinion.

Table of Contents

Chapter 1
What is Property? 1
Perspective 1
Outline 2
Case 4

Chapter 2
Attributes of Property 5
Perspective 5
Outline 6
Case 7

Chapter 3
Traditional Objects and
Classifications of Property 8
Perspective 8
Outline 9
Case 10

Chapter 4
Non-Traditional Objects and
Classifications of Property 11
Perspective 11
Outline 12
Case 13

Chapter 5
Role of Property in Society 15
Perspective 15
Outline 16
Cases 17

Chapter 6
Property Law: What Do Lawyers Do? 21
Perspective 21
Outline 22

Chapter 7
Finding 23
Perspective 23
Outline 24
Cases 25

Chapter 8
Creation of Bailments 35
Perspective 35
Outline 36
Case 37

Chapter 9
Bona Fide Purchase 39
Perspective 39
Outline 40
Cases 41

Chapter 10
Unauthorized Possession 45
Perspective 45
Outline 46
Cases 47

Chapter 11
Improving Another's Property
by Mistake (Accession) 53
Perspective 53
Outline 54
Cases 55

Chapter 12
Donative Transfers 60
Perspective 60
Outline 61
Cases 62

Chapter 13
Historical Development of
Estates Doctrine 68
Perspective 68
Outline 69
Cases 71

Table of Contents

Chapter 14
Freehold Estates 72
    Perspective 72
    Outline 73
    Cases 75

Chapter 15
Future Interests 92
    Perspective 92
    Outline 93
    Cases 96

Chapter 16
Concurrent Ownership 112
    Perspective 112
    Outline 113
    Cases 116

Chapter 17
Non-Freehold Estates:
   Landlord and Tenant 135
    Perspective 135
    Outline 136
    Cases 140

Chapter 18
Interests of Land of Another and in
   Natural Resources Affecting
   Another's Land 167
    Perspective 167
    Outline 168
    Cases 173

Chapter 19
Traditional Land Use Controls 218
    Perspective 218
    Outline 219
    Cases 220

Chapter 20
Administration of Land
   Use Controls 229
    Perspective 229
    Outline 230
    Cases 232

Chapter 21
Regulatory Takings 238
    Perspective 238
    Outline 239
    Cases 241

Chapter 22
Discrimination Against Groups
   of People 257
    Perspective 257
    Outline 258
    Cases 259

Chapter 23
The Real Estate Contract 269
    Perspective 269
    Outline 270
    Cases 274

Chapter 24
The Deed 323
    Perspective 323
    Outline 324
    Cases 326

Chapter 25
The Recording System 336
    Perspective 336
    Outline 337
    Cases 339

Chapter 26
The Methods of Title Assurance 351
    Perspective 351
    Outline 352
    Cases 355

Alphabetical Table of Cases

21 Merchants Row Corp. v.
Merchants Row, Inc. 166

Abo Petroleum Corporation v.
Amstutz 98
Adrian v. Rabinowitz 143
Allen v. Hyatt Regency-Nashville
Hotel 37
Anderson v. Gouldberg 47
Aquarian Foundation, Inc. v.
Sholom House, Inc. 133
Arlington Heights, Village of, v.
Metropolitan Housing
Development Corp. 259
Armory v. Delamirie 28
Armstrong v. Francis Corp. . . . 208

Bartos v. Czerwinski 295
Baseball Publishing Co. v.
Bruton 176
Beebe v. DeMarco 181
Belle Terre v. Boraas 261
Bleckley v. Langston 313
Boomer v. Atlantic Cement . . . 205
Braswell v. Braswell 102
Bridges v. Hawkesworth 29
Britton v. Town of Chester . . . 267
Brown v. Lober 358
Brown v. Southall Realty Co. . . 140
Burns v. McCormick 276
Bybee v. Hageman 332

Caccamo v. Banning 90
Capitol Federal Savings & Loan
Association v. Smith 106
Causby, United States v. 215
Centex Homes Corp. v.
Boag 129, 302
Chapin v. Freeland 49
Childs v. Warner Brothers
Southern Theatres 165
Clapp v. Tower 311
Clay v. Landreth 307
Cleburne, City of, v. Cleburne
Living Center, Inc. 265
Clevenger, v. Moore 331
Coffin v. Left Hand Ditch Co. . 211
Cohen v. Kranz 298
Cohn, In re 62

Cole v. Steinlauf 75
Commonwealth Building
Corp. v. Hirschfield 145
Cowling v. Colligan 202

Davis v. Smith 361
Doctorman v. Schroeder 285
Dolan v. City of Tigard 252
Duncan v. Vassaur 127
Durant v. Town of
Dunbarton 223
Dutcher v. Owens 131

Eads v. Brazelton 26
Earle v. Fiske 341
Eastlake, City of, v. Forest City
Enterprises, Inc. 236
Eastwood v. Shedd 345
Eddington v. Turner 312
Edwards v. Sims 10
Edwards v. Habib 159
Euclid, Village of, v. Ambler
Realty Co. 220
Evans v. Merriweather 209

Failoni v. Chicago & North
Western Railway Co. 374
Finn v. Williams 179
First National Bank of
Oregon v. Townsend 327
First English Evangelical Lutheran
Church of Glendale v. County
of Los Angeles 243
First American Title Ins. Co. v.
First Title Service Company of
the Florida Keys, Inc. 366
Foster v. Reiss 64
Foundation Development Corp.
v. Loehmann's, Inc. 157
French v. French 326

G-W-L, Inc. v. Robichaux 357
Gabel v. Drewrys Limited,
U.S.A., Inc. 347
Gallagher v. Bell 187
Gerruth Realty Co. v. Pire 287
Goddard v. Winchell 25

Granite Properties Limited
Partnership v. Manns 180
Grayson v. Holloway 328
Gruen v. Gruen 63

H & F Land, Inc. v. Panama
City-Bay County Airport and
Industrial District 379
Handler v. Horns 153
Handzel v. Bassi 300
Hannah v. Peel 31
Hardy v. Burroughs 59
Hawaii Housing Authority v.
Midkiff 227
Hickey v. Green 278
Howard v. Kunto 373

Indiana State Bar Association,
State ex rel., v. Indiana Real
Estate Association, Inc. 319
Isle Royal Mining v. Hertin 57

Jaber v. Miller 163
Jackson v. O'Connell 118
Jancik v. HUD 141
Johnson v. Wheat Ridge 87
Johnson v. McIntosh 17
Jones v. Alfred H. Mayer Co. 7
Jones v. Green 123
Joslin v. Pine River
Development Corp. 199

Kasten Construction Co. v.
Maple Ridge Construction . . . 284
King v. Wenger 281
Klamath Falls v. Bell 108
Kost v. Foster 96
Kramer v. Mobley 304

Laura v. Christian 117
Leach v. Gunnarson 360
Leeco Gas & Oil Company v.
County of Nueces 88
Lewis v. Searles 77
Lindh v. Surman 67
Lindsey v. Clark 186

Alphabetical Table of Cases

London County Council
  v. Allen 191
Loretto v. Teleprompter
  Manhattan CATV Corp. 247
Lucas v. South Carolina
  Coastal Council 248
Luette v. Bank of Italy Nat.
  Trust & Savings Ass'n 297

Madrid v. Spears 363
Mann v. Bradley 126
Marrone v. Washington
  Jockey Club 178
Martin v. City of Seattle 85
McAvoy v. Medina 32
McMillan v. Iserman 197
Mercer v. Wayman 375
Michael, In re Estate of 116
Miller, State Ex Rel., v.
  Manders 225
Mitchell v. Castellaw 173
Moore v. Regents of the
  University of California 13
Moore v. City of East
  Cleveland 263
Moore v. Phillips 79
Mortensen v. Lingo 343
Mountain States Telephone &
  Telegraph Co. v. Kelton 339
Mugaas v. Smith 342

National Audubon Society v.
  Superior Court 213
Nectow v. City of Cambridge . 222
Neponsit Property Owners'
  Ass'n v. Emigrant Industrial
  Sav. Bank 189
Niernberg v. Feld 283
Nogarr, People v. 124
Nollan v. California Coastal
  Commission 250
Noone v. Price 207

Oldfield v. Stoeco Homes, Inc. . 81
Osin v. Johnson 348
O'Connor's Estate, In re 71
O'Keeffe v. Snyder 50

Palazzolo v. Rhode Island 255

Palmer v. Flint 121
Parr v. Worley 335
Penn Central Transportation
  Co. v. City of New York 245
Pennsylvania Coal Co. v.
  Mahon 241
People v. (see opposing party)
Petersen v. Hubschman
  Construction Co., Inc. 355
Piggly Wiggly Southern, Inc. v.
  Heard 151
Porter v. Wertz 41
Prah v. Maretti 216
Pritchard v. Rebori 334

Raplee v. Piper 317
Rhue v. Cheyenne Homes . . . 201
Richard Barton Enterprises, Inc.
  v. Tsern 147
Robben v. Obering 365
Roberts v. Rhodes 83
Rose v. Chaikin 204
Russell v. Hill 48
Ryan, United States v. 368

S.S. Kresge Co. v. Winkelman
  Realty Co. 184
Sabo v. Horvath 350
Sakansky v. Wein 185
Sanborn v. McLean 193
Sanford v. Breidenbach 315
Scherer v. Hyland 66
Schley v. Couch 33
Shack, State v. 4
Shaughnessy v. Eidsmo 274
Shaver v. Clanton 110
Shay v. Penrose 309
Shelley v. Kraemer 19, 196
Sheridan Suzuki, Inc. v. Caruso
  Auto Sales 43
Short v. Texaco, Inc. 377
Simmons v. Stum 344
Sipriano v. Great Spring
  Waters of America, Inc. 212
Skendzel v. Marshall 289
Smith v. Warr 306
Snow v. Van Dam 194
South Staffordshire Water Co.
  v. Sharman 30

Sprague v. Kimball 192
Spur Industries, Inc. v. Del E.
  Webb Development Co. 206
State v. (see opposing party)
Stoller v. Doyle 104
Stone v. City of Wilton 234
Stone v. French 340
Stoner v. Zucker 177
Stratton v. Mt. Hermon Boys'
  School 210
Strong v. Whybark 346
Suttle v. Bailey 200
Sybert v. Sybert 100

Telluride, Town of, v. Lot
  Thirty-Four Venture, L.L.C. . . 149
Thornton, State Ex Rel.,
  v. Hay 182
Transamerica Title Insurance
  Co. v. Johnson 372
Tristram's Landing, Inc. v.
  Wait 321
Tulk v. Moxhay 190

Union Bond & Trust Co. v.
  Blue Creek Redwood Co. 291
United States v. (see opposing party)
United States National Bank of
  Oregon v. Homeland, Inc. . . . 161
Urbaitis v. Commonwealth
  Edison 175

Vadney, Matter of Estate of . . 120
Valatie, Village of, v. Smith . . . 232

Waldrop v. Town of Brevard . . 203
Wallach v. Riverside Bank 293
Walls v. Oxford Management . 155
Walters v. Tucker 333
Ward v. Mattuschek 279
Wetherbee v. Green 55
White v. Western Title
  Insurance Co. 369
Willard v. First Church of Christ,
  Scientist, Pacifica 174, 330
Wineberg v. Moore 349
Womack v. Stegner 329
Wronski v. Sun Oil Co. 214

Chapter 1

This introductory chapter tries to explain why the state would *want* to enforce property law, or private ownership.

The most compelling arguments for allowing property ownership, and protecting ownership rights through property law, are economic, dealing with people's monetary incentives under different rules. Economic theory and experience shows that, if people are not allowed to own property at all—that is, they have no guarantee of retaining the right to use and sell it—they will not invest in improving it, thus slowing economic growth. For example, would you build your house on property that you did not own, knowing that it could be taken away from you at any moment?

However, when property is owned collectively, people tend to take as much as possible for themselves, without maintaining it. For example, in college, if you ever shared a fridge with your suite mates, you know that everyone tries to eat as much as possible, and no one wants to spend money to re-stock the fridge, so you soon end up with an empty fridge. Similarly, if you have a common room that is not owned by anyone, no one will want to clean it. Thus, most countries have laws which protect ownership rights in property, if only because this is the only system that keeps the resources from being either neglected or depleted.

In reading this chapter (or outline), pay particularly close attention to the economic arguments behind property, since most teachers expect you to know them for the exam. Also, learn the few economic terms, like "efficiency," "external costs," and "tragedy of the commons."

Finally, your textbook emphasizes that property law is exceedingly complex. Don't worry; it's not, but if Prof. Cribbet admitted that, he'd be out of a job. True, the law is an amalgam of historical ideas about what property should be. True, the old theory of absolute ownership is being replaced by a case-by-case analysis, comparing the owner's right to privacy, peace, and security against the public's need to use or enter his property/land. However, in the end, property is mostly simple, black letter law, which you will have no problem learning.

Chapter 1

NOTE: THE PURPOSE OF THIS OUTLINE IS TO ORGANIZE THE CASES SO THAT ONE CAN QUICKLY UNDERSTAND THE RELEVANCE OF EACH CASE TO THE COURSE. NO ATTEMPT IS MADE IN THIS OVERVIEW TO ADDRESS EVERY CONCEPT THAT MUST BE STUDIED. BE SURE TO READ THE ENTIRE CASEBOOK AND/OR OTHER MATERIALS TO GAIN A FULL UNDERSTANDING OF ALL CONCEPTS.

I. Traditional Definitions: Traditional Definitions: "Property" law determines who can use resources, and how ownership rights are enforced by the government. Why should resources be owned privately? Here are some traditional theories.

  A. Blackstone

    1. Ancient English commentator Blackstone saw property law as the individual's absolute right to keep others from using a thing. *Blackstone, Commentaries on the Laws of England*.

    2. Yet property law balances individuals' interest against the community's. *Rose, Canons of Property Talk*.

  B. Efficiency Theory

    1. Ancient theorist Jeremy Bentham posits that most laws exist to protect property, to give people enforceable expectations of using goods. Without law, people are forced to always guard their possessions from others, thus lacking security and stability. *Bentham, Theory of Legislation*.

      a. However, defining property is complex, usually combining theories of contract, government, and economies. *Felix S. Cohen, Dialogue on Private Property*.

    2. Example: Many laws require that, when "property" is taken or damaged/destroyed, fair compensation be paid. Yet what constitutes compensable "property" is defined by law.

  C. "Tragedy of the Commons" refers to the proven observation that, when property is open to use by all, each person overuses it, thus depleting it.

    1. Example: In old England, "commons" were grasslands open to grazing by all. Each herder brought as many cattle as he could to graze there, since it was free, and any grass his cattle ate benefitted him alone. Soon, the commons were soon bare, since each had incentives to take as much as he could, and no one had incentives to conserve the resource.

    2. Example: Pollution presents the same incentives. Each factory has incentives to pollute rather than spend money to clean its emissions, because the cost/harm of each one's pollution is spread to others.

II. Economic Theories

  A. Economics Terminology: Economists say property law deals with "allocation of scarce resources."

  B. In economic terms, "tragedy of the commons" happens because people's "marginal utility" (benefit *to them* of adding one more cow to the common pasture) exceeds the cost to them (since the cost -- depletion -- is shared by all), which gives everyone incentives to keep adding cows.

  C. Put otherwise, problems arise when people's actions create "external costs" (which are borne by others).

  D. Generally, economists want property laws to promote *efficiency* (maximum production and minimum cost). Yet many criticize efficiency without "equity" or "justice" (fair distribution of the gains from efficiency).

  E. Solutions to "Tragedy of the Commons" Problems

    1. Privatization: "Privatizing" common property (assigning it to a single owner) reduces bad incentives, since private owners will bear all costs of their own overgrazing.

    2. Limited Use

      a. Overuse can be prevented by capping the maximum usage, then assigning the right to use the common property in limited quantities.

b. Note how important it is to decide *who* can use common property.

c. This can be done through various systems, e.g., lottery, first-come, first-served, merit, etc.

d. Such rationing usually creates more fairness and/or equality, but often causes inefficiency, since those selected to use the property are not necessarily the most skilled.

F. Law and Economics: The "law and economics" movement says law should maximize efficiency. Under it, property law must have:

1. Universality. All property should be owned by someone.

2. Exclusivity. People should usually get to keep the profits from their property, because this encourages them to invest in the property.

3. Transferability. Property should be sellable, to allow transfer to more productive users.

4. Example of Property Rights' Importance -- Broadcast Frequencies

   a. "Broadcast rights" mean the right to use a radio frequency.

   b. Frequencies are limited. They are owned by the government, but licensed to private broadcasters.

   c. They were previously NOT licensed like ordinary goods, by being sold to the highest bidder.

      (1) Instead, although scarce and valuable, they were distributed free to people who persuaded the government that they would promote the public interest.

      (2) The justification was that poor broadcasters providing socially valuable programming should not be outbid by tycoons.

   d. However, economists call the selection process inefficient, because:

      (1) The government can award frequencies to political favorites rather than the best users.

      (2) The rights are still available only to the rich, because instead of paying high licensing fees, they must pay equally high legal/lobbying fees to lobby the government.

      (3) Even tycoons end up paying more than if they bought the rights, because everyone hires lobbyists to compete for them, but only one wins, so everyone else's money is wasted.

   e. Today, frequencies are auctioned freely.

5. Example -- Future Rights. *Judge Richard Posner, Economic Analysis of Law*.

   a. The law does not always let you buy the right to use a resource later, without using it now.

   b. Example: You can buy land, then let it sit, hoping its price rises.

      (1) Yet the law often bans buying a water body, but not drawing water from it.

      (2) Economists say this is inefficient, because letting someone buy a lake and hold it would let him put it to better use later, when the time or economy is better.

      (3) They say such inefficient laws are based on irrational hostility to speculation (buying assets for resale rather than use), because society feels speculators reap windfalls for nothing, not realizing the value they add.

6. Generally, property law is rarely absolute. While some courts recognize owners' rights to do whatever they want, most weigh ownership rights against the public interest in access to the land. *State v. Shack* (N.J. 1971) [plantation owner cannot bar aid workers from visiting migrant farmworkers housed on his land].

State v. Shack

(New Jersey Prosecution) v. (Federal Human Rights Workers)
58 N.J. 297 (1971)

M E M O R Y   G R A P H I C

 ## Instant Facts

When federal human rights workers entered a private farm to help migrant workers housed there, the owner had them arrested for trespass.

 ## Black Letter Rule

State property laws cannot be applied to keep people from visiting migrant farmworkers.

Case Vocabulary

AMICUS CURIAE: ("Friend of the court.") In litigation, a non-party who files a supplementary "amicus" brief on behalf of a party, because the non-party (usually a government agency or interest group) has an interest in the case's outcome and precedent.

COMPANY TOWN: Historically, a town near a large employer, where all housing and services were privately owned by the employer. The company would force employees to live there, then charge monopolistic prices for all goods and services, and use private police to prevent unionization.

PENUMBRA: Hazy periphery. In constitutional law, refers to rights the Supreme Court decided people should have implicitly to enable their explicit constitutional rights.

SUPREMACY CLAUSE: Constitutional provision generally banning state governments from passing laws which interfere with federal laws, because the federal government is "supreme" over the states.

TRESPASS: Crime of entering private property without permission.

Procedural Basis: In (criminal, misdemeanor) prosecution for trespass, appeal from affirmed conviction.

Facts: New Jersey law forbids trespass on land whose owner objects, punishable by $50 fine ("[a]ny person who trespasses on any lands ... after being forbidden ... to trespass by the owner ... is ... disorderly ... and shall be punished by a fine [up to] $50]."). Plantation owner Tedesco housed his migrant laborers at a camp on his land. Federal public interest organization workers -- attorney Shack (D) and health inspector Tejeras (D) -- wanted to enter the camp to interview the laborers and tell them their legal rights. Tedesco refused to let Shack (D) and Tejeras (D) meet privately with the laborers. [Why?] When Shack (D) and Tejeras (D) insisted, Tedesco called a state trooper and had them charged with trespass. Shack (D) and Tejeras (D) were convicted. On appeal, they were again convicted. Shack (D) and Tejeras (D) appeal, claiming the anti-trespass statute is unconstitutional, because (i) First Amendment case law guarantees the right to pamphleteer in "company towns," and (ii) applying the state law to hinder federal employees authorized to aid laborers violates the Supremacy Clause. Interested observers -- the Federal Government and New Jersey public defender -- wrote amicus curiae briefs supporting Shack (D) and Tejeras (D), contending the anti-trespass law undermined the rights of union organizers and criminal attorneys.

Issue: Can state anti-trespass laws be applied against people visiting migrant farmworkers?

Decision and Rationale: (Weintraub) No. State property laws cannot be applied to keep people from visiting migrant farmworkers. I. The defendants' (D) constitutional claims are invalid, because unsupported by clear case law. II. However, trespass statutes should not isolate migrant farmworkers, for public policy reasons. Property rights serve human values, and should not subvert human rights of people on their property. Migrant farmworkers are socially disadvantaged, being isolated, unorganized, poor, ignorant, and voteless. Their plight justly requires federal aid to improve their living conditions and skills. If property owners could use property law to isolate farmworkers, the law would undermine the federal government's worthy mandate. Thus, it is recognized that necessity -- the public interest or private need -- may justify trespass. Applying property law requires balancing the rights of landowners and tenants. The relative importance of each one changes over time; historically, America moved from absolute ownership to greater recognition of the public interest. It is pointless to decide whether migrant farmworkers housed in on-site camps are technically "tenants." Whatever they are, they must not be isolated from visitors by property law, as long as visitors do not disrupt the landowner's business. However, landowners may still bar the general public and peddlers, and enforce security. Thus, when people enter private property to help migrant farmworkers, there is no trespass. Judgment against Shack (D) Tejeras (D) reversed.

Analysis:

This case is included to demonstrate that property rights are rarely absolute. Instead, they tend to be overshadowed by the courts' judgment of what the public interest requires. Ignore this case's constitutional points. Just be aware that the Supreme Court often allows intrusion on private property that has been historically a "public forum" (e.g., campuses, streets) to promote free speech and assembly. In each case, the court weighs the interests of the landowner (in privacy, productivity, and security) against the public interest. While a few courts still believe that owners have bought the right to do almost anything they want with their property, most courts increasingly consider the effect on the public interest.

Chapter 2

Recall that the last chapter explained *why* private property was desirable.

Chapter 2, another introductory "concepts" chapter, builds on that, by describing universal attributes of property law in all societies. This chapter contains only two main points: (i) All societies throughout history have allowed private property. (ii) More importantly, while every society allows private ownership, that right is never absolute.

All societies restricted owners' rights to use their own property (especially their land) when their intended use would harm neighbors or violate the public interest. Yesteryear's more absolute conception of property rights ("a man's home is his castle") are today increasingly subverted for the public good. This chapter includes a case which illustrates judges' increasing tolerance for government regulation of private individuals' right to use and sell their property.

After you finish this chapter's theory of property rights, you will start learning more substantive black letter law in the next chapter.

Chapter 2

NOTE: THE PURPOSE OF THIS OUTLINE IS TO ORGANIZE THE CASES SO THAT ONE CAN QUICKLY UNDERSTAND THE RELEVANCE OF EACH CASE TO THE COURSE. NO ATTEMPT IS MADE IN THIS OVERVIEW TO ADDRESS EVERY CONCEPT THAT MUST BE STUDIED. BE SURE TO READ THE ENTIRE CASEBOOK AND/OR OTHER MATERIALS TO GAIN A FULL UNDERSTANDING OF ALL CONCEPTS.

I.   Primitive Societies' Intangible Property
   A.   Some historians assume primitive societies had few property laws, because they had little property.
   B.   Yet in fact, most primitive societies recognized at least some private property, and also some shared property. *Lowie, Incorporeal Property in Primitive Society*.

II.   Historic Theories of Property Rights
   A.   Property was recognized by early Romans under the "occupation theory" (he who seizes land/ property owns it). Yet this is not necessarily fair.
   B.   Later theorists supported "natural rights theory" (the right to own property is a natural right). Unfortunately, this definition is meaningless.
   C.   Later came the "labor theory" (whoever labors to create property should own it). This theory describes goods, but is inapplicable to land or natural resources.
   D.   Then came "legal theory" (private property is whatever the law recognizes). This theory doesn't consider whether property law benefits society.
   E.   Today, most espouse "social utility theory"— that society allows private property because doings so benefits the social welfare. *Seligman, Principles of Economics*.

III.   Wealth Distribution
   A.   Roman theorists defined property as the exclusive right to use up a resource, or even misuse it.
   B.   However, exclusive property rights are not absolute; owners could never do anything they wanted. Property law always involved not just an "individual side" (right to use property), but also a "social side" (restrictions for the public good). *Ely, Property and Contract in Their Relation to the Distribution of Wealth*.

IV.   Sovereignty Versus Public Interest
   A.   Law has always balanced ownership rights against the public interest. For example:
      1.   The law does not always allow wills to convey property to whoever the dead person chooses.
      2.   Societies always restricted property rights when used for greedy, dangerous, dishonest, or unconscionable purposes.
      3.   All countries allow some confiscation without compensation. *Morris R. Cohen, Property and Sovereignty*.
      4.   In America, the government may regulate the sale of private property. *Jones v. Alfred H. Mayer Co.* (S.Ct. 1968) [Congress may ban white homeowners from refusing to sell to blacks].

V.   Property as Freedom: Some even claim that private property preserves democracy, because having property allows owners to resist the government without fearing impoverishment. *Lippmann, The Method of Freedom*.

Jones v. Alfred H. Mayer Co.

(Prospective Land Buyer) v. (Landowner)
88 S.Ct. 2186 (1968)

M E M O R Y   G R A P H I C

Instant Facts

When a white landowner refused to sell a house to a black buyer, the black buyer sued under a federal statute requiring blacks to be given property rights equal to whites.

Black Letter Rule

Congress may ban private owners from racially discriminatory sale of their property.

Case Vocabulary

COVENANT: Contract to do something related to land. Here, to not sell it to blacks.
BLACK CODES: Laws adopted in the post-Civil War South, intended to deprive newly-freed black slaves of basic rights.
PERSONAL PROPERTY: All property other than land.
REAL PROPERTY: Land; real estate.

Procedural Basis: In statutory civil rights action seeking injunction, appeal from affirmed judgment for defendant.

Facts: To combat discriminatory state laws banning blacks from owning property, Congress passed *42 U.S.C.A. § 1982* ("All citizens ... shall have the same right, in every state ....., as is enjoyed by white citizens thereof to inherit, purchase, ... sell, hold, and convey real and personal property"). After landowner Alfred H. Mayer Co. (D) refused to sell a Missouri home to black man Jones (P), Jones (P) sued Alfred H. Mayer Co. (D), seeking an injunction. Alfred H. Mayer Co. (D) defended, contending (i) § 1982 applies only to state action, not private refusals to sell, (ii) § 1982 was intended to apply only to Southern States' discriminatory "Black Codes," and (iii) § 1982 is unconstitutional, because banning discrimination exceeds Congressional authority under the Thirteenth Amendment [which bans slavery, and allows Congress to enforce this through "appropriate legislation"]. At trial, the District Court dismissed. On appeal, the Eighth Circuit affirmed. Jones (P) appeals, contending § 1982 applies to all racial discrimination in property ownership, public or private.

Issue: May Congress ban private owners from racially discriminating in the sale of their property?

Decision and Rationale: (Stewart) Yes. Congress may ban private owners from racially discriminatory sale of their property. I. This case does not implicate the *Fair Housing Title* (*Title VIII*) of the *Civil Rights Act*, a detailed law which prevents discrimination in many situations, including housing. II. Prior case law held § 1982 is violated when *the government enforces* a discriminatory private agreement. *Hurd v. Hodge* [state court cannot enforce private agreement to not sell houses to blacks]. Yet this is the first time we consider whether § 1982 bars purely private agreements, unassisted by government action. III. § 1982 facially grants all citizens "the same right" to purchase property "as is enjoyed by white citizens." This right might be subverted as effectively by private sellers as by the State; if whites agree not to sell to blacks, this violates § 1982's guarantee of equality. IV. Also, Congress clearly intended § 1982 to cover private discrimination, because § 1982 was originally part of the *Civil Rights Act*, which explicitly banned discrimination by "custom, or prejudice" as well as state action, and provides punishments for private violators. Congress's intent was to eliminate housing discrimination everywhere, not just in Southern states. V. § 1982 does not exceed Congress's Thirteenth Amendment authority to ban slavery, because banning slavery requires restricting private action [which would make blacks unable to own land, like slaves]. If Congress's aim is legitimate, it should be allowed broad power. Reversed; judgment for Jones (P).

Concurrence: (Douglas) [Omitted.]

Dissent: (Harlan) [Omitted.]

Analysis:

Again, since this is an introductory case, ignore the black letter law, instead focusing on the greater theme. Here, this case stands for the proposition that American law often subverts the individual's right to do whatever he wants with his property to the public good. Even "absolute" owners cannot use their property in some ways which undermine the law. At one time, ownership rights were more absolute, and less dependent on public policy. For example, a slave owner could kill his slave without committing murder. Back then, the feeling was that "a man's home is his castle," to do with as he pleases, more or less. Still, no society ever allowed owners absolute freedom to abuse their property. Today, modern law balances the individual's ownership rights against those of society and the public interest, with the latter often winning.

Chapter 3

Before learning the black letter law of property, you need to know how various types of property are categorized, because each category is regulated separately.

The first classification is land ("real property" a.k.a. "real estate") versus movable property ("chattels"). This distinction is vital in practice, because land is regulated much more heavily than other property, requiring extensive documentation to transfer it. This legal emphasis on land is a product of Britain's history. Britain was a feudal, agricultural country for many years, meaning that noble families were assigned specific tracts of land which became their ancestral home, and that most people's land ownership determined their wealth and status. Thus, in feudal England, determining the rights to a parcel of land was critically important. That legal tradition endures today, even though we are no longer a land-based economy; when a landowner is ousted, he can demand to be restored to his specific parcel, and cannot be forced to accept a similar tract elsewhere.

One type of property which defies such categorization is a "fixture," which is something built on the land, which can no longer be removed without damaging it, and often the land. While fixtures were movable property at one point, once installed, they are deemed to become part of the land, and belong to the owner. [Remember that before investing your own money in buying fixtures for your apartment.]

Another property type which does not fall into this ancient classification is "intangible" property, like a bond, which is usual a contractual right to payment. This is not accounted for by the ancient law because such contracts were rare in feudal England, but are vitally important today, as financial wealth eclipses the value of land.

Chapter 3

NOTE: THE PURPOSE OF THIS OUTLINE IS TO ORGANIZE THE CASES SO THAT ONE CAN QUICKLY UNDERSTAND THE RELEVANCE OF EACH CASE TO THE COURSE. NO ATTEMPT IS MADE IN THIS OVERVIEW TO ADDRESS EVERY CONCEPT THAT MUST BE STUDIED. BE SURE TO READ THE ENTIRE CASEBOOK AND/OR OTHER MATERIALS TO GAIN A FULL UNDERSTANDING OF ALL CONCEPTS.

I. Land Versus Items Versus Intangibles
   A. Almost all physical things can be owned.
      1. However, property law divides various types of property into different classifications.
      2. The most important is the division between "real property" (land) and "chattels" (movable items).
   B. Land
      1. Land ownership is regulated heavily, more than goods.
      2. Land transfers require extensive documentation, and laws provide that land passes to the next of kin.
      3. Land's regulation was based on English feudalism, when land ownership determined wealth and status, and families were attached to a specific tract of land.
   C. Chattels
      1. Historically, "chattels" (often cattle) were seen as less important, and also interchangeable.
      2. For example, if one lord stole another's cattle, the plaintiff lord would not insist on getting the same cows back; he would be equally happy with similar cattle, or cash.
   D. Intangibles
      1. Intangible property usually refers to a contractual right to payment.
      2. Examples of intangibles are bonds, entitling the bearer to dividends and repayment. These developed after feudalism, and are classified separately. *Brown on Personal Property*.

II. Fixtures Attached to Land
   A. Fixtures are items which are attached to land, which cannot be removed without damaging them.
   B. Examples of fixtures include wells built on land. They are classified separately. *Brown on Personal Property*.

III. Land Rights: Surface, Subsurface and Air
   A. Traditionally, landowners who buy the land's surface also own the "subsurface" (usually minerals) below their land and the "air rights" above it. *Edwards v. Sims* [neighbors may demand survey to determine who owns land a cave runs under].
      1. See also *United States v. 3,218.9 Acres of Land* [surface rights and air rights may be severed from surface rights].
   B. Water rights can also be owned.

Edwards v. Sims

(Cave Owner) v. (Neighboring Landowner)

2 Ky. 791, 24 S.W.2d 619 (Court of Appeals of Kentucky, 1929)

M E M O R Y   G R A P H I C

 Instant Facts

After a cave on landowner Edwards's (D) property became a tourist attraction, neighboring landowner Sims (P) sued for a survey to prove the cave ran under Sims's (P) land.

Black Letter Rule

Landowners also own the subsurface below their land and the air rights above it, but neighbors may demand a survey to determine who owns the subsurface.

Case Vocabulary

INTERLOCUTORY APPEAL: Appeal of a non-final court decision in the case. For example, an appeal challenging the court's ruling that certain evidence is inadmissible; the ruling does not end the case, but of course may influence it.

SUBSURFACE RIGHTS: Landowner's rights to any minerals found beneath his land.

Procedural Basis: Separate lawsuit seeking injunction against court-ordered survey from prior suit.

Facts: Edwards (D) owned land containing the entrance to a cave, which was a profitable tourist attraction. Adjoining landowner Lee (P) believed Edwards's (D) cave actually passed under Lee's (P) land. [Generally, landowners own anything under their land.] Lee (P) sued Edwards (D), winning a court-ordered survey to see whose land the cave lay under. Edwards (D) appealed, but his appeal was dismissed as "interlocutory" (not appealable until after final judgment). Edwards (D) then started a new lawsuit to enjoin the court order, nominally suing Judge Sims, claiming his ordering a survey was beyond his jurisdiction, and would damage Edwards's (D) privacy and possessory interests irreparably. [Privacy? Does he live in his cave?]

Issue: May a court order a survey of a cave, to see if it passes under another's land?

Decision and Rationale: (Stanley) Yes. Courts may order surveying of a cave, if there is evidence that it passes under another's land. Since case law on caves is sparse, we turn to mining law. The ancient rule is that landowners are entitled to the unfettered control of their land above, on, and beneath the surface, under the maxim "to whomsoever the soil belongs, he owns also to the sky and to the depths." Thus, whatever is in a direct line between the land's surface, down to the earth's center, and up into space, belongs to the land's surface's owner. Ordinarily, that ownership cannot be infringed. However, there are limitations on any owner's right to use his property, such as when its use harms a neighbor or burdens adjoining land. Under mining law, courts may compel surveys to reveal whether mining trespasses on adjoining land, as long as the plaintiff sues in good faith and presents evidence suggesting trespass, and the defendant has opportunity to be heard. We will apply this analogous law here. Here, these conditions were met, so the survey of Edwards's (D) land is valid. Also, a survey is the only way to determine whether the cave runs under Lee's (P) land. Judgment for Sims (D); injunction denied.

Dissent: (Logan) The traditional rule, while it is currently the law, should no longer be followed. Just because a person owns the land's surface does not mean he should have any claim on the limitless space above it into the reaches of the universe, nor the land below it, unto the Abyss. The rule should be that he who owns the surface should have ownership rights over everything that may be taken from the earth. Granting him ownership of air and subterranean land he cannot use is pointless. Here, mining law is not analogous. Here, Lee (P) has no legitimate reason to survey Edwards's (D) cave, because even if it runs under Lee's (P) land, Lee (D) cannot exploit it, since his land contains no entrance to the cave. Caves should belong absolutely to whoever owns their entrance, wherever they extend. Further, Edwards has the greater moral right to the cave, because he helped explore it and open it to tourists.

Analysis:

This case is included to illustrate the traditional rule that, when you buy land, you also acquire ownership of the airspace above it (to some degree) and all underground land below it, straight to Earth's core. Lawyers would say that, when you buy "surface rights," you also get rights to the "air" and "subsurface." Such rights can also be divided. For example, you can build a house on the surface, but sell subsurface rights to a mining company. This law especially comes up in mining disputes, when a mineral vein can run under two people's property. In this case, each owns the portion directly under his land.

Chapter 4

This chapter offers a brief introduction to a few of the new challenges occurring in property law. With the leading edge of technology constantly moving, the concepts of what the word "property" encompasses are evolving quickly. For instance, is an idea property? If not, at what point on its path to becoming something tangible does it become so? When the idea is written down? When it gives rise to a prototype? When it is copyrighted or patented?

Another newer issue is whether a patient has any property rights in tissue, cells, etc. removed during a medical procedure. When the patient attempts to assert property rights, may the situation be likened to slavery or indentured servitude? At least one court takes this position. This is but a small sample of the concepts introduced in this brief chapter.

Chapter 4

NOTE: THE PURPOSE OF THIS OUTLINE IS TO ORGANIZE THE CASES SO THAT ONE CAN QUICKLY UNDERSTAND THE RELEVANCE OF EACH CASE TO THE COURSE. NO ATTEMPT IS MADE IN THIS OVERVIEW TO ADDRESS EVERY CONCEPT THAT MUST BE STUDIED. BE SURE TO READ THE ENTIRE CASEBOOK AND/OR OTHER MATERIALS TO GAIN A FULL UNDERSTANDING OF ALL CONCEPTS.

I. Non-Traditional Property: Mental Constructs
  A. "Ideas," as such, cannot be owned; they must be manifested in some design or product in order to be protected as intellectual property.

II. Newly Developed and Developing Property Concepts
  A. Property interests have grown to encompass such diverse things as a job; income; benefits; professional licenses; contracts; and entitlements like use of public services and resources. Reich's *The New Property*.
  B. Some courts and commentators suggest legal recognition of a reliance interest, such as where a town gains a reliance interest in continued employment by a corporation which has for a long period of time provided a substantial portion of local employment.

  C. Rapidly developing medical technology has taken courts and lawmakers into new frontiers.
    1. An individual does not retain title or ownership rights in bodily fluid, tissue or organs taken from her body during medical procedures and thus cannot maintain a property tort action in conversion. *Moore v. Regents of the University of California*.
  D. Tennessee first recognized an individual's right to publicity, e.g., a celebrity's right to control the use of his image, under the common law in *Tennessee ex rel Elvis Presley International Memorial Foundation v. Crowell* (1987).

Moore v. Regents of the University of California

(Cancer Patient) v. (Hospital Operators)
51 Cal.3d 120, 271; Cal.Rptrt. 146; 793 P.2d 479 (Calif. 1990).

M E M O R Y   G R A P H I C

Instant Facts

A doctor repeatedly harvested Moore's body tissues and fluids under the guise of treatment, while using them for lucrative medical research without informing or compensating Moore.

Black Letter Rule

An individual does not retain title or ownership rights in bodily fluid, tissue or organs taken from her body during medical procedures and thus cannot maintain a tort action in conversion.

Case Vocabulary

SUI GENERIS: Unique; "of its own kind."

Procedural Basis: Appeal by Defendants to the State Supreme Court after the Appeals Court ruled that a cause of action in conversion was properly plead and could be sustained under the law.

Facts: John Moore (P) underwent a treatment regimen for hairy cell leukemia at the UCLA Medical Center (UCLA-MC) from October 1976 to September 1983. During this time he was treated by Dr. David Golde (D1), who withdrew extensive amounts of blood, bone marrow aspirate, and other [precious] bodily fluids and substances. Others involved in the suit are: the Regents of the University of California (Regents)(D2); Shirley Quan (D3), a researcher at UCLA-MC; Genetics Institute, Inc. (GI)(D4); and Sandoz Pharmaceuticals Corp. (Sandoz)(D5). All defendants knew at the time of Moore's (P) treatment that certain blood products and components were of great value for medical and scientific research. The treatment regimen proceeded as follows: On October 8, 1976, Dr. Golde (D1) recommended that Moore's (P) spleen be removed in order to slow down the progress of the disease. Based upon this recommendation, Moore (P) consented to the procedure and it was done. From November 1976 to September 1983, Moore (P) returned to the UCLA-MC several times based upon Golde's (D1) recommendations that the visits were needed for Moore's (P) health and well-being. During each of these visits, Dr. Golde (D1) withdrew samples of blood, blood serum, skin, bone marrow aspirate, and sperm. By using these tissue and fluid samples from Moore (P), Dr. Golde was able to develop a cell line for which a patent was issued with Dr. Golde (D1) and Quan (D3) as inventors and the Regents (D2) as assignee. The value of the cell line was estimated to be as high as $3.01 billion by 1990. Through various contractual agreements with GI (D4) and Sandoz (D5), Dr. Golde (D1), Quan (D3) and the Regents (D2) were able to reap great financial rewards. Upon discovering these facts, Moore (P) sued the defendants under several theories, including conversion.

Issue: Does a medical patient retain ownership rights in bodily tissue, fluids and organs such that a patient may rely on the tort theory of conversion in a suit against medical personnel for using the harvested or removed tissue, fluids and organs for pecuniary gain?

Decision and Rationale: (Panelli, J.) No. Moore (P) attempts to characterize the invasion of his rights as a conversion--a tort which protects against interference with possessory and ownership interests in personal property--because, he asserts, he continued to own his cells following their removal from his body and that he never consented to their use in potentially lucrative medical research. In addition, Moore (P) claims a proprietary interest in each of the products any of the defendants might ever create from his cells or the patented cell line. To establish a conversion, a plaintiff must show an actual interference with his ownership or right of possession. However, where a plaintiff has neither possession of or title to property alleged to have been converted, he cannot maintain an action for conversion. This Court is unaware of any reported decisions holding that a person retains sufficient interest in excised cells to support a cause of action for conversion. The laws governing such things as human tissue, fluid, etc. deal with human biological materials as objects sui generis, regulating their disposition to achieve policy goals rather than abandoning them to the general law of property. It is these specialized statutes to which courts ordinarily should and do look for guidance on the disposition of human biological materials. California statutory law drastically limits a patient's control over excised cells. Health and Safety Code section 7054.4 requires all excised human tissue, following scientific use, to be disposed of by approved methods in order to protect the public health and safety. Though it is clear the Legislature did not intend this provision to resolve the issue of whether a patient is entitled to compensation for the nonconsensual use of excised cells, a primary object of the statute is to ensure the safe handling of potentially hazardous biological waste materials. As such, one cannot escape the conclusion that the statute's practical effect is to drastically limit the patient's control over excised cells. It limits so many of the rights ordinarily attached to property that one cannot simply assume that what is left amounts to "property" or "ownership" for purposes of conversion law. Finally, the subject matter of the patent-- the patented cell line and the products derived from it--cannot be Moore's (P) property because the cell line is both factually and legally distinct from the cells taken from Moore (P). This brings us to the issue of whether the law of conversion should be extended. The threat of liability for conversion may help to enforce patients' rights indirectly in that physicians may be able to avoid liability by obtaining consent. But extending the law in this way would sacrifice the other goal of protecting innocent parties. Conversion is a strict liability tort and would thus impose liability upon all those into whose hands the cells come regardless of whether the particular defendant participated in or knew about the inadequate disclosures that violated the patient's right to make an informed decision. The fiduciary-duty and informed-consent protect the patient directly without punishing innocent parties or creating disincentives to the conduct of socially beneficial research. [The Court then describes the numerous benefits bestowed upon society by such research.] The extension of conversion law into this area will hinder research by restricting access to the necessary raw materials. We thus cannot make each cell sample the potential subject of a lawsuit. [The Court goes on to describe in some detail the potential negative impact an extension of conversion law might have.] For these reasons, we hold that the allegations of Moore's (P) third amended complaint do not state a cause of action for conversion. Reversed.

Concurrence: (Arabian, J.) The majority ignores the moral issue. Moore (P) asks us to enforce a right to sell one's own body tissue for profit; to regard the human vessel as equal with the basest commercial commodity. He urges us to commingle the sacred with the profane. He asks much.

Concurrence and Dissent: (Broussard, J.) If Moore's (P) doctor improperly interfered with his right to control the use of a body part, under traditional common law principles Moore (P) may maintain a conversion action to recover the economic value of the right to control the use of his body part. Accordingly, I dissent from the majority's rejection of the cause of action in conversion.

Dissent: (Mosk, J.) I disagree with the majority's rejection of Moore's (P) cause of action in conversion. There are two policy considerations which outweigh the majority's single policy. These two considerations recognize that every individual has a legally protectible property interest in his own body and its products. First, society acknowledges a profound ethical imperative to respect the human body as the physical and temporal expression of the unique human persona. One example of this is our prohibition against direct abuse of the body through economic exploitation like slavery and indentured servitude. Yet the specter of these institutions haunts the labs and boardrooms of today's biotechnological research-industrial complex. It arises wherever scientists claim, as defendants do here, the right to freely mine or harvest valuable physical properties of the patient's body. Research with human cells that results in significant economic gain for the researcher and no gain for the patient offends the traditional mores of our society in a manner impossible to quantify; it treats the human body as a commodity, a means to a profitable end. A second policy consideration adds notions of equity to those of ethics. We value fundamental fairness in dealings between the members of society and we condemn the unjust enrichment of any member at the expense of another, particularly when the parties are in unequal bargaining positions. No doubt there are extremely large pecuniary benefits to be gained in this new industry. However, it is from the patients that these benefits are primarily derived. Yet the defendants deny that Moore (P) is entitled to even the slightest gain from the use of his tissues and cells. This is both inequitable and immoral. It seems that this science has become a science for profit and I fail to see any justification for excluding the patient from participation in those profits.

Analysis:

Justice Arabian expresses the sentiment that Moore (P) is seeking judicial recognition of a right to sell his body tissue for profit. How valid is this point? Is it the idea of anyone gaining from the manipulation of human organs, tissue, fluid and cells that sticks in Justice Arabian's craw? If so, it seems Justice Arabian ignores the fact that the physicians, scientists and hospitals also gain from these things. So it is okay for persons who did the harvesting to profit, but the original owner cannot? This seems backward and is but one logical flaw in Justice Arabian's argument. The other stems from a misstatement of the facts. Moore (P) was not approached and asked if he would like to sell his tissue and cells; they were taken from him for the sole, albeit hidden, purpose of scientific research and, ultimately, pecuniary gain. It was not until after the fact that Moore (P), upon discovering the duplicity of Dr. Golde (D1), sought to share in the financial windfall which resulted from the use of his tissue and cells.

Chapter 5

This chapter discusses from what and how property rights in land in the United States were derived, as well as some limits on government enforcement of purported property rights. It includes—and largely is—two Supreme Court cases. The first is one of several seminal cases dealing with Native American property rights. Its underlying message is that the powerful are in control and will set rules with regard to property which are to their own benefit. Whether one agrees with this idea or not, the fact is that it helped set the stage for America's development into the nation it is today. The second case wrestles with the issue of race in the context of one's right to have and enforce restrictions on property rights and is set several years before the Civil Rights Movement of the 1960s.

Chapter 5

NOTE: THE PURPOSE OF THIS OUTLINE IS TO ORGANIZE THE CASES SO THAT ONE CAN QUICKLY UNDERSTAND THE RELEVANCE OF EACH CASE TO THE COURSE. NO ATTEMPT IS MADE IN THIS OVERVIEW TO ADDRESS EVERY CONCEPT THAT MUST BE STUDIED. BE SURE TO READ THE ENTIRE CASEBOOK AND/OR OTHER MATERIALS TO GAIN A FULL UNDERSTANDING OF ALL CONCEPTS.

I.   Origins of Title: *Johnson v. McIntosh*
   A.   Title to lands can be issued by and through the Sovereign or Government; indigenous peoples do not have legal authority to issue title notwithstanding their occupation of the lands long before their conquerors.
   B.   European discoverers of the New World gained title to discovered lands on behalf of their sovereign. This title was subject to the occupancy rights of Native Americans, who retained no rights to sell or otherwise alienate their rights except to the government.

II.   Restricting Uses of Property
   A.   Many property owners may, when they alienate the property or otherwise, attach restrictions to the title. These sometimes take the form of a restrictive covenant.
   B.   State judicial enforcement of private agreements is "state action" as that term is construed under the Fourteenth Amendment and is thus subject to all 14th Amendment-based limits on state action. *Shelley v. Kraemer*.
      1.   What *Shelley* holds is that private citizens who enter into agreements, such as a race-based restrictive covenant on property, may not rely on the courts or any other governmental entity to enforce the covenant.

Johnson v. McIntosh

(Property Claimant) v. (Actual Titleholder)
21 U.S. 543 (1823)

M E M O R Y   G R A P H I C

Instant Facts
Johnson (P) purchased title to some land from the Indians while McIntosh (R) gained title issued by and through the United States government. Johnson (P) seeks to gain legal recognition of his title.

Black Letter Rule
Title to lands can be issued by and through the Sovereign or Government; indigenous peoples do not have legal authority to issue title notwithstanding their occupation of the lands.

Case Vocabulary

EJECTMENT: An action to remove an occupier or owner from the property.
SEISIN: Possession of land.

Procedural Basis: Certification of an ejectment action to the U.S. Supreme Court after the District Court denied the claim.

Facts: Johnson (P) was granted land by two Indian Tribes, the Illinois and Piankeshaw nations, in 1773 and 1775. Johnson (P) now seeks to have these grants recognized by the courts in an ejectment action against McIntosh (R).

Issue: Is a title granted the holder by a Native American Tribe legally cognizable?

Decision and Rationale: (Marshall, Ch.J.) No. The facts show the authority of the chiefs who executed the conveyances and that particular tribes were in possession of the land at the time. The inquiry is therefore confined to the power of the Indians to give, and of private individuals to receive, a title which may be sustained in the courts of this country. The right of society to the rules by which property may be acquired and preserved cannot be drawn into question. The title to lands depends entirely on the law of the nation in which the lands lie. To trace the path to this conclusion, we must examine those principles of abstract justice which regulate the rights of civilized nations whose perfect independence is acknowledged; but those principles also which our own government has adopted in the particular case, and given us as the rule for our decision. When the nations of Europe began to conquer this New World they made ample compensation to its native inhabitants by bestowing on them civilization and Christianity in exchange for unlimited independence. In doing so it was necessary to establish a principle which all should acknowledge as the law by which the right of acquisition should be regulated. This principle was that discovery gave title to the government by whose subjects it was made, against all other European governments. The discovering nation, therefore, had the sole right to acquire the soil from the native inhabitants. With this right no European could interfere. The rights of the original inhabitants were not entirely disregarded, but were impaired to a degree. They were admitted to be the rightful occupants with a claim to retain this status. But their rights to complete sovereignty and power to dispose of the soil to whomsoever they pleased was denied by the original principle that discovery gave exclusive title to those who made it. The discoverer claimed and exercised, as a consequence of its ultimate dominion, a power to grant the soil while it was yet in the possession of the natives. These grants convey a title to the grantees, subject only to the Indian right of occupancy. As early as 1496, the English Monarch granted a commission to the Cabots who then discovered the continent of North America. To this discovery, the English trace their title. Thus has our whole country been granted by the crown, while in the occupation of the Indians. These grants purport to convey the soil as well as the right of dominion to the grantees. All nations of Europe have followed this principle. By the treaty which concluded our revolutionary war, Great Britain relinquished all claim to proprietary and territorial rights to the United States. By this treaty, the powers of government and the right to soil passed definitively to these states. It has never been doubted that the United States, or these several states, had a clear title to all the lands subject only to the Indian right of occupancy. The United States hold and assert in themselves the title by which the country was acquired. The authority flowing from the discovery includes the exclusive right to extinguish the Indian title of occupancy, either by purchase or conquest. The validity of the titles given by our government, or the crown before, has never been questioned in our courts. The existence of this power must negate the existence of any right which may conflict with and control it. An absolute title to lands cannot exist at the same time, in different persons, or in different governments. This is incompatible with an absolute and complete title in the Indians. Conquest gives a title which the courts of the conqueror cannot deny. It is not for the courts of this country to question the validity of this title, or to sustain one which is incompatible with it. Further, the conqueror prescribes the limits of the title. Humanity, however, demands that the rights of the conquered to property should remain

Johnson v. McIntosh (Continued)

unimpaired. The conquerors became such out of necessity; because the Indians were savages and it would not do for them to be assimilated into the society as a whole. European policy, numbers and skill prevailed in this struggle and by their victories gained title to the soil relinquished by the Indians. The absolute ultimate title has been considered as acquired by discovery, subject only to the Indian title of occupancy, which title the discoverers possessed the exclusive right of acquiring. Such a right is no more incompatible with a seisin in fee, than a lease for years, and might as effectually bar an ejectment. The Court is, therefore, decidedly of the opinion, that Johnson (P) does not exhibit a title which can be sustained in the courts of the United States. AFFIRMED.

Analysis:

What the Court basically holds here is that when North America was "discovered" by the Europeans, the discoverers gained title to the entirety of the discovered land, subject only to the right of Native Americans to occupy the land. The European sovereigns, or the United States, could gain actual possession of Native American-occupied land by either purchasing occupation rights from them or by conquering them and pushing them aside. In either case, the Native Americans could not and cannot transfer title to the lands they occupy to any person or entity other than the United States or the several states. In other words, proper legal title of land owned by Native Americans can be gained only through and from the government. All of these neat rules established by the Europeans and sustained by the United States are predicated upon discovery. What is obviously ignored in this, however, is the shear falsity of the idea that Europeans discovered the New World. The underlying truth of the matter, touched upon in the Courts somewhat rambling opinion, is that true power flows from the barrel of a gun. The strong shall survive and prevail [and make up their own self-serving rules].

STATE JUDICIAL ENFORCEMENT OF RACE-BASED RESTRICTIVE COVENANTS IS A VIOLATION OF THE 14TH AMENDMENT'S DUE PROCESS CLAUSE

Shelley v. Kramer

(African-American Home Buyers) v. (Party to Restrictive Covenant)
334 U.S. 1, 68 S.Ct. 836 (1948)

M E M O R Y   G R A P H I C

Instant Facts

Shelley (P) seeks to purchase a home that is subject to a restrictive covenant barring ownership or occupancy by non-Whites. They challenge state judicial enforcement of the covenant as a violation of equal protection and due process.

Black Letter Rule

State judicial enforcement of private agreements is "state action" as that term is construed under the Fourteenth Amendment and is thus subject to all 14th Amendment-based limits on state action.

Case Vocabulary

REAL PROPERTY: Land and any items attached to it.
RESTRICTIVE COVENANT: An agreement among private citizen property owners which sets forth guidelines on the use, size, layout, appearance, alienability, etc. of a parcel of real property.

Procedural Basis: Certification to the U.S. Supreme Court of two constitutionally-based challenges to judicial enforcement of a race-based restrictive covenants after the states' highest courts found the covenants enforceable.

Facts: [This opinion involves two cases appealed to the U.S. Supreme Court from the respective states' highest court.] On February 16, 1911, thirty of thirty-nine owners of property fronting both sides of Labadie Avenue in the city of Saint Louis signed an agreement which, for fifty years henceforth, restricted the owners of the district from allowing their lots to be purchased or occupied by any minorities, particularly "people of the Negro or Mongolian Race [s]." The entire district included fifty-seven parcels of land with the thirty owner-signatories holding title to forty-seven. At the time of the agreement, five of the parcels were owned by Negroes, one of which had been occupied since 1882. The trial court found that seven of the nine southside owners had failed to sign the covenant in 1911. On August 11, 1945, the Shelleys (P), who are Negroes, received from the Fitzgeralds and for valuable consideration a warranty deed to the parcel in question. On October 9, 1945, Kraemer (R) and other owners of property subject to the restrictive covenant brought suit seeking an order restraining Shelley (P) from taking possession of the property and that judgment be entered divesting Shelley (P) of title and re-vesting title in the immediate grantor. The trial court denied this relief on the ground that the covenant had never become final because it had not been signed by all owners as had been intended. The Supreme Court of Missouri reversed and held that enforcement of the provisions violated no rights guaranteed by the Constitution. Shelley (P) claims judicial enforcement of the restrictive covenant has violated rights guaranteed by the Fourteenth Amendment and Acts of Congress passed pursuant to that amendment, specifically equal protection of the laws, due process, and the privileges and immunities of citizens of the United States.

Issue: Does the Equal Protection Clause of the Fourteenth Amendment prohibit enforcement by state courts of race-based restrictive covenants?

Decision and Rationale: (Vinson, Ch.J.) Yes. This is a question with which this Court has not yet dealt. It cannot be doubted that the Fourteenth Amendment protects the rights to acquire, enjoy, own and dispose of property. Equality in the enjoyment of property rights was regarded by the Framers as an essential pre-condition to the realization of other basic civil rights and liberties which the Amendment was intended to guarantee. Thus, § 1978 of the Revised Statutes, from § 1 of the 1866 Civil Rights Act, provides: "All citizens of the United States shall have the same right, in every State and Territory, as is enjoyed by white citizens thereof to inherit, purchase, lease, sell, hold, and convey real and personal property." It is likewise clear that restrictions like the one sought to be created by the private agreements in these cases could not be squared with the requirements of the Fourteenth Amendment if imposed by state statute or local ordinance. But this is not the case here; these agreements do not involve action by the legislature or city councils, but by private citizens. Participation of the states is limited to enforcement of the restrictions. The question is whether this distinction removes these cases from the operation of the Fourteenth Amendment. The Fourteenth Amendment concerns itself with state action and, therefore, the restrictive covenants standing alone cannot be regarded as a violation of any rights guaranteed by the Amendment. But here there was more. Here, the purposes of the covenants were secured only by judicial enforcement by state courts of the restrictive terms. Kraemer (R) urges that this enforcement does not amount to state action. However, it has long been recognized that the action of state courts in their official capacities is action of the State within the meaning of the Fourteenth Amendment. This occurred in cases involving the exclusion of Negroes from jury service in criminal prosecutions, wherein we held such court-sponsored action to be as repugnant to the Fourteenth Amendment's guarantees as actions by the executive and legislative branches. This extends to the enforcement of substantive common law rules formulated by the courts even though all procedural due process requirements were enforced to the utmost. In short, from the time of adoption of the Fourteenth Amendment up to the present, actions of the states covered by the Amendment have included actions of state courts and judicial officials. It has never been suggested that state court action is immunized from the operation of those provisions simply because the act is that of the judicial branch of state government. We therefore have no doubt that there has been state action in these cases in the full and complete sense of the phrase. The facts show that Shelley (P) was a willing purchaser and the owners of the parcel were willing to sell, and that but for the intervention of the state courts, Shelley (P) would have been free to occupy the properties in question without restraint. States have made available the full coercive power of government to deny Shelley (P), on the ground of race or color, the full enjoyment of property rights. State action, as that phrase is understood for the purposes of the Fourteenth Amendment, refers to exertions of state power in all its forms, including this form. We hold that in granting judicial enforcement of the restrictive covenants in these cases, the States have denied the petitioners the equal protection of the laws and that, therefore, the action of the state courts cannot stand. Having so decided, we find it unnecessary to consider whether there has also been a deprivation of property without due process of law or denied privileges and immunities of citizens of the United States. Reversed.

Analysis:

This represents, in part, the way a court sometimes takes the easy way when dealing with a controversial subject. When one of the cases was before the trial court in Missouri, that court, rather than deal with the racial segregation/discrimination issue directly, instead chose not to enforce the covenant on the ground that its formation was procedurally defective; it lacked all signatures and was therefore void. The Missouri Supreme Court chose to not follow the trial court's easy approach, choosing instead to decide the case on its merits. Only it got the answer wrong, according to the U.S. Supreme Court. What other avenues might a court have relied upon to provide Shelley (P) the relief sought? One possible answer may have been to simply refuse to enforce the restrictive covenant on the ground that it was against public policy. This decision occurred long before the civil rights movement of the 1960s, but there were expressions of public policy upon which the court might have relied. On the other hand, at the time of the ruling, 1948, Jim Crow was alive and well in many regions of the nation. Public policy as expressed in the Jim Crow laws was most assuredly in full support of segregation. The greater significance of this case is the Court's ruling that judicial enforcement by state court's of the restrictive terms of an agreement or covenant is to be considered state action for purposes of the Fourteenth Amendment. The amendment does not reach private action by its very terms. This is why the parties to the covenant were free to exclude minorities in the first place—because they are private. This issue was left over to deal with, and was, during the 1950s and 1960s, by Congress's use of the commerce clause to ban discrimination in public accommodations.

Chapter 6

This extremely brief chapter offers a quick rundown on what property law lawyers do. Included is a short discussion of the tasks common to property law, like conducting a real estate closing or helping plan a construction project.

Also included is a short review of the practice of property law from the standpoint of the specialist vs. the general practitioner. Property law is so pervasive that unless you specialize in another area, at some point you will run into a property law problem.

The chapter closes with a short excerpt from an article titled 'Planning By Lawyers,' which reviews the historical importance of property and how lawyers have been key players in the evolution of the law of property.

Chapter 6

NOTE: THE PURPOSE OF THIS OUTLINE IS TO ORGANIZE THE CASES SO THAT ONE CAN QUICKLY UNDERSTAND THE RELEVANCE OF EACH CASE TO THE COURSE. NO ATTEMPT IS MADE IN THIS OVERVIEW TO ADDRESS EVERY CONCEPT THAT MUST BE STUDIED. BE SURE TO READ THE ENTIRE CASEBOOK AND/OR OTHER MATERIALS TO GAIN A FULL UNDERSTANDING OF ALL CONCEPTS.

I. Practicing Property Law: The Many Aspects of a Lawyer's Duties
   A. Litigation
   B. Drafting legal documents
   C. Examination of titles, abstracts of titles, title insurance policies....
   D. Creating plans for new real estate projects and developments.
   E. Counseling real estate clients, government agencies and developers.

II. Goals of the Property Law Practitioner
   A. Keep clients and clients' estates from becoming enmeshed in legal disputes if possible.
   B. Protect the client's interests at all times.

III. Specialization vs. General Practice
   A. Many attorneys choose to concentrate on property law and in doing so become property law specialists.
   B. Due to the high demand for legal work in property law, many general practitioners make it a substantial portion of their practice.

IV. Opportunities to Practice Property Law Are Everywhere.
   A. Land has long been an important factor in everyday life.
      1. Relationships between people, and between people and the government, have long been affected by land ownership.
      2. Land is not only finite; it is always unique and immovable.
      3. The uses to which land is put affect not just the owners or occupiers, but all those near or who come into contact with the land.
   B. Property law can often be extremely complex, involving planning and design, funding, construction, building codes, labor law, traffic planning, insurance, etc. The list literally goes on and on.

Chapter 7

Finders keepers? Well, sometimes.

This chapter explores the answer to that question, which depends primarily on how the law classifies the property that is found. It might be something nature dropped from the sky, or it might be a wallet that dropped from its owner's pocket. If the property once had an owner other than mother nature, and he somehow came to be parted with it, how did that happen? If a wallet did just drop from the owner's pocket without his intending or even knowing about it, the law would classify the wallet as lost. If the owner just put it down somewhere intending to pick it back up later, but then forgot about it, the law would call the wallet mislaid. If the owner threw it out of his car window as he was speeding down the interstate, never intending to return for it, the law would call the wallet abandoned. A finder might also find property that became embedded in the ground, or maybe even buried treasure.

In all these cases, the law treats the rights of the finder and the rights of the owner of the place where the property was found differently. This chapter will discuss the nature and rationale behind each of these categories.

Chapter 7

NOTE: THE PURPOSE OF THIS OUTLINE IS TO ORGANIZE THE CASES SO THAT ONE CAN QUICKLY UNDERSTAND THE RELEVANCE OF EACH CASE TO THE COURSE. NO ATTEMPT IS MADE IN THIS OVERVIEW TO ADDRESS EVERY CONCEPT THAT MUST BE STUDIED. BE SURE TO READ THE ENTIRE CASEBOOK AND/OR OTHER MATERIALS TO GAIN A FULL UNDERSTANDING OF ALL CONCEPTS.

I. Natural deposits to the soil are not movable objects, but part of the soil, and thus belong to the owner of the soil. *Goddard v. Winchell*.

II. Occupation or possession of lost or abandoned property requires the actual taking of the property by the finder with the intent to possess it. *Eads v. Brazelton*.

III. The finder of lost property has a title superior to all but the true owner. *Armory v. Delamirie*.
   A. When lost property is found in a shop that is open to the public, the finder's claim to the property is still greater than that of all but the true owner, including the shopowner. *Bridges v. Hawkesworth*.
   B. However, where a person has possession of land with a manifest intent to exercise control over it and the things on it, he also has possession of anything found on that land, and thus has a claim superior to that of the finder. *South Staffordshire Water Co. v. Sharman*.
      1. Ownership of a house does not include possession of lost property found there if the owner has not occupied or had prior control over the house. *Hannah v. Peel*.

IV. The finder has no title to property that is mislaid. The right of possession of mislaid property belongs to the owner of the premises where the property is found, and that right is superior to all but that of the true owner. *McAvoy v. Medina*.
   A. The classification of property as lost or mislaid depends on what the facts and circumstances of the case indicate about the intent of the owner and how the property came to be where it was found. *Schley v. Couch*.

V. Legislation
   A. Some scholars have suggested legislation to govern lost and found articles modeled on New York's law.
   B. This legislation merges mislaid and abandoned property into one catchall category of "lost" property unless someone proves that it was mislaid or abandoned within six months of the finding.
      1. The finder of lost property must either return it to the owner or deposit it with the police.
      2. The police then keep the property for six months if it is worth less than $500, or longer if it is worth more.
      3. If after the appropriate period no owner or other person with a right to possession has claimed the property, the police must give it back to the finder and title vests in him.

Goddard v. Winchell

(Land Owner) v. (Meteorite Buyer)
86 Iowa 71, 52 N.W. 1124 (1892)

MEMORY GRAPHIC

Instant Facts

After a meteorite fell onto Goddard's (P) land, Hoagland found it and dug it up, claimed it as his own, and sold it to Winchell (D).

Black Letter Rule

An object deposited on the soil through natural processes is part of that soil, not a movable object, and therefore is not subject to the rule of title by occupancy.

Case Vocabulary

ACCRETION: The gradual addition to land by natural causes, as a river adds soil to a riverbank.
AEROLITE: A meteorite.
ALIENATION: The voluntary transfer of property, especially by conveyance.
ESCHEAT: The reversion of property to the state when there is no one to inherit it.
FORFEITURE: The loss of property without compensation as a penalty for some illegality.
OCCUPANCY: The taking possession of a thing that belongs to nobody with the intention of becoming its owner.
PRESCRIPTION: The acquisition of property rights by continual possession or use for a certain term.
REPLEVIN: An action an owner may use to recover goods from one who has wrongfully taken them.
RIPARIAN: Relating to land that borders a river or stream.

Procedural Basis: Appeal from judgment in replevin action after bench trial.

Facts: Goddard (P) owned certain prairie land in Iowa, and leased the grass privileges for 1890 to Elickson. That year a 66-pound aerolite (meteorite) fell onto Goddard's (P) land and imbedded itself 3 feet into the ground. The next day Elickson saw Hoagland dig up the meteorite. Hoagland took the meteorite to his house and claimed to own it because he found it and dug it up. Two days later Hoagland sold the meteorite to Winchell (D) for $105, who knew that it had fallen onto the prairie south of Hoagland's land. The district court concluded that the meteorite became part of the soil on which it fell, which Goddard (P) owned, and that Hoagland's removing it was wrongful. Winchell (D) argues that the ancient rule "that whatsoever is affixed to the soil belongs to the soil" should be modified, or at least liberally construed. Further, Winchell (D) argues that Hoagland had "title by occupancy" according to the doctrine that movable things upon the surface of the earth that are unclaimed by any owner are deemed abandoned and belong to the first occupant or finder.

Issue: Is a meteorite that falls to earth and imbeds in the soil a movable object to which a person may claim title by occupancy?

Decision and Rationale: (Granger) No. The rule that "whatever is affixed to the soil belongs to the soil," or that "a permanent annexation to the soil, of a thing in itself personal, makes it a part of the realty," addresses only what becomes a part of the soil, and does not address the acquisition of property that exists independent of that soil. The rule of title by occupancy, on the other hand, addresses only such independent, movable property, which is not naturally part of the earth, but is on it. To take from the earth what nature has placed there through natural processes is to take a part of the earth, and not movables. The meteorite here came to its position in Goddard's (P) land through natural causes. It was a natural deposit, with nothing in its composition to make it unnatural to the soil. It was not a movable thing "on the earth" of the type to be thought of as "unclaimed by any owner" and "abandoned by the last proprietor." Winchell (D) states that one may acquire property by occupancy, escheat, prescription, forfeiture, or alienation. However, one who already owns property may also acquire more by accretion. The rules of accretion do not apply to riparian land owners only, as wind and other natural elements may also take soil from one man's property and deposit it on that of another. In such cases the deposit becomes the property of the owner of the soil on which it is made. Hundreds of meteorites fall from the heavens annually, and have done so for ages. It is difficult to understand why stones deposited in the earth as meteorites should be governed by a different rule from that which governs stones deposited by glacier action. While the meteorite here may have greater scientific value than other stones, that has little bearing on who should own it. Winchell (D) also cites the rule that the finder of lost articles is the owner thereof against all but the true owner, even if they are found on the property of a third person. This rule, however, does not apply to this case because the meteorite was never lost or abandoned. Rather, it became part of the earth, and we treat it as such. Affirmed.

Analysis:

The court relies on the doctrine of accretion to justify its conclusion that the meteorite became part of Goddard's (P) property. This doctrine usually applies to riparian landowners, who may gain land when water deposits soil onto their property. There is an exception to this rule in the riparian context: sudden changes such as those caused by a flood do not change property boundaries. However, whether or not this exception applies in the meteorite context, the change caused by the sudden addition of a meteorite to the soil would not change property boundaries. "Accretion" by meteorite deposits affects only the distribution of matter between the heavens and the earth, not between different landowners on the earth, as it does in the riparian context. To argue that the meteorite remains within the "boundaries" of the heavens (and therefore claimed by no owner and up for grabs), and does not shift to being within the boundaries of the soil on which it lands, is to misapply the exception. The exception preserves the status quo between landowners when sudden changes cause a loss of property by one owner and a reciprocal gain by another. Since meteorite deposits do not cause a loss to any landowner, this type of "sudden change" is distinguishable and the exception should not apply.

Eads v. Brazelton

(Actual Possessor) v. (Initial Finder)

22 Ark. 499, 79 Am.Dec. 88 (1861)

M E M O R Y   G R A P H I C

Instant Facts

Brazelton (P) found an abandoned shipwreck and marked it intending to return and recover it. Before he returned, Eads (D) began to recover the cargo.

Black Letter Rule

When property is lost, abandoned, or without an owner, occupation or possession of it requires an actual taking of it with the intent to possess it.

Case Vocabulary

BILL: Initial pleading in an equity action.
PIG: An oblong block of metal.

Procedural Basis: Appeal from decree granted in action in chancery to recover property and obtain injunctive and compensatory relief.

Facts: In 1827 the steamboat America sank in the Mississippi River. The boat and its cargo, including bundles and pigs of lead, were abandoned by their owners. Brazelton (P) sought the wreck, intending to retrieve the lead, and in 1855 discovered it and marked trees to indicate its location. When he thought he was ready to raise the lead, Brazelton (P) fastened a buoy to the wreck, intending to return with a boat for the lead the next day. However, other business, necessary repairs and other difficulties detained him. Several months later Eads and Nelson (Eads) (D), a wrecking firm, found the wreck and started raising the lead. Brazelton (P) argues that his discovery of the wreck and his marking it with the intent to return and recover it gave him a right of occupancy.

Issue: Is marking the location of abandoned property an act of possession that can give a person title by occupancy?

Decision and Rationale: (Fairchild) No. When Brazelton (P) placed his buoy over the wreck, he intended to use it for his work the next day, not to leave it there as a permanent fixture. He intended it only as a guide to find the wreck, just like the marks on the trees. Brazelton's (P) only claim to the wreck is by occupancy. This claim depends upon his finding the wreck; providing means to return to it by markings or buoys; and being near the wreck, continually asserting his claim and intending to make it good by future action, without anyone else appropriating it in the interim. It is clear that the lead was abandoned by its owners. Even without testimony to that effect, the law would imply abandonment from the time passed since the loss and from the fact that an island had formed upon the wreck on which trees had grown to 30 or 40 feet. Even before the island formed, the owners made no effort to recover the lead. When property is lost, abandoned, or is without an owner, occupation or possession of it depends upon an actual taking of it with the intent to possess it. While this actual taking need not be manual, Brazelton's (P) marking trees and attaching buoys to the wreck were not acts of possession under the law. These acts indicated Brazelton's (P) intent to possess the property, but they were not actual possession. Placing a boat over the wreck, with means and efforts to raise the lead, would have been the only way to keep an effective guard over it and would have been acts of possession that the law would protect. Reversed.

Analysis:

To acquire title by occupancy over a thing, a person must both intend to exert exclusive control over it and actually do so. Intent and actual possession must occur together. This case demonstrates that simply manifesting an intent to possess (using buoys to mark the wreck) is not an act of possession. Another important issue this case demonstrates relates to the degree of control a person must exert over a thing to take possession of it. A recent case that addressed this issue is *Popov v. Hayashi* [baseball battle], a California case decided December 18, 2002 after a bench trial by Judge McCarthy. On October 7, 2001, Barry Bonds hit his record-breaking 73rd home run. The ball sailed into the arcade and hit the upper webbing of Alex Popov's glove. Popov may have lost his balance in reaching for the ball, but in any event, before he was able to complete his catch and secure the ball, the crowd tackled him and knocked him to the ground. At some point the ball was knocked loose on the floor, and Patrick Hayashi, who was also knocked to the ground by the mob, saw it on the ground, scooped it up and put it in his pocket. After Hayashi revealed that he had the ball, probably worth more than $1 million, security guards took him to a secure area of the stadium, leaving Popov bruised and empty-handed. Major league baseball deems balls that are hit out of the field to be abandoned -- up for grabs. Who grabbed it? Who acquired possession? Who became the owner of the ball? It is unclear whether Popov had control of the ball as he fell under the mob, and it is unclear when or how the ball became loose. Did Popov acquire any right to possession in his attempt to catch and hold the ball? Judge McCarthy described possession as a process that includes the acts and thoughts of the person attempting to gain possession and culminates the moment he achieves it. Popov clearly intended to gain possession. Judge McCarthy found the question to be whether he did enough to reduce the ball to his exclusive dominion and control. Some authorities argued that to gain possession of a ball, the catcher must have complete control over it when the momentum of both the ball and the catcher cease. Others argued that it would suffice if the person manifests an intent to catch the ball and stops the momentum of the ball, even if he does not attain complete control over it. The precise rules for when a person achieves possession vary in different contexts and industries. As the court stated in *Eads*, a person need not always manually take control of a thing to take possession of it. In some industries, it suffices if a person is "actively and ably engaged in efforts to establish complete control," where the efforts are significant and complete control is expected in the near future. In *Eads*, for example, the court stated that it would suffice if Brazelton (P) put his boat over the wreck with means to raise the lead, and made efforts to do so. This makes good policy sense in the shipwreck salvaging context, since it would hardly encourage people to go to all the trouble and expense to recover shipwrecks if someone else could come along and grab the goods after they had done most of the recovery work, but before they had complete control. The general rule is that the degree of control possession requires as much control as the nature of the goods and the situation permit, considering the customs and practices of the industry. In the baseball context, full control over the ball is possible and generally expected. Judge McCarthy therefore concluded that possession of a ball hit into the stands requires full control once the momentum of the ball and the catcher cease, despite any incidental contact with other people or things. Popov gloved the ball, but he did not retain full control over it, and therefore did not acquire full possession, just as Brazelton (P) found and marked the wreck, but did not retain control over it and did not achieve full possession. However, the contact Popov encountered with the mob that tackled him was hardly incidental. Where Brazelton's (P) efforts to raise the wreck were interrupted by other business, repairs, and other difficulties, Popov's efforts were interrupted, while he was actually making those efforts, by violent unlawful activity. In Popov's case, therefore, Judge McCarthy found that although he did not have full possessory rights, he did have a pre-possessory interest in the ball sufficient to give him an action for conversion against Hayashi. As Judge McCarthy stated the rule, "[w]here an actor undertakes significant but incomplete steps to achieve possession of a piece of abandoned personal property and the effort is interrupted by the unlawful acts of others, the actor has a legally cognizable pre-possessory interest in the property. That pre-possessory interest constitutes a qualified right to possession which can support a cause of action for conversion." Hayashi, however, also had a possessory interest in the ball, since he was not one of the wrongdoers and he did gain full control of the ball. Judge McCarthy explained that if Popov had gained complete control of the ball before being attacked, Hayashi's subsequently gaining control over it would not have affected Popov's rights. However, Judge McCarthy explained that Popov's qualified, pre-possessory interest was not a full right to possession protected from Hayashi's subsequent legitimate claim. On the other hand, Popov's interest in the ball was enough to encumber Hayashi's right. As Judge McCarthy put it, when Hayashi grabbed the ball, it had a "cloud on its title." So, who owns the ball? Judge McCarthy, sitting in equity, found an equitable solution. He found that both Popov and Hayashi had claims of equal dignity, and therefore gave them an equal interest in the ball. He ordered them to sell the ball and split the proceeds.

Armory v. Delamirie

(Finder) v. (Subsequent Possessor)
(1722) 1 Strange 505

MEMORY GRAPHIC

Instant Facts
Armory (P) found a jewel and took it to Delamirie's (D) jewelry shop. Delamirie (D) refused to return the jewel.

Black Letter Rule
The finder of lost property has a title superior to all but the true owner.

Case Vocabulary
TROVER: A suit to recover the value of the plaintiff's chattel that the defendant has converted.

Procedural Basis: Appeal from judgment in action to recover property found by plaintiff.

Facts: Armory (P) found a jewel and took it to Delamirie's (D) jewelry shop to have it appraised. Delamirie's (D) apprentice removed the stones. Delamirie (D) offered three half pence to Armory (P) for the jewel. Armory (P) refused this offer and demanded the jewels to be returned to him. Delamirie (D) refused to return the stones. Armory (P) sues.

Issue: Does the finder of lost property have a title superior to all but the true owner?

Decision and Rationale: Yes. A finder of property does not acquire an absolute title; the true owner has absolute title. However, the finder does acquire a title superior to the rest of the world. Since Armory (P) found the jewel, and since Delamirie (D) is not the true owner, Armory (P) has a superior title. Judgment affirmed.

Analysis:

The rule announced in this case is called the prior possessor rule. It achieves several social goals: 1) It protects an owner who cannot prove that he is the true owner. Imagine how difficult it would be to prove that you own the blow dryer that you lent to your neighbor yesterday; 2) It protects individuals who entrust goods to others. Entrusting goods to others promotes social welfare. For example, an individual may entrust his clothes to the laundry without worrying that he may not get them back. Since he is the prior possessor, he will prevail over the laundry; 3) It protects the expectations of prior possessors, who expect to prevail; 4) It promotes peaceable possession. Were prior possessors not to prevail, individuals might begin to steal property, hoping that the law would protect them.

Bridges v. Hawkesworth

(Finder) v. (Shopowner)
21 L.J. Q.B. 75 (1851)

M E M O R Y   G R A P H I C

 Instant Facts

Bridges (P) found a lost parcel in Hawkesworth's (D) shop and let Hawkesworth (D) hold it for the owner, but when the owner failed to appear, Hawkesworth (D) refused to give the parcel back to Bridges (P).

Black Letter Rule

When lost property is found in a shop, the finder's claim to the property is greater than that of all but the true owner, including the shopowner.

Case Vocabulary

ANTECEDENT: Previous; an event that happens prior to another.

Procedural Basis: Appeal from judgment in action to recover property.

Facts: Bridges (P) visited Hawkesworth's (D) shop on business and found a small parcel containing bank notes on the floor. Bridges (P) told Hawkesworth (D) that he found the parcel of notes and asked him to hold it to deliver to their owner. After three years, no owner claimed the notes, so Bridges (P) asked Hawkesworth (D) for them. Hawkesworth (D) refused to give them up. Bridges (P) brought suit, and the judge decided Hawkesworth (D) had a greater claim to the notes than Bridges (P) and therefore let Hawkesworth (D) keep them.

Issue: Does a shopowner have a greater claim to lost property than the finder if the property is found in his shop?

Decision and Rationale: (Patterson) No. The general rule set forth in *Armory v. Delamirie* [finder's claim to lost goods is superior to all but the true owner], that a finder has a right to the property he found except against the true owner, would have given Bridges (P) a right to the notes if he found them outside Hawkesworth's (D) shop. Does the fact that the notes were found inside the shop rather than outside make any difference? If so, the location of the notes inside the shop would have had to give Hawkesworth (D) a claim to them even before Bridges (P) found them. However, this is not the case. The notes were never in Hawkesworth's (D) custody or protection before Bridges (P) found them. The general rule for lost property applies, even if the property is found inside a shop. Reversed.

Analysis:

This case makes clear that the general rule that a finder's claim to the property he finds is superior to all but the true owner is settled law, and that it holds regardless of where he finds the lost property. The court declines to create an exception to this rule for property found inside a shop. The shopowner never exercised control over the notes, since the shop was open to other customers who might find the notes, and he was unaware that the notes were even there. Bridges (P) was the first person to take possession of the notes, and Hawkesworth (D) had no claim that preceded that of Bridges (P). An exception might seem to make sense on policy grounds, since this would keep the lost property at the shop, which is where the true owner would be most likely to look for it. However, the fact that the notes were found on the floor is significant here. This fact indicates that the notes were *lost*, as opposed to *mislaid*. In *McAvoy v. Medina* [finder has no claim to mislaid property], discussed later in this chapter, the property at issue was found on a table rather than on the floor. The court there found that the property was not lost, but mislaid. If property is mislaid, the true owner might remember where he mislaid it and return to reclaim it. If property is lost, as when it falls out of a person's pocket onto the floor, the true owner will not remember where he laid it because he did not lay it anywhere. He would be unaware of when the property fell out of his pocket, or he would not have lost it. Still, an owner may "retrace his steps" once he discovers that his property is lost, and thus may still return to the shop in search of it. In this way the rule for lost property fails to serve the goal of returning the property to its true owner.

South Staffordshire Water Co. v. Sharman

(Finder) v. (Private Landowner)
2 Q.B. 44 (1896)

M E M O R Y   G R A P H I C

 Instant Facts

Sharman (P) hired South (D) to clean a pool on his land, and while doing so South (D) found two gold rings at the bottom of the pool.

Black Letter Rule

Where a person has possession of land with a manifest intent to exercise control over it and the things on or in it, he is presumed to also possess anything found on that land.

Case Vocabulary

DETINUE: Action to recover an item from a person who acquired it lawfully, as by finding, but who then kept it without right.

FEE SIMPLE: Generally, absolute ownership of land, with no restrictions.

FREEHOLDER: A person who has title to land; landowner.

LOCUS IN QUO: "The place in which" the cause of action arose.

Procedural Basis: Appeal from judgment in detinue action to recover property.

Facts: Sharman (P) owned the land with a pool, and hired South Staffordshire Water Co. (South) (D) to clean out the pool. South (D) found two gold rings in the mud at the bottom of the pool. Sharman (P) demanded the rings, but South (D) refused and gave them instead to the police, who searched for the true owner of the rings. The police did not find the owner and returned the rings to South (D). Sharman (P) sued South (D) in detinue to recover the rings. Since there was no contract between Sharman (P) and South (D) regarding any articles South (D) might find in the pool, the judge held that under *Armory v. Delamirie* [finder of lost property has a title superior to all but the true owner] and *Bridges v. Hawkesworth* [lost property that is found in a shop goes to the finder, not the shopowner], South (D), as finder, had good title against all the world except the true owner.

Issue: Does a finder have good title to property he finds on the private land of another?

Decision and Rationale: (Lord Russell of Killowen) No. Because Sharman (P), as freeholder, had the right to forbid anybody from entering or interfering with his land, he also had the right to direct the manner in which his pool would be cleaned and what would be done with anything found in it. South (D) argues correctly that Sharman (P) must show that he had actual control over the land and the things in it. Sharman (P) did have control over them. This is a case in which articles were found on private property, although the owner of the property did not know the articles were there. The possession of land includes possession of everything attached to that land, absent better title elsewhere, even if the possessor is unaware of a particular thing's existence. The possession of the thing stems from the power to exclude unauthorized interference with the land. This is different from the case in *Bridges*, where the shopowner did not exercise any control over the bank notes lost in his shop. The shop was open to the public, and the notes were lost in the public part of the shop. Before being found, the notes were never in the shopowner's custody or protection. Where, as here, a person has possession of a house or land, with a manifest intent to exercise control over it and the things on or in it, then anything found on that land, whether by an employee or even a stranger, is presumed to be owned by the owner of the land. Reversed.

Concurrence: (Wills) I agree. A contrary decision would only encourage dishonesty.

Analysis:

The court's rationale in *Bridges* seemed to indicate that the location in which lost property is found is irrelevant to who should own it. However, this case limits *Bridges* to those locations that are open to the public; private locations are relevant. Protecting private land does make sense. If I hired someone to mow my lawn and he found a necklace in my backyard that I did not know was there, I would certainly want him to give it to me. As the owner of private land, I would be the person most likely to own the necklace, especially from the point of view of the guy mowing the lawn. I would not want the law to encourage him to just pocket it without telling me. Even if I did not know about the necklace beforehand, since I am the person who controls who may enter my backyard, I would be the person most likely to know who might have lost the necklace, and therefore the person in the best position to return it to its true owner. This case makes good policy sense because it serves both the goal of protecting private property and that of returning lost property to its owner. *Parker v. British Airways Board* [lost bracelet found in executive lounge belongs to finder, not airline] involved a situation somewhere between the public location in *Bridges* and the private location in *South Stafforshire*. A lost bracelet was found in an airline's executive lounge. The lounge was not entirely private or entirely public. The airline permitted certain categories of people and excluded others, based on membership or ticket status. The court decided the case based on the type of control the airline exercised. While they exercised control to exclude certain people and things from the lounge and to clean and maintain it, they did not search for or assert control over lost articles. Since the airline did not assert control over lost articles, the court decided that any articles found should belong to the finder rather than the airline. This result is appropriate in light of the semi-public nature of the lounge. Any passenger with a first-class ticket or membership in the club was invited to enter the lounge. The exclusion of certain categories of people is not as important as the invitation to other categories of people to come and go freely. A shopowner might exclude certain individuals or dangerous items from his shop, but his shop will still be deemed open to the public. This case is therefore more akin to *Bridges* than to *South Staffordshire*, where the land was not open to any category of the public and the landowner had much stricter control over interference with property on his land.

Hannah v. Peel

(Finder) v. (House Owner)
K.B. 509 (1945)

M E M O R Y G R A P H I C

Instant Facts

Peel's (D) house, which he had never occupied, was requisitioned and used by troops, and Hannah (P), one of the troops, found a brooch there.

Black Letter Rule

Where a house owner has had no prior possession or control over property lost in his house, the property belongs to its finder, not the house owner.

Case Vocabulary

REQUISITIONED: Demanded and taken by the government for use by troops.

Procedural Basis: Writ for return of property or its value and damages for its detention.

Facts: Peel (D) bought a house in December 1938, but did not occupy it. In 1940 the government requisitioned the house for military use and compensated Peel (D) £250 per year. Hannah (P) was a lance-corporal stationed at the house, and while there he found a brooch. When he went home on leave, Hannah (P) took the brooch with him and showed it to his wife, who thought it might be of value. Hannah (P) then informed his commanding officer of his find and gave the brooch to the police. Two years later, having failed to find the owner of the brooch, the police gave it to Peel (D). Peel (D) sold the brooch for £66, and the buyers resold it a month later for £88. There was no evidence that Peel (D) knew of the brooch before Hannah (P) found it. Peel (D) offered Hannah (P) a reward for the brooch, but Hannah (P) refused, maintaining his right to possession against all but the true owner. Hannah (P) demanded that Peel (D) return the brooch. Peel (D) did not return it, so Hannah (P) brought this suit for the return of the brooch or its value, and damages for its detention. Peel (D) argues that he owned the brooch because he owned and had possession of the house.

Issue: If an owner has never occupied his house, does he possess lost property that is found there?

Decision and Rationale: (Birkett) No. We accept the argument that *South Staffordshire Water Co. v. Sharman* [landowner is presumed to possess anything found on his land] establishes that if a person finds a thing when acting as the servant or agent of another, he finds it for that other, not for himself. The authorities make clear that a man possesses everything attached to or under his land. On the other hand, *Bridges v. Hawkesworth* [lost property that is found in a shop goes to the finder, not the shopowner] makes clear that a man does not necessarily possess a thing that is lying unattached on the surface of his land, even if it is not possessed by someone else. Peel (D) never occupied the house and never possessed the brooch before Hannah (P) found it. The brooch was lost, Hannah (P) found it, and Peel (D) knew nothing of it before Hannah (P) found it. Under these circumstances, *Bridges* should apply. Peel (D) did not have prior possession of the brooch, so Hannah (P) acquired possession when he found it. Judgment for Hannah (P) for £66.

Analysis:

This decision was not based on principal-agent law, master-servant law, or on whether the lost property was attached or unattached to the land. While the court cites cases as establishing rules based on these principles, when it finally applied the law to the facts, it focused on the fact that Peel (D) never occupied the house or possessed the brooch before Hannah (P) found it. The decision in *South Staffordshire* was based on the landowner's control over the land he possessed. The court there reasoned that since the landowner had the right to exclude others and prevent their interference with things on his land, he had control over the things on his land and therefore was presumed to have possession of them. While here the court described *South Staffordshire* as focusing on the fact that the finder was the landowner's servant, the real basis for the decision was the landowner's control of his land. It is also on this basis that the court actually decides this case and distinguishes it from *South Staffordshire*. Because Peel (D) never occupied the house, he never exercised the kind of control over it that the landowner in *South Staffordshire* did. The house in this case was under the control of the troops that occupied it. Since Peel (D), though the owner of the house, exercised little, if any, control over it, the court found the case more akin to *Bridges* than to *South Staffordshire* and decided it accordingly. In *Bridges*, as here, the shopowner owned his shop, but exercised only limited control over it while it was open to the public, and he never knew of or exercised control over the notes that were lost there before they were found. Since the shopowner did not exercise prior control over the property lost on his premises, the finder had the superior claim to the property. The landowner in *South Staffordshire* did exercise prior control over the property lost on his land, so the landowner had a claim to the property superior to that of the finder. Here, as in *Bridges*, the owner of the house exercised no prior control over the lost brooch, so the finder had a claim superior to his.

McAvoy v. Medina

(Finder) v. (Shop Owner)

(1866) 93 Mass. (I 1 Allen) 548

M E M O R Y   G R A P H I C

Instant Facts

A customer of the shop owner placed his wallet on the counter, but neglected to remove it. McAvoy (P) found the wallet.

Black Letter Rule

A finder has no title to property that is mislaid.

Procedural Basis: Appeal from judgment in action to recover money found by plaintiff.

Facts: A customer of a shop placed his wallet on the counter but neglected to remove it; the customer had mislaid his wallet. McAvoy (P) found the wallet and gave it to the shop owner Medina (D) to keep until the true owner should claim it. If the true owner did not claim it, McAvoy (P) requested that Medina (D) advertise the lost money. The true owner was never found and Medina (D) refused to turn the money over to McAvoy (P).

Issue: Does the finder of mislaid property have title to that property?

Decision and Rationale: (Dewey). No. The ordinary rule is that a finder of lost property has title superior to all the world except the true owner. Here, however, the property was mislaid, not lost. When property is mislaid in a shop, the shop owner has a duty to safeguard the property until the true owner returns. Therefore, a finder can never gain title to mislaid property. *Bridges v. Hawkesworth* is distinguishable. In that case, the property was not voluntarily placed somewhere and then forgotten. Rather, in that case, the property was lost. In this case, since the property was not lost but mislaid, McAvoy (P) can claim no title. Judgment affirmed.

Analysis:

Lost property goes to the finder. Mislaid property goes to the shop owner. One way to understand this rule is to look to one of the goals of property law: Property law should promote the return of lost property to its true owner. If property is mislaid, the true owner will likely retrace his steps and return to the shop where he mislaid it. Thus, the rule that places mislaid property in the hand of the shop owner will more efficiently return mislaid property to the true owner. There are two criticisms to this rule. First, it is difficult to determine whether property has been mislaid or lost. For example, a wallet found on the floor could easily have fallen through a person's pocket and been lost. However, it also could have been mislaid on a counter and knocked to the floor by another customer. The second criticism is that individuals retrace their steps for both lost and mislaid property.

Schley v. Couch

(Finder) v. (Landowner)
155 Tex. 195, 284 S.W.2d 333 (1955)

M E M O R Y   G R A P H I C

Instant Facts
Schley (P), a workman, found money buried in a jar in Couch's (D) garage.

Black Letter Rule
Property found embedded in the soil under circumstances repelling the idea that is has been lost is mislaid property.

Case Vocabulary

LOST PROPERTY: Property which the owner has unintentionally left in some location unknown to him.
MISLAID PROPERTY: Property which the owner intentionally placed where he could return for it, but then forgot where that was.
TREASURE TROVE: "Treasure found"; money, coin, gold, silver, plate or bullion that was hidden by an unknown owner and later found.

Procedural Basis: Appeal from decision by court of appeals reversing judgment of trial court in action to recover property and damages.

Facts: Couch (D) owned land with a house with an attached garage. When Couch (D) moved in, the front half of the garage had a concrete floor and the rear half had a dirt floor. Couch (D) hired workmen, including Schley (P), to put a concrete floor in the rear half of the garage. While loosening the soil in the garage, Schley (P) found $1000 in currency buried in a glass jar in the ground. The owner of the money is unknown. Schley (P) sued Couch (D) for the money plus damages. The jury found that the money was mislaid rather than lost, and the trial court therefore rendered judgment for Couch (D) as bailee for the true owner. The appeals court reversed, holding that the money was neither lost nor mislaid, but instead was treasure trove, to which the finder has the right to possession. Neither party claims title to the money, but both claim the right to possession for the benefit of the true owner, should he ever appear.

Issue: Is property found embedded in the soil under circumstances repelling the idea that it has been lost to be considered mislaid property?

Decision and Rationale: (Griffin) Yes. We have decided not to recognize the "treasure trove" doctrine in Texas, an ancient doctrine that arose to govern treasure buried by Roman conquerors in the British isles. Although many states have applied this doctrine, Texas has never officially recognized it, and we see no reason to adopt it under present conditions in our nation. Instead we adopt the Oregon rule for treasure trove, as stated in *Jackson v. Steinberg* [the law of treasure trove has been merged with the law of lost goods], which treats treasure trove as lost goods for purposes of determining the rights of the finder. *Jackson* defines lost property as "that which the owner has involuntarily parted with through neglect, carelessness or inadvertence." The finder of lost property may retain it against the owner or possessor of the place where it is found. Mislaid property, on the other hand, is "property which the owner intentionally places where he can again resort to it, and then forgets." *Jackson* explains that mislaid property is presumed to be left in the custody of the owner or occupier of the place where it is found; and that owner or occupier generally has the right to possession of it against all but the true owner. Here, the true owner carefully placed the currency in a jar and buried it in the ground. This owner did not part with the money inadvertently, involuntarily, carelessly or through neglect. Rather, he did so by a deliberate, conscious and voluntary act, desiring to hide his money in a secure place with the intention of returning to claim it later. The evidence indicates that the owner buried the money in the garage after the garage was built, only four years before Couch (D) bought it and Schley (P) found the money, not long enough to establish that restitution to the true owner has become impossible. The facts show that this money was not lost property, and the jury found the property to be mislaid rather than lost. The finder of mislaid property has no right to it because the law presumes that possession of the property is in the owner of the locus in quo. Property found embedded in the soil under circumstances repelling the idea that it has been lost is mislaid property. The right to possession of mislaid property is therefore in the landowner, here Couch (D). Since no proof has been made as to who is the true owner of the money, we will presume that he has forgotten where he hid it or has since died. [What about four years not being so long?] Court of appeals reversed, trial court affirmed.

Concurrence: (Calvert) The majority fails to recognize a fourth category of found property, that of personal property found imbedded in the soil. The majority adopted the rule that applies to imbedded property, but defined it as mislaid property.

Concurrence: (Wilson) The distinctions between treasure trove, lost property and mislaid property are not worth preserving. In all these cases we should simply maintain the continuity of possession of the landowner until the true owner establishes his title.

Analysis:

As the cases in this chapter have shown, when a person finds and takes possession of personal property, his right to it depends on the way the law characterizes it. The common law classifies found property in five ways. It may be abandoned (the owner has intentionally discarded it); lost (the owner has unintentionally parted with it and does not know where it is); mislaid (the owner has intentionally placed it where he could return for it, but has forgotten where he put it); embedded (it has become part of the earth, like ancient pottery); or treasure trove (some type of money, usually very old, hidden away). Abandoned property belongs to the finder who has taken possession of it. The finder of lost property or treasure trove has a right to possession against all but the true owner. Possession of mislaid property goes to the owner of the premises on which it is found, whose claim is greater than all but the true owner. Embedded property belongs to the owner of the soil in which it was found. *Schley* demonstrates that the category to which particular property belongs depends on all the facts and circumstances of the case, particularly what they indicate about the true owner's intent and how the property came to be where it was found. This court also narrowed its work down by dismissing two of the five categories, treasure trove and embedded property. It merged treasure trove into the category of lost property, and merged embedded property into the category of mislaid property. Some scholars advocate dismissing the distinctions between the other three categories as well because they find it impossible to determine the intent of the owner, and thus impossible to determine whether they lost, mislaid or abandoned it. Justice Wilson, concurring in *Schley*, would merge treasure trove and lost property into mislaid property, leaving only the two categories of mislaid property and abandoned property.

Chapter 8

Suppose you give something you own to another, not to keep, but to hold onto for some period or for some purpose. When you do this, the law calls the relationship you create with the other person a bailment. You create a bailment when you give your keys to a valet to park your car, or when you give your laundry to a laundromat to wash, or when you check your coat or lend a book to a friend. You give another person possession and control of your property for some purpose until you come to reclaim it or the person returns it to you. When you do receive your property again, you expect it to be in the same condition as it was when you parted with it.

The law stands behind that expectation by holding the person you gave your property to, the bailee, responsible for the condition of your property. This chapter describes how a person might create a bailment by his conduct, despite his words, and discusses the legal consequences that stem from that relationship.

Chapter 8

NOTE: THE PURPOSE OF THIS OUTLINE IS TO ORGANIZE THE CASES SO THAT ONE CAN QUICKLY UNDERSTAND THE RELEVANCE OF EACH CASE TO THE COURSE. NO ATTEMPT IS MADE IN THIS OVERVIEW TO ADDRESS EVERY CONCEPT THAT MUST BE STUDIED. BE SURE TO READ THE ENTIRE CASEBOOK AND/OR OTHER MATERIALS TO GAIN A FULL UNDERSTANDING OF ALL CONCEPTS.

I. Creation of a Bailment
   A. A bailment is created when the owner of a thing allows another to lawfully possess it for a time.
   B. The owner then becomes the bailor and the person in possession of the thing becomes the bailee.

II. Control and Possession, a Matter of Degree
   A. The degree of control and posession a customer delivers to the operator of an enclosed, attended parking garage and the expectations of the parties suffice to create a bailment. A bailment relationship makes the bailee responsible for delivering the thing bailed to the bailor undamaged. *Allen v. Hyatt Regency-Nashville Hotel*.
   A. While a voluntary bailee has a duty to care for the thing bailed, an involuntary bailee does not. *Cowen v. Pressprich*.
   B. However, if an involuntary bailee exercises any dominion over the thing bailed, then he takes on the same duties as the voluntary bailee. *Cowen v. Pressprich*.

Allen v. Hyatt Regency-Nashville Hotel

(Car Owner) v. (Parking Garage)

668 S.W.2d 286 (1984)

M E M O R Y   G R A P H I C

Instant Facts

Allen's (P) husband parked her car in an enclosed garage with a booth attendant and security personnel, but the car was stolen.

Black Letter Rule

The degree of control and possession a customer delivers to the operator of an enclosed, attended parking garage and the expectations of the parties suffice to create a bailment.

Case Vocabulary

BAILMENT: The transfer of possession of personal property, without a transfer of ownership, from one person (bailor) to another (bailee) for a particular purpose, which leaves the bailee responsible for returning the thing bailed in good condition.

LICENSE: A privilege to use land, given to a person having no possessory interest in that land.

Procedural Basis: Appeal from judgment of appellate court after trial court judgment in negligence action for damages.

Facts: The Hyatt Regency-Nashville Hotel (Hyatt) (D) owns and operates a hotel with a multi-level parking garage. The garage is open to the public as well as hotel guests. Allen's (P) husband (Mr. Allen) parked her new car on the fourth floor of the Hyatt's (D) parking garage. Mr. Allen parked there because he felt the car would be safer in an attended garage than in an unattended outside lot. When Mr. Allen returned for the car, it was gone, and it has not been recovered. Mr. Allen reported the theft to the booth attendant and hotel security before reporting it to the police. The attendant said, "Well, it didn't come out here." A security guard told Mr. Allen that someone reported a person "messing with a car" that morning, but that he found nothing unusual when he went to investigate. The ticket Mr. Allen received from the dispensing machine when he arrived at the garage instructed the parker to keep the ticket and that it must be presented to the attendant upon leaving the garage. The ticket states that charges are for using the parking space. The ticket further states that the Hyatt (D) assumes no responsibility for loss due to fire, theft, collision or otherwise, and that the owners park their cars at the garage at their own risk. The Hyatt (D) uses the tickets to measure the time a vehicle is parked, but they do not identify particular vehicles.

Issue: Does parking a car in an enclosed, attended parking garage create a bailment?

Decision and Rationale: (Harbison) Yes. Several courts have struggled with the legal relationship created in park-and-lock cases. In one leading case, *McGlynn v. Parking Authority of City of Newark* [no bailment is created between a garage owner and its customer, but the garage owner does have a duty of reasonable care], the New Jersey Supreme Court decided that rather than consider the possession and control elements in the context of bailment, it was more useful to consider them in defining the duty of care of a garage operator to its customers. The Court found that garage owners are usually better situated to protect the parked car and to distribute the cost of protection through parking fees. Further, the Court found that owners usually expect to receive their cars back in the same condition in which they left them. Considering the control of the garage owners and the expectations of the car owners, the Court concluded that operators of parking garages have a duty of reasonable care to their customers. Since proof of negligence would be difficult because the car owner is generally absent when their loss occurs, the Court authorized a presumption of negligence from proof of damage to a car parked in an enclosed garage. [The progressive approach: bailment analysis without the bailment.] Tennessee courts, on the other hand, have generally looked to whether the evidence was sufficient to create a bailment for hire by implication. [The traditional, and majority, approach: go ahead and name names.] We find this approach, which is the majority view, to be the most satisfactory, unless the parties create some other relationship by their conduct or by contract. Here, Mr. Allen parked Allen's (P) car in an enclosed commercial garage that had an attendant controlling the exit and security personnel patrolling the premises. Under these circumstances we find that a bailment for hire was created, and that proof of nondelivery therefore entitled Allen (P) to the statutory presumption of negligence. We recognize that the fact that an owner locks his car and keeps the keys creates a question of whether there is sufficient delivery of possession and control to create a bailment. However, in these circumstances customers expect the garage operator to provide attendants and protection, and in practicality he does assume control of the parked vehicles since he limits access to the garage and requires the presentation of a ticket upon exit. The Hyatt (D) made no effort to rebut the presumption of negligence. The facts show that security personnel were aware of some vehicle tampering the day of the theft, and Allen's (P) car was somehow driven past the attendant's booth to exit the garage. Park-and-lock situations involve many different circumstances, and the expectations of the parties can create different legal relationships with different legal results. It is difficult to lay down one rule for all cases. The facts and circumstances of this case are consistent with the traditional concept of a bailment for hire. They amounted to more than a mere license or hiring a space to park a vehicle without any expectation of protection or obligation upon the garage operator. Affirmed and remanded.

Dissent: (Drowota) I find no bailment and that Allen (P) does not receive the benefit of the presumption of negligence. Allen (P) had the duty to affirmatively prove negligence and failed to do so. A bailment is created in parking lot or garage situations when the operator of the lot or garage knowingly and voluntarily assumes control, possession, or custody of a motor vehicle. If the operator has not done so, there may be a license to park or a lease of the parking space. The fact that a garage requires a ticket upon leaving does not create a basis on which to find a bailment. Most bailment receipts would identify the vehicle or its owner, but this ticket did not. The attendant was not performing the traditional bailee role of identifying and returning a particular article [he didn't return any article], but was only computing the amount due and accepting payment. Allen's (P) husband parked her car, locked it and kept the key. The Hyatt (D) attendant could not move it, did not know whose car it was, and did not know who would reclaim it or when. Anyone who obtained a ticket could drive out with any car he could operate. When the fee was paid, how could the Hyatt (D) reasonably exercise control?

Analysis:

The reason the designation of the relationship between the parking garage and its customers as a bailment is so significant is that it provides the bailor who sustains a loss with a presumption of negligence. In most cases, to overcome this presumption the bailee must prove that the loss did not result from his negligence. Even if he manages to do this, the case is not over; the bailee only succeeds in removing the presumption and shifting the burden back to the bailor. In some cases, a bailment may also give rise to strict liability. As explained in *Cowen v. Pressprich* [involuntary bailee has no duty to care for the subject of the bailment], bailments may be voluntary or involuntary, and voluntary bailments may be for hire, otherwise coupled with an interest, or gratuitous. A voluntary bailee, whether for compensation or gratuitous, has an absolute duty to deliver the thing bailed to the right person. Good faith or innocent mistake will not excuse delivery to the wrong person. An involuntary bailee, on the other hand, has no duty to care for the thing bailed or to deliver it to the right person as long as he does not exercise any dominion over it. Here, the Hyatt (D) was a voluntary bailee for hire. As a voluntary bailee, the Hyatt (D) had an absolute duty to deliver Allen's (P) car to the proper person. Under this rule, if the Hyatt (D) delivered the car to the wrong person, *i.e.*, if it accepted a ticket from the thief and let him leave with Allen's (P) car, it would be strictly liable for Allen's (P) loss.

Chapter 9

Ordinarily, only a person who owns something can pass good title to it to another. At common law, if someone stole the thing from the owner and then sold it to some third person who did not know it was stolen, the owner would still own the property. The thief, having no title himself, could not pass title to anyone else. There are many situations in which that innocent third party, a bona fide purchaser, can take good title, however. For example, if the owner does something that leads a bona fide purchaser to believe that the seller really owns the property, the true owner cannot then take the property back because he was partly responsible for the bona fide purchaser buying the property in the first place.

To smooth the flow of commerce, Congress has also passed several provisions that allow a bona fide purchaser to acquire good title even though someone other than the seller has a claim to it. If an owner gives possession of his hat to a merchant who is in the business of selling hats, and the merchant then sells his hat to a bona fide purchaser, Congress lets the bona fide purchaser keep the hat. After all, we need to be able to have confidence that when we walk into a store and buy something, we really get to own the thing we buy. [When you buy something from a guy in a back alley, that's a different story.]

This chapter explores several situations in which a bona fide purchaser can take good title to property that someone other than the seller owns, as well as what a bona fide purchaser might say if the owner turns up and wants his property back.

Chapter 9

NOTE: THE PURPOSE OF THIS OUTLINE IS TO ORGANIZE THE CASES SO THAT ONE CAN QUICKLY UNDERSTAND THE RELEVANCE OF EACH CASE TO THE COURSE. NO ATTEMPT IS MADE IN THIS OVERVIEW TO ADDRESS EVERY CONCEPT THAT MUST BE STUDIED. BE SURE TO READ THE ENTIRE CASEBOOK AND/OR OTHER MATERIALS TO GAIN A FULL UNDERSTANDING OF ALL CONCEPTS.

I. A bona fide purchaser is a person who buys property from a seller with no notice that a third person, not the seller, owns the property.
   A. The general rule is that title remains in the true owner, not the bona fide purchaser, since no one can convey better title than he has.
   B. There are, however, many exceptions to this rule. Title to property sold to a bona fide purchaser will shift from the true owner to the bona fide purchaser where:
      1. The owner's conduct estops him from asserting title against the bona fide purchaser;
      2. The owner is a beneficiary of the property which was held in trust, such that the owner had only equitable title, and the trustee had legal title, which he conveyed to the bona fide purchaser;
      3. The owner was fraudulently induced to sell his property to a person who then sold it to a bona fide purchaser, since the owner conveyed voidable title to the defrauder, and that title became absolute when the defrauder sold it to the bona fide purchaser; and
      4. The transaction falls under the *Uniform Commercial Code* [governs sales of goods], which gives "good title" to a "good faith purchaser" for value, even if the seller has only voidable title. *UCC § 2-403.*

II. Equitable estoppel and statutory estoppel are defenses available to a bona fide purchaser confronting a claim by the true owner.
   A. Equitable estoppel precludes a party from denying any material fact which he has induced another to rely upon.
      1. Thus, if an owner clothes another with indicia of ownership or apparent authority to sell his property, equitable estoppel will preclude him from denying the other's ownership or authority to sell, and he will not be able to recover against the bona fide purchaser.
      2. However, merely transferring possession of property to another, without more, is insufficient to induce reliance by a bona fide purchaser and therefore does not create an estoppel. *Porter v. Wertz.*
   B. Statutory estoppel may arise under the *UCC's* entrustment provision. When an owner entrusts his goods to a merchant who deals in goods of that kind, this gives the merchant power to transfer all the owner's rights to a buyer in the ordinary course of business. *UCC § 2-403(2).*
      1. A buyer in the ordinary course of business is a purchaser in good faith who buys from a merchant dealing in goods of that kind. A purchaser of a work of art is not a purchaser in good faith if he is indifferent as to the seller's status as an art merchant and his authority to sell the work of art. *Porter v. Wertz.*

III. Voidable Title
   A. The *UCC* allows a person with voidable title to pass good title to a bona fide purchaser for value even if that person acquired the goods through a bad check or through fraud criminally punishable as larceny. *UCC § 2-403(1).*
   B. However, more particularized statutes may impose other requirements that prevent good title from passing to a bona fide purchaser. For example, under a certificate of title statute, a person with only voidable title cannot pass good title to a motor vehicle to a bona fide purchaser if he does not have a title certificate because until he has the certificate, his voidable title is not perfected. *Sheridan Suzuki, Inc. v. Caruso Auto Sales.*

MERELY TRANSFERRING POSSESSION TO ANOTHER IS NOT ENOUGH TO EQUITABLY ESTOP AN OWNER FROM RECOVERING AGAINST A GOOD FAITH PURCHASER, BUT IT MAY STATUTORILY ESTOP HIM IF THE TRANSFER IS AN ENTRUSTMENT TO A MERCHANT AND THE PURCHASER REALLY IS IN GOOD FAITH

Porter v. Wertz

(Owner) v. (Defrauder)

68 A.D.2d 141, 416 N.Y.S.2d 254, aff'd 53 N.Y.2d 696, 439 N.Y.S.2d 105, 421 N.E.2d 500 (1981)

M E M O R Y   G R A P H I C

Instant Facts

Porter (P) gave Von Maker (D) a painting to hold while he decided whether to buy it, but Von Maker (D), through Wertz (D), a deli employee, sold it to Feigen (D).

Black Letter Rule

(1) A purchaser of art is not a purchaser in good faith under *UCC § 2-403* if he is indifferent as to the seller's status as an art merchant and his authority to sell the art. (2) Transferring possession of property to another, without more, is insufficient to equitably estop an owner from asserting his title against a purchaser in good faith.

Case Vocabulary

OBJECT D'ART: Usually "objet d'art," an object of artistic value.

PROVENANCE: Proof of past ownership of an objet d'art.

Procedural Basis: Appeal from judgment in bench trial in action to recover property or damages.

Facts: Samuel Porter and Express Packaging, Inc. (Porter) (P) owned a Maurice Utrillo painting (the Utrillo). After Porter (P) sold another painting to Harold Von Maker (Von Maker) (D), who was using the name of Peter Wertz (Wertz) (D), Von Maker (D) expressed an interest in the Utrillo. Porter (P) let Von Maker (D) hang the Utrillo in his home temporarily while he decided whether to buy it. When Porter (P) later sought the Utrillo's return, he was unable to reach Von Maker (D). The notes due on the other painting then started being dishonored. Porter (P) investigated and discovered that Von Maker (D) was using the name of Wertz (D); was subject to judgments; had been sued many times; had been arrested for several crimes involving fraud; and was convicted for one and was on probation. Porter (P) notified the FBI about the notes, but did not yet know that Von Maker (D) had already sold the Utrillo. Porter (P) had his attorney draw up a detailed agreement covering several paintings, including the Utrillo. Von Maker (D) executed this agreement, in which he acknowledged that he received the Utrillo from Porter (P); that the Utrillo belonged to Porter (P); that the Utrillo was on consignment with one of Von Maker's (D) clients; and that within 90 days Von Maker (D) would either return the Utrillo or pay $30,000 for it. Von Maker (D) never made any payment for the Utrillo. Even before Von Maker (D) executed the agreement, he had already had the real Wertz (D), a deli employee, sell the Utrillo to Richard Feigen (Feigen) (D) for $20,000. Feigen (D), who was in the business of buying and selling paintings, did not investigate Wertz's (D) status as an art dealer or whether he owned the Utrillo or was authorized by the owner to sell it. Feigen (D) sold the Utrillo to Brenner, and Brenner sold it to someone in Venezuela. Porter (P) seeks to recover his painting or the value thereof from Feigen (D). At trial Feigen (D) asserted the defenses of statutory estoppel under *UCC § 2-403* [gives good title to a good faith purchaser for value] and equitable estoppel. The trial court found statutory estoppel inapplicable, but dismissed the complaint as barred on equitable estoppel grounds.

Issue: (1) Is a purchaser of a work of art a purchaser in good faith under *UCC § 2-403* if he is indifferent as to the seller's status as an art merchant or his authority to sell the work of art? (2) Does transferring possession of property to another suffice to equitably estop an owner from asserting his title against a purchaser in good faith?

Decision and Rationale: (Birns) (1) No. Under *UCC § 2-403(2)* [entrustment to a merchant], "any entrusting of possession of goods to a merchant who deals in goods of that kind gives [the merchant] power to transfer all rights of the entruster to a buyer in the ordinary course of business." Under *UCC § 1-201(9)* [defines "buyer in the ordinary course of business"], a "buyer in the ordinary course of business" is a purchaser in good faith, who has no knowledge that the sale violates another's ownership rights, and who buys the goods from a person in the business of selling goods of that kind. To determine whether Feigen (D) may use the defense of statutory estoppel, we must first determine whether Feigen (D) is a buyer in the ordinary course of business. He is not. First, Feigen (D) bought the Utrillo from Wertz (D), who was not "a person in the business of selling goods of that kind." Wertz (D) worked at a deli and never held himself out as an art dealer. Second, Feigen (D) was not a purchaser in good faith. Under *UCC § 2-103(1)(b)* [defines good faith] "good faith" in the case of a merchant includes both "honesty in fact and the observance of reasonable commercial standards of fair dealing in the trade." Good faith cannot permit indifference as to the history of ownership or the right to possess or sell an object d'art. Feigen

Porter v. Wertz (Continued)

(D) did not confirm or even investigate whether Wertz (D) was an art merchant, and made no effort to verify whether Wertz (D) owned the Utrillo or was authorized by the owner to sell it. Feigen's (D) employee had a catalogue of the artist's work that would have raised a doubt as to Wertz's (D) right of possession, calling for further verification before completing the purchase, but the employee made no inquiry. Thus, Feigen (D) was not a buyer in the ordinary course of business, and the trial court correctly concluded that statutory estoppel was not a defense available to Feigen (D). (2) No. We disagree with the trial court's conclusion that equitable estoppel bars recovery. The Court of Appeals held in *Zendman v. Harry Winston, Inc.* [doctrine of equitable estoppel] that an owner may be estopped by his own acts from asserting his title against a bona fide purchaser for value if he has "clothed the vendor with possession and other indicia of title" or with apparent authority to sell. Here, Porter's (P) conduct was not blameworthy. When the first promissory note was dishonored, he investigated the matter, informed the FBI, and obtained an agreement to recover the Utrillo. Porter (P) did allow Von Maker (D) to possess the Utrillo, but he conferred no other indicia of ownership. Possession alone is insufficient to create an estoppel. Although Porter (P) knew Von Maker (D) was an art dealer, he did not consign the Utrillo to him for business purposes, but only for display in Von Maker's (D) home. Porter's (P) conduct did not contribute in any way to the deception Von Maker (D) and Wertz (D) practiced on Feigen (D). Finally, Feigen (D) was not a purchaser in good faith. Feigen (D) did not rely on any indicia of ownership in Von Maker (D) since he dealt with Wertz (D), and Feigen (D) and his employees made no inquiry into Wertz's (D) authority to sell the Utrillo. Feigen (D) claims that his failure to make this inquiry was consistent with the practice of the trade, but this does not excuse it. Commercial indifference to ownership or the right to sell facilitates traffic in stolen works of art and increases the culpability of the apathetic merchant. Porter (P) is the true owner of the Utrillo. Feigen (D) wrongfully detained the Utrillo and must return it or pay for its value. Reversed and remanded for an assessment of damages.

Analysis:

As the court explained in *Porter*, equitable estoppel is the principle which precludes a party from denying any material fact which he has induced another, excusably ignorant of the true facts, to rely upon such that he would suffer injury if the denial were allowed. Thus, if an owner invests another with indicia of ownership or apparent authority to sell his property such that a bona fide purchaser would be induced to rely upon that apparent ownership or authority, equitable estoppel will preclude the owner from denying the other's ownership or authority to sell, and he will not be able to recover against the bona fide purchaser. However, as this case shows, merely transferring possession is not enough to induce reliance by a bona fide purchaser. For equitable estoppel to bar recovery, the owner must be blameworthy in inducing reliance, *and* the buyer must be innocent and excusably ignorant. Here, neither was the case. Porter (P) did not induce reliance by a bona fide purchaser or do anything else blameworthy. Feigen (D), on the other hand, was blameworthy in that he did not investigate Wertz's (D) status as an art merchant or his ownership rights or authority to sell. He was not a good faith purchaser *excusably* ignorant of the true facts. Usually the good faith of a merchant is judged in part according to his compliance with the commercial standards of his industry. In the art world, however, the standards are not very strict. It has long been the practice in the art industry not only to decline to inquire into the ownership of works of art, but even to withhold details about ownership. Art dealers do this, at least in part, to protect the privacy of their sources. Unfortunately, this protects the privacy of not only legitimate owners, but also that of those who should be exposed. As this and many other courts have complained, protecting the privacy of thieves encourages theft and "facilitates traffic in stolen works of art." The court found this commercial standard unreasonably low, and therefore refused to allow compliance with it to give a merchant good faith status. On appeal from this case, the Court of Appeals declined to rule on the good faith issue. However, in 1991 in *Solomon R. Guggenheim Foundation v. Lubell* [declined to impose a duty of reasonable diligence on owners of stolen art for statute of limitations purposes], commenting again that in the New York City art market, "illicit dealing in stolen merchandise is an industry all its own," this Court concluded that "[t]o place the burden of locating stolen artwork on the true owner and to foreclose the rights of that owner to recover its property if the burden is not met would, we believe, encourage illicit trafficking in stolen art. . . . In our opinion, the better rule . . . places the burden of investigating the provenance of a work of art on the potential purchaser." Databases like the Art Loss Register now make it easier for buyers to investigate whether a painting has been stolen. As long as the owner is diligent in reporting the theft, a diligent search by the buyer will turn it up. Both the owner and the buyer should be held accountable for their lack of diligence in these areas. Under the doctrine of equitable estoppel, if an owner expressly or impliedly represents that the possessor of his goods has authority to sell them, then he is estopped to deny this authority. Under this doctrine, as *Porter* makes clear, merely giving possession of goods to another is not enough to imply an authority to sell; there must be some other indicia of this authority. Under the *UCC's* entrustment provision, on the other hand, the mere act of entrusting -- giving possession of -- goods *is* sufficient to imply authority to sell. This provision, however, is designed specifically for the commercial world. For entrustment to create a statutory estoppel, therefore, the entrustee must be a merchant dealing in goods of that kind, and the sale must be to a good faith purchaser in the ordinary course of business.

Sheridan Suzuki, Inc. v. Caruso Auto Sales

(Owner) v. (Bona Fide Purchaser)
110 Misc.2d 823, 442 N.Y.S.2d 957 (1981)

M E M O R Y   G R A P H I C

Instant Facts

Bouton "bought" a motorcycle from Suzuki (P) with a bad check, and then sold it to Caruso (D) the next day, before Bouton received his Certificate of Title.

Black Letter Rule

A person with only voidable title cannot pass good title to a motor vehicle to a bona fide purchaser for value if he does not have a Certificate of Title because until he has the certificate, his voidable title is not perfected.

Case Vocabulary

ABROGATE: To annul or set aside.
PERFECT: To make valid and effective, free from legal defects.

Procedural Basis: Motion for summary judgment seeking declaratory relief in dispute over ownership of property.

Facts: Sheridan Suzuki, Inc. (Suzuki) (P) "sold" a motorcycle to Bouton, giving him possession of the motorcycle, a signed bill of sale marked paid in full, and registration in Bouton's name. Suzuki (P) also applied for a Certificate of Title. The day after Bouton bought the motorcycle he offered to sell it to Caruso Auto Sales, Inc. (Caruso) (D). After examining Bouton's papers and calling Suzuki (P), who confirmed Bouton's purchase, Caruso (D) bought the motorcycle. Bouton gave Caruso (D) the motorcycle, signed over the registration and promised that he would transfer the Certificate of Title when he received it. Bouton's check to Suzuki (P) then bounced, and Bouton disappeared. Suzuki (P) informed authorities of the fraud and they did not issue the Certificate of Title. Suzuki (P) sued Caruso (D) to recover the motorcycle.

Issue: Can a person with only voidable title pass good title to a motor vehicle to a bona fide purchaser for value if he does not have a Certificate of Title?

Decision and Rationale: (Sedita) No. At common law, a thief could pass no title to stolen goods. Under *UCC § 2-403(1)* [good faith purchaser can acquire good title from a person with only voidable title], however, a person with voidable title can transfer good title to a good faith purchaser even if that person acquired the goods in exchange for a check that later bounced, or through fraud criminally punishable as larceny. [Commerce must go on, after all.] Since Bouton acquired this motorcycle with a bad check rather than through direct larceny or burglary, the title he gave to Caruso (D), a bona fide purchaser for value, cannot be void. Bouton received no more than voidable title, but under *UCC § 2-403(1)* a bona fide purchaser for value can receive good title from a person with voidable title. However, the *State Uniform Vehicle Certificate of Title Act (UVCTA)* [governs certificates of title for motor vehicles] comes into play here as well. Courts must give effect to all statutes and avoid interpretations that would create conflicts between them. Where a general and a more particularized statute overlap, courts usually give greater effect to the more particularized statute. The *UCC* establishes the general rule for commercial transactions. The *UVCTA* adds requirements to this general rule to address problems of fraud and theft for vehicles. *UVCTA § 2113(c)* [requires compliance to perfect a transfer of ownership] states that a transfer by an owner is only perfected when compliance with this section is complete. *UVCTA § 2105* [procedures for application for certificate of title] makes clear that this act is designed for more than mere record keeping and rubber-stamping. Rather, the commissioner must make a "quasi-judicial" determination of ownership after examining the documents submitted. The Department will not issue a new certificate of title until it satisfies itself that the owner/applicant has good title. Since the Department suspended issuance of the title certificate when it learned of Bouton's fraud, the voidable title Bouton received was never perfected and therefore could not pass to a bona fide purchaser for value. It is by requiring perfected title to make a transfer successful that the UVCTA accomplishes its goal of making improperly obtained transfers more difficult. To interpret *UVCTA § 2113(c)* differently would be to extract the teeth of this legislation. If Bouton had received a valid Certificate of Title, he could have passed his perfected voidable title to a bona fide purchaser for value. Since Bouton never had a perfected title, he could not pass good title to Caruso (D). Caruso (D) argues that Suzuki (P) is equitably estopped from denying Caruso's (D) title because Suzuki (P) represented that Bouton properly received ownership of the motorcycle. However, equitable estoppel does not create rights that do not exist, but only precludes the denial of rights claimed to have arisen otherwise. Since Caruso (D) never got any legal title or right to the motorcycle, it has no claim to assert. A person who buys a motor vehicle from a seller who does not have a Certificate of Title does so at his own risk. Suzuki's (P) motion granted and Caruso's (D) motion denied.

Analysis:

This court reached its decision by giving effect to state law. While many states follow this uniform law, some do not. The important thing to note here is that although the *UCC*, in an effort to smooth commercial transactions, allows title to pass to bona fide purchasers despite certain types of wrongdoing by the seller, more specific state laws may not, and they will trump the *UCC*. When particularized state or federal statutes exist to address particular problems, they get to define what is necessary to take good title as a bona fide purchaser for value. In practice, therefore, if you represent the owner trying to get his property back, do your research! If some statute regulates the particular industry or type of transaction in your case, you may be able to save the day.

Chapter 10

As the title suggests, this chapter will address the issue of unauthorized possession of property. More specifically, it will address the issues that arise when a person takes unauthorized control of property that belongs to another, how and when the original owner is permitted to retrieve or retake the property, and what happens when a second unauthorized possessor takes the property from the first such possessor. It will also briefly address the issue of adverse possession. An example is instructive.

Imagine the following scenario: X owns an enormous tract of land—so large, in fact, that he cannot always watch all of it. The land is perfect for growing corn, and Y, who believes that he is leasing the land from the true owner (when in fact he is leasing it from a shyster), uses ten acres for a small corn crop of his own. After the corn is harvested and sitting in storage waiting to be shipped, Z, without authorization, takes the corn and sells it for a very good price. Y, upon discovering the unlawful conversion, sues Z for the value of the corn.

Who should win the lawsuit in the above hypothetical? Who has a stronger title to the logs: Y, the one who leased the property (though from the wrong person), grew and harvested the corn, and then lost control of it to a thief; or Z, the person who, without permission, took the corn that had been mistakenly grown on X's land? Do either of them even have a recognizable title? What if X got involved? Would his claim be the strongest of all? If so, why? What if Y has been openly growing corn on the property every year for 10 years? Will that change anything? Somebody has to win the lawsuit. Who will it be?

These are the types of questions and issues addressed in this chapter. Read on to find out the answers.

Chapter 10

NOTE: THE PURPOSE OF THIS OUTLINE IS TO ORGANIZE THE CASES SO THAT ONE CAN QUICKLY UNDERSTAND THE RELEVANCE OF EACH CASE TO THE COURSE. NO ATTEMPT IS MADE IN THIS OVERVIEW TO ADDRESS EVERY CONCEPT THAT MUST BE STUDIED. BE SURE TO READ THE ENTIRE CASEBOOK AND/OR OTHER MATERIALS TO GAIN A FULL UNDERSTANDING OF ALL CONCEPTS.

I. Possession by Non-Owner Third Persons as a Form of Ownership
  A. When two non-owners are competing against one another for control of an item of property, some courts hold that the one who first acquired possession has a right to retain that possession against the other. *Anderson v. Gouldberg.*
    1. This is true even if the property is wrongfully obtained (such as when it is obtained while trespassing), though there is dispute as to whether the rule applies to thieves.
    2. Under the rule mentioned above, the only person who has better title to the property than the possessing party is the true owner. *Anderson.*
  B. A handful of other courts have ruled differently, holding that in order to recover the value of personal property from a party who unlawfully converts it for his own benefit, a suing party must show both title to and possession or a present right of possession of the property. In other words, a non-owner will not be able to recover, even if she was the first to have possession of the property. *Russell v. Hill.*

II. Acquiring Title by Adverse Possession
  A. The doctrine of adverse possession allows a person who has long-term possession of real or personal property to gain a title to the property that is good against the true owner.
    1. To gain title by adverse possession (called limitation title), certain elements must be present.
    2. Specifically, to establish title to property by adverse possession, a person's possession must be continuous, actual, hostile, visible, and exclusive, and must continue for the duration of a period of time established by the statute of limitations. *O'Keeffe v. Snyder.*
  B. In the majority of cases, adverse possession is used to gain title to real property. The doctrine is occasionally used in cases involving chattels, and at least one court has held that title to intangible interests, such as the rights to a song, can also be acquired by adverse possession. *Gee v. CBS, Inc.*
  C. When the statute of limitations for an action for replevin of property has run, the original owner of the property cannot circumvent the statute by physically repossessing the converted or taken property. *Chapin v. Freeland.*
  D. With respect to cases involving the replevin of personal property (i.e., chattels), some courts have replaced the doctrine of adverse possession with the discovery rule.
    1. Pursuant to the discovery rule, a cause of action for replevin does not accrue until the injured party discovers, or by exercise of reasonable diligence and intelligence should have discovered, facts that form the basis of the cause of action (i.e., finds out that someone else has his or her property). *O'Keeffe.*

Anderson v. Gouldberg

(Trespasser) v. (Converter)
(1892) 51 Minn. 294, 53 N.W. 636

M E M O R Y   G R A P H I C

Instant Facts

A dispute arose when Gouldberg (D) took possession of logs cut by Anderson (P) while he was trespassing on an unknown third party's land.

Black Letter Rule

One who has acquired possession of property, by whatever means, has a right to retain that possession against all but the rightful owner.

Case Vocabulary

REPLEVIN: A court order authorizing the retaking of personal property that has been wrongfully appropriated by another.

Procedural Basis: Appeal to the Minnesota Supreme Court of an order denying Gouldberg's (D) motion for a new trial.

Facts: During the winter of 1889-1890, Anderson (P) cut ninety-three pine logs and took them to a mill to be processed. While the logs were at the mill, Gouldberg (D) took the logs, claiming that they were taken from land belonging to the Ann River Logging Company and that he was taking them at the company's direction. A jury determined that the logs were not cut on Gouldberg's (D) land, but that Anderson (P) obtained the logs by trespassing on an unknown third person's property. Because the court had charged the jury that if Anderson (P) got possession of the logs as a trespasser his title would be good against anyone but the real owner, the jury found in favor of Anderson (P). Gouldberg (D) then appealed a denial of a motion for a new trial.

Issue: Is bare possession of property, though wrongfully obtained, sufficient title to enable the possessing party to maintain replevin against another non-owner who takes it away?

Decision and Rationale: (Mitchell, J.) Yes. To maintain an action for replevin, a person's possession must have been lawful against the person who deprived him of the property at issue; and possession is good title against all but those who have better title. Gouldberg (D) argues that possession only raises a rebuttable presumption of title. That is true, but he overlooks the fact that one who takes property from another's possession can only rebut the presumption of title by showing a superior title in himself, or in some way connecting himself with one who has. One who has acquired possession of property, by whatever means, has a right to retain that possession against a wrongdoer who is a stranger to the property. Any other rule would lead to an endless series of unlawful seizures and reprisals in every case where property has left the possession of the rightful owner. Affirmed.

Analysis:

A common phrase in lay-legal lingo is "possession is 9/10 of the law." The present case, which teaches that he who has possession of an item has a property interest in that item that can only be trumped by the true owner, provides some support for that commonly-stated proposition. Perhaps more important, however, is the fact that the underlying principle of *Anderson* is a good starting point for a study of the law of adverse possession, one of the subjects of this chapter. The doctrine of adverse possession, in brief, teaches that if a non-owner's possession of real or personal property is of such a nature and of such a duration that the requirements of the doctrine are satisfied, that possession can effect a legal transfer of title that trumps even the claims of the real owner. Simply stated, then, possession of an item or a piece of real property has a great deal of legal significance, the level of which will be demonstrated in subsequent cases in this chapter.

AN ACTION FOR TROVER CAN ONLY SUCCEED IF THE PLAINTIFF HAS GOOD TITLE TO THE CONVERTED PROPERTY

Russell v. Hill

(Not Stated) v. (Not Stated)
(1899) 125 N.C. 470, 34 S.E. 640

M E M O R Y   G R A P H I C

Instant Facts

Russell (P) filed suit against Hill (D) after Hill (D) unlawfully converted and sold $686.84 worth of timber that Russell (P) believed belonged to him.

Black Letter Rule

In order to recover the value of personal property from a party who unlawfully converts it for his own benefit, a suing party must show both title to and possession or a present right of possession of the property.

Case Vocabulary

TROVER: A common law cause of action through which damages are sought for the wrongful conversion of personal property; the usual measure of damages in an action for trover is the value of the converted property.

Procedural Basis: Appeal to the North Carolina Supreme Court of a ruling in favor of a party who unlawfully converted $686.84 dollars worth of timber.

Facts: In 1887, the state of North Carolina awarded F.H. Busbee a grant for a tract of land in Swain county, which Busbee properly registered with the state. Shortly thereafter, Iowa McCoy received a similar grant which mistakenly included some of the land previously awarded to Busbee. McCoy had no knowledge of the Busbee grant except for the implied knowledge which arises under the law from Busbee's registration. McCoy later sold some timber found on the land covered by both grants to Russell (P), which Russell (P) then harvested and prepared for sale. While the logs were lying on a river bank, Hill (D), without any claim of right or title in them, took the logs and sold them for $686.84. Russell (P) sued Hill (D) to recover the value of the logs and the trial court ruled for Hill (D). Russell (P) appealed.

Issue: Can a party who has possession but not ownership of certain personal property recover damages from another who unlawfully converts the property?

Decision and Rationale: (Montgomery, J.) No. The present action is in the nature of the old action of trover, and, before the plaintiff could recover in such an action, he had to show title and either possession or the right of possession. In *Barwick v. Barwick*, which addressed the issue of an action in trover, the court stated: "[I]f it appears . . . that the plaintiff, although in possession, is not in fact the owner, the presumption of title inferred from the possession is rebutted, and it would be manifestly wrong to allow the plaintiff to recover the value of the property; for the real owner may forthwith bring trover against the defendant, and force him to pay the value the second time, and the fact that he paid it in a former suit would be no defense. The *Barwick* court continued: "[T]rover can never be maintained unless a satisfaction of the judgment will have the effect of vesting a good title in the defendant. . . . Accordingly, it is well settled that to maintain trover, the plaintiff must show title and the possession, or a present right of possession." Busbee was the legal owner of the land, and McCoy was not in possession of it. If she had been in adverse possession, the title to the logs would have passed to Russell (P), and he could have maintained this action, but she had no such possession. Affirmed.

Analysis:

The North Carolina Supreme Court's decision in *Russell v. Hill* provides an interesting comparison with the prior case, *Anderson v. Gouldberg*. In both cases, a non-owner entered a third-party's tract of land and harvested some timber found thereon, and in both cases the harvested lumber was subsequently converted by someone else not related to the owner of the tract from which the logs were taken. The facts of the cases, then, are similar. The decisions rendered by the courts, however, are very different in their results. In *Anderson*, the Minnesota court held that one who has acquired possession of property, by whatever means, has a right to retain that possession against all but the rightful owner, meaning Anderson, the trespasser who cut the timber, was permitted to recover from Gouldberg, who subsequently converted the logs for his own benefit. In *Russell*, however, the court ruled that Russell (P), who was similarly situated with Anderson, could not recover because he could not show good title to the timber, something that Anderson could not but was not required to do. Why the discrepancy? The author of the text suggests that the difference possibly lies in the nature of the actions filed in the two cases. *Anderson* was an action for replevin while *Russell* was in the nature of an action for trover (or at least that is how the actions were viewed by the respective courts). The difference between the two causes of action, the author explains, is that replevin allows a party to take back or recover possession of the converted property while trover allows for the recovery of the value of the property as if the converter had purchased it from the original owner. The more important difference between the two causes of action has to do with title to the converted property; to succeed in an action for trover, the party bringing the action must be able to show good title to the converted property while a party bringing an action for replevin is not subject to such a requirement, but, as *Anderson* states, mere possession is enough so long as the converter is not the original owner of the property. Does this distinction make sense? Which case provides the better result? On a different note, the *Russell* court mentions that if Iowa McCoy had been in adverse possession of the land, Russell (P) would have succeeded; this is true because if McCoy had been in adverse possession of the land, she would have had good title to the timber (adverse possession gives good title) and that good title would have been passed on to Russell (P) at the time the logs were cut. Thus, the result of the action for trover would have been vastly different.

Chapin v. Freeland

(Not Stated) v. (Not Stated)

(1886) 142 Mass. 383, 8 N.E. 128, 56 Am.Rep. 701

M E M O R Y   G R A P H I C

Instant Facts

A lawsuit arose when the purported owner of a counter entered Chapin's (P) business, which was where the counter was located, and took it back without notice or permission.

Black Letter Rule

When the statute of limitations for an action for replevin of property has run, the original owner of the property cannot circumvent the statute by physically repossessing the converted or taken property.

Case Vocabulary

BILL OF EXCEPTIONS: A formal statement filed with an appellate court which lists a party's objections and exceptions taken during a trial and the basis for those objections and exceptions; the Federal Rules of Civil Procedure have replaced the use of bills of exceptions with direct appeals.

Procedural Basis: Appeal to the Supreme Judicial Court of Massachusetts (the state's highest court) of a ruling in favor of Freeland (D) in an action for replevin.

Facts: In 1867, Warner built a shop which included two counters that belonged to Freeland (D). In January of 1871, Warner mortgaged the premises to DeWitt, who later died. In April of 1879, DeWitt's executors foreclosed and sold the property to Chapin (P). In 1881, Freeland (D) took the counters from Chapin's (P) possession, and an action for replevin was filed. The trial court ruled for Freeland (D) and an appeal ensued.

Issue: When the statute of limitations for an action for replevin of property has run, can the original owner of the property circumvent the effect of the statute by physically repossessing the property?

Decision and Rationale: (Holmes, J.) No. It appears as if the trial court assumed that although the statute of limitations would have run in favor of Warner or DeWitt before the transfer of the property to Chapin (P), Freeland (D) could nevertheless lawfully self-repossess the property if she so desired. This is not the law. If a person cannot retake possession of an item by way of an action for replevin, he cannot take the item with his own hand. The principle that we lay down today is a necessary consequence of the enactment of the statute of limitations. As we understand the statutory period to have run before Chapin (P) acquired the counters, it is unnecessary to consider what would have happened if the timing and facts were different. A buyer who purchases an item from a seller against whom the remedy is already barred is entitled to stand in as good a position as the seller. Reversed.

Dissent: (Field, J.) The statute of limitations precludes the bringing of actions of replevin more than six years after the action accrues, but there is no statute or law that prohibits the owner of personal chattels from peaceably taking possession of them wherever he may find them. A debt barred by the statute of limitations is not extinguished; the statute only bars the remedy by action within the jurisdiction where the debtor resides. There is nothing in the statute which suggests any distinction between actions to recover chattels and actions to recover debts. Nor is their any case law in our jurisdiction, or in that of the majority of the United States or England, which holds that possession of chattels for the statutory period of limitations for personal actions creates a title.

Analysis:

In terms of the unauthorized possession of property—the subject of this chapter—the court's decision in *Chapin v. Freeland* teaches one important principle: physical repossession of property cannot be used to circumvent the effect of the statute of limitations. For example, if X takes Y's television set without Y's permission and keeps it for the duration of the limitations period for replevin actions, and Y, who knows about it, chooses to do nothing to get his television back, he cannot enter X's home after the statute has run and take the set back. When the limitations period runs, Y no longer has any legal right to take the television back and any repossession of it will be a theft. The same is true of Freeland's (D) counters in the present case. Chapin (P) gained ownership of and title to the counters when he purchased them from someone who had possessed them for the duration of the limitations period, and therefore any claim of right that Freeland (D) might have had to the counters was extinguished. The dissent disagrees with this outcome, and would hold that the running of the statute of limitations, while ending the right to use the courts to retake property, does not end the right to "peaceably" take the property from the converting party. Is that a good view? Won't it encourage too much physical repossession not supported by the law? Obviously the dissent doesn't think so, but that would have to be a concern. Allowing and/or encouraging people to circumvent the court system and take matters into their own hands with respect to the repossession of property can be a dangerous proposition—one which the law should (and the majority opinion does) seek to avoid.

O'Keeffe v. Snyder

(Artist) v. (Person in Possession of Art)

(1980) 83 N.J. 478, 416 A.2d 862

M E M O R Y   G R A P H I C

 Instant Facts

A lawsuit arose when three paintings, allegedly stolen from the artist thirty years prior, were discovered in the possession of an art collector who refused to give them up.

Black Letter Rule

In order to avoid a harsh application of the statute of limitations, a cause of action for replevin does not accrue until the injured party discovers, or by exercise of reasonable diligence and intelligence should have discovered, facts that form the basis of the cause of action.

Case Vocabulary

ACCRUAL OF A CAUSE OF ACTION: To arise or become a viable and enforceable cause of action.

ADVERSE POSSESSION: A way of obtaining good title to real or personal property by possessing the property in a certain manner (continuous, exclusive, hostile, open, and notorious possession) for a fixed period of time.

BONA FIDE PURCHASER: A person who buys something for value without notice that another person has a legitimate claim to the property and/or that the seller's title is defective.

DISCOVERY RULE: A rule of law under which a cause of action for replevin does not accrue until the injured party discovers, or by exercise of reasonable diligence and intelligence should have discovered, facts which form the basis of the cause of action.

EJECTMENT: A cause of action through which a rightful owner of property excludes a wrongful possessor from her property.

IMPLEADER: The process of brining a third party into an existing lawsuit, usually at the request of the defendant.

PROVENANCE: An item's history of ownership.

TACKING: The accumulation of consecutive periods of possession by parties in privity to each other.

THIRD-PARTY DEFENDANT: A party brought into an existing lawsuit at the request of the original defendant.

Procedural Basis: Appeal to the New Jersey Supreme Court of an Appellate Division decision granting summary judgment in favor of a painter who sought the return of some paintings by way of an action for replevin.

Facts: In March of 1976, Georgia O'Keeffe (P) filed suit against Barry Snyder (D) seeking to acquire three paintings that she had painted. The parties disagreed with respect to the facts of the case. According to O'Keeffe (P), the paintings were in her possession from the time that she painted them until 1946, when they were stolen from a gallery where they were on display. The paintings were uninsured and the theft was not reported until 1972, when O'Keeffe (P) authorized the reporting of the theft to the Art Dealers Association of America, Inc. (ADAA), which maintained a registry of stolen paintings. In September of 1975, O'Keeffe (P) learned that the paintings were on display in a New York gallery, and on February 11, 1976, she further discovered that Ulrich A. Frank (D) had sold the paintings to Barry Snyder (D) and the Princeton Gallery of Fine Art the prior year for $35,000. The defendants, Snyder (D) and Frank (D), offered a slightly different view of the facts. According to Frank (D), the paintings were in his family's possession from as early as 1941, a date prior to their alleged theft. Frank (D) did not know how his father obtained the paintings, but did claim a familial relationship to O'Keeffe's (P) deceased husband. According to Frank (D), his father gave him the paintings in 1965, and he later sold them to Snyder (D). The provenance of the paintings being in dispute, O'Keeffe (P) demanded the return of the paintings. When Snyder (D) refused, she initiated an action for replevin against him. Snyder (D) added Frank (D) to the lawsuit as a third-party defendant by way of impleader, and the case went in front of the court. In defense of his ownership, Snyder (D) asserted that he was a purchaser for value, that he had title to the paintings by adverse possession, and that O'Keeffe's (P) action was barred by the statute of limitations. The trial court granted summary judgment for Snyder (D) on the ground that the action was barred by the statute of limitations because it had not been commenced within six years of the theft. The Appellate Division reversed, with the majority concluding that the paintings were stolen, and that the defenses of the expiration of the statute of limitations and title by adverse possession were identical and neither had been satisfactorily proven. One dissenting judge argued that the statute of limitations did not begin to run until the discovery of the paintings' whereabouts and that the case should be remanded to decide factual issues in that respect. The case was then appealed to the New Jersey Supreme Court.

Issue: Is application of the doctrine of adverse possession the most appropriate way to determine the outcome of an action for replevin of a work of art?

Decision and Rationale: (Pollock, J.) No. On the limited record before us, we cannot determine who has title to the paintings; that determination will be made at trial. Nonetheless, it may aid the trial court if we resolve questions of law that may become relevant at trial. The critical legal question on appeal is when did O'Keeffe's (P) cause of action accrue, as the statute of limitations provides that an action for replevin of chattels must be commenced within six years after the accrual of the cause of action. A statute of limitations bars a cause of action after the statutory period has ended. To avoid the harsh results that might arise from a mechanical application of the statute, the courts have developed a concept known as the discovery rule, which provides that, in an appropriate case, a cause of action will not accrue until the injured party discovers, or by exercise of reasonable diligence and intelligence should have discovered, facts which form the basis of the cause of action. Today we conclude that the discovery rule applies to an action for replevin of a painting. Thus, O'Keeffe's (P) cause of action accrued when she first knew, or reasonably should have known through the exercise of due diligence, of the cause of action, including the identity of the possessor of the paintings. Regarding adverse possession, the acquisition of title to real and personal property by adverse possession is based on the expiration of a statute of limitations. To establish title to chattels by adverse possession, the possession must be hostile, actual, visible, exclusive, and continuous. There is an inherent problem with works of art that raises questions whether their possession has been open, visible, and notorious—works of art are readily moved and easily concealed. O'Keeffe (P) argues that nothing short of public display should be sufficient to alert the true owner and start the statute running. Although there is merit in that contention from the perspective of the original owner, it imposes a heavy burden on the purchasers of paintings who wish to enjoy them in the privacy of their homes. With respect to the application of adverse possession to the situation at hand, the divergent conclusions of the lower courts suggests that the doctrine no longer provides a reasonable means of resolving this kind of dispute. The record provides a brief glimpse into the world of art sales where paintings worth vast sums of money are sometimes bought without inquiry about their provenance. There does not appear to be a reasonably available method for an owner of art to record the ownership or theft of paintings or for a purchaser to ascertain the painting's provenance. Although we cannot mandate the initiation of a registration system, we can develop a rule for the commencement and running of the statute of limitations that is more responsive to the needs of the art world than the doctrine of adverse possession. The introduction of equitable considerations through the discovery rule provides a more satisfactory response than does the use of adverse possession. The discovery rule shifts the emphasis from whether the possessor has met the tests of adverse possession to whether the owner has acted with due diligence in pursuing his property. The rule permits an artist who uses reasonable efforts to report, investigate, and recover a painting to preserve the rights of title and possession. Properly interpreted, the discovery rule becomes a vehicle for transporting equitable considerations into the statute of limitations for replevin. If a chattel is concealed from the true owner, fairness compels tolling the statute during the period of concealment. The discovery rule is also consistent with the law of replevin. In an action for replevin, the period of limitations ordinarily will run against the owner of lost or stolen property from the time of the wrongful taking, absent fraud or concealment. Where the chattel is fraudulently concealed, the general rule is that the statute is tolled. A bona fide purchaser who purchases a painting entrusted to an art dealer in the ordinary course of business should be able to acquire good title against the true owner. Under the U.C.C., entrusting possession of goods to a merchant who deals in that kind of goods gives the merchant the power to transfer all the rights of the entruster to a buyer in the ordinary course of business. The interplay between the statute of limitations as modified by the discovery rule and the U.C.C. should encourage good faith purchases from legitimate art dealers and discourage trafficking in stolen art without frustrating an artist's ability to recover stolen works. In short, the discovery rule will fulfill the purposes of a statute of limitations and accord greater protection to the innocent owner of personal property whose goods are lost or stolen. Before the expiration of the statute, the possessor has both the chattel and the right to keep it except as against the true owner. The only imperfection in the possessor's right to retain the chattel is the original owner's right to repossess it. Once that imperfection is removed, the possessor should have good title for all purposes; the expiration of the six-year period should vest title as effectively under the discovery rule as under the doctrine of adverse possession. To summarize, the operative fact that divests the original owner of title to either personal or real property is the expiration of the period of limitations. Our adoption of the discovery rule does not change that principle. We next consider the effect of transfers of a chattel from one possessor to another during the period of limitations under the discovery rule. The majority and better view is to permit tacking. Treating subsequent transfers as separate acts of conversion could lead to absurd results. It is more sensible to recognize that on expiration of the period of limitations, title passes from the former owner by operation of the statute. Needless uncertainty would result from starting the statute running anew merely because of a subsequent transfer. Reversed.

Analysis:

Although it discounted the principle and chose not to apply it in this case, the O'Keeffe court provides the reader with an introduction to one of the more important legal doctrines that arises in cases involving the unauthorized possession of property—the doctrine of adverse possession. Under the doctrine of adverse possession, a person who possesses a piece of property in a certain manner for a specified period of time can acquire good title to the property, thereby taking title away from the true owner. As the New Jersey Supreme Court wrote in the present case, to establish title to property by adverse possession, a person's possession must be continuous, actual, hostile, visible, and exclusive, and must continue for the duration of a period of time established by the statute of limitations. Continuous possession is possession that is more than sporadic, though not necessarily constant, depending on the circumstances. For example, a person who builds a structure and resides on another person's property for the entirety of the statutory period has continuous possession. So too does a person who lives on another's property for nine months of the year, leaving each winter when the snow is too deep to allow a person to come and go as one would when living at a certain location. Actual possession is just that, actual possession of the property. A person cannot simply claim that property belongs to her, but she must actually possess it. For example, a person who regularly maintains that a certain piece of property is his but never actually sets foot on the property is not in actual possession of the property. On the other hand, a person who houses and grazes his cattle on a parcel of land as if it belonged to him is in actual possession of the property. Hostile possession is possession that is actually adverse to the ownership of the true owner; it is possession taken without permission. Thus, if a person is present on the land with the blessings of the true owner, there is no hostile possession. Similarly, if a person is trying to gain title to a piece of land by adverse possession, the true owner can thwart those plans by simply granting the person permission to stay; as soon as the true owner says that the adverse possessor has her permission to possess the land, the person's chance to gain title by adverse possession ends. Visible possession, often referred to as open and notorious possession, is possession that is visible to the true owner if he or she takes the time to look. For example, a person cannot gain title to a piece of property by adverse possession if she intentionally tries to hide herself such that the true owner will not know that she is there. Thus, a person who wants to gain title to a tract of land by adverse possession cannot live in a small structure obscured by bushes and trees in such a way that the true owner could regularly return to the property and not see that someone else is living there. The possession must be visible to the true owner who checks on the land. This is not to say that the owner is required to check on the land for title to pass; an owner who simply chooses not to ever check on his land cannot use that lack of knowledge as a defense to a claim of adverse possession. Along these same lines, the adverse possessor has no duty to notify the true owner of her possession of the property. And finally, possession must be exclusive, meaning the adverse possessor must act as a true owner and exclude all those who do not have his or her permission to enter the land. For example, a person who regularly allows others to possess part of the land without her permission and does not eject them when they do will not be able to claim exclusive possession. On the other hand, the fact that she may have regular guests come and stay with her will not prevent a claim under the doctrine. There are a handful of other important concepts that apply to the doctrine of adverse possession. First, the hostile, actual, visible, exclusive, and continuous possession must continue uninterrupted for the duration of the limitations period as set forth in the statute of limitations for an ejectment action. Thus, if the statute of limitations is ten years and the true owner ejects the wrongful possessor on the anniversary of the ninth year, the wrongful possessor cannot return to the land and claim title by adverse possession after just one year because his possession was interrupted by the actions of the true owner. A second concept that often arises in cases of adverse possession is that of tacking, which is defined as the accumulation of consecutive periods of possession by parties in privity to one another. Tacking occurs when one party who has been in hostile, actual, visible, exclusive, and continuous possession of a piece of land transfers his possession to another person. Instead of causing the other person to have to start counting from the beginning of the limitations period, the principle of tacking allows the new possessor to begin her time at the time the previous possessor began his possession. Finally, the doctrine of adverse possession applies to chattels the same way that it applies to land, though, as this court did, many jurisdictions have, in the context of chattels, abandoned adverse possession in exchange for the discovery rule. Moving to a slightly different topic, in addressing the reasoning behind the abandonment of the common law doctrine of adverse possession in exchange for the discovery rule, the basics of which are explained in the opinion, the New Jersey Supreme Court cites issues of equity and fairness. Indeed, in more than one place in the opinion, Justice Pollock writes that the implementation of the discovery rule serves to mitigate the harsh and unjust results that may occur from a strict application of the doctrine of adverse possession. (In the present case, that harsh result is O'Keeffe's (P) likely inability to make any legitimate claim to her painting.) It can be argued, however, that the implementation of the discovery rule also makes it easier for the court to decide cases such as this one. At one point in the opinion, Justice Pollock notes that "there is an inherent problem with many kinds of personal property that will raise questions whether their possession has been open, visible, and notorious." He later adds that "[t]he problem is even more acute with works of art." By implementing the discovery rule, New Jersey's highest court is able to avoid deciding whether, in this case, Frank's (D) possession and almost exclusively in-home display of the paintings met the statutory requirements for adverse possession. This would arguably be a difficult call for the court to make, as Frank (D) acted as the owner of the paintings, displayed them publicly (though anonymously) on at least one occasion, and really did nothing to hide the fact that he had them.

Chapter 11

Imagine the following fact scenario: X, a well-known carpenter and piano-maker, enters a piece of property that he believes is his and cuts down a number of trees. He then harvests the lumber and uses it two build two things: (1) a modest home for his family which he builds on the spot where he cut the wood, and (2) an exquisite grand piano which he was commissioned to build for the local symphony. Everything goes well until the projects are done and X is ready to move into his new home, when, out of the blue, Y appears and stakes claim to X's home and the tract of land that it is on. After some research, X discovers that he harvested wood from and built his home on the wrong tract of land, and that Y is in fact the owner of the land.

A number of issues arise from this not-so-hypothetical situation. X's home and the symphony's piano are built from wood taken from Y's land without Y's permission. What does X owe to Y with respect to the piano? Should X have to pay Y the value of the wood, or should Y be able to lay claim to the piano itself, since it is built with his wood? What about the house? Should X be permitted to live there? If not, should Y have to pay something to X to compensate for the house and the labor? If yes, is it fair to require him to do so?

The answers to these questions, as well as fact scenarios very similar to that used above, are found in this chapter, which addresses the doctrine of title by accession.

Chapter 11

NOTE: THE PURPOSE OF THIS OUTLINE IS TO ORGANIZE THE CASES SO THAT ONE CAN QUICKLY UNDERSTAND THE RELEVANCE OF EACH CASE TO THE COURSE. NO ATTEMPT IS MADE IN THIS OVERVIEW TO ADDRESS EVERY CONCEPT THAT MUST BE STUDIED. BE SURE TO READ THE ENTIRE CASEBOOK AND/OR OTHER MATERIALS TO GAIN A FULL UNDERSTANDING OF ALL CONCEPTS.

I. The Doctrine of Title by Accession
   A. The doctrine of title by accession holds that a person who either converts another's personal property or performs labor on another person's real property which benefits the owner can gain title to the converted property if certain requirements are met.
   B. The doctrine applies where the trespasser has, in good faith, expended his own labor on the property and the circumstances are such that it would be grossly unjust to permit the other party to receive the full benefit of that labor with nothing being paid to the laborer. *Wetherbee v. Green*.

   1. In determining whether the doctrine applies, courts will also consider whether the nature of the converted property is different enough from that of the original property that the original property cannot simply be retaken.
   C. When it would not be grossly unjust to permit the other party to receive the full benefit of the labor, such as when there is no great disparity in value between the pre-conversion and post-conversion property, the doctrine of accession does not apply. *Isle Royal Mining Co. v. Hertin*.

II. Improvements Built Upon Another's Land
   A. Where an occupant has, in good faith, made improvements to real property prior to eviction (such as the building of a building on the land), he is permitted to sue in equity for the value of those improvements. *Hardy v. Burroughs*.

Wetherbee v. Green

(Tree Harvester) v. (Landowner)
(1871) 22 Mich. 311, 7 Am.Rep. 653

M E M O R Y   G R A P H I C

Instant Facts

Green (P) sued Wetherbee (D) when he discovered that Wetherbee (D) was making a profit harvesting timber from his land.

Black Letter Rule

When nature of converted property is changed enough that it becomes a different species of property, and the conversion is not an intentional wrong, the appropriating party is only required to make satisfaction to the former owner for the materials converted and does not have to turn over the property.

Case Vocabulary

CONVERSION: A wrongful appropriation or possession of another person's tangible personal property, which appropriation or possession can be the basis for a lawsuit under tort law.

DEFENDANTS IN ERROR: An archaic term for the party who, in a case that has been appealed, prevailed in the lower court.

DOCTRINE OF TITLE BY ACCESSION: A principle of law under which a person who converts another's property can gain title to the converted property; the doctrine applies where the trespasser has, in good faith, expended his own labor upon the property under circumstances that would make it grossly unjust to permit the other party to receive the benefit of that labor.

REPLEVIN (REPLEVIED): A court order authorizing the retaking of personal property that has been wrongfully appropriated by another.

Procedural Basis: Appeal to the Supreme Court of Michigan of a judgment in favor of the plaintiff landowner in a lawsuit over another party's conversion of trees on the plaintiff's land.

Facts: Wetherbee (D), who was under the impression that he had permission to do so, harvested a number of trees from Green's (P) land and, by his own labor, used the wood to make hoops. Upon discovering what Wetherbee (D) had done, Green (P) sued to gain ownership of the hoops. Wetherbee (D) objected to the lawsuit on the ground that the standing timber was worth only $25 while the hoops that he had made were worth $700. The trial court rejected Wetherbee's (D) assignment of value and ruled in favor of Green (P). Wetherbee (D) appealed.

Issue: Can a party who in good faith reliance upon a supposed right takes another's property and improves it ever acquire an interest in the improved property such that the owner cannot reclaim it in its improved condition?

Decision and Rationale: (Cooley, J.) Yes. As a general rule, one whose property has been appropriated by another without authority has a right to follow and recover it; and if, in the meantime, it has been increased in value by the addition of labor or money, the owner may still reclaim it. There must, however, be some limit to the right to follow and reclaim materials which have undergone a process of manufacture. According to Justice Blackstone, that limit is reached when the converted property is changed into a different species of property. In those instances, if the conversion is made in good faith and is not an intentional wrong, the party appropriating the property is only required to make satisfaction to the former owner for the materials converted, and not to turn over the newly-converted property. In this case, the important question appears to be whether the standing trees, when cut and manufactured into hoops, are to be regarded as so far changed in character that their identity has been destroyed. It is difficult to discover any test which can be applied to all cases involving a change in the nature of goods. Some cases have given the former owner the right to reclaim converted property when it can be identified as being his, but this is a very unsatisfactory test which, in many cases, would defeat the purpose of the law. For example, it would not be appropriate to allow a former owner to take a piece of wood that has been used to build a church organ; no one would defend a rule of law which, because the identity could be determined, would permit the owner of the wood to appropriate or destroy such a musical instrument a hundred times the value of the original materials. Thus, when the right to the improved article is the point in issue, the question of how much the property or labor of each has contributed to make it what it is must always be of first importance. Additionally, any test applied in the adjustment of questions of title to chattels by accession must take into account the circumstance of relative values. When we bear in mind that what the law seeks to do in good faith cases of accession is the accomplishment of substantial equity, we shall readily perceive that the fact of the value of the materials having been increased a hundred fold is more important in the adjustment than any chemical change or mechanical transformation. There may be complete changes with so little improvement in value that there could be no hardship in giving up the improved article; but in the present case, where Wetherbee's (D) labor appears to have given the timber nearly all of its present value, equity requires a change in title. The lower court erred in rejecting the proffered testimony regarding Wetherbee's (D) belief that he had authority to use the timber to make hoops, and if he can make such a showing, he is entitled to have the jury instructed that the title to the timber was changed by a substantial change of identity and that Green's (P) remedy is an action to recover damages for unintentional trespass. Reversed.

Analysis:

The case of *Wetherbee v. Green* introduces the doctrine of title by accession, which doctrine holds that a trespasser who has in good faith expended his own labor upon converted property can gain title to the converted property when the circumstances are such that it would be grossly unjust to permit the true owner to receive the full benefit of that labor. In this case, the court determined that the doctrine applied for two reasons: (1) the nature of the converted property was different enough from that of the original property that the original timber could not simply be retaken; and (2) there was such a great disparity in value between the standing timber and the hoops that Wetherbee (D) had made (the pre-conversion and post-conversion property) that it would have been unfair to allow Green (P) to take the hoops in payment for his lost timber. With regard to the second reason listed above, Justice Cooley wrote: "[To] inflict upon a person who has taken the property of another, a penalty equal to twenty or thirty times its value, and to compensate the owner in a proportion equally enormous, is so opposed to all legal idea of justice and right and to the rules which regulate the recovery of damages generally, that if permitted by the law at all, it must stand out as an anomaly and must rest upon peculiar reasons." In other words, the court determined that it would be inappropriate to give Green (P) $700 worth of hoops as repayment for his loss of $25 worth of timber. As this case demonstrates, the doctrine of title by accession is one of fairness—it applies when equity and principles of fairness dictate that it should apply. In describing the purpose of the doctrine, the *Wetherbee* court wrote: "[The doctrine's] purpose is not to establish any arbitrary distinctions . . . but to adjust the redress afforded to the one party and the penalty inflicted upon the other, as near as circumstances will permit, to the rules of substantial justice." To put it another way, the purpose is to achieve an appropriate degree of fairness. And in describing the principles underlying the doctrine, the *Wetherbee* court further focused on the idea of fairness when it wrote: "In the redress of private injuries the law aims not so much to punish the wrong-doer as to compensate the sufferer for his injuries; and the cases in which it goes farther and inflicts punitory or vindictive penalties are those in which the wrong-doer has committed the wrong recklessly, willfully, or maliciously." In short, in situations involving the conversion and subsequent change in the nature of property, one should look to whether the value of the property was increased by the conversion in determining the appropriate remedy for the unlawful conversion.

Isle Royal Mining Co. v. Hertin

(Landowner) v. (Tree Harvester)
(1877) 37 Mich. 332, 26 Am.Rep. 520

M E M O R Y   G R A P H I C

Instant Facts

A tree harvester filed suit against a land owner when the land owner took control of a quantity of wood mistakenly harvested from his land.

Black Letter Rule

When a person mistakenly performs labor on another person's property and that other person receives a benefit from that mistake, the laborer is not entitled to compensation for the benefit received unless the doctrine of accession is found to apply.

Case Vocabulary

REMUNERATION: Payment.

Procedural Basis: Appeal to the Supreme Court of Michigan of a lawsuit involving the mistaken conversion and subsequent retaking of trees harvested from the defendant's property.

Facts: During the winter of 1873-74, Hertin (P), a landowner, mistakenly left his land and entered onto a tract belonging to the Isle Royal Mining Co. (D). While on Isle Royal's (D) land, Hertin (P) cut a quantity of cord wood which he eventually piled on the bank of a nearby lake. During the spring of 1874, the mining company took possession of the wood and used it. Shortly thereafter Hertin (P) filed suit against Isle Royal (D) seeking compensation for his labor, which he claimed was $1.87½ per cord. At trial, the judge instructed the jury that if Hertin (P) had cut the wood by mistake and without any willful negligence or wrong, he was to prevail. The jury, presumably relying on this instruction, found in favor of Hertin (P), and Royal Isle (D) appealed.

Issue: When a person mistakenly performs labor on another's property and the owner receives a benefit from that mistake, is the laborer entitled to compensation for the benefit received?.

Decision and Rationale: (Cooley, C.J.) No. At common law, a person who enters another's land on an assumption of ownership can be held responsible as a trespasser, even if he does so in good faith and under an honest mistake as to his rights. If a person can be ordered to pay damages for a good faith trespass, then it seems unlikely that he can gain any title or right to the property through his unlawful encroachment upon the owner's rights. There is one exception to this rule that applies where the trespasser has, in good faith, expended his own labor upon the land under circumstances which would render it grossly unjust to permit the other party to receive the benefit of such labor. This exception is known as the doctrine of title by accession, and though it has not been claimed that the present case falls within the purview of the doctrine, Hertin (P) insists that this case is within its equity, and that there would be no departure from settled principles of law in giving Isle Royal (D) the benefit of it. There is, however, no great disparity in value between the standing trees and the cord wood in this case as was found to exist in *Wetherbee v. Green* [holding that when the nature of converted property is changed enough that it becomes a different species of property, and the conversion is not an intentional wrong, the appropriating party is only required to make satisfaction to the former owner for the materials converted and does not have to turn over the property]. The trees are not only susceptible of being traced and identified in the wood, but the difference in value between the two is not so great but that it is conceivable that the owner may have preferred the trees standing to the wood cut. We cannot assume that a man prefers his trees cut into cord wood rather than left standing, and if his right to leave them uncut is interfered with even by mistake, it is just that the consequences fall upon the person committing the mistake. Nothing could more encourage carelessness than the acceptance of the principle that one who, by mistake, performs labor on the property of another should lose nothing by his error, but should have a claim against the owner for remuneration. It is highly probable that Isle Royal (D) would suffer no hardship if compelled to pay Hertin (P) for his labor, but a general principle is tested not by its operation in a individual case, but by its general workings. Reversed.

Analysis:

At this point in the text, *Isle Royal Mining Co. v. Hertin* provides an important comparison with the prior case, *Wetherbee v. Green*, which comparison helps to clarify when the doctrine of title by accession applies and when it does not. As stated in the analysis portion of that case's brief, the *Wetherbee* court determined that the doctrine of title by accession applied to the dispute between Wetherbee and Green for two reasons: (1) the nature of the converted property was different enough from that of the original property that the original timber could not simply be retaken; and (2) there was such a great disparity in value between the pre-conversion and post-conversion property that it would have been unfair to allow Green to take the hoops in payment for his lost timber. In this case, written by the same Justice Cooley (now Chief Justice of the Michigan Supreme Court), the court does not address the degree of change in the property, but focuses solely on the disparity or lack of disparity in value between the standing timber and the cord wood produced by Hertin's (P) labor. Specifically, the court determines that there is "no such disparity in value between the standing trees and the cord wood . . . as was found to exist between the trees and the hoops in *Wetherbee*," and, as such, the doctrine of title by accession does not apply in this case. In short, the court's holding demonstrates the need for a disparity in value between pre-conversion and post-conversion property if the doctrine of title by accession is to apply—a disparity which is present in *Wetherbee* and not present here.

Hardy v. Burroughs

(Home Builder) v. (Landowner)
(1930) 251 Mich. 578, 232 N.W. 200

M E M O R Y   G R A P H I C

Instant Facts

A lawsuit arose when a party mistakenly built a home on another person's property and the landowner both refused to pay for the construction and to sell the property to the builder.

Black Letter Rule

Where an occupant has, in good faith, made improvements to property prior to eviction, he is permitted to sue in equity for the value of those improvements.

Procedural Basis: Appeal to the Michigan Supreme Court of a lower court's denial of the defendants' motion to dismiss.

Facts: Hardy (P) mistakenly built a home on a tract of land that belonged to Burroughs (D). Upon discovery of the mistake, Burroughs (D), who permitted another party to occupy the house, refused to pay Hardy (P) for the cost of construction ($1,250). Hardy (P) filed suit seeking reimbursement for his expenses.

Issue: When a person has made good faith improvements to property prior to being evicted therefrom, is she permitted to sue in equity for the value of the improvements that she made?

Decision and Rationale: (Clark, J.) Yes. Hardy (P) does not contend that there can be recovery at law, but seeks recovery in equity. The issue is whether, absent any allegations of fraud or evidence that Burroughs (D) knew of Hardy's (P) mistake at the time of construction and did nothing about it, Hardy (P) can legally sustain the suit that has been filed. The authorities are divided. According to some, an occupant's right in equity to compensation for improvements made prior to eviction applies only when he is a defendant in a lawsuit, and therefore does not give him the right to reimbursement by way of a direct suit against the owner unless the owner has engaged in some type of fraud. According to others, however, where an occupant has, in good faith, made improvements to property prior to eviction, he is permitted to sue in equity for the value of the improvements regardless of whether there are allegations of fraud or misconduct by the owner. The better reasoning supports Hardy's (P) lawsuit. It is not equitable that Burroughs (D) should profit by Hardy's (P) innocent mistake, or that Burroughs (D) should take all while Hardy (P) gets nothing. The fact that Burroughs (D) did not initiate the lawsuit or otherwise seek relief should not bar Hardy's (P) right to relief in equity. If Hardy (P) can make a case for equitable relief, Burroughs (D) should either pay Hardy (P) the fair value of the improvements or give Hardy (P) ownership of the lot upon receipt of its fair value. Affirmed.

Analysis:

This particular case presents some of the interesting policy issues that have to be weighed in cases arguably involving the doctrine of title by accession. On the one hand is the right of a landowner to choose what is done with his or her land. In this case, Burroughs' (D) right to decide what structures were to be built on his land was taken away from him by the court's decision. As you will recall, Burroughs (D) was ordered either to pay for the value of the house or sell the land to Hardy (P). But what if Burroughs (D) did not have enough money to pay for the entire house? That would leave him no choice but to sell the land to make good on the debt the court says was owed for the construction of the house that he did not ask to be built. Is it appropriate for the court to order, in such a case, the owner to sell his land to another person? What if the land had some sort of sentimental value that could not be recouped by means or a sale price? Is it fair, in that situation, to order the sale of the land? At least one judge didn't think so. In *Somerville v. Jacobs*, a West Virginia case with similar facts, Judge Caplan, in dissent, wrote: "This is nothing less than condemnation of private property by private parties for private use. . . . It clearly is the accepted law that as between two parties in the circumstances of this case he who made the mistake must suffer the hardship rather than he who was without fault." Is that too harsh (as a dissenter he is in the minority), or is Judge Caplan correct? On the other hand, would it be fair to allow Burroughs (D) to keep the home that Hardy (P) had built without some sort of remuneration to Hardy (P)? $1,250 was a pretty hefty sum in 1930 (and, for some of us, still is today), the year when this case was adjudicated. Would it really be appropriate to give Hardy (P) nothing because of a simple mistake? Chief Justice Cooley didn't think so, and other courts have agreed. These are difficult cases because someone is going to be forced to do something that they did not want to do because of one party's mistake, and either way someone is going to be treated at least a little bit unfairly.

Perspective
Donative Transfers

Chapter 12

"Donative transfer" just means "gift," but the law of gifts is rather complicated.

One reason is that gifts are viewed differently from most other transfers, and sometimes not enforced as readily by courts. As you know, generally, gifts are not enforceable as contracts, because there is no consideration exchanged for the gift. Similarly, property law tends to view gifts as windfalls, and courts have fewer qualms about denying beneficiaries their expected gifts.

Another reason is that gifts are often spontaneous, undocumented transfers. Unfortunately, they can be exceedingly hard to prove afterwards, especially if the donor dies. In such cases, courts are often hesitant to enforce alleged gifts without extensive proof, for the same reason they will not accept oral wills: they fear that it is too easy for plaintiffs to claim the deceased gave them generous gifts, when the departed are no longer around to corroborate their claims. Similarly, deathbed gifts by dying people represent a situation akin to wills, so courts must demand at least some documentation to avoid undermining the Statute of Wills' writing requirement.

A final reason why enforcing gifts is complicated is that some gifts are conditional. For example, what if I promise to give you a painting, but only on condition that I get to hang onto it until I die? Is that a gift, or does it essentially trespass into the realm of wills? Or, take another example: if you give/get a wedding ring, what happens if the wedding gets called off? Is the gift of the ring conditional on the marriage happening?

These are some issues involving gifts which you will study in this chapter. While the rules are complex, knowing them is important, because gifts are rather common in our society. Think of all the gifts you have made to friends, family, loves, etc. However, if made improperly, your generous gifts may cause the intended beneficiary to receive a troublesome lawsuit instead, and deny him/her the benefit of your kindness. Knowing the law of gifts will help you avoid such unwanted problems, for you and your clients alike.

Chapter 12

NOTE: THE PURPOSE OF THIS OUTLINE IS TO ORGANIZE THE CASES SO THAT ONE CAN QUICKLY UNDERSTAND THE RELEVANCE OF EACH CASE TO THE COURSE. NO ATTEMPT IS MADE IN THIS OVERVIEW TO ADDRESS EVERY CONCEPT THAT MUST BE STUDIED. BE SURE TO READ THE ENTIRE CASEBOOK AND/OR OTHER MATERIALS TO GAIN A FULL UNDERSTANDING OF ALL CONCEPTS.

I. Future Gifts Invalid: The intent, or promise, to "donate" (give) a gift *later* is invalid, without more.

II. Gift Requirements: A gift is valid if:
    A. accompanied by an instrument of gift, and
    B. made with (proven) intent to make a gift. (The property need not be delivered at that time, if there is a reasonable and satisfactory excuse.) *In re Cohn* [dying man's birthday gift locked in his company's vault is valid].

III. Gifts Effective After Donor's Death: Donors may make living gifts while reserving the right to keep the item for their lifetime. *Gruen v. Gruen* [gift of painting only after donor's death is valid].

IV. Deathbed Gifts Valid Without Will: A gift causa mortis ("gift in contemplation of death") is usually made by a dying person. It is valid without a formal will, but only if it meets strict requirements.
    A. A gift causa mortis is valid if it is:
        1. A gift,
        2. Of personal property,
        3. Made in imminent expectation of death,
        4. By a competent donor,
        5. With the intent ...
        6. ... And upon the condition that the property should belong to the donee if:
            a. The donor dies,
            b. The donee accepts,
            c. The delivery is "actual, unequivocal, and complete" during the donor's lifetime, wholly divesting the owner of control, AND
            d. The donor dies of the anticipated peril.

    B. The gift must be returned to the donor if:
        1. The donor survives,
        2. The donor changes his mind before dying, OR
        3. The donee dies before the donor. *Foster v. Reiss* [dying woman's note to ex-husband to take property she stashed in the house they share is not valid "delivery"] [Overruled in part].
    C. Imperfect Delivery: Some courts impute constructive delivery if:
        1. Donative intent is proven by concrete, undisputed evidence,
        2. The donor intended to transfer possession immediately, AND
        3. The donor took steps he believed sufficient to effectuate transfer. *Scherer v. Hyland* (N.J.) [suicidal woman's endorsement of check to boyfriend is valid under circumstances]; *but see Woo v. Smart* (Va.) [dying man's personal check is not valid gift causa mortis until accepted by bank].

V. Engagement Rings: What happens when a suitor gives a wedding ring, but the wedding is called off?
    A. Fault-Based: Some jurisdictions' courts decide the issue based on who was responsible for the engagement failing.
    B. Modified No-Fault: In others, the groom is entitled to his ring back only if he did not break off the wedding.
    C. No-Fault Approach: In some states, engagement rings must be returned to the donor anytime the marriage does not occur. *Lindh v. Surman* [adopting no-fault approach in Pennsylvania].

In re Cohn

(Gift Recipient) v. (Prior Owners)
176 N.Y.S. 225

M E M O R Y   G R A P H I C

Instant Facts

A dying man wrote a promise to give his wife his shares for her birthday, as soon as they were formally transferred to his name, but his business partners challenged the gift as an invalid promise to donate a gift later.

Black Letter Rule

A gift is valid if accompanied by an instrument of gift and proof of the intent to make a gift, and the property need not be delivered at that time, if there is a reasonable and satisfactory excuse.

Case Vocabulary

EXECUTRIX: Female "executor" (person who administers a dead or bankrupt person's "estate," or remaining possessions). Here, apparently Sara (P) was executrix of Leopold's estate.
IN RE "[In the] matter of." Used to introduce cases in certain specialty courts. E.g., probate court.
PROBATE: Matter of handling a dead person's will and estate; done in a specialty "probate court."
SURROGATE: The judge in probate court.
TESTATOR: Person who leaves a will, or otherwise transfers property, usually after death.

Procedural Basis: In probate case, appeal from judgment for plaintiff.

Facts: Husband Leopold Cohn, on wife Sara Cohn's (P) birthday, wrote out a note saying, "I give this day to my wife, Sara ... Cohn, as a present for her ... birthday ... 500 ... shares of American Sumatra Tobacco Company common stock." Leopold did not give the stock certificates to Sara (P) then, because his shares were held in the name of his family company (D), and locked in its safe. Leopold needed to transfer title (formal ownership) of the shares to his personal account to give them to Sara (P). Leopold said he would give Sara (P) the shares as soon as he got them. Leopold died days later, before getting possession of the shares. Apparently, Company (D) refused to honor the gift to Sara (P). Sara (P) sued Company (D), claiming Leopold's note and intent constituted a legally binding gift. Company (D) defended, claiming the promise was an invalid promise to give a gift in the future, whenever he got the shares. [By law, promises to give a gift later are unenforceable as contracts, because there is no consideration in exchange for the promise.] In probate court, the surrogate (probate judge) held for Sara (P). Company (D) appeals.

Issue: If a donor intends to give a gift, and gives a written instrument of gift because he does not have the property in his possession, is the gift valid?

Decision and Rationale: (Shearn) Yes. A gift is valid if accompanied by an instrument of gift and proof of the intent to make a gift, and the property need not be delivered at that time, if there is a reasonable and satisfactory excuse. Here, the excuse was valid, because Leopold needed to go through formalities to gain possession from Company (D). These circumstances excuse manual delivery, and make a symbolical delivery effective. There is no evidence that Leopold intended a future gift instead of a present one. Though Leopold said he would give the shares "as soon as he could get it," he wrote, "I give this day," and clearly intended to give it to her on her birthday. Judgment for Sara (P) affirmed.

Dissent: (Page) This is not a valid gift inter vivos (while the giver is still alive). Leopold could have delivered the stock to Sara (P) immediately, but chose to keep the shares in Company's (D) name, to allow formation of a new partnership, and to let that partnership have a controlling block of American Sumatra's shares.

Analysis:

This case illustrates the prevailing rule that the intent, or promise, to "donate" (give) a gift *later* is invalid, without more. The rationale is usually given that a promise to give a gift is unenforceable as a contract, because unsupported by consideration. However, this rationale makes no sense, since a gift given now is valid, even though similarly without consideration. Other reasons given to support the rule include: that donors should be allowed to re-think hasty impulse promises, and that delivery helps disprove false claims. (Lesson: if you plan to give a gift, and want to spare the object of your generosity a lawsuit, transfer the property right away, and avoid cases like this one.)

Gruen v. Gruen

(Donee Stepson) v. (Donor's Wife)
68 N.Y.S.2d. 849 (Court of Appeals of New York, 1986)

M E M O R Y   G R A P H I C

Instant Facts

When a donor gave his son a painting on condition the donor could keep it for his lifetime, his wife challenged the gift, claiming a living gift cannot include a life estate.

Black Letter Rule

Donors may make living gifts while reserving the right to keep the item for their lifetime.

Case Vocabulary

INTER VIVOS [GIFT]: "between the living." [Gift] made by a person while still alive.

LIFE ESTATE: Right to property for the person's lifetime.

REMAINDER: Right to acquire property after its current owner dies.

SPECIAL TERM: An extra session of court, outside its normal schedule. (It makes no difference here.)

TESTAMENTARY: By will, i.e., after the donor's death.. The issue here is that, if this gift is ruled testamentary (as opposed to inter vivos), then it is invalid, for failure to follow a will's formalities.

Procedural Basis: In probate suit seeking specific performance, judgment for defendant, reversed on appeal, appealed again.

Facts: Victor Gruen owned a valuable painting. He wrote his Son (P), saying he wanted to give Son (P) the painting for his birthday, but wanted to retain possession for his lifetime. Son (P) never took possession during Father's lifetime. After Father died, his wife ("Stepmother" (D)) refused to give it to Son (P). Son (P) sued Stepmother (D), claiming a valid gift with a life estate. Stepmother (D) defended, claiming the gift was invalid, because (i) the gift was actually a testamentary transfer, but invalid because it lacked the formalities, and (ii) an inter vivos gift of a chattel, with a life estate and complete right of possession, is invalid. At trial, Special Term found for Stepmother (D), holding such a gift is invalid, and finding insufficient evidence the gift was made. On Son's (P) appeal, the Appellate Division reversed, holding such gifts are valid, and finding evidence that it was made. Stepmother (D) appeals.

Issue: Is an inter vivos gift, made on condition the donor may keep it until his death, valid?

Decision and Rationale: (Simons) Yes. An inter vivos gift may specify that the donor may possess the object until his death. Prior cases hold that donors may make gifts within their lifetime of remainder interests in real estate and intangibles. The same principle should apply to similar gifts of chattels. The cases do not require that gifts of goods must include a present right to possess them. If the evidence proves an intent to make a present and irrevocable transfer of title or ownership, the gift is effective immediately, because it represents the transfer of some interest. *Speelman v. Pascal* [gift of future royalties on George Bernard Shaw's yet-unwritten play "My Fair Lady" is valid]. This holding will not interfere with will requirements, and we need not require physical possession when the donor wants otherwise. Technically, acceptance by the recipient is required, but when the gift is valuable to him, we presume it. Judgment for Son (P) affirmed.

Analysis:

The last case, *In re Cohn* [dying man's birthday gift locked in his company's vault] showed the principle that, while inter vivos (living) gifts should ideally involve transfer on the spot, courts will sometimes recognize a valid transfer even when the item is not delivered immediately. This case goes one step further, holding that a current promise to transfer an item is valid, even if the transfer does not happen until the donor's death. Note that this comes very close to violating a cardinal maxim, that promises to give a gift later are not valid. Of course, in practice, there is little difference between the future promise and the promise in this case. Courts' increasing tolerance of deferred gifts may signal that they will eventually recognize future gifts.

Foster v. Reiss

(Decedent's Children's Representatives) v. (Decedent's Ex-Husband)
18 N.J. 41 (1955)

M E M O R Y   G R A P H I C

Instant Facts

After a dying woman tells her once-estranged husband to take property she stashed in the house they shared, her children challenged the deathbed gift as invalid.

Black Letter Rule

A "gift in contemplation of death" is valid if it is (i) a gift, (ii) of personal property, (iii) made in imminent expectation of death, (iv) by a competent donor, (v) with the intent (vi) and upon the condition that the property should belong to the donee if the donor dies, (vii) where the donee accepts, (viii) the delivery is "actual, unequivocal, and complete" during the donor's lifetime, "wholly divesting him of its possession, dominion, and control," and (ix) the donor dies of the anticipated peril.

Case Vocabulary

DEFEASIBLE: For property, that which will not necessarily pass to another, or which may not pass if certain conditions arise.
DONATIO CAUSA MORTIS: Same as "gift causa mortis," the [slightly] more modern term.
GIFT CAUSA MORTIS: Transfer of chattels by a person expecting to die soon, which may be valid without a formal will.
LEGACY: Gift by will.

Procedural Basis: In probate action, judgment for plaintiffs, reversed on appeal, now appealed.

Facts: Adam (D) and Ethel Reiss were married, with each having prior children. Later, Adam (D) and Ethel apparently quarreled, and Ethel removed Adam (D) from her will, in favor of her children. Adam (D) and Ethel separated. Later, they reconciled and cohabited in Ethel's house. Eventually, Ethel went in for major surgery. Fearing death, Ethel wrote a note to Adam (D), granting Adam (D) some cash, shares in a building and loan association (represented by a building loan book), and a savings account (represented by a bank passbook), all of which were stashed in her house (which they cohabited). Adam (D) learned of the note and got the items. After surgery, Ethel apparently became comatose, could not recognize or talk with visitors (this point is disputed by the parties), and soon died. Ethel's Children (P) sued Adam (D) to recover possession, claiming the note was invalid, and Adam (D) was entitled only to what he was assigned by will ($1). Adam (D) defended, claiming the note was a valid gift causa mortis ("in contemplation of death"). At trial, the trial court held for Children (P), finding the note invalid. On appeal, the Appellate Division reversed, finding the note valid, and finding delivery of the property to Adam (D) was unnecessary because Adam (D) had possession of the property in her/their house. Children (P) appeal.

Issue: Is a gift causa mortis valid when the donor, instead of giving the item, directs the donee to take it from its hiding place?

Decision and Rationale: (Vanderbilt) No. The ancient doctrine of gift causa mortis, derived from Greek, Roman, and old English law, applies when a person anticipating death, gives another his chattels to keep in case he dies. The modern doctrine is similar: a donatio causa mortis is a (i) gift, (ii) of personal property, (iii) made in imminent expectation of death, (iv) by a competent donor, (v) with the intent (vi) and upon the condition that the property should belong to the donee if the donor dies, (vii) where the donee accepts, (viii) the delivery is "actual, unequivocal, and complete" during the donor's lifetime, "wholly divesting him of its possession, dominion, and control," and (ix) the donor dies of the anticipated peril. Traditionally, the property must be returned to the donor if (A) the donor survives, (B) the donor changes his mind before dying, or (C) the donee dies before the donor. This doctrine is necessarily an exception to will requirements. First, we consider whether there was actual delivery during the donor's lifetime, wholly divesting him of control. State case law holds that the property must actually be delivered by the donor's affirmative act, unless delivery is (A) impossible, or (B) incompatible with the gift. Ex. For a savings account, delivery is impossible, so delivery of the passbook is acceptable. The delivery requirement is absolute, because without it, any writing would constitute a testamentary transfer, undermining the statute of wills' requirements. Here, there was no delivery, because Ethel never gave the cash and books to Adam (D), just indicated where they are. We disagree with the appellate court's finding that delivery was unnecessary because Adam (D) had possession. Even if this doctrine were valid, Adam (D) did not have actual possession, because he did not own the house or know the location of the cash and books. Further, the note is not valid proof of Ethel's intent, since when Adam (D) got the note, Ethel was under the influence of ether (anaesthetic) and unable to transact. Thus, Ethel's incompetence rendered her unable to authorize Adam (D) to take possession as her agent, under the *Restatement of the Law of Agency § 122*. Reversed; judgment for Children (P).

Dissent: (Jacobs) Here, the facts require us to deem that delivery was proper, since Adam (D) had possession of the items by virtue of living in the house where they lay, so that a note telling him to take them should be sufficient. Also, we note that some other states' courts do not require stricter rules for gifts causa mortis than for gifts inter vivos.

Analysis:

This case illustrates the ancient doctrine of gifts causa mortis, which essentially allows deathbed transfers to be valid without a will's formalities. However, this is a rare exception to the statute of wills, and thus the gift must meet many strict requirements to be valid. The most contentious of these requirements is delivery. As the dissent indicates, state courts are split on this rule. The majority impose stricter definitions of delivery for such deathbed gifts than for living gifts, perhaps to discourage challenges, which are difficult to prove once the donor is dead. However, this can have the effect of invalidating the dying person's intent, as seems to be the case here.

Scherer v. Hyland

(Suicide's Boyfriend) v. (Suicide's Executor)
75 N.J. 127 (1977)

MEMORY GRAPHIC

Instant Facts

After a suicidal woman endorsed a check to her live-in boyfriend before killing herself, executor claimed this delivery was invalid as a gift causa mortis.

Black Letter Rule

Constructive delivery may be imputed if (i) donative intent is proven by concrete, undisputed evidence, (ii) the donor intended to transfer possession immediately, and (iii) the donor took steps he believed sufficient to effectuate transfer.

Case Vocabulary

AD LITEM: "For the [purposes of] litigation."
ADMINISTRATOR: Person appointed by the court to represent the estate of people who die without leaving wills. [Some representation here!]
PER CURIAM: "By the court." Collective court opinion, not ascribed to any single judge.

Procedural Basis: In probate action, summary judgement for plaintiff, affirmed on appeal, appealed again.

Facts: Mr. Scherer (P) and Ms. Wagner lived together in Scherer's (P) apartment. Both were involved in a car crash, in which Wagner was disfigured and disabled. Scherer (P) took care of Wagner. Wagner became depressed and attempted suicide once. Later, Wagner killed herself by jumping from the roof. That morning, she had received a settlement check for the accident for $17,400. Before jumping, Wagner endorsed the check and left it on the table, and next to it wrote a note saying she "bequeathed" all her possessions, including the check, to Scherer (P). The check was taken by the police, and apparently claimed by Wagner's executor Hyland (D) ("Executor"). Scherer (P) sued Executor (D), claiming the check was his as a valid gift causa mortis. Executor (D) defended, claiming (i) the gift was invalid for lack of delivery, under *Foster v. Reiss* [dying woman's note to ex-husband to take property she stashed in the house they share is not valid "delivery"], (ii) a suicide's gift causa mortis is invalid, because the person retains control of the peril, and (iii) there was no acceptance. At trial, Scherer (P) won summary judgement. On appeal, the court affirmed. Executor (D) appeals again.

Issue: If a suicidal person endorses a check and leaves it for her cohabitant to find, is this a valid gift causa mortis?

Decision and Rationale: (Per Curiam) Yes. Constructive delivery may be imputed if (i) donative intent is proven by concrete, undisputed evidence, (ii) the donor intended to transfer possession immediately, and (iii) the donor took steps he believed sufficient to effectuate transfer. Under our wills statute, Wagner's note is invalid as a will, and thus must be analyzed as a gift causa mortis. (i) The primary issue here is whether "delivery" was valid. Delivery is required mainly for evidentiary purposes, to prevent fraud, perjury, and mistaking a donative impulse for a completed gift. *Foster* required strict manual delivery, except in rare cases. However, we overrule this approach. Instead, we will impute constructive delivery if (i) donative intent is proven by concrete, undisputed evidence, (ii) the donor intended to transfer possession immediately, and (iii) the donor took steps he believed sufficient to effectuate transfer. This approach reflects the realities of such transfers, without enabling fraud. Here, these requirements are met. Wagner clearly intended to transfer the check to Scherer (P), so there is no possibility of fraud. We find that Wagner's affirmative steps were sufficient to transfer; she endorsed the check, which is the only act needed to transfer it, and universally understood to mean this. Also, it is clear she meant it for Scherer, since he was the only person she expected to enter his apartment. Her leaving constituted a total surrender, since she left to kill herself. (ii) Next, Executor (D) argues suicide is not "peril" sufficient to sustain gifts causa mortis, because it is voluntary. While some other jurisdictions support this view, we reject it. Suicides' death is no less imminent once a suicidal fixation is formed, and it is unrealistic to believe that someone who is depressed enough to commit suicide can freely renounce it. (iii) Finally, acceptance is present here. Though the issue is rarely litigated, there is authority indicating that acceptance is implied if the gift is unconditional and benefits the donee. Judgment for Scherer (P) affirmed.

Analysis:

While this case effectively overrules *Foster v. Reiss* [dying woman's note to ex-husband to take property she stashed in the house they share is not valid "delivery"], remember that this is only the new rule for one jurisdiction. States are still split over whether to allow some form of constructive delivery. Note that the *Scherer* approach tries to honor the intent of the dying person, even going so far as to add a *subjective* element; it essentially says the delivery is deemed valid if the donor *intended it* as such. Of course, this approach inevitably creates some of the dangers that *Foster*'s majority intended to avert: the risk of fraud, and the difficulty of determining what a dead person intended.

Lindh v. Surman

(Suitor) v. (Bride-to-be)
560 Pa. 1 (1999)

M E M O R Y   G R A P H I C

Instant Facts
When a man proposed, but kept breaking their engagement, his fiancée finally refused to return the ring.

Black Letter Rule
In Pennsylvania, engagement rings must be returned to the donor anytime the marriage does not occur.

Procedural Basis: In civil action seeking restitution or damages, judgment for defendant, reversed on first appeal, then affirmed on second appeal, now appealed again..

Facts: Roger Lindh (P) proposed to Janis Surman (D), offering her an engagement ring worth about $21,400. Janis (D) accepted. Two months later, Roger (P) broke the engagement, and demanded the ring. Janis (D) returned it. Later, they reconciled, and Roger (P) again proposed, offering the ring. Janis (D) accepted. Five months later, Roger (P) called off the engagement. Janis (D) refused to return the ring. Roger (P) sued Janis (D) to recover the ring (or its value), claiming an engagement ring is conditional on the marriage happening. Janis (D) defended, claiming (i) the ring is conditional only on the engagement, and (ii) Roger (P) was at fault for the marriage's non-occurrence. At arbitration, the arbitrators held for Janis (D). Roger (P) appealed. After trial, the court awarded Roger (P) the money. Janis (D) appealed. The appellate court affirmed. This appeal followed.

Issue: If a person gives an engagement ring, but then breaks off the wedding, must the donee return the ring?

Decision and Rationale: (Newman) Yes. In Pennsylvania, engagement rings must be returned to the donor anytime the marriage does not occur. Pennsylvania law treats an engagement ring as a conditional gift. (i) However, the gift is implicitly conditional on the marriage occurring. Mere acceptance of the proposal is insufficient. (ii) Whether the donor is entitled to the ring back when s/he ended the engagement is an issue of first impression. We can adopt one of three approaches: (A) the fault-based theory, which considers who broke the engagement and why, (B) the no-fault theory, which automatically requires return of the ring if the marriage does not occur, or (C) the modified no-fault position, which lets the donor get the ring back, but not if s/he broke the engagement. The fault-based approach may seem equitable. However, it is inappropriate to assess complex personal relationships in terms of who is "right" or "wrong." Also, requiring near-spouses to justify themselves would invite bitter, unpleasant accusations, and courts would have to decide the issue without clear guidance. However adopting the modified no-fault approach would wrong the person who broke off the engagement for good cause. Thus, we adopt the no-fault principle. We note that this accords with many states' no-fault divorce statutes. Judgment for Roger (P) affirmed.

Dissent: (Cappy) Courts could easily assess fault in such situations, since they hear equally sordid matters daily.

Dissent: (Castille) I do not believe a no-fault policy should be applied to broken engagements. Instead, we should apply the approach in the *Restatement of Restitution § 58*, which states that gifts made in the hope of marriage are not recoverable, absent fraud or fault by the donee.

Analysis:
Honestly, the issue of engagement rings is not likely to come up on your final exam, and cannot be such a commonly-litigated issue. Apparently, it is included in this chapter more for its novelty value than its ultimate legal importance. As you can see, wedding rings are treated differently from other gifts, whether by this court's ruling, or by the *Restatement of Restitution*.

Perspective
Historical Development of Estates Doctrine

Chapter 13

American property law developed from English law. In turn, British property law developed historically and haphazardly, based on the feudal system in place at the time. Thus, to understand why American law is what it is, it helps to have a basic knowledge of how English law reflected feudal circumstances. This chapter is a brief summary of some feudal factors which influenced modern law. The conclusion you should draw is that modern law is *still* founded on extremely ancient law, even though its feudal focus is no longer suited to our modern commercial economy.

This chapter is interesting for your personal knowledge, and may help you understand the logic behind seemingly random laws, but remember, this chapter will NOT be on your final exam. The English feudal history, and the ancient rules explained in it, are just too complex and archaic to remember, or even to study too closely. For this chapter, consider skipping the text itself, and reading just the outline; the text goes into too much detail on ancient rules, which are no longer useful to know.

As a final warning, reading this entire chapter may make you not want to practice law anymore. One public interest lawyer told me that he abandoned any ambition for corporate law after reading the following nonsense, taken from this very chapter: "If we now take stock of the feudal tenures . . . we shall find the position to have been as follows: the greater part of English land was held by socage tenure, a considerable part was subject to copyhold tenure, while the remainder was held either in grand sergeanty or in frankalmoin, or was affected by the peculiar customs of gavelkind, borough-English, or ancient demesne." Consider thyself warned, young squire, and proceedeth at thine own risk.

Chapter 13

NOTE: THE PURPOSE OF THIS OUTLINE IS TO ORGANIZE THE CASES SO THAT ONE CAN QUICKLY UNDERSTAND THE RELEVANCE OF EACH CASE TO THE COURSE. NO ATTEMPT IS MADE IN THIS OVERVIEW TO ADDRESS EVERY CONCEPT THAT MUST BE STUDIED. BE SURE TO READ THE ENTIRE CASEBOOK AND/OR OTHER MATERIALS TO GAIN A FULL UNDERSTANDING OF ALL CONCEPTS.

I. Feudalism: British property law developed historically and haphazardly, based on the feudal system in place from the 11th to 19th Centuries.
   A. In Europe
      1. "Feudalism" means land is *held* (managed) by residents, but *owned* by a higher-ranked lord/ king.
      2. Feudalism replaced common ownership as post-Roman Empire barbarian invasions forced people to accept a centralized, hierarchical, quasi-military organization to guarantee adequate armies for mutual protection.
      3. Under feudalism, ownership was given to the overlord/king, and delegated back to individuals. Each was bound reciprocally; the tenant was required to give the lord certain services and soldiers, while the lord was required to protect his vassals.
   B. In England
      1. English feudalism was more centralized; *all* land belonged to the king, and was delegated and re-delegated to lesser people. This is historical; since the Norman King William had to take England by force from rebellious Saxons, he felt he had won the land as his own, but allowed resident Saxons to "buy" it back through services.
      2. Thus, British feudalism required "tenure," meaning that land residents owed various specified services to the king. Tenure was universal in England. (Elsewhere, tenure only applied to knights.)
      3. With time, each lord subdivided his land, creating contractual relationships with lesser lords, and delegating to them some responsibilities owed to the king.
   C. Feudal "tenures": The "tenure" (services required of a lord) varied. They include:
      1. "Knight service" (providing for the army)
         a. Originally, lords had to provide knights for the King's army.
         b. Later, this was replaced by cash payment, used to hire armies.
         c. Eventually, lords made more onerous demands on their sub-tenants, in the name of knight service, even though these were not used for military purposes. These include:
            (1) "Relief" (payment when the tenant died, and was succeeded) [akin to modern inheritance taxes].
            (2) "Aids" (extraordinary payment, collected when the lord was imprisoned for ransom, or needed money to make his son a knight, or pay his daughter's marriage costs).
            (3) "Escheat" (confiscation of property if the tenant committed a major crime).
            (4) "Wardship" (the right to manage lands inherited by underage children, usually for the lord's own benefit).
            (5) Right to marry wards off to the person of the lord's choice. [And you thought *your* lease was oppressive.]
      2. These quasi-military tenures gradually turned into personal services, then into cash payment. There were two types of non-military tenure.
         a. "Socage" (paying rent and/or harvesting the crops) became the dominant form of landholding tenure. This was more economically efficient, and less onerous to tenants. It became the most common form of landholding.
         b. "Copyhold" was a variant instituted around a lord's manor. Tenants essentially paid the same cash or labor, but inherited the land subject to *fixed*, cus-

tomary duties. Importantly, lords could no longer demand services arbitrarily.

(1) If the lord demanded more than was due, tenants could go to court against him.

(2) Further, tenants had their customary duties written down in a "court roll" (paper), and each successor got a "copy." [Again, the ancestor of your lease.]

II. American Abolition of Tenures: Fortunately, complicated land tenures were abolished in America, though some aspects endured.

III. "Escheat" (reversion of uninherited land to the state)

A. State and federal law provides that, if a land-owner dies without suitable heirs, his property "escheats" (reverts to ownership of) the state or federal government. [So, if you own land, make a will.]

B. Usually, in such cases, the state need not pay inheritance tax on the land . *In re O'Connor's Estate* (Neb. 1934) [Nebraska inheritance tax laws inapplicable to escheat]; *but see In re Estate of O'Brine* (N.Y. 1975) [when *personal* property escheats to *federal* government, the state can first collect inheritance taxes].

In re O'Connor's Estate

(County) v. (State)
126 Neb. 182 (1934)

M E M O R Y   G R A P H I C

Instant Facts

When a landowner died without a will or heirs, and the property escheated (reverted) to the state, the county demanded the state pay inheritance tax on it.

Black Letter Rule

If property escheats to the state, the state need not pay inheritance taxes.

Case Vocabulary

ESCHEAT: To [have land] revert back to the state, if its owner does not leave it to capable heirs.
FEE: The grant of ownership in land.
PROBATED: Litigated in probate (will/inheritance) court.
REVERSION: Right to reclaim property, granted to another for his lifetime, upon the holder's death.
TENURE: [Archaic] Duties required of vassals (landholders) in old England as a condition of keeping land granted to them by the Crown (e.g., providing soldiers or money for the army, harvesting crops, doing housework for the king/lord).

Procedural Basis: Appeal from judgment for plaintiff.

Facts: Nebraska landowner O'Connor died, without a will or heirs. Thus, O'Connor's land escheated to Nebraska (D), by law. Adams County (P), where the property was apparently located, sued Nebraska (D) to collect an inheritance tax, contending the escheat is a taxable transfer. Nebraska (D) defended, claiming escheat is different from a taxable transfer, and is not covered by inheritance tax laws. At trial, the District Court held for Adams County (P). Nebraska (D) appeals.

Issue: If a landowner dies without will or heirs, and the land escheats to the state, must the state pay county inheritance taxes on it?

Decision and Rationale: (Yeager) No. If property escheats to the state, the state need not pay inheritance taxes. Whether the escheat constitutes a taxable transfer depends on the meaning of "escheat." In feudal England, escheat meant the falling back, or reversion, of land to the lord if the grantee lacked capable heirs. Today, escheat means the lapsing or reverting of property to the state, as original and ultimate proprietor of real estate, for failure of persons legally entitled to hold it. The theory is that the state is the original proprietor of all land, and the final one; what is termed land "ownership" is really just tenancy, contingent upon legally-recognized rights of tenure, transfer, and succession. Nebraska law has continued to recognize this doctrine; its Constitution recognizes escheat. The relevant inheritance tax law shows it intended a tax upon a right of succession by inheritance, will, or transfer in contemplation of death. This is distinguishable from reversion, where the title holder dies without will, without heirs, and without such transfer. We cannot interpret the tax statutes to abridge the right to reversion, because it is a longstanding right clearly guaranteed in our Constitution, and should not be surrendered without clear legislative intent. This holding renders moot all other issues in this case. Judgment for Adams County (P) reversed.

Analysis:

Basically, this case is included to illustrate the ancient right of escheat, which holds that, since land was originally granted by the Crown/State, the government automatically reclaims it if the land "owner" lacks heirs. Originally, this happened because the Norman (French) King William, after conquering the Saxons (English) by force, announced that he was now sole owner of all land in England, but would essentially give select families the right to live there. However, it was thought that, if the original family died out, they had no further claim to the land, and the king should be free to reassign it. This case demonstrates that, antiquated as this notion may be, it is still the law. However, its holding on the secondary issue -- whether inheritance taxes must be paid on escheated property -- is not definitive; other cases have held otherwise. See In re Estate of O'Brine (N.Y. 1975) [when *personal* property escheats to *federal* government, the state can first collect inheritance taxes].

Chapter 14

In the present day, we often take for granted what it means to "own" land or property. Property is "ours" in the sense that we have a right to enjoy and profit from it, to exclude others in most cases, and – perhaps most importantly – to sell the property or pass it on to our descendants or loved ones through our wills. When one tries to strip away our assumptions and really delve into the question of why we treat property in these ways, it is not at all self-evident that this is the natural or only system. In fact, even a short review of the history of property law shows that our modern property rules evolved from a very, very different situation in which the land was all owned by the sovereign or nobles and most land owners were not "owners" in our conception of the word, but just tenants making use of the land at the nobles' pleasure.

This historical situation changed dramatically in England with the passage of laws that facilitated the inheritability of interests in land. This is the origin of our modern "estates" in land that determine who takes title, for how long and under what conditions. This chapter examines the more extensive "freehold estates" as opposed to the "non-freehold estates," which could not be inherited under the common law. The most important part of the freehold estates is thankfully the easiest to understand. The fee simple, or fee simple absolute, has a potentially infinite duration, because the holder may sell or gift the property or provide for its devise in his will. If he dies without a will, however, the estate will pass to his legal heirs. For reasons of simplicity and certainty, modern law favors the fee simple estate over all others. The other freehold estates, which the chapter treats in detail, are the life estate (which lasts only as long as a specified person is alive), the defeasible fees (which may revert to the grantor if a certain event or action occurs) and the fee tail (which can pass only to certain natural heirs of the grantee).

Even this quick list of the features of freehold estates gives a clue as to some of the most important questions that courts have to consider with respect to them. First, how does one know which type of estate is being conveyed in a deed or will? In the past, the common law required very specific terms of art to be used to create a given estate. Today, most courts will follow the expressed intent of the parties even if the typical language of a given estate is not used. Of course, discerning the intent of parties from sometimes sloppily drafted deeds or wills can lead to disputes and many of the cases in this chapter have their origins in such documents. Second, does the holder of a freehold estate owe any duties to others who might take the land in the future? Courts answer this question quite differently depending on the type of estate at issue in the case. Owners of fee simple estates, for example, are restricted pretty much only by nuisance or zoning laws. Life tenants, on the other hand, have quite strict duties to maintain their property for the person who will take over the property after the life tenancy expires. With the defeasible fees, the holder of the estate does not owe any particular duties to those with possible future interests, but is restricted in her use of the land by conditions which could trigger a reversion or forfeiture of the estate. Third, if someone dies without a will, who, if anyone, inherits his property? This question is really answered more by statute than by case law these days, but is none-the-less an important issue to discuss with respect to freehold estates. Finally, since property cases often deal with deeds executed years or even decades before the controversy, when will the passage of time bar a particular challenge to an estate? Or conversely, when will the intent of the parties be honored and enforced regardless of the passage of time? This is a difficult issue since it overlaps with many policy considerations – certainty, putting land to its best use, protecting families – that we hold quite dear. Although the jargon and concepts of freehold estates can be daunting at first, the underlying principles really do explain a lot about American law, and therefore, about American culture and values as well.

Chapter 14

NOTE: THE PURPOSE OF THIS OUTLINE IS TO ORGANIZE THE CASES SO THAT ONE CAN QUICKLY UNDERSTAND THE RELEVANCE OF EACH CASE TO THE COURSE. NO ATTEMPT IS MADE IN THIS OVERVIEW TO ADDRESS EVERY CONCEPT THAT MUST BE STUDIED. BE SURE TO READ THE ENTIRE CASEBOOK AND/OR OTHER MATERIALS TO GAIN A FULL UNDERSTANDING OF ALL CONCEPTS.

I. The greatest estate in land is the *fee simple absolute*, which may last indefinitely, and which, if not sold or passed by will, passes to the owner's heirs.

  A. Traditionally, to create a fee simple under the common law, a deed or conveyance used the words "to A and his heirs."

    1. In modern practice, almost all states have statutes that favor fee simple title and give fee simple effect to any conveyance that expresses the grantor's intention to pass a fee simple.

    2. In a common law jurisdiction, the lack of the words "and his heirs" in a deed in the chain of title is sufficient to make title unmarketable. *Cole v. Steinlauf.*

    3. As used in the law of wills and estates, the word "heirs" is a term of art that refers to persons who take property under relevant statutes of descent (usually when a person dies without a valid will); individuals who take property under a will are not "heirs."

  B. Prior to the passage of the Statute of Wills (1540), English law did not usually allow freehold estates in land, unlike personalty, to be passed by will.

    1. The differences between the treatment of real and personal properties was accentuated by the jurisdiction of the Ecclesiastical Courts over probate.

    2. Primogeniture, the idea that a person had only one legal heir (usually the oldest male descendent), was the primary rule of inheritance developed in England.

    3. The development of primogeniture tended to prefer passing property to successors rather than wives or ancestors, even if the latter were closer relations than the successors.

  C. Under modern statutes, if a person dies intestate (without a will), the property will usually be divided by giving half of the estate to a surviving spouse and dividing the other half between surviving descendants per stirpes.

    1. When there is a surviving spouse but no descendants, the entire estate goes to the spouse; when there are descendants, but no surviving spouse, the entire estate goes to the descendants per stirpes.

    2. When there is neither a surviving spouse nor descendants, the property passes to collaterals or ancestors through a statutorily determined calculation of degrees of relatedness to the deceased.

    3. Most state statutes provide that someone causing a wrongful death cannot inherit from the deceased.

  D. At common law, illegitimate children inherited nothing if their natural parent died intestate, but modern statutes usually include illegitimate children to inherit from their mothers and fathers, where the father has acknowledged paternity or paternity has been proved.

  E. Although we take for granted that property is inheritable and devisable, it is important to consider the policy considerations that may or may not justify using the law to aid the wishes of persons in controlling the use or ownership of land after he or she is deceased.

II. Although it gives the owner the right to enjoy his or her land and to reap the profits of its use, the *life estate* is not inheritable, and upon the death of the life tenant either reverts to the grantor or passes to remaindermen named in the deed.

  A. The common law required no special words to create the life estate.

1. A will creates a fee simple estate absent express language limiting the devise to a life estate, since the law (often due to statute) disfavors forfeitures. *Lewis v. Searles*.

2. A will may make a devise contingent upon the devisee's marital status for a legitimate reason, such as the devisee's support or protection. *Lewis v. Searles*.

B. A life tenant has a fiduciary duty to reasonably maintain her property for the benefit of the remainderman, so, absent prejudice to the life tenant, laches will not bar the remainderman's suit for waste. *Moore v. Phillips*.

C. In the past, under common law, life tenancies were not inheritable, but now, a life estate *pur autre vie* (where the estate terminates upon the death of someone other than the holder) may be inherited in some cases.

III. Defeasible Estates
  A. There are two important *defeasible estates:*
    1. The fee simple determinable, which will automatically revert to the grantor upon the occurrence of a certain event
    2. The fee simple subject to a condition subsequent, which gives the grantor the right to reenter and terminate the estate upon the occurrence of a certain event.
  B. Generally, a court will look at the language of the will or deed to determine the intention of the parties to create a particular defeasible fee.
    1. Where the intent of the parties is unclear from the language of a deed, the court will look to the circumstances to determine the type of defeasible fee created by the deed. *Oldfield v. Stoeco Homes, Inc.*

2. Because of the principle that forfeitures are disfavored, courts generally prefer to interpret an unclear deed as creating a fee simple subject to a condition subsequent rather than a fee simple determinable. *Oldfield v. Stoeco Homes, Inc.*

C. By itself, a clause providing that a conveyance is made for certain purposes will not create a limited estate in a grant of land. *Roberts v. Rhodes*.

D. The passage of time alone does not terminate grantor's rights or grantee's obligation to perform under a condition subsequent. *Martin v. City of Seattle*.

E. A statute of limitations may bar grantor's untimely lawsuit to reenter lands under a condition subsequent. *Johnson v. City of Wheat Ridge*.

F. A governmental entity that holds a defeasible fee cannot condemn the grantor's reversionary interest and pay merely nominal damages. *Leeco Gas & Oil Company v. County of Nueces*.

IV. At common law after the year 1285, a conveyance "to A and the heirs of his body" created a *fee tail* estate, which may be inherited only by specified natural decedents of the grantee; the *fee tail* lasts until the holder dies without issue.
  A. Most states have statutes which abolish the fee tail and make a conveyance "to A and his heirs" into a fee simple in A.
  B. Where a will conferred a fee simple with the qualification that if grantee died without issue, then the land passed to another, grantee received a fee tail. *Caccomo v. Banning*.

Cole v. Steinlauf

(Not Stated) v. (Not Stated)
136 A.2d 744 (Conn. 1957)

M E M O R Y   G R A P H I C

Instant Facts

Plaintiffs-purchasers of property sued Defendant-seller for return of their earnest money on the grounds that a previous deed in the chain of title that lacked the words "and heirs" made the title unmarketable.

Black Letter Rule

Purchasers are justified in rejecting as unmarketable a deed that is preceded in the chain of title by another deed that lacks the specific language necessary to create a fee simple.

Case Vocabulary

FEE SIMPLE ABSOLUTE: This is the greatest estate in land someone can have and it can potentially last forever; it passes to the heirs of the owner if he dies without a will.

Procedural Basis: Plaintiffs-purchasers' appeal from a trial court ruling that seller had delivered marketable, fee simple title to property despite a prior deed that conveyed the property to grantee "and assigns" rather than "and heirs."

Facts: The prospective purchasers (P) and seller (D) of a property located in Norwalk agreed to a contract that stated that if seller (D) could not deliver good and clear title to the property, purchaser (P) could reject the deed. If the purchasers (P) rejected the deed, seller (D) would repay any deposit money plus the reasonable fees for the title search. The purchasers (P) put down a $420 deposit and hired an attorney to review the title before the July 1, 1955 closing date. The title examination turned up a 1945 deed, from New York, conferring title to one of the seller's (D) predecessors. That deed conferred the property to grantee "and assigns forever," rather than the standard – in Connecticut – fee simple terms, to grantee "and his heirs." The purchasers (P) rejected the seller's (D) deed and sought return of their deposit plus $50 for the title examination fee. Seller (D) refused to pay the purchasers (P), and purchasers brought suit. The trial court found that the 1945 deed constituted a full fee simple title and ruled in favor of seller (D). The purchasers (P) appealed.

Issue: Does a deed that runs to grantee "and his assigns" create a fee title without any flaw or defect that would render the title unmarketable?

Decision and Rationale: (Wynne, C.J.) Yes. Although the language of the 1945 deed – to grantee "and his assigns" – may create a full fee title, this is not without reasonable doubt such that the purchasers (P) in this case had a right to reject the seller's (D) deed and recoup their deposits. In common law jurisdictions, like Connecticut, a deed granting title "to grantee 'and his assigns forever' vests only a life estate in the grantee." Deeds where the term "and his heirs" has been left out can be reformed to convey fee simple title if that was the parties' clear intention. Since the court did not have the parties to the 1945 deed present, it could not determine those parties' intentions. Although the seller (D) cited many cases indicating that the title was in fact a fee simple, this is not the issue. The more important question is whether the 1945 deed could cause the purchasers (P) reasonable doubt about the marketability of the title. In essence, to say as the trial court did, that the purchasers (P) must accept this title, puts the purchasers (P) in position of having to take a risk that a court in the future would agree that this was an unrestricted fee simple deed. The trial court erred by treating this as a case in which its role was to judge the title rather than to determine whether the purchasers (P) were justified in refusing the deed. Since the title is not marketable, the trial court decision is reversed and seller (D) is ordered to pay purchasers (P) $470.

Concurrence: (Baldwin, A.J.) Although it was not within the purview of the court in this case, "the true intent of the parties to convey [a fee simple] may be shown in equity. Absent an action appropriate to make that determination, the purchasers (P) are justified in rejecting the title offered by seller (D).

Analysis:

Although the study of freehold estates is complicated and sometimes confusing, the law of the fee simple estate illustrates how far removed modern American property law is from its medieval and common law origins. In the past, a deed had to contain the language "to A and his heirs" to create a fee simple. Now, almost every state has statutes and case law indicating that courts will first try to determine the grantor's intention to determine whether he intended to convey a fee simple even if the deed does not contain the "magic words." Even when courts cannot discern an explicit intention of the grantor, the law favors fee simple estates because they are more certain and permanent. This focus on intentions may show the influence of contract law on American property law. In contracts, we generally prefer to allow the parties to determine the details of their promises and performance, but courts will step in when contracts lack key provisions or to determine uncertain provisions. The permanent nature of real property makes certainty all the more crucial. One interesting question that arises from Cole is how a court decides when it can discern the intentions of parties? In Cole itself, the court does not need to determine the intentions of the parties

Cole v. Steinlauf (Continued)

to the 1945 deed because the court is not judging what estate was conveyed but only whether or not the title is marketable. Nevertheless, the court does state at one point that determining the intent of the parties "is impossible . . . in this proceeding, for the reason that the necessary parties are not all before the court." But won't this often be the case in property law, where deeds made years and sometimes generations earlier still affect the title to the property? Where the parties' intentions are not clear from the document they created, other evidence will be necessary to determine their states of mind. If the parties are not available to testify, where will the court go for such evidence? In this light, we can perhaps see why the standard language of deeds and estates has persisted. If a deed is "to A and his heirs," then it clearly conveys a fee simple estate, and courts and parties are spared the rigors of interpreting the intentions of a distant grantor.

A WILL CREATES A FEE SIMPLE ESTATE ABSENT EXPRESS LANGUAGE LIMITING THE DEVISE TO A LIFE ESTATE. A WILL MAY MAKE A DEVISE CONTINGENT ON THE DEVISEE'S MARITAL STATUS FOR A LEGIMATE REASON, SUCH AS THE DEVISEE'S SUPPORT OR PROTECTION

Lewis v. Searles

(Niece of Testatrix and Devisee) v. (Children and Grandchildren of Other Deceased Nieces and Nephews)
452 S.W.2d 153 (Mo. 1970)

M E M O R Y   G R A P H I C

Instant Facts

An unmarried devisee who inherited "all of [testatrix's] real and personal property . . . so long as she remains single" sought a declaratory judgment that she took a fee simple estate and not a life estate.

Black Letter Rule

(1) A will provision that limits a devise upon the marriage of the devisee is valid when the purpose is to provide support for the devisee. (2) [By statute] A devise will be considered a fee simple absent express language indicating a life estate or creating a further devise following the devisee's death.

Case Vocabulary

LIFE ESTATE: An estate in land that lasts for the duration of a specific person's life; the holder of the life estate has a duty to maintain the property in good condition for the remainderman, the person to whom the property will pass at the end of the life estate.

FEE SIMPLE DETERMINABLE: A fee simple estate in land that in the event of a certain, specified occurrence or action automatically ends and reverts to the grantor.

CONDITION: In Property law, a condition attached to a conveyance of land is language stating that in the event of a certain occurrence the size, extent or nature of the estate conveyed will change.

LIMITATION: In Property law, a limitation or "words of limitation" in a will create an estate less extensive than a fee simple.

TESTATOR/TESTATRIX: A person who has died leaving a will. Testatrix, the feminine version, is now considered old-fashioned.

Procedural Basis: Appeal from a trial court decision that a will granted Lewis (P) a life estate, but only one-third of the fee simple estate in the land on which she resided.

Facts: Leticia G. Lewis, the testatrix in this case, died in 1926. Surviving her were two nieces, Hattie L. Lewis ["Lewis"] (P) and Letitia A. LaForge ["Letitia"], and a nephew, James R. Lewis ["James"]. The relevant provision of the testatrix's will stated: "'Second, I devise to my niece, Hattie L. Lewis, all of my real and personal property . . . so long as she remains single and unmarried.'" The provision continued by stating that if Lewis (P) were to marry, "'then and in this event I desire that all of my property . . . be divided equally between my nieces and nephews as follows [with each of the three to receive "an undivided one third" of the testatrix's property].'" Lewis (P) took possession of the property when she was around 53 years old and remained unmarried. At age 95, Lewis (P) brought a declaratory judgment suit to quiet her title to the property in fee simple. By the time of the suit, both Letitia and James were deceased, survived by children and grandchildren (D), who were the respondents to the quiet title action. The respondents admitted Lewis's (P) right of possession but argued that she received only a life estate, not a fee simple, under the terms of the testatrix's will. The trial court ruled in favor of the respondents (D), finding that the testatrix had intended Lewis (P) to have a life estate. The trial court therefore entered judgment that each of Lewis (P), Letitia and James, or their heirs, owned an undivided one-third share of the property in fee simple, subject to the life estate of Lewis (P). The trial court denied Lewis's (P) motion for a new trial, and Lewis (P) appealed.

Issue: (1) Is a provision that devises real property to a person as long as he or she remains unmarried void as against public policy? (2) Did testatrix intend to devise to Lewis (P) a determinable fee interest in testatrix's real property?

Decision and Rationale: (Eager) (1) No. Although will provisions restraining marriage are generally disfavored, such a provision may be valid where, as in this case, the purpose is to provide support for a single person. In fact, recent case law has created so many exceptions to the general rule against provisions in restraint of marriage that the exceptions are consuming the rule. Searles (D) argued that the Winget decision controls the present case. In Winget, the testator was a widower with three stepchildren and no children of his own. Two of the stepchildren were adults, living on their own, while the third, who was disabled, continued to live with the testator. In Winget, the will devised all of the testator's property to the disabled stepdaughter "as long as she remains single, and if she marry it is my will that she share equally with the other heirs." It was also clear from the will that the "other heirs" were the other stepchildren. In Winget, the court held that the marriage provision was valid because its intent was to provide support for the devisee should she remain unmarried. Lewis (P) attempted to distinguish Winget from the present case by arguing that, in Winget, the court heard evidence concerning the circumstances under which the marriage provision was drafted. Lewis (P) argued that without similar evidence here, the court could not uphold the marriage provision. In the present case, however, the wording of the will itself evinces the testatrix's intent to protect and support Lewis (P). Since the marriage provision is not a penalty for marrying and has a legitimate purpose not against public policy, it is valid. (2) Yes. The will, construed as a whole, indicates the testatrix's intent to create a fee simple determinable for Lewis (P) and the will does not contain any language that shows a clear intent to limit Lewis' (P) estate upon her death. In interpreting a will, the intent of the testator is the court's ultimate guideline. Moreover, Missouri statute [Section 474.480] states that a devise is in fee simple absent either the *expressed* intent to create a life estate or stipulation of a further devise to be made after the death of the devisee; neither of these is present in the will at issue in this case. Searles (D) and the other defendants, however, again argue that *Winget* should control this case. In *Winget*, after concluding that the marriage provision was valid, the court held that the language of the will created a life estate, not a fee simple, for the disabled stepdaughter. The *Winget* court ruled that the provision ["as long as she remains single"] provided a limitation and duration. The *Winget* court concluded that since the stepdaughter might remain single until her death, the provision created a life estate. In essence, in *Winget* and similar cases, the courts have added the words "or upon her death" onto the ends of marriage provisions. Ostensibly, this was done to prevent intestacy in the case that the devisee died unmarried, but that is unnecessary, since upon her death, the devisee's heirs would simply inherit her fee simple. Furthermore, the *Winget* case made no mention of the predecessor statute of Section 474.480, which was in effect when the testatrix died. In cases decided under statutes similar to Section 474.480, the key question is whether the will in question contains "express words" contrary to the creation of a fee simple. In the present case, the will contains no language indicating an intention to create a life estate. In the will at issue in this case, the testatrix provided that upon Lewis's (P) marriage, Lewis (P) and two other named persons would receive "undivided" one-third shares in fee simple (no further limitation being stipulated). It is also clear that the testatrix intended Lewis (P) to have a greater estate if she remained single, and that the testatrix was thinking only in fee estates here. The "gift over" in this will was conditioned only on Lewis's (P) getting married, not on her death, and the court will not add or insert "or death" into the will. It is held that Lewis (P) inherited a fee simple in the testatrix's property subject to divestiture of undivided two-thirds interest should she marry, in which case the two-thirds interest would be devised to the heirs of the other niece and nephew per stirpes. The trial court's decision is reversed. [The court, writing per curiam, adopted the Special Commissioner's decision.]

Analysis:

Probably the first thing that will strike most readers of *Lewis v. Searles* is the complicated and somewhat confusing array of parties. Alas, this is often the case with property cases involving wills because of the great lengths of time that often pass between the writing of a will and its interpretation. This means that people originally named in a will may be deceased and their shares will have passed to heirs who are only vaguely aware of the original relationships. For this reason, the court in *Lewis* is careful to note that all parties to the case received proper service or publication. Once the reader sorts out the relationships between the plaintiff, testator and other parties, however, a few relatively straightforward rules for interpreting wills surface. The first two such rules, highlighted repeatedly by the *Lewis* decision, are (1) that it is the overall intention of the testator that controls the meaning of will, and (2) that the will must be viewed as a whole by the court attempting to discern the testator's intentions. This pair of rules illustrates how far modern property law has come from its medieval origins. In the past, courts would look for the existence of specific terms or phrases, such as "to A and his heirs," to determine the type of estate created by the will. The absence of these "magical" phrases could result in a lesser estate being transferred. Nowadays, on the other hand, courts will look to the overall document to determine the testator's intentions. Additionally, in many states, such as Missouri in the present case, statutes create a presumption that a will devises a full fee simple estate absent explicit language to indicate otherwise. The Missouri statute plays an interesting role in *Lewis* because, although the statute's predecessor was in existence at the time of the *Winget* case, the authority on which the respondents in *Lewis* relied so heavily, the *Winget* decision made no mention of the statute. The *Lewis* decision makes clear, however, that this court was influenced by the policy considerations underlying the statute. One other general rule for interpreting wills bears mention in light of *Lewis*, that courts will avoid interpretations that would create a partial intestacy. It is interesting to note that while the *Winget* court employed this rule to reach a decision that the will in that case created a life estate, the *Lewis* court drew on the same rule to determine that the will here created a fee simple. But note that in *Lewis*, the court claims that the reasoning used in *Winget* about this rule does not withstand scrutiny since if the devise is, as the *Lewis* decision has it, a fee simple determinable upon the marriage of the devisee, then upon her death, it would pass to her heirs the same as any other fee simple estate.

A LIFE TENANT HAS A FIDUCIARY DUTY TO REASONABLY MAINTAIN HER PROPERTY FOR THE BENEFIT OF THE REMAINDERMAN, SO, ABSENT PREJUDICE TO LIFE TENANT, LACHES WILL NOT BAR REMAINDERMAN'S SUIT FOR WASTE

Moore v. Phillips

(Remaindermen) v. (Executor of Life Tenant's estate)
627 P.2d 831 (Kan.App. 1981)

M E M O R Y   G R A P H I C

Instant Facts
Remaindermen filed a suit against the estate of a deceased life tenant for damages stemming from the life tenant's neglect of the property.

Black Letter Rule
Absent prejudice to the tenant or his estate, the passage of time will not bar a remainderman's suit for damages due to tenant's waste.

Case Vocabulary

WASTE: Damage to a property beyond normal depreciation due to a tenant's affirmative acts (COMMISSIVE WASTE) or neglect of upkeep (PERMISSIVE WASTE).

REMAINDERMAN: The person who has the right to a future interest in land, typically, the person to whom the land will pass upon the death of a life tenant.

Procedural Basis: Appeal from a district court decision overturning a district magistrate's ruling that the defenses of laches or estoppel could be used against plaintiff-remainderman's suit alleging waste.

Facts: Leslie Brennan, the original owner of the property at issue in this case, died in 1962. In his will, Brennan gave his wife Ada C. Brennan ["Ada"] a life estate in a parcel of farmland with a farmhouse. The remainder interest went to Ada's daughter Dorothy Moore ["Moore"] (P) and Kent Reinhardt ["Reinhardt"] (P). From 1964 until Ada's death in 1976, Ada and Moore (P) were estranged. After her husband's death, Ada lived in the farmhouse until August 1965. After that, no one lived in the farmhouse, although Ada rented out the farmland. During Ada's lifetime, Moore (P) and Reinhardt (P) inspected the farm property on occasion and they rented the farmhouse from 1969 to 1971, but did not live there. Due to poor health, Ada asked for a voluntary conservatorship in 1973. Ada died testate, leaving no property to Moore (P) or Reinhardt (P). After Ada's death, Moore (P) and Reinhardt (P) sued Ada's estate, the executrix of which was Ruby F. Phillips ["Phillips"] (D), for $16,159 for damages to the farmhouse due to Ada's neglect of its upkeep. Phillip (D) argued that Moore (P) and Reinhardt's (P) suit was barred by the statute of limitations, and offered the affirmative defenses of laches, estoppel and abandonment. Although the magistrate allowed the defenses of laches and estoppel, the district judge ruled that they did not apply in this case. After inspecting the house, the district court ruled for Moore (P) and Reinhardt (P) but set actual damages at $10,433. Phillips (D) appealed.

Issue: Is a suit by a remainderman alleging that a life tenant's permissive waste caused damage to a property barred by laches or estoppel where remainderman waited eleven years until the life tenant's death to file the suit?

Decision and Rationale: (Prager, J.) No. Because Ada, the life tenant, had a fiduciary duty to Moore (P) and Reinhardt (P), the remainderman, to maintain the property in good condition, the timing of their lawsuit did not prejudice Ada's estate. Phillip (D) argued that Kansas has a statute allowing remaindermen to bring a suit for waste during the life of a life tenant and that the only reason that Moore (P) and Reinhardt (P) did not bring such a suit was to avoid Ada's damaging testimony. Phillips (D) noted that Moore (P) and Reinhardt (P) had inspected the property, but had never brought any demands for repair in the past. In response, Moore (P) and Reinhardt (P) argue that they did express their worries over the farmhouse's deterioration over the years, but that most of the damage had occurred in the last two years. Moore (P) and Reinhardt (P) say that the reason they waited to file the suit was to avoid the upsetting contact between Ada and Moore (P). In property law, the life tenant, although she may use the property for her benefit, is like a trustee in that she has a fiduciary duty to the remaindermen to reasonably maintain the property. When, through her neglect or misconduct, a life tenant causes damage *in excess* of ordinary depreciation to the value of remainderman's interest, the legal term is "waste." "Permissive Waste," as alleged in this case, is waste caused by "the failure of the tenant to exercise ordinary care." The remainderman may seek damages, injunctive relief, or – in special cases – a receivership as remedies for a tenant's waste. As Phillips (D) noted, a Kansas statute permits a remainderman to sue during the tenant's lifetime. In most states, it is the tenant's death or the expiration of the tenancy, not the commission of waste, that triggers the statute of limitations. There is case law that holds that an action for waste may be barred by laches or estoppel. Laches, sometimes referred to as "sleeping on one's rights," bars a lawsuit when the delay of a party in bringing a suit acts to prejudice the opposing party. Neither laches nor estoppel is triggered simply by the passage of time. In the present case, since Ada owed a continuing duty to Moore (P) and

Reinhardt (P), the plaintiffs decision to wait until Ada's death to bring the suit does not act to prejudice her estate. The applicability of laches must be decided on a case-by-case basis. Since the delay did not act to the detriment of Ada or her estate, the trial court did not err in declaring the defense of laches inapplicable in this case. The plaintiffs' reasons for delaying the suit, to avoid further upsetting Ada and to avoid taking money she might need during her last years, are legitimate and the law should not compel them to bring suit during Ada's lifetime in this case. The district court is affirmed.

Analysis:

The most important principle to take away from *Moore* is that the duty that the life tenant owes to the remainderman is very strong. The court in *Moore* refers to the life tenant as a fiduciary of the remainderman and analogized the tenant's duty to that of a trustee. A trustee will be liable if, because of his negligence or unreasonable actions, the trust loses material value. The same is true of the life tenant if her failure to keep up the property causes a reduction in its value. The court notes one very important difference between the duties of the trustee and the life tenant. That is that the life tenant, unlike the trustee, may use the property for her exclusive benefit and keep any profits derived from the property. These kinds of actions, of course, would be strictly forbidden for a trustee. One interesting question that may occur to the reader of *Moore* is whether and how much weight the court put on the fact that Moore and Reinhardt had checked up on their property from time to time over the years. Would the court have decided any differently if they had not seen the property at all until after Ada Brannan's death? In this case, the court might have decided the same way since most of the damage was shown to have happened during the last couple of years. But what if the property had been deteriorating slowly over a decade or more? Would the court hold to its line that since the tenant's duty is continuing, there was no prejudice to the tenant from the delay or would the court think that the remainderman's failure to check up on the property was somewhat responsible for the damage? Would it make any difference whether the tenant was actually living on the property? Would it or should it make any difference that the life tenant was very elderly and unable to personally inspect the property? One item that the case does not really address is whether Ada's estate would have any recourse against the conservator, since he or she should have been protecting Ada's interests, or indeed, whether the remaindermen could seek damages from a conservator, if the conservator's negligence was the reason for the waste. Like so many cases in this section, *Moore* underlines the complexity of relationships with regard to property passed down by will.

Oldfield v. Stoeco Homes, Inc.

fee simple subject to con. sub.

(Resident and Taxpayer of Ocean City) v. (Purchaser of Land from Ocean City)

139 A.2d 291 (N.J. 1958)

M E M O R Y   G R A P H I C

 ## Instant Facts

City residents and taxpayers sued to invalidate city resolutions extending the time under which a purchaser of land from the city had to complete obligations and to have the purchaser forfeit the land back to the city.

Black Letter Rule

A deed provision stating that purchaser's failure to perform certain requirements would "automatically cause title . . . to revert" was not sufficient to create a fee simple determinable where other deed provisions and surrounding circumstances indicated that the parties intended to create a fee simple subject to a condition subsequent.

Case Vocabulary

FEE SIMPLE SUBJECT TO A CONDITION SUBSEQUENT: This is a fee estate under which the grantor may take affirmative action to have the land forfeited back to him if a certain condition occurs; it is usually created by using language such as "To A on the condition that. . . ." or "To A provided that. . . ."

grantor must act

Procedural Basis: Appeal from a trial court decision that a land deed requiring defendant-purchaser to perform certain work for the seller-city created a fee simple subject to a condition subsequent.

Facts: In 1951, the City of Ocean City, New Jersey [the "City"] (D) decided to sell large segments of lots in low-lying swampy areas to developers for the benefit of the community. Within part of the land to be sold, the City (D) planned to retain 226 lots, but to have the purchaser fill and grade these lots, as well as the lots sold to the purchaser, as a condition of the deed. The City (D) sold the land to Stoeco Homes, Inc. ["Stoeco"] (D) and confirmed the sales by city resolutions. The deed for the land outlined the conditions and restrictions on the sale, including a provision for the filling and grading mentioned above to be completed within one year. In the deed, the City (D) reserved the right "to change or modify any restriction, condition or other requirements hereby imposed in a manner . . . permitted by law." The deed went on to state that "[a] failure to comply with the covenants and conditions of [the filling and grading provisions] will automatically cause title to all lands to revert to the City of Ocean City; and a failure of other restrictions and covenants may cause title to revert to the City as to any particular land, lot or lots involved in any violation." Because of unexpected problems encountered in dredging the land in question in this case, Stoeco (D) could not complete the filling and grading within the one year time period. The City (D), still wanting the areas to be redeveloped, passed a resolution to modify the terms of the deed to extend until December 31, 1954 the date for Stoeco (D) to perform the filling and grading. On December 30, 1954, the City (D) passed another resolution extending the time for completion of the original provisions until 1958 for one part of the land and until 1960 for another. As a result, residents and taxpayers (P) of Ocean City brought suit against Stoeco (D), the City (D) and other financial institutions involved in the sale seeking to have the City's (D) time-extending resolutions declared invalid and to have the lands forfeited back to the City (D). Among their many allegations, the plaintiff residents (P) argued that the deed under which the lands were transferred created a fee simple determinable, such that Stoeco's (D) failure to perform the grading provisions would cause the lands automatically to revert to the City (D). The Defendants argued that the estate created was a fee simple subject to a condition subsequent, requiring the City (D) to take affirmative action to re-enter the lands. The trial court agreed with the Defendants that the deed created a fee simple subject to a condition subsequent. The residents and taxpayers (P) appealed.

Issue: Does a deed from a city under which a purchaser is obligated to perform certain work for the city within a time certain create a fee simple subject to a condition subsequent?

Decision and Rationale: (Burling, J.) Yes. The deed from the City (D) to Stoeco (D) created a fee simple subject to a condition subsequent because the whole of the deed indicates that this was the City's (D) intention and because deeds should be interpreted to avoid forfeitures whenever possible. The primary difference between a fee simple determinable and a fee simple subject to a condition subsequent is that in the former, the reversion of the land to the grantor is automatic, while in the latter, reversion requires the affirmative action of the grantor. Thus, the interest retained by the grantor in a fee simple determinable is called the "possibility of reverter," while that retained in a fee simple subject to a condition subsequent is called a "power of termination." The plaintiff residents (P) argued that the deed provision that Stoeco's (D) failure to comply with the filling and grading provisions "will automatically cause title to all lands to revert to the City. . . ." unequivocally created a fee simple determinable. Thus, argue the Plaintiffs, the City (D) had no ability to waive Stoeco's (D) duty to perform. Although language is the court's main guide to interpreting the intentions of the parties to the deed, such language must be viewed within the context and purpose of the document in question. If the intentions of the parties are clear from the deed itself, the court's inquiry is over. But if there is any ambiguity, the court should construe the deed to avoid forfeiture. This rule of construction, therefore, favors the fee simple subject to a condition subsequent to the fee simple determinable. In the deed at issue here, the phrase "automatically causes title to revert" must be set against the deed's repeated use of the word "conditions" to describe the performance provisions and the clause by which the City (D) reserves the right to modify "any restriction, condition or other requirements" of the deed. Since the language of the deed is not unequivocal as to the intentions of the parties, the court will examine the larger circumstances to determine which estate the parties intended to create. It is important to note that the filling and grading provisions really create two

obligations for Stoeco (D): first, to complete the grading and filling as outlined in the deed and second, to do so within one year. It is really only the second of these requirements that the city has chosen to amend. The parties surely did not consider the time provision so vital that they intended its violation "by a day would result in an immediate and automatic forfeiture of the estate." Nothing in the deed or the surrounding circumstances indicates that the City (D) considered time to be of the essence in the performance of the grading and filling. Large-scale redevelopment projects often encounter unexpected delays and difficulties that require different (and costlier) methods than were originally anticipated. Indeed, such an unexpected development is one reason to include the clause allowing the City (D) to modify its requirements. Since the parties did not intend an automatic reversion of the property after one year, the deed created a fee simple subject to a condition subsequent. The trial court's decision is affirmed.

Analysis:

This case is very useful for illustrating how courts examine the language of deeds to determine the type of estate the parties intended to create. At first blush, the automatic reversion clause of the deed at issue in *Oldfield* might seem cut and dry; if the purchaser fails to perform, the land goes back to the City. The court, however, placed this term within the larger context of the deed, especially the clause allowing Ocean City to modify the terms of the deed, and concluded that the plain language of the deed was unclear as to the parties' intentions. This analysis may cause some raised eyebrows among readers of the decision. Why, for example, would the court be willing to give a looser interpretation to the phrase "automatically cause title . . . to revert to the City" but then claim that the use of the word "condition" really does indicate the parties' intent to create an estate subject to a condition subsequent. Remember, however, that the court does not claim that the language of the deed clearly indicates the desire to create a fee simple subject to a condition subsequent, but only that the deed as a whole is unclear. It is for this reason that the court is willing to examine the conditions and circumstances surrounding the land transfer and to enlist the canon of construction preferring the creation of an estate subject to a condition subsequent. Nevertheless, the legal scholar is right to ask what the limits of interpreting language are with regard to deeds and other, similar documents. One interesting aspect of the deed language that the court appears to overlook is that the automatic reversion language was directly applied to the grading and filling requirements, while the deed provided that "failure of any other restrictions and covenants *may* cause title to revert to the City. . . ." (emphasis added). One might interpret this sentence either to indicate that the parties specifically intended the grading and filling provision to carry special weight and cause an automatic reversion, or to indicate that overall, Ocean City did intend a condition subsequent estate. In either case, the existence of that second, discretionary reversion clause shows the difficulty of discerning the parties' intentions from the often imperfect documents that ostensibly create estates in land.

Roberts v. Rhodes

(Conveyee From Heirs of Original Grantor) v. (Conveyee From Original Grantee)
643 P.2d 116 (Kan. 1982)

M E M O R Y   G R A P H I C

Instant Facts

The heir of the original grantor of property conveyed to a school district for "school purposes" sued to claim title to the property now that it was no longer being used by the school district.

Black Letter Rule

Where a deed conveyed property for "school purposes," but without provision for reversion, and the grantee-school district used the property appropriately for sixty years, the grantee has a fee simple estate in the property.

Procedural Basis: Appeal to the Supreme Court of Kansas of a Court of Appeals decision reversing a trial court decision that plaintiff, heir of the original grantor, had a reversionary interest in land conveyed to a school district for "school purposes," but no longer used for a school.

Facts: In 1902, D.W. and Margaret Smith, for consideration of one dollar, executed a quitclaim deed to the Montgomery County, Kansas school district. The deed used typical quitclaim language: "[The Smiths] . . . remise, release and quitclaim unto the parties of the second part [i.e., the school district], their heirs and assigns, all the following described real estate. . . ." But, after the description of the property, the deed continued, "it being understood that this grant is made only for school or cemetery purposes." In 1908, T.A. and Louella Stevens, this time for $75, made an almost conveyance of another property to the same school district. Again, typical quitclaim language was used with the exception of a clause stating: "It being understood that this grant is made for school and cemetery purposes only." Neither deed contained any language of reversion or other limitation relating to the stated purposes of the conveyances. The school district took possession of the properties described in the deeds and used them for school purposes for over sixty years. Since the school district could not legally operate a cemetery, the properties were never used for cemetery purposes. Rhodes (D) acquired the land after the school district sold it in 1971. Roberts (P) sued, claiming that he acquired title to the property through a deed from the heirs of the original grantors on the theory that title reverted to the heirs of the grantors when it ceased being used for school purposes. The district court agreed with Roberts (P). However, on appeal, the Court of Appeals reversed, holding that the school district had acquired fee simple title under the 1902 and 1908 deeds. Roberts (P) filed a petition for review with the Supreme Court of Kansas.

Issue: Did a school district take unrestricted fee simple title in lands under deeds that conveyed the lands for "school purposes" without other language of limitation or reversion?

Decision and Rationale: (Fromme, J.) Yes. Since the deeds contained no language indicating a reversionary interest or limitation triggered by the cessation of school use for the property, the school district acquired fee simple title in the property conveyed by the deeds. Roberts (P) argued that the school's estate was a fee simple determinable. The Restatement of Property clearly states that a fee simple determinable is created by words of limitation providing "that the estate shall automatically expire upon the occurrence of a stated event." Neither deed contained such a reversion or termination. Moreover, in Kansas, the court is directed by statute to prefer a fee simple absolute "unless the intent to pass a less estate shall expressly appear or be necessary implied in the terms of the grant" (K.S.A. 58-2202). This statute reflects the otherwise generally accepted principles of property law that (1) forfeitures are disfavored, and (2) mere statements of purpose for which the property is to be used do not create a fee simple determinable. The Restatement notes that when a deed attaches limiting words such as "until," "so long as," and "during" to its purpose provision, courts have found intent to create a determinable estate. But again, none of these words or terms is present in the deeds at issue in this case. Kansas's courts have been guided by these principles since the 1890 case of *Curtis v. Board of Education*. In Curtis, the court held that a deed granting land to a school district "for the erection of a school-house thereon, and for no other purposes" gave the school district fee simple title. In light of these rules and precedents, deeds that state that the land is to be used for school purposes, but without language of reversion or limitation, convey "fee simple title when the land has been accepted and used by the grantee for school purposes for more than sixty years." The Court of Appeals is affirmed and the case is remanded for the district court to enter judgment for Rhodes (D).

Analysis:

The *Roberts v. Rhodes* decision illustrates the law's preference for passing the greatest estate possible by showing that the Restatement of Property, Kansas case law and Kansas statutes all follow this general principle. To put it a different way, as the *Roberts* court does, forfeitures are disfavored. There are many reasons why this general rule has been adopted, but two in particular stand out. First, the law favors predictability and certainty. If a person, or business or institution, receives an estate in land, he will want to know that he can benefit from long-term plans and improvements without fear of losing the land to a reversion or future interest. It is usually in the best interest of society to have each piece of real estate put to its optimal use, and a person will hesitate to make expensive developments on land he is uncertain of keeping. Second, although the courts will enforce a grantor's will to have a piece of land used for certain purposes, they will also insist that the consequences of any other use are very clearly articulated. This is especially important when a substantial amount of time has passed since the original grant. The more attenuated one's situation is from that under which the original grant was made, the more likely it is that the land will now best serve other purposes. A deed must be quite clear about who will make decisions about its use or land may languish since a holder will not want to give up the land but may wish to use it for other purposes. This brings us to the most interesting question raised in the *Roberts* decision. Why does the court note, near the end of the decision, that the school district has used the land for school purposes for more than sixty years? The court appears to be limiting its ruling only to cases where the grantee has used the land for the purpose stated in the deed for more than sixty years. But does the court really mean sixty years and not, more generally, some substantial amount of time? Even if the court means the latter, the rules articulated by the court in the decision do not seem to indicate that the grantee must use the property for the stated purpose for any particular length of time unless the deed contains language of limitation or reversion. Perhaps the court was simply noting that the school district seems to have taken the property in utmost good faith, as indicated by their use of the property for the stated purpose for several decades. It is interesting to consider how a court might view a case in which a school district took property under an identical deed, but sold or leased it within a few months or years to someone interested in building a mall. Could the court order a reversion of the property without an explicit reversionary clause in the deed?

THE PASSAGE OF TIME DOES NOT TERMINATE GRANTOR'S RIGHTS OR GRANTEE'S OBLIGATION TO PERFORM UNDER A CONDITION SUBSEQUENT

Martin v. City of Seattle

(Successor of Grantor) v. (Grantee)
728 P.2d 1091 (Wash. Ct. App. 1986)

M E M O R Y   G R A P H I C

Instant Facts

Successors of grantor sued to compel the grantee-city to perform a condition subsequent under a seventy-five year old deed.

Black Letter Rule

(1) Absent prejudice to the grantee, the passage of time does not terminate the grantee's obligations to perform or grantor's rights to forfeit lands under a fee simple subject to a condition subsequent. [On appeal, however, the Washington Supreme Court ruled that the grantor must act within a reasonable time after grantee's breach of the condition.] (2) When a city's refusal to perform a condition subsequent destroys the value of a grantor's rights under a deed, the city has committed an unconstitutional taking, and owes the grantor the fair value of his right.

Case Vocabulary

IMPOSSIBILITY: Impossibility of performance may be advanced as a defense for failure to perform under a contract or deed when a material change in circumstances outside the control of the non-performing party or a change in the law makes it impossible to perform the terms of the contract.

Procedural Basis: Appeal and cross-appeal from a trial court decision finding for plaintiff but awarding reduced damages.

Facts: In 1908, the C.B. Dodge Company quitclaimed a strip of land to the City of Seattle [the "City"] (D) so that the City (D) could construct Lake Washington Boulevard. The deed for the land contained conditions that obligated the City (D) to allow the Dodge Company or its successors and assigns to build a boathouse on the Lake Washington shore, to acquire the land for the boathouse, and to allow building and access for its use. The deed made the City's (D) breach of these conditions grounds for the grantor to reenter and forfeit the land granted to the City (D). Substantial evidence showed that from 1908 to 1983, no boathouse was built. In 1983, the Martins (P) and other successors to the Dodge grant (P) demanded that the City (D) allow them to build a boathouse, but the City (D) refused. As a result, the Martins (P) brought suit for a declaratory judgment that the deed was valid and to forfeit the City's (D) estate in the Lake Washington Boulevard lands or, alternatively, to have the City (D) pay damages. The trial court found in favor of the Martins (P), holding that the deed was valid and setting damages at $50,000, but also held that the Martins (P) could not reenter the lands, and denied the Martins (P) attorney fees. The City (D) appealed the decision, claiming that the trial court erred in finding the deed and its conditions valid. The Martins (P) cross-appealed, seeking higher damages, the right to reenter the land, and attorney fees. The City (D) argued that the passage of time, the doctrine of laches, and changes in the lake's water levels made the conditions of the deed unenforceable. The Martins (P) argued that the City's (D) denial of the Martins' (P) right to build a boathouse constituted an unconstitutional taking.

Issue: (1) Does the passage of seventy-five years render unenforceable the grantee's obligations in a condition subsequent in a deed of land? (2) Does a city's refusal to allow a grantor to exercise a right conferred as a condition of a deed constitute an unconstitutional taking?

Decision and Rationale: (Dore, J.) (1) No. Because the deed did not contain a time limit and since the passage of time has not prejudiced the City (D), the deed and its conditions are valid. The City (D) argued that the passage of time made the Martins' (P) rights under the condition subsequent unenforceable. There is no direct case law on this question. The City (D) cited cases in which the grantor's failure to exercise a forfeiture within a reasonable time constituted a waiver of the right to forfeiture. The City also cited contract cases with similar rulings, requiring performance within a reasonable time when the contract is silent as to time. The City (D) also cited the doctrine of laches, which provides that a party who sleeps on his rights may lose those rights if the delay prejudices the other party. In this case, however, the City (D) did not prove any prejudice as a result of the passage of time. Moreover, the deed itself contemplates that successors of the Dodge Company, not the Company itself, would exercise the right to build the boathouse. If the boathouse had been built shortly after the deed, its owners would certainly still be allowed to maintain the boathouse. Since the passage of time would not affect the right to access and maintain a boathouse, it should affect the right to build the boathouse. Finally, the City (D) advanced the affirmative defense of impossibility, citing a change in the water levels of Lake Washington since the deed was made. The water level in the lake has decreased, uncovering new lands along the shore. The State owns those lands and gave them to the City (D) for use as a park, but the City (D) has not shown that it could not get the State's permission for a boathouse. Increased difficulty or cost is not sufficient to prove impossibility as a defense for non-performance. (2) Yes. The City's (D) refusal to permit the boathouse is an unconstitutional taking because the deed gives the Martins (P) a property right, the value of which is destroyed by the

government's action. Case law establishes that "property includes the unrestricted right to use, enjoy and dispose of the land." By bringing suit praying compensation for the lost value of their property, the Martins (P) "are bringing an action for inverse condemnation," and their remedy should be payment for the full value of their damages.

Since testimony at trial established the value of the right to build the boathouse at $60,000, the trial court erred in lowering the damage amount to $50,000. The trial court is reversed and the case is remanded for the calculation of reasonable attorney fees.

Analysis:

While this case is illustrative of many difficult issues involved in the creation of defeasible fee estates, it is important to note that the Washington Supreme Court overturned the ruling here in *Martin v. Seattle*, 765 P.2d 257 (1988). In that decision, the Washington Supreme Court held that a grantor must act to reenter and forfeit the land within a reasonable time *after the grantee's breach*. The Washington Supreme Court found that the breach had actually occurred in 1913, the date that the City first received the parkland property from the State. Thus, the Supreme Court ruled against the Martins because they had waited too long to seek forfeiture of the lands. As following cases will show, some states have adopted statutes that limit the time for a grantor to reenter. Other aspects of this case, however, are still quite useful in showing the many considerations that the property law practitioner must consider when creating a fee simple with a condition subsequent. The unconstitutional taking issue, in particular, is interesting because it reminds us that anytime a transfer of land is made between a private party and a governmental entity, the property lawyer drafting the deed will have special issues to consider and about which her client must be informed. The court in Martin was able to sidestep one interesting (and potentially very thorny) issue, whether the Martins could have declined money damages and insisted on reversion of the property. Here, the takings issue is very important because the remedy for condemnation is fair money damages. It is interesting to consider whether the result would be different if the original grantor had acted to build the boathouse shortly after the conveyance and had asked only for forfeiture of the lands.

Johnson v. City of Wheat Ridge

(Grantor's Executor and Heir) v. (Grantee)
532 P.2d 985 (Colo. Ct. App. 1975)

WELL, THERE ARE NO BATHROOMS, SO I GUESS I OWN THIS LAND AGAIN!

JOHNSON PARK

M E M O R Y   G R A P H I C

Instant Facts

Several years after grantee-city's alleged breach of a condition subsequent, the grantor's heir sued to terminate city's estate in deeded property.

Black Letter Rule

Grantor's suit to reenter and take possession of lands due to grantee's breach of a condition subsequent is barred when not filed within the statutory limitation period.

Procedural Basis: Plaintiff appealed the trial court's dismissal of his suit to quiet title to lands as an heir of the grantor.

Facts: In 1955 and 1957, Judge Johnson, an elderly man, made the two land conveyances at issue in this case. In 1955, he conveyed five acres to the Wheat Ridge Lions Foundation, under the condition that it be used for a public park named after the grantor. In 1957, he conveyed roughly fourteen acres to Jefferson County, to be used for the Wheat Ridge Recreation District, also under the condition that it be used for "Johnson Park." The deed for the fourteen-acre parcel was conditioned on the grantee's timely completion of a road to the land, the clearing of fire hazards, and installation of public lavatories and water. Both deeds contained a clause stating that the failure to comply with the conditions "shall constitute a condition subsequent terminating the estate of the Grantee" in the property and that "the Grantor, his heirs or assigns may re-enter and take possession of said premises." In 1958, Judge Johnson gave written consent for the five-acre parcel to be transferred to the County, again on behalf of the Recreation District, subject to the original deed. Both parcels were transferred to the City of Wheat Ridge [the "City"] upon its incorporation in 1969. In 1971, Paul Johnson ["Johnson"] (P), Judge Johnson's executor and heir, brought suit to quiet his title in the above property claiming that Judge Johnson was unduly influenced when making the original conveyances and that the grantees, including the City (D), had failed to perform under the deeds' conditions. After taking evidence, the district court dismissed Johnson's (P) suit for the following reasons: (1) the grantees had performed all but one condition of the deeds, (2) the suit was barred by the statute of limitations, (3) the suit was barred by laches, and (4) the evidence was insufficient to sustain the undue influence allegation.

Issue: Is a grantor's (or grantor's heir's) suit to reenter and terminate grantee's estate for failure to perform a condition subsequent barred for failure to file within the statutory limitations period after grantee's alleged breach?

Decision and Rationale: (Enoch, J.) Yes. Johnson (P) sought to have the district court enforce his right to terminate a grantee's estate due to the grantee's breach of a condition subsequent. Such judicial proceedings are governed by the statute of limitations. The limitations statute relevant to this case states that an action "to enforce the terms of any restriction concerning real property" must be "commenced within one year from the violation. . . ." The evidence showed that the only condition of the original deeds not met by the grantees was the timely installation of lavatories on the fourteen-acre parcel. This breach does not effect an automatic reversion of title to the grantor or his heirs. In this case, the breach occurred in 1959 and the limitations period began to run from that time. This lawsuit is barred by the statute of limitations. The trial court's conclusion that there was insufficient evidence of undue influence will not be overturned. Thus, the trial court's decision is affirmed.

Analysis:

This relatively straightforward case clearly illustrates that a court may apply a limitations statute quite strictly to a defeasible fee case. In comparison to the more in-depth analysis that the passage of time received in *Martin v. City of Seattle*, the statute of limitations rule seems cut and dry. The advantages of this simpler analysis are easy to see, especially for grantees who want certainty concerning their interest in a parcel of land. It is important to realize, though, that the possibly short duration of the limitations period means that the grantor may have to keep closer tabs on the grantee's progress in fulfilling any required conditions or forego the right of reentry and forfeiture. This concern is interesting to consider in the *Johnson* case, although the court did not address it directly. While the court did not find enough evidence to support an allegation that Judge Johnson was unduly influenced in making his original conveyances, the court did note that he was quite elderly at that time. One wonders if he was aware that a statute of limitations would apply to any suit seeking to reenter the lands conveyed to the city, and whether he was able to monitor the grantee's progress in creating and improving the park lands. Similar concerns could apply to a grantor who lived a great distance from the land and thus had difficulty checking up on the performance of any conditions. In most cases, the grantor probably assumes at the time of the conveyance that the grantee intends to fulfill the conditions of the deed, and may not be as diligent as necessary in following up on the grantee's progress. Thus, in a jurisdiction where a statute of limitations – the period was only one year in *Johnson* – may cut off a grantor's suit to terminate the grantee's estate, it is very important that a lawyer preparing the deed inform his client of the need to stay abreast of any developments affecting the deed.

Leeco Gas & Oil Company v. County of Nueces

(Grantor) v. (Grantee)

736 S.W.2d 629 (Tex. 1987)

M E M O R Y   G R A P H I C

Instant Facts

Grantor appealed a trial court decision that the grantee-county needed to pay grantor only nominal damages when it condemned the grantor's future interest in land the county wanted to develop without restriction.

Black Letter Rule

To condemn a grantor's reversionary interest in property for which it holds the defeasible fee, a governmental entity must pay grantor the difference between the fee simple and the defeasible fee interests in that land.

Procedural Basis: Appeal to the Texas Supreme Court of a court of appeals decision affirming a trial court ruling that grantee-County could condemn grantor's reversionary interest and pay only nominal damages.

Facts: In 1960, Leeco Gas ["Leeco"] (P) gave fifty acres to Nueces County [the "County"] (D) by gift deed, with the condition "so long as a public park is constructed and maintained" on the property. The County (D) built and kept a park on the property, but initiated condemnation proceedings against Leeco's (P) reversionary interest in 1983. Leeco (P) was awarded $10,000 in the condemnation proceedings. Leeco (P) appealed the condemnation commissioners' decision to county court. The county court entered summary judgment against Leeco (P) on all issues except damages. Although Leeco (P) experts testified at a trial to determine damages that Leeco's (P) interest was worth $3 to 5 million, the trial court awarded Leeco (P) only $10, designated nominal damages. Leeco (P) appealed and the court of appeals affirmed the trial court decision. Leeco (P) appealed to the Texas Supreme Court, arguing that the County's (D) knowing acceptance of a deed with a reversionary interest estopped the County (D) from condemning the property. Leeco (P) also challenged the damage amount.

Issue: May a grantee-county condemn the reversionary interest in a gift deed subject to a condition subsequent and pay only nominal damages?

Decision and Rationale: (Gonzalez, J.) No. Although the County (D) is not estopped from condemning Leeco's (P) reversionary interest, the possibility that the County (D) would breach the conditions of the deed were not so remote as to justify an award of merely nominal damages. Since the acquisition of land for parks and recreation is a governmental function and since case law establishes that a governmental entity is not subject to estoppel when conducting legitimate governmental functions, the County (D) is not estopped from condemning the land. Resolution of the damages issue, however, requires a longer analysis and a look at the County's (D) testimony regarding the park property. The general rule is that "a possibility of reverter has no ascertainable value" when the triggering event is not "probable within a reasonably short period of time." The court of appeals decision affirming the nominal damages found that the County (D) was unlikely to ever breach the deed conditions while Leeco (P) had its reversionary interest. The court of appeals then applied *City of Houston v. McCarthy*, which held that when a grantee was unlikely to ever breach the applicable condition, the reversionary interest had a merely speculative value. The present case, however, is distinguishable from *McCarthy*. Although the County (D) may not have breached the deed conditions while Leeco (P) retained its possibility of reverter, there was ample evidence – from county officials' testimony and in the County's (D) condemnation statement – to indicate that the County (D) was contemplating plans for the property that would be inconsistent with the deed restrictions. In the present case, the County (D) saw Leeco's (P) reversionary interest as a "burden" to be removed to facilitate flexibility in future plans for the land. Moreover, in *McCarthy* and related cases, the condemning governmental entity owned neither the possessory nor reversionary interests in the land and had to pay the full value of the property in damages. Those cases were to decide whether the damages would be paid to the owner of the possessory interest or to the owner of the future interest. In the present case, on the other hand, the condemning entity, the County (D), owns the defeasible fee, the conditions of which restrict the County's (D) possible future plans for this multi-million dollar property. It would be bad public policy to allow the County (D) to pay only nominal damages to Leeco (P) because this would discourage further gift deeds for the public good. Thus, when a grantee-governmental entity condemns the future interest in land for which it holds the defeasible deed, damages will be the difference between the values of an unrestricted fee simple and the defeasible fee interests. The court of appeals decision is reversed and the case is remanded for a trial to determine the damage calculation set out above.

Concurrence: (Campbell, J.) While there is precedent for the majority decision in this case, future cases should hold that a governmental entity's attempt to condemn future interests in gifted land should be treated as a renunciation of the gift. The land would simply revert to the grantor in an unrestricted fee simple estate.

Analysis:

One of the most striking aspects of the Leeco decision is the Texas Supreme Court's analysis of the testimony indicating that the County would use the park property in a manner inconsistent with the gift deed. The lower courts do not appear to have been much concerned with the County's plans for the property after it had terminated Leeco's reversionary interest. The supreme court's decision characterizes the court of appeals as having ended its inquiry once it determined that the County would not breach the deed so long as Leeco kept its possibility of reverter. This raises a number of interesting questions. How influenced was the supreme court by the likelihood of the County acting in a way that would violate the deed restrictions? Was the fact that the County wanted out from under the defeasible fee itself evidence that it was contemplating a plan that would have triggered Leeco's reversionary interest under the deed? The lower courts' decisions certainly seem simpler in many ways, but the supreme court's decision seems more equitable under this set of circumstances. It is an interesting exercise to try to hypothesize a situation where a governmental entity might want to condemn a grantor's future interest even though the government had no reason to think its future plans would risk a reversion. The other interesting set of questions related to this case are raised by the concurrence. Justice Campbell apparently agreed with most of the majority's reasoning, but suggested a different resolution to the problem. Rather than a scheme for calculating damages, the concurrence simply suggests that when a governmental entity that has a gift deed subject to a condition subsequent takes action to condemn the grantor's reversionary interest, the property automatically reverts to the grantor in fee simple. Presumably, the governmental entity could then use its power of eminent domain to condemn the fee interest and take the land for its proposed use anyway. When compared with the majority decision's remedy, this solution raises a couple of questions. Would the value to the grantor or to the grantee-governmental entity be identical under the two proposals? If not, under which solution would the value to the grantor be greater? The majority's method really tries to account for the value of the reversionary interest, which is, after all, what is being condemned in this case. The concurrence, on the other hand, would have condemnation constitute the rejection of the gift. Presumably, the governmental entity would have to pay the fair market value of a fee simple estate if it used eminent domain to condemn the property after it had reverted to the grantor. While the concurrence seems to protect the interest of the grantor, does it deprive the governmental entity of some of the value of the gift of land?

WHERE A WILL CONFERRED A FEE SIMPLE WITH THE QUALIFICATION THAT IF GRANTEE DIED WITHOUT ISSUE, THEN THE LAND PASSED TO ANOTHER, GRANTEE RECEIVED A FEE TAIL

Caccamo v. Banning

(Seller of Real Property) v. (Purchaser of Real Property)
75 A.2d 222 (Del. 1987)

ACTUALLY, HE WAS BORN WITH A TAIL, BUT WE HAD IT CUT OFF!

M E M O R Y G R A P H I C

Instant Facts

Plaintiff-seller of property brought suit to compel defendant-buyer to accept the tendered deed, which buyer has rejected on grounds that title was unmarketable, and to pay the purchase price.

Black Letter Rule

Absent language indicating grantor's conflicting intentions, a deed that gives grantee "a fee simple except if grantee should die without issue of her body," gives grantee a fee tail estate.

Case Vocabulary

FEE TAIL: Title to land that can pass only to certain natural descendants of the grantor; if the grantee dies without having had natural issue, the title will pass to the heirs of another. Originally a medieval estate, the fee tail is now illegal in a large majority of states.

DISENTAILMENT: The process, usually created by statute, allowing a person to bar a fee tail and prevent another person from asserting his rights under the fee tail; disentailment usually results in the creation of a fee simple absolute in the grantee.

ISSUE: In the law of wills and property, issue refers to natural offspring; in many cases, the term "issue" is interpreted to exclude adopted children.

Procedural Basis: Lawsuit filed by seller of property to determine whether seller has a fee simple interest in land and can compel buyer to pay the agreed purchase price.

Facts: In his will, Benjamin F. Potter, gave his wife a life estate in certain real property. The will instructed that, after his wife's death, the property was to go to his granddaughter, Anna Naomi Coverdale [now married as "Caccamo"] (P), "in fee simple and absolutely forever; but in case [Caccamo (P)] should die without leaving lawful issue of her body begotten then and in that case I give, devise and bequeath all the same over unto [others]." After Potter's widow died, Caccamo (P) tried to statutorily disentail the estate. In April 1950, Caccamo (P) auctioned the property to Delema W. Banning ["Banning"] (D) for $2,025. Banning (D) put down a $405 deposit and promised to pay the difference when Caccamo (P) delivered good title. In June 1950, Caccamo (P) tendered a deed for fee simple title, but Banning (D) rejected the deed as failing to give good, marketable title. Caccamo (P) argues that Potter's will conveyed a fee tail estate to her and that through disentailment she now has a fee simple. Banning (D), on the other hand, argues that Potter's will conveyed to Caccamo (P) a fee simple that is rendered void should she die without having left lawful issue, i.e., that Caccamo's (P) interest in the land would end at the time of her death. Another way to state Banning's (D) contention is that Potter's will limits Caccamo's (P) interest to a "definite rather than an indefinite failure of issue." Both Caccamo (P) and Banning (D) agree that if the court finds that Potter's will gave Caccamo (P) a fee simple or a fee tail that she has successfully disentailed, Banning (D) will take the land and pay Caccamo (P) the balance of the purchase price. The parties also agree that if the court finds that Caccamo (P) has any other estate, she will return Banning's (D) $405 in earnest money.

Issue: Does a will granting a fee simple estate to a granddaughter "but in the case that [granddaughter] should die without leaving lawful issue of her body begotten" then to another convey a fee tail estate to the granddaughter?

Decision and Rationale: (Wolcott, Judge) Yes. Case law establishes that a will containing a gift of land "to A and her heirs forever, 'except she should die without heir born of her own body', with a remainder in that event over to B" creates a fee tail estate in A (Roach v Martin's Lessee). The present case falls within the purview of this rule unless something in Potter's will indicates that he intended the property to pass to others at the time of Caccamo's (P) death without issue, that is, that he intended a definite failure of issue to trigger the gift over. The only item in the entire will or codicil that might indicate intent on Potter's part to indicate a definite failure of issue is the word "leaving" in the phrase "should die without leaving lawful issue of her body." In a previous case, the state supreme court interpreted similar language to create a fee tail estate. Because Caccamo's (P) interest had been disentailed by statute, she had a fee simple estate when she tendered the deed to Banning (D) in June. Therefore, judgment is entered in favor of Caccamo (P) and Banning (D) is ordered to pay the remainder of the purchase price plus costs.

Analysis:

The fee simple conditional and its descendant, the fee tail, are among the most difficult and confusing topics in property law (or any other type of law, for that matter). The crucial feature of the fee tail is that it could only be inherited by designated natural descendants of the grantee. The fee tail estate would expire when its holder died without having had any offspring that qualified to inherit the estate. This situation is termed a "failure of issue." Fortunately, the fee tail estate is almost entirely a thing of the past. Unfortunately, the language "to A and the heirs of his body" still lurks among many a deed or conveyance. As was the case in *Caccamo*, many states now have statutes that transform fee tail estates into fee simple estates in the grantee. One element of the *Caccamo* decision that warrants elaboration is the court's distinction between definite and indefinite failure of issue. Originally, in England, the estate "to A and the heirs of his body" lasted as long as the natural descendants of the grantee continued to have more such natural descendents. Since it was uncertain when the estate would expire, the event that would trigger the gift over to B was dubbed an "indefinite failure of issue." This is the archetypal *fee tail* estate. The alternative interpretation, advanced by the defendant in *Caccamo*, is that the deed specifies a "definite failure of issue," meaning that one looks at the time of the grantee's death to see if she had issue. If so, the gift over to B is defeated once and for all. This was important in *Caccamo*, since the Connecticut disentailment statute apparently created a fee simple in the case of a deed with indefinite failure of issue language but not where the deed contained a definite failure of issue provision. Once the court had decided that the deed language indicated a classic fee tail with an indefinite failure of issue provision, the statutory process gave Caccamo a fee simple absolute, which meant she could transfer good, marketable title to Banning.

Perspective
Future Interests

Chapter 15

When the first four words of the chapter are "Future Interests is tough," you know it will definitely *not* be "a piece of cake."

When the first paragraph says, "This course is not by any to be entered into inadvisably or lightly..." you know the subject matter will definitely *not* be a "walk in the park."

The analysis of "Future Interests" is correct—it is *extremely* difficult to comprehend. But enough of the negativity. . . .

The subject of future interest is just what it says—an interest in property that comes into possession in the future. The interest in the property is a present interest, with the right to possession occurring in the future. There are five kinds of future interests: (1) Possibility of Reverter; (2) Power of Termination; (3) Executory Interest; (4) Remainder; and, (5) Reversion.

You will learn what each of these means, but keep in mind that the manner in which the future interest is classified depends upon the type of estate that precedes it and whether the future interest is in the grantor or a third person.

You will also learn about various rules and doctrines, most originating in England. Examples include the Doctrine of Destruction of Contingent Remainder, the Rule In Shelley's Case, the Doctrine of Worthier Title, and the Rule Against Perpetuities.

They all pertain in some fashion to future interests, whether destroying certain estates, prohibiting their creation, or voiding certain transfers.

If you plot out each factual scenario into a simple example such as, "O to A for life and then to B," it will help greatly in identifying the interests held by each party and understanding the concepts introduced.

Chapter 15

NOTE: THE PURPOSE OF THIS OUTLINE IS TO ORGANIZE THE CASES SO THAT ONE CAN QUICKLY UNDERSTAND THE RELEVANCE OF EACH CASE TO THE COURSE. NO ATTEMPT IS MADE IN THIS OVERVIEW TO ADDRESS EVERY CONCEPT THAT MUST BE STUDIED. BE SURE TO READ THE ENTIRE CASEBOOK AND/OR OTHER MATERIALS TO GAIN A FULL UNDERSTANDING OF ALL CONCEPTS.

I. Overview of Future Interests
  A. Definition of Future Interest: A present property interest that entitles the holder to possession of the property in the future.
  B. The holder of the future interest cannot enter possession until the termination of the preceding estates.
  C. Future interests are inheritable, and may be conveyed by deed or will, even before the taking of possession occurs.

II. Future Interests in the Grantor or in a Third Person
  A. A "reversion" is a future interest retained by the grantor.
     1. Example—Grantor A, owner of a fee simple absolute, conveys to B a life estate or a term for years. A retains a reversion in fee simple.
  B. A "remainder" is a future interest created in a third person.
     1. Example—A is granted immediate possession for life, and then to B and his heirs. B has a remainder in fee simple absolute.
  C. Not all future interests in third persons are remainders; some are considered "executory interests"—an interest granted to a third person when the grantor has conveyed a defeasible estate to another grantee.
     1. Example—To A and her heirs, but if liquor is sold on the premises, then to B and his heirs.

III. Vested and Contingent Remainders
  A. A "vested" remainder exists when:
     1. It is given to a born and ascertained person, and
     2. It is not subject to a condition precedent.
        a. "Vested remainders may be:
           (1) Indefeasibly vested—not subject to defeat.
           (2) Vested subject to partial divestiture, or subject to open.

(3) Vested subject to total divestiture.
  B. A "contingent" remainder exists when:
     1. It is given to a person who is unborn or unascertained, or
     2. It is subject to a condition precedent.
     3. Thus, a remainder in real property is "vested" when there is a person capable of being ascertained and ready to take, who has a present right of future enjoyment, which is not dependent upon any uncertain event or contingency, while in the case of a "contingent" remainder the right itself is uncertain. *Kost v. Foster*.
        a. At common law, a contingent remainder was an inalienable interest, and could not be levied upon by judicial process.
        b. Most courts now favor alienability of interests in land, including both vested and contingent remainders.

IV. Doctrine of Destruction of Contingent Remainder
  A. A common law rule providing for the destruction of a contingent remainder, which fails to vest at or before the termination of the preceding freehold estate.
  B. Originating in England in the Sixteenth Century, the doctrine was based upon the feudal concept that seisin of land could never be in abeyance. From that principle, the rule developed that if the prior estate terminated before the occurrence of the contingency, the contingent remainder was destroyed for lack of a supporting freehold estate.
     1. The one instance in which this could happen was when the supporting life estate merged with the reversionary interest.
  C. The destructibility doctrine is now almost universally regarded as obsolete by legislatures, courts, and legal writers.
     1. Thus, the merger of a life estate with the reversionary interest does not destroy contingent remainder. *Abo Petroleum Corporation v. Amstutz*.

V. The Rule In Shelley's Case
  A. The Rule In Shelley's Case provides that when a person takes a freehold estate and in the same instrument there is a limitation, by way of remainder, of an interest of the same legal or equitable

quality, to his heirs, or heirs of his body, as a class of person, to take in succession, from generation to generation, the limitation to the heirs entitles the ancestor to the whole estate. *Sybert v. Sybert.*

B. A majority of the states has abolished the Rule, as has England from where it originated.

C. The rule's name comes from the old English case of *Wolfe v. Shelley* (1581).

D. The effect of the Rule was prohibiting the creation of a contingent remainder in the heirs of one to whom the same will or deed gave a life estate.

VI. The Doctrine of Worthier Title

A. It is also known as the rule against a remainder to the grantor's heirs, or the conveyor-heir rule.

B. It prohibits the creation of a remainder in the grantor's heirs by deed.

C. Thus, a limitation contained in a deed conveying real property, which provides that the land shall revert back to the grantor, or to his lawful heirs, if the life tenant should die without heirs, is a remainder subject to the rule against a remainder to the grantor's heirs (i.e., the Doctrine of Worthier Title) thereby causing the grantor to retain a reversion in the land. *Braswell v. Braswell.*

D. The Doctrine of Worthier title exists in most states, although some states (such as California) have recommended abolishing it as to both inter vivos and testamentary transfers because:

1. It is based upon the false premise that the grantor does not really intend to give the property to his heirs, but instead intends to retain a reversion with full power to dispose of the property again in the future.

2. It breeds litigation.

3. It can create estate and inheritance tax problems.

VII. Executory Interests

A. Statute of Uses

1. Historical Rise

a. Feudal lawyers developed a scheme of transferring land to two or more joint tenants to hold "for the use of" the grantor or other persons as specified.

b. "Feoffee to uses" was the term for the transferee, and he had legal title (i.e., he was seised of the fee simple estate.)

c. "Cestui que use" was the term for the person for whose benefit the transferee was to hold the land, and he had only a beneficial interest.

d. Since wills were not permitted long ago, the feoffment to uses allowed for the passing of land at death to non-heirs.

e. However, if the feoffee to uses were dishonest to his "trust," the cestui que use had no remedy.

f. The King of England intervened and the feoffee to uses were ordered to carry out the "trust" or be held in contempt.

2. The Statute of Uses was created in 1535 by the English parliament, and it read:
"Where any person or persons stand or be seised ... to the use, confidence or trust of any other person or persons or to any body politic ... that in every such case all and every such person or persons and bodies politic that have ... any such use in fee simple, fee tail, for term of life or for years ... or in remainder or reverter shall stand and be seised ... in lawful seisin estate and possession of the same ... lands ... to all intents of and in such like estates as they had or shall have in the use."

3. The Statute did not abolish or prohibit conveyances to uses, but rather *executed* the use—the seisin (and therefore the legal estate) vested in the cestui que use, passing through the feoffee to uses (a conduit through which legal title passed).

4. Because the Statute destroyed the use as a method of devising property on death, the Statute of Wills was passed five years later in 1540.

5. Loopholes were eventually discovered in the Statute of Uses, mainly:

a. It did not apply to a use on a use;

b. It did not apply to personal property; and,

c. It did not apply to active uses (as opposed to passive).

6. Called the most important single piece of legislation in Anglo-American law of property, the Statute of Uses led to the rise of the modern trust, new methods of conveying real property, and new estates in land.

a. New methods of conveying land included the modern day "bargain-and-sale" form of a "deed" and the "covenant to stand seised" derived from "good" consideration through a legal relationship based on blood or marriage.

b. New estates in land resulted from the expansion of the freehold estates by permitting certain types of future interests.

c. The Statute resulted in changing the common law so that it was possible to:

(1) Limit a freehold to begin *in futuro*;

(2) Limit a remainder after the grant of a fee simple;

(3) Limit a remainder so as to vest in possession prior to the normal ending of the preceding estate; and,

(4) Use a power of appointment to vest in a third party an interest greater than that owned by the donee of the power.

B. Rule Against Perpetuities

1. As stated by Professor Gray:

"No interest is good unless it must vest, if at all, not later than twenty-one years after some life in being at the creation of the interest."

2. If an interest violates the Rule, it is void for remoteness, but the rest of the gift is valid. *Cribbet and Johnson, Principles of the Law of Property.*

C. Executory Interests

1. The statute of uses resulted in the recognition of executory interests—an interest held by a third person that follows an estate subject to executory interest.

a. Shifting executory interests exist where the possessory right shifts from one grantee to another.

b. Most executory interests today are "shifting" executory interests.

2. Shifting Executory Interests

a. Where the fee in the first taker created by a deed is made determinable, as upon the happening of a valid condition subsequent, followed by a limitation over of the fee or use to another upon the happening of the prescribed event, the fee or use shifts from the first to the second taker, whereby the deed is a conveyance under the statute of uses, and is a clear case of shifting use. *Stoller v. Doyle.*

3. Springing Executory Interests

a. It is an interest or use that comes about upon the happening of a future event.

b. An anti-racial restrictive covenant between property owners, with forfeiture clause if agreement is violated, was not an enforceable executory interest, but instead was a racial restriction in violation of the Fourteenth Amendment. *Captiol Federal Savings & Loan Association v. Smith.*

VIII. Another Look At The Rule Against Perpetuities

A. It originated in the late 17th century to deal with donative transfers of land among family members that resulted in remote vesting.

B. The rule against remote vesting in future generations protected the public's interest in land development and controlled undue concentration of wealth and power.

C. It struck a balance, however, by allowing landowners to provide for known family members and those within the first generation thereafter.

D. The common-law Rule is now a minority rule, with many states having created their own variations of the rule, some abandoning it all together, and others adopting the Uniform Statutory Rule Against Perpetuities.

E. If a violation of the Rule Against Perpetuities occurs, it does not void the entire conveyance, just that portion that violates the Rule. *The City of Klamath Falls v. Bell.*

1. When an executory interest, following a fee simple in land is void under the Rule Against Perpetuities, the prior interest becomes absolute unless the language of the creating instrument makes it very clear that the prior interest is to terminate whether the executory interest takes effect or not. *The City of Klamath Falls v. Bell.*

F. The Uniform Statutory Rule Against Perpetuities does not apply to commercial transactions. *Shaver v. Clanton.*

Kost v. Foster

(Children of Grantor) v. (Purchaser of 1/7th Interest)
(1950) 406 Ill. 565

M E M O R Y   G R A P H I C

Instant Facts

Grantee children (Kost) unsuccessfully argued that the conveyance of a deed of 1/7th of the family's property to a third party (Foster) was void because the bankrupt child from whom the interest derived held only a contingent remainder in the property, rather than a vested remainder.

Black Letter Rule

A remainder in real property is "vested" when there is a person capable of being ascertained and ready to take, who has a present right of future enjoyment, which is not dependent upon any uncertain event or contingency, while in the case of a "contingent" remainder the right itself is uncertain.

Case Vocabulary

CONTINGENT REMAINDER: A future interest created in a third person who is unborn or unascertained, or is made subject to a condition precedent.

COUNTERCLAIM: A court pleading, like a complaint, by defendant against plaintiff or others.

DECREE FOR PARTITION: A court order that divides property held by two or more persons.

RULE OF DESTRUCTIBILITY OF CONTINGENT REMAINDERS: A common law rule which provided that a contingent remainder will be destroyed unless the future interest vests by the time it is to become possessory.

VESTED REMAINDER: A future interest created in a third person who is born and ascertained, and that is not subject to a condition precedent.

WARRANTY DEED: A deed to real property that contains covenants of good, clear title.

Procedural Basis: Appeal from a decree of partition of real property entered following court trial.

Facts: In 1897, husband and wife grantors, John and Catherine Kost, executed a warranty deed conveying certain real property to their son, Ross Kost, "to have and to hold use and control for and during his natural life only, at his death to his lawful children…." Ross Kost took possession and occupied the real property until his death in 1949. Ross Kost had seven living children at the time of his death. Five of the children were born prior to the execution of the deed of John and Catherine Kost—including Oscar Kost (P and counter-D)—and two were born subsequent thereto. In 1936, prior to the death of Ross Kost, a trustee in bankruptcy of the estate of Oscar Kost (P and counter-D), bankrupt, executed a deed of conveyance of the 1/7th interest in the real property of Oscar Kost (P and counter-D) to Foster (D and counter-P). The Kost children (P and counter-D) filed a complaint seeking to declare the trustee's deed as void and removed as a cloud on the title, and that the real property be partitioned according their rights and interests in the property. [The kids said "hey, Oscar only had a contingent remainder in the property, not a vested remainder, so the trustee should not have deeded Oscar's interest to Foster." Keep reading to find out what all this means!]. Foster (D and counter-P) filed a counterclaim asserting that he was the owner of the undivided 1/7th interest which Oscar had because he had purchased such interest and the deed was not subject to collateral attack. The trial court ruled in favor of Foster (D and counter-P). The Kost children (P and counter-D) appeal from the decree of partition entered on the counterclaim of Foster (D and counter-P).

Issue: Is a vested remainder created in an estate in real property where it is vested in quality, but contingent in quantity?

Decision and Rationale: (Daily) Yes. We must decide whether or not the interest of Oscar Kost (P and counter-D) was a vested remainder at the time of the purported sale by the trustee in bankruptcy, because if the interest was not vested and was instead a contingent remainder, it would not pass to a trustee in bankruptcy of the remainderman. The chief characteristic that distinguishes a vested from a contingent remainder is the present capacity to take effect in possession should the possession become vacant, with the certainty that the event upon which the vacancy depends will happen sometime, and not upon the certainty that it will happen or the possession become vacant during the lifetime of the remainderman. In the case of a vested remainder, there is a person capable of being ascertained and ready to take, who has a present right of future enjoyment that is not dependent upon any uncertain event or contingency, while in the case of a contingent remainder the right itself is uncertain. The uncertainty that distinguishes a contingent remainder is the uncertainty of the right and not of the actual enjoyment. If the language has the conditional element incorporated into the description or into the gift to the remainderman then the remainder is contingent, but if, after words giving a vested interest, a clause is added making it subject to being divested, the remainder is vested. Thus, on a devise to A for life, the remainder to his children, but if any child dies in the lifetime of A his share to go to those who survive, the share of each child is vested, subject to be divested by its death, but on a devise to A for life, remainder to such of his children as survive him, the remainder is contingent. When a conveyance of a particular estate is made to support a remainder over, the tenant for the particular estate takes it, and if the remainderman is in being he takes the fee. In such a case the remainder is not contingent as to its becoming a vested remainder, because the title vests in the remainderman on the delivery of the deed. The title thus vested becomes an estate of inheritance. When John and Catherine Kost executed the deed, there were five children of Ross Kost (the life tenant) in being, including Oscar Kost (P and counter-D), and designated as remainderman and capable of taking immediate possession upon termination of the life estate. The remainders, while vested in the children already born to the life tenant, are contingent in quantity until the death of the life tenant because of the possibility of the birth of other children, who will have a right to share in the estate. We find no authority for the contention that the rule as to the destruction of contingent remainders should be applied when the estate is vested in quality but contingent in quantity. The estate in remainder vested in the five children of Ross Kost upon the execution and delivery of the deed, and it vested in each of the other children as each of them was born. We reject the contention that the gift over to the children of any deceased child of Ross Kost indicated an intention of the grantors to create a contingent remainder in the children of Ross Kost; since if the remainders were vested it would descend to the issue of any child who might die during the lifetime of Ross Kost, and, therefore, no substitution would have been necessary. Applying Gray's Rule Against Perpetuities test, we find that the gift over was a condition subsequent, and no conditional limitation was incorporated into the description of or into the gift to the remainderman. The remainder is subject to being divested on the contingency of one of the children of Ross Kost dying before the life tenant and leaving lawful children. Thus, we conclude that language contained in the deed meets every test for the creation of a vested remainder in the lawful children of Ross Kost. Since Oscar Kost (P and counter-D) had a vested remainder, a trustee in bankruptcy could properly convey his interest, and Foster (D and counter-P) acquired an undivided $1/7^{th}$ interest in the fee of the real estate, subject to the life estate of Ross Kost. Decree affirmed.

Analysis:

The reason the parties to this case were arguing as to whether the remainder was vested or contingent was because, at common law, a contingent remainder was an inalienable interest, and could not be levied upon by judicial process. See, *Goodwine State Bank v. Mullins.* Thus, if the court had held that the remainder was contingent, the trustee's deed conveying the $1/7^{th}$ interest to Foster (D and counter-P) would have been void. However, most courts now favor alienability of interests in land, including both vested and contingent remainders. Note that the Kost children (P and counter-D) attempted to apply the rule as to the destruction of contingent remainders—a common law rule providing for the destruction of a contingent remainder, which fails to vest at or before the termination of the preceding freehold estate. Although the doctrine is infrequently applied today, the next case shows that attempts are still made to have it applied.

Abo Petroleum Corporation v. Amstutz

(Fee Simple Grantee of Prior Estate) v. (Contingent Remainder Grandchildren)

(1979) 93 N.M. 332

M E M O R Y   G R A P H I C

Instant Facts

Deed to real property was challenged by Abo (P) on the grounds that the contingent remainders of the grandchildren, Amstutz (D), were destroyed by the merger of the grantee-daughters' life estates with the reversionary interest of the grantor-parents.

Black Letter Rule

Merger of life estate with the reversionary interest does not destroy contingent remainder.

Case Vocabulary

CONDITIONAL DEEDS: A conveyance of real property that is based on the occurrence of a certain event or conduct.

DOCTRINE OF DESTRUCTIBILITY OF CONTINGENT REMAINDERS: If a prior estate terminates before the occurrence of the contingency, the contingent remainder is destroyed for lack of a supporting freehold estate, e.g., where the supporting life estate merges with the reversionary interest.

QUIET TITLE: Court action that seeks to show who has title to land, by compelling the adverse party to prove he has a right to the property or be estopped from asserting such right in the future.

REVERSIONARY INTEREST: A future estate retained by the grantor because an estate of a lesser quantity has been conveyed, such as estates for years or life estates.

SEISIN OF LAND: Ownership; possession of a freehold estate in land.

Procedural Basis: Appeal from partial final judgment entered following the granting of motion for summary judgment in action to quiet title.

Facts: In 1908, Mr. and Mrs. Turknett (the parents), owners in fee simple of certain real property, conveyed, by separate conditional deeds, life estates in two separate parcels to their two daughters, Beulah and Ruby. Each deed provided that the property would remain the daughter's during her life, and upon her death, to her children, but if she dies without an heir(s), then to her estate, and pass as provided by law at the time of her death. At the time of these 1908 deeds, neither daughter had any children. In 1911, the parents gave another deed to Beulah, which covered the same land as in the previous deed, and which purported to convey absolute title to the grantee. In 1916, the parents executed another deed to Beulah, granting a portion of the property included in her two previous deeds. A second deed was also executed to Ruby, as a correction deed for the 1908 deed. Thereafter, Beulah and Ruby had children, three and four, respectively, and collectively referred to herein as "grandchildren" Amstutz (D). After the execution of the deeds, the daughters, Beulah and Ruby, attempted to convey fee simple interests in the property to the predecessors of Abo (P). The grandchildren (D) [most likely not wanting to lose their inheritance] defended Abo's (P) lawsuit for quiet title to the property by contending that the 1908 deeds gave their parents (the "daughters" herein) life estates in the property and thus only life estates could have been conveyed to the predecessors in interest of Abo (P). On the other hand, Abo (P) contends that the subsequent 1911 and 1916 deeds vested the daughters with fee simple title, and that such title was conveyed to Abo's (P) predecessors in interest, thereby giving Abo (P) fee simple title to the property. [Why such contention you ask? Well,...] It asserts that by conveyance to the daughters through the 1911 and 1916 deeds, the parents' reversionary interest merged with the daughters' life estates, thus destroying the contingent remainders in the grandchildren (D) and giving the daughters fee simple title to the property. After the court granted Abo's (P) motion for summary judgment and entered partial final judgment in its favor, the grandchildren (D) appealed.

Issue: Is the doctrine of destructibility of contingent remainders still viable in modern society so as to destroy a contingent remainder when a life estate merges with the reversionary interest?

Decision and Rationale: (Payne) No. We hold that because the doctrine of destructibility of contingent remainders is but a relic of the feudal past, which has no justification or support in modern society, it should not apply in New Mexico. To reach our conclusion, we first begin by examining the conveyance by the first deed executed by the parents in 1908. Because the deeds gave each of the daughters property "during her natural life," these words conveyed only a life estate. Each deed provided that upon the daughter's death, the property would pass to "her children if she have any at her death." The deeds created contingent remainders in the daughters' children, which could not vest until the death of the daughter holding the life estate, because it was impossible at the time of the conveyance to determine whether the daughters would have children, or whether the children would survive them. The deeds also provided that if the contingent remainder failed [no grandkids at daughters' deaths], the property would become part of the daughter's estate, and pass by law at the time of her death. Because one's heirs are not ascertained until death, the grant over to the daughter's estate created a second, or alternative, contingent remainder. The issues that remain for us to decide are (1) whether the parents retained any interest, (2) whether by their subsequent deeds to their daughters they conveyed any interest that remained, and (3) whether those conveyances destroyed the contingent remainders in the grandchildren. The grantor-parents divested themselves of the life estate and contingent remainder interest upon delivery of the first deed. Because both remainders are contingent, however, the parents retained a reversionary interest in the property. In order to determine whether Abo's (P) position is valid—that by conveyance to the daughters through the 1911 and 1916 deeds, the parents' reversionary interest merged with the daughters' life estates, thus destroying the contingent remainders in the grandchildren (D) and giving the daughters fee simple title to the property—we must decide whether the doctrine of destructibility of contingent remainders is applicable in New Mexico. Originating in England in the Sixteenth Century, the doctrine was based upon the feudal concept that seisin of land could never be in abeyance. From that principle, the rule developed that if the prior estate terminated before the occurrence of the contingency, the contingent remainder was destroyed for lack of a supporting freehold estate. The one instance in which this could happen was when the supporting life estate merged with the reversionary interest. The destructibility doctrine is almost universally regarded as obsolete by legislatures, courts, and legal writers. It has been renounced by virtually all jurisdictions in the United States, either by statute or judicial decision, and was abandoned by England over a century ago. [What's taken New Mexico so long?] Although there is support for the argument that the doctrine promotes alienability of land, it does so only arbitrarily and oftentimes by defeating the intent of the grantor. Because the doctrine of destructibility of continent remainders is but a relic of the feudal past, which has no justification or support in modern society, we decline to apply it in New Mexico. We hold that the conveyances of the property to the daughters did not destroy the contingent remainders in the grandchildren (D). The daughters acquired no more interest in the property by virtue of the later deeds than they had been granted in the original deeds. Any conveyance by them could transfer only the interest they had originally acquired even if it purported to convey a fee simple. Reversed.

Analysis:

This case demonstrates the abolishment of the doctrine of destructibility of contingent remainders. It also, however, discusses "reversionary interests,"—a future estate retained by the grantor because an estate of a lesser quantity has been conveyed. Common examples are conveyances for years and life estates. A "remainder" is a non-reversionary future estate, which is created in favor of someone other than the grantor. The grantor-parents divested themselves of the life estate and contingent remainder interest when they executed the first deed, but because the remainders are contingent, the parents retained a reversionary interest in the property. Had the court applied the doctrine of destructibility of contingent remainders, then the daughters would have had fee simple title to the property and would have been able to properly convey the property to Abo's (P) predecessor in interest. The court noted that even though the doctrine may promote the alienability of land, it does so often times in an arbitrary manner, and inconsistent with the grantor's intent.

Sybert v. Sybert

(Brothers of Devisee) v. (Wife of Devisee)
(1953) 152 Tex. 106

M E M O R Y   G R A P H I C

Instant Facts

Testators' wills gave son a life estate in property, and then in fee simple to his heirs, but when he died childless with a surviving wife, the Rule In Shelley's Case was applied giving son a fee simple estate, rather than only a life estate.

Black Letter Rule

The Rule In Shelley's Case provides that when a person takes a freehold estate and in the same instrument there is a limitation, by way of remainder, of an interest of the same legal or equitable quality, to his heirs, or heirs of his body, as a class of person, to take in succession, from generation to generation, the limitation to the heirs entitles the ancestor to the whole estate.

Case Vocabulary

ANCESTOR: Referring to ascendant and meaning one who precedes in a family tree, such as a parent or grandparent.
FEOFF: Also called "enfeoff" and referring to giving possession of a freehold interest to someone.
FREEHOLD: Representing possession of a fee simple estate, or a life estate.
INTESTATE: Where one dies without a will.
RULE IN SHELLEY'S CASE: Where a single document gives a person a freehold estate and a remainder to that person's heirs, then the remainder interest is shifted back to the person, rather than the heirs.
TESTATORS: One who dies with a will.

Procedural Basis: Appeal to Texas Supreme Court from affirming of judgment in action challenging the devise of real property under a will.

Facts: J. H. Sybert died leaving a will, which left all of his property to his wife, for life, and after her death, to his sons, including to his son Fred Sybert, a "tract of land (a life estate only, to manage, control and use for and during the term of his natural life and after the death of my said son, Fred Sybert, to vest in fee simple in the heirs of his body)." Thereafter Mr. Sybert's wife died, leaving a will disposing of the land in the same manner and by identical words copied from the will of Mr. Sybert. The son, Fred Sybert, died childless and intestate, survived by his wife, Eunice Sybert (D). Fred's two brothers (P) challenge the devise of property to Fred contending that the will vested a life estate only in Fred, while Fred's wife, Eunice (D) contends that the Rule In Shelley's Case operated to vest a fee simple estate in him. (Meaning she can keep the land!) The trial court ruled in favor of Eunice (D) and judgment was affirmed by the appellate court. The matter was appealed to the Texas Supreme Court.

Issue: Does the Rule In Shelley's Case apply when the language in a will bequeaths real property to a person for life and then after the person's death to the "heirs of his body" in fee simple?

Decision and Rationale: (Hickman) Yes. We hold that the Rule In Shelley's Case applies when the language in a will bequeaths real property to a person for life and then after the person's death to the "heirs of his body" in fee simple, unless there is language showing that the words "heirs of his body" were not used in their usual and technical sense. The Rule In Shelley's Case has been abolished by the legislatures in a majority of the states, however, the rule is still in force in Texas. The rule, as quoted from the landmark case of *Hancock v. Butler*, provides: "When a person takes an estate of freehold, legally or equitably, under a deed, will, or other writing, and in the same instrument there is a limitation, by way of remainder, either with or without the interposition of another estate, of an interest of the same legal or equitable quality, to his heirs, or heirs of his body, as a class of persons, to take in succession, from generation to generation, the limitation to the heirs entitles the ancestor to the whole estate." This result would follow, even if the deed might state that the first taker should have a life estate only. The rule is founded on the use of the technical words, "heirs" or "heirs of his body" in a deed or will. Because the rule is a rule of law, it must apply in this case, unless there is language qualifying the words "heirs of his body" in the Syberts' wills, showing that they were not used in their technical sense; that is, to signify an indefinite succession of takers from generation to generation. We conclude that there is no such qualifying language. Fred's two brothers (P) rely upon other cases that are clearly distinguishable. In one case, the remainder was "to his bodily heirs equally," and it was held that the word "equally" qualified the word "heirs." In another case, the language in one deed was "to the issue of her body," and we held that "issue" was a word of purchase, meaning children. In the case now before us, the word "heirs" is used, to which the Rule in Shelley's Case is peculiarly applicable. The second deed in the other case contained the words "to her bodily heirs, share and share alike." We held that "share and share alike" qualified the word "heirs" and took the case from out of the rule. The language in the Sybert will brings it squarely within the rule, and whether or not the testator so intended is immaterial. [The testator's lawyers should have done a better job in will drafting!] Judgment affirmed.

Concurrence: (Griffin) The case forcibly points out the anomaly brought about by the Rule In Shelley's Case. The Rule is a relic, not of the horse and buggy days, but of the preceding stone cart and oxen days. It was devised in feudal times to insure feudal landlords the receipt of their rents from their feoffs, or tenants. The reason for the Rule has long since passed, and it should be repealed. A reading of the two wills leaves no doubt that it was the intention of the two testators to leave a life estate only to their son Fred. The application of the Rule results in setting aside this intention. The Rule is only a trap and snare for the unwary, and should be repealed. However, repeal is the duty of the legislative branch, and the judiciary cannot legislate by refusing to follow the Rule. [The old "our hands are tied" approach to deciding cases!]

Analysis:

In this case, we learn about the legendary Rule In Shelley's Case. Although at least 39 states have abolished the Rule, as did England from where it originated, the Texas Legislature had not done so at the time this case was decided. However, Texas finally abolished the rule in 1964. The rule's name comes from the old English case of *Wolfe v. Shelley* (1581), and it provided that when a will or deed gave a remainder to the "heirs" of a person who received a prior freehold estate by the same will or deed, that person also took the remainder. The effect was prohibiting the creation of a contingent remainder in the heirs of one to whom the same will or deed gave a life estate. In other words, the remainder interest is shifted to the ancestor, rather than to the heirs. Simply put, although a deed or will "to A for life, and then to his heirs" creates a remainder in A's heirs, the rule shifts the remainder interest to A, the heirs' ancestor. The issue in this case was whether the words "heirs of his body" were used in their technical sense, which the court held they were. If the will had said to Fred's children, the Rule would not apply, since the language applied to specific persons, rather than heirs in general.

Braswell v. Braswell

(Devisee of Life Tenant) v. (Remainder Heirs of Grantor)
(1954) 195 Va. 971

M E M O R Y   G R A P H I C

Instant Facts

Grantor, upon the execution of a deed retained a reversion in the land, and upon his death, his reversion passed to his three sons, one of whom devised his 1/3 share to Charles Braswell (P).

Black Letter Rule

A limitation contained in a deed conveying real property, which provides that the land shall revert back to the grantor, or to his lawful heirs, if the life tenant should die without heirs, is a remainder subject to the rule against a remainder to the grantor's heirs (i.e., the Doctrine of Worthier Title) thereby causing the grantor to retain a reversion in the land.

Case Vocabulary

BILL: A complaint in equity requesting relief.
DEVISEE: The person to whom real property is given under the terms of a will.
DOCTRINE OF WORTHIER TITLE: An inter vivos conveyance for life, with remainder to the heirs of the conveyor is ineffective to create a remainder, but leaves in the conveyor a reversion which will pass by operation of law upon his death, unless he otherwise disposes of it.
INTER VIVOS: Latin for, "between the living", and referring to conveyance during life, and not by will.
SEIGNIORY: The retained right held by the grantor (lord) in land.

Procedural Basis: Appeal from suit for partition involving claim of ownership of real property.

Facts: James J. Braswell (grantor) conveyed, by deed, land which he owned in fee simple to his son, Nathaniel, "during his natural life and to his lawful heirs at his death, and if [he] should die leaving no lawful heir from his body, then the land … shall revert back to the said James J. Braswell or to his heirs." Grantor James died, intestate, leaving as his sole heirs three sons, one of whom was Nathaniel the life tenant. Nathaniel died, testate, without issue, devising all his real property to Charles Braswell (P) (devisee of Nathaniel). Charles Braswell (P) brought suit against the other two sons of the grantor James Braswell (remainder heirs) for partition, contending that he was the owner as tenant in common of a 1/3 undivided interest in the land conveyed in the deed by grantor James. The trial court upheld this claim of ownership, and the two sons (D) of grantor James appealed asserting that the Doctrine of Worthier Title did not apply.

Issue: Is a limitation contained in a deed conveying real property, which provides that the land shall revert back to the grantor, or to his lawful heirs, if the life tenant should die without heirs, a remainder subject to the rule against a remainder to the grantor's heirs (i.e., the Doctrine of Worthier Title) thereby causing the grantor to retain a reversion in the land?

Decision and Rationale: (Smith) Yes. The first limitation of the deed from grantor James created a life estate in Nathaniel with a contingent remainder in fee simple in his unborn issue. However, the contingent remainder never vested because the life tenant Nathaniel died without issue. The second aspect of the limitation is what is at issue in this case. The deed provided that the land shall revert back to James or to his lawful heirs, if the life tenant should die without heirs. We must determine whether this aspect of the limitation is a reversion or a remainder. A remainder is what is left of an entire grant of lands after a preceding part of the same grant has been disposed of in possession, whose regular expiration the remainder must await. A reversion is the remnant of an estate continuing in the grantor, undisposed of, after the grant of a part of his interest. It differs from a remainder in that it arises by act of the law, whereas a remainder is by act of the parties. A reversion moreover, is the remnant left in the grantor, while a reminder is the remnant of the whole estate disposed of, after a preceding part of the same has been given away. Common law discriminates between the acquisition of land by descent and by purchase. [A form of *legal* discrimination!] English common law provided that an inter vivos conveyance for life, with remainder to the heirs or next of kin of the conveyor is ineffective to create a remainder, but leaves in the conveyor a reversion which will pass by operation of law upon his death, unless he otherwise disposes of it. It is known as the Doctrine of Worthier Title, or rule against a remainder to the grantor's heirs, or the conveyor-heir rule. The rule against a remainder to the grantor's heirs had its origin in feudal custom which preferred to have real property pass by the "worthier" channel of descent, rather than by the less worthy channel of purchase. Although previously a rule of law, it is now regarded as a rule of construction. For the rule against remainders to heirs of grantors to be applied: (1) there must be an inter vivos transfer, (2) if the subject matter be realty there must be a limitation to the grantor's heirs (used in its technical meaning of indefinite succession) or an equivalent limitation. There is a presumption in favor of reversions, which may be rebutted by a contrary intent gathered from the instrument as a whole. The rule does not apply if the limitation is construed to mean that the property was intended to pass to the heirs of the grantor, or upon an equivalent limitation, determined at some time other than the death of the grantor. Here it is contended that the rule against remainders does not apply because by the use of the word "then" the grantor meant to fix the time of the ascertainment of his heirs at the date of the life tenant's death rather than the date of the grantor's death. The only language used in the limitation in the deed before us which might tend to indicate the word "heirs" was not used to embrace those persons who corresponded to the description at the time of the grantor's death, is the word "then." The grantor said if Nathaniel should die leaving no heir from his body *then* the land conveyed shall revert back to James or his heirs. This use of the word "then" only fixes the time when it is determined whether the life tenant died without issue of his body and does not fix the time for ascertaining the heirs of the grantor. Also, by using the word "then" in conjunction with the word "revert" and without other language to the contrary, the grantor clearly intended that if the life tenant should die without issue of his body, "in that case" the land should "come back" and pass as if no conveyance had been made. Thus, we are unable to find in the language of the deed anything which would warrant disregarding the rule against remainders to the grantor's heirs, nor any valid basis for holding the word "heirs" to signify anything other than its normal and technical meaning of indefinite succession as determined at the death of the grantor. We therefore hold that grantor James upon the execution of the deed retained a reversion in the land. Upon his death intestate, his reversion passed to his three sons in equal share, and upon son Nathaniel's death testate and without issue, his 1/3 interest in the reversion which he inherited from grantor James passed to his devisee, Charles Braswell (P). Affirmed.

Analysis:

Recall in the preceding case involving the Rule In Shelley's case, that the rule was a rule of law. The Doctrine of Worthier Title involves a rule of construction, and the court in this case was faced with the issue of whether the deed's limitation was a reversion or a remainder. Since the sons of the grantor (D) where faced with having the Doctrine of Worthier Title applied, they asserted that the grantor James, by using the word "then" (if Nathaniel should die leaving no heir from his body *then* the land conveyed shall revert back to James or his heirs) meant to fix the time of the ascertainment of his heirs at the date of the life tenant's death (Nathaniel) rather than the date of his death. There is a presumption that the law is in favor of reversions, which may be rebutted by evidence showing a contrary intent. The sons (D) were attempting to rebut the presumption, but the court property rejected their argument and ruled in favor of Nathaniel's devisee, Charles Braswell (P). The Doctrine of Worthier title exists in most states, although some states (such as California) have recommended abolishing it as to both inter vivos and testamentary transfers because (1) it is based upon the false premise that the grantor does not really intend to give the property to his own heirs, but instead intends to retain a reversion with full power to dispose of the property again in the future, (2) it breeds litigation, and, (3) it can create estate and inheritance tax problems.

Stoller v. Doyle

(Grantee of Subsequent Conveyance Deed) v. (Children of First Grantee Holding Executory Interest)

(1913) 257 Ill. 369

M E M O R Y   G R A P H I C

Instant Facts

Stoller (P), grantee of a conveyance deed from Frank Doyle and his wife, sued the Doyle children (D) and sought to declare himself the owner in fee simple free and clear of any claims of the children (D).

Black Letter Rule

Where the fee in the first taker created by a deed is made determinable, as upon the happening of a valid condition subsequent, followed by a limitation over of the fee or use to another upon the happening of the prescribed event, the fee or use shifts from the first to the second taker, whereby the deed is a conveyance under the statute of uses, and is a clear case of shifting use.

Case Vocabulary

ABSTRACT: ("Abstract of Title") A document prepared for the buyer of land that shows the history of the land and revealing good and marketable title.

DEED OF BARGAIN AND SALE: A deed conveying land for valuable consideration but it does not guarantee the validity of the title.

DEFENDANT [OR PLAINTIFF] IN ERROR: A defendant in error is a term used on appeal that refers to the prevailing party in the lower court from which the appeal has been taken, which is the respondent on appeal. [Plaintiff in error refers to the appellant.]

DEMURRER: A challenge to the legal sufficiency of the pleading, such as a complaint.

LIQUIDATED DAMAGES: Where parties to a contract agree to a fixed amount of damages to be recovered should one party breach the contract, regardless of the actual damages incurred due to the breach.

PRAYER: Usually the last provision of a civil complaint where the damages and relief sought are plead.

SEVERANCE: Referring herein to the separation of certain parties from the action.

SHIFTING USE: A use that comes about after a certain event terminates the preceding estate.

WRIT OF ERROR: A writ from the appellate court to the lower court requesting the record be delivered for review; it is instigated by the unsuccessful party in the lower courts who seeks to have the appellate court review the judgment for error.

Procedural Basis: Review by Illinois Supreme Court pursuant to writ of error of action to quiet title to real property.

Facts: In 1882, Lawrence Doyle and his wife executed a warranty deed to Frank Doyle for certain land, with the following restrictions and limitations: "… Frank Doyle shall not have power to reconvey this land, unless it be to the grantor. He shall not have power to mortgage the land, and in case the said Frank Doyle should die before his wife dies, and any children survive him, the surviving children and his wife shall have the use of the land … during the lifetime of his wife, when it shall go to his children, if any are living, but, if at the death of the grantee no children survive him, the title shall be in the grantors. Should any children survive the grantee and his wife survive him, she shall have no [an?] interest in the land only so long as she remains unmarried and is his widow." [Said another way, there was one contingency that would terminate Frank's fee simple, and that was if his wife should survive him. If the contingent future event of the death of the Frank before his wife should occur, and any children should survive him the wife and surviving children would have the use of the land during the lifetime of the wife, the interest of the wife to terminate if she remarried, and after her death the fee was to go to the children; but, if at the death of Frank no children should survive him, there would be a reversion to the grantor.] Fifteen years later, in 1897, Lawrence Doyle, then a widower executed a second deed of the same land, in the same form to Frank Doyle, but omitting the restrictions and conditions, so as to give him an absolute title to the premises. Five years later, in 1902, Frank Doyle and his wife executed a warranty deed to Stoller (P). The following year, Stoller (P) entered into a contract with Bauman wherein Stoller (P) agreed to convey to Bauman in fee simple, free of all encumbrances on said land (and another tract as well). The contract provided a purchase price of $1,500, plus a liquidated damage clause in the amount of $1,500 to be paid by the party failing to perform. Bauman refused to accept the deed to the land from Stoller (P) because the abstract did not show a merchantable title. Stoller (P) sued to compel specific performance (Stoller v. Bauman), but the lawsuit was dismissed. Bauman then sued Stoller (P) (Bauman v. Stoller) to recover the $1,500 purchase price, and the $1,500 liquidated damages. The court held that by the first deed of 1882, a contingent interest was conveyed to Frank's children, and the later deed to Frank could not affect that interest, and therefore the abstract did not show merchantable title. Judgment was entered for Bauman, and after an unsuccessful appeals by Stoller (P), the case came to an end. Thereafter, Stoller (P) [not wanting to give up the fight] filed the present lawsuit against Frank Doyle's children (D), alleging that by the first deed Frank did not take an estate in fee simple, but only an estate for life; that his wife took an estate for life, contingent upon her outliving him; that his children took a contingent remainder in fee; that there was an ultimate reversion in fee to the grantor in the event that no children survived Frank; and that the second deed to him conveyed the reversion, whereby the life estate was merged in the fee and the intervening contingent interest were destroyed. Stoller (P) sought to be declared the owner in fee simple of the land, free and clear of any claims of the children (D), and that his title should therefore be quieted. The trial court held that Stoller (P) was the owner in fee simple and quieted his title. Three of the children (D) sought review of the decree before Supreme Court of Illinois.

Issue: Did the statute of uses result in the recognition of executory interests?

Decision and Rationale: (Cartwright) Yes. The statute of uses resulted in the recognition of executory interests. A remainder cannot be created without a precedent estate, which is said to support the remainder. Where the particular estate, supporting a remainder, comes to an end before the happening of the event upon which the remainder is to take effect, the remainder is defeated. Under that rule, where the reversion and life estate come together in the same person, the life estate merges in the reversion and comes to an end, and a contingent remainder is destroyed. Looking at the 1882 deed to determine what estate was granted, we find that, under the pertinent sections of the conveyance act, a statutory warranty deed is to be deemed a conveyance in fee simple, although words formerly necessary to transfer an estate of inheritance are not contained in it. At common law, in order to create an estate in fee simple it was necessary that the grant should be to the grantee and his heirs without limitation. A deed in the statutory form under the conveyance act is a conveyance in fee simple, however, a less estate may be limited by express words, or may appear to have been granted or conveyed by construction or operation of law. Here, the estate granted to Frank Doyle was therefore a fee simple, except as limited by the deed. It was subject to conditional limitations, which might terminate it; but, unless the contingent events took place, it would last forever. If the contingency that the grantee's wife survive him should occur, it would cease to be a fee. If the contingent future event of the death of the grantee before his wife should occur, and any children should survive him, the wife and surviving children were to have the use of the land during the life of the wife, (unless she remarried upon which her interest would terminate), and after her death the fee was to go to other children; but, if at the death of the grantee no children should survive him, there was a reversion to the grantor. The grantor conveyed the whole estate, except a contingent reversion dependent on the grantee dying without leaving children surviving him. The future interest of the wife and children under that deed will take effect, if at all, in derogation of the estate of the grantee conveyed by the granting clause of the deed. Although not permitted at common law, under the statute of uses, a deed of bargain and sale that creates such a limitation is valid. As was argued in the case of *Abbott v. Abbott,* where the fee in the first taker created by a deed is made determinable, as upon the happening of a valid condition subsequent, followed by a limitation over of the fee or use to another upon the happening of the prescribed event, the fee or use shifts from the first to the second taker, whereby the deed is a conveyance under the statute of uses, and is a clear case of shifting use. The estate of the children was limited to take effect in derogation of the estate of the grantee, created by the granting clause. The deed operated as a conveyance of the fee, with the limitations over, which may terminate the estate granted upon the conditions specified in the deed, and did not create a contingent remainder destructible by the act of the grantor in subsequently conveying the reversion to the grantee. The second deed to Frank Doyle did not affect the contingent interest of his children. Reversed.

Analysis:

This is a *very complicated and confusing* case. It demonstrates that the statute of uses resulted in the recognition of executory interests, and specifically, in this case, *shifting* executory interests. An executory interest is an interest held by a third person that follows an estate subject to executory interest. Shifting executory interests exist where the possessory right shifts from one grantee to another. Most executory interests today are "shifting" executory interests. Example: To A, but if A marries B, then to B. A has a fee simple subject to limitation, and B has a shifting executory interest in fee simple absolute. The court also considers the issue of destructibility of contingent remainders, a common law rule that has mostly been abolished in modern times. The court in this case held that the deed did not create a contingent remainder, which was destructible by the grantor later conveying the reversion to the grantee. Thus, the second deed to Frank, without limitations, did not affect the contingent interests of the children (D), and thus, the children were entitled to claim an interest in the property.

Capitol Federal Savings & Loan Association v. Smith

(Financial Institution Concerned With Title) v. (Owners of Property)

(1957) 136 Colo. 265

M E M O R Y   G R A P H I C

Instant Facts

Smiths (P), minority owners of real property, challenged private covenant prohibiting the sale or lease of real property to Negroes as a cloud on their title, and the court rejected argument it was an enforceable executory interest that vested upon the sale to the Smiths (P).

Black Letter Rule

Anti-racial restrictive covenant between property owners, with forfeiture clause if agreement is violated, is not an enforceable executory interest, but instead is a racial restriction in violation of the Fourteenth Amendment.

Case Vocabulary

DECLARATORY JUDGMENT: A form of a judgment whereby the court declares the rights of parties or renders its opinion concerning issues of law.

Procedural Basis: Writ of error before Colorado Supreme Court from trial court decree quieting title to real property and entering declaratory judgment.

Facts: The Smiths (P) are owners of certain lots of real property. Prior to the Smiths (P) becoming owners of the property, their predecessors in title along with owners of other lots within the block entered into an agreement among themselves that the lots should not be sold or leased to colored persons, and providing for forfeiture of any lots sold or leased in violation of the agreements to such of then owners of other lots in said block who might place notice of their claims of records. In their amended complaint seeking to quiet title and obtain declaratory judgment, the Smiths (P) alleged that they were colored persons of Negro extraction and that any interest, or claim of any interest of any defendants (D) under said agreement was without foundation of right and in violation of the U.S. Constitution, and that said agreement was a cloud on their title and should be removed. Certain other owners (D) recorded a "Notice of Claim" with the recorder's office asserting that they were owners of the lots and asserting title and possession to the property by virtue of the forfeiture provision of the agreement. The trial court found that the Smiths (P) were the owners in fee simple and quieted their title thereto free and clear of any right of enforcement of the restrictive covenant or the Notice of Claim filed by the owners of the other lots (D). The court further adjudged and decreed that the restrictive covenant may not be enforced by the court as a matter of law, and to enforce the same would be a violation of the equal protection clause of the Fourteenth Amended. Capitol Federal Savings & Loan Association and the owners of the other lots (D) sought review by the State Supreme Court.

Issue: Is an anti-racial restrictive covenant between property owners, containing a forfeiture clause if the agreement is violated, an enforceable executory interest, which vests automatically upon the happening of the specified events and without need for judicial action by the court?

Decision and Rationale: (Knauss) No. We hold that the anti-racial restrictive covenant between property owners, containing a forfeiture clause if the agreement is violated, is not an enforceable executory interest, but instead is a racial restriction in violation of the Fourteenth Amendment. The covenant or agreement under consideration was dated May 9, 1942 and provided that the signatories to the contract agreed for themselves, their heirs, and assigns "not to sell or lease [the lots] to any colored person or persons, and covenant and agree not to permit any colored person or persons to occupy said premises during the period from this date to January 1, 1990." It further provided that if any of the lots were conveyed or leased in violation of the agreement, the right, title or interest of the owner so in violation of the agreement would "be forfeited to and rest in such of the then owners of all of said lots and parcels of land not included in the conveyance or lease who may assert title thereto by filing for record notice of their claim." Counsel for the owners of the other lots and interested financial institutions (D) contend that prior U.S. Supreme Court cases—holding unconstitutional state judicial action which had affirmatively enforced a private scheme of discrimination against Negroes—did not involve an agreement "for automatic forfeiture, nor the creation of future interest in land," and thus are not controlling here. They argue that the agreement here entered into between the predecessors in interest of the Smiths (P) and the other lot owners (D) did not create a "private anti-racial restrictive covenant," but instead it created a future interest in the land known as an executory interest. They further argue that such interest vested automatically in the other lot owners (D) upon the happening of the events specified in the original instrument of grant, and the validity of the vesting did not in any way depend upon judicial action by the courts. [They're trying to have racial discrimination upheld without the need for judicial action.] We do not agree with these contentions. It is still a racial restriction in violation of the Fourteenth Amendment. High-sounding phrases or outmoded common-law terms cannot alter the effect of the agreement. Because the language in the U.S. Supreme Court decision in *Shelley v. Kraemer* [state judicial action which had affirmatively enforced a private scheme of discrimination against Negroes held unconstitutional] suggested that private racially restrictive covenants were not invalid per se, it was believed for some time that an action for damages might lie against one who violated such a covenant, and, in fact, a number of lower courts awarded such damages. However, in *Barrows v. Jackson,* the Supreme Court held that although such a grantor's constitutional rights were not violated, nevertheless the commodious protection of the Fourteenth Amendment extended to her and she could not be made to respond in damages for treating her restrictive covenant as a nullity. As a result, there can be no rights, duties, or obligations under such a covenant. Judgment affirmed.

Analysis:

Although it may be difficult to ascertain at first blush, the transaction involved an executory interest, called a "springing" executory interest, because it springs from the grantor's possessory estate at some time in the future upon the occurrence of a future event. Compare the executory interest to a remainder—the remainder awaits the natural termination of the prior estate, but the executory interest becomes possessory when breach of a condition terminates the fee simple. The court rejected the argument that the agreement between the Smiths' (P) predecessors in interest and the other lot owners (D) created an executory interest, the termination of a fee simple that did not involve state action. The argument was an attempt to avoid the unconstitutional anti-racial restrictive covenant. Noting that it did not matter what terms were used to describe it, the court held that it remained a racially restrictive covenant in violation of the Fourteenth Amendment.

VIOLATION OF RULE AGAINST PERPETUITIES DOES NOT VOID ENTIRE CONVEYANCE, JUST THAT PORTION THAT VIOLATES THE RULE

The City of Klamath Falls v. Bell

(City That Closed Library) v. (Heirs of Shareholders of Grantor-Corporation)
(1971) 7 Or.App. 330

M E M O R Y   G R A P H I C

Instant Facts

City (P), which was deeded land in fee simple on limitation, "so long as" it used the land for a library, sued to determine the rights to the land after library was closed.

Black Letter Rule

When an executory interest, following a fee simple in land, is void under the Rule Against Perpetuities, the prior interest becomes absolute unless the language of the creating instrument makes it very clear that the prior interest is to terminate whether the executory interest takes effect or not.

Case Vocabulary

AB INITIO: Latin meaning, from the beginning.
AGREED NARRATIVE STATEMENT: Referring to a statement of facts that the parties have agreed upon and that the court considers when making its ruling.
FEE SIMPLE ON A CONDITION SUBSEQUENT: (also called fee simple subject to a condition subsequent, fee simple subject to a power of termination, fee simple upon condition.) An estate that is subject to the grantor's ability to terminate it (power of termination) upon the occurrence of a certain condition.
FEE SIMPLE ON A SPECIAL LIMITATION: (also called fee simple determinable, base fee, qualified fee, determinable fee, estate on limitation.) An estate that will automatically terminate upon the occurrence of a certain event, and revert to the grantor (possibility of reverter).
GIFT OVER: A gift of property that occurs when the prior estate terminates.
POSSIBILITY OF REVERTER: A future interest in the grantor that takes effect after conveying a fee simple on a special limitation and upon the occurrence of the terminating event.
RULE AGAINST PERPETUITIES: No interest is good unless it must vest, if at all, not later than twenty-one years after some life in being at the creation of the interest.

Procedural Basis: Appeal from declaratory judgment adjudicating rights under deed of real property.

Facts: In 1925, Daggett-Schallock Investment Company ("the corporation") conveyed, by deed, certain land to the city of Klamath Falls ("the City") (P) as a gift for use as a city library, "so long as it complies with the conditions" set forth with regard to its use, and thereafter to Fred Schallock and Floy Daggett, their heirs and assigns. The following year, the City (P) built and operated a library on the land in compliance with the conditions in the deed. One year after, in 1927, the corporation was voluntarily dissolved, and all creditors were paid and all assets distributed to the sole shareholders of the corporation, Messrs. Schallock and Daggett. In 1969, the library was closed and the building became vacant. The City (P) filed a complaint for declaratory judgment seeking to have the court adjudicate the respective rights of the parties under the deed. [It was not about to try to determine who should get the land because of that famous and often criticized Rule Against Perpetuities!] Named as defendants in the complaint were heirs of Schallock and Daggett, including Bell (D-1), the sole heir of Schallock, and Flitcraft (D-2) and Crapo (D-3), the sole heirs of Daggett. In 1970, Bell (D-1) and Crapo (D-3) conveyed their interest in the property to Flitcraft (D-2). The trial court found that title to the property was vested in the City (P), based on a finding that the gift over to Schallock and Daggett was void under the Rule Against Perpetuities. Flitcraft (D-2) appealed contending that the termination of use as a library caused title to pass to the descendents of Schallock and Daggett, the shareholders of the donor-corporation (now dissolved.)

Issue: (1) Does the Rule Against Perpetuities apply to executory interests? (2) When a deed reveals an unquestionable intent to limit the interest of the first grantee to a fee simple on a special limitation, and a subsequent executory interest is void under the Rule Against Perpetuities, does the grantor retain a possibility of reverter? (3) Does an attempt by the grantor to alienate a possibility of reverter destroy it?

Decision and Rationale: (Schwab) (1) Yes. (2) Yes. (3) No. We must first determine the nature of the estate that passed to the City (P) under the deed from the corporation. The "magic" words "so long as" have generally been held to create a fee simple on a special limitation, also known as a fee simple determinable, or a base or qualified fee. Other common words used to create such an estate are "until" or "during," or any other language that indicates an intent that the estate shall automatically end upon the occurrence of a designated event (i.e., a breach of condition.) Upon breach of the condition, the deed provided for a gift over to Schallock and Daggett, or their heirs and assigns. This gift over was an attempt to grant an executory interest since only an executory interest can follow an earlier grant in fee simple. However, the trial court correctly found that the gift over to Schallock and Daggett, their heirs and assigns, was void *ab initio* under the Rule Against Perpetuities, which applies to executory interests. Grays' classic statement of the rule is: "No interest is good unless it must vest, if at all, not later than twenty-one years after some life in being at the creation of the interest." Clearly, the City (P), as first grantee under the deed, could have continued in possession in perpetuity by maintaining the library on the land. Thus, the gift over to Schallock and Daggett violates the Rule Against Perpetuities. We next must determine whether under the deed there was a possibility of reverter in the grantor-corporation. When a deed reveals an unquestionable intent to limit the interest of the first grantee (the City) to a fee simple on a special limitation, the courts do not create an indefeasible estate in the first grantee when a subsequent executory interest (in Schallock and Daggett) is void under the Rule Against Perpetuities. Instead, the grantor (the corporation) retains an interest known as a possibility of reverter. The general rule provides that when an executory interest, following a fee simple in land is void under the Rule Against Perpetuities, the prior interest becomes absolute unless the language of the creating instrument makes it very clear that the prior interest is to terminate whether the executory interest takes effect or not. Moreover, it is well settled that the Rule Against Perpetuities does not apply to possibilities of reverter. However, before we can follow this general rule, we must consider an unusual Oregon rule that holds that the possibility of a reverter cannot be alienated. But, the Oregon Supreme Court has never held that an attempt to alienate a possibility of reverter destroys it, and in the case at bar, the grantor-corporation did attempt to alienate the possibility of reverter with its gift over to Schallock and Daggett. Thus, we must decide this issue of first impression on appeal in the case before us. The Oregon Supreme has decided two cases that dealt with the consequences that follow a grantor's attempt to transfer the interest that remains in him when he grants a defeasible fee. In *Wagner v. Wallowa County,* the grantors gave land to the county for a high school, but prior to an electorate vote abolishing the school, the grantors deeded the land to the school district. The court, in considering the fee simple estate on a condition subsequent, held that the grantors destroyed their right to re-enter when they attempted to convey it before the breach of the condition. In *Magness v. Kerr,* the court was faced with a fee simple determinable, when a canning company was divested of its estate for failing to use the property for its intended purposes, and the property therefore reverted before the transfer of the future interest. Neither

of these cases is conclusive in determining whether an attempt to alienate a possibility of reverter destroys it. We note language from an Iowa case, *Reichard v. Chicago, B. & Q.R. Co.,* which involved a conveyance after termination of a fee simple subject to a special limitation: "It seems rather fantastic to us, that a conveyance which is ineffective to convey what it attempts to convey is nevertheless an effective means of destroying it." We thus hold that an attempt by a grantor to transfer his possibility of reverter does not destroy it. The final issue we must consider is the City's (P) contention that the grantor-corporation, upon dissolution, was civilly dead and without a successor to whom the possibility of reverter could descend. Oregon statutes make it clear that corporate assets no longer escheat or revert to the original grantor upon dissolution. When the sole shareholders of the corporation, Schallock and Daggett, received all the remaining assets of the corporation, one such asset was the possibility of reverter in the land. We hold that a possibility of reverter is descendable, and since the defendants in this case were all of the heirs of Schallock and Daggett, Flitcraft (D-2) acquired all rights to the property when the other defendants (D-1 and D-3) conveyed their interests to her in 1970. Reversed.

Analysis:

The significance of this case is that it demonstrates the difference between executory interests and possibilities of reverter and powers of termination. An executory interest is subject to the Rule Against Perpetuities but possibilities of reverter and powers of termination are not. A review of the various estates held by the parties is helpful. The City (P) had a fee simple on a special limitation, because the estate would automatically end if the land were not used as a library. An attempt was made to grant an executory interest to Schallock and Daggett, their heirs and assigns (a future interest that vests automatically upon the land not being used as a library.) However, because an executory interest is subject to the Rule Against Perpetuities, the gift over to Schallock and Daggett, their heirs and assigns, was void. (A library could have remained on the land forever.) Because the gift over to Schallock and Daggett, their heirs and assigns, was void, the grantor-corporation had a "possibility of reverter," an estate that is not subject to the Rule. Furthermore, because Oregon had a rule that the possibility of reverter cannot be alienated, the court had to determine whether the *attempt* to alienate the possibility of reverter actually destroyed it. The court, in holding that it did not, acknowledged the reasoning of another court that it made no sense to conclude that the deed, which is ineffective to convey what it attempts to convey is effective to destroy the possibility of reverter in the grantor. Thus, the grantor-corporation had a possibility of reverter, except for the fact that Oregon law did not permit corporate assets to revert to the original grantor upon dissolution of the corporation. Nevertheless, because the possibility of reverter was an asset of the corporation, and as such was distributed to the shareholders upon dissolution, the heirs of Schallock and Daggett took the possibility of reverter through descent. We therefore learn that even though the Rule Against Perpetuities may be violated, the entire conveyance is not void, rather only that interest that violates the Rule is stricken from the deed. The result in this case was to create a new interest in the heirs of the grantor's shareholders.

Shaver v. Clanton

(Heir of Lessor) v. (Lessees With Option to Renew)
(1994) 31 Cal. Rptr.2d 595

M E M O R Y   G R A P H I C

Instant Facts
Shaver (P) challenged trial court's ruling declaring amendment to lease void because it violated the Rule Against Perpetuities.

Black Letter Rule
The Uniform Statutory Rule Against Perpetuities does not apply to commercial transactions.

Case Vocabulary

UNIFORM STATUTORY RULE AGAINST PERPETUITIES: A rule that modified the common law Rule Against Perpetuities by providing an alternative 90-year perpetuities period.

Procedural Basis: Appeal from trial court ruling declaring amendment to commercial lease void.

Facts: Mr. and Mrs. Clanton (D) entered into a 10-year lease with Mr. Stanley for shopping center space, effective May 1, 1971. The lease contained a renewal option for another 10 years. The parties amended the lease in 1988, and again in 1989. The last amendment granted the Clantons (D) options to extend the lease for additional five-year periods beginning at the end of each prior lease period (perpetual options) and gave them a right of first refusal if the property were offered for sale. After Mr. Stanley died, his sole heir, daughter, Donna Shaver (P), brought suit challenging the validity of the lease amendments on the ground that they violated the Rule Against Perpetuities. The trial court held that the 1988 amendment was valid, but the 1989 amendment was not because it provided for option renewals into infinity, which they could not do, and therefore, because the provision was an integral part of the amendment the whole amendment is voided. The Clantons (D) appealed.

Issue: Does the Uniform Statutory Rule Against Perpetuities apply to commercial transactions?

Decision and Rationale: (Soneshine) No. This case of first impression requires us to determine whether a lease amendment, which provides for perpetual options to renew, is void because it violates the Rule Against Perpetuities. Until it adopted the Uniform Statutory Rule Against Perpetuities in 1991, California law applied the Rule Against Perpetuities to commercial transactions, including options to renew. Now, under the Uniform Statutory Rule, commercial, nondonative transactions are expressly exempt from the Rule. The Rule provides: "A nonvested property interest is invalid unless one of the following conditions is satisfied: (a) When the interest is created, it is certain to vest or terminate no later than 21 years after the death of an individual then alive. (b) The interest either vests or terminates with 90 years after its creation." The common law policy favoring alienation of property led to the establishing of the Rule Against Perpetuities—"No interest is good unless it must vest, if at all, not later than 21 years after some life in being at the creation of the interest." From the earliest stages of the doctrine's development, the English courts and many American courts found covenants to renew leases exempt from the rule on two grounds: (1) Such covenants, without time limits, do not suspend the power to alienate, since the lessee always has in himself the legal as well as the practical power to convey that which is substantially a fee simple; on the other hand, when the lessee gives up his right to renew the lessor will resume complete ownership; and, (2) The perpetual renewal covenant should never have been classified as an "exception" to the Rule, but instead should have been considered to be outside the province of the Rule. In summary, the purpose of the Rule was found to be inapt to commercial transactions. California is now one of twenty jurisdictions that have adopted the Uniform Statutory Rule, which supersedes the common law Rule Against Perpetuities, and applies to nonvested property interests regardless of whether they were created before or after its effective date of January 1, 1992. Shaver (P) makes two arguments: (1) that the Uniform Rule should not apply to commercial transactions between individuals where free alienability of property is clearly desirable and only large commercial or governmental entities should be excluded from the common law rule, and (2) even if the Uniform Rule does apply to commercial transactions it should not apply in this case because the nature of the transaction was "at least quasi-donative." The former argument is not persuasive because the California Law Revision Commission Comment to the Uniform Rule cited the case relied upon by Shaver (P) to point out the inappropriateness of the period of a life in being plus 21 years to commercial transactions since the rule can invalidate legitimate transactions in such cases. The latter argument is also not viable. Although it is asserted that the Clantons (D) and Mr. Stanley were close personal friends, whom Mr. Stanley wanted to help out, and that Stanley considered the Clantons' (D) son as the son he never had, the transaction cannot be considered gratuitous in nature, accompanied by donative intent. The lease amendment did give the Clantons (D) favorable terms, but there is no evidence of any detriment to Stanley that would characterize the amendments as donative, nor that either party had donative intent. Thus, the Rule Against Perpetuities does not apply. California Civil Code section 718 provides that no lease or grant of any town or city lot, which reserves any rent or service of any kind, and which provides for a leasing or granting period in excess of 99 years, shall be valid. The 1989 amendment, when read in context with this section, should have been construed to avoid a violation of the Rule Against Perpetuities. A lease in violation of section 718 would not be void except as to the excess of the period. By adopting the Uniform Rule while preserving section 718, we conclude the Legislature intended the two statutes to be read together—thus, the rule is clear, commercial, nondonative transactions such as options to renew, right of first refusal, and commercial leases are exempt form the Uniform Rule, but if they involve a lease or grant of a town or city lot, they are limited to 99 years. Therefore, the 1989 amendment is valid and gives the Clantons (D) a series of options to renew. The total term of the lease, however, is limited to 99 years from its effective date, May 1, 1971. [Reversed.]

Concurrence: (Crosby) I concur with the majority, but the holding is hornbook law and hardly worthy of publication. Moreover, open-ended leases and options in perpetuity must be about as common as polar bear sightings in Death Valley. The Court of Appeal is not likely to see another such case in the next 99 years.

Analysis:

This case discusses the Uniform Statutory Rule Against Perpetuities, which has been adopted by a majority of the States. We learn that it expressly exempts commercial, nondonative transactions, and applies to nonvested property interests created both before and after its enactment. So what was the issue? [The concurring justice certainly didn't believe there was any unique issue of first impression that justified a formal published opinion.] Shaver (P) desired to have the lease amendments declared void so that the Clantons (D) could not continue renewing the lease. The court correctly noted that the Uniform Rule did not apply to commercial transactions, and rejected Shaver's (P) arguments that the transaction was "quasi-donative." Some courts have held that an option to purchase in gross—where the optionee does not own any other interest in the specific land—may violate the rule if the option can be exercised beyond the period of perpetuities. However, if the optionee also is the lessee of the land—which the Clantons (D) were in this case—then the option is exempt from the rule. Similar rulings exist with respect to an option to renew a lease. Legal commentators have noted that the rule against perpetuities is clearly not suited to commercial transactions, because lives in being plus 21 years has no purpose in the commercial arena.

Chapter 16

As the name implies, this Chapter is about "concurrent ownership," where two or more people own property concurrently. There are different types of concurrent ownerships, the most common of which include "tenants in common," "joint tenants," and "tenancy by the entirety."

The distinguishing factor about joint tenancy is its "right of survivorship," which means that upon the death of a joint tenant, the surviving joint tenants own the property. Many disputes arise concerning ownership interests in real property, especially when individuals are not entitled to property that they otherwise believed they were entitled to, usually based upon a misunderstanding of the laws concerning concurrent ownership. Many examples of such disputes are set forth in the cases presented in this Chapter.

The law today favors tenancy in common, but joint tenancy will be upheld if there is a clear expression of intent to create such an estate. Whether or not an intent to create a joint tenancy is *clear* is the subject matter of many lawsuits. Just as disputes arise concerning the creation of concurrent estates, there are a vast array of disputes concerning severance of the estates, including whether *murder* severs a joint tenancy estate! If a joint tenancy is severed, a tenancy in common is created, which does not entail a right of survivorship.

The last section of the Chapter pertains to "condominiums" and the issues that arise from that unique form of concurrent ownership.

Chapter 16

NOTE: THE PURPOSE OF THIS OUTLINE IS TO ORGANIZE THE CASES SO THAT ONE CAN QUICKLY UNDERSTAND THE RELEVANCE OF EACH CASE TO THE COURSE. NO ATTEMPT IS MADE IN THIS OVERVIEW TO ADDRESS EVERY CONCEPT THAT MUST BE STUDIED. BE SURE TO READ THE ENTIRE CASEBOOK AND/OR OTHER MATERIALS TO GAIN A FULL UNDERSTANDING OF ALL CONCEPTS.

I. "Concurrent Ownership" in the legal sense refers to two or more persons who concurrently have equal rights in real or personal property.

II. Types of Concurrent Ownership
  A. Tenants In Common
    1. "Tenants In Common" are individuals each owning fractional undivided interests—equal or unequal.
    2. "Undivided interest" refers to an ownership interest where none own an identifiable segment of the property, and none can assert a paramount right of possession of any segment.
    3. When disputes arise among tenants in common, available legal remedies include partition, leasing and apportioning the rent, or purchase by one cotenant of the other's interest.
  B. Joint Tenancy
    1. "Joint Tenancy" means individuals comprising a single legal entity which owns the property.
    2. Joint tenancy involves "right of survivorship"—upon the death of a joint tenant, the surviving joint tenants own the property.
    3. Prior to the nineteenth century, joint tenancy existed, unless there was evidence of a clear intent by the transferor to create a tenancy in common. Today, statutes often declare that a tenancy in common will be created unless there is an intent to create a joint tenancy.
    4. It is often said that joint tenants are "seised pur my et pur tout"—each joint tenant is an owner of an undivided interest and an owner of the whole as well.
    5. Joint tenants may compel partition, either "in kind"—through physically dividing the property—or "by sale"—with proceeds of the sale paid to the joint tenant.
    6. Joint tenants may effect a "severance" of their interest—by conveying the interest by deed to another. The grantee becomes a "tenant in common," with no right of survivorship.
    7. Four Unities of Joint Tenancy
      a. Unity of *Interest*—each has equal undivided interest in the property.
      b. Unity of *Title*—each has derived their interest in the property through the same event, such as a single will or conveyance.
      c. Unity of *Time*—the interests vest at the same time (a limitation to a class will create a joint tenancy even if the members of the class come into being at different times.)
      d. Unity of *Possession*—each is seised of the whole estate, not just an undivided interest therein.
  C. Tenancy By The Entirety
    1. "Tenancy by the entirety" is concurrent ownership available only to a married couple.
    2. At common law, a married woman was subject to the husband's control and power of disposal of the property of the marital estate. Now, through legislation and judicial action, husband and wife have equal rights in the control and enjoyment of their property.
    3. Husband and wife are "seised pur tout et non pur my"—neither is an individual owning an undivided interest. Thus, neither can effect a severance by conveying an undivided interest and neither can compel a partition.
  D. Other Marital Estates
    1. "Dower and Curtesy"
      a. Although generally abolished today, "curtesy" gave the husband control over his wife's property and "dower" gave the wife right to a one-third estate for life in the real property upon the death of her husband—the wife was not considered an heir and the eldest son inherited the estate.)
    2. "Homestead Rights"
      a. It applies to any posessory interest in real property that is used as a home or a means of supporting a family.
      b. It is protected from creditor's claims.
    3. "Community Property"
      a. Created by statute, the concept is derived from Civil Law and varies from state to state.
      b. In general, property owned by a spouse before marriage and that acquired by gift or testate or intestate succession thereafter, is

that spouse's separate property, and all other property acquired during marriage is community property.

    c.   Upon dissolution of marriage by death of a spouse, the decedent spouse may make a testamentary disposition of all separate property and half of the community property.

    d.   Upon dissolution of marriage by divorce, generally the community property is divided equally, unless there is a property settlement agreement providing otherwise.

E.   Nontraditional "Marital" Estates

    1.   "Common Law" Marriage—no longer recognized by the courts in most states.

    2.   "Unmarried Cohabitation"—the property rights of parties who live together without marriage vary from state to state, and may be based on contract law, rules of equity or fairness, or public policy considerations.

    3.   "Same Sex Unions"—generally, same sex marriages are not available under existing laws, although the modern trend is to give some legal rights and protections similar to that afforded to married couples.

III.   General Aspects of Concurrent Ownership

A.   At common law, joint tenancies were favored. The courts of the United States, however, favor the presumption of all tenants holding jointly as tenants in common, unless there is a clear showing of an intention to create a joint tenancy with the right of survivorship. *In re Estate of Michael.*

    1.   Where one seeks the court's assistance in interpreting a deed, the court will only look to the deed, and will not consider any other evidence, such as language from a will, to determine the intention of the party.

B.   Cotenants who have mortgage obligations concerning their real property are obligated to pay their pro rata share of the expenses. However, if one cotenant does not pay, and the other prevents the property from being lost through sale, the nonpaying co-tenant retains a right of redemption.

    1.   A co-tenant who pays more than his share of a debt secured by a mortgage or other lien on the common property is entitled to reimbursement (contribution) from his cotenants to the extent to which he paid their shares of the

indebtedness. *Laura v. Christian.*

    2.   A cotenant who pays a mortgage or taxes to avoid a foreclosure sale usually cannot obtain a personal judgment for contribution from the nonpaying cotenant because the nonpaying cotenant is not personally liable for the nonpayment—e.g., a mortgagee obtains the property through foreclosure proceedings, rather than obtaining personal liability against the nonpaying mortgagor.

C.   The right to compel partition is an inherent right of joint tenancy and tenancy in common.

D.   If a partition suit is filed to terminate a co-tenancy, there must be an accounting.

IV.   Creation of Concurrent Estates and Severance Thereof

A.   If two joint tenants exist, and one transfers his interest to a *third person*, the joint tenancy is severed and a tenancy in common is created between the grantee and former joint tenant.

B.   If there are three joint tenants, and one conveys his interest to a *third party*, the joint tenancy is destroyed as to the part conveyed, and the third party becomes a tenant in common with the other two joint tenants; however, the latter still holds the remaining two-thirds as joint tenants.

C.   If three or more joint tenants exist, the conveyance by one joint tenant to *another joint tenant* does not sever the entire joint tenancy; the grantee remains a joint tenant as to his original interest but becomes a tenant in common as to the interest conveyed by the grantor joint tenant. *Jackson v. O'Connell.*

D.   In an action for reformation of the deed (as opposed to judicial interpretation of a deed), if clear and convincing evidence exits showing that the grantor intended for a deed conveying real property to contain language concerning joint tenancy with right of survivorship, but such language was absent due to the scrivener's negligence, the deed can be reformed to include the omitted language. *Matter of Estate of Vadney.*

E.   The express language often used to create joint tenancy estates is: "as joint tenants and not as tenants in common."

    1.   Some courts hold that a deed from the grantor to two grantees containing the phrase, "as joint tenants, and not as tenants in common, to them and their assigns and to the survivor, and

the heirs and assigns of the survivor forever" conveys a joint tenancy, and not a joint life estate to the grantees with a contingent remainder in fee to the survivor. *Palmer v. Flint*.

2. However, other courts hold that a deed conveying property "as joint tenants with full rights of survivorship and not as tenants in common" does not create a joint tenancy, but instead joint life estates followed by a contingent remainder in fee to the survivor. *Jones v. Green*.

F. Whether a mortgage severs a joint tenancy depends upon the particular jurisdiction.

1. If a jurisdiction treats a mortgage as a lien, the execution of a mortgage by one of two joint tenants will not sever the joint tenancy.

   a. However, if the jurisdiction treats a mortgage as a conveyance of title, then a severance will result.

2. In those jurisdictions that treat mortgages as a lien, a mortgage upon real property executed by one of two joint tenants is not enforceable after the death of that joint tenant. *People v. Nogarr*.

G. A divorce alone does not sever a joint tenancy estate.

1. The provisions of a divorce property settlement agreement may, however, convert a joint tenancy into a tenancy in common. *Mann v. Bradley*.

H. Murder

1. In some states, murder by one joint tenant of another joint tenant severs a joint tenancy. *Duncan v. Vassaur*.

2. Other states have contrary views, such as:

   a. A murderer is deprived of the entire interest except for a life interest in one-half;

   b. A murderer is entitled to keep all the property;

   c. A murderer holds upon a constructive trust to the extent of the computed value of one-half of the property as of the date of the victim's death for the period of the victim's expectancy;

   d. A murderer is chargeable as constructive trustee of the entire property for the benefit of the victim's estate;

   e. A murderer is chargeable as constructive trustee of one-half of the property for the benefit of the victim's estate;

   f. By the murder, the joint tenancy has separated and terminated and one-half of the property should go to the heirs of the murdered person and the other one-half to the murderer, or to his heirs, when deceased.

V. Condominiums

A. Condominium ownership is a form of concurrent ownership.

B. Except upon a showing of unusual circumstances or a change in the vendor's position, the vendor's damages for breach of a condominium purchase agreement are usually measurable, and the remedy at law is adequate and there is no jurisdictional basis for the equitable remedy of specific performance of the purchase agreement. *Centex Homes Corp. v. Boag*.

C. A condominium co-owner is not jointly and severally liable for tort claims arising out of the ownership, use and maintenance of the common elements of a condominium project, but instead is liable only for a pro rata portion of the damages. *Dutcher v. Owens*.

D. Condominium associations usually have rules and restrictions that govern condominium living.

1. Most often, the rules and restrictions pertain to maintenance, prohibited activity, budgets, and restrictions on transfers of individual units.

2. Associations are generally afforded a pre-emptive right, which gives it right of first refusal when an owner indicates an intent to sell a unit. The association is usually given the right to match the purchase price. This type of restraint on alienation has been upheld by the courts.

3. However, a declaration of condominium provision that gives the condominium association power to arbitrarily, capriciously, or unreasonably withhold its consent for a unit owner to transfer his interest in the unit is an unreasonable restraint on alienation, notwithstanding a reverter clause, which mandates compensation by the association to the owner in the event of a transfer of the unit in violation of the consent requirement. *Aquarian Foundation, Inc. v. Sholom House, Inc.*

In re Estate of Michael

(Deceased Owner of King Farm)

(1966) 421 Pa. 207

M E M O R Y   G R A P H I C

Instant Facts

Surviving son challenged lower court's ruling that deed to his mother created a joint tenancy with right of survivorship, and urged that a tenancy in common was created.

Black Letter Rule

A presumption exists in favor of tenants in common, unless there is a clear intention to create a joint tenancy with the right of survivorship.

Case Vocabulary

BEHOOF: Part of a conveyance that provides a use, profit, or advantage.

HEREDITAMENTS: Referring to real property, and was used in wills and deeds as part of the phrase "lands, tenements, and hereditaments."

INDENTURE: A formal written agreement among parties with different interests, traditionally having distinguishing edging to prevent forgery.

JOINT TENANCY WITH RIGHT OF SURVIVORSHIP: Individuals comprising a single legal entity which owns the property and upon the death of a joint tenant, the surviving joint tenants own the property.

TENANTS BY THE ENTIRETIES: Concurrent ownership available only to a married couple; it is similar to joint tenancy except that a tenant by the entirety is not permitted to terminate the other spouse's right of survivorship by conveyance or transfer to another.

TENANTS IN COMMON: Individuals each owning fractional undivided interests—equal or unequal.

Procedural Basis: Appeal from a decree of declaratory judgment in action interpreting deed to real property.

Facts: In 1947, Joyce King deeded certain real property, known as "King Farm," to Harry Michael and Bertha Michael, his wife, tenants by the entireties, and Ford Michael (son of Bertha and Harry) and Helen Michael, his wife, tenants by the entireties, with right of survivorship. After Harry died, Bertha created a will leaving her estate to her two sons, Ford and Robert (appellant herein), with each to receive equal shares. With respect to King Farm, Bertha's will provided that her interest therein should go to Robert and the sum of $1,000 to Ford to balance the gift. Bertha died and Ford and Robert were appointed executors of their mother's estate. A dispute arose as to what, if any, interest Bertha had in King Farm, based upon the construction of the language of the 1947 deed. The lower court held that the deed created a joint tenancy with right of survivorship between the two sets of husbands and wives (Michael and Bertha and Ford and Helen.) Robert (appellant) contends that the deed created a tenancy in common, with each couple holding its undivided one-half interest as tenants by the entireties. The appellees, conceding that the respective one-half interests were held by husband and wife as tenants by the entireties, contend, that as to each other the couples held as joint tenants with a right of survivorship.

Issue: Is there a presumption in favor of tenancy in common?

Decision and Rationale: (Jones) Yes. At common law, joint tenancies were favored, and the doctrine of survivorship was a recognized incident to a joint estate. The courts of the United States, however, favor the presumption of all tenants holding jointly as tenants in common, unless there is a clear showing of an intention to the contrary. Pennsylvania, by the Act of 1812, eliminated the incident of survivorship in joint tenancies unless the instrument creating the estate expressly provides that such incident should exist. The intent must be expressed with sufficient clarity to overcome the statutory presumption that survivorship was not intended. In construing the language of the 1947 deed, we cannot find a sufficiently clear expression of intent to create a right of survivorship to overcome the presumption. Nowhere in the deed is the term "joint tenants" employed. The normal procedure would be to employ the phrase "joint tenants, with a right of survivorship, and not as tenants in common." [Simple enough!] The deed also uses the term "their heirs and assigns forever." The use of the plural would tend to indicate a tenancy in common. If "his or her" heirs and assigns had been used, a strong argument could be made that the grantor intended a right of survivorship and that the survivor of the four named grantees would have an absolute undivided fee in the property. We cannot find within the four corners of the deed a clearly expressed intention to create a joint tenancy with the right of survivorship. Thus, the Act of 1812 compels us to find that the deed created a tenancy in common as between the two sets of married couples, each couple holding its undivided one-half interest as tenants by the entireties. Decree reversed.

Analysis:

Prior to the nineteenth century, joint tenancy existed, unless there was evidence of a clear intent by the transferor to create a tenancy in common. Today, statutes often declare that a tenancy in common will be created unless there is an intent to create a joint tenancy. Pennsylvania had such a statute—the Act of 1812—and the court was required to construe the language of the deed to determine if there was an intent to create a joint tenancy. Note that the court only looks to the deed, and does not consider any other evidence that may have been provided, such as language from Bertha's will wherein she indicated that she expected her interest to pass under her will. Thus, it is crucial to make sure that the language of a deed adequately (and legally) complies with the grantor's intent. However, note the holding in *Matter of Estate of Vadney* later in the Chapter wherein a deed was reformed to comply with the grantor's intent, based upon extrinsic evidence rather than the express language of the deed. The difference in the two holdings has to do with the type of action—one seeks judicial interpretation of a deed and the other seeks reformation of the deed to comply with the grantor's intent. This case also demonstrates the different types of tenancies, such as "tenancy by the entireties"(available only to married persons), "tenants in common," and "joint tenancy." The difference between tenants in common and joint tenancy is that the later involves "right of survivorship"—upon the death of a joint tenant, the surviving joint tenants own the property.

Laura v. Christian

(Mortgage Paying Co-tenant) v. (Co-tenant Offering Contribution)
(1975) 88 N.M. 127

M E M O R Y   G R A P H I C

Instant Facts

Christian (D) knew that real property was subject to foreclosure, but he let Laura (P) make the payments to stop the sale, and thereafter he agreed to contribution to maintain his interest in the property.

Black Letter Rule

Co-tenant who pays more than his share of a debt secured by a mortgage or other lien on the common property is entitled to reimbursement (contribution) from his cotenants to the extent to which he paid their shares of the indebtedness.

Case Vocabulary

CONSTRUCTIVE TRUST: Involuntary trust created by operation of law where one gains a thing by fraud, accident, mistake, undue influence, etc., and imposed by a court of equity to prevent unjust enrichment.
MORTGAGEE: The creditor who possesses the mortgage on property, as a lien to secure payment of an obligation by the mortgagor.
PERFECT AN APPEAL: Exercising all steps necessary to pursue an appeal.

Procedural Basis: Appeal from judgment in quiet title action concerning interests held in real property.

Facts: Laura (P) [a guy] brought an action to quiet title concerning real property known as Fireside Lodge. Although there were several defendants involved in the trial, the appeal only concerns defendant Christian (D), who claims a ¼ interest as a tenant in common with Laura (P) in the Fireside Lodge. Laura (P) and Christian (D) made some payments on the mortgage lien, but subsequent payments called for by the mortgage instruments were not paid, and the mortgagee instituted a foreclosure action, which resulted in an order for sale of the property. Laura (P), in order to protect the property from sale, paid the mortgagee the sum of $17,288.40, which represents the amount of the judgment, interest, and expenses owing to the mortgagee. Although Christian (D) had knowledge as early as nine months prior to the order for sale that foreclosure was being threatened, he did not pay his proportionate share of the mortgage indebtedness as it became due, and failed to take action to avoid the sale. [What prompted his later interest in contributing his share? Read on …] After learning that the value of the property had been greatly enhanced, Christian (D) was willing to pay a share of the indebtedness discharged by Laura's (P) payment to the mortgagee. On the day of commencement of trial, Christian (D) agreed to pay his proportionate share of the expenditures made by Laura (P) to protect his ¼ interest in the property. Judgment was entered in favor of Laura (P) quieting title. Christian (D) appealed.

Issue: Is a co-tenant who pays more than his share of a debt secured by a mortgage or other lien on the common property entitled to reimbursement (contribution) from his cotenants to the extent to which he paid their shares of the indebtedness?

Decision and Rationale: (Oman) Yes. Christian (D) claims a ¼ interest as a tenant in common with Laura (P) in the Fireside Lodge. The general rule as to reimbursement or contribution from a cotenant is as follows: A co-tenant who pays more than his share of a debt secured by a mortgage or other lien on the common property is entitled to reimbursement (contribution) from his cotenants to the extent to which he paid their shares of the indebtedness. It is also a general rule that a cotenant has a right to redemption or prevention from loss of common property by payment of an obligation, which should be discharged proportionately by cotenants, subject to the right of contribution. However, the option must be exercised within a reasonable time. Although we do not applaud Christian's (D) delay in assuming his obligation, we conclude that his election to contribute was timely. The judgment of the district court should be reversed with instructions to enter a new judgment quieting title to a 3/4ths interest in the property in Laura (P), and establishing a ¼ interest in Christian (D), subject to lien thereon in favor of Laura (P) to secure repayment to him of all amounts expended for the benefit of Christian (D).

Analysis:

We learn from this case that cotenants who have mortgage obligations concerning their real property are obligated to pay their pro rata share of the expenses. However, if one cotenant does not pay, and the other prevents the property from being lost through sale, the nonpaying co-tenant retains a right of redemption. Christian (D), realizing the enhanced value of the property, exercised his right of redemption, and offered to contribute his pro rata share of the costs paid by Laura (P). The court was unwilling to declare that he waited too long, and thus, allowed him to redeem the property. Note that the court's judgment established Christian's (D) ¼ interest in the property, but gave Laura (P) a lien thereon to secure repayment from Christian (D). A cotenant who pays a mortgage or taxes to avoid a foreclosure sale usually cannot obtain a personal judgment for contribution from the nonpaying cotenant because the nonpaying cotenant is not personally liable for the nonpayment—e.g., a mortgagee obtains the property through foreclosure proceedings, rather than obtaining personal liability against the nonpaying mortgagor. In addition, when Laura (P) prevented the foreclosure sale by paying the sum due, the effect was to maintain the title for all cotenants, including Christian (D). Thereafter, Christian (D) had the option of exercising his right to redemption, within a reasonable time, and reimbursing Laura (P) for his pro rata share.

Jackson v. O'Connell

(Nieces Claiming Interest) v. (Original Joint Tenant)
(1961) 23 Ill.2d 52

MEMORY GRAPHIC

Instant Facts

Jackson and her fellow three nieces (P) sued an original joint tenant (D) contending that the entire joint tenancy was severed by one joint tenant conveying her interest to one of two other joint tenants.

Black Letter Rule

Where three or more joint tenants exist, the conveyance by one joint tenant to another joint tenant does not sever the entire joint tenancy; the grantee remains a joint tenant as to his original interest but becomes a tenant in common as to the interest conveyed by the grantor joint tenant.

Case Vocabulary

MASTER: A quasi judicial officer who has been appointed to help the judge and court, by acting as a referee, hearing officer, person who resolves discovery issues, or makes calculations, etc.

QUITCLAIM DEED: A deed that conveys real property but without warranty of title and without covenants.

SEVERANCE OF JOINT TENANCY: Conduct by a joint tenant that destroys the joint tenancy and converts it into a tenancy in common without right of survivorship.

UNITY OF INTEREST: One of the four "unities" of a joint tenancy, where each tenant has equal undivided interest in the property.

UNITY OF POSSESSION: One of the four "unities" of a joint tenancy, where each tenant is seised of the whole estate, not just an undivided interest therein.

UNITY OF TIME: One of the four "unities" of a joint tenancy, where the interests vest at the same time (but note that a limitation to a class will create a joint tenancy even if the members of the class come into being at different times.)

UNITY OF TITLE: One of the four "unities" of a joint tenancy, where each tenant has derived their interest in the property through the same event, such as a single will or conveyance.

Procedural Basis: Appeal from decree of partition in action to determine interests of cotenants following conveyance of real property.

Facts: Upon Neil Duffy's death, his will devised certain parcels of real estate to his three sisters Nellie Duffy, Anna Duffy, and Katherine O'Connell (D), as joint tenants. [Even though the court says the facts are simple, start diagramming the parties NOW!] Thereafter, Nellie quitclaimed all her interest in the properties to Anna. Nellie subsequently died, and eight years later Anna died. Anna's will devised her interest in the property to four nieces, Beatrice Jackson, Eileen O'Barski, Catherine Young, and Margaret Miller (hereinafter "the nieces") (P). The nieces (P) brought suit against Katherine O'Connell (D) and others to partition the real estate, contending that Nellie's quitclaim deed to Anna severed in its entirety the joint tenancies existing between Nellie, Anna, and Katherine (D), and that as a result Anna became the owner of an undivided two-thirds interest and Katherine (D) an undivided one-third interest, as tenants in common. The nieces (P) further contend that they, as successors in interest to Anna, each own an undivided one-sixth and Katherine (D) an undivided one-third, as tenants in common. Katherine (D) counterclaimed contending that Nellie's quitclaim deed to Anna severed the joint tenancies only so far as Nellie's one-third interest was concerned, and that the two-thirds joint tenancies between Anna and Katherine (D) remained in effect, so that upon Anna's death, Katherine (D) succeeded to that two-thirds interest as surviving joint tenant and the nieces (P) are each entitled to a one-twelfth interest as devisees of the one-third interest which passed to Anna by Nellie's quitclaim deed. [Simple enough?] A master found for Katherine (D) and the nieces (P) appealed.

Issue: Does a conveyance by one of three joint tenants to another joint tenant destroy the joint tenancy in its entirety?

Decision and Rationale: (Klingbiel) No. In this appeal we must determine whether a conveyance by one of three joint tenants to another of the joint tenants destroyed the joint tenancy in its entirety or merely severed the joint tenancy with respect to the undivided third interest so conveyed, leaving the joint tenancy in force and effect as to the remaining two-thirds interest. Common law rules of joint tenancy provide that the following four unities are necessary for the creation and continuance of a joint tenancy: unity of interest, unity of title, unity of time, and unity of possession. Any act of a joint tenant that destroys any of these unities operates as a severance of the joint tenancy, thereby extinguishing the right of survivorship. It is well settled that where there are three joint tenants, and one conveys his interest to a *third party*, the joint tenancy is destroyed as to the part conveyed, and the third party becomes a tenant in common with the other two joint tenants; however, the latter still holds the remaining two-thirds as joint tenants. The nieces (P) contend that this rule should not apply where the conveyance is to a fellow joint tenant and that in such a case, the interest of the grantee becomes different in quantity from that of the remaining joint tenant, and that unity of interest is destroyed and severance of the entire joint tenancy results. We find no authority to support such a view. Although a joint tenancy may be terminated by destroying the unity of interest, such is not the case here. Even though Nellie's quitclaim deed resulted in the interest of Anna (the grantee) and Katherine (D) being unequal, it must be noted that their interests in the undivided two-thirds, which formed the subject matter of the joint tenancies here in question, remained the same. Unity of interest exists with respect to the undivided interest which forms the subject matter of the joint tenancy. It is the interests of the joint tenants in the subject involved in the joint tenancy that must be equal. Therefore, we conclude that where three or more joint tenants exist, the conveyance by one joint tenant to another joint tenant does not sever the entire joint tenancy; the grantee remains a joint tenant as to his original interest but becomes a tenant in common as to the interest conveyed by the grantor joint tenant. Decree affirmed.

Holding! →

Analysis:

To better understand this case, it is helpful to review the general rules concerning creation and continuance of joint tenancies as applied to different factual scenarios. At common law, four unities were required to create a joint tenancy: (1) unity of interest—each tenant has equal undivided interest in the property; (2) unity of title—each tenant has derived their interest in the property through the same event, such as a single will or conveyance; (3) unity of time—the interests vest at the same time; and (4) unity of possession—each is seised of the whole estate, not just an undivided interest therein. If only two joint tenants existed, and one transferred his interest to a third person, the joint tenancy is severed and a tenancy in common is created between the grantee and former joint tenant. If three or more joint tenants existed, and one transferred his interest to a third person, the third person is a tenant in common with the remaining joint tenants; however, the remaining joint tenants continue as joint tenants among themselves. In this case, one of the three joint tenants conveyed her interest not to a third person, but to a fellow joint tenant. The court rejected the argument that such a conveyance severed the entire joint tenancy because the unity of interest would be destroyed. Why? Because the grantee remains a joint tenant as to her original interest. She also is a tenant in common as to that interest conveyed by the grantor, which will not destroy the entire joint tenancy.

Matter of Estate of Vadney

(Decedent Who Intended Joint Tenancy)

(1994) 83 N.Y.2nd 885

M E M O R Y   G R A P H I C

Instant Facts

Son of decedent sought to have deed reformed to include omitted language concerning joint tenancy with right of survivorship to conform to grantor's intent.

Black Letter Rule

If clear and convincing evidence exits showing that grantor intended for a deed conveying real property to contain language concerning joint tenancy with right of survivorship, but such language was absent due to the scrivener's negligent, the deed can be reformed to include the omitted language.

Case Vocabulary

REFORM A DEED: Referring to "reformation" of a legal document wherein the court orders the document modified according to the parties' intent, usually based upon fraud or mistake.

CLEAR AND CONVINCING EVIDENCE: Evidence that proves something by more than a preponderance of the evidence but less than proof beyond a reasonable doubt.

Procedural Basis: Appeal from order reversing Surrogate Court and granting petition for partition of deed.

Facts: Decedent Vadney deeded her real property to herself and her son Peter Vadney (P) but the deed did not describe the type of tenancy created or contain any survivorship language. Peter (P) assumed that the deed created a joint tenancy with right to survivorship that passed to him upon his mother's death without having to go through probate. As a result, Peter (P) excluded the property from the list of estate assets when his mother's will was admitted to probate. The decedent's three other children (D) contended that the deed created a tenancy in common based upon a statute that provides that a tenancy in common is created unless the instrument *expressly* declares the disposition to be a joint tenancy. They sought an interest in the property through the residual clause of their mother's will. Peter (P) filed a petition to reform the deed, contending that the absence of survivorship language was contrary to his mother's intent and due solely to a scrivener's error. [A fancy way of saying that the lawyer screwed up!] The court denied the petition after ruling that extrinsic evidence of the grantor's intent was not admissible to vary the terms of the deed. The Appellate Division reversed and the Court of Appeals accepted the case for review.

Issue: If clear and convincing evidence exits showing that grantor intended for a deed conveying real property to contain language concerning joint tenancy with right of survivorship, but such language was absent due to the scrivener's negligent, can the deed be reformed to include the omitted language?

Decision and Rationale: (Name of justices not provided) Yes. There was uncontroverted testimony of the attorney who drafted the deed indicating that he had received oral instructions from the decedent to prepare a deed conveying the property to herself and Peter (P) as joint tenants, and that he neglected to include survivorship language in the deed through oversight. He also produced a copy of his notes taken during a meeting with the decedent, which indicated an intent to create by the deed a right of survivorship. The attorney's wife also testified that when she witnessed the signing of the will, the decedent stated that she wanted Peter (P) to have the house. We therefore conclude that Peter (P) has met his very high burden of proving by clear and convincing evidence that the decedent intended to create a joint tenancy rather than a tenancy in common, and that the language manifesting such an intent was mistakenly omitted from the deed by the scrivener. Thus, the deed should be reformed to include the omitted language. Order affirmed.

Analysis:

In this action for reformation of the deed, the court concluded that due to substantial uncontroverted extrinsic evidence, the petitioner, Peter (P), had met the burden of proving by clear and convincing evidence that the decedent intended to create a joint tenancy with right of survivorship, rather than a tenancy in common. Recall that the statute requires express language to establish joint tenancy. In one of the previous cases in the chapter, *In re Estate of Michael*, the court refused to look beyond the "four corners" of the deed. However, that action involved obtaining a decree of declaratory judgment, which requires the court to interpret the language of the legal document. In this case, Peter (P) sought to have the deed reformed due to the attorney's mistake and the very strong evidence of the grantor's true intent. Contrary to the common law, the presumption now is against joint tenancy. Many states have statutes requiring a clear expression of intent to create a joint tenancy with right of survivorship. The court, faced with overwhelming evidence of the grantor's intent, obviously made the right decision. However, even if the court found against Peter (P), he would not be left without a remedy—he could sue the attorney for malpractice for the damages sustained.

Palmer v. Flint

(Subsequent Grantee) v. (Original Grantee)
(1960) 156 Me. 103

M E M O R Y   G R A P H I C

Instant Facts

Palmer (P) sought to have court declare original deed to Nathan and Flint (D) as creating joint tenancy and not joint life estate.

Black Letter Rule

A deed from the grantor to two grantees containing the phrase, "as joint tenants, and not as tenants in common, to them and their assigns and to the survivor, and the heirs and assigns of the survivor forever" conveys a joint tenancy, and not a joint life estate to the grantees with a contingent remainder in fee to the survivor.

Case Vocabulary

BILL OF COMPLAINT: A written petition submitted to the court requesting certain relief from the defendant.
GRANTING CLAUSE: The language in a deed or other document that expresses the transfer of an interest.
HABENDUM CLAUSE: Also called a "to have and to hold clause," and referring to that portion of a deed that describes the interest granted and any conditions relating thereto.

Procedural Basis: Appeal from declaratory judgment in action concerning rights to real property under a deed.

Facts: Federal Land Bank (D1) conveyed real property to Nathan Palmer and his wife Alice Palmer (now Alice Flint) (D2). The deed conveyed the property to Nathan and Alice (D2) "as joint tenants, and not as tenants in common, to them and their assigns and to the survivor, and the heirs and assigns of the survivor forever." Alice (D2) divorced Nathan and, by quitclaim deed, conveyed the premises to Nathan. Thereafter, Nathan conveyed the property to Frank [a strawman perhaps], who reconveyed to Nathan and his sister Roxa Palmer (P), "as joint tenants and not as tenants in common, to them and their heirs and assigns, and to the survivor of them, and to the heirs and assigns of such survivor forever." After Nathan died, Palmer (P) filed suit to have the court determine rights or status of the parties to the premises, and if it should be determined that the deed from the Bank (D1) did not convey an estate of which the grantor intended to convey, that the deed be reformed in accordance with the parties' true intention. The lower court found that said deed was according to the parties' intent; that the quitclaim deed of Alice (D2) to Nathan was inoperative to convey her contingent remainder; and that the state of the title in the premises was an estate for the life of Alice (D2) in Roxa Palmer (P), remainder in fee to Alice (D2). Palmer (P) appealed contending that Alice (D2) conveyed her entire interest in the property by quitclaim to Nathan, and upon his death, Palmer (P) became the owner.

Issue: Does a deed from the grantor to two grantees containing the phrase, "as joint tenants, and not as tenants in common, to them and their assigns and to the survivor, and the heirs and assigns of the survivor forever" convey a joint life estate to the grantees with a contingent remainder in fee to the survivor?

Decision and Rationale: (Siddall) No. The real controversy in this case is between Palmer (P) and Alice (D2), with Palmer (P) contending that the deed from Alice (D2) to Nathan was intended to convey her interest in the remainder and that Nathan was thereby seized in fee simple of the entire interest so that upon his death, Alice (D2) acquired no interest. Alice (D2) contends that the deed from the Bank (D1) to Nathan and Alice (D2) conveyed a joint life estate to the grantees with a contingent remainder in fee to the survivor, and that the quitclaim deed from Alice (D2) to Nathan was inoperative to convey to him her contingent remainder. The problem before us is the determination of the respective estates of the grantees in the fee conveyed to them by the Bank (D1). Our state has enacted legislation modifying the common law that favored joint estates. It provides that devisees of land to "two or more or persons, create estates in common, unless otherwise expressed. Estates vested in survivors upon the principle of joint tenancy shall be so held." There are numerous divergent views taken by courts of other jurisdictions concerning the construction of deeds involving the issue of joint tenancy. Generally, under statutes favoring the creation of tenancies in common but not abolishing joint tenancies it is held that any language clearly indicating an intention to create a joint tenancy will be sufficient regardless of where it appears in the deed. In our jurisdiction, an estate in joint tenancy is well recognized, and the statute does not abolish such an estate; however, the intent to create it must be clear and convincing. In order to create a joint tenancy, there must be unities of time, title, interest, and possession. A joint tenant has a right of severance. Any joint tenant who conveys to a stranger destroys the unity of title and the unity of time, and the grantee becomes a tenant in common with the others, although the others remain joint tenants as between themselves. We cannot find that the use of the word "heirs" in the phrase "and the heirs of the survivor forever" in the deed's granting or habendum clauses precludes a severance of the property, thereby creating a life estate in the grantees with a contingent fee in the survivor, as claimed by Alice (D2). If such an estate had been desired, the parties could have indicated such intent by apt language. The deed contained no reference to a life estate, nor did it refer to any estate in remainder. We hold that the essential unities of time, title, interest, and possession were present in the estate created by the deed, and that the deed conveyed the entire estate disposed of by the grantor, a fee, to the grantees as joint tenants with all of the incidents and attributes of such tenancy. Thus, reformation of the deed is unnecessary. The conveyance from Alice (D2) to Nathan disposed of her entire interest in the property and he thereby became the owner of the fee, which is now in Palmer (P). Appeal allowed. Bill of complaint sustained. Case remanded for entry of a decree of declaratory judgment for Palmer (P).

Analysis:

This is another case that analyzes whether a joint tenancy estate was created. The required express language was used—"as joint tenants and not as tenants in common"—but Alice (D2) placed reliance upon the phrase "heirs and assigns of the survivor forever" to assert that a joint life estate was created, with a contingent remainder to the survivor, rather than a joint tenancy. If Alice's (D2) contention were upheld, it would have affected the ability to sever the estate. The court correctly held that had the grantor intended to create a joint life estate it would have so indicated in the deed. Keep in mind that different jurisdictions have different statutes and judicial decisions concerning the adequacy of language in a deed to create joint tenancies, and the type of evidence that will be permitted to establish such tenancy.

Jones v. Green

(Party Seeking Partition) v. (Party Opposing Partition)
(1983) 126 Mich. App. 412

M E M O R Y   G R A P H I C

Instant Facts

Deed to two grantees did not create joint tenancy, despite express language of joint tenancy with right of survivorship and not tenants in common, and resulting joint life estates could not be partitioned by only one life tenant.

Black Letter Rule

(1) Language in a deed conveying property "as joint tenants with full rights of survivorship and not as tenants in common" will not create a joint tenancy, but instead joint life estates followed by a contingent remainder in fee to the survivor. (2) A joint life estate is indestructible by the voluntary act of only one of the life tenants.

Case Vocabulary

INTER ALIA: Latin for among other things.
MOIETY: A small segment of an interest, half or less than half.
MOTION FOR SUMMARY JUDGMENT: A legal motion requesting the judge to enter judgment, before trial, on the grounds that the action has no merit or there is no defense to the action.
PER CONTRA: Latin for by contrast.
PER CURIAM: An opinion by the whole court, rather than one judge.
REVERSIBLE ERROR: An error that is significant enough to possibly cause prejudice to a party so as to require the reversal of a judgment.

Procedural Basis: Appeal from order denying motion for partial summary judgment in action to partition real property.

Facts: Jones (P) and Green (D) bought a residence and the deed provided that the seller conveyed to them "as joint tenants with full rights of survivorship and not as tenants in common." Thereafter, Jones (P) filed suit to partition the property that she and Green (D) had purchased. Green (D) moved for summary judgment, arguing that property conveyed to unmarried persons as joint tenants with full right of survivorship and not as tenants in common cannot be partitioned under Michigan law. The trial court (D) denied the motion, and Green (D) appealed.

Issue: Does language in a deed conveying property "as joint tenants with full rights of survivorship and not as tenants in common" create an indestructable joint estate?

Decision and Rationale: (Per Curiam) Yes. We first note that all land held jointly is generally subject to partition. [But it's not so easily done in Michigan!] We held in *Ames v. Cheyne* that where property stands in the name of joint tenants with the right of survivorship, neither party may transfer the title to the premises and deprive the other of such right of survivorship. We further held that joint life estates are created followed by a contingent remainder in fee to the survivor, indestructible by the voluntary act of only one of the life tenants. We reject Jones' (P) argument that *Ames* is not applicable because it was decided before the enactment of M.C.L. §600.3304. The committee comment to the statute provides that the court could find that property was subject to partition since the statement "with right of survivorship" would reasonably be considered merely a statement of an incident of joint tenancy rather than a contract. However, said statute is substantially the same as its predecessor, which provided that all persons holding land as joint tenants or tenants in common may have partition. In addition, following enactment of §600.3304, the Supreme Court and this Court have reaffirmed the holding in *Ames*. Therefore, the real property held by Jones (P) and Green (D) cannot be partitioned. Reversed.

Analysis:

Even though Michigan courts hold that express language conveying property "as joint tenants with full rights of survivorship and not as tenants in common" creates an indestructible estate, not all courts follow this view. Many, if not most, courts view the language "with right of survivorship" as merely extra assurance of the intent to create a joint tenancy. Compare the holding in the previous case, *Palmer v. Flint*, wherein very similar language was held to create a joint tenancy. It would seem that the *Palmer* holding is the better view, since it is consistent with the grantor's intent. The *Jones* court found that the language created a contingent remainder, which cannot be destroyed by severance. Had the court found a joint tenancy, severance would have been permitted.

People v. Nogarr

(State) v. (Joint Tenant and Mortgagees of Deceased Joint Tenant)

(1958) 164 Cal.App.2d 591

M E M O R Y   G R A P H I C

 ## Instant Facts

Mortgagees of deceased joint tenant sought to have mortgage satisfied after death of joint tenant.

Black Letter Rule

A mortgage upon real property executed by one of two joint tenants is not enforceable after the death of that joint tenant.

Case Vocabulary

CONDEMNATION: An action by the government to determine if property should be declared for public use upon reasonable compensation to the owners of the property.

DOCTRINE OF EQUITABLE CONVERSION: Where equity acts to make that which out to be done; for example, real property will be treated as personal property in order to acknowledge transfer of real property based upon written agreement to sell, but where party dies before title is transferred.

JUSTICE PRO TEM: Pro tem is the abbreviation for "pro tempore"—Latin, for "the time being"—and as applied to "justice" refers to appointing one to act temporarily as a justice.

Procedural Basis: Appeal from judgment following trial concerning rights of joint tenants to real property.

Facts: Elaine Wilson ("Elaine") (D2) and her husband Calvert acquired certain real property as joint tenants. Four years later, Elaine (D2) and Calvert separated, and thereafter Calvert executed a promissory note to his parents, Mr. and Mrs. Frank Wilson (D1), and also gave them a mortgage to the property. Elaine (D2) did not have knowledge or consent to the execution of the mortgage. Eight months later, Calvert died. Approximately one year after his death, the State of California (P) commenced an action to condemn the property, alleging that Elaine (D2) was the owner and the Wilsons (D1) were mortgagees thereof. Elaine (D2) answered the complaint and alleged that she was the owner and the Wilsons (D1) had no right, title, or interest therein. The Wilsons (D1) answered and alleged that they were the owners and holders of the mortgage and sought to have the mortgage satisfied from the proceeds of the condemnation award. The State (P) paid the amount of the fair market value of the property into court [for safekeeping] and a trial was had as to the interests of Elaine (D2) and the Wilsons (D1). The court found for the Wilsons (D1), and Elaine (D2) appealed. On appeal, Elaine (D2) contended that the mortgage did not terminate the joint tenancy and sever Calvert's interests from that of Elaine (D2), but that the mortgage was a lien upon his interest as a joint tenant only and thus, upon his death, his interest having ceased to exist the lien of the mortgage terminated and Elaine (D2) was entitled to the distribution of the entire award. [In other words, the parents should have called due the note before Calvert died.]

Issue: Is a mortgage upon real property executed by one of two joint tenants enforceable after the death of that joint tenant?

Decision and Rationale: (Nourse) No. It is undisputed that a joint tenancy existed between Elaine (D2) and Calvert at the time of the execution of the mortgage, and that upon the death of Calvert, Elaine (D2) became the sole owner of the property. Under the doctrine of equitable conversion, Elaine (D2) is entitled to the entire condemnation award, unless the execution by Calvert of the mortgage destroyed one of the four unities required for joint tenancy and thus severed the joint tenancy and destroyed the right of survivorship. Under the law of this state, a mortgage is but a lien upon the property mortgaged, and does not pass title to the mortgagee. Thus, inasmuch as the mortgage was but a lien upon Calvert's interest, and as it did not operate to transfer the legal title or any title to the mortgagees or entitle the mortgagees to possession, it did not destroy any of the unities. Thus, the joint tenancy estate was not severed and Elaine (D2) and Calvert did not become tenants in common. It necessarily follows that, as the mortgage lien attached only to such interest as Calvert had in the real property, when his interest ceased to exist the lien of the mortgage expired with it. In jurisdictions where a mortgage operates to transfer the legal title, a mortgage by a joint tenant causes a severance of the joint tenancy. Also, in some states where a mortgage is regarded as mere security, a mortgage by a joint tenant brings the tenancy to an end. The authorities cited by the Wilsons (D1) are from other jurisdictions and all, except one, were rendered in jurisdictions where a mortgage operated not merely as a lien or charge upon the mortgagor's interest but as a transfer or conveyance of his interest. In those jurisdictions where title is conveyed by the mortgage, the unity of title is destroyed. We reject these authorities. There is nothing inequitable in holding that the lien of the Wilsons' (D1) mortgage did not survive Calvert's death. The note was payable upon demand, and they could have enforced the lien and mortgage by foreclosure and sale prior to Calvert's death, and thus have severed the joint tenancy. By choosing not to do so, they awaited the contingency of which joint tenant would die first at their own risk. Judgment reversed.

Analysis:

This case shows that the issue of whether a mortgage severs a joint tenancy depends upon the particular jurisdiction. If a jurisdiction treats a mortgage as a lien, the execution of a mortgage by one of two joint tenants will not sever the joint tenancy. However, if the jurisdiction treats a mortgage as a conveyance of title, then a severance will result. California treats mortgages as a lien and thus, Calvert's execution of the mortgage did not sever the joint tenancy. As a result, the Wilsons (D1) lost their lien against the property because it was destroyed upon Calvert's death. Although California treats mortgages as liens, there are still a number of jurisdictions retaining the "title theory" of the mortgage, derived from early English law.

Mann v. Bradley

(Divorced Husband) v. (Administratrix of Deceased Ex-Wife's Estate and Children)
(1975) 188 Colo. 392

NOW THAT YOUR MOTHER IS DEAD, I AM THE SOLE OWNER OF THE HOME!

M E M O R Y   G R A P H I C

Instant Facts

Mr. Mann (D) argued, unsuccessfully, that the provisions of the divorce property settlement agreement did not indicate an intent to terminate joint tenancy ownership.

Black Letter Rule

The provisions of a divorce property settlement agreement may convert a joint tenancy into a tenancy in common.

Case Vocabulary

ADMINISTRATRIX: A female administrator who is appointed to handle the estate of one who dies intestate.
SINE QUA NON: Latin for "without which not."

Procedural Basis: Petition for writ of certiorari granted to review court of appeal's decision affirming the judgment to quiet title to real property following trial.

Facts: Betty Mann and Aaron Mann (D) acquired the family residence as joint tenants during their marriage. Thereafter, they divorced and in connection therewith, they entered into a property settlement agreement. The agreement, which was adopted as an order of the court in the divorce action, provided that the family residence should be sold and the proceeds equally divided between the Manns upon the happening of any of the three following events: (1) The remarriage of Mrs. Mann; (2) When their youngest child attains the age of 21; or (3) The mutual agreement of the parties to sell. Mrs. Mann continued living in the residence with her children until her death. Shortly thereafter, Mr. Mann (D) claimed that the residence belonged to him based upon right of survivorship in the joint tenancy with Mrs. Mann. [Nice dad!] Thereupon, the administratrix of Mrs. Mann's estate and the children (P) filed an action to quiet title to the property, contending that the property settlement agreement converted the joint tenancy into a tenancy in common with the result that Mrs. Mann's interest passed to her children upon her death. After trial, judgment was entered quieting title in the children as tenants in common in fee simple of an undivided one-half interest in the resident. Mr. Mann (D) appealed and the court of appeal held that the joint tenancy was terminated. Mr. Mann (D) sought review before the state supreme court.

Issue: May a divorce property settlement agreement convert a joint tenancy into a tenancy in common?

Decision and Rationale: (Hodges) Yes. Mr. Mann (D) contends that the provisions of the property settlement agreement demonstrate a clear intent that the residence remain in joint tenancy until the occurrence of one of the three contingencies. Since none occurred prior to Mrs. Mann's death, Mr. Mann (D) reasons that the property passed to him by right of survivorship. [The court's response—the contention has no merit!] The modern tendency is to not require that the act of the co-tenant be destructive of one of the essential four unities of time, title, possession, or interest before a joint tenancy is terminated. The joint tenancy may be terminated by mutual agreement, as here, where the parties treated their interest as belonging to them in common. An agreement between the joint tenants to hold as tenants in common may be inferred from the manner in which the parties deal with the property. In this case, the agreement, which provides for the ultimate sale of the property, evinces the parties' intent not to hold the property in joint tenancy as of the effective date of the agreement. The entire tenor of those provisions of the agreement pertaining to the property is inconsistent with any purpose of the parties to continue the right of survivorship, which is the *sine qua non* of joint tenancy. The portion of the agreement, which states that the property "shall remain in the joint names of the parties," does not change our opinion, since the wording is consistent with any form of concurrent ownership. In fact, the language strongly supports the intent to change from joint tenancy, and since the Manns were going to sell and divide the proceeds, the property would remain in their joint names—the way tenants in common hold property. Affirmed.

Analysis:

Duncan v. Vassaur

(Father of Joint Tenant Murderer) v. (Father of Murdered Joint Tenant)

(1976) 550 P.2d 929

M E M O R Y   G R A P H I C

Instant Facts

Father of joint tenant murderer sought to quiet title to real property that was conveyed to him shortly after the murder.

Black Letter Rule

A murder by one joint tenant of another joint tenant is inconsistent with the continued existence of the joint tenancy so as to terminate the joint tenancy.

Case Vocabulary

APPELLEE: Party who is responding to an appeal, rather than initiating it.

BONA FIDE INNOCENT PURCHASER FOR VALUABLE CONSIDERATION: One who purchases property, in good faith, for valuable consideration and without notice of any defect in title.

JUDGMENT ON THE PLEADINGS: Deciding the case as a matter of law based upon the allegations contained in the complaint.

Procedural Basis: Appeal from dismissal of cross petition and granting of motion for judgment on the pleadings in action to quiet title to real property.

Facts: Edgar Vassaur, Jr. ("Jr.") owned real property prior to his marriage to Betty. Jr. conveyed the property to himself and Betty, as joint tenants. Betty, while married to Jr., shot and killed him. [She must have wanted the property all for herself.] Approximately 45 days after Jr. was shot and killed, Betty, having been charged with first-degree manslaughter, conveyed the real property to her father, William Duncan (P). Thereafter, Duncan (P) filed an action against Jr.'s estate (D) to quiet title to the property. Jr.'s father, Edgar Vassaur, Sr. ("Sr."), as the administrator of Jr.'s estate (D), answered and cross petitioned claiming an ownership interest of one-half of the property, a lien on the balance in the amount of the proceeds of a credit life insurance policy on Jr.'s life, and another lien in the amount of a home improvement loan which had been repaid by the estate. Duncan (P) demurred to the answer and cross petition and moved for judgment on the pleadings. The trial judge sustained the demurrer, dismissed the cross petition and granted Duncan's (P) motion for judgment on the pleadings. Sr. (D) appealed.

Issue: Is a murder by one joint tenant of another joint tenant inconsistent with the continued existence of the joint tenancy so as to terminate the joint tenancy?

Decision and Rationale: (Davison) Yes. We must interpret and apply the Oklahoma "slayer statute" which provides in pertinent part: "No person who is convicted of murder or manslaughter in the first degree … shall inherit from [the deceased victim], or receive any interest in the estate of the decedent, or take by devise or legacy, or descent or distribution, from him, or her, any portion of his or her, estate…." We have held that a joint tenant can terminate the joint tenancy by an act that is inconsistent with its continued existence. We are of the [obvious] opinion that the murder here involved was inconsistent with the continued existence of the joint tenancy and that at the time the murder was committed, the joint tenancy was terminated and separated. Other states and other courts have reached different contrary views, such as holding that (1) a murderer is deprived of the entire interest except for a life interest in one-half; (2) a murderer is entitled to keep all the property; (3) a murderer holds upon a constructive trust to the extent of the computed value of one-half of the property as of the date of the victim's death for the period of the victim's expectancy; (4) a murderer is chargeable as constructive trustee of the entire property for the benefit of the victim's estate; (5) a murderer is chargeable as constructive trustee of one-half of the property for the benefit of the victim's estate; (6) by the murder, the joint tenancy has separated and terminated and one-half of the property should go to the heirs of the murdered person and the other one-half to the murderer, or to his heirs, when deceased. We believe that the most equitable solution is to hold that by the murder, the joint tenancy is separated and terminated and one-half of the property should go to the heirs of the deceased murdered person and the other one-half to the murderer, wife, or to her heirs, when deceased. By such holding, the joint tenancy is changed to a tenancy in common. Although it is inconceivable that Duncan (P) did not know of the fact that his daughter had murdered her husband shortly before he received the deed from her, he should be given an opportunity, upon remand, to prove that he was a bona fide innocent purchaser for a valuable consideration and that he was without knowledge that his grantor daughter had murdered her husband at the time of the execution and delivery of the deed. Judgment reversed and the cause remanded. In the absence of proof of bona fide innocent purchase without knowledge of the murder, then the trial court is directed to enter judgment in favor of Sr., as administrator of Jr.'s estate (D), as follows: That one-half of the property should go to Duncan (P) and the other one-half to Sr. as the administrator of the deceased's estate (D) to be distributed to the heirs of the deceased. Also, Duncan (P) should account to the administrator for one-half the rents collected by him less necessary money paid out for upkeep and taxes. Also that a lien should be fixed on Duncan's (P) one-half of the property for one-half of the insurance paid to release the mortgage and also one-half of the amount paid by the estate for release of the improvement mortgage.

Analysis:

Yet another way to sever a joint tenancy—murder! The court concluded that the law of the state—Oklahoma's slayer statute—required it to hold that a joint tenancy is terminated by murder by one joint tenant of the other joint tenant. A tenancy in common is thereupon created, whereby one-half of the property goes to the heirs of the murdered joint tenant and the other one-half to the murderer, or heirs when deceased. The court mentioned the various ways that different states address the issue presented by murder of one joint tenant by the other. It is interesting that the Oklahoma Supreme Court found it "inconceivable" that Duncan (P) could not have known about his daughter's murder at the time of the execution and delivery of the deed to him; nevertheless, it remanded the case to the trial court to give him the opportunity to prove that he was a bona fide innocent purchaser for value, but at the same time indicating how the judgment should be entered if he was unable to so prove.

Centex Homes Corp. v. Boag

(Condo Developer) v. (Condo Purchaser)
(1974) 128 N.J. Super. 385

M E M O R Y   G R A P H I C

 ## Instant Facts

Centex (P) sued the Boags (D) for specific performance of the condominium purchase agreement, or in the alternative, for liquidated damages.

Black Letter Rule

Except upon a showing of unusual circumstances or a change in the vendor's position, the vendor's damages for breach of a condominium purchase agreement are usually measurable, and the remedy at law is adequate and there is no jurisdictional basis for the equitable remedy of specific performance of the purchase agreement.

Case Vocabulary

VENDEE: The buyer of something such as real property.
VENDOR: The seller of something such as real property.

Procedural Basis: Motion for summary judgment in trial court in action for specific performance of real estate purchase agreement and liquidated damages.

Facts: Centex Homes Corporation (P) is a developer of a condominium project in New Jersey. Mr. and Mrs. Boag (D) executed a contract for the purchase of a certain condominium unit in the building under construction by Centex (P). Prior to signing the contract, they gave Centex (P) a deposit in the amount of $525, and at, or shortly after, signing the contract, they gave Centex (P) $6,870 which, together with the deposit, represented approximately 10% of the total purchase price of the unit. Shortly thereafter, Boag (D) was notified by his employer that he would be transferred out of state to the Chicago, Illinois area. Boag (D) thereupon advised Centex (P) that he would be unable to complete the purchase agreement and he stopped payment on the $6,870 check. [Trying hard to get that money] Centex (P) deposited the check for collection two weeks after receiving Boag's (D) notice, but the check [not surprisingly] was not honored by the bank. Thereafter, Centex (P) filed suit for specific performance of the purchase agreement or, in the alternative, for liquidated damages in the amount of $6,870. The matter is presently before the Superior Court on the motion of Centex (P) for summary judgment.

Issue: Is a vendor who sells condominium units entitled to specific performance to compel the vendee to buy the property pursuant to the purchase agreement?

Decision and Rationale: (Gelman) No, absent unusual circumstances. No court has determined in any reported decision whether the equitable remedy of specific performance will lie for the enforcement of a contract for the sale of a condominium apartment. Under a condominium housing scheme, each condominium apartment unit constitutes a separate parcel of real property, which may be dealt with in the same manner as any real estate. The apartment unit owner receives a recordable deed conferring upon him the same rights and subjects him to the same obligations as in the case of traditional forms of real estate ownership, the only difference being that the condominium owner receives in addition an undivided interest in the common elements associated with the building and assigned to each unit. Centex (P) argues that since the subject matter of the contract is the transfer of a fee interest in real estate, the remedy of specific performance is available to enforce the agreement under principles of equity. The principle underlying the remedy of specific performance is equity's jurisdiction to grant relief where the damage remedy at law is inadequate. The early English precedents suggest that the availability of specific performance to a vendor was an outgrowth of the equitable concept of mutuality, i.e., that equity would not specifically enforce an agreement unless the remedy was available to both parties. Our present Supreme Court has squarely held, however, that mutuality of remedy is not an appropriate basis for granting or denying specific performance. The disappearance of the mutuality of remedy doctrine from our law dictates the conclusion that specific performance should no longer be automatically available to a vendor of real estate, but should be confined to those special instances where a vendor will otherwise suffer an economic injury for which his damage remedy at law will not be adequate, or where other equitable considerations require that the relief be granted. The subject matter of the real estate transaction in this case is a condominium apartment unit, which has no unique quality since it is but one of hundreds of virtually identical units being offered for sale. One must therefore conclude that the damages sustained by the vendor resulting from the breach of the sales agreement are readily measurable and the remedy of damages is wholly adequate. There is no compelling reason for granting specific performance. Thus, the complaint is dismissed as to the first count for specific performance. With respect to the count for liquidated damages, the agreement (which was authored by Centex (P)) provides that liquidated damages are limited to such moneys as

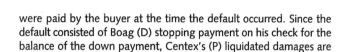
were paid by the buyer at the time the default occurred. Since the default consisted of Boag (D) stopping payment on his check for the balance of the down payment, Centex's (P) liquidated damages are limited to the moneys paid prior to that date, i.e., the initial $525 deposit. Thus, the second count of the complaint will also be dismissed.

Analysis:

This case introduces us to the specific characteristics of a condominium housing scheme, and demonstrates that it is another form of concurrent ownership. However, to fully understand the case, one must have some general knowledge concerning "remedies." Centex (P) wanted to enforce the purchase agreement by the equitable remedy of "specific performance," which would result in a court order compelling Boag (P) to purchase the property. Centex (P) did plead in the alternative for liquidated damages, a remedy at law. Generally, equitable remedies are available when remedies at law are inadequate, and because of the unique nature of real estate, specific performance is generally available. However, this case concerned a condominium unit and whether specific performance can be obtained to enforce the purchase agreement. Because a condominium unit has no unique quality, with many identical units offered for sale, the damages sustained by the vendor due to the vendee's breach are measurable and the damages remedy at law is sufficient to make the vendor whole. Thus, specific performance is not available.

Dutcher v. Owens

(Condo Owner) v. (Lessees)
(1983) 647 S.W. 948

M E M O R Y   G R A P H I C

Instant Facts

Dutcher (D) was sued along with other defendants by Owens (P), lessees of condo who sustained property damage from fire, and he contended that his liability should be limited to the percent of his pro rata ownership of the common elements.

Black Letter Rule

A condominium co-owner is not jointly and severally liable for tort claims arising out of the ownership, use and maintenance of the common elements of a condominium project, but instead is liable only for a pro rata portion of the damages.

Case Vocabulary

IN PARI MATERIA: Latin for, "in the same matter" and, as applied to judicial construction of statutes, it means that where inconsistencies in statutes exist, the court will look to other statutes regarding the same matter for assistance in properly construing the statutes.

JOINT AND SEVERAL LIABILITY: A form of liability where the injured party may sue one or more wrongdoers separately, or all together, and enforce the judgment obtained against one or all.

PRO RATA: To assess in equal quantities.

VICARIOUSLY LIABLE (VICARIOUS LIABILITY): Where one is liable for the conduct of another due to the relationship between the two, such as employer and employee or principal and agent.

Procedural Basis: Appeal to Texas Supreme Court to review judgment in action for negligence and damages sustained to real and personal property following a jury trial.

Facts: Dutcher (D), a resident of California, owned a condominium unit located in Texas, which he leased to Ted and Christine Owens (P). Ownership of the unit included a 1.572% pro rata undivided ownership in the common elements of the project. [Also called common areas.] A fire, which began in a light fixture in a common area, caused the Owens (P) to suffer substantial property loss. The Owens (P) sued Dutcher (D), the Condominium Association, the electric company, the developer, and a class of co-owners of the condominiums. [They couldn't think of any more defendants to sue!] All defendants except Dutcher (D) obtained a change of venue to a different county. The case against Dutcher (D) was tried before a jury which found the following: (1) the fire was proximately caused by a lack of an insulating box behind the light fixture; (2) the homeowners' association knew of the defect; (3) the homeowners' association was negligent in failing to install the insulating box; and (4) the negligence of the association resulted in damage to the Owens' property in the amount of $69,150. The trial court rendered judgment against Dutcher (D) in the amount of $1,098.04, which represents the amount of damages multiplied by Dutcher's (D) 1.572% pro rata undivided ownership of the common elements of the project. The court of appeals reversed in part holding that each unit owner, as a tenant in common with all other unit owners, is jointly and severally liable for damage claims arising in the common elements. [This equates to Dutcher (D) being on the hook for the whole $69,150, unless the other defendants contribute. Needless to say, Dutcher (D) appealed to the state Supreme Court.]

Issue: Is a condominium co-owner jointly and severally liable for tort claims arising out of the ownership, use and maintenance of the common elements of a condominium project?

Decision and Rationale: (Ray) No. In enacting the Texas Condominium Act, the Texas Legislature intended to create a new method of property ownership. A condominium is an estate in real property consisting of an undivided interest in a portion of a parcel of real property together with a separate fee simple interest in another portion of the same parcel. In essence, condominium ownership is the merger of two estates in land into one: the fee simple ownership of an apartment or unit in a condominium project and a tenancy in common with other co-owners in the common elements. General common elements consist of, inter alia, the land upon which the building stands, the foundations, bearing walls and columns, roofs, halls, lobbies, stairways, and entrances and exits, and all other elements of the property of common use or necessary to its existence. The condominium association is a legislatively created unincorporated association of co-owners having as their common purpose a convenient method of ownership of real property in a statutorily created method of ownership which combines both the concepts of separateness of tenure and commonality of ownership. Given the uniqueness of the type of ownership involved, the onus of liability for injuries arising from the management of condominium projects should reflect the degree of control exercised by the defendants. To rule that a condominium co-owner had any effective control over the operation of the common areas would be to sacrifice reality to theoretical formalism, for in fact a co-owner has no more control over operations than he would have as a stockholder in a corporation which owned and operated the project. While the Texas Act creates a new form of real property ownership, it does not address the issue of the allocation of tort liability among co-owners. We are nevertheless guided by other provisions in the Act which appear in pair materia, and which proportionately allocate various financial responsibilities, such as pro rata contributions by co-owners toward expenses of administration and maintenance, insurance, taxes and assessments. Owens (P) argues that since two bills previously submitted to the legislature, which contained provisions for re-apportionment of liability on a pro rata basis, did not pass, we should not impose liability on a pro rata basis. However, we cannot infer that the pro rata provisions were the reason for bills not passing, since each bill involved a complete revision of the Act. The theories of vicarious and joint and severally liability are judicially created vehicles for enforcing remedies for wrongs committed. Since the Act is silent as to tort liability, we are dealing with rights and liabilities that are not creatures of statutes but with the common law. We hold that because of the limited control afforded a unit owner by the statutory condominium regime, the creation of the regime effects a reallocation of tort liability. The liability of a condominium co-owner is limited to his pro rata interest in the regime as a whole, where such liability arises from those areas held in tenancy-in-common. The judgment of the court of appeals is reversed and the judgment of the trial court is affirmed.

Analysis:

Whereas the previous case required some basic knowledge concerning "remedies," this condominium case requires some basic understanding of tort liability. The decision by the trial court was that pro rata liability was appropriate, thus limiting the damages imposed against Dutcher (D) to his specific ownership interest in the common elements (i.e., 1.572%). The court of appeals, however, held that joint and several liability was the appropriate means of imposing liability, thus potentially requiring Dutcher (D) to pay the entire judgment. In other words, a plaintiff can be made whole and collect the judgment from just one defendant. The Texas Supreme Court reversed the court of appeals, and affirmed the judgment of the trial court. In so doing, it acknowledged the two forms of ownership that exist in condominiums: a fee simple in the particular unit and a tenancy in common among the co-owners of the common elements. The court also based its holding on the degree of control (or lack thereof) that a co-owner has in the common areas. Clearly, Dutcher (D) living in a different state lacked the control to deal with maintenance of the common areas, a responsibility assigned to the homeowners' association. The court construed the condominium Act in Texas and determined that their holding was not inconsistent with the Act or its intent.

Aquarian Foundation, Inc. v. Sholom House, Inc.

(Purchaser of Condo) v. (Homeowners' Association)
(1984) 448 So.2d 1166

M E M O R Y   G R A P H I C

Instant Facts
Condominium homeowners' association, Sholom (P), sued purchaser of condo unit, Aquarian (D), to set aside conveyance because written consent was not obtained from association (P) prior to sale in accordance with declaration of condominium.

Black Letter Rule
A declaration of condominium provision that gives the condominium association power to arbitrarily, capriciously, or unreasonably withhold its consent for a unit owner to transfer his interest in the unit is an unreasonable restraint on alienation, notwithstanding a reverter clause, which mandates compensation by the association to the owner in the event of a transfer of the unit in violation of the consent requirement.

Case Vocabulary

DECLARATION OF CONDOMINIUM: A document setting forth the rights and obligations involved in condominium ownership.
ILLUSORY: As referring to an unenforceable "illusory contract," wherein one party's consideration is so lacking as to result in no obligation at all.
PRE-EMPTIVE RIGHT: As applied to corporations it means giving shareholders the right to purchase newly issued stock prior to the stock being offered for sale to the public; as applied to condominiums, it means giving the association right of first refusal in connection with purchasing a unit that the owner intends to sell.

Procedural Basis: Appeal following non-jury trial in action to set aside conveyance of condominium unit based upon illegal restraint on alienation.

Facts: Bertha Albares sold her condominium unit at the Sholom House, Inc. (P) to Aquarian Foundation, Inc. (D) without obtaining the written consent of the condominium association's board of directors, as required by the declaration of condominium. The declaration gave the association (P) the right to arbitrarily, capriciously, or unreasonably withhold its consent to a sale, lease, assignment, or transfer of a unit owner's interest. Eschewing its right to ratify the sale [and wanting to show who had real power and control], the association (P) sued to set aside the conveyance, to dispossess Aquarian (D), and to recover damages. A "reverter clause" in the declaration provided that upon a violation thereof, title to the unit shall revert to the association, subject to it paying to the unit owner the fair appraised value. After a non-jury trial, the trial court found that Albares had violated the declaration of condominium, thus triggering the reverter clause. It entered judgment for the association (P), and declared the conveyance to Aquarian (D) null and void. Aquarian (D) appeals.

Issue: Is a declaration of condominium provision that gives the condominium association power to arbitrarily, capriciously, or unreasonably withhold its consent for a unit owner to transfer his interest in the unit an unreasonable restraint on alienation, notwithstanding a reverter clause, which mandates compensation by the association to the owner in the event of a transfer of the unit in violation of the consent requirement?

Decision and Rationale: (Pearson) Yes. It is well settled that increased controls and limitations upon the rights of unit owners to transfer their property are necessary concomitants of condominium living. Thus, restrictions on a unit owner's right to transfer his property are recognized as a valid means of insuring the association's ability to control the composition of the condominium as a whole. Indeed, a restriction contained in a declaration of condominium may have a certain degree of unreasonableness to it, and still withstand attack. However, such restrictions will be invalidated when found to violate some external public policy or constitutional right of the individual. Where the restriction constitutes a restraint on alienation, condominium associations are not immune from the requirement that the restraint be reasonable. Thus, while a condominium association's board of directors has considerable latitude in withholding its consent to a unit owner's transfer, the resulting restraint on alienation must be reasonable. Where the restraint does not impede the improvement of the property or its marketability, it is not illegal. Accordingly, where a restraint on alienation, no matter how absolute and encompassing, is conditioned upon the restrainer's obligation to purchase the property at the then fair market value, the restraint is valid. In the present case, the declaration of condominium permits the association to reject perpetually any unit owner's prospective purchaser for any or no reason. Such a restraint on alienation provision can be valid only if the association has a corresponding obligation to purchase or procure a purchaser for the property from the unit owner at its fair market value. In other words, it must be accountable to the unit owner by offering payment or a substitute market for the property. The language in the declaration, however, does not contain anything requiring the association (P) to provide another purchaser, purchase the property itself from the owner, or approve the transfer. What it does contain is the reverter clause, which the association (P) contends is the functional equivalent of a preemptive right and, as such, makes the restraint on alienation lawful. The problem with this position is that the reverter clause imposes no obligation upon the association (P) to compensate the unit owner within a reasonable time after the association (P) withholds its consent to transfer. Thus, the clause is not the functional equivalent of a preemptive right. Instead, the clause and the association's (P) obligation do not come into effect until a violation of the restriction on an unapproved transfer occurs. The association's (P) accountability to the unit owner is illusory. There is no reasonable likelihood that a potential purchaser, apprised by the condominium documents that the consent of the association is required and that a purchase without consent vitiates the sale, would be willing to acquire the property without the association's (P) consent. Without a sale, there is no violation of the reverter clause. Without such a violation, the association (P) has no obligation to pay the unit owner. The power of the association (P) to withhold its consent to transfer arbitrarily, capriciously, and unreasonably effectively prevents the activation of the reverter clause and eliminates the accountability of the association (P) to the unit owner. We therefore conclude that such power of the association (P) is not saved by the reverter clause from being declared an invalid and unenforceable restraint on alienation. Reversed.

Analysis:

This case is an example of condominium association's rules and restrictions that govern condominium living. Most often, the rules and restrictions pertain to maintenance, prohibited activity, budgets, and, as in this case, restrictions on transfers of individual units. The pre-emptive right generally afforded associations gives a right of first refusal when an owner indicates an intent to sell a unit. The association is generally given the right to match the purchase price. This type of restraint on alienation has been upheld by the courts. In this case, the association (P) unsuccessfully argued that the reverter clause was the equivalent of a pre-emptive right, and therefore lawful. The court rejected the argument because the reverter clause did not require the association (P) to compensate the unit owner within a reasonable time after it withholds consent. Instead, the only time the association (P) was obligated to compensate the unit owner was after a violation of declaration of condominium occurred, i.e., a sale without consent by the association. The court noted that a potential purchaser would not be willing to purchase the property without the association's (P) consent, if apprised that consent is required, and without it, the sale is void. Thus, under normal circumstances, a sale would not ordinarily be expected to occur, which caused the court to conclude that the power of the association (P) to withhold its consent to transfer was an illegal restraint on alienation.

Chapter 17

One of the most common legal relationships in the United States today is the landlord-tenant relationship. Indeed, a significant percentage of the population of the United States lives in, or at some point has lived in, rented housing. Similarly, a good portion of the businesses that Americans frequent on a daily basis rent the premises on or in which they operate. Because renting is such a common practice, and because such a large number of rental agreements for both residential and commercial premises are signed into effect each day, it is important for lawyers, law students, and the general public to have a basic understanding of the law that governs the landlord-tenant relationship. This chapter addresses this important relationship.

The first issue addressed in the chapter is the creation of leasehold estates, or, in other words, the formation of the landlord-tenant relationship, including the dual nature of the relationship. The next issue addressed in this chapter is that of access to the rental market, or how it is that the government provides ways for all (or at least many) citizens to obtain safe and decent housing. The third issue addressed is that of the tenant's right to possession of the leasehold. Specifically, the chapter addresses the tenant's right to take physical possession of the premises at the commencement of the rental period, and the responsibilities that the landlord and tenant each have with respect to guaranteeing that the tenant will be able to gain that possession in a timely manner. The next section of the text addresses some of the miscellaneous provisions found in lease agreements that govern the landlord-tenant relationship. This includes a discussion of the duration of the lease, the physical condition of the rental premises, the all-important concept of rent, and, finally, any restrictions that might apply to the tenant's use of the premises. Fifth, the chapter addresses the responsibilities of both landlord and tenant with respect to avoiding and paying for injuries caused to person and property on the rental premises. Sixth, the chapter addresses the various remedies available to the landlord in the event that the tenant somehow breaches the lease agreement, including the ability of the landlord to seek termination of the lease, eviction of the tenant, or the payment of damages. And finally, the last portion of the chapter addresses the abilities of both the landlord and the tenant to transfer their respective interests in the leasehold to other parties and the responsibilities of each that do and do not continue on after the transfer.

In short, this chapter addresses a number of significant issues that arise in the context of the landlord-tenant relationship. It is obvious from the above summary of the topics addressed in the chapter that there is a lot to learn, but the landlord-tenant relationship is such a common one in the world today that making an effort to understand all of the concepts taught, and more, will undoubtedly pay off at some point in the future.

Chapter 17

NOTE: THE PURPOSE OF THIS OUTLINE IS TO ORGANIZE THE CASES SO THAT ONE CAN QUICKLY UNDERSTAND THE RELEVANCE OF EACH CASE TO THE COURSE. NO ATTEMPT IS MADE IN THIS OVERVIEW TO ADDRESS EVERY CONCEPT THAT MUST BE STUDIED. BE SURE TO READ THE ENTIRE CASEBOOK AND/OR OTHER MATERIALS TO GAIN A FULL UNDERSTANDING OF ALL CONCEPTS.

I. The Creation of Leasehold Estates
    A. A leasehold is created in the same manner as other contractual relationships—by means of an oral, written, or implied agreement.
    B. Leases are both contracts and conveyances, and because lease agreements are, at least in part, contractual, the landlord-tenant relationship is subject to principles of contract law. *Brown v. Southall Realty Co.*
    C. A rental contract is unenforceable when the property rented does not meet government safety and habitability regulations (housing codes) and the landlord is aware of the violations at the time the lease is executed. *Brown.*

II. Gaining Access to the Rental Market: The Federal Fair Housing Act (FHA)
    A. The federal FHA was enacted "to provide, within constitutional limitations, for fair housing throughout the United States." 42 U.S.C. § 3601.
        1. Many states have enacted their own fair housing acts.
    B. The FHA prohibits various types of discrimination in the sale or rental of housing units. The types of discrimination prohibited include discrimination, among other things, based on race, religion, gender, familial status, and national origin. 42 U.S.C. § 3604.
    C. The penalties for violating the FHA can be very severe. *Jancik v. Department of Housing and Urban Development.*

III. The Tenant's Right to Possession of the Leasehold
    A. A majority of courts hold that a lessee is entitled to receive both actual and legal possession of a leased premises at the beginning of the lease period. As such, unless there is some agree-

ment to the contrary, it is the lessor's duty to deliver such possession at the beginning of the term. *Adrian v. Rabinowitz.*
        1. A handful of other courts have held that it is the tenant's duty to expel unwanted holdover tenants, and to place that burden on the landlord is unfair.
    B. When a tenant is wrongfully dispossessed of the leasehold, his or her obligation to pay rent is suspended. In some cases, the tenant has been permitted to withhold rent even when he or she is dispossessed of only a portion of the leasehold.

IV. Provisions Governing Tenancy
    A. The Duration of a Leasehold
        1. Introduction
            a. Leaseholds are generally classified according to their duration.
            b. Where no duration is specified in a lease agreement, the lease will be considered a tenancy at will.
            c. A tenancy that has a definite start date and end date is called a tenancy for years (even if it is less than one year in duration).
            d. And a tenancy which continues from one specified period (week, month, year, etc.) to another until either party gives notice of intent to terminate the lease is a periodic tenancy.
        2. Holdover Tenants
            a. A holdover tenant (a tenant at sufferance) is one who wrongfully remains in possession of a leasehold after the expiration of the lease.
            b. Under the common law, it was a general principle of landlord-tenant law that a holdover tenant may, at the election of the landlord, be held to be a tenant for a term identical to that of the original lease (i.e., a tenant for a year if the original lease was for a year), even if the holdover was for a matter of hours.
            c. In recent years, however, courts have moved away from a strict application of this doctrine. For example, in *Common-*

wealth Building Corp. v. Hirschfiel, the court determined that a holdover tenant may be held to be a tenant for another term only when

    (1) Either his actions are such that the landlord may rightfully assume that he intends to create a second tenancy, *or*

    (2) When the action of the tenant is such that the court, as a matter of law and in the interest of justice, deems it appropriate to hold him liable for a second lease under the principle of quasi contract.

3. Renewals and Extensions of Lease Agreements

  a. In order to avoid a holdover situation, many landlords and tenants seek to include in the lease agreement express provisions for dealing with renewals and extensions of the lease.

  b. If a tenant does choose to invoke its right to remain in possession beyond the expiration of the lease in accordance with a prearranged agreement, he or she has a duty to notify the landlord of that intention.

4. The Right to Extend One's Occupancy of Certain Housing

  a. In the majority of cases, a lessee's right to occupy and possess a leasehold ends with the termination of the lease. In some residential tenancies, however, such as those involving federally subsidized housing, the lessee may arguably have a right to remain in possession.

  b. Some states have enacted laws to protect certain groups' rights to housing. To protect the elderly and the disabled, for example, New Jersey passed a Senior Citizens and Disabled Protected Tenancy Act, which seeks to prevent the forced eviction and relocation of senior citizen tenants.

B. The Condition of the Leased Premises

1. The law implies a number of covenants into lease agreements that involve the condition of the leased premises.

2. Perhaps most significant, the implied warranty of habitability is a promise to the tenant that the rented premises is one fit for human

habitation; it further guarantees that the premises will stay fit for human habitation for the duration of the lease.

3. A covenant of quiet enjoyment is a promise to the tenant that his or her possession of the rental premises will not be interrupted by one with superior title.

4. Finally, some courts imply a covenant of suitability into commercial leases, which requires that the premises be suitable for its intended commercial purpose.

5. Under each of these covenants or warranties, only a significant breach material to the purpose for which the lease was consummated justifies a lessee in withholding the payment of rent. *Richard Barton Enterprises, Inc. v. Tsern*.

C. Rent

1. One of the key ingredients in the landlord-tenant relationship is the concept of rent.

2. The amount of rent that a tenant is required to pay can be determined in a number of different ways. In some cases, it will be a fixed amount per month. In other cases, however, it may depend on store sales or a specific index such as the Consumer Price Index.

3. In some states and cities, the government has the power to impose a cap on the amount of rent that a tenant can be required to pay. The establishment of this type of cap is generally referred to as rent control.

  a. Some states have made rent control illegal. Others still permit it in certain areas.

  b. Local laws and ordinances which require commercial developers to generate affordable housing in conjunction with commercial developments are violative of general laws prohibiting rent control. *Town of Telluride v. Lot Thirty-Four Venture, L.L.C.*

D. The Tenant's Use of the Premises

1. The Duty of Continuous Operation

  a. Some commercial lease agreements contain covenants of continuous operation. A covenant of continuous operation is a covenant or promise to operate a business in the leased premises for the duration of the lease (i.e., a promise not to leave the building empty at any time during the rental period).

b. A covenant of continuous operation will not be implied in a lease agreement when the contract as a whole indicates that no such covenant was intended by the parties. *Piggly Wiggly Southern, Inc. v. Heard.*

2. Physically Altering the Premises

a. In some cases it is important that a tenant make physical alterations to a leased premises. This is particularly true in commercial leases, where the carrying on of a business requires that certain fixtures be installed or premises otherwise be changed.

b. When changes of this type are going to be necessary, the lease agreement should specify which party is responsible for making the changes and the controls that each has once those changes are made.

c. When a tenant has made physical changes or added fixtures to a rented premises, he or she may want to remove them at the end of the lease. Under the common law of fixtures, the tenant is free to remove whatever he or she has erected or installed for the purpose of carrying on a business as long as the fixtures can be removed without causing injury to the premises. *Handler v. Horns.*

V. Injuries to Persons and Property

A. Criminal Injuries

1. Where a landlord has made no affirmative attempt to provide security for her tenants and is not responsible for any physical defect that enhances the risk that a crime may be committed, she cannot be held liable for a criminal attack perpetrated upon a tenant on the leased premises. *Walls v. Oxford Management Co.*

B. Non-Criminal Injuries

1. Under the traditional view, landlords generally have immunity with respect to injuries suffered on the leased premises. There are, however, a few exceptions to this rule.

a. The first exception applies when an injury results from a landlord's failure to use reasonable care in maintaining a common area, such as a sidewalk, driveway, or play area.

b. The second exception deems a landlord potentially liable for injuries caused by latent defects that exist at the time of the signing of the lease and that are known or should have been known to the landlord.

c. The third exception makes landlords potentially liable for breaches of express covenants to repair the premises.

d. Under the fourth exception, there is potential liability for injuries caused because of negligently-made repairs.

2. In recent years, however, some courts have moved away from landlord immunity and held that landlords are, in all aspects of their occupations, liable for failures to use reasonable care.

VI. The Lessor's Remedies Against a Defaulting Tenant

A. Introduction

1. When a tenant defaults on certain obligations or breaches certain covenants contained in the lease agreement, the law permits the landlord to seek either termination of the lease, eviction of the tenant, and/or damages in an appropriate amount.

2. The most common type of default or breach is the non-payment of rent. There are other tenant actions, however, that can also be construed as a default or breach, such as wrongfully holding over past the end of the lease.

B. Terminating the Lease

1. While the modern law often provides them with the right to terminate a lease in certain situations (the ability of a landlord to terminate a lease was significantly less under the common law), a landlord's right to terminate a commercial lease is not without limits. *Foundation Development Corp. v. Loehmann's, Inc.*

a. Specifically, a forfeiture or termination sought because of a trivial or immaterial breach of a commercial lease often will not be enforced by the courts. *Foundation.*

C. Eviction
1. Another remedy available to landlords for dealing with a tenant breach of the lease agreement is eviction, or physically dispossessing the tenant of the property.
2. There are a number of different scenarios in which a landlord can have a tenant evicted. However, a landlord may not evict a tenant in retaliation for the tenant's decision to report housing code violations to the proper authorities (a retaliatory eviction). *Edwards v. Habib*.
D. Damages
1. When a landlord chooses to seek damages for a tenant breach of the lease agreement, the landlord has a responsibility to mitigate damages. *United States National Bank of Oregon v. Homeland, Inc.*
    a. Under this principle, when a tenant abandons the leased premises prior to the expiration of the lease, the landlord has a duty to attempt to relet the premises prior to the end of the abandoning tenant's term so as to minimize losses attributable to the tenant. *Bank of Oregon*.
2. Because collecting damages can be difficult, many landlords require security deposits to be paid at the time of the signing of the lease, thus giving the landlord at least some money if there is a breach that causes the need for an order for damages.

VII. The Transfer of Leaseholds
A. If a landlord transfers his interest in a leasehold to another party, that party, with a few exceptions, is bound by the lease and has the ability to enforce it.
B. Unless the terms of the lease prohibit it, tenants too may transfer their leasehold estates. However, unless the landlord specifically releases the first tenant from the obligation to pay rent, it is still bound by that and other covenants included in their contractual agreement. Thus, the landlord has two sources from which he or she may collect the rent (the first and second tenant).
1. Some leases contain clauses which require landlord permission before a tenant can transfer his or her interest in the leasehold estate.
2. Under the majority view, when a lease contains this type of clause, the lessor's consent to one assignment does not waive the need to obtain lessor permission for subsequent assignments, and does not waive the lessor's ability to object to a proposed second assignment. *Childs v. Warner Brothers Southern Theatres*.
3. Similarly, the existence of this type of clause does not imply, as a mater of law, an obligation on the part of the landlord to act reasonably in withholding consent. In fact, the landlord may generally act unreasonably in denying consent without consequence. *21 Merchants Row Corp. v. Merchants Row, Inc.*
    a. In recent years, some courts and legislatures have attempted to move away from this particular view and impose a reasonableness requirement on the landlord. This altered position, however, is still the minority view.
C. There are two types of tenant transfers of a leasehold estate: assignments and subleases.
1. In most jurisdictions, the question of whether a transfer of the tenant's interest in the leasehold estate is an assignment or a sublease is determined by the English rule. Under that rule, if the instrument purports to transfer the lessee's estate for the remainder of the term, it is an assignment, and if the transfer is for less than the remainder of the term, it is a sublease. The intention of the parties is irrelevant.
    a. A minority of courts have held that the English rule is unjust and that when determining whether a particular conveyance is an assignment or a sublease, courts should look to the intention of the parties. *Jaber v. Miller*.
2. Under the common law, a sublessee (subtenant) is not liable to the original or head landlord for rent, as there is no privity of contract or estate between the two. Assignees, on the other hand, share privity of estate with the head landlord and therefore are liable for rent.

Brown v. Southall Realty Co.

(Tenant) v. (Landlord)
(1968) 237 A.2d 834

M E M O R Y   G R A P H I C

Instant Facts
A lawsuit arose when a tenant refused to pay rent because her apartment was in such bad physical condition.

Black Letter Rule
A rental contract is unenforceable when the property rented does not meet government safety and habitability regulations and the landlord is aware of the violations at the time the lease is executed.

Case Vocabulary

ACTION FOR POSSESSION: A legal action initiated by a landlord in an attempt to regain possession of her property from a tenant.
LEASEHOLD: A tenant's possessory interest in land or other property.

Procedural Basis: Appeal to the District of Columbia Court of Appeals of an action for possession filed when a tenant refused to pay rent.

Facts: Sometime prior to 1968 (the date of the lawsuit), Brown (D) entered into a rental agreement with Southall Realty Co. (P). The dwelling that Brown (D) rented from Southall (P) had some serious problems such as a broken toilet, a broken railing, and an insufficient ceiling height in the basement, all of which were violations of the District of Columbia Housing Code. Southall (P) knew of the Housing Code violations at the time that it entered into the lease agreement with Brown (D). The conditions were so bad that Brown (D) eventually chose not to pay rent. Shortly thereafter, Southall (P) filed suit for possession of the premises and for $230 in back rent. Brown (D) refused to agree to Southall's (P) demands, arguing that the rental agreement was void because it was an illegal contract.

Issue: Can a landlord enforce a rental agreement entered into in contravention of government housing regulations?

Decision and Rationale: (Quinn, J.) No. Ms. Brown (D) contends that the lease should have been declared unenforceable because it was knowingly entered into in contravention of the District of Columbia Housing Regulations. Section 2304 of the Regulations reads: "No persons shall rent . . . any habitation . . . unless [it is] in a clean, safe and sanitary condition, in repair, and free from rodents or vermin." Section 2501 reads: "Every premises . . . shall be maintained and kept in repair so as to provide decent living accommodations for the occupants." The purpose of these regulations is to ensure that housing within the District is healthy and safe. It appears that the violations at issue, known by Southall (P) to exist at the time of the signing of the lease agreement, were such that they made the premises unsafe and unsanitary. The lease contract was, therefore, entered into in violation of the regulations referenced above. In *Hartman v. Lubar*, we stated that "[t]he general rule is that an illegal contract, made in violation of [a] statutory prohibition designed for . . . regulatory purposes, is void and confers no right upon the wrongdoer" where the statute appears to "imply a prohibition or render a prohibited act void." In this case, to uphold the validity of the lease agreement in light of the defects known to exist prior to the agreement would be to flout the purposes of the referenced regulations. Reversed.

Analysis:

The present case holds that a lease agreement that is based on an illegal contract is unenforceable. Two basic yet significant principles underlying this holding are: (1) the law of contracts plays a significant role in the governance of the landlord-tenant relationship, and (2) a leasehold is created in the same manner as other contracts—by means of an oral, written, or implied agreement. (It must be remembered that the Statute of Frauds will sometimes affect one's ability to enter into an oral lease.) Because the law of contracts governs the validity and execution of lease agreements, some basic principles of contract law apply to these agreements. First, to enter into an enforceable lease agreement, both parties must have the legal capacity needed to enter into a contract. Thus, for example, a child cannot legally enter into a lease agreement. Additionally, most courts recognize that an enforceable lease agreement must contain certain terms, such as the identity of the parties entering into the agreement, a description of the premises to be leased, a statement of the duration of the proposed lease, and, in some cases, a statement of the amount of rent that will be required. If any of these terms are missing, there may be an argument that the lease agreement is void or voidable. Finally, as the present case demonstrates, when a landlord enters into a lease with a tenant knowing that the premises to be leased are not habitable and/or are in serious disrepair, the lease will not be enforced by the courts. To hold otherwise would simply not make sense.

Jancik v. Department of Housing and Urban Development

(Apartment Owner) v. (United States Government Agency)

(1995) 44 F.3d 553

M E M O R Y   G R A P H I C

Instant Facts

A landlord was ordered to pay a large sum of money in damages, civil penalties, and attorney fees when it was determined that he was illegally discriminating against potential tenants on the basis of race and familial status.

Black Letter Rule

It is unlawful for a landlord to discriminate against potential tenants on the basis of race or familial status.

Procedural Basis: Petition for review to the Seventh Circuit Court of Appeals of a Department of Housing and Urban Development (HUD) decision which found that Stanley Jancik (P) had discriminated in the rental of an apartment on the basis of both family status and race—both violations of the Fair Housing Act (FHA).

Facts: In August of 1990, Stanley Jancik (P), the owner of a building in a large housing complex in Northlake, Illinois, placed a rental ad in a local newspaper which included the words "mature person preferred." Concerned that this request was a violation of the Fair Housing Act, the Leadership Council for Metropolitan Open Communities (LCMOC) decided to test Jancik's (P) ad. In doing so, they chose two volunteers, Cindy Gunderson, who was white, and Marsha Allen, who was African American, to speak with Jancik (P) about the ad. Gunderson telephoned Jancik (P) first. During their conversation, Jancik (P) stated that he did not want any teenagers in his building. Later, when asking about the origin of Gunderson's name, Jancik (P) asked if it was "white Norwegian or black Norwegian," and then admitted that he was inquiring about race. Two hours later, Marsha Allen spoke with Jancik (P). During their conversation, Jancik (P) stated that he did not want any tenants with children, and, after inquiring about Allen's race and being asked the question's relevance, admitted that he asked for the purpose of screening applicants. Based on these conversions, LCMOC filed a complaint with HUD, charging that Jancik (P) had violated § 804(c) of the FHA (codified at 42 U.S.C. § 3604(c)). That section makes it unlawful to: "make . . . or publish . . . any notice, statement, or advertisement, with respect to the sale or rental of a dwelling that indicates any preference, limitation, or discrimination based on race, color, religion, sex, handicap, familial status, or national origin." Specifically, the complaint charged that Jancik (P) was discriminating on the basis of familial status and race. The issue was eventually taken before an Administrative Law Judge (ALJ) who determined that Jancik (P) had violated the FHA. Jancik (P) was ordered to pay $57,228.64 in damages, civil penalties, and attorney fees. Jancik (P) petitioned the Seventh Circuit Court of Appeals for review.

Issue: Can a landlord lawfully discriminate against potential tenants on the basis of race or family status?

Decision and Rationale: (Rovner, J.) No. Section 3604(c) prohibits the publishing of any advertisement that "indicates" any preference or limitation based on race, family status, and other factors. We have not previously dealt with the "indicates" aspect of this section, but the other circuits which have done so have all applied an objective "ordinary reader" standard. Under this standard, "the statute [is] violated if an ad for housing suggests to an ordinary reader that a particular [protected group] is preferred or dispreferred for the housing in question. In applying this test, courts have held that the statute is violated by "any ad that would discourage an ordinary reader of a particular [protected group] from answering it." Significantly, no showing of a subjective intent to discriminate is necessary to establish a violation, though evidence of such intent is not irrelevant. Evidence that the author intended his words to indicate a prohibited preference obviously bears on the question of whether the words do so. Thus, if such proof exists, it may provide an alternative means of establishing a violation. In view of these guidelines, the ALJ's finding that Jancik (P) expressed a preference based on family status is supported by substantial evidence. First, Jancik (P) told Allen that he did not want to rent to any families with children and told Gunderson that he did not want any teenagers in the building. Both of these statements quite clearly suggest to an "ordinary" listener that Jancik (P) had a preference or limitation based on family status. The advertisement indicating a preference for a "mature person" is similarly problematic as the implementing regulation notes that the term is among "the most often used in residential real estate advertising to convey either overt or tacit discriminatory preferences or limitations." 24 C.F.R. § 109.20(b)(7). Certainly the use of the listed terms does not violate the Act per se, but it does indicate a possible violation and establish a need for further proceedings. Here, the context makes clear that there existed an unlawful preference. The determination that Jancik (P) violated section 3604(c) by asking questions about race is also supported by substantial evidence. Jancik (P) did not expressly indicate a preference based on race, but merely asked the testers about their race. However, the context of the questions makes it clear that they did indicate an intent to discriminate on the basis of race. First, each question came in the midst of observations in which Jancik (P) was expressing other impermissible preferences. Further, when Allen asked Jancik (P) the purpose of his question about race, he admitted that he was screening applications. Jancik's unlawful purpose was similarly revealed in his conversation with Gundersen in which he inquired whether she was "white Norwegian or black Norwegian." Finally, the fact that Jancik (P) had never rented to an African-American further bolsters the ALJ's conclusion that his question reflected an intent to exclude tenants on the basis of race. For these reasons, Jancik's (P) petitions for review are denied.

Analysis:

An important part of landlord-tenant law, and the subject of the *Jancik* case, is access to the rental market. Access to the rental market is an important issue for a number of reasons, one of which is the fact that a good percentage of Americans rent the space in which they live (whether it be apartments, condominiums, trailers, etc.). This being the case, Congress has made efforts to make residential rentals available to as many Americans as possible. One such attempt is the Fair Housing Act, a portion of which is addressed in this case. Specifically, *Jancik* addresses § 3604(c), which makes it unlawful to "make, print, or publish, or cause to be made, printed, or published any notice, statement, or advertisement, with respect to the sale or rental of a dwelling that indicates any preference, limitation, or discrimination based on race, color, religion, sex, handicap, familial status, or national origin, or an intention to make any such preference, limitation, or discrimination." Other subsections make it unlawful to refuse to rent or sell to any person based on the above discriminatory criteria (§ 3604(a)), to discriminate for any of the above-listed reasons with respect to the terms or conditions of a sale or rental (§ 3604(b)), to lie about the availability of a rental property based on discriminatory criteria (§ 3604(d)), or to induce the sale or rental of property by means of discriminatory representations (§ 3604(e)). As this case makes clear, the federal government is very serious about equal access to housing, which is why one advertisement and two brief conversations about the race of potential tenants cost Stanley Jancik $57,228.64, a hefty sum. In addition to the federal Fair Housing Act, many states have created their own versions of the Act, which often include a different spectrum of potential discriminations that are made unlawful. Thus, a person may be in violation of a state statute only, a federal statute only, or both, depending on the discriminatory practice being employed.

Adrian v. Rabinowitz

(Tenant) v. (Landlord)
(1936) 116 N.J.L. 586, 186 A. 29

M E M O R Y   G R A P H I C

Instant Facts

A lessee filed suit when his landlord failed to give him actual possession of a commercial rental property on the day that the lease was to begin.

Black Letter Rule

Unless there is some agreement to the contrary, the lessor has a duty to deliver to the lessee both actual and legal possession of the demised premises at the beginning of the term.

Case Vocabulary

DEMISED PREMISES: The leased premises.
LESSEE: A tenant.
LESSOR: A landlord.
VENIRE DE NOVO: The granting of a new jury panel because, for whatever reason, the original jury's determination cannot be acted upon.

Procedural Basis: Appeal to the Supreme Court of New Jersey of a lawsuit involving the untimely delivery of rental property to the lessee.

Facts: On April 30, 1934, Rachel Rabinowitz (D) and Goodwin Adrian (P) entered into a lease agreement under which Adrian (P) agreed to rent a commercial space from Rabinowitz (D) for the purpose of opening a shoe store. The lease was to begin on June 15 and run for six months, yet when June 15 arrived, Rabinowitz's (D) prior tenant had not yet vacated the premises. To evict the tenant, Rabinowitz (D) filed a lawsuit seeking his removal. Upon taking possession of the premises approximately one month later, Adrian (P) filed suit against Rabinowitz (D) for her untimely delivery of the property. The court awarded Adrian (P) $500 in damages and $25 for rent paid when the premises was unavailable. Rabinowitz (D) appealed.

Issue: Does a lessor have an affirmative duty to provide the lessee with actual and exclusive possession of the premises at the beginning of a lease?

Decision and Rationale: (Heher, J.) Yes. There are two different views on the question at issue. Under the English rule, when the term is to commence in the future, the lessor undertakes an implied duty to provide the lessee with legal and actual possession upon the commencement of the lease period. This rule has the support of respectable American authority, and in an early case in this state, *Kerr v. Whitaker*, this court construed the stipulation for possession at the commencement of the term "as an express covenant to let the premises, and give possession" on the first day, and held that the lessor, having failed to deliver possession, was liable to the lessee. The English rule is the better rule. It has the virtue of effectuating the common intention of the parties—to give actual and exclusive possession of the premises to the lessee at the commencement of the term. As such, there is no reason to place upon the lessee, without express stipulation to that effect, the burden of ousting the holdover tenant, and thus to impose upon him the consequences of the delay incident to the adjudication of the controversy and the obligations to pay rent during that period. Therefore, Rabinowitz's (D) motions for a nonsuit and a directed verdict on the ground that there was no evidence of a breach of undertaking to deliver possession of the demised premises were properly denied. There was, however, error in the measurement of the damages. The judge found that Adrian (P) "would have disposed of at least $2,800 worth of seasonable merchandise," had delivery of the premises occurred at the commencement of the lease, and that he was compelled to sacrifice his merchandise at 25 percent below cost because of the delay. The measure of damages for the breach of a lease agreement, in the absence of special circumstances, is the difference between the actual rental value and the rent reserved for the period of non-possession. The damages recoverable are those fairly and reasonably within the contemplation of the parties to the contract, at the time of its making, as the probable consequence of the breach. The law, in the estimation of the damages, applies that formula which makes for the greater definiteness and certainty; and, in a case such as this, the difference between the rental value and the rent reserved measures the damages with that degree of certainty which the law terms reasonable, while the evidence of possible profits during the period in question, and, by the same reasoning, losses resulting from the depreciation in value of seasonable merchandise which might have been sold, do not provide a definite standard. Furthermore, granting that the depreciation in the value of the merchandise may fairly and reasonably be supposed to have been within the contemplation of the parties to the contract as the probable result of the breach, and that the making of the contract under the asserted special circumstances may be established by parol, the proofs offered do not warrant the application of that standard. Reversed. Venire de novo awarded.

Analysis:

There are two schools of thought regarding the issue before the *Adrian* court. The first, which is generally referred to as the English rule, holds that unless there is some agreement to the contrary, the lessor has a duty to deliver to the lessee both actual and legal possession of the demised premises at the beginning of the term. In other words, the landlord or lessor has a duty to make sure all prior tenants have evacuated the premises before the beginning of a new lease term. The English rule, which has been accepted by a number of American jurisdictions, is based upon the idea that the tenant bargains for possession of the land, not for a chance at a lawsuit to demand possession. Additionally, proponents of the English rule frequently argue that the landlord is in a much better position to eject a wrongful holdover than the lessee ever would be. The second school of thought adheres to what is termed the American rule. Under the American Rule, the landlord has no duty to deliver actual possession and thus the lessee is on his or her own if there is a problem. This school of thought adheres to the principle that the tenant can eject the wrongful holdover as easily as the landlord by means of an ejectment action. Furthermore, there is also a belief that it is unfair to charge the landlord with the responsibility of ejecting the wrongful holdover as he has no other authority over the holdover tenant. In the United States, the jurisdictions are split between these two schools of thought, some accepting one and others accepting the other.

Commonwealth Building Corp. v. Hischfield

(Landlord) v. (Tenant)
(1940) 307 Ill. App. 533, 30 N.E.2d 790

M E M O R Y   G R A P H I C

Instant Facts

A landlord sought to have a tenant pay an additional year's worth of rent when the tenant did not finish moving out until the day after the expiration of the lease..

Black Letter Rule

A holdover tenant may be held to be a tenant for another term when either his actions are such that the landlord may rightfully assume that he intends to create a second tenancy, or when the action of the tenant is such that the court, as a matter of law and in the interest of justice, holds him liable for a second lease under the principle of quasi contract.

Case Vocabulary

HOLDOVER TENANT: A tenant who wrongfully remains in possession of a leasehold after the expiration of the tenancy.

INSTRUCTED VERDICT: A directed verdict, or a judgement entered by a trial judge who replaces the jury as the fact-finder because, based on the evidence presented, either there is only one decision that can reasonably be made, or because the evidence failed to establish a prima facie case.

JUDGMENT NON OBSTANTE VEREDICTO: A judgment notwithstanding the verdict, or a judgment entered in favor of one party even though the jury decided in favor of the other party.

TENANCY AT SUFFERANCE: The type of tenancy created when a tenant holds over past the termination of the original lease; the duration of a tenancy at sufferance depends on the terms of the original lease and local law.

Procedural Basis: Appeal to the Appellate Court of Illinois of a trial court's denial of a motion for a judgment notwithstanding the verdict and its granting of a motion for a new trial.

Facts: Hischfield (D) and his family leased an apartment from CBC (P) for $275 a month. The lease expired at the end of the day on September 30, 1938, and two months prior to that date, Hischfield (D) informed CBC (P) that he would be leaving upon the expiration of the lease. On September 27, three days before the expiration of the lease, Hischfield (D) began moving his belongings from the apartment. By midnight on the morning of October 1, 1938, the majority of Hischfield's (D) belongings had been moved out, though some carpets and bed furniture remained. These remaining items were moved out on October 1, the day after the expiration of the lease. Later that day, a representative of CBC (P) served Hischfield (D) with a notice which stated that because he had not vacated the apartment before the end of the lease period, he was being considered a holdover tenant and therefore owed CBC (P) rent for the month of October. A lawsuit over the rent soon followed.

Issue: When a tenant is a few hours late moving out of a leased residence, can he be held to be a holdover tenant and therefore made responsible for additional rent?

Decision and Rationale: (Matchett, J.) No. While the law is otherwise in England, in New York a tenant who holds over after the expiration of his term may, at the election of the landlord, be held to be either a trespasser or tenant for another similar term. The New York rule was adopted by the Illinois Supreme Court in the case of *Clinton Wire Cloth Co. v. Gardner*, and has been followed in subsequent cases with the caveat that the rule is to be applied only where the holding-over is voluntary. Upon a consideration of the record as a whole, we are of the opinion that the motion for an instructed verdict in favor of Hischfield (D) should have been granted, and that after the trial his motion for a judgment notwithstanding the verdict should also have been allowed. An examination of similar cases demonstrates that, in a holdover situation, a new tenancy can be presumed in two situations: first, when the voluntary action of the tenant is such that the landlord may rightfully assume an intention on the tenant's part to create a second tenancy, or second, when the action of the tenant is such that the court will, as a matter of law, hold the tenant liable for a second lease upon the principle of quasi contract so that justice may prevail. In this case, we think that CBC (P) is not entitled to recover under either theory. The uncontradicted evidence shows no grounds on which a voluntary agreement for a new tenancy could be inferred. Hischfield (D) was vacating the premises with reasonable speed and in good faith. The landlord's representatives were present and assisted Hischfield (D) in getting his goods out of the apartment. There is not a scintilla of evidence from which the jury could reasonably find any intention on the part of Hischfield (D) to continue the lease. Unfortunately, notwithstanding good faith, the removal of the last piece of furniture was delayed for a few hours. The tenant and his family did not arise at midnight and move out. They waited until dawn, and shortly thereafter CBC (P) availed itself of this supposed ancient rule of law and served notice of its intention to collect $3,300 from Hischfield (D). There is nothing either in word or deed of the tenant that indicates an intention on his part to renew. Every action indicated the contrary intention. Hischfield (D), therefore, cannot be held on the theory of a voluntary contract. Nor can he be held on the theory of quasi contract. The lease provided that if the tenant failed to move at the expiration of the lease, he should pay double the usual rent for the actual time of his occupancy. This is the agreement of the parties and it is reasonable. We therefore hold that Hischfield's (D) motion for judgement in his favor notwithstanding the verdict should have been granted. The order granting

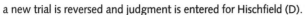
a new trial is reversed and judgment is entered for Hischfield (D).

Concurrence: (O'Connor, J.) I agree with the outcome and the opinion. I only write to add that the $3,300 claim made by CBC (P) shocks the conscious, is wholly without merit, and should not be entertained by any court. In cases such as this one, the "rule of reason" must always be kept in mind. Under that rule, some derelictions do not give rise to a cause of action.

Analysis:

The present case addresses an important issue in landlord-tenant law—the holdover tenant, also known as a tenant at sufferance. A tenancy at sufferance arises when a tenant remains in possession of the leasehold after the lease has expired or been terminated; the duration of the tenancy at sufferance, as will be seen, depends on the terms of the original lease and local law. Thus, for example, a tenant of a residential apartment who chooses not to move at the expiration of his or her lease, is a holdover tenant and is bound by a tenancy at sufferance. As the *Commonwealth* court explains, it is a general principle of landlord-tenant law that a holdover tenant may, at the election of the landlord, be held to be a tenant for a term identical to that of the original lease. Thus, for example, if a business owner leases a space for a six month period of time, but at the end of the six months does not vacate the premises, the landlord has the power to impose another six month lease with the same terms and conditions as the original lease, and the law will require the business owner to be bound by that lease. As the *Commonwealth* court further points out, the purpose behind this rather strict rule is to impose certainty as between landlords and tenants with regard to their respective rights. As you might be able to see, if the holdover rule were applied in as strict a manner as possible, landlords might be able to misuse it to their benefit. That appeared to be the case in *Commonwealth*, where the landlord sought to obtain an entire year's rent for an apparently unavoidable twelve hour holdover. This brings up the second lesson taught by this opinion, which is that many courts have sought to lessen the harshness of the rule and the potential for misuse that it creates by imposing limitations on its use. In this case, the harshness of the rule was diminished by the imposition of a voluntariness requirement. Specifically, the court held that the traditional holdover rule would only come into play if the tenant acted in such a way that the landlord could rightly assume that the tenant intended to stay, or the tenant acted in such a way that justice would only prevail if another tenancy were imposed. By imposing this caveat or restriction on the holdover rule, the court was able to avoid ruling in favor of CBC (P), which it would have had to do had it strictly followed the common law holdover rule. Finally, it should be noted that some states have taken amelioration of the rule even further and modified the rule by statute. For example, Arizona statutory law makes any holdover situation a month-to-month lease, meaning in the example give above, the business owner would not be bound by a six month lease, but a lease for a month that would be automatically renewed if not terminated. Such a rule would, of course, be beneficial to one who wishes to remain in a lease for a period of time, but not for as long a period of time as the original lease.

Richard Barton Enterprises, Inc. v. Tsern

(Tenant) v. (Landlord)

(1996) 928 P.2d 368

M E M O R Y   G R A P H I C

Instant Facts

A tenant filed suit against his landlord when, after repeated requests, the landlord, in violation of the lease agreement, failed to repair an elevator on the premises.

Black Letter Rule

A commercial lessee's obligation to pay rent is dependent on the lessor's performance of those covenants that have a significant effect on the purpose for which the lessee entered into the lease.

Case Vocabulary

A FORTIORI: Latin phrase meaning "even more so" or "more certainly."

CONSTRUCTIVE EVICTION: A situation in which a leased premises is so unfit for habitation and/or occupancy that the tenant is, for all intents and purposes, forced to leave.

DOCTRINE OF MUTUALLY DEPENDENT COVENANTS: Doctrine of contract law which holds that if one party does not live up to his contractual obligations, the other party does not need to live up to hers.

IMPLIED WARRANTY OF SUITABILITY: An implied covenant in commercial rental agreements which requires that the premises be suitable for its intended commercial purpose.

RENT ABATEMENT: A reduction in the amount of rent owed or paid.

Procedural Basis: Appeal to the Utah Supreme Court of a lower court judgment awarding Barton (P), a commercial tenant, an abatement in rent and the cost of repairing an elevator that was located on the leased premises.

Facts: On November 27, 1991, Richard Barton (P), an antiques dealer, entered into an agreement with John Tsern (D) regarding the lease of a commercial building in downtown Salt Lake City. The lease was to run for one year at a cost of $3,000 per month. The lease contained a provision requiring Tsern (D) to fix a leaky roof and repair the freight elevator such that it would be in "good working order." Barton (P) had difficulty with the premises from the beginning. First, though he was able to set up shop on the first floor at the beginning of the lease, he did not gain access to the second floor until almost three weeks later, when a holdover tenant finally left. Additionally, no repairs were made to the freight elevator for over a month, and when repairs were finally made, Tsern (D) paid for only those repairs necessary to make the elevator "go up and down." When the elevator repair company suggested that additional repairs were necessary to make the elevator safe, Tsern (D) refused to pay for the extra repairs. Thereafter the elevator was shut down by government inspectors and, because Tsern (D) refused to pay for the repairs, it was deemed inoperable. Over the course of the first few months, Barton (P) refused to pay the full amount of rent that was due because of his inability to use the entirety of the premises and Tsern's (D) failure to repair the elevator. Eventually lawsuits were filed. Barton (P) sued to have the elevator repaired and Tsern (D) counterclaimed seeking the remainder of the rent. The trial court ruled in favor of Barton (P), ordering Tsern (D) to pay the cost of repairing the elevator, abating the rent to $2,000 per month, awarding Barton (P) damages, and requiring Tsern (D) to pay Barton's (P) attorney fees in the amount of $100,000. Tsern (D) appealed.

Issue: Does a commercial lessee's obligation to pay rent depend in any way on the lessor's performance of the covenants which he or she has undertaken in the lease agreement?

Decision and Rationale: (Stewart, J.) Yes. The trial court found that the parties agreed to the concept of a rent credit but did not agree on an amount, so it took it upon itself to fix an amount. Tsern (D) argues that the trial court erred in supplying a required term of the proposed modifications. We agree. Courts may not impose a modification of a lease to which the parties have not agreed, and, a fortiori, may not do so when the parties have explicitly disagreed as to the essential terms thereof. A valid modification of a contract or lease requires a meeting of the minds, and Barton (P) and Tsern (D) did not agree as to the amount of the abatement. As an alternative to the lease modification ground for abating rent, the trial court also ruled that the covenant to pay rent was dependent on the lessor's compliance with its covenant to repair the elevator. Tsern (D) argues that the trial court erred in so ruling and that a lessee's covenant to pay rent is independent of a lessor's obligations once the lessee takes possession of the premises. He argues that the trial court erred in ruling that the contract doctrine of mutually dependant covenants governed and that Barton's (P) obligation to pay rent was dependent on Tsern's (D) covenant to repair the elevator. Tsern (D) specifically relies on *King v. Firm*, which held that a lessee's covenant to pay rent was wholly independent of the lessor's covenant to make repairs. Under the common law a lease was considered primarily a conveyance of an interest in land, and the lessor's covenants were independent of the lessee's covenant to pay rent. As such, the lessee was required to pay rent even if the lessor failed to comply with an obligation imposed by the lease. The doctrine that lease covenants are independent obligations was established prior to the development of the doctrine of mutually dependent covenants in contract law and often caused harsh results. Eventually, the common law rule was mitigated to some extent by the fiction of constructive eviction, which allowed a lessee to stop paying rent if a lessor's breach of warranty was tantamount to removal of the tenant from the premises. Although the fiction of constructive eviction served the useful purpose of ameliorating the harshness of the rule of independent covenants, even the doctrine of constructive eviction has limited capacity to achieve fairness. With the evolution from an agrarian to an urbanized, industrialized society, courts have had to reassess the doctrines that underlie and define the legal rights and liabilities of parties to a lease. In 1985, this Court recognized that certain property law rules that historically governed the leasing of land had become obsolete. Specifically, in *Williams v. Melby*, we observed that the realities of the expectations of lessors and lessees had so changed from earlier times that it was necessary to recognize that a "residential lessee does not realistically receive an estate in land. Rather, the lessee's rights, liabilities, and expectations are more appropriately viewed as governed by contract and general principles of tort law." Four years after deciding *Williams*, we held in *Reid v. Mutual of Omaha Ins. Co.*, that principles of contract law rather than property law govern in computing a lessee's liability for damages for breach of a lease. And later, in *Wade v. Jobe*, we held that the covenant to pay rent was dependent on the lessor's compliance with the implied warranty of habitability. We find that the principles announced in *Wade* in the context of residential leases are equally applicable to the commercial context. In addition, several other states have held that under certain circumstances, commercial lessees may withhold rent. One group of states holds that covenants in commercial leases are mutually dependant. Texas offers the most expansive protection for commercial leases, extending to commercial lessees all protections available to residential lessees, including an implied warranty of suitability. A second group of states does not recognize implied warranties in commercial leases, but nevertheless holds that covenants in commercial leases may be mutually

dependant. Both groups of cases recognize that the covenant to pay rent under a commercial lease is dependent on the lessor's compliance with those covenants necessary to provide the lessee with the benefits that were the essence of the bargain. By making the lessee's covenant to pay rent dependent on the lessor's performance of essential covenants, the legal analysis can focus on the essential elements and purposes of the bargain between the lessor and the lessee. This approach should provide a more fair, realistic, and forthright analysis of whether a lessee may abate rent. To the extent that *King v. Firm* is inconsistent with this conclusion, it is overruled. Not all breaches of covenants by a lessor justify a lessee in withholding rent. Only a significant breach of a covenant material to the purpose for which the lease was consummated justifies a lessee in abating rent–temporary or minor breaches of routine covenants do not. In sum, we hold that the lessee's covenant to pay rent is dependent on the lessor's performance of covenants that were a significant inducement to the consummation of the lease. Tsern (D) knew that an operable elevator was essential to Barton's (P) use of the second floor and that the lack of an operable elevator was more than an inconvenience. Tsern's (D) promise to repair the elevator was a significant inducement to Barton (P) to enter into the lease. The absence of an operable and safe elevator had more than a peripheral effect on Barton's (P) use of the premises; it impaired his ability to conduct his business. It follows that Tsern (D) was entitled to receive rent equal to the value of the premises without an operable freight elevator. In computing the amount of rent abatement or reimbursement, the lessee is entitled to abate rent by an amount equal to the reduced value of the premises due to the lessor's breach. Affirmed in part and reversed in part.

Analysis:

Placed in a section of the text entitled "Condition of the Premises," the present case addresses or refers to a number of important legal concepts that directly relate to the condition of the leasehold. These include the implied warranty of suitability, the implied warranty of habitability, and the covenant of quiet enjoyment. As these are all very important concepts, they will be addressed in turn. The implied warranty of suitability is a covenant, implied in some commercial rental agreements, that the premises is suitable for its intended commercial purpose. As it was explained by one Texas court, "[t]his warranty means that at the inception of the lease there are no latent defects in the facilities that are vital to the use of the premises for their intended commercial purpose and that these essential facilities will remain in a suitable condition." *Davidow v. Inwood North Professional Group–Phase I.* The concept of an implied warranty of suitability is not accepted in all jurisdictions. As the *Richard* opinion points out, some states do not recognize implied warranties of suitability in commercial leases. As such, an attorney dealing with landlord-tenant issues and commercial leases will need to research the law of the state in which he or she is practicing to determine whether the protections afforded a tenant under the implied warranty of suitability are available. The implied warranty of habitability, which began its proliferation in the 1960's, is a much more widely-accepted doctrine of property law. Similar in nature to an implied warranty of suitability, the implied warranty of habitability is a warranty given by residential landlords to their tenants that the residential premises are fit for human habitation. There is certainly room for argument over the meaning of "fit for human habitation," and lawyers dealing with these issues will have to research local law to determine the extent of the protection, but it is safe to say that the warranty provides that at least some minimum standards of safety and decency must be met before a landlord can lease an apartment, home, or other residential premises. It should be noted that the source of the warranty is different in different states. Specifically, some states have adopted statutory provisions which imply the warranty in residential leases while in other states the warranty is judicially created and enforced. The covenant of quiet enjoyment is a two-fold promise. First, it is a promise to a tenant, whether commercial or residential, that no one with superior title to the premises will appear and dispossess the tenant. Second, it is a promise that the landlord will not evict the tenant, whether actually or constructively. The majority of American jurisdictions accept and imply a covenant of quiet enjoyment in residential and commercial leases. Finally, mention should be made of the doctrine of mutually dependent covenants. As the *Richard* opinion points out, for many years leases were considered to be more like conveyances than contractual agreements, and, as such, contract law doctrines such as the doctrine of mutually dependent covenants were not available in landlord-tenant disputes; thus the view that a tenant is obligated to pay rent regardless of whether the landlord lives up to his or her end of the bargain. In recent years, however, leases have come to be viewed as being more like contracts than actual conveyances of land. As such, courts such as the Utah Supreme Court in *Richard* have begun to make contract law doctrines available in landlord-tenant situations. Specifically, in the present case the Utah Supreme Court allowed Barton (P) to use the contract law doctrine of mutually dependent covenants to secure a rent abatement based on Tsern's (D) refusal to perform the covenants that he had promised to perform. As courts continue to recognize the contractual nature of the landlord-tenant relationship, this and other doctrines will continue to protect the interests of both the landlord and the tenant.

ORDINANCES WHICH REQUIRE BUILDERS AND DEVELOPERS TO CREATE AFFORDABLE HOUSING IN CONJUNCTION WITH OTHER PROJECTS ARE IN THE NATURE OF RENT CONTROL ORDINANCES

Town of Telluride v. Lot Thirty-Four Venture, L.L.C.

(Town Government) v. (Construction Company)
(2000) 3 P.3d 30

M E M O R Y   G R A P H I C

Instant Facts

A developer challenged a city ordinance requiring it to generate affordable housing units in conjunction with commercial developments.

Black Letter Rule

Local laws and ordinances which require commercial developers to generate affordable housing in conjunction with commercial developments are potentially violative of general laws prohibiting rent control.

Case Vocabulary

RENT CONTROL: A system under which the amount of rent that a landlord can demand is capped at a fixed rate with only limited increases.

Procedural Basis: Appeal to the Colorado Supreme Court of a trial court's decision granting summary judgment in favor of a town whose affordable housing ordinance was challenged by a company involved in the construction of residential housing.

Facts: In September 1994, the Town of Telluride (D) enacted Ordinance 1011, an "affordable housing" ordinance which required all new developments within the town to create affordable housing for forty percent of the employees generated by the development. The ordinance provided four ways in which developers could satisfy the requirements of the ordinance. Specifically, developers could: (1) construct new housing units with fixed rental rates; (2) impose deed restrictions on existing free market units such that rental rates could be fixed; (3) pay fees to the Town (D) in lieu of creating affordable housing; or (4) convey land to the Town (D) which could be used for building affordable housing. Lot Thirty-Four Venture, L.L.C. (P), a developer, challenged the ordinance on the ground that it constituted rent control, which was generally prohibited by Colorado state law.

Issue: Does the Town of Telluride's (D) affordable housing ordinance violate the State of Colorado's general prohibition of rent control?

Decision and Rationale: (Kourlis, J.) Yes. This appeal requires us to determine whether Telluride's (D) affordable housing scheme falls within Colorado's prohibition of rent control. Colorado's prohibition reads, in part: "[N]o county or municipality may enact any ordinance or resolution which would control rents on private residential property." The Colorado General Assembly did not define rent control, so we must interpret the meaning of the phrase using standard rules of statutory construction. In doing so, we find the term to be clear on its face. Rent control is commonly understood to mean allowable rent capped at a fixed rate with only limited increases, and we accept this definition. Because Ordinance 1011 sets a base rental rate per square foot and then strictly limits the growth of the rental rate, the ordinance constitutes rent control and thus violates the plain language of the prohibition. The scheme as a whole operates to suppress rental values below their market values, and unlawfully restricts the property owner's ability to develop his land as he sees fit. Ordinance 1011 cannot be saved on the grounds that it applies only to new construction while existing housing units are not subject to the controls. The salient fact is that the ordinance caps rental rates for a class of housing at a price below what the market can bear. The effect of the ordinance is the same, regardless of whether new or existing units are exempt. In addition, the statutory ban on rent control makes no distinction between existing units and those subsequently developed. Furthermore, the fact that the ordinance offers developers several options for satisfying the affordable housing requirement does not change the character of, or redeem, the rent control provision. Once owners decide to develop their property, they must engage in a program that effectively redistributes the value of the rental property from landlord to tenant—a hallmark of rent control. Because Ordinance 1011 imposes a base price for rental values, and thereafter limits the rate growth, we conclude that the ordinance constitutes rent control within the meaning of Colorado's general ban. The Court of Appeals' reversal of the trial court's decision granting Telluride's (D) motion for summary judgment is affirmed.

Analysis:

At issue in the present case is the concept of rent control, and whether the Telluride (D) ordinance at issue constituted rent control. (The court, obviously, found that it did.) Rent control can be a very emotional and divisive issue, and arguments based on economic theory, public policy, and a number of other theories are regularly made for or against the practice. Tenants, of course, are often in favor of rent control because it allows them to have affordable access to housing in times of housing shortages or other emergencies when demand might increase the price of housing beyond what they can afford. Landlords, on the other hand, are generally opposed to rent control because it places a limit on the profitability of their rental housing. In some cases, landlords have even complained that rent control so limits their ability to make profitable use of their property that the rent control amounted to an unlawful taking. When this is true, and a landlord can back up his or her claims with evidence, courts have ruled in favor of the landlord challenging the rent control system. (In one such case, *Pennell v. City of San Jose*, the United States Supreme Court seemingly accepted the proposition that a rent control ordinance can amount to a taking if it truly limits the landlord's ability to profitably use his or her land.) Rent control has an interesting and now somewhat cyclical history. Rent control is said to have begun in the District of Columbia during World War I, when there was a major wartime housing shortage in the District. It became more widely used during World War II for similar reasons, and in many areas continued in effect after the war. During the 1970's, many peacetime rent control ordinances were adopted throughout the United States, and in cases such as *Bowles v. Willingham* [addressing rent control during wartime], *Block v. Hirsh* [addressing rent control just following the conclusion of a war], and *Pennell v. City of San Jose* [addressing rent control during a peacetime housing shortage], the United States Supreme Court has clearly held that both wartime and peacetime rent controls are constitutionally permissible in particular situations. In more recent years, however, state legislatures and some courts have begun to scale back and in many cases abolish rent control statutes. Such was the case in *Town of Telluride v. Lot Thirty-Four Venture, L.L.C.*, as the only reason the ordinance was challenged was that Colorado had clearly enacted a state-wide ban on rent control. As long as rent control ordinances exist—and they still do—the debates will likely continue.

Piggly Wiggly Southern, Inc. v. Heard

(Tenant) v. (Landlord)
(1991) 261 Ga. 503, 405 S.E.2d 478

M E M O R Y   G R A P H I C

Instant Facts

A lawsuit was filed when a commercial tenant vacated a leased premises (though continued to pay rent) three years prior to the end of the lease and refused to sublease the vacant premises to any other business.

Black Letter Rule

A commercial lease agreement which provides that the tenant's use of the premises is not limited to the purpose for which it is leased, but can be assigned without the consent of the landlord or used for any other lawful business, does not create an implied covenant of continuous operation.

Case Vocabulary

ANCHOR TENANT: The most significant or largest commercial tenant in a multi-tenant area; the tenant whose existence draws large amounts of commercial traffic off of which smaller businesses in the area feed.
COVENANT OF CONTINUOUS OPERATION: A covenant or promise made by a party to a commercial lease that it will operate a business in the leased premises for the duration of the lease.

Procedural Basis: Appeal to the Georgia Supreme Court of a lawsuit regarding Piggly Wiggly's (D) refusal to sublease a recently-vacated commercial premises to another business.

Facts: In 1963, Piggly Wiggly (D), a supermarket chain, entered into an agreement with another party under which the other party would construct a supermarket building that Piggly Wiggly (D) would then lease. The terms of the lease called for rent of $29,053.60 per year plus a certain percentage of any gross sales exceeding $2,000,000; the original lease was for 15 years with subsequent extensions being agreed to. In the early 1980's, with three years left to go on the lease, Piggly Wiggly (D) closed its operation and moved to a different location. After moving, Piggly Wiggly (D) continued to pay the base rent, but made no efforts to sublet the recently vacated store. Hardy (P), who had taken ownership of the building from the original builder, filed suit seeking damages for an alleged breach of the lease agreement. The pertinent part of the agreement at issue read: "Lessee's use of the leased building and the leased property shall not be limited nor restricted to [use for a super-market, etc.], and said building and property may be used for any other lawful purpose, without the consent of the Lessor." Specifically, Hardy (P) claimed that the lease should be read to contain a covenant of continuous operation.

Issue: Does a commercial lease agreement which provides that the tenant's use of the premises is not limited to the purpose for which it is leased but can be assigned without the consent of the landlord or used for any other lawful business create an implied covenant of continuous operation?

Decision and Rationale: (Name of Authoring Judge Not Stated) No. The lease agreement at issue in this case does not contain an express covenant of continuous operation. In fact, the language of the agreement is plainly to the contrary, and we cannot construe it otherwise. There is also nothing in the agreement that would create an implied covenant of continuous operation. The agreement's provision for free assignability by the tenant, without consent of the lessor, weighs strongly against a construction of the contract that would require the tenant to continue its business throughout the term of the lease. Similarly, the existence of a substantial minimum base rent suggests the absence of such a covenant. In sum, there is no express covenant of operation and we will not rewrite the contract to create one. Reversed.

Dissent: (Benham, J.) I disagree that the language of the lease expressly negates a requirement of continuous operation. Although the language with regard to Piggly Wiggly's (D) obligation to continue business operations in the leased premises during the term of the lease is not as clear as it might be, any ambiguity is dispelled by application of the rules governing the construction of contracts. Specifically, under Georgia law, any ambiguity in a document is to be construed against its draftsman, which, in this case, is Piggly Wiggly (D). Furthermore, considering the percentage rental provision together with the provision which references business use of the premises, and construing the lease most strongly against Piggly Wiggly (D) as the drafter, I conclude that the lease contains an express covenant by Piggly Wiggly (D) that it would conduct "business" operations in the leased premises during the entire period of the lease. Holding the premises empty cannot reasonably be construed as using the premises for a business. I would affirm the trial and appellate courts.

Analysis:

Placed in the section of the text that addresses use of the leased premises, *Piggly Wiggly*, as the opinion makes clear, addresses the issue of covenants of continuous operation. Covenants of continuous operation, generally inserted into commercial leases by the landlord, benefit the landlord in a number of ways (and thus provide him or her with a number of reasons to include them). First, as may well have been the case in *Piggly Wiggly*, if a portion of the rent is determined by a percentage of business done by the tenant, a covenant of continuous operation benefits the landlord in that it may guarantee a higher amount of rent for each rental period. Perhaps more important, if a landlord owns more than one commercial property in a given area, the abandonment of a commercial premises by one party may adversely affect the other tenants in the area, and a covenant of continuous operation can preclude abandonment. For example, what if, in the present case, Heard (P) owned the entire shopping plaza in which the Piggly Wiggly store originally operated. And what if, like many such shopping plazas, the supermarket was the anchor tenant. In such a case, the loss of Piggly Wiggly (D) without any replacement (remember, Piggly Wiggly (D) vacated the premises but refused to sublease to anyone) would potentially be a huge loss to Heard (D). It is conceivable that the loss of Piggly Wiggly (D) without any replacement would mean significantly less consumer traffic and, therefore, less business for the smaller shops in the plaza. That would, in turn, mean less income for everyone, and less reason for the other tenants to stay or renew an existing lease. In short, it is conceivable that the loss of Piggly Wiggly (D) might mean the financial ruin of the shopping plaza. In such a case, it is easy to see why a commercial landlord would want to include a covenant of continued operation in a lease. An important issue tackled in the present case is the implication or non-implication of a covenant of continuous operation when there is no such covenant expressly contained in the lease. In other words, when should such a covenant be implied? *Piggly Wiggly* does not provide a whole lot of information on this issue, other than to say that in the present case, there is no reason to imply such a covenant. Other cases are more helpful. Likely the most significant of any other cases is *Lippman v. Sears Roebuck & Co.*, a 1955 decision by the California Supreme Court. In that case, California's highest court determined that a covenant of continuous operation will only be implied if "the implication [that such a covenant exists] arise[s] from the language used or it [is] indispensable to effectuate the intention of the parties; [and it] appear[s] from the language used that [the existence of such a covenant] was so clearly within the contemplation of the parties that they deemed it unnecessary to express it." How would the case come out if this standard were applied to the facts of *Piggly Wiggly*? The outcome would probably be the same, since the majority determined that the contract as a whole negates the idea that any such covenant was meant to be implied.

Handler v. Horns

(Landlord) v. (Landlord/Tenant)
(1949) 2 N.J. 18, 65 A.2d 523

M E M O R Y   G R A P H I C

Instant Facts

A lawsuit arose when a tenant (who was also a 1/3 owner of the leasehold) claimed a right to remove certain trade fixtures from the building that he was renting.

Black Letter Rule

A tenant is permitted to remove whatever he has erected or installed on the rental premises for the purpose of carrying on a trade or business so long as it can be severed from the estate before the lease expires and without causing material injury to the premises.

Case Vocabulary

DOCTRINE OF ACCESSIONS: Doctrine under which a fixture built or installed on the land of another becomes the property of the landowner.

FORFEITURE RULE: Common law rule which held that if a tenant, at the end of his term, renews his lease and thereby acquires a new interest in the premises, his right to remove improvements is forfeited unless he reserves this right in the renewal lease.

QUICQUID PLANTATUR SOLO, SOLO CEDIT: Latin phrase meaning whatsoever is fixed to the land is part of the land.

TRADE FIXTURE: An item erected or installed by a commercial tenant on the property being rented for the purpose of furthering the tenant's trade or business.

TRADE-FIXTURE DOCTRINE: Doctrine under which a tenant is permitted to remove trade fixtures that he or she has affixed to the land for the purpose of carrying on a trade or business; generally, the doctrine only applies if the trade fixtures can be removed prior to the expiration of the lease and without damaging the premises.

Procedural Basis: Appeal to the Supreme Court of New Jersey of a lawsuit involving a tenant's ability to remove business-related fixtures from the leasehold; the lower courts ruled for the landlord and the tenant appealed.

Facts: In 1929, Henry and Augusta Horns leased a building, which they owned, to their son, Fred Horns, to be used as a plant for the processing, refrigeration, and sale of meat. To equip the building for that particular business, Fred made $89,000 in improvements and alterations, which included installing a number of meat-related pieces of equipment and fixtures. During his lifetime, Fred signed two leases for the premises. In the first lease, he agreed that "at the end or other expiration of the term, [he would] deliver up the demised premises and its fixtures in as good condition as on the date" the lease was executed. In the second lease, Fred made two important covenants: (1) that "all additions and improvements made by the Tenant shall belong to the landlords," and (2) that "at the expiration of this lease or any renewal thereof, the Tenant shall have the right to remove any and all trade fixtures that may belong to it or which may have been installed in the premises, with the exception, however, of any fixtures that may be so affixed to the building as to become a part of the realty and not removable without causing material damage to the premises." When Augusta Horns died in 1937, her husband having predeceased her, the building was left to their three children, including Fred, the tenant. Thereafter, Fred and one of his sisters, passed away, and their 1/3 shares in the building were passed on to their surviving children. Thus, the building eventually came to be owned by Henry Horns (D) (Fred's son and Henry and Augusta's grandson), Clara Horns (Henry and Augusta's daughter and Fred's sister), and Hazel Handler (P) (Henry and Augusta's granddaughter and Fred's niece). At some point a dispute arose between Hazel (P) and Henry (D) over Henry's (D) ability, under the terms of the lease, to remove certain fixtures from the property prior to its sale. The matter was taken to court and, eventually, ended up in front of the New Jersey Supreme Court.

Issue: When a tenant affixes something onto rental property to assist in the carrying on of a trade or business, and the item can be severed from the property without causing any material injury to the property, can the item lawfully be removed before the tenant quits the premises?

Decision and Rationale: (Ackerson, J.) Yes. There is an ancient maxim–quicquid plantatur solo, solo cedit–which means whatsoever is fixed to the land is part of the land. Over the years this maxim has given way to numerous exceptions, one of which involves fixtures installed by tenants. As between landlord and tenant, the presumption is that the tenant's motive in placing a fixture on the rental property is to benefit himself and not the landlord. This is particularly true where the item is affixed for the purpose of carrying on a trade or business. It is also sound public policy to allow the tenant great latitude to remove fixtures so as to encourage trade and industry. These considerations have led courts to place special emphasis on the element of intention as to the ownership of the fixtures where the claimants are landlord and tenant. As such, the general rule today is that a tenant is permitted to remove whatever he has erected or installed on the rental premises for the purpose of carrying on a trade (referred to as trade fixtures), provided it can be severed from the estate before the lease expires and without causing the estate material injury. As a general rule, an article can be regarded as a trade fixture if it is annexed for the purpose of furthering the tenant's trade or business. Referring to the second lease, made on April 14, 1939, Handler (P) asks us to apply the rule that if a tenant, at the end of his term, renews his lease and thereby acquires a new interest in the premises, his right to remove improvements is forfeited, unless he reserves this right in the renewal lease. This rule is generally referred to as the forfeiture rule, and has been much criticized in modern judicial literature and rejected or limited in its application. In any event, today's holding is inconsistent with the forfeiture rule, which is therefore repudiated. We note that the original lease contained a provision that at the end of the term the tenant "will deliver up the demised premises and its fixtures in as good condition as on the date hereof." Obviously this does not apply to fixtures installed by the tenant after the date of the lease, but only those on the premises at the time it was executed. The sixth paragraph of the second lease, which provides that "additions and improvements" shall belong to the landlord, is not only confined to those thereafter made, but also distinguishes this type of permanent structural addition to the building from the trade fixtures placed there by the tenant which, according to the twenty-seventh paragraph, may be removed if such removal "does not materially damage the premises." Since there was no prohibition against the removal of such fixtures by the tenant in the original lease, and the second lease provides for removal under the stated condition, Horns (D) has a right to such trade fixtures as can be so removed. As it appears from the testimony presented that much of the fixtures in question could be removed without causing material damage to the freehold, the decree below is modified so as to exclude from the sale of the premises those trade fixtures that can be so removed. Reversed.

Analysis:

Under the doctrine of accessions, if a person builds or installs a permanent fixture onto the land of another, and certain conditions are met, the fixture becomes the property of the landowner. In determining whether the doctrine applies, courts generally look at the degree to which the fixtures are attached or connected with the land; whether the fixtures are specially adapted to the premises; whether removal of the fixtures would destroy or damage the premises; and the interest each of the parties has in the land. One widely-recognized exception to the doctrine of accessions is the trade-fixture doctrine, which, as stated in the opinion above, permits a tenant to remove trade fixtures that he or she has affixed to the land for the purpose of carrying on a trade or business, so long as the trade fixtures can be removed prior to the expiration of the lease and without damaging the premises. In the present case, that involved the removal of items used to process and store meat—relatively small items. In other cases, however, the trade-fixture doctrine has been used to justify and permit the removal of larger things such as a house (*Van Ness v. Pacard*, 27 U.S. 137 (1829)), small farm buildings (*Old Line Life Ins. Co. v. Hawn*, 275 N.W. 542 (1937)), and service station buildings (*Cameron v. Oakland County Gas & Oil Co.*, 269 N.W. 227 (1936)). As these other cases make clear, the term "trade fixture" can be broadly defined to include a number of different items. Two additional things should be noted. First, in the *Handler* opinion above, the second lease contained an important provision which gave Henry Horns (D) the right and ability to remove certain trade fixtures from the land. Many issues such as the one that arose in this case can and are addressed by the lease agreement, thus potentially avoiding a fight over ownership. Indeed, if there is the potential for a dispute over the ownership of fixtures that a tenant intends to install, it would behoove the tenant to have those issues addressed squarely in the lease agreement. Second, the opinion references the presentation of testimony as to the removal of the trade fixtures at issue. Henry (D) apparently had to present testimony regarding the damage or lack thereof which would result from a removal of the meat processing and storage equipment. If a similar dispute were to arise today, a tenant might very well be required to provide similar testimony to a court of competent jurisdiction.

Walls v. Oxford Management Co.

(Tenant) v. (Apartment Management Company)

(1993) 137 N.H. 653, 633 A.2d 103

M E M O R Y   G R A P H I C

Instant Facts

A woman filed suit against her landlord and the company charged with managing the apartment complex after she was sexually assaulted in the parking lot.

Black Letter Rule

Where a landlord has made no affirmative attempt to provide security for her tenants and is not responsible for any physical defect that enhances the risk that a crime may be committed, she cannot be held liable for a criminal attack upon a tenant.

Procedural Basis: Not stated.

Facts: On December 5, 1988, Deanna Walls (P) was sexually assaulted in the parking lot of the Bay Ridge Apartment Complex. Walls (P) lived with her mother in the complex at the time of the attack, and thus was a resident of Bay Ridge. Following the attack, Walls (P) filed suit against her landlord and Oxford Management Company (Oxford) (D), which was in charge of managing the 412-apartment complex. Walls (P) argued that Oxford (D) "had a duty to provide reasonable security measures for the protection of residents of bay Ridge, a duty to warn residents of its lack of security, as well as a duty to warn residents of the numerous criminal activities which had taken place on the premises of Bay Ridge and in the vicinity of Bay Ridge." Walls (P) further alleged that Oxford (D) breached these duties and that the breach was a proximate cause of the sexual assault.

Issue: Does the mere creation of a landlord-tenant relationship alone impose on the landlord a duty to protect tenants from criminal activity?

Decision and Rationale: (Horton, J.) No. At one time landlords enjoyed considerable immunity from rules of conduct that governed others. In the case of *Sargent v. Ross*, however, we abolished landlord immunity and held that a landlord has a duty to act as a reasonable person under the circumstances. While we can state that landlords owe a duty of reasonable care to tenants, we must also consider the rule that private citizens have no duty to protect others from criminal activity. We agree that landlords generally have no duty to protect tenants from criminal activity. Without question, there is much to be gained from efforts at curtailing criminal activity. Yet, we will not place on landlords the general burden of insuring their tenants against harm from criminal attacks. There are, however, two important exceptions to this rule. Under the first exception, a party who does or should realize that his conduct has created a condition which involves an unreasonable risk of harm to another has a duty to exercise reasonable care to prevent the risk from taking effect. Accordingly, in the majority of cases in which a landlord has been held liable for a criminal attack upon a tenant, a known physical defect, such as a defective deadbolt or window latch, foreseeably enhanced the risk of that attack. Under the second applicable exception, landlords who provide security have been found liable for removing the security in the face of a foreseeable criminal threat. Thus, we hold that while landlords have no general duty to protect tenants from criminal activity, such a duty may arise when a landlord has created or is responsible for a known defective condition on a premises that foreseeably enhanced the risk of criminal attack. Moreover, a landlord who undertakes to provide security will thereafter have a duty to act with reasonable care. Where, however, a landlord has made no affirmative attempt to provide security, and is not responsible for a physical defect that enhances the risk of crime, we will not find such a duty. In short, we reject liability based solely on the landlord-tenant relationship. It must be noted that a finding that an approved exception applies is not dispositive of the issue of the landlord's liability. Where a landlord's duty is premised on a defective condition that has foreseeably enhanced the risk of criminal attack, the question whether the defect was a proximate or legal cause of the tenant's injury remains one of fact. Moreover, where a landlord has voluntarily assumed a duty to provide some degree of security, that duty is limited by the extent of the undertaking. For example, when a landlord has chosen to provide lighting in a parking lot, there is no additional duty to provide security personnel. Walls (P) argues that a landlord's implied warrant of habitability to provide reasonably safe premises requires the landlord to secure tenants against criminal attack. Until now, this court has not considered whether a landlord's failure to provide security against criminal activity renders a dwelling "unsafe" or "unfit for living" and is thus a breach of the implied warranty of habitability. Other jurisdictions, however, have held that it does not, and we agree. The warranty of habitability implied in residential lease agreements protects tenants against structural defects, but does not require landlords to take affirmative measures to provide security against criminal activity. Remanded.

Analysis:

The particular portion of the text in which the present case is found addresses the issue of injuries to person and property, and the extent of landlord liability for injuries that happen on a leased premises. This particular case, *Walls v. Oxford Management Co.*, directly addresses only one small part of the larger issue of liability for injury—that of landlord liability for criminal activity that occurs on a leased premises. As the *Walls* court states, it is the general rule that landlords are not liable for criminal attacks on tenants. Furthermore, it is undisputed that there is no strict liability for criminal activity, meaning no courts have held that a landlord is strictly liable for criminal activity occurring on the leased premises. There are some exceptions, however, to the general rule of non-liability, which exceptions place a duty upon the landlord to protect against criminal activity. The two major exceptions to this rule are mentioned in the opinion. When either of these exceptions applies, the landlord has a duty to protect against criminal activity. When the landlord fails to do so, or when a crime occurs, general negligence principles apply to the determination of landlord liability. One of the more important principles that applies to these types of cases is that of foreseeability, meaning the criminal activity must be a foreseeable result of the landlord's breach of duty. If there is no such foreseeability, courts will be hesitant to hold landlords responsible for criminal attacks. As stated above, liability for criminal activity is only a small portion of the general principle of landlord liability for injury to persons or property. There are other non-criminal forms of injury as well, such as personal injury, for which a landlord might possibly be liable. In brief, there are a number of different views on landlord responsibility for personal injuries that occur on a leased premises. Under the traditional view, as the *Walls* court briefly alludes to, landlords generally enjoy immunity with a handful of exceptions. With respect to personal injuries, the first exception applies when an injury results from a landlord's failure to use reasonable care in maintaining a common area, such as a sidewalk, driveway, or play area. The second exception deems a landlord potentially liable for injuries caused by latent defects that exist at the time of the signing of the lease and that are known or should have been known to the landlord. The third exception makes landlords potentially liable for breaches of express covenants to repair the premises, and fourth, there is potential liability for injuries caused because of negligently-made repairs. In more recent years, some courts such as the *Walls* court have moved even farther away from landlord immunity and held that landlords are, in all aspects of their occupations, liable for failures to use reasonable care. In other words, general negligence principles apply to all aspects of the landlord's duties, and not just to the exceptions enumerated above. On a different note, while the *Walls* court clearly held that the implied warranty of habitability does not require protection from all criminal activity, at least one court has accepted Walls' (P) creative argument. In *Trentacost v. Brussel*, the New Jersey Supreme Court held that a landlord was liable for a breach of the implied warranty of habitability when he failed to secure the front entrance to the building. That holding, however, is truly a minority holding, as most courts agree that the implied warranty of habitability does not apply to protect against criminal activity.

Foundation Development Corp. v. Loehmann's, Inc.

(Landlord) v. (Tenant)
(1990) 163 Ariz. 438, 788 P.2d 1189

M E M O R Y   G R A P H I C

Instant Facts

A commercial landlord filed suit seeking termination of the lease agreement when the tenant failed to make a timely rent payment.

Black Letter Rule

A forfeiture for a trivial or immaterial breach of a commercial lease should not be enforced.

Case Vocabulary

FORFEITURE: The termination of a lease agreement.
SUMMARY EVICTION STATUTE: A statute which permits a landlord to terminate a lease agreement upon a breach by the tenant.

Procedural Basis: Appeal to the Arizona Supreme Court of an appellate court reversal of a trial court's decision in favor of a tenant in a suit by a landlord seeking termination of the lease.

Facts: In 1978, Loehmann's (D) entered into a commercial lease with Foundation's (P) predecessor in interest. Under the terms of the lease, Loehmann's (D) paid a base monthly rent plus additional common area charges. Additionally, if Loehmann's (D) failed "to pay any installment of minimum annual rental or additional rental or other charges [and did not cure] within ten (10) days after receipt . . . of notice of such neglect or failure," Foundation (P) could elect to terminate the lease. In February of 1987, Foundation (P) sent Loehmann's (D) a statement regarding common area charges which stated that the balance due was $3,566.44. Loehmann's (D) disagreed with the amount requested and sent correspondence back to Foundation (P) to that effect. On April 10, 1987, Foundation (P) sent a demand letter stating that payment had to be made within ten days. Loehmann's (D) received the letter seven days later, on April 17. On April 24, Loehmann's (D) issued a check for $3,566.44, which it sent out the next day. Then, on April 28, Foundation (P) filed a lawsuit against Loehmann's (D) alleging a breach of the obligation to pay the common area charge in a timely manner. In response to the allegations, Loehmann's (D) argued that the breach was not only trivial, but was a mistake, and therefore did not warrant termination of the lease. The trial court ruled in favor of Loehmann's (D), and the court of appeals reversed. Loehmann's (D) then appealed the matter to the Arizona Supreme Court.

Issue: Does the law permit a landlord to terminate a lease when the tenant commits a minor breach of the lease agreement?

Decision and Rationale: (Name of Authoring Judge Not Stated) No. Before deciding whether the breach in this case can support a forfeiture, we must first examine the common law nature of the landlord-tenant relationship so as to determine the legislative objective behind the century old statute that is now A.R.S. § 33-361. Because of its historical underpinnings, landlord-tenant law is infused with principles of both real property and contract law. Though logically it is correct to say that a lease is both a conveyance and a contract, the modern law traditionally viewed it as a conveyance. As such, the remedy of recission of a contract upon breach, available in contract law situations, was not made available to landlords and tenants. Consequently, in the absence of a statue or lease clause authorizing it, neither landlord nor tenant was empowered to terminate a leasehold because of the other's breach, but merely had to sue for damages. Thus, at common law a landlord could not dispossess a tenant who failed to keep his promise to pay rent. In Arizona, A.R.S. § 33-361(A) confers the right of re-entry and termination to the landlord for the violation of a commercial lease; the landlord may also commence an action for recovery of possession of the premises. We join Foundation (P) in reading the statue to have a legislative intent to confer on the landlord a right to terminate for breach. We do not, however, read it as broadly as Foundation (P) urges—to express a legislative intent that any breach, at any time, of any provision, would give the landlord the right to forfeit the leasehold. Foundation (P) argues that so long as the lease provides that violation of a covenant is grounds for termination, the court must enforce the lease according to its terms. It also contends that because the lease provides for forfeiture and ARS § 33-361(A) permits the landlord to re-enter and take possession for a violation of any lease provision, the trial court has no discretion regarding the enforcement of the forfeiture. In claiming A.R.S. § 33-361 prevents judicial consideration of equitable defenses to forfeiture of Loehmann's (D) leasehold interest, Foundation (P) ignores the important interplay of property and contract law that preceded the enactment of the statute. The concept that a lease is a conveyance was essential to maintain economic equilibrium in an agrarian environment, and the fact that leasehold interests now prevail in the urban business world does not diminish their importance. Furthermore, public policy militates in favor of assuring the stability of such economic relationships. Accordingly, absent some express statement of legislative intent, we are hesitant to believe that the legislature intended to permit forfeitures under any and all circumstances, no matter how trivial, inadvertent, non-prejudicial, or technical the breach. Other courts have refused to enforce a forfeiture when both lease and statue permitted one. Moreover, an overwhelming majority of courts have concluded that a lease may not be forfeited for a trivial or technical breach, even where the parties have specifically agreed that "any breach" gives rise to the right of termination. Nearly all courts hold that, regardless of the language of the lease, to justify forfeiture the breach must be material, serious, or substantial. Thus, well reasoned authority from other states also refutes the arguments advanced by Foundation (P) in this case. In short, we decline to hold that any breach, no matter how trivial or insignificant, can justify a forfeiture. Trivial or not, the delay in paying the rent here was at most three days. Therefore, we now join the overwhelming majority of jurisdictions that hold the landlord's right to terminate is not unlimited. A court's decision to permit termination must be tempered by notions of equity and common sense, and, under this principle, a forfeiture for a trivial or immaterial breach of a commercial lease should not be enforced. The court of appeals is reversed and the trial court's judgment is affirmed.

Analysis:

The present case introduces the concept of the termination of a lease agreement. Under the common law, landlords had a very limited ability to terminate lease agreements, and in many cases involving a breach of the agreement by the tenant, landlords were limited to recovering damages; they could not terminate the lease and re-take possession of the leasehold. That being said, the common law did permit the termination of lease agreements when the agreement itself contained a forfeiture or termination clause which permitted termination of the leasehold for certain types of breaches such as the non-payment of rent. In situations where the lease agreement does allow for termination, termination is not an automatic occurrence. Instead, it is a process that must be initiated by the landlord. Thus, if a landlord chooses to do so, it can ignore the breach and thus waive its right to seek termination of the lease. When such a waiver is made, however, it is generally only for past breaches. For example, by accepting a late rent payment when the lease agreement authorizes termination upon the late payment of rent, a landlord waives the right to terminate for that particular late payment, but generally will not be held to waive the right to terminate for future late payments. In such a situation, the doctrine of estoppel is the one doctrine that might deem a current waiver to be a future waiver of the right to terminate a lease for breach of the lease agreement. For estoppel to apply, there must generally be a pattern of past toleration of breaches of the agreement. Thus, if a party is two weeks late paying rent every month for the first three years of a lease, and, after three years, the landlord finally seeks termination for late payment of rent, the tenant may be able to claim that the landlord, based on a prior pattern of waivers, is estopped from terminating the lease under those facts. The present case deals with a termination situation slightly different from those involving termination clauses, though the lease at issue did have such a clause. In the present case, termination is sought to be effected by way of Arizona's summary eviction statute. Summary eviction statutes are statutes that, upon the discovery of a breach of the lease agreement, permit a landlord to evict a tenant or terminate a lease by way of a special summary proceeding. The statute at issue in the present case is a typical summary eviction statute. It reads, in pertinent part: "When a tenant neglects or refuses to pay rent when due and in arrears for five days, or when tenant violates any provision of the lease, the landlord . . . may re-enter and take possession, or without formal demand or re-entry, commence an action for recovery of possession of the premises." This is a typical summary eviction statute because the remedy under the statute is limited to possession of the premises. Additionally, most statutes, like this one, set forth what breaches are actionable, and what time frame the tenant has to cure the breach. Finally, it should be noted that most courts dislike termination proceedings. Thus, like the Arizona Supreme Court did in the present case, many courts will overlook minor breaches, particularly when the breaching party has made an attempt to cure the breach (such as paying the rent that is overdue).

Edwards v. Habib

(Tenant) v. (Landlord)
(1968) 397 F.2d 687

M E M O R Y   G R A P H I C

Instant Facts
A lawsuit arose when a tenant was evicted from her rental property immediately after she reported a number of housing code violations to the proper authorities.

Black Letter Rule
A landlord may not evict a tenant in retaliation for the tenant's report of housing code violations to the proper authorities.

Case Vocabulary
EVICTION: The act of legally dispossessing a tenant or other person of property.
RETALIATORY EVICTION: An eviction made in retaliation against a tenant who does something that the landlord disapproves of, such as report housing code violations.

Procedural Basis: Appeal to the United States Court of Appeals for the District of Columbia Circuit of a lower trial court decision not to allow Edwards (P) to present evidence of retaliatory motive during an action for eviction.

Facts: In 1965, Yvonne Edwards (P) began renting housing from Nathan Habib (D) on a month-to-month basis. Shortly after moving in, Edwards (P) made a handful of complaints regarding the safety and sanitariness of the property. A government inspection was initiated and more than forty housing code violations were discovered, all of which Habib (D) was ordered to fix. Habib (D) did fix the violations, but at the same time he also gave Edwards (P) a notice of eviction. In a lawsuit that followed, Edwards (P) claimed that she was being evicted by Habib (D) because she reported the violations. At a trial, however, Edwards (P) was not permitted to present evidence of retaliation and a directed verdict was entered on behalf of Habib (D). Appeals were thereafter made and, eventually, the case reached the United States Court of Appeals for the District of Columbia Circuit.

Issue: May a landlord evict a tenant in retaliation for the tenant reporting housing code violations to the proper authorities?

Decision and Rationale: (Wright, J.) No. Edwards (P) challenges the constitutionality of using the D.C. Code to aid a landlord in evicting a tenant because the tenant reported housing code violations to the government. We need not decide the constitutionality of such a procedure, however, because we are confident that Congress did not intend such a use. 45 D.C. Code § 910 provides: "Whenever . . . any tenancy shall be terminated by notice as aforesaid, and the tenant shall fail or refuse to surrender possession of the leased premises, . . . the landlord may bring an action to recover possession before the District of Columbia Court of General Sessions." This is a procedural provision. It neither says nor implies anything about whether evidence of retaliation or other improper motive should be available or unavailable as a defense to a possessory action. It is true that in making a case for possession the landlord need only show that his tenant has been given the statutory notice, and he does not have to give a reason for evicting a tenant who does not occupy the premises under a lease. But while the landlord may evict for any legal reason, or for no reason at all, he cannot evict in retaliation for a reporting of housing code violations. As a matter of statutory construction and for reasons of public policy, such an eviction cannot be permitted. The housing and statutory codes indicate a strong congressional desire to provide citizens with decent, or at least safe and sanitary, places to live. Effective enforcement of the codes depends in part on private initiative in reporting violations. To permit retaliatory evictions, then, would clearly frustrate the effectiveness of the housing code as a means of upgrading the quality of housing in Washington. Furthermore, in light of the appalling conditions and shortage of housing in Washington, the expense of moving, the inequality of bargaining power between tenant and landlord, and the social and economic importance of assuring at least minimum standards in housing conditions, we cannot tolerate retaliatory evictions. Clearly a tenant such as Edwards (P), even though her home is marred by housing code violations, will pause before she complains if she fears eviction as a consequence. Hence an eviction under the circumstances of this case would not only punish Edwards (P) for making a complaint which she had a right to make, but would also stand as a warning to others that they dare not be so bold. All of this being said, we do not hold that if the tenant can prove a retaliatory purpose she is entitled to remain in possession in perpetuity. If the illegal purpose is dissipated, the landlord can, in the absence of legislation or a binding contract, evict his tenants or raise their rents for economic or other legitimate reasons, or even for no reason at all. Reversed.

Analysis:

The present case deals with the issue of eviction in general and retaliatory eviction in particular. In short, eviction is the process of physically dispossessing a tenant of property. The landlord's ability to evict a tenant depends, in part, on the nature of the lease. For example, a tenancy at will can be terminated at the will of either party without reason or justification. So too can a periodic tenancy such as a month-to-month tenancy be terminated without justification. In such a case, the landlord can evict by simply giving the tenant notice that the lease agreement is no longer in effect and the tenant must vacate the premises within a specified period of time. Things are slightly more complicated when a tenancy is for a longer period of time. If, for example, a tenant signs a year lease, the landlord generally cannot evict without reason after just a month. Instead, the landlord would need a valid reason to evict the tenant. The most valid reason would be that the tenant is not living up to or is defaulting on certain important covenants, such as the covenant to pay rent. In such a case, the law would permit the landlord to seek to have the lease terminated or the tenant evicted. When a written lease agreement is signed, it will generally set forth the procedures for and times when a landlord can seek to have the tenant evicted. Evictions are not always appropriate, and in some cases a tenant can get damages for wrongful eviction. For example, if the landlord, without any valid reason, decides to evict a tenant and has the tenant and his or her belongings physically removed from the premises, the tenant will be permitted to seek damages. Similarly, under the theory of constructive eviction, if a leased premises becomes uninhabitable, the tenant can claim eviction and get damages from the landlord. Another type of wrongful eviction, addressed directly in the present case, is the retaliatory eviction. Prior to the decision in the present case, the general rule of law was that in the type of month-to-month tenancy at issue here, the landlord could, without explanation, end the tenancy and evict the tenant. The tenant really had no defense to the eviction and simply had to follow the wishes of the landlord. In the present case, however, the Court entered into new territory and created a prohibition against retaliatory evictions under which an eviction made in retaliation for the tenant's doing something that the landlord does not approve of will be held to be invalid. The decision is based almost solely on public policy grounds—grounds that make a great deal of sense. The Court is absolutely correct that if Habib (D) were permitted to do what he was trying to do—evict Edwards (P) because she reported housing code violations—many such violations would go unreported because tenants would be afraid to report them for fear that homelessness might be the result. This would be particularly true of poor tenants who could not afford to move at the drop of a hat. Furthermore, the resultant lack of reporting would result in even more rundown housing as the government would never be made aware of the housing code violations. In short, the public policy grounds on which the *Edwards* decision is based are very sound. Since the decision in the present case, a number of courts and legislatures around the country have adopted the reasoning and principle of this decision; additionally, many have used the same reasoning to enact prohibitions against retaliatory rent increases. In that regard, the *Edwards* decision can be considered a real pioneer in the area of landlord-tenant law.

United States National Bank of Oregon v. Homeland, Inc.

(Not Stated) v. (Abandoning Tenant)
(1981) 291 Or. 374, 631 P.2d 761

M E M O R Y   G R A P H I C

Instant Facts

A commercial landlord filed suit against a tenant when the tenant prematurely abandoned the leased premises and stopped paying rent.

Black Letter Rule

When a tenant abandons a leased premises prior to the expiration of the lease, the landlord has a duty to mitigate damages by attempting to relet the premises prior to the end of the abandoning tenant's term so as to minimize losses attributable to the abandoning tenant's actions.

Case Vocabulary

ABANDONING TENANT: A tenant who physically abandons the leasehold prior to the expiration of the lease.
RECEIVER: A neutral party appointed to assist in the protection or collection of property that is the subject of claims put forth by two or more adverse parties.

Procedural Basis: Appeal to the Oregon Supreme Court of a lower court decision limiting a landlord's ability to seek damages against a tenant who prematurely abandoned the leased premises.

Facts: In April of 1971, Ralph and Bernice Schlesinger leased space in an office building in downtown Portland to Homeland for a five-year term running from April 1, 1971, to March 31, 1976. Homeland's rent was $1,175 per month for the first six months, $1,275 per month for the second six months, and $1,415 per month for the remainder of the lease. In July of 1973, with 32 months remaining on the lease, Homeland abandoned the premises. Shortly thereafter a receiver was appointed for Homeland. It took some time, but in February of 1974 the Schlesingers, after months of trying, were finally able to relet the premises to Sebastian's International. The lease to Sebastian's was on the same terms as other tenants in the building and at a rental rate competitive with similar office space available in Portland–$1,500 per month. The lease to Sebastian's began on February 1, 1974, and was to end on January 31, 1977, ten months after the scheduled end of the Homeland lease. In July of 1974, Sebastian's too vacated the premises. Following these events, the Schlesingers filed suit against Homeland's receiver (D) for unpaid rent. It sought rent for the 32 months that Homeland did not stay in the lease. At trial, Homeland's receiver sought to have the Schlesingers' claim limited to a period between Homeland's abandonment and the beginning of the Sebastian's lease. The trial court agreed and so limited the claim. The Court of Appeals affirmed and the matter was appealed to the Oregon Supreme Court.

Issue: When a tenant abandons the leased premises prior to the expiration of the lease, does the landlord have a duty to mitigate damages by attempting to relet the premises within a reasonable period of time, and, if the landlord does so, does that affect the amount of damages the landlord can seek from the abandoning tenant?

Decision and Rationale: (Peterson, J.) Yes and yes. The resolution of this case turns, in part, on the rules of law enunciated in three recent Oregon cases. First, in *Wright v. Baumann*, we rejected the previously accepted view that a lessor is not required to mitigate damages when the tenant abandons the leasehold. Specifically, we stated that "whether [the landlord-tenant relationship is] regarded as arising out of contract or conveyance, a court of equity should require the [landlord] to do equity by making a reasonable effort to avoid damages." Two years later, in *Kulm v. Coast-to-Coast Stores*, we adopted the rule that in the event of an abandonment, the lessor's measure of damages is "not the full amount of the stipulated rent but an amount which represents the difference between the stipulated rent and the rent which [the landlord] would receive upon leasing the premises to others." This holding gives the landlord the benefit of the bargain on the theory that if the fair rental value was less than the agreed rent, the landlord could relet the premise at fair rental value and then be made whole by receiving the fair rental value from the new tenant plus the difference between the fair rental value and the abandoning tenant's agreed rental price from the abandoning tenant. *Kulm* also held that if, after a reasonable effort, the landlord was unable to relet the premises, the landlord would be entitled to receive the entire amount of the rent reserved for the period during which the premises could not be rented. Furthermore, the landlord is entitled to the entire amount of agreed-upon rent during the time that he or she is attempting to relet the premises. Finally, in *Foggia v. Dix*, we held that in mitigating damages, the landlord is not required to rent the premises below the fair rental value. To determine the appropriate resolution in the present case, we must address two additional issues in conjunction with the law just stated. Specifically, we must determine the effect of the landlord's reletting or attempting to relet the premises for a different term than the unexpired portion of the abandoning tenant's lease and at a higher rent. In the present case, there is no claim that the Schlesingers attempted to rent other space in the building so as to protect any claim for damages against Homeland's receiver (D). Homeland's receiver's (D) sole claim is that the Schlesingers' "attempt to relet the premises for a term and rent in excess of that provided for in the original lease" terminated any claim for damages. We do not hesitate to conclude that attempting to relet for a different term does not, of itself, bar the Schlesingers' claim for damages, for to insist that it relet only for the unexpired term of the lease might well inhibit the marketability of the premises. The Sebastian's lease was for a term slightly longer than the unexpired term of the Homeland lease. There is no evidence that the reletting or the attempts to relet which preceded the reletting prejudiced the receiver (D). We also conclude

that reletting or attempting to relet at a higher rate does not bar the Schlesingers' claim for damages. Although any increase in rent may have a theoretical effect in limiting marketability, a lessor's duty to mitigate damages does not compel the reletting at less than the then fair rental value. Additionally, in the present case, the premises was relet to Sebastian's at a rate of $1,500 per month, a mere six percent higher than Homeland's $1,415 per month rental rate. Finally, there is substantial evidence that similar premises were then renting at $1,500 per month, and that $1,500 per month was competitive. In the absence of any claim or evidence that $1,500 per month is not a fair rental value, we conclude that the increase in rent from $1,415 per month to $1,500 per month is consistent with a reasonable effort on the Schlesingers' part. Reversed and remanded.

Analysis:

In addition to terminating the lease and seeking to have the defaulting tenant evicted, a landlord can also seek damages from a tenant who, in one way or another, breaches the lease agreement. The present case addresses one aspect the process of seeking damages: the landlord's duty to mitigate damages. As this opinion makes clear, when a tenant prematurely abandons the premises and stops paying rent, the landlord has a right to seek damages from the abandoning tenant. Those damages are generally the full amount of rent that the tenant would have paid had he or she honored the lease agreement. As this case also makes clear, however, the landlord has a duty to attempt to mitigate damages. In the case of an abandoning tenant, that means the landlord must make a reasonable attempt to re-let the premises, and must do so within a reasonable period of time. This is exactly what the landlord did in this case. Instead of waiting for the lease to expire thirty-two months from the time of Homeland's abandonment, the Schlesingers advertised the space and found a new tenant within a few months. In doing so, they lived up to their obligation to mitigate damages. When a landlord does seek to mitigate damages in an abandoning tenant situation, what, then, is the landlord entitled to recoup from the abandoning tenant? As this case makes clear, the landlord is entitled to the full amount of rent that he or she would have received had the tenant honored the agreement. To determine what the abandoning tenant owes, the courts will come up with a total monetary figure that the landlord would have received had the abandoning tenant honored the agreement and subtract anything that is to be paid by the newly-found tenant. The abandoning tenant is then held to be responsible for the difference and no more. Specifically, once the premises is re-let, the landlord cannot seek monthly rent from the abandoning tenant, but only the appropriate amount of damages. As the present case further demonstrates, a landlord is not bound to find a tenant who will take the exact lease that was abandoned. He or she can lease the premises for a different period of time, whether longer or shorter, without forfeiting a right to damages. Furthermore, the fact that a landlord enters into a new lease with a different monthly rent than that imposed on the abandoning tenant similarly does not preclude a claim for damages, even if the new monthly rent is higher than the prior rent. If the landlord did have an obligation to find a tenant at the same rental price for the same duration, he or she might have a more difficult time leasing the premises, and it would be unfair to impose such a burden on the landlord when it was the abandoning tenant's breach that created the problem in the first place.

Jaber v. Miller

(Assignor) v. (Assignee)
(1951) 219 Ark. 59, 239 S.W.2d 760

M E M O R Y   G R A P H I C

Instant Facts

The assignee of a lease sought to have the courts invalidate fourteen promissory notes, executed in favor of the assignor, when the premises covered by the lease burned to the ground in a fire.

Black Letter Rule

Courts should look to the intention of the parties when determining whether an instrument is an assignment or a sublease.

Case Vocabulary

ASSIGNEE: A person to whom property rights are transferred in the course of an assignment.

ASSIGNMENT: A transfer of the right of possession of a leasehold for the entirety of the time remaining on the lease.

ASSIGNOR: A person who gives up property rights and powers in the course of an assignment.

HEAD LANDLORD: The original landlord, or the landlord in the primary landlord-tenant relationship; thus, if X leases to Y, and Y subleases to Z, X is the head landlord.

HEAD TENANT: The original tenant, or the tenant in the primary landlord-tenant relationship; thus, if X leases to Y, and Y subleases to Z, Y is the head tenant.

SUBLANDLORD (SUBLESSOR:): The secondary landlord, or the landlord in the secondary landlord-tenant relationship; thus, if X leases to Y, and Y subleases to Z, Y is the sublandlord.

SUBLEASE: A transfer of the right of possession for a time less than the full duration of the lease (even one day less).

SUBLESSEE (SUBTENANT): The secondary tenant, or the tenant in the secondary landlord-tenant relationship; thus, if X leases to Y, and Y subleases to Z, Z is the sublessee.

Procedural Basis: Appeal to the Arkansas Supreme Court of a lower court ruling finding fourteen promissory notes to be representative of monthly rent payments and therefore invalid as no more rent was to be paid on the lease.

Facts: In 1945, Jaber (D) rented a building from its owner for a five-year term which was to expire in March of 1951. The lease provided that if the building were to be destroyed by fire, the lease would terminate. In 1949, Jaber (D) transferred his lease to Norber & Son (Norber). The form of the transfer appeared to be an assignment rather than a sublease. The document of transfer was entitled "Contract and Assignment," and spoke of assigning the lease to Norber. Additionally, the transfer was for the duration of the lease period. As a part of the transfer, Norber agreed to execute five $700 promissory notes in favor of Jaber (D). Finally, under the agreement, Norber undertook the payment of the monthly rent and granted Jaber (D) the right to reenter and possess the leasehold if Norber failed to pay the rent or make good on the promissory notes. Norber later transferred its lease to Miller (P). Miller (P) was unable to pay the promissory notes as per the original plan, so he and Jaber (D) agreed that payments would be made each month in the amount of $175, and new promissory notes to that effect were created. After the transfer to Miller (P) but prior to the expiration of the lease, the building burned to the ground. Following the burning of the building, Miller (P) filed suit seeking to have fourteen promissory notes for $175 each cancelled. In doing so, Miller (P) argued that the original transfer was a sublease instead of an assignment, and that the notes represented monthly rent and that the obligation to pay rent had terminated with the fire. Jaber (D), on the other hand, argued that the notes were given not for rent, but as deferred payments for the assignment of the lease to Norber. The chancellor ruled in favor of Miller (P) and Jaber (D) appealed.

Issue: When distinguishing between subleases and assignments, should a court take into consideration more than just the duration of the transfer?

Decision and Rationale: (Smith, J.) Yes. In most jurisdictions, the question of whether an instrument is an assignment or a sublease is determined by the English rule. Under that rule, if the instrument purports to transfer the lessee's estate for the remainder of the term, it is an assignment, and if the transfer is for less than the remainder of the term, it is a sublease. The intention of the parties had nothing to do with the matter. This arbitrary common law distinction is at variance with the usual conception of assignments and subleases. We think of an assignment as the outright transfer of all or part of an existing lease, the assignee stepping into the shoes of the assignor. A sublease, on the other hand, involves the creation of a new tenancy between the sublessor and the sublessee, so that the sublessor is both tenant and landlord. The injustice of the English rule has often been pointed out. Suppose A makes a lease to B, and B then executes to C what both intend to be a sublease, but the sublease is for the entire term. If C in good faith pays rent to B, he does so at his peril because under the English rule the contract is really an assignment, and therefore C's primary obligation is to A if the latter elects to accept C as his tenant. Consequently A can collect the rent from the subtenant even though the sublessor has already been paid. The English rule can be equally harsh upon the sublessor. Suppose that A makes a lease to B. B then makes to C what B considers a profitable sublease for twice the original rent, but B makes the mistake of attempting to sublet for the entire term instead of retaining a reversion. Under the English rule, the instrument is an assignment, and if the original landlord acquires the subtenant's rights there is a merger which prevents B from being able to collect the increased rent. That has been the situation in a handful of cases. While a majority of American courts have adopted the English rule, a minority have made attempts to soften the harshness of the rule. In several jurisdictions the courts look solely to the intention of the parties to determine whether a transfer is a sublease or an assignment. In other jurisdictions, the courts have gone as far as possible to find something that might be said to constitute a reversion in what the parties intended to be a sublease. In some states, notably Massachusetts, it has been held that if the sublessor reserves a right of re-entry for nonpayment of rent, this is a sufficient reversionary estate to make the instrument a sublease. Miller (P) urges us to follow the Massachusetts rule and hold that since Jaber (D) reserved the right of re-entry, his transfer to Norber & Son was a sublease. We cannot do so. The Massachusetts rule was adopted to carry out the intention of the parties who thought they were making a sublease rather than an assignment. The instrument at issue is in the form of an assignment, and it would be an obvious perversion of the rule to apply it as a means of defeating the parties' original intention. In Arkansas, the distinction between a sublease and an assignment has been considered in only one case, and in that case the litigants were in agreement that the traditional English view was the appropriate law. No precedent other than this being set, we do not feel compelled to adhere to an unjust rule which was logical only in the days of feudalism. The execution of leases is a practical matter that occurs a hundred times a day without legal assistance. The layman appreciates the common sense distinction between a sublease and an assignment, but would never even suspect the existence of the common law distinction. Furthermore, the English rule is not a rule of property in the sense that titles or property rights depend on its continued existence. A lawyer trained in common law technicalities can prepare either instrument without fear that it will be construed to be the other, but for the less skilled lawyer or the layman, the common law rule is a trap that leads to hardship and injustice by refusing to permit the parties to accomplish the result they seek. For these reasons we adopt the rule that the intention of the parties is to govern in determining whether an instrument is an assignment or a sublease. The duration of the primary term, as compared to the length of the sublease, may be a factor in arriving at the parties' intention, but it should not be the sole consideration. In the present case, it cannot be doubted that the parties intended an assignment. The document is so entitled, and all its language is that of an assignment. The consideration is stated to be in payment for the lease and not in satisfaction of a tenant's debt to the landlord. Finally, the deferred payments are evidenced by promissory notes, which are not ordinarily given by one making a lease. For these reasons, the lower court's decision is reversed.

Analysis:

The present case, *Jaber v. Miller*, introduces the two types of transfers applicable to leasehold estates: subleases and assignments. It is important for any student of property law to understand the difference between these two types of transfers because the legal rights and responsibilities that go with each are vastly different. Under the majority view, which is rejected by the *Jaber* court, one must look to the duration of a transfer to determine whether it is a sublease or an assignment. To the majority of courts, a transfer of the right of possession of a leasehold for the entirety of time remaining on the lease is an assignment. A similar transfer of the right of possession for a time less than the full duration of the lease (even one day less) is a sublease. In the view of most courts and commentators, and under the terms of the traditional English rule, the intent of the parties with respect to the nature of the transfer is irrelevant. This being the case, *Jaber* clearly represents the minority view and its holding should therefore not be accepted as the law in all jurisdictions. As stated above, the legal rights and responsibilities applicable in subleases and assignments have some significant differences. The major difference between the two transfers has to do with the transferee's rent obligation. Under the majority view, a subtenant is not liable to the head landlord for rent. This is because the subtenant, having less than the full tenancy, has no privity of estate or privity of contract with the head landlord. This does not mean that the subtenant has no duty to pay rent, however, because she does have a landlord-tenant relationship with the head tenant and therefore must pay rent to that person (who, in turn, will pay it to the head landlord, thus fulfilling his still-existent obligation); she just has no obligation to the head landlord. The same lack of liability enjoyed by the subtenant to the head landlord with respect to the issue of rent applies to other covenants undertaken by the head tenant in the original lease as well. The rules are different for assignments. In the case of an assignment, the subtenant shares privity of estate with the head landlord, and is therefore liable to the head landlord for rent just as the head tenant is. Thus, there is co-responsibility for rent. (The head tenant can only be relieved of liability for rent if the head landlord excuses his responsibility; additionally, the only way for an assignee to be relieved of liability is to fully reassign his interest in the leasehold to another assignee and thereby end his privity of estate with the head landlord.) Finally, it should be noted that while the Arkansas Supreme Court changed the test for distinguishing between subleases and assignment, because the transfer in this case was for the duration of the leasehold, it would have been held to be an assignment under the traditional English rule.

Childs v. Warner Brothers Southern Theatres

(Landlord) v. (Assignee)
(1931) 200 N.C. 333, 156 S.E. 923

M E M O R Y   G R A P H I C

Instant Facts

The owner of a movie theater filed suit against a tenant when tenant's assignee stopped paying rent.

Black Letter Rule

When a lease contains a clause that prohibits assignment of the lease without the permission of the lessor, the lessor's consent to one assignment does not waive the need to obtain lessor permission for any subsequent assignments, and does not waive the lessor's ability to object to a proposed second assignment.

Case Vocabulary

HABENDUM CLAUSE: A clause in a lease that sets forth any conditions or restrictions upon the lessor's use of the premises.

MULTIPLE COVENANT: A covenant in a lease that operates upon both the lessee and the lessee's heirs and assigns.

SINGLE COVENANT: A covenant in a lease that operates only upon the lessee and does not extend to the lessee's assigns and heirs.

UNDERLET: To sublease.

Procedural Basis: Appeal to the North Carolina Supreme Court of a trial court's decision holding the assignee of a lease liable for rent.

Facts: Sometime between 1923 and 1925, R.A. Childs (P) became the owner of a piece of land on Main Street in Columbia, North Carolina. At the time, the property was being leased to R.D. Craver who, in 1925, with Childs' (P) consent, assigned the lease to Warner Brothers Southern Theatres, Inc. (Warner Brothers) (D). The pertinent portion of the original lease agreement stated: "[I]t is agreed that the said R.D. Craver shall not convey this lease or underlet the premises without the written consent of the lessors." In 1926, the lease again changed hands when Warner Brothers (D) reassigned the lease to Carolina Theatres, Inc. At the time of the reassignment, Childs (P) informed Warner Brothers (D) that "I shall continue to recognize you as the lessee of the property . . . and expect you to see that the [rent] payments are made promptly in accordance with the lease." Shortly thereafter Carolina Theatres stopped paying rent for the property and Childs (P) filed suit against Warner Brothers (D). Childs (P) won at the trial level and Warner Brothers (D) appealed.

Issue: If a lease provides that the lessee cannot assign or sublease the premises without the lessor's consent, and the lessor does consent to an assignment, can the assignee subsequently make a valid reassignment without the lessor's consent?

Decision and Rationale: (Brogden, J.) No. In 1603, the English courts decided *Dumpor's Case*, in which it was held that once a lessor gives his assent to an assignment, such assent is deemed to be a waiver of any provision prohibiting assignment without the lessor's consent, and the lessor's control over his property is gone. This rule was thereafter followed in England and by some early American courts. Later, however, some American courts began to avoid application of the rule by making a distinction between single multiple covenants, holding that the rule did not apply to multiple covenants. Without entering into any discussion of the distinctions between single and multiple covenants, it is sufficient to say that a reasonable construction of the lease in the present case leads to the conclusion that the restriction against assignment and subletting operated upon both the original lessee and his heirs and assigns, including Warner Brothers (D). In the present case, the clause at issue expressly included the lessee and his assigns. Moreover, Warner Brothers (D) and his assigns agreed to pay rent, and, upon failure to do so, Childs (P) expressly reserved the right of re-entry. The covenant to pay rent is continuous in its nature, and is binding by express provision upon the lessee's assigns. Furthermore, all persons occupying the premises under the assignment from the original lessee were charged with notice of the conditions imposed by the lease. Therefore, we hold that by consenting to one assignment, the Childs (P) did not waive the conditions of the lease and did not consent that thereafter any subsequent assignee could turn his property over to any undesirable or irresponsible person without his approval. Affirmed.

Analysis:

In the present case, the North Carolina Supreme Court rejects the Rule in *Dumpor's Case*, which, again, holds that once a lessor who has the power to reject assignments consents to an assignment of the tenant's leasehold, he or she thereafter has no ability to reject any further assignments of the lease. Despite the ruling in the present case, however, the Rule in *Dumpor's Case* is still the law in a number of jurisdictions. This is not to say, however, that courts have not attempted to change the rule, which is often said to be illogical and unsupported by reason. A handful of courts have held that the Rule applies only to assignments, and not to subleases, and have therefore limited its application to only one kind of transfer of a leasehold. Additionally, some courts have held that if, in giving consent to an assignment, the lessor makes it clear that there is no waiver of the future right to reject assignments, the Rule does not apply. Finally, some other courts have held that if the original lease agreement states that the giving of consent to one assignment does not waive the lessor's right to require consent to future assignments, the Rule does not apply. In short, it is clear that the Rule in *Dumpor's Case*, while still arguably on the books, is an unpopular rule that appears to be on its way out.

21 Merchants Row Corp. v. Merchants Row, Inc.

(Commercial Tenant) v. (Commercial Landlord)

(1992) 412 Mass. 204, 587 N.E.2d 788

M E M O R Y   G R A P H I C

Instant Facts

A commercial tenant filed a lawsuit when its landlord refused to consent to an assignment of the lease, and thereby prevented the tenant from completing the sale of its business.

Black Letter Rule

A clause in a commercial lease which requires the tenant to obtain the landlord's permission before assigning or otherwise transferring the lease does not imply, as a mater of law, an obligation on the part of the landlord to act reasonably in withholding consent.

Procedural Basis: Appeal to the Supreme Judicial Court of Massachusetts of a lower court decision granting damages to a tenant who, because of the landlord's unwillingness to agree, was unable to assign its interest in a lease.

Facts: In 1974, 21 Merchants Row Corp. (21 Merchants) (P) entered into a lease agreement with Merchants Row, Inc.'s (Row) (D) predecessor it title. The lease agreement provided that 21 Merchants (P) could not assign or sublease the premises without the express written permission of the landlord. In 1983, Row (D) acquired the premises subject to the lease. Four years later, in 1987, 21 Merchants (P) entered into an agreement for the sale of its business, which sale was contingent upon Row (D) consenting to an assignment of the lease. 21 Merchants (P) sought Row's (D) consent and got it with the limitation that Row (D) had the ability to reject any future assignments or proposed assignments. When 21 Merchants (P) later asked Row (D) to consent to an assignment of the lease to the purchaser's bank with the caveat that there would be no restrictions on the bank's ability to transfer or assign the lease, Row (D) refused. A lawsuit followed. At trial, 21 Merchants (P) presented the theory that Row (D) wrongfully and unreasonably refused to consent to the assignment of the lease, and 21 Merchants (P) thereby suffered. The jury ruled in favor of 21 Merchants (P) and awarded it $3,300,000.00 in damages. Row (D) appealed.

Issue: Does a clause in a commercial lease which requires the tenant to obtain the landlord's permission before assigning or otherwise transferring the lease imply, as a mater of law, an obligation on the landlord's part to act reasonably in withholding consent?

Decision and Rationale: (Lynch, J.) No. In *Slavin v. Rent Control Bd. of Brookline*, we held that, with respect to residential leases, "a lease provision requiring the landlord's consent to an assignment or sublease permits the landlord to refuse arbitrarily or unreasonably." We see no reason to depart from this rule and grant commercial tenants greater protection than is given to residential tenants, particularly when, if we were to differentiate between residential and commercial leases, we would do so in favor of residential tenants. Reversed.

Analysis:

The holding in the present case—that a landlord whose consent must be obtained to make an assignment or sublease can arbitrarily and unreasonably withhold consent to a proposed transfer—is the majority view among American jurisdictions. It is a holding, however, that has been under attack for some time by both the courts and the legislatures of some states. Opponents of the rule argue that it too strongly goes against the general prohibition of restraints on the alienation of property, and for that reason should be abolished. Because courts and legislatures in some states are attempting to lessen the harshness of the rule, many landlords have begun to include clearly worded consent clauses into their lease agreements which expressly grant the landlord the right to arbitrarily withhold consent as to assignments or subleases of the premises. Tenants, of course, often seek clauses which require a withholding of consent to be reasonable. When a tenant makes a transfer of his or her interest in a leasehold without the required consent, the transfer will nevertheless be valid unless the landlord has granted to himself the power to terminate a lease if an assignment or sublease is made without consent. If no such reservation of power has been made, the landlord must simply settle for a suit for damages, whatever they may be, and the transfer remains in effect.

Chapter 18

You've learned a lot so far about how people own their property. In this chapter, you will learn about how people may own rights in other people's property. For example, they might have the right to drive over their neighbor's lot to get to a road or they might have the right to take water from a stream on their neighbor's property. A less tangible right is the right of owners in a subdivision to require their neighbors to use their property for residential purposes only. Landowners may also have the right to prevent their neighbors from removing the lateral support from under their land. The examples in this chapter range in scope from a dispute over whether a neighbor can build a house that will block sunlight on a homeowner's solar panels to whether the city of Los Angeles can continue to take water from Mono Lake, thereby depriving it of its natural resources.

This chapter discusses the ways these rights are created, how they are administered once they are created, and how they may be terminated. Like in property law generally, you'll see a trend in these cases in which courts reject common law rules for a more flexible rule of reason.

Also included in this chapter is a discussion of nuisance law. In essence, nuisance law may be seen as an ownership interest that one landowner has to prevent noxious activities on nearby property.

It's helpful when reading these cases to make a diagram of the facts. For example, draw a picture of the lots in *S.S. Kresge Co. v. Winkelman Realty Co.* and in *Lindsey v. Clark*. The diagrams will help you visualize what the landowners are doing on each other's property.

Chapter 18

NOTE: THE PURPOSE OF THIS OUTLINE IS TO ORGANIZE THE CASES SO THAT ONE CAN QUICKLY UNDERSTAND THE RELEVANCE OF EACH CASE TO THE COURSE. NO ATTEMPT IS MADE IN THIS OVERVIEW TO ADDRESS EVERY CONCEPT THAT MUST BE STUDIED. BE SURE TO READ THE ENTIRE CASEBOOK AND/OR OTHER MATERIALS TO GAIN A FULL UNDERSTANDING OF ALL CONCEPTS.

I. Interests Created by Volition, Implication and Prescription
  A. Easements, Profits a Prendre and Licenses
    1. Definitions
      a. Easement: An interest in real property which gives the holder the right to use another's land for a specific purpose.
      b. Easement Appurtenant: An easement which benefits a specific parcel of land, regardless of the owner's identity.
      c. Easement in Gross: An easement that benefits the holder without regard to whether the holder owns an adjoining or nearby parcel; it does not belong to any particular parcel of land.
      d. Profits a Prendre: An easement that confers the right to enter someone else's land and remove timber, minerals, oil, gas, game or other substances.
      e. License: A right to use land that is subject to termination at the will of the possessor of the land.
    2. Express Creation
      a. Specific words of inheritance or words of art are not necessary to create a valid appurtenant easement, even of unlimited duration. *Mitchell v. Castellaw.*
      b. Contrary to the common law rule, a grantor may reserve an interest in property for a third party. *Willard v. First Church of Christ, Scientist, Pacifica.*
      c. The words "right-of-way" in a deed do not necessarily mean that the grantor granted an easement rather than a fee simple; the grantor's intent must be determined from the deed as a whole. *Urbaitis v. Commonwealth Edison.*
      d. Language that gives "an exclusive right and privilege" to use land conveys an easement rather than a lease or a license. *Baseball Publishing Co. v. Bruton.*
      e. An easement may be created by estoppel when the grantee expended substantial money in reliance on the fact that the grant would be continuous. *Stoner v. Zucker.*
        (1) An agreement may be taken out of the statute of frauds when one party partially performs his or her part of the agreement, if the equities of the situation so require. The contract will be enforced if the party seeking enforcement acted in reliance on the oral contract, suffered a substantial detriment for which there is no other remedy, and the other party would reap an unearned benefit if the statute of frauds were applied. *Restatement (Third) of Property.*
      f. A ticket creates a revocable license, not an easement or other property right. *Marrone v. Washington Jockey Club.*
    3. Implied Creation
      a. Easement of Necessity:
        (1) Where an owner of land conveys a parcel which has no outlet to a highway except over the grantor's property or over a third party's property, an easement by necessity is created over the grantor's property. *Finn v. Williams.*
        (2) The right may be asserted by the grantor or grantee. The easement is implied over only the land with privity and it may lie dormant until the necessity arises.
      b. An easement may be created by implication if there was a prior existing use that

was apparent and continuous and if there was unity of ownership. *Granite Properties Limited Partnership v. Manns*.

4. Creation by Prescription

   a. To establish a prescriptive easement, a claimant must show an open and notorious use of the defendant's land adverse to the defendant's rights, for a continuous and uninterrupted period. *Beebe v. DeMarco*.

     (1) Many courts disagree about whether presumptions should be used to determine whether the use of the easement is adverse.

     (2) Some courts require the neighbor to acquiesce to the adverse use.

   b. The public may acquire an easement over private land by custom. *State Ex. Rel. Thornton v. Hay*. For there to be a custom:

     (1) The use must be ancient.

     (2) The right must be exercised without interruption.

     (3) The use must be peaceable and free from dispute.

     (4) The use must be reasonable.

     (5) The use must be limited by visible boundaries and to specific uses.

     (6) The use must be obligatory, i.e., not left to each landowner to decide the public's rights.

     (7) The custom must not be repugnant or inconsistent with other customs or laws.

5. Scope and Transferability

   a. An easement may be used only in connection with the estate to which it is appurtenant. *S.S. Kresge Co. v. Winkelman Realty Co.*

   b. Easements in gross are assignable and divisible. *Miller v. Lutheran Conference & Camp Association*.

   c. If the location of an easement is specified in a deed, the easement may not be relocated, even if the relocation is rea-

sonable. *Sakansky v. Wein*.

     (1) Parties may create a "floating easement" for an express purpose, that burdens a whole estate until the parties determine where it will be located.

   d. The scope of an easement by prescription is based on how it was originally used.

6. Termination

   a. Abandonment of an easement requires intent, whether express or implied, but mere non-use is not enough. *Lindsey v. Clark*. There must be acts or circumstances clearly showing the intent to abandon.

   b. Prescription: There must be adverse use by the owner of the servient estate that is acquiesced in by the owner of the dominant estate for a period sufficient to create a prescriptive right.

   c. The easement may terminate under its own terms. For example, it may have been created for only a limited time. If no time period is stated, easements are presumed to last forever.

   d. Easements may be terminated by merger. This occurs when the dominant estate and the servient estate are owned by the same owner.

B. Covenants and Equitable Servitudes

1. Traditional Elements of Covenants

   a. A covenant runs with the land if the parties so intended, there is vertical privity, and the covenant "touches and concerns" the land; the original covenantors' liability ends when they convey the burdened property. *Gallagher v. Bell*.

   b. A property owners association has privity of estate with a property owner for the purpose of a covenant running with the land. *Neponsit Property Owners' Ass'n v. Emigrant Industrial Sav. Bank*.

2. Equitable Servitudes

   a. A covenant is enforceable in equity as an equitable servitude against a person who purchases land with notice of it. *Tulk v. Moxhay.*

b. A restrictive covenant does not run with the land if the covenantee does not own any land which the covenant may benefit. *London City Council v. Allen.*

c. An equitable servitude is not reciprocal when a subdivider includes a restriction in most deeds in a subdivision but forgets to include it in one deed, if the buyer without the restriction had no actual or constructive notice of it. *Sprague v. Kimball.*

d. An equitable servitude can be implied, even if it is not created by a written instrument, where there is a scheme for development of a residential subdivision and the purchaser of the lot has notice of it. *Sanborn v. McLean.*

e. If lots are part of a common scheme, restrictions in some deeds are enforceable against owners of other lots as well; they are considered implied reciprocal negative easements or servitudes. *Snow v. Van Dam.*

f. The Restatement (Third) of Property allows third-party beneficiary covenants that benefit a parcel that was not part of the original scheme at the time the covenant was entered into.

3. The Restatement (Third) of Property combines covenants, equitable servitudes and reciprocal negative easements into a single category of covenants.

4. Constitutional and Public Policy Limitations

a. Judicial enforcement of a restrictive covenant constitutes state action for purposes of the Fourteenth Amendment. *Shelley v. Kraemer.*

b. A restrictive covenant may not be imposed against persons who acquired property in reliance on the nonexistence of the covenant and who would suffer prejudice if the covenant were enforced. *McMillan v. Iserman.*

5. Construction, Administration and Termination

a. Some courts hold that restrictions in a deed should not be strictly construed; they look at the parties' intent and the surrounding circumstances to interpret the restrictions more broadly. *Joslin v. Pine River Development Corp.*

b. Other courts hold that nothing will be deemed a violation of a restriction that is not in plain disregard of its express words. *Jones v. Park Land for Convalescents, Inc.*

c. In order for a covenant to run with the land, it must be mutual and not capable of being altered without the consent of adjacent owners. *Suttle v. Bailey.*

d. A restrictive covenant that requires building plans to be approved by a homeowners association is enforceable, but the association must act reasonably and in good faith. *Rhue v. Cheyenne Homes, Inc.*

e. A restrictive covenant will become unenforceable only if changed conditions affect the entire subdivision that is subject to the covenant. *Cowling v. Colligan.*

f. A restrictive covenant may estop a neighboring landowner from suing for damages. *Waldrop v. Town of Brevard.*

II. Non-Volitional Interests

A. Nuisance

1. A private nuisance is an unreasonable interference with the use and enjoyment of land. *Rose v. Chaikin.*

2. Courts can grant an injunction conditioned on the payment of permanent damages to a complaining party in order to compensate him for the impairment of property rights caused by a nuisance. *Boomer v. Atlantic Cement Co.*

3. If a party comes to a nuisance, it may sue to abate the nuisance but be liable for the

damages to do so. *Spur Industries, Inc. v. Del E. Webb Development Co.*

4. Nuisance law has declined as a result of the increase in zoning laws.

B. Support of Land

1. Under theories of strict liability and negligence, adjoining landowners have a duty to provide lateral support to each other's land. *Noone v. Price.*

   a. Strict liability for removal of lateral support is limited to land that would subside while in its natural state.

2. If the land subsides from removal of lateral support because of the additional weight of a building, the adjacent landowner is only liable in cases of negligence.

   a. Adjacent lateral support may be removed provided that artificial support, such as a retaining wall, is provided to replace such support.

   b. The duty to maintain the artificial support becomes a covenant that runs with the land.

C. Drainage. Courts apply three different rules (*Armstrong v. Francis Corp.*):

1. Common Enemy Rule: A landowner has the unrestricted right to rid his lands of surface waters, without liability for harm it may cause others.

2. Civil Law Rule: A landowner who interferes with the natural flow of surface waters so as to cause an invasion of a neighbor's interests in the use and enjoyment of his land is subject to liability to the other.

3. Reasonable Use Rule: A landowner is legally privileged to make alterations to the natural flow of surface water until there is an unreasonable interference with a neighbor's use of his land. Courts look at the following factors:

   a. The utility of the possessor's use of his land.

   b. The degree of harm that results.

   c. The forseeablility of harm that results.

   d. The feasibility of alternatives.

D. Rights to Water

1. Water in Watercourses

   a. A riparian landowner may use all the water in a stream to satisfy natural needs for water, such as thirst. But for artificial needs for water, such as manufacturing and irrigation, it is up to a jury to decide on a case-by-case basis how the water should be divided. *Evans v. Merriweather.*

   b. In Colorado and other western states, the first appropriator of water from a natural stream for a beneficial purpose has a prior right to the water to the extent of the appropriation. *Coffin v. Left Hand Ditch Co.*

2. Groundwater

   a. Under the rule of "capture," landowners may pump as much groundwater as they want without liability to neighbors who claim that the pumping depleted their wells. *Sipriano v. Great Spring Waters of America, Inc.*

   b. In the western states, where the ground is more arid, courts usually apply the reasonable use doctrine or an appropriation rule.

   c. California applies a "correlative rights" rule. Under this rule, landowners may use only their reasonable share when water is insufficient to meet everyone's needs. Any water not needed for beneficial use is surplus water that may be appropriated for non-riparian land. As between the appropriators, the one first in time is the first in right. *City of Barstow v. Mojave Water Agency.*

3. The Public Trust

   a. Under the public trust doctrine, private rights to water may be subject to the public's rights of navigation, commerce, fishing, and preservation; the state has a duty to take the public trust into account when it allocates water resources. *National Audubon Society v. Sup. Ct.*

E. Oil and Natural Gas
1. Under the fair share doctrine, landowners have the right to a reasonable opportunity to produce their fair share of oil in a pool. *Wronski v. Sun Oil Company.*
2. Under the rule of capture, a landowner may pump oil that migrated from adjoining lands without liability.

F. Airspace, Air, Sunlight
1. Under the common law, *cujus est solum, ejus est usque ad coelum et ad inferos*: "to whomsoever the soil belongs, he owns also to the sky and to the depths."
2. The modern rule is that flights over private land are a taking under the Fifth Amendment if they are so low and frequent as to directly and immediately interfere with the enjoyment and use of the land. *United States v. Causby.*

3. The private nuisance doctrine applies to determine whether a landowner has a right to protect his access to sunlight. *Prah v. Maretti.*
a. Under the common law doctrine of "ancient lights," if a landowner had received sunlight for a specified period of time, the landowner acquired a negative prescriptive easement to receive sunlight. American courts have rejected this doctrine based on the needs of development.

Mitchell v. Castellaw

(Landowner) v. (Owner of Adjoining Land)
151 Tex. 56, 246 S.W.2d 163 (1952)

M E M O R Y   G R A P H I C

Instant Facts

A landowner sued an adjacent landowner to establish an easement for a driveway.

Black Letter Rule

Specific words of inheritance or words of art are not necessary to create a valid appurtenant easement, even of unlimited duration.

Case Vocabulary

EASEMENT: An interest in real property which gives the holder the right to use another's land for a specific purpose.
EASEMENT APPURTENANT: An easement which benefits a specific parcel of land, regardless of the owner's identity.
EASEMENT IN GROSS: An easement that benefits the holder without regard to whether the holder owns an adjoining or nearby parcel; it does not belong to any particular parcel of land.
SERVITUDE: An easement.

Procedural Basis: Appeal of quiet title action establishing easement.

Facts: Mrs. Stapp owned three adjacent lots. She leased one for use as a filling station. [An easement for a wash rack next to the filling station is not at issue in the excerpt in your casebook.] She sold another lot to Smith. That lot had a driveway connecting the filling station to the street. The deed to Smith provided that "It is expressly agreed and understood that grantors, their heirs or assigns, shall not build or permit any one else to construct any type of building or anything else on the portion of lot described as follows; and that grantor shall have the right to use this part of said lot as a driveway." That was the only reference in the deed to the driveway. When Mrs. Stapp died, her daughter, Mrs. Castellaw (P) became owner of the filling station property and renewed the lease. Smith conveyed his lot to Mitchell (D) and Powers (D). The deed contained the same clause reserving the driveway, but corrected the first reference to "grantors" to "grantees." Castellaw (P) filed a quiet title action to determine whether she owned an easement for a driveway over Mitchell (D) and Powers' (D) lot. The lower courts held in Castellaw's (P) favor. Mitchell (D) and Powers (D) appealed to the Texas Supreme Court.

Issue: Are specific words of art necessary to create a valid appurtenant easement of unlimited duration?

Decision and Rationale: (Garwood, J.) No. There is no question that an easement may be validly reserved in a deed of fee simple title. However, Mitchell (D) and Powers (D) argue that there is no easement because (1) the easement was Mrs. Stapp's personal right and did not pass to Castellaw (P) and (2) the provision is "repugnant" [not disgusting, but so conflicting with the rest of the deed that Mrs. Stapp could not have intended it] to the grant of the whole lot and should be ignored. With respect to the "repugnant" argument, if the clause in the deed actually granting the lot had provided that it was subject to the reservation, there would have been no question that the reservation was intended. Here, though, an ordinary reader would understand what Stapp meant. The reservation is specific and is consistent with the prior usage. We also disagree that the easement was personal to Mrs. Stapp, i.e., an easement in gross, despite the fact that the words "reserve" or "and her heirs" were not used. Even Smith used the driveway into the filling station when Stapp sold the lot to him. Neither words of inheritance nor words of art are necessary to create a valid appurtenant easement even of unlimited duration. Affirmed.

Analysis:

Here the court looked at the surrounding facts and circumstances to determine whether Mrs. Stapp intended to reserve a permanent easement over the lot next to the filling station. The clause at issue prohibited the grantees, their heirs or assigns from building on the driveway, but it only referred to the grantees, and not their heirs and assigns when it stated that the grantor had the right to use the driveway. Rather than basing its decision on a technicality in the language used in the deed, the court held that Mrs. Stapp did intend to reserve the easement as a driveway forever. In fact, even if the deed from Smith to Mitchell (D) and Powers (D) did not mention the driveway at all, the law is that appurtenant easements pass by grant without specific mention. In addition, when it is not clear whether an easement is appurtenant (attached to a specific lot) or in gross (personal to its holder), courts tend to hold that an easement is not in gross if it can fairly be construed to be appurtenant.

Willard v. First Church of Christ, Scientist, Pacifica

(Property Owner) v. (Third Party)

7 Cal. 3d 473, 102 Cal. Rptr. 739, 498 P.2d 987 (1972)

M E M O R Y   G R A P H I C

Instant Facts

A purchaser of a lot sought to invalidate an easement for church parking.

Black Letter Rule

Contrary to the common law rule, a grantor may reserve an interest in property for a third party.

Case Vocabulary

CONVEYANCE BY DEED: Transferring property by a written document for the transfer of land or other real property from one person to another.

Procedural Basis: Appeal of quiet title action.

Facts: Genevieve McGuigan owned two adjacent lots, lots 19 and 20, across the street from the First Church of Christ, Scientist (Church) (D). Lot 19 contained a building and lot 20 was vacant. McGuigan let the Church (D) use lot 20 for parking. She sold lot 19 to Petersen. Willard (P) expressed an interest in buying both lot 19 and lot 20 from Petersen. Petersen delivered a deed for both lots into escrow, and then approached McGuigan with an offer to purchase lot 20 [pretty presumptuous!]. McGuigan was willing to sell lot 20, so long as the Church (D) could continue to use it for parking. The Church's (D) attorney drew up a provision for the deed, and McGuigan sold the property to Petersen, who recorded the deed. [Not surprisingly] The deed from Petersen to Willard (P) did not mention the Church's (D) parking easement. Petersen apparently told Willard (P) that the Church (D) wanted to use lot 20 for parking, but did not tell him about the easement clause in the deed from McGuigan. When Willard (P) learned about the easement clause, he sued the Church (D) in a quiet title action. The trial court held that McGuigan intended to convey an easement to the Church (D) but the clause was invalid under the common law because one cannot reserve a property interest for a third party. The Church (D) appealed.

Issue: May a grantor reserve an interest in property for a third party?

Decision and Rationale: (Peters, J.) Yes. A grantor may reserve an interest in property for a third party. The common law prohibition was based on the courts' mistrust of conveyance by deed and their desire for livery by seisin. This mistrust is out of date. Now we are concerned with trying to follow the grantor's intention. Grants are now interpreted like contracts rather than based on rigid feudal standards. To deny McGuigan her intent would be inequitable because she discounted the price she charged Petersen by about one-third for the easement. Other courts have either circumvented or abolished the common law rule. Willard (P) argues that the common law rule should be applied here because title insurers and he himself relied on it. However, he has presented no evidence that a title insurance policy was issued. In addition, he himself did not read the deed containing the reservation. The Church (D) used the lot for parking before and after Willard (P) acquired it, so he was not prejudiced by lack of use for an extended period of time. When looking at grants made prior to this decision, we must balance the equitable and policy considerations, including the grantor's intent and reliance on the old rule. Any ambiguity or conflict in the clause granting the right to park to the Church (D) is resolved in favor of the grantor's intent. Reversed.

Analysis:

Courts are about evenly split on the issue in this case. About half the courts have abolished the common law rule prohibiting reserving easements for third parties and about half still follow it. The New York Court of Appeals, in *Estate of Thomson v. Wade*, held that the common law prohibition may easily be circumvented if the grantor conveys the easement to the third party first and then conveys the property to the grantee in a separate deed. The court concluded that the common law rule protects the rights of bona fide purchasers and avoids conflicts of ownership. But the question remains that if the common law rule can be circumvented so easily, why keep it? Although this procedure avoids frustrating the grantor's intent, there is no reason to force the grantor to do in two steps what could otherwise be done in one. The common law rule appears to be nothing more than a trap for the unwary and serves only to frustrate the grantor's intent. The common law rule seems to function solely as an obstacle to conveying interests in land, but serves no purpose. This is not a function consistent with our modern preference for effecting the grantor's clear intent.

Urbaitis v. Commonwealth Edison

(Property owner) v. (Adjacent Easement Owner)
143 Ill.2d 458, 575 N.E.2d 548 (1991)

M E M O R Y   G R A P H I C

Instant Facts
Landowners filed a quiet title action to determine whether an adjacent strip of land was conveyed to a railway as an easement for the railroad's use or as a fee simple estate.

Black Letter Rule
The words "right-of-way" in a deed do not necessarily mean that the grantor granted an easement rather than a fee simple; the grantor's intent must be determined from the deed as a whole.

Procedural Basis: Appeal of quiet title action.

Facts: In 1909, Benjamin Dodson conveyed a long thin strip of land to a railway company. The land was subsequently conveyed to Commonwealth Edison (D). The deed provided that Dodson "conveys and warrants" the land to the railway. The deed also referred to the land as "said right-of-way." Railway operations on the land stopped in 1946. Urbaitis and others (P) owned residential properties next to the strip of land. They sued Commonwealth Edison (D) in a quiet title action. Urbaitis (P) claimed that the conveyance to Commonwealth Edison (D) was an easement that became theirs when the railway operations ceased. Alternatively, they claimed that when the railway operations ceased the easement reverted to Dodson's heirs, who deeded their interests to Urbaitis (P). Commonwealth Edison (D) claimed Dodson conveyed a fee simple, not an easement. The trial court and the court of appeals held that Commonwealth Edison (D) owned the parcel of land in fee simple. Urbaitis (P) appealed to the Supreme Court of Illinois.

Issue: Does the use of the word "right-of-way" in a deed mean that the deed coveys an easement rather than a fee simple?

Decision and Rationale: (Bilandic, J.) No. The use of the words "convey and warrant" in a deed indicate the grantor's intention to convey a fee simple estate. When a deed conveys only a "right" in land, it conveys an easement. Here, the Dodson deed used the words "convey and warrant" and was in the form of a warranty deed. Thus, we presume the deed granted a fee simple, unless additional language indicates a different intent. The term "right-of-way" was not used in the deed to limit or define the estate granted. Rather, it was used as a shorthand reference to the land itself. It is important to note that the term is not used in the granting clause of the deed. While other cases have held that deeds using the term "right-of-way" negate the possibility that a fee simple estate was granted, there is no per se rule. In those cases, more than a mere reference to a "right-of-way" was required. In those cases, the grant itself was of a right-of-way. We must give effect to the intentions of the parties based on the deed as a whole. Affirmed.

Analysis:

This case makes sense in that the court looks to the deed as a whole to determine whether Dodson intended to convey an easement or a fee simple estate. The court held that the incidental use of the term "right-of-way" was not determinative. While this makes sense generally, think about the practical effect in this case. The railroad now owns a long thin strip of land next to a housing development. Can the railroad sell it to someone who might put it to an annoying use? Can the railroad divide the strip and sell each homeowner the strip next to their property? With respect to cases like this involving railroad tracks, courts often interpret deeds more strictly to construe them as conveying easements rather than fee simples because they don't want railroads to own long strips of land that they may abandon and later sell for purposes perhaps obnoxious to adjoining owners. The existence of the long strip of land may also interfere with land development.

Baseball Publishing Co. v. Bruton

(Billboard Company) v. (Landowner)
302 Mass. 54, 18 N.E.2d 362 (1938)

M E M O R Y   G R A P H I C

Instant Facts

A billboard company sued a landowner to force him to allow the company to place a billboard on his property.

Black Letter Rule

Language that gives "an exclusive right and privilege" to use land conveys an easement rather than a lease or a license.

Case Vocabulary

LICENSE: A privilege to go upon land belonging to the licensor, that is revocable at the will of the licensor.
SPECIFIC PERFORMANCE: A remedy sought in an action that requires the defendant to actually perform the duties in the contract at issue.

Procedural Basis: Appeal of decisions overruling demurrer and granting specific performance.

Facts: Bruton (D) owned a building in Boston. Baseball Publishing Co. (Baseball) (P) was a billboard company. In 1934, Bruton (D) gave Baseball (P) a signed writing, headed "Lease No. ___," agreeing to give Baseball (P) the exclusive right to maintain a billboard on the wall of his building. The agreement provided that the right was granted for one year with the right to renew for four years. The consideration was $25 per year. Baseball (P) sent Bruton (D) a check for $25. Bruton (D) returned the check. Baseball (P) still erected a sign on Bruton's (D) property. Baseball (P) kept the sign there until 1937 and each year sent Bruton (D) $25, which Bruton (D) returned. In 1937, Bruton (D) removed the sign. Baseball (P) sued Bruton (D) for specific performance, arguing that the agreement was a lease rather than a revocable license. Bruton (D) filed a demurrer, which the court denied. The court ruled that the writing was a contract to give a license, but entered a final decree for specific performance. In 1937, Baseball (P) sent Bruton (D) $25 to renew its right for another year but Bruton (D) refused the money. Bruton (D) appealed the court's ruling.

Issue: Does language that gives "an exclusive right and privilege" to use land convey an easement, rather than a lease or a license?

Decision and Rationale: (Lummus, J.) Yes. A lease conveys an interest in land and transfers possession of the land. A license merely allows acts on land that would otherwise be trespass and does not convey possession of the land. The fact that the writing here is called a "Lease" does not make it a lease. A license is revocable at the will of the person who possesses the land, even though the revocation may constitute a breach of contract. Thus, there can be no specific performance of a license. Here, the writing grants "the exclusive right and privilege to maintain" the sign. This is more than a license. It grants Baseball (P) an easement in gross. Affirmed.

Analysis:

Stoner v. Zucker

(Landowner) v. (Land User)
148 Cal. 516, 83 P. 808 (1906)

M E M O R Y   G R A P H I C

Instant Facts
A landowner permitted another person to take water from his land, withdrew his permission, and then sued him for trespass.

Black Letter Rule
An easement may be created by estoppel when the grantee expended substantial money in reliance on the fact that the grant would be continuous.

Case Vocabulary

PAROL: Oral, as opposed to written.
STATUTE OF FRAUDS: A law that provides that certain promises and agreements are not enforceable unless they are in writing and signed by the person to be charged or by someone lawfully authorized to sign for him or her.

Procedural Basis: Appeal of action for trespass.

Facts: In 1899, Stoner (P) allowed Zucker (D) to enter his land and build a ditch for carrying water. Zucker (D) spent about $7000 to build and maintain the ditch. In 1900, Stoner (P) served notice on Zucker (D) that Zucker (D) was no longer permitted to enter his land. Nonetheless, Zucker (D) continued to enter the land. Stoner (P) sued Zucker (D) for trespass, seeking to prohibit Zucker (D) from entering his land. The trial court held that Stoner (P) granted to Zucker (D) a right-of-way, which Zucker (D) owns. The court held that consideration for the right-of-way consisted of Zucker's (D) provision of water to Stoner (P). Stoner (P) appealed.

Issue: May a license become an easement based on estoppel when the licensee expended substantial money in reliance on the fact that the license would be continuous?

Decision and Rationale: (Henshaw, J.) Yes. Stoner (P) argues that a license is always revocable and that Zucker (D) should have known Stoner (P) could revoke it at any time. He also argues that the license was granted orally, and that to convert it to an easement would violate the statute of frauds. Most courts have held that a license becomes an easement when the licensee spends money in reliance on the license. To hold otherwise would allow the licensor to defraud the licensee. Where a licensee has expended money or labor to execute a parol license, the license becomes irrevocable for as long as the nature of the license requires. Here, Zucker (D) spent money and time in reliance on his reasonable expectation that the license would be continuous. Affirmed.

Analysis:

The statute of frauds requires that certain promises and agreements are not enforceable unless they are in writing and signed by the person to be charged. In most states, contracts for the sale of real estate and leases for more than one year must be in writing to be enforceable. Thus, under the statute of frauds, an agreement to convey an easement must be in writing, whereas a license to use property need not. However, here, the court makes an exception to that rule, holding that a license may become an easement by operation of law, even if there is no writing. This is based in large part on the doctrine of part performance. An agreement may be taken out of the statute of frauds when one party partially performs his or her part of the agreement, if the equities of the situation so require. The contract will be enforced if the party seeking enforcement acted in reliance on the oral contract, suffered a substantial detriment for which there is no other remedy, and the other party would reap an unearned benefit if the statute of frauds were applied. The part performance must be meant solely to fulfill the particular agreement to be enforced. Thus, this case illustrates an exception to the rule that conveyances of real estate must be in writing.

Marrone v. Washington Jockey Club

(Ticket Holder) v. (Race Track Owner)

22 U.S. 633, 33 S. Ct. 401 (1913)

M E M O R Y   G R A P H I C

 Instant Facts

A man sued a race track after he bought a ticket and was denied entry.

 Black Letter Rule

A ticket creates a revocable license, not an easement or other property right.

 Case Vocabulary

IN REM: Pertaining to a "thing," such as property.

Procedural Basis: Appeal to U.S. Supreme Court of action for trespass.

Facts: Marrone (P) purchased tickets for the race track on two days. On both days, the owner of the track, Washington Jockey Club (the Club) (D), forcibly prevented Marrone (P) from entering. Marrone (P) sued for trespass, claiming the ticket he bought entitled him to a property interest in the race track. He also claimed that the Club (D) conspired to ruin Marrone's (P) reputation by claiming that he drugged a horse he entered in a race. The lower courts ruled in the Club's (D) favor. Marrone (P) appealed to the U.S. Supreme Court.

Issue: Does a ticket create a property right?

Decision and Rationale: (Holmes, J.) No. The common law rule is that tickets do not create an in rem right. Although a ticket creates a contract, it does not create a property right, unless it operates as a conveyance. It is commonly understood that a ticket does not operate as a conveyance. Because the ticket did not create a property interest, Marrone's (P) only remedy was to sue for breach of contract, not specific performance. The ticket was a license subject to revocation. Affirmed.

Analysis:

A license is a privilege to go upon land belonging to another, that is revocable at the will of the possessor. An easement, on the other hand, is not revocable at the will of the grantor. The revocation of the license may, however, constitute a breach of contract, but is still effective. Thus, when you buy a ticket to a movie or concert, management has the right to bar you from entering because they don't like the way you're dressed. You may be able to sue for breach of contract and get back the money you paid for the ticket, but you can't sue for specific performance. While the Court decides here that licenses are revocable, courts have held that licenses coupled with an interest are irrevocable.

Finn v. Williams

(Landowner) v. (Adjacent Landowner)
376 Ill. 95, 33 N.E.2d 226 (1941)

M E M O R Y   G R A P H I C

Instant Facts

A landowner sued an adjacent landowner for an easement of necessity to reach a highway.

Black Letter Rule

Where an owner of land conveys a parcel of it which has no outlet to a highway except over the grantor's property or over a third party's property, an easement by necessity is created over the grantor's property.

Case Vocabulary

DOMINANT ESTATE: The land that benefits from an easement.
EASEMENT OF NECESSITY: An implied easement that is created when a parcel of land is conveyed with no means of ingress and egress.
MESNE CONVEYANCE: Intervening conveyances.
SERVIENT ESTATE: The land that is burdened by an easement.

Procedural Basis: Appeal of action for declaratory relief.

Facts: In 1895, Charles Williams owned 140 acres of land. He conveyed about 40 acres to Bacon, who, in 1937, sold the 40 acres to the Finns (P). Zilphia Williams (Williams) (D) inherited the remaining 100 acres. When the Finns (P) bought the property, they could get to the highway over the land of third parties. However, each of these private ways to the highway were closed. The only way the Finns (P) could reach the highway was by going over Williams' (D) land. Beginning in 1939, Williams (D) refused to permit the Finns (P) to travel on her property to reach the highway. The Finns (P) sued Williams (D) for the declaration of an easement of necessity. The trial court held in favor of the Finns (P). Williams (D) appealed.

Issue: Where an owner of land conveys a parcel of it which has no outlet to a highway except over the grantor's property or over a third party's property, does an easement by necessity exist over the grantor's property?

Decision and Rationale: (Wilson, J.) Yes. The law here is firmly established: Where an owner of land conveys a parcel thereof which has no outlet to a highway except over the grantor's property or over a third party's property, an easement by necessity exists over the grantor's property. If one person once owned the entire parcel, the easement may be dormant through several transfers of the property. Here, the right of way easement was implied when Charles Williams conveyed a parcel to Bacon in 1895. It passed by mesne conveyances to the Finns (P) in 1937. It is immaterial that Bacon and the Finns (P) had been able to get to the highway over other roads. When those roads were no longer available, the Finns (P) could use the dormant easement implied in the deed severing the dominant and servient estates. Affirmed.

Analysis:

As this case demonstrates, an easement by necessity is created when a piece of land is conveyed with no means of ingress and egress. The right may be asserted by the grantor or grantee. The easement is implied over only the land with privity and it may lie dormant until the necessity arises. A common rationale for the easement is that the parties could not have intended to make an inaccessible estate. However, this does not explain the dormancy provision, because the estate may not have been inaccessible when the property was originally conveyed. Another rationale is that land should be accessible, whether for government use or for private economic use. Land without access is useless, except to the adjoining landowners who would then have extreme bargaining power to negotiate an easement. On the other hand, by implying an easement, the court is inferring an intent that may not have been there. Moreover, the easement burdens the servient estate without compensation. Many states have laws providing for a right of access over another's land with compensation regardless of privity when that land completely surrounds the land of the person seeking access. However, one state statute that allowed access without compensation was held unconstitutional.

Granite Properties Limited Partnership v. Manns

(Landowner) v. (Adjacent Landowner)
117 Ill.2d 425, 512 N.E.2d 1230 (1987)

M E M O R Y   G R A P H I C

⚡ Instant Facts
One landowner sued to prevent an adjacent landowner from interfering with its use of an easement on the adjacent landowner's land.

⚖ Black Letter Rule
An easement may be created by implication if there was a prior existing use that was apparent and continuous and if there was unity of ownership.

Procedural Basis: Appeal of action for permanent injunction.

Facts: For about 20 years, Granite Properties Limited Partnership (Granite) (P) owned several adjoining lots. In 1982, it sold Parcel B to the Manns (D). Granite (P) owned Parcel A which contained a shopping center and Parcel E which contained an apartment complex. Parcel B was undeveloped. Granite (P) used a gravel driveway on Parcel B to gain access to the rear of the shopping center for deliveries, trash storage, and utility repair. Without the driveway, there would not be enough room for trucks to make deliveries to the shopping center. Granite (P) also used a driveway on Parcel B to access the parking lot for the apartments on Parcel E. Both of the easements were in use before Granite (P) sold Parcel B to the Manns (D). Granite (P) sued the Manns (D) to permanently enjoin them from interfering with Granite's (P) use and enjoyment of the easements. The trial court entered final judgment in favor of Granite (P) as to the apartment complex easement, but denied the shopping center easement. The appellate court held that Granite (P) was entitled to both easements, based primarily on the element of prior use. The Manns (D) appealed.

Issue: May an easement be created by implication by a prior existing use?

Decision and Rationale: (Ryan, J.) Yes. An easement may be created by implication if there was a prior existing use that was apparent and continuous and if there was unity of ownership. There are two types of easements: easements by necessity and easements implied from a pre-existing use. An easement implied from a pre-existing use requires three elements: (1) Common ownership of the dominant and servient parcels and a conveyance of one of the parcels; (2) Before the conveyance, the common owner used part of a parcel for the benefit of another, and this was apparent, obvious, continuous, and permanent; and (3) The easement is necessary and beneficial. The easement is inferred from the prior use in order to fill the parties' likely intention. On the other hand, an easement by necessity does not require a prior use, just necessity. This conforms to the view of the Restatement of Property. Section 474 sets forth eight circumstances from which an inference of intention may be drawn: (1) whether the claimant is the conveyor or the conveyee; (2) the terms of the conveyance; (3) the consideration for the conveyance; (4) whether the claim is made against a simultaneous conveyee; (5) the extent of the necessity for the easement; (6) whether reciprocal benefits will result; (7) the manner in which the land was used prior to the conveyance; and (8) the extent to which the manner of prior use was known to the parties. Here, the factors that favor easements include the fact that Granite (P) had used the driveways since the 1960's, the driveways were permanent, and the Manns (D) were aware of the prior use before they purchased Parcel B. The Manns (D) argue that Concrete (P), as the grantor, should not be permitted to modify its own grant unless absolutely necessary and that alternative reasonable means of ingress and egress are available. While more necessity is needed to infer an easement for a conveyor than for a conveyee, the necessity requirement is met by an apparent previous use. And less necessity is required when there was a prior use. Given the strong evidence of prior use in this case and the Manns' (D) knowledge of it, we affirm the appellate court decision.

Analysis:

This case succinctly explains the implied easement by prior use doctrine. However, not all courts agree with this doctrine. Some courts have held that easements may not be implied because they violate the statute of frauds [law requiring that certain agreements are not enforceable unless they are in writing and signed by the person to be charged] and recording laws. Other courts hold that necessity should be looked at only at the time the parcel is sold. Also at issue later in this chapter is whether easements can be implied for sewers, utilities, and views.

Beebe v. DeMarco

(Landowner) v. (Neighboring Landowner)
157 Or. App. 176, 968 P.2d 396 (1998)

M E M O R Y   G R A P H I C

 Instant Facts

A landowner sued for an easement by prescription over her neighbor's land, after she had regularly driven over the land for 35 years.

Black Letter Rule

To establish a prescriptive easement, a claimant must show an open and notorious use of the defendant's land adverse to the defendant's rights, for a continuous and uninterrupted period.

Case Vocabulary

EASEMENT BY PRESCRIPTION: An easement that is acquired through use over an extended period of time without contest by a possessor with an enforceable right to bar the use.

Procedural Basis: Appeal of action to declare an easement and for specific performance.

Facts: In 1957, Beebe (P) and her husband bought lot 11 in a subdivision. The Wolfs (D) owned lot 14, three lots west. In 1958, owners of an adjacent subdivision built a six-feet-wide alley along the rear of Beebe's (P) and the Wolfs' (D) lots. Beebe (P) had access to a road through the back alley. In 1959, Beebe (P) and her husband began using the alley to take out their boat. The alley wasn't wide enough for the boat, so they drove over the unfenced back portions of other lots, including lot 14. Beebe (P), her husband, and their guests and contractors drove over these lots frequently until 1993. The Wolfs (D) never gave Beebe (P) permission to drive over their land. In 1994, the Wolfs (D) entered into an agreement with DeMarco (D) to build a house on lot 14 next to the alley. During the construction, they built a fence which blocked Beebe (P) from driving across the lot. Beebe (P) sued, claiming an easement by prescription across lot 14. The trial court ruled in favor of Beebe (P), required the Wolfs (D) and DeMarco (D) to remove the fence, allowed Beebe (P) to use the easement, and to grade, level, drain, build, maintain, or repair the roadway. The Wolfs (D) and DeMarco (D) appealed.

Issue: May a claimant establish a prescriptive easement by showing an open and notorious use of the defendant's land adverse to the defendant's rights for a continuous and uninterrupted period?

Decision and Rationale: (Riggs, P.J.) Yes. To establish a prescriptive easement, a claimant must show an open and notorious use of the defendant's land adverse to the defendant's rights for a continuous and uninterrupted period of ten years. Beebe's (P) use of the roadway meets all these elements. The Wolfs (D) and DeMarco (D) argue that the trial court erred in including the use of the roadway by Beebe's (P) guests and contractors to meet the requirement of continuous use. We need not reach this argument, because we hold that the use by Beebe (P) and her husband was enough to satisfy the requirement. Continuous use need only be use that is consistent with the user's needs. The Wolfs (D) and DeMarco (D) also argue that the trial court erred in finding that Beebe's (P) use of the roadway was adverse. A use that is open and continuous for ten years is presumed to be adverse. Moreover, there is no evidence of an existing road, permissive use, or use of the roadway by the Wolfs (D) or DeMarco (D). The Wolfs (D) and DeMarco (D) further argue that the trial court erred in allowing Beebe (P) to pave the roadway, which would create a greater burden on their estate. Easement owners are required to maintain their easements. While the judgment does not expressly allow paving, there is no evidence that Beebe (P) intends to pave it. We are not deciding whether paving is an appropriate means of repairing the easement. Affirmed.

Analysis:

The doctrine of easement by prescription was created by the courts as a type of adverse possession. Almost every state has adverse possession statutes, but many do not allow prescriptive easements. Many courts disagree about whether presumptions should be used to determine whether the use of the easement is adverse. Some courts require the neighbor to acquiesce to the adverse use. Note that a prescriptive easement does not require necessity. Prescriptive easements tend to be allowed only for limited types of easements, such as right-of-ways, support, water, and fences. Prescriptive easements in light and air are not permitted. This is due to the fact that looking out at a view is not an open and obvious use, and that the owner has no cause of action to start the statute of limitations running. In addition, such an easement would violate the historical encouragement of development. Easements by prescription are beneficial because they encourage use of the land by giving rights to those that use it, and encourage care and oversight of the land by the owner. Others oppose prescriptive easements on the basis that easements should be in writing to prevent unfair surprise to successors in title.

State Ex. Rel. Thornton v. Hay

(Public) v. (Landowner)
254 Or. 584, 462 P.2d 671 (1969)

M E M O R Y   G R A P H I C

Instant Facts

The state of Oregon brought an action on the public's behalf against a beachfront landowner, arguing that the public had an easement to use the dry-sand area of the beach.

Black Letter Rule

The public may acquire an easement over private land by custom.

Case Vocabulary

DEDICATION: Solemn appropriation of property to public use, either express or implied.

EJECTMENT: An action to recover possession of real estate and damages.

SUI GENERIS: Latin for "of its own kind;" unique.

Procedural Basis: Appeal of state court action for injunctive relief.

Facts: The Hays (D) owned an ocean-front resort on Cannon Beach. They built a fence around the "dry-sand" area [the area between the high tide point and the vegetation line] in front of their resort for use only by resort guests. The area was included in the legal description of the Hays' (D) property. The State of Oregon (Oregon) (P) sued them for specific performance to prevent them from building a fence or other improvements on that area. Oregon (P) claimed either that the public had an easement over the area or that Oregon (P) had the power to prevent the construction pursuant to its zoning laws. The Hays (D) agreed that the area lying seaward of the high tide line, the wetland area, was state recreation area. The trial court found that the public had acquired an easement for recreational purposes on the dry-sand area. The Hays (D) appealed.

Issue: Can the public acquire an easement by custom?

Decision and Rationale: (Goodwin, J.) Yes. The public has used the dry-sand area of Oregon's beaches since aboriginal times. Owners can not use the area for any other purpose. The area's seaward boundaries are unstable, unsafe during winter storms, and unfit for construction of permanent structures. Early cases held that landowners owned land only above the vegetation line. A U.S. Supreme Court decision that held otherwise did not stop Oregonians from regularly going to the beach. While many cases support the trial court's decision here, their holdings are based on different theories. Many cases hold that the public may acquire easements in private land by implied dedication. However, dedication requires the owner's intent, and it is unlikely that the Hays (D) intended to dedicate anything. Another set of cases rely on prescriptive easements. In Oregon, an easement can be created by uninterrupted use and enjoyment of the land for ten years if the use is open, adverse, under claim of right, and without permission. Here, the public used the beach under a claim of right for more than 60 years. The Hays (D) claim that the public cannot acquire rights by prescription because they are not subject to trespass and ejectment actions. While an owner cannot sue the public, the owner can use signs and fences to prevent public use. In any event, we think a better basis for affirming the trial court's decision is the English doctrine of custom. Prescription applies only to the specific tract of land at issue, whereas custom applies to all the beachfront property in Oregon. A custom is such usage as by common consent and uniform practice has become the law of the place. According to Blackstone, the first element of a custom is that it must be ancient. Here, the public has always freely used the dry-sand area of Oregon's beaches. Second, the right must be exercised without interruption. Third, the use must be peaceable and free from dispute. These elements are satisfied here because the public's use has never been interrupted by someone with superior rights. Fourth, the use must be reasonable. Here, the public has used the beaches in appropriate ways; when inappropriate uses have been detected, the police have stopped them. Fifth, the visible boundaries of the dry-sand area limit the use of it to recreational uses connected to the wetland areas. Sixth, the use must be obligatory, i.e., not left to each landowner to decide the public's rights. Here, the public has used the dry-sand area consistently and that use has never been challenged by a landowner so long as the public stayed on the dry sand. Finally, the custom here is not repugnant because it does not violate a law. The Hays (D) argue that custom is unprecedented in this state and that because our legal history is brief it is inappropriate to rely upon an English doctrine that requires greater antiquity. We disagree. Here, the custom meets all of Blackstone's requirements. Other states have relied on custom too. With respect to antiquity, even European settlers were not the first people to use the dry-sand area. The public's use of the area is so notorious that buyers of beachfront property must know that the public uses it. Affirmed.

Concurrence: (Denecke, J.) I do not believe the public's easement should be based on custom. I believe it should be based on the public's long usage of the dry-sands area, the public's long held belief of its right to such use, acquiescence by the landowners of such use, and the desirability to the public of such use.

Analysis:

Custom is a unique basis for a court decision. Most of our law is created by legislation or the courts. But here it was based on the fact that the public had been doing something for generations. Custom as a basis for creating easements has passed federal Constitutional scrutiny. After this case, the Hays (D) argued in federal court that the outcome here constituted a taking of their property in violation of the Fifth Amendment [requires compensation for government taking of property]. However, the court ruled against them. Nonetheless, the doctrine of custom has not necessarily been followed, and has been criticized. Other courts have allowed the public to use beaches based on implied dedication. But, as the court in *Hay* stated, for dedication, the landowner's intent is required. Some courts infer that intent from the landowner's apparent acquiescence while the public uses the beach. Why didn't the court here base its decision on easement by prescription? An easement by prescription would apply only to the land at issue in the suit, and would not apply to all of Oregon's beaches. Thus it would have been of limited use to assert wide public rights.

S.S. Kresge Co. v. Winkelman Realty Co.

(Owner of Servient Estate) v. (Easement Owner)
260 Wis. 372, 50 N.W.2d 920 (1952)

M E M O R Y   G R A P H I C

Instant Facts

The owner of a servient estate sued to prevent the easement owner from using the easement for additional parcels of property.

Black Letter Rule

An easement may be used only in connection with the estate to which it is appurtenant.

Procedural Basis: Appeal of action to quiet title and for specific performance.

Facts: A tract of land consisted of eight lots. S.S. Kresge Co. (Kresge) (P) owned parts of lots 5 and 6. Prior to 1936, Max Tisch owned lot 2 and on it had built a commercial building which consisted of a plumbing shop, a garage, and a retail plumbing store. Albert Dern owned the adjacent western portion of lot 3 and used the lower floor of his building for a barber shop and the second floor for living quarters. In 1934, Tisch bought Dern's property, remodeled it, and leased it and the west half of lot 3 to Sears Roebuck & Co. (Sears). Sears used the entire property as a store. In 1936, Kresge (P) tried to close an alleyway that ran along its property that provided access to a road from lot 3. Dern had used this alley for access to his building. When Tisch sued Kresge (P) in 1936, the court ruled that Tisch had a perpetual right-of-way across the alley to and from the west half of lot 3. In 1943, Winkelman Realty Company (Winkelman) (D) bought lot 2 and the west half of lot 3 from Tisch, along with the appurtenant easement. Winkelman (D) used the properties for various stores and used the basement of the Tisch buildings and the areas under the sidewalks and alleyway as a storeroom for all its stores. Wilkelman (D) used the alleyway and the former Dern building on lot 3 to distribute merchandise to the stores. Kresge (P) sued Winkelman (D) to prohibit Winkelman (D) from using the easement for any purpose other than access to the west half of lot 3 and from using the Dern property to convey merchandise. The trial court held that the easement was appurtenant only to the west half of lot 3 and that Winkelman's (D) use of the easement for its other properties was an unauthorized use and an added burden upon Kresge's (P) estate. Winkelman (D) appealed the judgment, and Kresge (P) asked for modification of the judgment to prohibit any use of the easement by Winkelman (D) on the ground that it is difficult to distinguish the increased burden from the lawful use of the easement.

Issue: May an easement be used only in connection with the estate to which it is appurtenant?

Decision and Rationale: (Broadfoot, J.) Yes. While it is true that the owner of land has a right to use it to its fullest economic value, it is also true that an easement can be used only in connection with the estate to which it is appurtenant. A person who acquires a prescriptive right based on a particular use cannot use the property in a manner that is far different from that original use. The easement was originally established because Dern used the alley for access to his barber shop and living quarters. Winkelman (D) now uses the property as a retail outlet and a storage warehouse. Winkelman (D) argues that it has not unreasonably changed the nature of the alley's use. However, Kresge (P) is not required to wait until the use is unreasonable in order to sue. Waiting could lead to Winkelman (D) acquiring additional rights by prescription. With respect to Kresge's (P) motion for review, the trial court granted all the relief Kresge (P) prayed for in its complaint. The trial court could have granted Kresge (P) additional relief, but did not. This was not an abuse of discretion, so there is no basis for Kresge's (P) motion for review. Affirmed.

Analysis:

Up until now in this chapter, you've been reading about how easements are created. In this case, the easement already existed, and at issue was the scope of the easement. What was the holder of the easement allowed to do on it? When an easement is expressly created for a particular purpose, the language creating the easement controls. For example, in *Willard v. First Church of Christ, Scientist, Pacifica*, the easement was expressly created for church parking. Parking for nearby stores would have violated the easement. Here, the easement was created by prescription. Apparently Dern used the alley for access when he owned the western half of lot 3. [Recall from *Granite Properties L.P. v. Manns*: an easement may be created by prescription if there was a prior existing use that was apparent and continuous and if there was unity of ownership.] When an easement is created by prescription, only the type of use that created the easement may continue. In addition, the dominant estate may not be enlarged so that the easement benefits more land. This makes sense. Winkelman (D) bought an easement that was appurtenant only to part of lot 3. It would fly in the face of basic property law to allow Winkelman (D) to get more than it paid for.

Sakansky v. Wein

(Easement Owner) v. (Servient Estate Owner)
86 N.H. 337, 169 A. 1 (1933)

M E M O R Y   G R A P H I C

Instant Facts
The owner of an easement sued the owner of the servient estate to prevent him from building over the old easement and creating a new one.

Black Letter Rule
If the location of an easement is specified in a deed, the easement may not be relocated, even if the relocation is reasonable.

Procedural Basis: Appeal of master's recommendation and of evidentiary issue in action for injunctive relief.

Facts: Sakansky (P) owned a piece of land with buildings on it. He also owned an 18-foot wide right-of-way over the land owned by Wein (D). The deed originally granting the right-of-way did not specify what it could be used for, but did specify its location. Before trial Sakansky (P) conveyed his property and the right-of-way to J.J. Newberry Co. (Newberry) (P) and took back a mortgage. Wein (D) wanted to build a building on his land. He proposed leaving an 8-foot tall opening in his new building for Sakansky's (P) right-of-way. Wein (D) also proposed creating a new right-of-way that would go around his building and provide access to the same point. This new right-of-way would be for vehicles that could not fit in the 8-foot tall opening. Sakansky (P) and Newberry (P) sued Wein (D) for injunctive relief. A master heard the case. Sakansky (P) objected to the admission of any evidence regarding the new right-of-way. The master decided that the parties' rights were to be determined based on reasonableness. He recommended that Wein (D) be permitted to build over the old right-of-way so long as Wein (D) also built the new right-of-way.

Issue: If the location of an easement is specified in a deed, may the easement be relocated, even if the relocation is reasonable?

Decision and Rationale: (Woodbury, J.) No. Here we apply the rule of reason, rather than rely on technicalities. We look at the locations and uses of the servient and dominant estates and the advantages and disadvantages each derives. The parties are bound by a contract that specifies the location of the right-of-way. Sakansky (P) and Newberry (P) have the unlimited right to travel over this land. They do not have the right to use another part of Wein's (D) land, even if the use would be necessary and not inconvenient to Wein (D). Wein (D) similarly may not require Sakansky (P) and Newberry (P) to use other land. It is reasonable for Sakansky (P) and Newberry (P) to approach the rear of its building with vehicles over 8-feet high. Thus, Sakansky (P) and Newberry (P) have the right to use only the existing right-of-way and may insist on that right whether reasonable or not. Wein (D) may still build over the right-of-way, but he must leave a reasonable amount of headroom. Because the rule of reason is not applicable to require Sakansky (P) and Newberry (P) to travel over the proposed new right-of-way, we hold that evidence concerning the proposed new right-of-way is irrelevant and inadmissible. We are not required to determine reasonableness based only on what was reasonable back in 1849 when the right-of-way was originally conveyed. Sakansky (P) and Newberry (P) are not required to use only vehicles that were available in 1849. They may use any vehicles which their reasonable needs may require in the development of their estate. Reversed.

Analysis:

This case allows the owner of the easement to expand the use of his easement. Apparently Sakansky (P) and Newberry (P) are now driving trucks on the easement, possibly many of them, whereas the original owner of the easement might have driven a few cars on it. The deed here was silent regarding the uses to which Sakansky (P) and Newberry (P) could use the easement. Thus, the court allowed them to do anything on it that was reasonable. However, the deed was specific about where the easement was located. Therefore, the court held that this location could not change, even if changing it was reasonable. Presumably, if the proposed new right-of-way was as convenient and comparable as Wein (D) suggested, Sakansky (P) and Newberry (P) would have consented to it and not gone through the expense of suing. Courts assume that normal development will take place on an estate. Thus, whether the owner of the dominant estate may use a truck instead of a car on an easement depends on how necessary and reasonable the change is and how troublesome the change is to the owner of the servient estate.

Lindsey v. Clark

(Owner of Dominant Estate) v. (Easement Owner)
193 Va. 522, 69 S.E.2d 342 (1952)

M E M O R Y   G R A P H I C

 ## Instant Facts
The owner of a dominant estate argued that an easement had been abandoned because the owner did not use it.

 ## Black Letter Rule
Abandonment of an easement requires intent, whether express or implied, but mere non-use is not enough.

Case Vocabulary

GENERAL WARRANTY: A statement in a deed that grantor agrees to defend the title from claims of others. In general, the seller is representing that he or she fully owns the property and will stand behind this promise.

Procedural Basis: Appeal of action for injunction and declaratory relief.

Facts: In 1937, the Clarks (D) owned four adjoining lots, lots 31, 32, 33, and 34. The Clark's (D) home was on lots 31 and 32. In 1937, the Clarks (D) deeded the front two-thirds of lots 33 and 34 to the Sixes. The deed reserved a right-of-way along the south of the lots for the benefit of the property behind it. On the rear of those lots, Clark (D) built a rental house and garage. The house the Sixes built on their property encroached on the right-of-way by about two feet. In 1939, the Sixes conveyed their property to the McGhees with the same reservation. In 1944, the McGhees conveyed the property to the Lindseys (P) without any reservation. The deeds were all duly recorded. Despite the reservation of the right-of-way on the south side of the property at issue, Clark (D) used a right-of-way along the north side of the property without objection by the Sixes, the McGhees, or, until recently, the Lindseys (P). There is some evidence that Clark (D) orally reserved the right-of-way on the north. The Lindseys (P) sued the Clarks (D) claiming that the Clarks (D) had no right-of-way at all because the one on the north side was never reserved and the one on the south side was abandoned and therefore extinguished. The trial court held that the right-of-way on the south side was not abandoned. However, it held that it would be expensive to remove the encroachment on the easement, and that such removal would not be necessary if the Lindseys (P) allowed Clark (D) to use the right-of-way on the north side. It also held that Clark (D) had to stop using the right-of-way for any purpose other than for access to the rear one-third of lots 33 and 34.

Issue: Is an easement considered abandoned if the holder does not use it?

Decision and Rationale: (Buchanan, J.) No. Abandonment of an easement requires intent, whether express or implied, but mere non-use is not enough. There must be acts or circumstances clearly showing the intent to abandon. Or, there must be adverse use by the owner of the servient estate that is acquiesced in by the owner of the dominant estate for a period sufficient to create a prescriptive right. Use of another right-of-way does not manifest an intent to abandon the original one. Clark (D) was clearly mistaken about where his right-of-way was located. He could not have intended to abandon the easement when he didn't know where it was. The fact that the house encroaches on the easement does not mean that Clark (D) knew about the encroachment and acquiesced to it. Indeed, he thought the easement was on the other side of the property. When the Lindseys (P) bought their property they had both actual and constructive knowledge of the situation. They saw that Clark (D) was using the right-of-way on the north side of the property. They are charged with the information that was available to them in the recorded deeds. Affirmed.

Analysis:

So far in this chapter, we have learned about the life of an easement, from creation, modification, and now termination. In this case, we learn that it takes a lot to terminate an easement. Like a fee simple estate, an easement may last forever, even if it isn't used. However, there are ways to terminate an easement. First, it may have been created for only a limited time. For example, the deed conveying the easement may provide that the easement exists for 20 years and then returns to the servient estate. If no time period is stated, easements are presumed to last forever. Second, easements may be terminated by merger. This occurs when the dominant estate and the servient estate are owned by the same owner. Separating the estates later does not recreate the easement. Third, an easement may be terminated by abandonment and a statement of release by the owner of the dominant estate. For example, here, if Clark (D) had not used the right-of-way on the south side of the Lindseys' (P) lot and told the Lindseys (P) that he no longer needed it, then he would have abandoned the easement. An easement may also be terminated by prescription. Just like an easement may be created by prescription [see Beebe v. DeMarco in your casebook], an easement may be terminated by prescription if the owner of the dominant estate fails to enforce its rights against interference with the easement by the owner of the servient estate within the statutory time period.

Gallagher v. Bell

(Covenantee) v. (Covenantor)
69 Md. App. 199, 516 A.2d 1028

M E M O R Y   G R A P H I C

Instant Facts

Landowners sued previous owner who had agreed to share the cost of building streets, but who no longer owned the affected land.

Black Letter Rule

A covenant runs with the land if the parties so intended, there is privity, and the covenant affects the value or use of the land; the original covenantors' liability ends when they convey the burdened property.

Case Vocabulary

COVENANT RUNNING WITH THE LAND: An agreement that may be enforced by the original contracting parties and also by and against the successors of either party.

INDEMNITY: An agreement to reimburse another for loss or to protect him against liability.

IN ESSE: A now-rejected doctrine requiring a covenant to expressly bind successors or assigns if the covenant addressed something that was not yet in existence.

Procedural Basis: Appeal of jury verdict in action for breach of covenant.

Facts: The Sisters of Mercy (the Sisters) owned about 35 acres of land. On the land were a mansion house and a tenant house. In 1959, the Sisters sold the mansion house and some of the acreage to the Franciscans [holy property!]. Later in 1959, the Sisters sold the rest of the land, except the half acre on which the tenant house stood, to the Bells (P) for a proposed subdivision. The contract between the Sisters and the Bells (P) provided that the subsequent purchaser of the tenant house would agree to dedicate half of the street adjoining the lot and share pro rata the cost of installing a street and utilities. In 1960, the Gallaghers (D) bought the half-acre parcel and tenant house from the Sisters. In a written contract, Mr. Gallagher (D) agreed to dedicate half of the streets bounding the lot and share pro-rata the cost of installing streets and utilities with the Bells (P). The contract provided that it would be binding on the parties' heirs, successors, and assigns, and would survive the execution of the deed. In 1961, the Gallaghers (D) and the Bells (P) entered into an agreement whereby the Bells (P) granted to the Gallaghers (D) a temporary right-of-way over the Bells' (P) property. In consideration, the Gallaghers (D) agreed to dedicate half of the streets bounding their lot and share pro rata in the cost of installing the street and utilities. In 1979, the Gallaghers (D) sold their property to Camalier. Upon learning about the 1961 agreement between the Gallaghers (D) and the Bells (P), Camalier insisted on an indemnity agreement from the Gallaghers (D). In 1983, the Bells (P) finally started on the roads. They demanded $18,000 from Camalier. Camalier rejected their demand, relying on the indemnity agreement. The Gallaghers (D) also rejected the Bells' (P) demand. In 1983, the Bells (P) recorded a declaration of covenant stating that because of the sale of the property to Camalier, Camalier was bound by the covenant. In 1983, Camalier sold the property to the Sindelars. The Bells (P) sued the Gallaghers (D) for their share of the cost of building the streets. The Gallaghers (D) argued that the 1961 covenant ran with the land, and that their liability for it ended when they sold to Camalier. The court submitted the issue to a jury, which decided that the Gallaghers (D) were liable to the Bells (P) for $7000. The Gallaghers (D) appealed, arguing that the issue should have been decided by the judge, not a jury, and that the covenant ran with the land.

Issue: Does a covenant run with the land?

Decision and Rationale: (Willner, J.) Yes. A covenant runs with the land if the parties so intended, there is privity, and the covenant affects the value or use of the land. Covenants may be either personal or run with the land. The difference is based on whether the original covenanting parties' rights and duties can devolve upon their successors. Normally this issue arises when parties other than the original contracting parties seek to determine whether they are bound by an existing covenant. But here, the Gallaghers (D) are being asked to perform on a promise they made directly to the Bells (P). Most courts hold that if a covenant runs with the land, the covenantor's liability ends when he conveys the burdened land. This law developed from *Spencer's Case* in 1583. For a covenant to run with the land: (1) the covenant must "touch and concern" the land; (2) the original parties must have intended the covenant to run; and (3) there must be some form of privity of estate. Some courts also require that the covenant be in writing. The "touch and concern" test requires that the thing to be done affect the quality, value, or mode of enjoying the affected land. Here, the Bells' (P) interest in their land would be rendered more valuable by performance of the covenant, and the Gallagher's (D) interest in their property was rendered less valuable by the covenant. The transaction also benefitted the Gallaghers (D) because they received a right-of-way that they did not otherwise have. Accordingly, the transaction here touched and concerned the land. The second factor, intent, is usually a fact issue

Gallagher v. Bell (Continued)

to be determined by a jury, unless all reasonable inferences favor one party. Here, lots of evidence leads to the conclusion that the parties intended the covenant to run with the land: Both the contract between the Gallaghers (D) and the Sisters and the contract between the Gallaghers (D) and the Bells (P) provided that they extended to the Gallaghers' (D) successors. The time for performance was uncertain and would not necessarily occur while the Gallaghers (D) owned the land. The Gallaghers (D) consistently maintained that the covenant ran with the land. The declaration of covenant sets forth the Bells' (P) intent that the covenant run with the land. At trial Bell (P) and his counsel acknowledged that the covenant ran with the land. However, the Bells (P) argue that the 1961 covenant was personal because a similar covenant was included in the agreement with the Sisters and because of the indemnity agreement between the Gallaghers (D) and Camalier. However, the contract with the Sisters

was not signed by Mrs. Gallagher (D), who became directly bound only by the 1961 agreement with the Bells (P). The existence of the indemnity agreement means only that Camalier may be able to recover from the Gallaghers (D) if she is liable for the covenant. With respect to privity, only vertical privity is required. This means that the person presently claiming the benefit or being subjected to the burden of the covenant must be a successor to the estate of the original person who was benefitted or burdened. Requiring other types of privity, such as mutual privity or horizontal privity, could create artificial results. Thus, we hold that the covenant at issue here runs with the land. Accordingly, the Gallaghers' (D) liability ended when they conveyed their property to Camalier. Any liability under the indemnity agreement would flow to Camalier, not to the Bells (P). Reversed.

Analysis:

A covenant running with the land requires three elements: intent, privity, and that the covenant "touch and concern" the land. Intent is fairly straightforward. As this case holds, only vertical privity is required. That is, the burden runs only to persons who succeed to the covenantor's estate. This is opposed to horizontal privity, which requires that the covenant be made in connection with the conveyance of the estate from one of the parties to the other. In this case, horizontal privity would exist if the Bells (P) had originally owned all the land and sold a parcel to the Gallaghers (D). The Restatement (Third) of Property eliminates any requirement of horizontal privity and, therefore, allows neighbors to enter into covenants that run with the land.

Neponsit Property Owners' Ass'n v. Emigrant Industrial Sav. Bank

(Property Owners' Association) v. (Property Owner)
278 N.Y. 248, 15 N.E.2d 793 (1938)

M E M O R Y   G R A P H I C

Instant Facts

A property owners association sued to foreclose a lien on an owner's property based on the owner's failure to pay the association fees as required by a covenant.

Black Letter Rule

A property owners association has privity of estate with a property owner for the purpose of a covenant running with the land.

Case Vocabulary

JUDICIAL SALE: A sale made without the consent of the owner of the property by some officer appointed by law, usually after the owner failed to pay the mortgage on the property. This sale transfers all the rights the owner had in the property, but it does not guaranty title to the property; it merely transfers the rights of the person from whom it was seized.

Procedural Basis: Appeal of denial of motion for judgment on the pleadings in action to foreclose lien.

Facts: In 1911, Neponsit Realty Company (Neponsit) owned a tract of land from which it sold lots to various purchasers. In 1917, Neponsit sold a lot to the Deyers. The deed to the Deyers contained a covenant which required the Deyers, their heirs, successors, and assigns to pay Neponsit or its assignee, the Neponsit Property Owners' Association (the Association) (P), a certain amount of money every May. The Association (P) would use the money to maintain roads, parks, sewers, etc. for the development. The deed provided that the payment would become a lien on the property until it was paid. The deed also provided that the covenant would run with the land until January 1940. Every subsequent deed contained the same covenant. Emigrant Industrial Savings Bank (Emigrant) (D) purchased the Deyers' property through a judicial sale and failed to pay the charge. The Association (P) sued Emigrant (D) to foreclose its lien on the property. Emigrant (D) moved for judgment on the pleadings on the ground that the Association (P) had no standing to enforce the covenant. The trial court denied Emigrant's (D) motion. The appellate court affirmed. Emigrant (D) appealed to the New York Court of Appeals.

Issue: Does a property owners association have privity of estate with a property owner for the purpose of a covenant running with the land?

Decision and Rationale: (Lehman, J.) Yes. Neponsit clearly intended that the covenant would run with the land and would be enforceable by a property owners association. For a covenant to run with the land, there must be intent, the covenant must "touch and concern" the land, and there must be privity of estate. With respect to privity between the Association (P) and Emigrant (D), the Association (P) was organized for the purpose of receiving the charges from the property owners and using the money for the owners' benefit. The relationship between the Association (P) and Emigrant (D) does not fit into any traditional definition of privity of estate. However, enforcing covenants is based on equitable principles. The Association (P) was formed as a convenient instrument by which the property owners could advance their common interests. It is the agent of the property owners. We will not adhere to an ancient formula here to hold that the Association (P) owns no property which would benefit from the covenant. In substance, if not in form, there is privity of estate here. Affirmed.

Analysis:

Here the court takes a more relaxed view of the privity requirement for a covenant to run with the land. While technically, the Association (P) did not ever own any of the relevant property, it was formed on behalf of the property owners to collect money and maintain the properties. One way to get around the privity requirement would have been to convey the common areas to the Association (P), thereby creating privity of estate. In this excerpt, the court did not discuss the "touch and concern" requirement. In another part of the opinion, the court held that "touch and concern" is a question of degree. Normally, a promise to pay money is not related to the land because the burden of paying money and the benefit of paying money could be performed by nonlandowners. Here, the covenant required the payment of money to be used to maintain common areas, rather than the land actually owned by Emigrant (D). However, the court held that maintaining the common areas increased the value of Emigrant's (D) property and therefore did touch and concern it. Covenants that have been held not to touch and concern land include non-compete agreements and a requirement to pay club membership fees. Note that the Restatement (Third) of Property eliminates the touch and concern requirement and provides only that covenants are valid unless they are illegal, unconstitutional, or violate public policy.

Tulk v. Moxhay

(Garden Seller) v. (Garden Buyer)

(1848) 2 Phillips 774, 41 Eng. Rep. 1143

M E M O R Y   G R A P H I C

Instant Facts

Tulk had a covenant which required maintenance of a garden on some land, but Moxhay later tried to put buildings on it after buying it.

Black Letter Rule

A covenant will be enforceable in equity against a person who purchases land with notice of the covenant.

Case Vocabulary

ASSIGNS: Another name for assignees.

ASSIGNEE: Person to whom one's property is transferred to.

DIVERS: Various.

MASTER OF THE ROLLS: An assistant judge of the English court of equity (known as court of chancery).

MESNE CONVEYANCE: A conveyance which is between the first grantee and the present holder in the chain of title.

Procedural Basis: Appeal from injunction granted by Master of the Rolls.

Facts: In 1808, Tulk (P) sold a vacant piece of land in Leicester Square to Elms. Tulk (P) also owned several of the houses that formed the Square. The deed of conveyance contained a covenant by which Elms, his heirs, and assigns would keep and maintain the property as a pleasure ground and square garden, enclosed by an iron railing. The covenant also stated that the property was to be "uncovered with any buildings." This property passed by various mesne conveyances [intermediate conveyances between the first grantee and the current holder of title] from Elms to Moxhay (D). Moxhay's (D) purchase deed contained no similar covenant against building on the Square. Moxhay (D) did admit, however, that he (D) purchased the land with notice of the original covenant in the 1808 deed. Moxhay (D) tried to assert the right to build structures on the garden as he (D) saw fit, and Tulk (P) filed for an injunction to prevent Moxhay (D) from using the pleasure ground and garden for any purpose other than as an open area, uncovered with buildings.

Issue: Is a covenant enforceable against a purchaser of land when that purchaser acquired the land with knowledge of the covenant?

Decision and Rationale: (Cottenham) Yes. Here, there was a clear contract between Tulk (P) and Elms, by which Elms promised not to use the land adjoining Tulk's (P) houses in the Square for anything other than a square garden. If Moxhay (D) were allowed to purchase this land from Elms and violate this contract, then any owner of land who tried to sell part of his land, like Tulk (P), would risk having his remaining land be rendered worthless. This is because the sale price of the land in question would be affected by the covenant. Moxhay (D) likely paid less for the land than he would have had to pay for land unburdened by such a covenant. If Moxhay (D) were allowed to build on the land, he (D) would have effectively received unburdened land for the lower price of burdened land. Nothing could be more inequitable than allowing this, for Moxhay (D) could then resell the unburdened land at a higher price, and thus would be unjustly enriched. If a covenant is attached to property by its original owner, no one with notice of that covenant can purchase that property and not be bound by the covenant. Decision affirmed.

Analysis:

This case created the equitable servitude. An equitable servitude is a covenant regarding the use of land which is enforceable against subsequent possessors in equity, even if the covenant itself is not enforceable at law. The traditional difference between this and a real covenant relates to the available remedies. When a real covenant is breached, the remedy is damages in a suit a law. When an equitable servitude is breached, however, the remedy is either an injunction or enforcement of a consensual lien, which secures a promise to pay money, in a suit in equity.

London County Council v. Allen

(Covenantee) v. (Covenantor's Successor)
L.R. [1914] 3 K.B. 642, Ann. Cas.1916C 932

M E M O R Y   G R A P H I C

Instant Facts
A government body sued a successor in interest to a party with which the government body had entered into an agreement not to develop certain land.

Black Letter Rule
A restrictive covenant does not run with the land if the covenantee does not own any land which the covenant may benefit.

Procedural Basis: Appeal of ruling denying a demurrer.

Facts: In 1907, the London County Council (London) (P) and Morris Allen (D), the owner of certain land, agreed that no buildings or structures would be placed on Plot 1 and Plot 2 without London's (P) consent. The plots were to be used for roads. London (P) and Allen (D) further agreed that every conveyance of the land would include notice of the restriction. In 1911, Mrs. Allen (D) acquired Plot 1 from Allen (D) and built three houses on it. Allen (D) built a wall on Plot 2. Norris (D) was the mortgagee (the lender) of Plot 1 and apparently had no notice of the restrictive covenant. London (P) sued Mrs. Allen (D) and Norris (D). Mrs. Allen (D) and Norris (D) filed a demurrer arguing that there was no privity of contract between London (P) and Allen (D), and that any restrictive covenant was personal and bound only Allen (D). Mrs. Allen (D) and Norris (D) also argued that they had no notice of the covenant and therefore were not bound by it. The lower court held that London (P) had the power to bind Allen (D) and his assigns pursuant to the London Building Act. Mrs. Allen (D) and Norris (D) appealed.

Issue: Does a restrictive covenant run with the land if the covenantee does not own any land which the covenant may benefit?

Decision and Rationale: (Scrutton, J.) No. Counsel has agreed that the covenant would not run with the land at law, so here we will look at equity. In *Tulk v. Moxhay* [covenant enforceable in equity against person who purchases land with notice of the covenant], the court did not hold that the covenantee must continue to hold land in order to enforce the covenant. That case was based solely on notice of the covenant. No case has held that a covenantee without ever owning land benefitted by the covenant could enforce the covenant against subsequent owners of the burdened land. It is regrettable that London (P) cannot enforce a covenant meant to benefit the public against persons who bought the property knowing of the restriction. But I am forced to hold this way. Therefore, I am granting the demurrer of Norris (D) and Mrs. Allen (D) and dismissing the action against them with costs. I regret that I cannot deprive Mrs. Allen (D) of her costs because I am not impressed with her conduct. Reversed.

Analysis:

While the language in this case may be hard to decipher, the judge's feelings certainly are not. This case sets forth the rule that in order for a covenant to run with the land, "both ends" of the covenant, the benefit and the burden, must touch and concern the land. Here, the benefit did not touch and concern any specific land. London (P) did not own any land that the covenant benefitted. The judge was clearly upset by the outcome but, under the law as it stood at the time, he had no choice. The Restatement (Third) of Property has rejected the requirement that the benefit of a covenant touch and concern land. Under the Restatement, the benefit of a covenant may be in gross (i.e., personal) so long as there is a legitimate interest in enforcing the covenant.

PROPERTY OWNERS WITH RESTRICTIVE COVENANT IN THEIR DEEDS MAY NOT ENFORCE THE COVENANT AGAINST OTHER OWNERS WITHOUT WRITTEN NOTICE OF IT

Sprague v. Kimball
(Buyers) v. (Seller)
213 Mass 380, 100 N.E. 622

M E M O R Y   G R A P H I C

Instant Facts
Buyers of lots in a subdivision sued the seller and a subsequent buyer to enforce a restrictive covenant in their deeds, but not in the deed to the subsequent buyer.

Black Letter Rule
An equitable servitude is not enforceable against buyers who had no written notice of it.

Procedural Basis: Appeal of motion to dismiss action for specific performance.

Facts: Kimball (D) sold Sprague and others (P) several lots within a plan. The deeds for the lots contained a clause prohibiting any building within 23 feet of Bassett Street and completely prohibiting any stables or commercial businesses on the lots for 20 years. Several years later, Kimball (D) sold a lot to Grossman (D) without any restrictions. The plan does not refer to the restrictions. The deed to Sprague (P) did not state that other lots in the plan would be similarly restricted. Sprague (P) sued Kimball (D) and Grossman (D) to enjoin any commercial building on lots within the plan.

Issue: Is an equitable servitude enforceable against a buyer who had no written notice of it?

Decision and Rationale: (Braley, J.) No. An equitable servitude is not enforceable against buyers who had no written notice of it. I hold that Kimball (D) intended to subject all the lots in the plan to the same restrictions. Sprague (P) bought the lots in reliance on Kimball's (D) promise that the entire neighborhood would be restricted for residential use. Accordingly, the restrictions attached to each lot for the mutual benefit of each buyer. The restrictions are an equitable servitude, rather than a covenant running with the land at law. However, equitable interests as well as legal interests in land must be evidenced by a sufficient writing. If the plan referred to the restrictions, Kimball (D) would be estopped to deny that all the grants included the restriction. However, any agreement by Kimball (D) to restrict Grossman's (D) lot to residential use was oral only. Sprague (P) argues that to require a writing in this case would be to condone fraud. However, the mere nonperformance of an oral contract where no fiduciary duty exists does not constitute fraud. The suit must be dismissed.

Analysis:

This case looks at reciprocal negative easements. The question is whether an easement is reciprocal when a subdivider includes the covenant in most deeds in a subdivision but forgets to include it in one deed. If all the elements are met, every deed after the first one sold with the covenant will be held to contain the reciprocal negative easement. The first element is vertical privity, which was present in this case; Kimball (D) was the common owner of all the lots. The second element is intent. The court here held that the parties intended the restriction to be binding upon the entire subdivision. Third, the restriction must touch and concern the land. Here, the limitation on using the land for residential purposes only related to the use of the land. Fourth, the buyer without the restriction in his deed must have notice of the restriction. The notice can be actual, constructive, or inquiry notice. Actual notice means that the purchaser actually knew of the restriction. Constructive notice means that the buyer should reasonably have known about the restriction from the circumstances. Inquiry notice means that the purchaser had or should have had enough knowledge to suspect that there might be some restriction, thus putting the purchaser in a position under which he should have inquired. Once on notice of a possible restriction, a person may be required to inspect other deeds to find out if a restriction exists. This requirement may weigh even more heavily when the property is in a subdivision that appears to be uniform. The requirement might be less important when the homes are all independent from one another and the deeds are unrelated. Here the court held that Grossman (D) had no notice, either actual, constructive, or inquiry notice, about the restriction in his neighbors' deeds. The court looked at whether the plan itself made any reference to the restriction. The court didn't look at any other factors, at least in the excerpt in your casebook. For example, were there houses on all the other lots? Had the restriction been enforced consistently? While we don't know the answers to these questions, we do know that Sprague (P) and the other homeowners were out of luck. The plaintiffs in *Sanborn v. McLean*, the next case in your book, had better luck.

Sanborn v. McLean

(Neighbor) v. (Gas Station Builder)
(1925) 233 Mich. 227, 206 N.W. 496, 60 A.L.R. 1212

M E M O R Y   G R A P H I C

Instant Facts

The McLeans tried to build a gas station on their lot in a residential district, but were enjoined from doing so by their neighbors.

Black Letter Rule

An equitable servitude can be implied on a lot, even when the servitude is not created by a written instrument, if there is a scheme for development of a residential subdivision and the purchaser of the lot has notice of it.

Case Vocabulary

NUISANCE PER SE: An act that would produce public annoyance and inconvenience regardless of the circumstances surrounding it.
PLAT: A map of a specific area of land, such as a subdivision.
RECIPROCAL NEGATIVE EASEMENT: An easement created when the owner of two or more lots sells one with restrictions on it that benefit the land retained by the owner. This sale creates a mutual servitude, and while it is in effect, the original owner cannot use his or her retained land in any way that is forbidden to the buyer of the other lot.

Procedural Basis: Appeal from decree providing injunctive relief for violation of reciprocal negative easement.

Facts: In 1891, ninety-one lots were subdivided along Collingwood Avenue in Detroit. Each lot was designed for and sold solely for residence purposes. In December 1892 , Robert J. and Joseph R. McLaughlin, then the owners of the lots on Collingwood, deeded lots 37 to 41 and 58 to 62, inclusive, with restrictions that provided "No residence shall be erected ...which shall cost less than $2,500, and nothing but residences shall be erected upon said premises." In July 1893, they conveyed lots 17 to 21 and 78 to 82, both inclusive, and lot 98 with the same restrictions. On September 7, 1893, the McLaughlins sold lot 86 to the McLeans (D) by a deed which did not contain these restrictions. The McLeans (D) occupied a house on the lot. They (D) later started to erect a gasoline filling station at the rear of their (D) lot. Sanborn (P), who owned the neighboring lot, filed for an injunction. The McLeans (D) were enjoined by decree, and appealed.

Issue: Can a restriction on the use of property be implied on a lot purchased in a subdivision when the restriction is not contained in the deed, but is contained in the deeds of other lots in the subdivision that were previously sold?

Decision and Rationale: (Wiest) Yes. A negative servitude, such as a covenant restricting a lot to residential use, can be implied on a lot if a developer has set up a scheme for a residential subdivision and if the purchaser of the lot has notice of the covenants used to set up the scheme. Here, the McLaughlins imposed the restrictions on the Collingwood lots for the benefit of the lands they retained, namely to carry out the scheme of a residential district. Because they sold these lots with restrictions in order to benefit themselves, the servitude became a mutual one, and so the McLaughlins were bound by the same restrictions as their buyers. This restriction is thus considered a reciprocal negative easement, and this reciprocal negative easement attached to lot 86 before the McLeans (D) acquired the land. Such an easement was still attached to lot 86 after the sale to the McLeans (D) and can still be enforced by Sanborn (P) if the McLeans (D) had actual or constructive knowledge of it. Because the abstract of title to lot 86 showed that lot 86 was part of a much larger subdivision, and because the deeds resulting in reciprocal negative easements were on record, the McLeans (D) were bound by constructive notice to follow that easement. Furthermore, the general plan for the residential district had been observed by all lot purchasers, whether explicitly restricted or not, for over thirty years. The McLeans (D) could not have avoided noticing the strictly uniform residential use of the neighboring lots, and therefore were on inquiry notice to learn why all the lots conformed with each other. The least inquiry by the McLeans (D) would have revealed the easement on lot 86. Decree affirmed.

Analysis:

Most jurisdictions follow this case and imply negative restrictions from a common scheme. A few, however, closely follow to the Statute of Frauds [contracts for land sales must be in writing] in such matters. Courts in these jurisdictions say that an equitable servitude will not be implied from the presence of restrictions on other lots in a subdivision, from developer's oral promise to impose such restrictions, or from a general scheme not included in the deed to the lot in question.

Snow v. Van Dam

(Lot Owners) v. (Lot Owner)
291 Mass. 477, 197 N.W. 224

M E M O R Y   G R A P H I C

 Instant Facts

Lot owners in a subdivision sued another lot owner for violating a restriction in their deeds against building commercial buildings.

Black Letter Rule

If lots are part of a common scheme, restrictions in some deeds are enforceable against owners of other lots as well.

Case Vocabulary

VICTUALLER: One who sells food, especially one who supplies food to an army, navy, or ship.

Procedural Basis: Action for injunction for violation of restriction in deed.

Facts: In 1906, Luce owned a tract of land. Title soon passed to Shackelford. The northen part of the tract, the entrance to the tract, was marshy and was considered unsuitable for building. In 1907, the whole tract, except the northerly part, was divided into about 100 lots. Snow and the other plaintiffs (collectively Snow) (P) each owned a lot on which they built a summer house. The deed to each lot contained a restriction providing that only one dwelling house could be built on each lot at a cost of not less than $2500 and that no outhouses could be built without the consent of the grantor and his heirs. In 1923, Shackelford sold the unsold lots, except the northerly part, to J. Richard Clark, subject to the same restrictions. The northerly part was divided into three parcels, C, D, and E. In 1923, Shackelford sold those lots to Robert C. Clark. The deed to those lots provided that only one dwelling house could be built on each lot at a cost of not less than $2500, that the plans for any dwelling costing less had to be approved by the grantor, and that no outhouses could be built without the grantor's consent. In 1927, the city zoned Lot D for business purposes. In 1933, Clark sold lot D to Van Dam (D). The deed to Van Dam (D) contained the same restriction "in so far as the same may be now in force and applicable." Van Dam (D) erected a building on Lot D for selling ice cream, dairy products, and other foods. Snow (P) sued Van Dam (D) for an injunction, claiming a violation of the restrictions.

Issue: If two lots are part of a common scheme or plan, does a restriction in one deed restrict the other lot?

Decision and Rationale: (Lummus, J.) Yes. A restriction must benefit the land and be intended to be appurtenant to that land. If the restriction was not intended to benefit a particular dominant estate, the restriction is considered a personal contract and will not run with the land. An intention that a restriction is appurtenant may be inferred from a subdivision plan. Here, unless Snow's (P) lots and Van Dam's (D) lot were part of a single scheme, there is nothing to show that the restrictions upon Van Dam's (D) lot was intended to be appurtenant to Snow's (P) lots. In England and some American jurisdictions the law is that a grantee subject to restrictions acquires an enforceable right to have the remaining land within a scheme bound by similar restrictions. However, in Massachusetts, the law as set forth in *Sprague v. Kimball* is that the statute of frauds prevents the enforcement of any oral agreement that the vendor's remaining lots will be bound by similar restrictions. But the existence of a scheme is important for determining the land to which the restrictions apply. A scheme can be established by a recorded plan or by uniformity of restrictions. Extensive omissions or variations of the restrictions tend to show that there is no scheme. Here, the only evidence of a scheme is a list of conveyances of different lots from 1907 to 1923 with similar restrictions. The existence of a scheme is also important to enable the restrictions to be made appurtenant to a lot within the scheme that was conveyed earlier by a common vendor. Here, some of the lots were sold before and some were sold after Shackelford conveyed Lot D to Robert C. Clark on January 23, 1923 and first imposed a restriction on the lot now owned by Van Dam (D). While persons who bought their lots before January 23, 1923 do not succeed to any rights of Shackelford, earlier purchasers in land developments have long been able to enforce restrictions against a later purchaser. The rationale for this rule is hard to find without conflicting with *Sprague v. Kimball*. The burden is on Snow (P) to establish that Snow's (P) lots and Van Dam's (D) lot were part of the same scheme. Van Dam's (D) lot lies at the entrance of the development and sets the character of the entire tract. That lot was shown on all the plans from the beginning. When Van Dam's (D) lot was restricted in 1923, the restriction was part of an original scheme and gave rights to earlier as well as later purchasers.

Analysis:

This case looks at the doctrine of implied reciprocal negative easements. This doctrine often arises in the context of subdivisions. Generally, the subdivider can enforce the covenant against any parties that are violating it. However, once the subdivider has sold all the property, he or she no longer has the power (or the interest) to enforce a covenant. Thus, other owners in the subdivision may enforce it. The issue in this case is whether people who bought their property after and before Van Dam (D) bought his lot may enforce the covenant against Van Dam (D). Subsequent purchasers certainly can enforce it. When Shackelford sold the lot to Van Dam (D), the covenant in Van Dam's (D) deed was appurtenant to all Shackelford's remaining lots. The covenant ran with the land when Shackelford sold the subsequent purchasers their lots. However, it is more difficult to establish that prior owners may enforce the covenant. This case looks at the issue from a third party beneficiary perspective. It holds that the covenant in the deed to Van Dam (D) benefits prior purchasers as third party beneficiaries. The court infers the intent to make the prior purchasers third party beneficiaries from the existence of a general scheme to keep the development residential.

Shelley v. Kraemer

(Black Property Buyer) v. (White Neighbors)
334 U.S. 1, 68 S.Ct. 836, 92 L.Ed. 1161 (1948)

M E M O R Y   G R A P H I C

Instant Facts

A black person bought property in violation of a restrictive covenant providing that only whites could own or occupy the property. When the white neighbors sued to enforce the covenant, the black buyer claimed the judicial enforcement of the covenant was unconstitutional state action.

Black Letter Rule

Judicial enforcement of a restrictive covenant constitutes state action for purposes of the Fourteenth Amendment.

Procedural Basis: Appeal of judgment for injunctive relief in Fourteenth Amendment equal protection claim.

Facts: In 1911, 30 property owners signed an agreement stating that for the next 50 years they would not sell or rent their property to anyone who was not white. At the time the agreement was signed, five of the parcels in the district were owned by blacks. Not all the owners in the district signed the agreement. In 1945, Shelley (D), a black person, bought a parcel covered by the restrictive covenant with no actual knowledge of it. Owners of other parcels covered by the covenant (collectively Kraemer) (P) sued Shelley (D) seeking an injunction divesting Shelley (D) from title to the property and revesting title in the immediate grantor. The trial court held in favor of Shelley (D) on the ground that the agreement had never become enforceable because the parties intended that it would not be enforceable until all the owners in the district signed it. The Supreme Court of Missouri reversed, holding that the agreement was enforceable and did not violate the U.S. Constitution. Shelley (D) appealed to the U.S. Supreme Court on the ground that judicial enforcement of the restrictive covenant violated the Fourteenth Amendment to the U.S. Constitution.

Issue: Does the Fourteenth Amendment prohibit judicial enforcement of restrictive covenants based on race?

Decision and Rationale: (Vinson, C.J.) Yes. The Fourteenth Amendment protects the right to acquire, enjoy, own, and dispose of property. The restrictive covenant at issue here would clearly be unconstitutional if imposed by statute. The Fourteenth Amendment applies only to government action. It does not apply to private agreements no matter how discriminatory or wrongful. However, participation by the state consisted of judicially enforcing the agreements. The purposes of the agreements were obtained by judicial enforcement. This Court has long held that judicial action is considered state action for purposes of the Fourteenth Amendment. This is true not just in cases addressing the procedural unfairness of the judicial proceedings. The actions of state courts in enforcing substantive common law rights may violate the Fourteenth Amendment even if the proceedings rigorously conformed with due process. In any event, it has never been suggested that state court action is immune from the Fourteenth Amendment. Here, there has been active state action in enforcing the restrictive covenants, and this action denied Shelley (D) equal protection. It is clear that Shelley (D) suffered discrimination at the hands of the courts. Kraemer (P) argues that state courts can enforce restrictive covenants excluding whites from owning property so they should therefore be able to exclude blacks. First, Kraemer (P) has not directed us to any opinion where this was true. Second, equal protection applies to individuals, not to groups. It is no defense to the violation of Shelley's (D) rights that other groups have been treated unequally. In addition, Kraemer's (P) rights are not violated by denying them access to the courts to enforce their covenant. The Constitution does not confer the right to deny another's equal protection. The fundamental intent of the framers of the Fourteenth Amendment was to establish equality in enjoying basic civil and political rights regardless of race or color. Having decided that the state courts violated Shelley's (D) rights, we need not consider whether Kraemer (P) was denied property without due process of law or denied privileges and immunities. Reversed.

Analysis:

It makes sense that judicial action should be considered state action for Fourteenth Amendment purposes. It certainly is considered state action for procedural purposes. Otherwise, state courts could discriminate against blacks and deny certain races due process of law. However, here, the Court takes a further leap and holds that, while private citizens are free to discriminate with impunity, they cannot use the courts to enforce their discrimination. The breadth of this holding is potentially infinite. Nearly all private activity can be made the subject of a court case. An agreement that is unenforceable is the functional equivalent of no agreement at all. However, the Court has not extended the holding of *Shelley* beyond racial restrictions. In the next case in your book, *McMillan v. Iserman*, you'll see how the court skirted the Fourteenth Amendment issue to determine that land owners could not prohibit a neighbor from building a home for mentally handicapped people pursuant to a restrictive covenant.

McMillan v. Iserman

Homeowners) v. (Builder of Proposed Home for Mentally Impaired)
120 Mich. App. 785, 327 N.W.2d 559 (1982)

M E M O R Y   G R A P H I C

⚡ Instant Facts

Homeowners in a subdivision sued another owner who wanted to build a facility for mentally impaired persons, claiming that the facility violated a new restriction in their deeds.

⚖ Black Letter Rule

A restrictive covenant may not be imposed against persons who acquired property in reliance on the nonexistence of the covenant and who would suffer prejudice if the covenant were enforced.

📖 Case Vocabulary

EQUAL PROTECTION CLAUSE: Portion of the Fourteenth Amendment to the U.S. Constitution that prohibits discrimination by state government institutions. The clause grants all people "equal protection of the laws," which means that the states must apply the law equally and cannot give preference to one person or class of persons over another.

Procedural Basis: Appeal of grant of motion for summary judgment in action for injunction.

Facts: McMillan and others (collectively McMillan) (P) owned lots in a subdivision. Iserman (D) also owned a lot and contracted with Alternate Living Programs and Health Assistance, Inc. (ALPHA) (D) to build a state-licensed group residential facility. In 1958, a restrictive covenant was included in the deeds for the subdivision providing that a vote by 3/4 of the property owners in the subdivision could amend the deed restrictions at any time. After Iserman (D) bought his property and contracted with ALPHA (D), 3/4 of the owners agreed to restrict such facilities. McMillan (P) sued Iserman (D) for an injunction, claiming the facility would violate the amended deed restriction. Iserman (D) filed a motion for summary judgment, arguing that the deed restriction discriminated against mentally impaired people and therefore violated the Fourteenth Amendment to the U.S. Constitution. The trial court granted the motion. McMillan (P) appealed. Iserman (D) also appealed, challenging the court's finding that the deed restriction could be applied retroactively.

Issue: (1) May a restrictive covenant be imposed against a person who acquired property in reliance on the nonexistence of the covenant and who would suffer prejudice if the covenant were enforced? (2) Does a restrictive covenant prohibiting facilities for the mentally handicapped violate public policy?

Decision and Rationale: (Cavanagh, J.) (1) No. (2) Yes. The 1958 deed restriction was validly included in the deeds when the subdivision property was owned by a common owner. Therefore, the amended restriction is not an invalid retroactive reciprocal negative easement. A retroactive reciprocal negative easement is a new restriction that is applied retroactively, rather than a new restriction stemming from a preexisting amending clause. We have not previously determined whether amended deed restrictions may be more restrictive than any original deed restrictions. On fairness grounds, however, we hold that an amended deed restriction does not apply to a lot owner who, prior to the amendment, committed himself to a certain land use which the amendment seeks to prohibit, so long as (1) the owner justifiably relied on the existing restrictions; and (2) the owner would be prejudiced if the amendment were enforced against his lot. Here, Iserman (D) justifiably relied on the existing restrictions when he contracted with ALPHA (D). To enforce the amended deed restriction would be to force Iserman (D) to breach that contract. Therefore, McMillan (P) is estopped from asserting the amended deed restriction against Iserman (D). We also hold that the deed restriction is unenforceable on public policy grounds. While it is established public policy to uphold land use restrictions, it is also settled policy to promote the development of facilities for the mentally handicapped. On balance, we find that the scales tip in favor of the mentally handicapped. In light of our holding on these two issues, we need not address the constitutional argument.

Dissent: (MacKenzie, J.) The court was wrong to apply estoppel here. Nothing McMillan (P) did misled Iserman (D). Iserman (D) was on notice at all times that the deed restrictions could be amended at any time by 3/4 of the property owners. Iserman (D) did not claim that he would suffer any damages if the facility were forbidden. If ALPHA (D) sued Iserman (D) for breach of contract, Iserman (D) could assert frustration of purpose and impossibility of performance as defenses. The court based its public policy argument on zoning laws. However, the legislature expressly limited its declaration of policy to zoning, not to restrictive covenants. The restrictions here prohibit a particular use of the property; they do not exclude a class of persons from owning or using the properties. The restriction would not be a denial of equal protection if a statute imposed it.

Analysis:

As you saw in *Shelley v. Kraemer* [judicial enforcement of private agreement constitutes state action for purposes of the Fourteenth Amendment], a covenant that property will not be sold to members of certain racial groups is not enforceable. This case upholds the basic premise that a covenant must be an enforceable promise in order to be protected by the courts. Thus, a covenant to commit crimes on property would not be enforceable. Here, the court avoided the constitutional argument and held that the covenant was not enforceable against Iserman (D) based on equitable estoppel. Ignoring the public policy argument for a moment, the covenant would be enforceable against purchasers who bought lots in the subdivision after the deed restriction was added. However, the court's pubic policy holding would bar enforcement of the restriction against subsequent purchasers as well.

Joslin v. Pine River Development Corp.

(Landowners) v. (Landowner Using Property for Beach Access)
116 N.H. 814, 367 A.2d 599

M E M O R Y   G R A P H I C

Instant Facts
Homeowners in a subdivision sued the owner of one lot to prohibit owners in an adjoining subdivision to use that lot for beach access.

Black Letter Rule
Restrictions in a deed are not strictly construed; look at the parties' intent and the surrounding circumstances to interpret the restrictions more broadly.

Procedural Basis: Appeal of order granting permanent injunction.

Facts: The Scribners developed 48 beachfront lots, including Lot #26, and other back lots. They conveyed some of the lots to Joslin and others (collectively Joslin) (P). Pine River Development Corp. (Pine River) (D) bought Lot #26 and other lots without beach access. All of the deeds to the beachfront lots contained restrictions limiting the number of cottages to be built on the lots, prohibiting mobile homes, requiring permanent buildings and modern plumbing, and imposing set back requirements. Pine River (D) subdivided the back lots it bought and sold them to various buyers. Those buyers formed the Pine River Association (the Association) (D), a homeowners association. Pine River (D) conveyed Lot #26 to the Association (D) so that association members could use it for swimming, boating, and accessing the water. Joslin (P) sued Pine River (D) and the Association (D) for an injunction prohibiting them from using Lot #26 for beach access. The trial court granted the injunction.

Issue: Should restrictions in a deed be strictly construed?

Decision and Rationale: (Kension, J.) No. Courts previously construed covenants strictly based on a prejudice against them. However, the modern view is that private land use regulations are important for maintaining the character of a neighborhood. Even courts that strictly construe restrictions mitigate that rule by looking at the parties' intent. Courts also look at the location and character of the tract, the purpose of the limitation, whether the restriction benefits the grantor, the grantee, and subsequent purchasers, and whether the restriction is pursuant to a general business plan. Here, although the restrictions in the deed for Lot #26 refer only to buildings, they clearly were meant to require the property to be used only for residential purposes. The trial court was not required to find that the use of Lot #26 by hundreds of people at all hours of the day and night for boating, sunbathing, and swimming was within the scheme of the development. Affirmed.

Analysis:

This opinion looks favorably upon land use restrictions and upholds the one at issue, even though Pine River's (D) use of the land did not technically violate the restriction. Technically, the restrictions limited the number of cottages to be built on the lots, prohibited mobile homes, required permanent buildings and modern plumbing, and imposed set back requirements. They did not restrict using the land for other homeowners to swim, boat, and play. However, the court looked at the spirit rather than the letter of the restrictions. Other cases hold the opposite, holding that land use restrictions are not favored and should be strictly interpreted.

Suttle v. Bailey

(Land Owner) v. (Adjacent Land Owner)

68 N.M. 283, 361 P.2d 325

M E M O R Y   G R A P H I C

Instant Facts

An owner in a subdivision sued the owner of an adjacent lot for an injunction when the adjacent owner built commercial property on the land in violation of a deed restriction.

Black Letter Rule

In order for a covenant to run with the land, it must be mutual and not capable of being altered without the consent of adjacent owners.

Procedural Basis: Appeal of granting of injunction against defendant.

Facts: In 1937, the Dickasons dedicated property to the city of Albuquerque. The property was subdivided and covenants in the deeds restricted the land to residential use only. The restrictions also provided that the covenants would run with the land until January 1, 1970, except that they could be altered or annulled before that date by written agreement of the grantor, his successors, or assigns, and the grantee, his successors, or assigns. The restriction provided that the agreement would be effective without the consent of the owners of the adjacent properties. The Baileys (D) purchased two lots that adjoin Suttle's (P) property. The Baileys (D) built an office building and an insulation business on their property. Suttle (P) sued the Baileys (D) for an injunction prohibiting them from using their property for commercial purposes. The trial court granted the injunction.

Issue: If a grantor reserves the right to void deed restrictions without the consent of other owners, do the restrictions run with the land?

Decision and Rationale: (Carmody, J.) No. The right to void the deed restrictions was reserved only for the grantor, the Dickasons. Subsequent grantees had no assurance that the restrictions on any other parcels would not be altered or annulled. Covenants that run with the land must be mutual. Because there was no mutuality here, we hold that the reservation in the deeds was a personal covenant between the Dickasons and their individual grantees. The individual grantees do not have the right to enforce the covenant against others. Reversed.

Analysis:

The court here had a hard choice to make. No matter how it ruled, it had to change the basis of someone's bargain. The court chose to invalidate the restriction completely, thereby terminating the requirement that the lots be used only for residential purposes. Thus, Suttle (P) and all the other owners who relied on the assumption that the restriction probably would stay in effect until 1970 were out of luck. If the court had invalidated only the grantor's reservation of the right to modify or terminate the restrictions, the court would have changed the Baileys' (D) purchase, a deed restriction that could be amended.

Rhue v. Cheyenne Homes, Inc.

(Landowner) v. (Owners' Association)

168 Colo. 6, 449 P.2d 361 (1969)

M E M O R Y   G R A P H I C

Instant Facts

A homeowners association sued a landowner who wanted to move onto his lot an old house that substantially differed from the neighborhood houses.

Black Letter Rule

A restrictive covenant that requires building plans to be approved by a homeowners association is enforceable, but the association must act reasonably and in good faith.

Procedural Basis: Appeal of decision granting injunction.

Facts: Leonard Rhue (D) owned a lot in a new subdivision. The deeds for properties in the subdivision provided that no building could be built, placed or altered on any lot until the architectural control committee approved the construction plans and specifications. The subdivision contained primarily two-year old ranch style and split-level homes. Rhue (D) sought to move a thirty-year old Spanish style house onto his lot. Rhue (D) did not submit his plans to the architectural committee. Cheyenne Homes, Inc. (P), the neighborhood homeowners association, sued Rhue (D) seeking an injunction barring Rhue (D) from moving the house onto the lot. At trial, two of the three members of the architectural committee testified that they would not have approved the plans. The house was substantially older than those in the neighborhood. It had a stucco exterior and a red tile roof, whereas the other houses were predominantly brick with asphalt shingle roofs. There was testimony that the house would devalue the surrounding properties. The trial court entered the injunction on the grounds that failure to submit the plans breached the restrictive covenant and the house was not in harmony with the neighborhood and would depreciate property values. Rhue (D) appealed, arguing that the restriction was not enforceable because no specific standards guided the architectural committee.

Issue: Is a restrictive covenant that requires building plans to be approved by a homeowners association enforceable?

Decision and Rationale: (Pringle, J.) Yes. It is no secret that subdividers use restrictive covenants to attempt to maintain property values. Modern courts recognize that plan approval by architectural committees is one way to accomplish this. The clear intention of the covenant is to protect property values. So long as the intention is clear, cases have upheld restrictions like this one even if no specific restrictions guide the architectural committee. Nonetheless, a purchaser is protected by the fact that a refusal to approve plans must be reasonable and made in good faith. Here, the committee's likely refusal to approve the plans was reasonable. Affirmed.

Analysis:

You've probably seen those housing developments where every house looks the same. Maybe you live in one. The houses are the same color with the same landscaping and even the same color curtains. Ever wonder how people find their houses there? This case upholds the restrictions that maintain a neighborhood's uniformity. Whether you agree with this decision depends on whether you think neighborhood uniformity should be encouraged.

Cowling v. Colligan

(Subdivision Landowners) v. (Subdivision Landowner)
158 Tex. 458, 312 S.W.2d 943 (1958)

M E M O R Y   G R A P H I C

Instant Facts

Landowners in a subdivision sued another owner for violating a restrictive covenant requiring the land to be used only for residential purposes.

Black Letter Rule

A restrictive covenant will become unenforceable only if changed conditions affect the entire subdivision that is subject to the covenant.

Procedural Basis: Appeal of action for declaratory judgment and injunction for violation of restrictive covenant.

Facts: The Post Oak Gardens subdivision contained 49 tracts of land. The tracts contained a covenant restricting the use of the lots for residential use only. Several churches had been built on various tracts. One half of the remaining lots had residences on them. Tract No. 2 was owned by Mrs. Colligan (D) and leased by Falkenbury (D). Tract No. 2 contained 5 acres, had only a small frame building on it, and was used for pipe storage. It was adjacent to various lots that were outside the subdivision and which were used for commercial purposes. It also fronted a road that was a quiet country road when the subdivision was platted, but had become a busy main thoroughfare. The market value of Tract No. 2 with the residential restriction was $10,000 per acre, and without the restriction it was $35,000 to $43,000 per acre. Cowling and 17 other owners in the subdivision (collectively Cowling) (P) sued Colligan (D) and Falkenbury (D) to obtain a declaratory judgment that the restrictive covenant was enforceable and to enjoin them from using Tract No. 2 for commercial purposes. The trial court held that the covenant was valid and had not been waived or abandoned. However, the court also held that the conditions surrounding Tract No. 2 had changed so much that it would be unjust and inequitable to enforce it against that tract. The Court of Appeals affirmed the trial court's judgment.

Issue: May a court refuse to enforce a residential-only restriction against a lot on the ground that a change of conditions has rendered the lot unsuitable for residential purposes and it would be inequitable to enforce it?

Decision and Rationale: (Calvert, J.) No. A court may refuse to enforce a residential use only restriction if surrounding lot owners have acquiesced in the violations and have effectively abandoned the covenant or waived their right to enforce it. A court may also refuse to enforce a covenant if the surrounding conditions have changed substantially or if it is no longer possible to achieve the benefits the covenant was intended to promote. The trial court held that the covenant had not been waived or abandoned. The only contrary evidence was the fact that churches had been built in the subdivision, but this is a trivial violation. A court may not refuse to enforce a residential-only restriction against a lot on the ground that a change of conditions has rendered the lot unsuitable for residential purposes and it would be inequitable to enforce it. A court must also look at the interests of the other owners who acquired their property based on the restriction. The court did not make a finding that removing Tract No. 2 from the restriction would not harm Cowling (P). The changed conditions were outside the subdivision. The covenant still protected the interior lots. Otherwise, if lots on the border of the subdivision were omitted from the covenant, then the next row of lots would soon be omitted, until the restriction was removed from the entire subdivision. The trial court judgment is reformed to strike the portion stating that it is inequitable to enforce the restriction against Tract No. 2.

Analysis:

Here the court discusses ways a restrictive covenant may be terminated. For example, subdivision owners may waive the right to enforce the covenant by their acquiescence in previous violations. But, as this case holds, changed conditions alone may not be enough to terminate a covenant. Changed conditions must affect the entire development, not just some of the tracts. The equities favoring the lot owner who opposes the restriction must be weighed against the equities favoring the other lot owners who purchased their property in reliance on the restriction. Otherwise, if a court lifts the restriction with respect to some of the tracts, a domino effect that may destroy the entire subdivision is likely. Indeed, this is the reason that lots on the edge of a subdivision tend to be less expensive than lots in the interior. It's impossible to know what will happen in the future in the areas surrounding the subdivision.

Waldrop v. Town of Brevard

(Landowner) v. (Nearby Dump Owner)

233 N.C. 26, 62 S.E.2d 512 (1950)

M E M O R Y   G R A P H I C

Instant Facts

A landowner sued a town that was operating a dump nearby for nuisance, despite the fact that a covenant in the deed to the town provided that the landowner released and waived all claims against the town.

Black Letter Rule

A restrictive covenant may estop a neighboring landowner from suing for damages.

Case Vocabulary

NONSUIT: A type of judgment given against a plaintiff who is unable to prove his case or when he has not presented sufficient evidence upon which a jury could find a verdict.

Procedural Basis: Appeal of decision granting motion for nonsuit in action to abate nuisance and for damages.

Facts: In 1938, the Town of Brevard (Brevard) (D) bought five acres of land from the Shipmans for a garbage dump. The land was in the middle of a 120-acre tract of land the Shipmans owned. The duly recorded deed from the Shipmans to Brevard (D) provided that Shipman released Brevard (D) from any liability for using the land as a dump. The deed also provided that the release and waiver ran with the Shipman's land. At the time, only the Shipmans and one other family lived on the tract. In 1939, the Tinsleys bought a lot from Shipman. In 1940 they sold the lot to the Waldrops (P). The Waldrops (P) sued Brevard (D) to abate a nuisance and for special damages. At trial, the court granted Brevard's (D) motion for a nonsuit. The Waldrops (P) appealed.

Issue: May a restrictive covenant estop a neighboring landowner from suing for damages?

Decision and Rationale: (Denny, J.) Yes. The Waldrops (P) are estopped from asserting any claim for damages against Brevard (D) so long as Brevard (D) is operating the dump in a reasonably prudent manner. The waiver or release in the deed from the Shipmans to Brevard (D) constitutes a waiver not to sue that binds the Shipman's heirs and assigns. The Waldrop's (P) contention that the conditions surrounding the dump have changed so that the covenant should not be enforced is without merit. The change here is not sufficient to affect the duly recorded easement. The Waldrops (P) do not claim that Brevard (D) operated the dump negligently. Affirmed.

Analysis:

Here, the court held that the Waldrops (P) were estopped from suing Brevard (D). This makes sense. The dump was there before the Waldrops (P) bought their land. [The Waldrops (P) probably could have smelled it.] The Waldrops (P) could have gone to the county clerk's office to read the deed from the Shipmans to Brevard (D) and see that there was no right to sue Brevard (D) for operating the dump. The fact that only a few people lived near the dump at the time Brevard (D) acquired it and later a lot of people lived nearby was not sufficient to terminate Brevard's (D) rights. This growth in population was to be expected and, unfortunately for the Waldrops (P), as the neighboring population grew, the use of the dump probably grew too. Note that this case presumes that Brevard (D) was operating the dump properly. Of course, if there was evidence that Brevard (D) was mismanaging the dump and creating more odors and other problems than were reasonably expected from a dump, the Waldrops (P) would probably have been able to recover damages.

Rose v. Chaikin

(Homeowners) v. (Adjacent Windmill Owner)

187 N.J. Super. 210, 453 A.2d 1378

M E M O R Y   G R A P H I C

Instant Facts

Homeowners sued a neighbor who was operating a noisy windmill on his property.

Black Letter Rule

A private nuisance is an unreasonable interference with the use and enjoyment of land.

Case Vocabulary

TEMPORARY RESTRAINING ORDER: An order prohibiting a person from an action that is likely to cause irreparable harm. This differs from an injunction in that it may be granted immediately, without notice to the opposing party, and without a hearing. It is intended to last only until a full hearing on an injunction can be held.

Procedural Basis: Claim and cross-claim for injunctions against nuisances.

Facts: In 1981, the Chaikins (D) built a 60-foot windmill on their property in an effort to save on electric bills and conserve energy. The windmill was extremely noisy. Neighboring homeowners (collectively Rose) (P) sought relief from the city council. The city council restricted the hours during which the Chaikins (D) could operate the windmill. Rose (P) sued the Chaikins to enjoin them from using the windmill at all. The court granted a temporary restraining order restricting the use of the windmill to no more than two hours a day. The evidence at trial showed that the windmill produced sounds that exceeded the 50 decibels permitted under the city ordinance. Other sounds in the area include the sounds of the ocean, birds, the wind, boat traffic, and the Rose's (P) heat pump. Rose (P) suffered tension, nervousness, dizziness, loss of sleep, and fatigue. The Chaikins (D) sued the Roses (P) to enjoin the operation of their heat pump. Evidence at trial showed that the heat pump sound exceeded 50 decibels, but that it was used for short periods of time and did not affect the Chaikins' (D) health or comfort. The Chaikins (D) asserted three arguments against Rose (P): (1) Noise alone cannot constitute a nuisance; (2) Even if noise could constitute a nuisance, the noise from their windmill did not exceed a threshold level; and (3) The circumstances did not warrant the extraordinary relief of an injunction.

Issue: Does a noisy windmill in a quiet neighborhood constitute a private nuisance?

Decision and Rationale: (Gibson, J.S.C.) Yes. A private nuisance is an unreasonable interference with the use and enjoyment of land. Courts must balance the competing interests and determine whether the use is unreasonable. Noise is an actionable private nuisance if it injures the health and comfort of nearby people and if it is unreasonable under the circumstances. Relevant circumstances include the character, volume, frequency, duration, time, and location of the noise. Other factors include the availability of alternative means of achieving the defendant's objective, the social utility of the conduct, and whether the use complies with government regulations. Here, these factors indicate that the windmill noise is an actionable nuisance. The sound is distinctive, constant, and louder than other sounds. It is intrusive in a quiet residential neighborhood with close proximity to the ocean. It is disturbing to ordinary persons and injuriously affects their health. Alternative ways to save on electric bills are available. While there is some social utility in using a renewable source of power, this does not mean that it is permissible at any cost. The benefits of the windmill are small and the harm is substantial. The windmill is a nuisance and an injunction is warranted. The Chaikins (D) have failed to prove that the Rose's (P) heat pump is an actionable nuisance. The operation of the pump is limited in duration and frequency and the sound is less alien. In addition, the Chaikins (D) have not proved that the heat pump unreasonably affects their health and comfort.

Analysis:

This case sets forth the basic elements of a nuisance claim. A private nuisance is an unreasonable interference with the use and enjoyment of land. As you can see in this opinion, the determination as to whether a nuisance exists is fact-specific and must be determined on a case-by-case basis. Thus, a noisy windmill in an industrial area may not constitute a nuisance.

Boomer v. Atlantic Cement Co.

(Neighbor) v. (Cement Plant Operator)
(1970) 26 N.Y.2d 219, 257 N.E.2d 870, 309 N.Y.S.2d 312

M E M O R Y   G R A P H I C

Instant Facts

A court found that a cement plant constituted a nuisance to neighbors, but denied an injunction.

Black Letter Rule

Courts can grant an injunction conditioned on the payment of permanent damages to a complaining party in order to compensate him or her for the impairment of property rights caused by a nuisance.

 ## Case Vocabulary

METALLURGICAL: Having to do with the science of metals.

Procedural Basis: Appeal from judgment in actions for injunction and damages.

Facts: Atlantic Cement Company (D), or ACC (D), runs a large cement plant near Albany. Boomer (P) and other neighboring land owners (Ps) claimed that their property interests were injured because of the high levels of dirt, smoke, and vibration that the plant produced. The trial court found this constituted a nuisance, and temporary damages were allowed in various specific amounts up to the time of trial to the respective neighbors. An injunction, however, was denied on the grounds that the total damages to Boomer and the other neighbors (Ps) was small compared to the value of ACC's (D's) operations and the damage that an injunction would inflict upon ACC (D). Boomer and the other neighbors (Ps) were also awarded $185,000 in permanent damages.

Issue: Can the courts grant an injunction as a remedy for a nuisance when such an injunction would have greater economic consequences for the nuisance-causing party than the nuisance itself has for the complaining party?

Decision and Rationale: (Bergan) Yes. Courts can grant an injunction conditioned on the payment of permanent damages to a complaining party in order to compensate him or her for the harm caused by a nuisance. The trial court denied an injunction because of the large disparity in economic consequences between imposing the injunction and allowing the nuisance to continue. This reasoning, however, contradicts the longstanding doctrine that an injunction should be granted where a nuisance has been found and the complaining party has sustained substantial damage. Granted, following this rule literally would result in the closing of the plant. The trial court's awarding of damages, however, violates this longstanding rule. One option would be to grant the injunction, but postpone its effect until after a specified period of time. This way, technological advances would allow ACC (D) to eliminate the nuisance without shutting down its (D's) plant. There is no guarantee, however, that ACC could even make such advances on its own. Further, any such advances in eliminating dust and pollution by cement plants would likely result from industry-wide efforts, and the rate of research and development by the entire cement industry is clearly out of ACC's (D's) control. For these reasons, the best option is to grant the injunction on condition that ACC (D) pays Boomer and the other neighbors (Ps) a level of permanent damages as may be fixed by the court. This court undoubtedly has the power to grant such an injunction on these conditional grounds. Also, permanent damages are allowable when the loss a complaining party could recover would be smaller than the cost of completely removing the nuisance. In essence, ACC (D) would be purchasing a servitude on the neighbors' (Ps') land. This action would preclude future recovery by Boomer and the other neighbors (Ps) or their grantees. Judgment reversed.

Dissent: (Jasen) Though a reversal is required here, an award of permanent damages should not be allowed in place of an injunction where substantial property rights have been impaired by the creation of a nuisance. The majority essentially allows ACC (D) to continue causing harm to the surrounding community for a fee set by the court. Moreover, once all those who complain about the nuisance are paid off, there will no longer be any incentive to correct the nuisance, and the air pollution and blasting noise will simply continue.

Analysis:

This case reflects an almost classic conflict between environmental and economic interests. In addition to the dirt, smoke, and vibration mentioned by the court, there are even greater injuries to neighboring landowners that were not mentioned. ACC also owned a quarry less than a mile away. Blasting operations there had frightened the neighborhood children and cracked the walls and ceilings of many of the nearby homes. This practice also contributed heavily to the level of air pollution. Moreover, the blasting conducted by ACC was arguably unnecessary, as it only served to completely shatter the stones in the quarry. This step could have been easily bypassed in the production of cement in favor of less explosive and violent means. At the same time, however, ACC's plant undoubtedly provided hundreds of jobs to the local population. Those same employees certainly stimulated the local economy, and contributed to the property tax base of the community.

Spur Industries, Inc. v. Del E. Webb Development Co.

(Cattle Farm) v. (Nearby Residential Development)
108 Ariz. 178, 494 P.2d 700 (1972)

M E M O R Y   G R A P H I C

Instant Facts
An owner of a residential development sued a nearby cattle feedlot for creating a public nuisance.

Black Letter Rule
If a party comes to a nuisance, it may sue to abate the nuisance but be liable for the damages to do so.

Procedural Basis: Appeal from granting of permanent injunction in action for public nuisance.

Facts: In 1956, Spur Industries, Inc.'s (Spur) (D) predecessor established cattle feedlots in a rural area several miles from Phoenix. In 1959, Del E. Webb (Webb) (P) built a nearby residential development know as Sun City. Webb (P) sued Spur (D) for an injunction, arguing that the feedlot produced flies and odors that constituted a public nuisance for the residents of the southern portion of Sun City and that it reduced sales. The trial court granted an injunction permanently enjoining Spur (D) from operating the feedlot near Sun City. Spur (D) seeks damages for its cost of moving.

Issue: If a party comes to a nuisance, is it liable for damages for abating the nuisance?

Decision and Rationale: (Cameron, V.C.J.) Yes. A private nuisance affects a single individual or a small group of people. A public nuisance affects an entire community or neighborhood. Under Arizona law, any condition that constitutes a breeding place for flies is a public nuisance. Spur (D) is clearly operating a public nuisance. If Webb (P) were the only party injured, Webb (P) could not recover, based on the doctrine of "coming to the nuisance." This means a homeowner may not recover if he knowingly came into a neighborhood reserved for industrial or agricultural endeavors. Spur (D) could not have known that a new city would develop near its feeding operation. Spur (D) is required to move not because it did anything wrong, but because of a regard for the public's rights and interests. Webb (P) is entitled to relief not because it is blameless, but because of the damage to the people in Sun City. However, this does not mean that Webb (P) is not required to compensate Spur (D) if Webb (P) caused Spur's (D) damage. Webb (P) took advantage of the reduced land values in a rural area and foreseeably brought people to the nuisance. Webb (P) should be required to indemnify Spur (D) for forcing Spur (D) to leave. We remand to the trial court for a hearing on the damages Spur (D) suffered as a result of the permanent injunction. Affirmed in part, reversed in part.

Analysis:

Webb (P) certainly won a pyrrhic victory here. Yes, it was able to force Spur (D) to move its operations, but it had to pay Spur's (D) costs to do so. The court came up with a compromise solution. It balanced the rights and needs of the people of Sun City to live free from the smells and flies of a feedlot against the social utility of raising cattle. Now Webb (P) must decide whether the cost of moving Spur's (D) operations outweigh the costs to Sun City if Spur (D) stays. This makes sense. Spur (D) began its cattle operations in a remote area several years before Webb (P) began its development. Spur (D) could not have reasonably foreseen that a large community would pop up nearby. The result would have been different of course if Sun City were in existence first and then Spur (D) decided to locate its feedlot nearby.

Noone v. Price

(Uphill Homeowner) v. (Downhill Homeowner)
171 W.Va. 185, 298 S.E.2d 218 (1982)

M E M O R Y   G R A P H I C

Instant Facts

A homeowner on the side of a mountain sued the homeowner at the bottom for damages arising from failure to provide lateral support.

Black Letter Rule

Under theories of strict liability and negligence, adjoining landowners have a duty to provide lateral support to each other's land.

Case Vocabulary

LATERAL SUPPORT: Support that exists when the supported and supporting lands are divided by a vertical plane.

Procedural Basis: Appeal of partial grant of summary judgment motion in action for damages for failure to provide lateral support.

Facts: In 1960, the Noones (P) bought a house located on the side of a mountain. The house was built in 1928 or 1929. In 1955, Mrs. Price (D) bought a house below the Noones (P) at the foot of the hill in a house built in 1912. Between 1912 and 1919, a retaining wall was built behind Price's (D) house. Before 1955, the wall had fallen into disrepair. Price (D) sold her house in 1972. In 1964, the Noones (P) became aware that their house was slipping down the hill. They complained to Price (D) that the problem was the result of the deteriorating retaining wall. Price (D) did nothing. The Noones (P) paid $6000 to repair their house. In 1968, the Noones (P) sued Price (D) for $50,000 for Price's (D) failure to provide lateral support for their land. Price (D) denied that her wall caused the Noones' (P) damage and argued that the Noones (P) were negligent for failing to take proper precautions to protect their land and were estopped from suing because they were aware of the wall's condition when they bought their house. Price (D) filed a motion for summary judgment. The trial court granted the motion in part, holding that there was a duty to support the land but not the structures on the land.

Issue: Do adjoining landowners have a duty to provide lateral support to each other's land?

Decision and Rationale: (Neely, J.) Yes. Support is lateral when the supported and supporting lands are divided by a vertical plane. Withdrawing lateral support may subject the landowner to strict liability or liability for negligence. Strict liability applies only to damage to land in its natural state. However, most jurisdictions hold that if the land in its natural state would support the weight of a building, and the building is damaged because of subsidence of the land itself, the landowner may recover damages for the injury to the land and to the building. Likewise, if an adjacent landowner provides sufficient support for the land in its natural state, but the land slips as a result of the weight of a building, there is no cause of action against the adjoining landowner for damage to the land or to the building. Here the Noones (P) should have been allowed to prove that their land was strong enough in its natural state to support the weight of their house and that the house was damaged when the land in its natural state at the bottom of the hill slipped as a result of failing lateral support caused by the deterioration of the retaining wall. If the weight of the Noones' (P) house caused the subsidence, and the land would not have subsided without the weight of the house, the Noones (P) cannot recover. A retaining wall becomes a burden on the land upon which it is constructed which runs with the land; subsequent owners have an obligation to maintain it. Here, Price's (D) predecessor built the retaining wall before there was a house on the Noones' (P) property. Therefore, Price (D) had only the obligation to maintain the wall to support the Noones' (P) land in its natural condition, not with a building. Under a negligence theory, while a neighbor has no obligation to support the buildings on a neighbor's land, if those buildings are actually being supported, a neighbor who withdraws support must do so in a non-negligent way. This case rests on the question of strict liability. The wall was constructed before the construction of the Noones' (P) house. There is no allegation that Price (D) did anything to cause the collapse of the wall. For the Noones (P) to recover, they must prove that the disrepair of the retaining wall would have caused their land to subside in its natural condition. If the land would not have subsided but for the weight of the Noones' (P) house, they cannot recover. Reversed.

Analysis:

Armstrong v. Francis Corp.

(Downstream Landowner) v. (Upstream Developer)
20 N.J. 320, 120 A.2d 4 (1956)

M E M O R Y   G R A P H I C

Instant Facts

A downstream landowner sued an upstream developer for an injunction due to the increased volume of water and flooding in a stream caused by the developer's expulsion of surface waters.

Black Letter Rule

Landowners may reasonably use their land, even if they alter the flow of surface water thereby, and cause some harm to others, but they incur liability if their interference with the flow of surface water is unreasonable.

Case Vocabulary

DAMNUM ABSQUE INJURIA: Latin for "a loss or damage without injury."

SURFACE WATER: Water coming from rain, snow, and streams that spreads over the ground or collects in ponds, as opposed to stream water that runs in defined channels.

Procedural Basis: Appeal of action granting injunctive relief.

Facts: Francis Corp. (Francis) (D) owned 42 acres of land. A stream flowed across the land and emptied into a lake. The stream was the natural drainage area for 85 acres, including Francis' (D) land. Francis (D) built 185 small homes on its land. It also built 14 homes on adjacent land. It built a drainage system for both developments. The drainage system emptied into pipes below the level of the stream and followed the course of the stream. The pipe joints were designed to receive percolating waters in order to provide a drier terrain for the housing development. When the stream passed Francis' (D) land it formed the boundary between the Armstrongs' (P) land and the Klemps' (D) land. It passed through a culvert under the Klemps' (D) driveway, across the Union County Park Commission's land to the lake. As a result of the housing development, the water coming from the culvert was more voluminous, smellier, and silted, and flooded regularly. The water eroded the bank on the Armstrongs' (P) property and was within 15-feet of their septic tank system. The water loosened rocks and boulders which caused damage to the Klemps' (D) property. The other 40 acres are likely to be developed soon, which will likely cause further erosion, silting, and flooding. The Armstrongs (P) sued Francis (D) for an injunction. Francis (D) sued the Klemps (D) in a cross-claim. The trial court ordered Francis (D) to pipe the brook for the entire distance to the lake within 60 days.

Issue: Is a landowner liable to another landowner for conducting surface water onto the other's land?

Decision and Rationale: (Brennan, J.) Yes. Francis (D) argues that it should not be liable because it is conducting the water where it otherwise would have flowed. This argument fails because Francis (D) has augmented the volume of water passing through the culvert. In cases involving the casting of surface water from one's own land onto the land of another, only New Hampshire and Minnesota apply tort liability. Under the "reasonable use" rule, a landowner is allowed to reasonably use his land, even if the flow of surface waters is altered and causes some harm to others. Liability is incurred when the landowner's actions are not reasonable. All other states apply property law principles, rather than tort principles. The first property law is the "common enemy" rule. Under this rule the landowner is permitted to rid his lands of surface waters in any possible way. Under the "civil law" rule, a person may not alter the natural flow of surface waters so that it interferes with another's right to use and enjoy their land. However, states that apply these rules never apply them strictly. They all temper the rules with a reasonableness requirement, essentially applying the reasonable use rule. Under this rule, a landowner may not discharge upon adjoining land, by artificial means, large quantities of surface water in a concentrated flow except through natural drainways, regardless of the means by which the surface water is collected and discharged. We too will adopt the reasonable use rule, as does the Restatement of Torts. This rule is flexible. Society has a great interest in developing the land. Therefore it is proper to consider whether the landowners' use of the land outweighs the gravity of the harm which results from altering the flow of surface waters. While residential developments are beneficial, there is no reason why adjacent landowners should bear the cost of expelling surface waters. Affirmed.

Analysis:

Under the common law, landowners could do whatever they wanted with the surface water on their land even if they damaged adjacent properties. Later laws developed that applied the rules set forth in this case, the common enemy rule and the civil law rule. As this court explains, while these two rules are theoretically polar opposites, in application, courts made exceptions to the rules based on reasonableness. Thus, in essence, all courts apply the reasonable use rule. This case involves water that is unwanted or undesirable. In the next cases, the parties will be fighting about capturing the water.

Evans v. Merriweather

(Upstream Mill Operator) v. (Downstream Mill Operator)
4 Ill. 492 (1842)

M E M O R Y   G R A P H I C

Instant Facts

A downstream mill operator sued an upstream mill operator when the upstream mill operator dammed the stream and blocked the water from reaching the downstream mill.

Black Letter Rule

A riparian landowner may use all the water in a stream to satisfy natural needs for water, such as thirst. But for artificial needs for water, such as manufacturing and irrigation, it is up to a jury to decide on a case-by-case basis how the water should be divided.

Case Vocabulary

EX JURE NATURAE: Latin for "by natural right."
RIPARIAN: Adjacent to a stream.
USUFRUCTUARY: Pertaining to the right to use property of another and of drawing the profits it produces without wasting its substance.

Procedural Basis: Appeal of jury verdict for plaintiff in action for damages caused by diversion of stream.

Facts: In 1834, Smith & Baker bought six acres of land, through which a stream ran, from Carlin. Smith & Baker built a steam mill on the land, relying on the stream and a well. About a year or two later, Evans (D) bought the adjoining six acres of upstream land from Carlin on which he too built a steam mill. Smith & Baker then sold its mill to Merriweather (P). Ordinarily, there was enough water for both mills to operate, but in 1837 there was a drought. There was not enough water for Evans (D) to operate his mill. One of his employees built a dam just below Evans' (D) mill, thereby diverting all the water in the stream into his well. There is evidence that Evans (D) was aware of the dam. As a result of the dam, Merriweather's (P) mill could not run more than one day a week. Merriweather (P) sued Evans (D) and obtained a jury verdict of $150.

Issue: May riparian landowners use all the water of a stream to the detriment of other riparian landowners?

Decision and Rationale: (Lockwood, J.) Yes. Riparian landowners may use all the water of a stream to satisfy only their natural needs, such as thirst. Early English cases held that water courses may not be diverted. Riparian landowners may use the water, and even diminish the natural current, but the use must be reasonable. To determine whether consuming all of the water in a stream is reasonable, we must look at whether one's wants in water are natural or artificial. Quenching the thirst of people and cattle and household uses are natural uses of water. Artificial uses of water include irrigating land, propelling machinery, and manufacturing. A riparian landowner may use all of a stream to satisfy his natural needs for water. But for artificial needs for water, it is up to a jury to decide on a case-by-case basis how the water should be divided. Here, Evans (D) illegally obstructed the water by a dam. Affirmed.

Analysis:

Here we see that a riparian landowner may take water from the stream in two situations: (1) When taking the water will not affect the flow of water in the stream; and (2) When the water is used for "natural" purposes, such as for drinking and household purposes. When taking the water for artificial purposes affects downstream users, the old minority view is the "natural flow" theory, that the downstream owner could always sue the upstream user for an injunction. The majority view is the "reasonable use" theory, that the upstream user may use the water reasonably. The reasonable use theory involves balancing the landowners' respective needs. Relevant factors include: the utility of the possessor's use of his land; the degree of harm that results; the foreseeability of harm that results; and the feasibility of alternatives.

Stratton v. Mt. Hermon Boys' School

(Downstream Landowner) v. (Upstream Landowner)
216 Mass. 83, 103 N.E. 87 (1913)

M E M O R Y   G R A P H I C

Instant Facts

A downstream landowner sued an upstream landowner for diverting stream water to land that was not connected to the stream.

Black Letter Rule

If a riparian landowner diverts water to un-connected land, he is liable for any actual injury to other riparian landowners.

Case Vocabulary

NOMINAL DAMAGES: Damages that are recoverable when the defendant has violated a legal right, but the plaintiff has not sustained an actual loss, such as $1 in recognition that technically the defendant injured the plaintiff.

WATERSHED: The region from which a river receives its water supply.

Procedural Basis: Appeal of jury verdict in action for damages for wrongful diversion of water.

Facts: Stratton (P) owned a mill on a stream. Mt. Hermon Boys' School (the School) (D) owned land upstream from Stratton (P). The School (D) diverted water from the stream to its school about a mile away and in a different watershed. In 1911, the School (D) housed 525 students, 100 employees, 103 cattle, 28 horses, and 90 pigs. The School had a pool, laundry, canning factory, and electric power plant. The diversion of water substantially diminished the volume of water that would have come to Stratton's (P) land. Stratton (P) sued the School (D) for damages resulting from the diversion. At trial, the court instructed the jury that the School (D) could use the water only for its land adjoining the stream, not for other premises. The court also instructed the jury that if the School (D) used the water for other premises, Stratton (P) could recover nominal damages even if he did not suffer any actual loss. The jury found for Stratton (P) for substantial damages.

Issue: May a riparian landowner use stream water for land that is not adjoining the stream if there is no damage to downstream riparian landowners?

Decision and Rationale: (Rugg, C.J.) Yes. A landowner may make reasonable use of the water in connection with his riparian land, provided he leaves the current diminished by no more than is reasonable. If he diverts the water to unconnected land, he is liable for any actual injury to other riparian landowners. Nominal damages are not available. Although the trial court's instruction did not conform with this rule, the School (D) did not suffer any harm from the error. The jury held that the School (D) was liable for substantial damages and ample evidence supported this conclusion. Affirmed.

Analysis:

Other courts have held that a riparian owner may obtain an injunction against any person who diverts water to non-riparian lands even if the riparian owner is not damaged. The rationale for this rule is that the riparian owner may be damaged in the future and the injunction prevents the non-riparian owner from acquiring any rights by prescription. On the other hand, the Restatement (Second) of Torts provides that a non-riparian owner may make reasonable and beneficial use of stream water so long as the use does not harm a riparian owner.

Coffin v. Left Hand Ditch Co.

(Water User) v. (Riparian Landowners)
6 Colo. 443 (1882)

M E M O R Y   G R A P H I C

Instant Facts

A company that diverted stream water to irrigate nonriparian land sued riparian landowners who damaged its dam for trespass.

Black Letter Rule

In Colorado and other western states, the first appropriator of water from a natural stream for a beneficial purpose has a prior right to the water to the extent of the appropriation.

Case Vocabulary

PATENT: A grant of government land, including the official certificate granting the land.

Procedural Basis: Appeal of action for damages for trespass and for an injunction.

Facts: George Coffin (D) acquired land by a government patent near the margin of the St. Vrain creek but not on it. The patent to Coffin (D) contained no reservation or exception for vested water rights. Before Coffin (D) acquired his land, the Left Hand Ditch Co. (Left Hand) (P) built a dam to divert water from the south fork of the St. Vrain creek. The water then followed a series of ditches and creeks and was used to irrigate land near the Left Hand creek. In 1879, the St. Vrain did not have sufficient water to supply Left Hand's (P) ditch and to irrigate Coffin's (D) land. Coffin (D) therefore destroyed Left Hand's (P) dam, interfering with Left Hand's (P) diversion of water. Left Hand (P) sued Coffin (D) for damages for trespass and for an injunction barring future damage to the dam. The trial court held for Left Hand (P).

Issue: May a nonriparian landowner acquire the right to use water by prior appropriation?

Decision and Rationale: (Helm, J.) Yes. The doctrine of priority of right to water by priority of appropriation has always existed in Colorado. In this part of the country where the climate is dry and the soil is arid, water rights are extremely valuable. The government has always encouraged the diversion and use of water for agriculture. If the doctrine of priority of appropriation is not protected, property values will be destroyed. The right to use water must be protected even after the land over which the water flows is conveyed to a third party. Therefore the common law doctrine giving a riparian owner a right to the flow of water over his land is inapplicable in Colorado. Instead, in the absence of statutes to the contrary, we hold that the first appropriator of water from a natural stream for a beneficial purpose has a prior right to the water to the extent of the appropriation. Coffin (D) argues that he has a better right to the water, even if Left Hand (P) was first in time, because his land lies near the St. Vrain and Left Hand (P) is diverting the water to an area near another creek. However, the right to use water acquired by priority of appropriation does not depend on where the water is being used. This doctrine is based on the imperative necessity for irrigation. It would be unfair to deny someone the right to use water after they have spent a lot of time and money diverting the water a long distance. Affirmed.

Analysis:

The court here essentially holds "first come, first served." Prior to this case, you have learned about riparian rights to water, meaning that a landowner has the right to the water flowing on his land. This is generally the rule in eastern states where the climate is wetter and water is more abundant. In western states, where the climate is drier, riparianism has been rejected and prior appropriation applies. In the 1800s, when this case arose, prior appropriation meant that water rights were acquired by being the first to use the water. In modern times, rights to use water are acquired by permit, with permits going to the first ones who apply. About eight western states follow the Colorado rule set forth here abolishing riparian rights. About nine states follow the California doctrine which applies riparian rights and appropriation rights.

Sipriano v. Great Spring Waters of America, Inc.

(Landowner) v. (Neighboring Landowner)
1 S.W.3d 75 (1999)

M E M O R Y   G R A P H I C

Instant Facts
A landowner sued a neighboring landowner when the landowner pumped all the underground water.

Black Letter Rule
Under the rule of "capture," landowners may pump as much groundwater as they want without liability to neighbors who claim that the pumping depleted their wells.

Case Vocabulary
GROUNDWATER: Water that has percolated through the soil and does not flow in an underground stream or in a defined channel.

Procedural Basis: Appeal of summary judgment in negligence action.

Facts: Sipriano (P) and other landowners sued Great Spring Waters of America, Inc. (Great Springs) (D) for draining their water wells. Great Springs (D) filed a motion for summary judgment based on the common law rule of "capture." Under this rule, landowners may pump as much groundwater as they want without liability to neighbors who claim that the pumping depleted their wells. The trial court granted the motion for summary judgment and the court of appeals affirmed.

Issue: May a landowner pump as much groundwater as it chooses without liability to neighbors?

Decision and Rationale: (Enoch, J.) Yes. Sipriano (P) asks us to abandon the rule of capture and adopt a reasonable use rule which would impose liability on landowners who unreasonably use groundwater to their neighbors' detriment. We do not think such a sweeping change in the law is appropriate at this time. Affirmed.

Concurrence: (Hecht, J.) The legislature has established a policy encouraging conservation of groundwater, but most of Texas has not complied with this policy. Texas is the only western state that still follows the rule of capture. The reasons for adopting the rule no longer exist. The Restatement (Second) of Torts applies a reasonable use rule. I agree with the Court that for now the rule of capture should not be abolished before the 1997 legislative changes have a chance to take effect. But I believe the rule of capture will soon become obsolete.

Analysis:

Under the rule of capture, each landowner is presumed to own all of the water under its land. There is no liability for taking all the groundwater except where the taking is malicious. This rule generally applies in the eastern states where water is more plentiful. In the western states, where the ground is more arid, courts usually apply the reasonable use doctrine or an appropriation rule, like in *Coffin v. Left Hand Ditch* Co. [the first appropriator of water from a natural stream for a beneficial purpose has a prior right to the water to the extent of the appropriation]. As the concurrence states in this opinion, Texas is the only western state that still applies the capture rule.

National Audubon Society v. Superior Court

(Environmental Organization) v. (City Water District)

33 Cal.3d 419, 189 Cal. Rptr. 346, 658 P.2d 709 (1983)

M E M O R Y   G R A P H I C

Instant Facts

An environmental organization sued a water district that was permitted to take almost all the water flowing into Mono Lake, thereby damaging the lake's beauty and ecology.

Black Letter Rule

Under the public trust doctrine, private rights to water may be subject to the public's rights of navigation, commerce, fishing, and preservation; the state has a duty to take the public trust into account when it allocates water resources.

Case Vocabulary

WRIT OF MANDATE: A court order requiring the performance of a specified act, or giving authority to have it done; they are available only in extraordinary circumstances and courts are vested with discretion to accept or reject petitions for them.

Procedural Basis: Petition for mandate to review summary judgment in action for declaratory and injunctive relief.

Facts: In 1940, the state water resources department granted a permit to the Department of Water and Power of the City of Los Angeles (DWP) (D) to appropriate virtually all of the water that flows into Mono Lake. As a result, the level of the lake had dropped, the salinity had increased, and gulls no longer bred there. The National Audubon Society (Audubon) (P) sued for declaratory relief and to enjoin the DWP's (D) diversion of the water on the ground that Mono Lake was protected by a public trust. The trial court granted the DWP's (D) motion for summary judgment, holding that the public trust doctrine was subsumed in the state's water rights system. Audubon (P) filed a petition for mandate with the California Supreme Court.

Issue: Does the public have any rights against private rights to water?

Decision and Rationale: (Broussard, J.) Yes. This case brings together two conflicting doctrines: the appropriative water rights system and the public trust doctrine. We must balance the needs to preserve the environment against the habitability and prosperity of much of California. Let's review a little history. In 1913, Los Angeles (D) built an aqueduct to carry water from the Owens River 233 miles to Los Angeles (D). This water supply was soon strained. Extending the aqueduct to Mono Lake made sense because it was only 50 miles from the Owens River. Los Angeles (D) purchased the riparian rights along four streams that flow into Mono Lake and to Mono Lake. The city (D) then applied for permits to appropriate the waters. Based on a Water Code statute that declared the use of water for domestic purposes to be the highest use of water, the water board felt it had no choice but to grant the permits, despite the evidence that Mono Lake would be impaired. The DWP (D) and Audubon (P) have very different projections about what effect the continued diversion of water from Mono Lake will have in the future. DWP (D) believes the lake will eventually stabilize and no longer shrink. Audubon (P) believes the lake will continue to shrink out of existence and that diversion of the water will drastically increase its salinity and thereby injure the food chain. The public trust doctrine is based on Roman law, providing that the government owns the navigable waters and land lying beneath them for the public's benefit. The purpose of the public trust is to protect navigation, commerce and fishing on the water, along with preserving the land's natural state. Here, Audubon (P) seeks to protect Mono Lake's recreational and ecological uses. Protection of these values is among the purposes of the public trust doctrine. The public trust covers all tidelands and navigable lakes and streams, including Mono Lake. Although the streams diverted by DWP (D) are not navigable, we hold that the public trust doctrine protects navigable waters from harm caused by diverting nonnavigable tributaries. We reach the following three conclusions: (1) The public trust doctrine prevents any party from acquiring the right to appropriate water that harms the interest protected by the public trust. (2) The legislature may grant permits for using waters in ways that may not promote the public trust. (3) The state has a duty to take the public trust into account when it allocates water resources. Once it has granted a permit for using water, the state must supervise the appropriation and may reconsider its decisions. Reconsideration is particularly important where, as here, the board did not take the public trust into account. Some responsible body must weigh the needs of Los Angeles (D) against the duty to protect Mono Lake. Let a peremptory writ of mandate issue ordering the trial court to vacate its summary judgment and enter a new judgment consistent with this opinion.

Analysis:

This case sets forth the public trust doctrine. Basically, it provides that in allocating water resources the state must balance the private interests at issue, here those of the thirsty people of Los Angeles, and the public's right to scenic, ecologically sound natural treasures. This is related to servitudes that you learned about earlier in this chapter; the government has a servitude over navigable waterways. All private rights to water are subject to this servitude.

Wronski v. Sun Oil Company

(Landowner) v. (Oil Company)
89 Mich. App. 11, 279 N.W.2d 564 (1979)

M E M O R Y   G R A P H I C

Instant Facts
Landowners claimed an oil company drilled oil from beneath their land.

Black Letter Rule
Landowners have the right to a reasonable opportunity to produce their fair share of oil in a pool.

Case Vocabulary

ACCOUNTING: A cause of action seeking an order requiring the opposing party to produce a detailed list of the receipts and disbursements related to the claim.

CONVERSION: The wrongful taking of the personal property of another, when in his actual possession, or taking of the goods of another who has the right of immediate possession.

PRORATION ORDER: An order specifying the maximum number of barrels of oil that may be produced each day per well.

WELL SPACING ORDER: An order specifying how many acres there must be between each well.

Procedural Basis: Appeal of action for accounting or for damages for conversion of oil.

Facts: Wronski (P) owned 200 acres of land, along with the mineral rights. The land was over the Columbus 3 pool, an oil field. The state established a uniform well spacing pattern for the pool and limited production to a maximum of 75 barrels of oil per day per well. Sun Oil Company (Sun Oil) (D) leased property over the pool and had drilled several oil wells that were subject to the proration order. Wronski (P) claimed that Sun Oil (D) over-drilled oil from these wells and drained the oil from beneath his land. Wronski (P) sued Sun Oil (D) for an accounting or for compensatory and exemplary damages. The trial court held that Sun Oil (D) had violated Wronski's (P) common law rights by illegally, unlawfully and secretly draining oil from beneath his property.

Issue: Does pumping oil from under another's land constitute conversion?

Decision and Rationale: (Holbrook, J.) Yes. In Michigan we follow the ownership-in-place theory. This means that the owner of land also owns the oil and gas beneath it. Because oil and gas may migrate across property lines, the rule of capture developed. Under this rule, a landowner may pump oil that migrated from adjoining lands without liability. The injured landowner's remedy was to "go and do likewise." To mitigate the harshness of this rule, the "fair share" doctrine emerged. Under this theory, a landowner is entitled to that share of oil in the common pool in the proportion which the reserves underlying his land bear to the recoverable reserves in the pool. In Texas, the rule of capture is modified to take into account conservation rules. Wronski (P) had the common law right to have a reasonable opportunity to produce its just and equitable share of oil in the pool. If Sun Oil (D) deprived Wronski (P) of this right, Sun Oil (D) is liable for conversion. We hold that any violation of a proration order constitutes conversion. Sun Oil (D) violated this order and is liable to Wronski (P) for conversion. Affirmed.

Analysis:

At common law, oil and gas were considered like wild animals, that is, beyond the control of the landowner. Thus, courts applied the law of capture, which they first applied to wild animals (you own any wild animals you capture on your land), to oil and gas. Under this rule, the first person to extract the oil or gas owned it, even if it came from under a neighbor's land. The only way a neighboring landowner could respond when reserves under his land were being drained by a well on the land of another was by counterdrilling. Note that you learned about the rule of capture in an earlier case in your casebook, *Sipriano v. Great Spring Waters of America, Inc.* In that case, the court held that landowners may pump as much groundwater as they want without liability to neighbors who claim that the pumping depleted their wells. The *Sipriano* court refused to abandon this rule and adopt a reasonable use rule instead. But in *Wronski,* the court rejected the rule of capture and instead held that landowners had the right to a reasonable opportunity to produce their fair share of oil in a pool.

United States v. Causby

(Government Airport Lessor) v. (Nearby Landowner)

328 U.S. 256, 66 S.Ct. 1062, 90 L.Ed. 1206 (1946)

M E M O R Y   G R A P H I C

Instant Facts

A landowner sued the U.S. for flying airplanes very low and frequently over his land.

Black Letter Rule

Flights over private land are a taking under the Fifth Amendment if they are so low and frequent as to directly and immediately interfere with the enjoyment and use of the land.

Case Vocabulary

CUJUS EST SOLUM EJUS EST USQUE AD COELUM: Latin for "to whomsoever the soil belongs, he owns also to the sky and to the depths."

TAKING: When the government acquires private property and fails to compensate an owner fairly.

Procedural Basis: Grant of writ of certiorari in action to determine whether federal government violated Fifth Amendment of U.S. Constitution.

Facts: Causby (P) owned land near an airport. The U.S. (D) leased the airport on a month-to-month lease. Airplanes passed directly over Causby's (P) land, about 67 feet over his house, blowing the leaves off his trees. As a result of the noise, Causby (P) had to give up his chicken business. Causby (P) and his family suffered from anxiety, fear, and lack of sleep. Causby (P) sued the U.S. (D) for taking its property without compensation in violation of the Fifth Amendment to the U.S. Constitution. The Court of Claims held that the U.S. (D) had taken an easement over Causby's (P) property and that the value of the property was $2000. The U.S. (D) filed a petition for writ of certiorari with the U.S. Supreme Court, which the Court granted.

Issue: Are flights over private land a taking under the Fifth Amendment?

Decision and Rationale: (Douglas, J.) Yes, if they are so low and frequent as to directly and immediately interfere with the owner's enjoyment and use of the land. The U.S. (D) argues that it has the right to travel through the navigable airspace without compensating the owner of the land beneath it. At common law, a landowner owned his land and all the space to the periphery of the universe. With modern air travel, that rule can no longer apply. But here, if the flights made Causby's (P) land completely uninhabitable, there would be a taking. It wouldn't matter that the planes never touched Causby's (P) land. Causby's (P) beneficial ownership of the land would be destroyed. It is not like a nuisance case where incidental damages could be recovered. While Causby's (P) use and enjoyment of his land is not completely destroyed, it is limited and the value is diminished. The fact that the Civil Aeronautics Authority approved the flight path is not relevant. Congress has determined that navigable airspace in the public domain is airspace above the minimum safe flight altitude, not the lower altitude that is needed for taking off and landing. A landowner owns at least as much of the space above his land as he can use for things like buildings, trees, and fences. The fact that he is not actually using that airspace for anything other than light and air does not mean he does not have a right to it. The damages here are not just consequential, but are the result of a direct invasion of Causby's (P) property. North Carolina law also holds that landowners own the space above their land, subject to the right to flight at regular altitudes. Flights over private land are not a taking unless they are so low and frequent as to be a direct and immediate interference with the enjoyment and use of the land. The Court of Claims did not specify the easement which the U.S. (D) took. It did not describe the frequency of flights, permissible altitudes, or types of airplane. Therefore, we reverse and remand the case to the Court of Claims to make these necessary findings.

Dissent: (Black, J.) Air transportation should not be made into a constitutional issue. Courts should only award damages and grant injunctions. Congress is in a better position to develop solutions for new national problems. I would reverse on the ground that there has been no taking in the constitutional sense.

Analysis:

Under the common law, *cujus est solum, ejus est usque ad coelum et ad inferos*: "to whomsoever the soil belongs, he owns also to the sky and to the depths." In other words, a landowner had complete control over everything above and below his property. For hundreds of years, there were no airplanes to interfere with a landowner's piece of the sky. But in the early 1900s, the emerging airline industry realized that air travel would be impossible if air carriers had to get permission from every owner of private property they flew over. In 1926, Congress passed the Air Commerce Act, which declared that the "navigable air space" of the U.S. was a public highway, open to all citizens. Navigable air space was defined as the sky above "the minimum safe altitudes of flight" as determined by federal regulators, usually 500 to 1,000 feet above the ground. In *Causby*, the Supreme Court officially abolished the principle of *usque ad coelum* and set forth a new rule: a landowner has air rights only insofar as they are essential to the use and enjoyment of the land. It's interesting to note that *usque ad coelum* didn't completely disappear; it was given to nations rather than to individual landowners. The 1944 Chicago Convention on International Civil Aviation declared that each country controlled the airspace over its territory.

Prah v. Maretti

(Landowner) v. (Adjacent Landowner)
108 Wis.2d 223, 321 N.W.2d 182 (1982)

M E M O R Y   G R A P H I C

Instant Facts

A landowner with solar heating sued a neighbor when the neighbor's proposed construction threatened to block the sunlight across his property.

Black Letter Rule

The private nuisance doctrine applies to determine whether a landowner has a right to protect his access to sunlight.

Case Vocabulary

SPITE FENCE: A fence or wall put up to spite a neighbor, usually to detract from the desirability or value of the neighbor's property.

Procedural Basis: Certified appeal to state supreme court of summary judgment in action for injunctive relief and for damages.

Facts: Glenn Prah (P) owned a house with a solar heating system. Panels on the roof supplied energy for heat and hot water. Maretti (D) subsequently bought a lot next to Prah's (P) and began plans for building a home. When Prah (P) learned of Maretti's (D) plans, Prah (P) told Maretti (D) that the house would create a shadow on Prah's (P) solar system and asked him to build the house a few feet over. They didn't reach an agreement. The subdivision architectural committee and the city planning commission approved Maretti's (D) plans and planned location for his house. There is some dispute about whether the proposed grade of the property was approved. Prah (P) sued Maretti (D) for injunctive relief and for damages. Prah (P) moved for a temporary injunction, which the court denied. Maretti (D) filed a motion for summary judgment, which the court granted. Prah (P) appealed to the court of appeals which certified the appeal to the Wisconsin supreme court.

Issue: Does a landowner have a right to access to sunlight on his property?

Decision and Rationale: (Abrahamson, J.) No, if the other landowner's use of his land is reasonable. Prah (P) makes three arguments: (1) Maretti's (D) construction constitutes a common law private nuisance; (2) Maretti's (D) construction constitutes a statutory violation; and (3) the construction interferes with Prah's (P) solar easement he acquired by prior appropriation. With respect to the first argument, a private nuisance is when one landowner's use of his property unreasonably interferes with another's enjoyment of his property. The Restatement (Second) of Torts defines private nuisance as a nontrespassory invasion of another's interest in the private use and enjoyment of land. The Restatement's broad definition of "interest in the private use and enjoyment of land" would include access to sunlight. Maretti (D) argues that his right to develop his land is per se superior to Prah's (P) right to sunlight. He cites the maxim "cujus est solum ejus est usque ad coelum," the owner of the land owns up to the sky and down to the center of the earth. However, a landowner's rights are not unlimited. Even at common law, a landowner could acquire the right to receive sunlight by an express agreement or by the doctrine of "ancient lights." Under this doctrine, if a landowner had received sunlight for a specified period of time, the landowner acquired a negative prescriptive easement to receive sunlight. American courts are less receptive to protecting sunlight and have rejected the ancient lights doctrine based on the needs of development. Many states apply the private nuisance doctrine to protect access to light. Courts had been reluctant to protect access to light based on three policy considerations: (1) Guarding landowners' right to use their property as they wish; (2) Valuing sunlight only for aesthetic enjoyment rather than for any practical purpose; and (3) Not restricting development. But these reasons no longer apply. Society has increasingly regulated land use. Sunlight is now seen as a source of energy. Unhindered private development is no longer as important. The flexible law of private nuisance is suited to resolving modern property development issues, as opposed to a rigid rule denying rights to sunlight. The right to sunlight depends on whether the conduct complained of is unreasonable. Thus, we hold that Prah (P) has stated a claim upon which relief can be granted. The trial court must decide whether Prah (P) is entitled to relief in this case. The fact that Maretti's (D) house conforms with zoning regulations, building codes, and deed restrictions is entitled to some weight in determining whether he has acted reasonably, but it is not controlling. The court must also look at the extent of harm to Prah (P), the suitability of solar heat in that neighborhood, the remedies available to Prah (P), and the cost to Maretti (D) of avoiding the harm. Summary judgment is not appropriate here. Reversed.

Dissent: (Callow, J.) Policy considerations should be left to the legislature

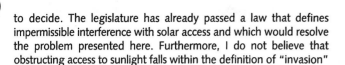

to decide. The legislature has already passed a law that defines impermissible interference with solar access and which would resolve the problem presented here. Furthermore, I do not believe that obstructing access to sunlight falls within the definition of "invasion" as that word is used in the Restatement's definition of nuisance. Otherwise all construction would constitute a nuisance because it impacts adjacent property.

Analysis:

By applying the nuisance doctrine to the right to access to sunlight, the court takes a middle road approach between completely denying the right and absolutely protecting it. Under the nuisance doctrine, the issue is reasonableness. Here Prah (P) will be able to keep his solar panels and his access to sunlight if the fact finder holds that Maretti's (D) acts are unreasonable. Prah (P) will not be able to access the sun, if the fact finder holds that Maretti's (D) use of his land is reasonable. Under this approach, the issues must be determined based on a case-by-case basis, rather than based on an absolute rule.

Chapter 19

This chapter introduces the student to some basic land-use controls. Governments have needed to exert some control over land uses since their inception. Indeed, one of the reasons governments exist is to control the use of land. The reasons for this are many and varied, and range from protecting the health and safety of inhabitants to promotion of commercial interests.

Zoning and similar land-control schemes are an elementary part of all town and city planning. When settlements were begun in the early American West, the establishing pioneers would plat out a town long before any significant numbers of people arrived to settle. Their motives were most always financial in nature, since a lot could not be sold and profits made until the land had been platted and recorded. Because of this, many town founders and platters were often mere land speculators; scurrilous individuals. Their occupation matters little, however, to the people who now live in their namesake towns.

Zoning and related matters often involve constitutional issues over property rights. Sometimes, when land is zoned, the land loses some or all of its value. When this happens, the town or municipality may be compelled by law to compensate the landowner. This chapter will discuss this and other basic concepts in land-use controls.

Chapter 19

NOTE: THE PURPOSE OF THIS OUTLINE IS TO ORGANIZE THE CASES SO THAT ONE CAN QUICKLY UNDERSTAND THE RELEVANCE OF EACH CASE TO THE COURSE. NO ATTEMPT IS MADE IN THIS OVERVIEW TO ADDRESS EVERY CONCEPT THAT MUST BE STUDIED. BE SURE TO READ THE ENTIRE CASEBOOK AND/OR OTHER MATERIALS TO GAIN A FULL UNDERSTANDING OF ALL CONCEPTS.

I. Zoning
  A. Zoning does not violate constitutional protections of property rights; zoning ordinances are a valid use of the police power.
    1. Zoning may be used to accomplish many different goals, such as attracting industry and commercial business, slow or increase growth, preserve the environment, etc.
    2. The prevailing view is that actions based upon aesthetic concerns should be construed as being in the public good. *See, e.g., Berman v. Parker.*
    3. Some zoning ordinances are vulnerable to challenge based upon First Amendment freedom of speech grounds.
  B. The zoning power may not be used to restrict a landowner's rights to freely utilize her land unless the restriction is substantially related to the public health, safety, morals or general welfare. *Nectow v. City of Cambridge.*

II. Subdivisions
  A. Regulation of subdivisions has been a part of American urban planning since the 19th Century.
  B. Subdivision zoning is similar to individual lot zoning, but goes one step further by creating larger tracts out of individual lots.
  C. Most subdivision plans attempt to make the subdivision mesh well with the comprehensive plan for the area which includes the subdivision.
  D. Many subdivision plans require developers to at least share the cost of installing facilities to service the new subdivision, such as sewer and water supply, streets, sidewalks and lights.

  E. Local governments have broad authority to deny zoning subdivision requests for valid health and safety factors so long as they have governing regulations, enacted pursuant to state law, which allow or require consideration of these factors. *Durant v. Town of Dunbarton.*

III. Official Planning Maps
  A. Many cities have official maps which depict all sorts of features, including both present and future streets.
    1. Zoning decisions are often made based upon features depicted on the map, but not yet installed.
  B. Protection of the public's financial interests is part of promoting the public welfare and will therefore support an exercise of the police power. *State Ex. Rel. Miller v. Manders.*
  C. Where government action substantially harms a property owner's interests, the property owner must be fairly compensated.

IV. Public Ownership
  A. A state or local government may employ public ownership as a tool in reaching zoning goals.
  B. A government taking of private property is constitutionally valid, and the process by which the taking is effectuated is irrelevant, so long as its purpose is to promote the public welfare. *Hawaii Housing Authority v. Midkiff.*
  C. Often, a zoning authority may condemn land in order to transfer it to another private party who will develop it in a manner which promotes the public good.

Village of Euclid v. Ambler Realty Co.

(Suburb) v. (Landowner)

(1926) 272 U.S. 365

M E M O R Y   G R A P H I C

Instant Facts

A realty company challenged a municipal ordinance which established a zoning plan restricting the use and size of buildings in various districts.

Black Letter Rule

Zoning ordinances are a valid exercise of the police power and thus do not violate the constitutional protection of property rights.

Case Vocabulary

CLEW: Old English spelling of "clue."

DEROGATION: Act of discrediting or belittling.

MUNICIPALITY: A legally incorporated association of residents in a relatively small area for governmental or other public purposes; another term for town, village or city.

PARALLELOGRAM: A geometric figure with two pairs of parallel and equal sides, such as a rectangle or square.

SANITARIUM: A medical institution for the care of invalids or convalescing patients.

Procedural Basis: Appeal from order granting injunction against enforcement of ordinance.

Facts: The Village of Euclid (D) is essentially a suburb of the City of Cleveland. Most of this land is used for farms or undeveloped. Ambler Realty Co. (P) owns a 68-acre tract of land in the western end of the village. This tract is bordered by a principal highway, Euclid Avenue, to the south, and by a major railroad, the Nickel Plate, to the north. There are residential lots with buildings to the east and west of Ambler Realty's (P) land. In 1922, the Village Council (D) adopted a comprehensive zoning plan to regulate and restrict the use of land, as well as the size of the lots and the heights of buildings. This ordinance divided the village into six use districts, U-1 to U-6. Each higher-numbered district included the uses of the district below it. Thus, U-1 districts allowed only single-family dwellings, while U-2 districts were extended to include two-family dwellings along with U-1 uses; U-3 districts were extended to include public buildings like churches, schools, hospitals with U-2 uses, and so on. U-6 districts could be used for sewage plants and junkyards, as well as for all residential and industrial operations below this level. The ordinance also divides the village into three height districts, H-1 to H-3, and four area districts, A-1 to A-4. The zone map attached to this ordinance shows that the use, area, and height districts are all allowed to overlap one another. The ordinance is enforced by the inspector of buildings under the board of zoning appeals. This board is authorized to make rules in order to implement the ordinance, as well as impose penalties for violations. The board can also interpret the ordinance in harmony with its general purpose and intent, so that the public health, safety, and general welfare may be protected. Ambler Realty's (P) land itself falls under the U-2, U-3, and U-6 districts. Ambler Realty (P) claims this land is vacant and that it has been held in order to sell and develop it for industrial uses. If Ambler Realty's (P) land is used for industrial purposes, it is worth about $10,000 per acre, but if it is kept for residential use, it is only worth roughly $2,500 per acre. The records indicate the normal and reasonably expected use of the land facing Euclid Avenue is for industrial and trade purposes. Ambler Realty (P) claims the ordinance violates its (P) constitutional rights, at both the state and federal levels, against deprivation of property and liberty without due process of law and denies it (P) the equal protection of the law.

Issue: Is it unconstitutional to enact an ordinance which establishes a comprehensive zoning plan regulating the use of property?

Decision and Rationale: (Sutherland) No. Zoning ordinances are a valid exercise of the police power and thus do not violate the constitutional protection of property rights. It is not necessary to decide separately if this ordinance violates the Ohio Constitution, as the question is substantively the same. Building zone laws are relatively new, yet are clearly necessary and valid. The increasing urbanization of modern life has required the use of regulations which, fifty years ago, would have been considered arbitrary or oppressive. While the meaning behind constitutional guarantees is constant, they must be applied in ways to meet the new conditions of life. The ordinance under review, then, must be justified through some aspect of the police power. This line is not a clear one, but must vary with circumstances and conditions. As with the law of nuisances, the maxim *sic utere tuo ut alienum non laedas* can serve as a guide. The building of a structure should be considered after the building itself is looked at in connection with the circumstances and its surroundings. No one has doubted the validity of regulations regarding the height of buildings within reasonable limits, the materials used in construction, the exclusion of certain trades from residential areas, etc. The Village (D), though essentially a suburb of Cleveland, is nonetheless a separate political body. As such, it has the power to govern itself as it sees fit within the limits of the Ohio and Federal Constitutions. Here, the serious question is over the exclusion of apartment houses, stores and shops, and other similar establishments from residential areas. The state courts that deny or narrow this power are greatly outnumbered by the state courts that sustain it. Various commissions and experts have reported for the separation of residential, business, and industrial buildings. They have pointed to the ease of providing appropriate firefighting measures in each section; increased safety, especially for children, by reducing traffic in residential areas; and increased home security. Also, the distracting of apartment houses helps preserve the quiet, open character of single-family neighborhoods, while preventing heavy traffic, overcrowding, and excessive noise. If nothing else, these reasons are enough to counter any arguments that the ordinance is arbitrary, unreasonable, or not substantially related to the public health, safety, morals, or general welfare. Unless such arbitrariness and unreasonableness is proven, the ordinance cannot be declared unconstitutional. Granted, it is entirely possible that the provisions set forth in a zoning ordinance may be found to be clearly arbitrary or unreasonable in a specific situation. When an injunction is sought, however, because the mere existence or threat of enforcement of the ordinance may cause an injury, the court will not go over the ordinance, sentence by sentence, to find which parts are constitutional and which parts are not. Without a specific complaint of actual injury, a land owner cannot challenge the constitutionality of such an ordinance. Decree reversed.

Analysis:

The seeds of four dominant themes in legislative zoning are planted in this opinion. First, there is the idea that a city or municipality is allowed to exclude some uses of property in certain circumstances. Second, the court essentially allows the same government body to control the economic markets, in a way, by designating where areas of trade can be set up. Third, the court places emphasis on local control in zoning measures, particularly when it establishes early in its opinion that Euclid is a separate governing entity. Finally, the court places some emphasis on aesthetic values, and how these can be a valid basis for a zoning ordinance in the appropriate context. This concept can be found in the discussion on separating apartment buildings from other residences. These concepts are mentioned throughout various judicial opinions and treatises on legislative zoning.

Nectow v. City of Cambridge

(Landowner) v. (Municipality)
277 U.S. 183, 48 S.Ct. 447 (1928)

M E M O R Y   G R A P H I C

Instant Facts

The City zoned residential a narrow strip of the landowner's tract. The landowner sued claiming the land was of no value zoned residential.

Black Letter Rule

The zoning power may not be used to restrict a landowner's rights to freely utilize her land unless the restriction is substantially related to the public health, safety, morals or general welfare.

Case Vocabulary

DISSEISED: Stripped of the ownership of land; to have land taken away.
LOCUS: Location or parcel.

Procedural Basis: Appeal to the Supreme Court after the lower court, upon consideration of the facts as reported by the master, sustained the ordinance as applied.

Facts: [The following facts are as reported by the master appointed by a justice of the lower court.] The City of Cambridge (Cambridge) (R) passed a zoning ordinance dividing the city into three districts: residential, business and unrestricted. Each district is subclassified to restrict the types and kinds of buildings which may be erected. Nectow's (P) land was zoned R-3, permitting only dwellings, hotels, clubs, churches, schools, etc. The parcel in question is about 29,000 square feet and is in the shape of a long strip, 100 feet in width. There is an auto assembly plant and other industrial facilities as well as a few residences surrounding the parcel. Before passage of the ordinance, Nectow (P) had a contract for sale of the parcel but after passage the would-be purchaser backed out due to the ordinance. The ordinance excludes business and industry from the parcel while the remainder of Nectow's (P) tract is unrestricted. Moreover, it appears that the street adjacent to the parcel will be widened in the near future, thus further narrowing the parcel to 65 feet. The master expressly found that "no practical use can be made of the land… for residential purposes…." Further, that "the districting of [Nectow's] land in a residence district would not promote the health, safety, convenience, and general welfare of the inhabitants of that part of [Cambridge]." And that "the [parcel] is of… little value for the limited uses permitted by the ordinance."

Issue: May a governmental authority restrict, through a zoning ordinance, a landowner's property rights where such ordinance is not related to the public health, safety, morals or general welfare.

Decision and Rationale: (Sutherland, J.) No. An inspection of the plat shows that the inclusion of the parcel in question is not indispensable to the general plan and could actually have been easily excluded by a small adjustment of the zoning boundaries. There does not appear to be any reason why this should not be done. Nevertheless, if that were all, we should not be warranted in substituting our judgment for that of the zoning authority. But that is not all. The governmental power to interfere by zoning regulations with the general rights of the landowner by restricting his use is not unlimited. Such restriction may not be imposed if it does not bear a substantial relation to the public health, safety, morals, or general welfare. Here, the finding of the master, confirmed by the court below, is that the health, safety, convenience, and general welfare of the inhabitants of the part of the city affected will not be promoted by the disposition imposed by the zoning ordinance. The finding of the master, supported by other findings of fact, is determinative of the case. The action of the zoning authorities thus comes within the ban of the Fourteenth Amendment and, therefore, cannot be sustained. Reversed.

Analysis:

The Due Process Clause of the Fourteenth Amendment is construed in this case to impose the general welfare requirement upon government in the zoning context. The Amendment includes the following language from which this construction is drawn: "nor shall any State deprive any person of life, liberty, or property, without due process of law." This clause, in laymen's terms, simply requires governments to treat their citizens fairly. This principle was embodied very early on in the Magna Carta, signed by King John (under some duress) of England in 1215, while his brother, Richard I, a.k.a. Richard the Lionhearted, was away fighting and dying in the Third Crusade. The Magna Carta guaranteed, among other things, that one could not be disseised without due process of law. Here, the Supreme Court employed the general welfare test, but many state courts simply ask whether the zoning ordinance is unreasonable, arbitrary or capricious. This language may give a court more leeway, but is generally applied in a same or similar manner as the Supreme Court applied the general welfare test.

Durant v. Town of Dunbarton

(Developer) v. (Zoning Authority)

121 N.H. 352, 430 A.2d 140

M E M O R Y   G R A P H I C

Instant Facts

A landowner applied to the planning board for approval of a subdivision plan. The planning board denied the request, citing potential problems with flooding, sewage and lines of sight for drivers of the adjacent street.

Black Letter Rule

A local government has broad authority to deny zoning subdivision requests for valid health and safety factors so long as it has governing regulations, enacted pursuant to state law, which allow or require consideration of these factors.

Procedural Basis: Appeal to the State's highest court from the trial court's affirmation of the Planning Board's denial of the application for subdivision.

Facts: Durant (P) owned a tract of land fronting Jewett Road, a State Highway. Desiring to divide this tract into several lots, Durant (P) submitted a subdivision plan (The Plan) to the State Water Supply and Pollution Control Commission (WSPCC), which approved it. Durant (P) then submitted her plan, along with the WSPCC's approval, to the Dunbarton Planning Board (Board)(R), which denied it after a hearing, citing three reasons for the denial: (1) potential disruption of natural water courses, (2) potential sight distance problems from the driveways exiting onto a State highway, and (3) potential problems with subsurface septic systems due to an extremely high water table in the area. Durant (P) appealed the denial to the trial court, which affirmed.

Issue: May a local government zoning authority deny approval of a development request pursuant to its zoning regulations due to potential health and safety hazards?

Decision and Rationale: (Douglas, J.) Yes. Durant (P) first argues that the Board (R) did not have authority under its subdivision regulations to deny the plan for the reasons given. If any of the Board's (R) reasons support the denial, Durant's (P) appeal must fail. State law authorizes municipalities to grant their planning boards discretion to approve or deny subdivision plans in accordance with the subdivision regulations it has previously adopted. The scope of those regulations may be quite broad and may include provisions promoting health, safety, convenience, or prosperity. In 1965, the Board (R) adopted its current subdivision regulations. The regulation upon which the Board (R) based its denial reads, in part, as follows: "Land of such character that it cannot be safely used for building purposes because of exceptional danger to health or peril from fire, flood or other menace shall not be platted for residential occupancy, nor for such other uses as may increase danger to health, life or property or aggravate the flood hazard, until appropriate measures have been taken by the subdivider to eliminate such hazards...." The regulation also places the burden of showing that the lot size is adequate for installation of a sewage disposal system and an on-lot water supply system. The State statutory delegation is thus quite broad and certainly allows for the regulation of septic tanks and sewerage systems. Durant's (P) next argument is that the regulations are impermissibly vague in that they do not contain standards for the evaluation of on-site systems. But the regulations, when read as a whole, inform the subdivider that her plan must contain adequate information to enable the planning board to conclude that future development of the land will not pose an exceptional danger to health. This language provides sufficient notice to developers of what is expected of them. The regulations with regard to potential disruption of water courses, though less specific, are also adequate. Under its subdivision regulations, a planning board may consider any characteristics of the land that relate to the current and future fitness of the land for building purposes. Water courses over land clearly affect the desirability and suitability of construction on a particular piece of property, and consideration of such factors is within the ambit of the Board's (R) delegated authority. Next Durant (P) argues that the Board's (R) findings of potential problems with water courses and waste disposal systems are inadequate because the regulations require "exceptional danger to health or peril from fire, flood, or other menace." Subdivision regulations are a tool for promoting the orderly and planned growth of a municipality. In evaluating a subdivision plan, such as Durant's (P) plan here, a board must consider current as well as anticipated realities. It may, therefore, deny a plan based on potential conflicts with its regulations. Although the Board (R) did not state that those potential dangers were exceptional, the record indicates that it found them to be so and we agree with the master's conclusion

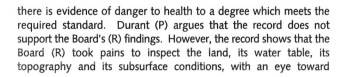

there is evidence of danger to health to a degree which meets the required standard. Durant (P) argues that the record does not support the Board's (R) findings. However, the record shows that the Board (R) took pains to inspect the land, its water table, its topography and its subsurface conditions, with an eye toward ascertaining its suitability for Durant's (P) proposed subdivision. Though the WSPCC approved the plan, the Board (R) is certainly entitled to rely in part on its own judgment and experience in acting upon applications for subdivision approval. Affirmed.

Analysis:

Just like many other areas of the law, zoning law has a uniform model, the Standard Zoning Enabling Act (SZEA). The SZEA includes a provision which authorizes legislative bodies at the local level to regulate the uses of land and set boundaries for different districts with different rules. The majority of these local legislative bodies appoint a group of citizens to a "planning board" or "planning commission." This planning commission is a panel of individuals, usually having experience in some nuance of real estate, which makes recommendations to the legislative body. To complete its task, the commission commonly holds hearings, conducts or commissions studies, etc. All of this in an effort to inform its recommendations. The largest ongoing responsibility of the commission is usually considering applications from landowners to have their land rezoned. Most wish to have their parcel rezoned to allow for a more intensive use; one that raises the value of the land. A few even ask to have neighboring property rezoned to a less intensive use. Similar to, but different, is the board of adjustment. The board of adjustment is a quasi-judicial body and hears landowners' requests to be allowed to use their land in a way not contemplated by the particular zoning regulation. While a few municipalities make rulings from the board of adjustment appealable directly to the legislative body before it goes to the local county court, most send appeals directly to court. As you can tell from the procedural basis, this is what happened here.

State Ex Rel. Miller v. Manders

(Would-be Builder) v. (Building Inspector)
2 Wis.2d 365, 86 N.W.2d 469 (1957)

M E M O R Y   G R A P H I C

Instant Facts

A landowner purchased a tract of land through which, unbeknownst to him, the City planned to install a street. When the landowner applied for a permit to erect a building on the planned street route, the City denied his application.

Black Letter Rule

1) Protection of the public's economic interests is within the scope of promoting the public welfare and will therefore support an exercise of the police power. 2) Where government action substantially harms a property owner's interests, the property owner must be fairly compensated.

Case Vocabulary

CERTIORARI: A writ or order employed by an appellate court, instructing the lower court to forward the record of a case to the appellate court for its review.
EX REL: Language employed in the title of a case, signifying that the government has taken up a case at the instigation of or on behalf of a private party.
MANDAMUS: A writ issued by a court, requiring a government official or a lower court to perform some task or function, usually of the ministerial variety.

Procedural Basis: Appeal to the State's highest court after the trial court dismissed the appeal from the local planning board's rejection of the appeal from the building inspector's denial of a building permit.

Facts: In 1947, the City of Green Bay, pursuant to the State's enabling statute and city ordinances, adopted an official map of the city showing established and proposed streets and other urban accoutrements. In 1953, Miller (P) purchased a tract of land lying to the north of Velp avenue in Green Bay. It was Miller's (P) intent to devote the parcel to industrial purposes and in order to do so, he planned to erect a building on a portion of the parcel fronting on Velp avenue. According to the official city map, however, Green Bay planned to put in an 80-foot wide street going north from Velp avenue, directly through the portion on which Miller (P) planned to erect his building. When Miller (P) applied for a building permit, building inspector Manders (R1), citing the planned street, refused to issue it. Miller (P) appealed the denial to the Zoning and Planning Board of Appeals (Board)(R2), challenging the constitutionality of the enabling statute and the city ordinances pursuant to which the City established its official map. After a hearing, the Board sustained Manders' (R1) denial of the permit application. Miller (P) then sought a mandamus order requiring Manders (R1) and the Board's (R2) to issue the building permit. This appeal was also denied and the action dismissed. Miller (P) has appealed.

Issue: 1) Does protection of the taxpayer's interests by considering the cost to the city when making zoning decisions constitute promotion of the public welfare thus making it a proper exercise of the police power? 2) Must a government fairly compensate a landowner where zoning and planning decisions result in substantial harm to the landowner's interests?

Decision and Rationale: (Currie, J.) 1) Yes. 2) Yes. The issue is whether Wisconsin's Official Map Law, § 62.23(6) (the statute), and the ordinances of the City of Green Bay enacted pursuant thereto, are unconstitutional as being a taking without just compensation. Section 62.23(6) provides for the adoption by the common council of any city of an official map showing existing streets, highways, parkways, etc. and also the exterior lines of planned new streets, etc. Subdivision (d) bars a permit from issuing for any building in the bed of any street shown or laid out on the map with a few exceptions. A person wishing to build in a street bed may apply for a building permit. One who fails to apply, or does but is turned down, and constructs a building anyway is not entitled to compensation for any damage sustained by the building due to the street construction. If land within the area of the planned street is not yielding a fair return, the board of appeals may go ahead and grant a building permit or variance covering the area of the planned street so long as the increased cost of opening such street is as small as practicable. Reasonable requirements may be also be imposed for granting such permit so long as they are designated to promote the health, safety, convenience or general welfare of the community. However, subdivision (d) also requires the granting authority to refuse a permit where the applicant will not be substantially damaged by placing his building outside the mapped street. Having reviewed the provisions at issue, the first question becomes clear. It is whether the enactment of § 62.23(6) may be sustained as a valid exercise of the police power on the ground that it tends to promote the general welfare. One of the objectives of the statute is to promote orderly city growth and development so as to prevent the haphazard erection of buildings. The are practical reasons why a city should be able to enforce such advanced planning. For one, a requirement that a city acquire title to land in the bed of planned streets and compensate the owner would create practical difficulties which would limit drastically any power conferred upon a city to adopt a general map which includes streets and highways that may be needed in the future. There is little doubt that an objective which seeks to achieve better city planning is within the concept of promoting the general welfare. The Constitution accommodates a wide range of community planning devices to meet the pressing needs and problems of a growing community. A second objective of the statute is to protect as much as possible the financial interests of the city's taxpayers by allowing a permit to be granted so long as it will increase the cost of opening the street as little as practicable. Protection of the economic interests of the general public falls within the scope of promoting the general welfare, and thereby affords a basis for the exercise of the police power. Indeed, without such a saving clause, it is very doubtful the statute would be constitutional. This saving clause requires refusal of a permit application where the applicant will not be substantially damaged by placing his building outside the zone of the planned street. Subdivision (d) must be so construed that the converse of this is true, i.e., it is the duty of the issuing authority to grant the permit if the applicant property owner would be substantially damaged were the permit denied. This construction is necessary to sustain the constitutionality of the statute, something the Court must do with all provisions of law if possible. Were the issuing authority to deny an application where the result would be substantial damage to the property owner, or were to grant a permit subject to a condition which would result in substantial damage, the aggrieved applicant may secure court review by certiorari. Affirmed.

Analysis:

This case represents a somewhat convoluted statement of the general law regarding takings. The basic rule when it comes to takings is that the landowner must be fairly and justly compensated where government action with respect to a parcel of land will essentially render the parcel valueless, or close to it. In other words, were you to own a piece of prime real estate upon which you plan to construct a skyscraper, the government would be perfectly within the law and would not have to make any compensation were it to build an overpass which makes it impossible to go through with the skyscraper, but nonetheless leaves the real possibility that you could put up a snow cone stand. The reason for this is that the parcel, while certainly not as valuable as it would have been with the skyscraper, still retains some value. Here, the Court prefers to use language like "substantial damage to the property owner." Regardless of the language employed, the meaning remains the same.

Hawaii Housing Authority v. Midkiff

(Government Agency) v. (Large Landowner)
467 U.S. 229, 104 S.Ct. 2321 (1984)

M E M O R Y   G R A P H I C

 Instant Facts

Hawaii decided to force owners of very large amounts of Hawaiian property to sell much of their property in order to increase land ownership rates. Midkiff (R) sued claiming the scheme was unconstitutional.

Black Letter Rule

A government taking of private property is constitutionally valid, and the process by which the taking is effectuated is irrelevant, so long as its purpose is to promote the public welfare.

Case Vocabulary

EMINENT DOMAIN: The power of the government to take property from a private individual in order to use it for a public purpose.
FEE SIMPLE: The most unrestricted and broadest interest in land one may possess. It lasts until the current fee holder dies without leaving any heirs behind to inherit the land.

Procedural Basis: The U.S. Supreme Court granted certiorari after the Circuit Court of Appeals reversed the District Court's ruling that the taking scheme was constitutional. This after Miller's (R) refusal to arbitrate.

Facts: The Hawaiian Islands were originally settled by Polynesian immigrants. In their society, all land was held at the will of the king of the islands; there was no private ownership of land. Despite early efforts to spread land ownership among the crown, the chiefs, and the common people, the land remained in the hands of a few. In the mid 1960s, the Hawaiian Legislature discovered that 49% of land in the islands was owned by the state or federal government, while 47% was in the hands of 72 private landowners. The Legislature concluded that concentrated land ownership was responsible for skewing the State's residential fee simple market. As a remedy, the Legislature decided to force the large landowners to break up their estates. In order to avoid the landowners having to pay significant federal taxes incurred by selling their land, the Legislature enacted the Land Reform Act (the Act), which allowed residential tracts to be condemned and the fee simple for the condemned land to be transferred to the existing lessee of the land. This scheme made the land sales involuntary and thus allowed the owners to avoid a significant portion of the potential tax liability. The Act allowed lessees living on single-family residential lots within tracts at least five acres in size to ask the Hawaii Housing Authority (HHA) (P) to condemn the leased property. When a set number of tenants on a tract make requests, the Act authorizes the HHA (P) to hold a public hearing to determine whether acquisition by the State of all or part of the tract will "effectuate the public purposes" of the Act. If the HHA (P) finds that these public purposes will be served, it is authorized to designate the tract for acquisition. The HHA (P) then acquires title to the tract at prices set by condemnation trial or by negotiation between lessors and lessees. After compensation has been set, the HHA (P) may sell the land titles to tenants. The HHA (P) may not operate for profit and may not sell or lease more than one lot to any one purchaser or lessee. In practice, funds to purchase the tracts has been supplied entirely by the lessees. This process was followed with respect to Midkiff's (R) land. Midkiff (R) sued claiming the Act violates the Fifth Amendment's Public Use Clause and asking that its enforcement be enjoined.

Issue: May the government force a landowner to negotiate with and sell land to private individuals without violating the Public Use Clause of the Fifth Amendment?

Decision and Rationale: (O'Connor, J.) Yes. Our starting point is the Court's decision in *Berman v. Parker*, wherein we held constitutional the District of Columbia Redevelopment Act, which provided for both the use of the eminent domain power to redevelop slum areas and the possible sale or lease of the condemned lands to private interests. In that case, we dealt with what has traditionally been known as the police power. An attempt to define its reach or outer limits is fruitless, for each case must stand on its own facts. It is the product of legislative determination addressed to the purposes of government, which have never been capable of complete definition. When the legislature has spoken, the public interest has been declared. The legislature, not the judiciary, is the main guardian of the public needs. This is so whether one is talking about Congress or a state legislature. Once the object is within the authority of the legislature, the right to realize it through the exercise of eminent domain is clear. The means by which the object is attained is also for the legislature to determine. It is argued that the Act allows a taking from one private citizen for the benefit of another private citizen. But the means of executing the project are for the legislature to determine, once the public purpose has been established. The "public use" requirement is thus coterminous with the scope of a sovereign's police powers. The role of the courts is thus to review the legislature's judgment as to what constitutes a public use, even when the eminent domain power is equated with the police power. This role is, however, an extremely narrow one. Deference to the legislature's "public use" determination is required until it is shown to involve an impossibility. Any departure from this judicial restraint would result in courts deciding on what is and is not a governmental function. The Court will not substitute its judgment as to what constitutes a "public use" unless the use be palpably without reasonable foundation. Of course, the Act, like any other, may not achieve its intended goals, but when the legislature's purpose is legitimate and its means are not irrational, our cases make clear that empirical debates over the wisdom of takings are not to be carried out in the federal courts. Redistribution of fees simple to correct deficiencies in the market as determined by the legislature is a rational exercise of the eminent domain power. Therefore, the Act must pass the scrutiny of the Public Use Clause. Government does not itself have to use property to legitimate the taking; it is only the taking's purpose, and not its mechanics, that must pass scrutiny under the Public Use Clause. Reversed.

Analysis:

Notice the Court's extreme deference to the determination of the Hawaii Legislature. What the Court has said is that no matter what a state does in using its eminent domain power, a court will not question the state's actions if the purpose behind the state's scheme is a public one. This leaves a court with one task when reviewing a state's use of eminent domain: examining whether the purported use is indeed a public use. Once again, the Court extends significant deference to the legislature's determination of public uses. This is akin to rational basis review, which the Court applies to most legislative determinations. It asks whether there could be a reasonable ground or basis for legislative action. If there could be, then the action will be sustained. Notice that there does not have to be a stated rational basis; just a potential rational basis. In other words, a court may come up with one on its own. When this type of very limited scrutiny is applied, the government action under examination is very rarely rejected as unconstitutional.

Chapter 20

This chapter offers a brief illustration of how the devices employed to control land uses are administered. It opens with a section on nonconforming uses and discusses how such uses are put to an end. The most prevalent manner in which this occurs is the amortization period. Instead of making payments to the bank for your mortgage, however, an amortization period in the land use regulatory context is a period of time at the end of which the nonconforming use must be terminated. Like most if not all zoning determinations, the arbitrary and capricious standard is applied to amortization periods.

We also have a case, *Stone v. City of Wilton*, in which the local zoning authority denied a developer permission to construct a multi-family, low-income housing project. Properly zoned for such a project when the developer purchased the tract, it was rezoned to a designation not allowing the project. The cited reasons were inadequate city services for such a project, but there is strong suggestion that the City had other, perhaps discriminatory motives. This is not an uncommon thread in zoning and developer-related cases.

The middle section discusses the means by which local governments can be flexible in their zoning approach. It also briefly talks about new and innovative zoning schemes. One of these is the Planned Unit Development or PUD. A PUD is a large section of land with mixed use zoning. All the things an individual needs to survive in our modern society are contained within the PUD. It has residential, retail, commercial, recreation and other designations all within a relatively small area. PUDs help foster a closer community and cut down on transportation problems because people do not have to drive to everywhere they need to go.

The final section briefly illustrates how zoning decisions can be made directly by the people through things like referenda and initiatives. The key to such means is the premise that power is derived and flows upward from the people; a referendum or initiative is looked at as a reservation of a small part of that power.

Chapter 20

NOTE: THE PURPOSE OF THIS OUTLINE IS TO ORGANIZE THE CASES SO THAT ONE CAN QUICKLY UNDERSTAND THE RELEVANCE OF EACH CASE TO THE COURSE. NO ATTEMPT IS MADE IN THIS OVERVIEW TO ADDRESS EVERY CONCEPT THAT MUST BE STUDIED. BE SURE TO READ THE ENTIRE CASEBOOK AND/OR OTHER MATERIALS TO GAIN A FULL UNDERSTANDING OF ALL CONCEPTS.

I. Nonconforming Uses: Existing Nonconformities
  A. An existing nonconformity is one that had been allowed, but was prohibited by a change in or enactment of zoning regulations.
    1. Many zoning amendments and/or initial enactments provided for a period during which a nonconformity could continue. These are often called an "amortization period."
  B. An amortization period for a nonconforming use is constitutional so long as it does not unreasonably inflict a substantial loss on the owner or fail to comport with the reasonableness requirement of due process. *Village of Valatie v. Smith.*
    1. Several courts have declared any amortization of nonconformities unconstitutional.
    2. Some municipalities establish an individual amortization period appropriate for each nonconformity.
  C. A landowner gains a vested right in an existing zone classification when she takes substantial steps in developing her parcel in conformity with the existing classification. *Stone v. City of Wilton.*
    1. Some states simply provide that the right to develop vests at the time the developer files for a building permit.
      a. This has been referred to as a "date certain vesting rights doctrine."
    2. A municipality may be barred on equitable estoppel grounds from rezoning land upon which it had assured a developer it could build. *Town of Largo v. Imperial Homes Corp.*
    3. A building permit issued in error and then

relied upon may be revoked in the majority of jurisdictions. The minority estop the issuing authority from revoking such a permit issued in good faith.

II. Adapting Regulations to Development Proposals
  A. Planning Ahead
    1. It is always impossible to plan perfectly for all uses to which a tract of land may be put in the future.
    2. Flexibility is thus built into all land-use regulatory schemes.
      a. Even so, the shear size and number of development plans at odds with existing regulations often overwhelms the system.
  B. Amending the Zoning Map
    1. One wishing to use land in a way not permitted by regulation usually must file an application for a zoning amendment with the local planning commission.
    2. Planning commissions will usually hold public hearings at which all those affected, including neighbors, may be heard.
    3. The high volume of such proposals leads to a zoning map which appears to be the result of whim and caprice. This is often called "spot zoning."
    4. Most courts will defer to the local regulatory body when it comes to rezoning decisions.
  C. Variances and Other Exceptions
    1. Where a proposed nonconforming use is compatible with established uses, a local zoning board of adjustment may issue special exception, sometimes called a "conditional use" permit, which spells out the requirements for the nonconformity to be allowed.
    2. Courts reviewing special exceptions often require the board to state its reasons for granting or denying a request and to base its decision on substantial evidence.

3. A variance from a zoning regulation is not confined to a specific use as is a special exception. They are given only to avoid unnecessary hardship

D. New Flexibility Tools

1. Despite great use of special exceptions and variances, zoning regulators need more flexibility. Other measures have been used to meet this demand, but are still subject to all constitutional restrictions against arbitrary action.

2. Some legislative bodies of local governments have taken to granting special exceptions, sometimes without conditions, themselves, in addition those issued by the planning board. Such special exceptions are more vulnerable to abuse because they are not subject to standards or procedural requirements as are those of the planning board.

3. Contract zoning is sometimes used whereby an owner wanting a different use will create covenants running with the land which restrict its use in accordance with an agreement between the owner and other interested parties.

4. Planed Unit Developments (PUD) allow several different uses to be allowed on one large tract.
   a. These uses are usually residential, commercial (professional offices, retail establishments), schools, churches, etc.
   b. These uses must meet certain performance standards. A PUD reduces the need for extensive transportation because all needs are in one area.

5. Euclidean zoning segregates different uses into separate districts with distinct boundaries.
   a. The often significant distance between uses in Euclidean zones leads to a greater reliance upon transportation and the problems that come with it.

6. Some states have implemented schemes to supervise local rezoning problems in an effort to achieve consistency with established goals and guidelines.

7. In some states, municipalities allow their citizens to participate in zoning regulation through the referendum process.
   a. Zoning decisions are legislative in nature and may be made by the general populace through referendum, but must not be arbitrary or capricious. *City of Eastlake v. Forest City Enterprises, Inc.*
   b. Not all state courts have determined zoning decisions to be legislative in nature, meaning they may not be made by referendum.
   c. Using the initiative process to rezone has been held proper. *Arnel Development Co. v. City of Costa Mesa.*

Village of Valatie v. Smith

(Municipality) v. (Mobile Home Owner)
83 N.Y.2d 396, 610 N.Y.S.2d 941 (NY. Ct. App. 1994)

M E M O R Y   G R A P H I C

Instant Facts

Smith (D) inherited a mobile home in Valatie. It was considered a non-conforming use by the Village of Valatie (P) who are forcing Smith (D) to move the home.

Black Letter Rule

An amortization period for a nonconforming use is constitutional so long as it does not unreasonably inflict a substantial loss on the owner or fail to comport with the reasonableness requirement of due process.

Case Vocabulary

AD HOMINEM: An argument that plays on personal prejudices rather than reason and logic based upon facts.
AMORTIZATION: Procedure by which zoning nonconformities are eliminated over time, usually by employing some mechanism which, when triggered by a certain event or lapse of time, requires the nonconformity to cease.

Procedural Basis: Appeal to the State's highest court from the Appellate Division's affirmation of the Supreme Court's grant of summary judgment to the mobile home owner.

Facts: In 1968, the Village of Valatie (Village) (P) enacted an ordinance prohibiting the placement of mobile homes outside mobile home parks. The ordinance also provided that any pre-existing mobile homes outside a park could remain as a nonconforming use until either ownership of the land or ownership of the mobile home changed. According to the Village (P), at the time of enactment there were six mobile homes within the exception. In 1989, Smith (D) inherited her father's mobile home. The Village (P) subsequently instituted this action to enforce the ordinance and have the unit removed. The Supreme Court granted Smith's (P) summary judgment motion, reasoning that the right to continue a nonconforming use runs with the land and , therefore, setting a termination point at the transfer of ownership was unconstitutional. The Appellate Division affirmed on the ground that the ordinance was unreasonable in that the amortization period bears no relationship to the use of the land or the investment in that use. The Village (P) appeals.

Issue: Must an amortization period for a nonconforming use bear some relationship to the land's use?

Decision and Rationale: (Simons, J.) No. First, it is important to note that Smith (D) does not challenge the ordinance as applied; that it effects an unconstitutional taking. Nor does Smith (D) challenge the government's authority to regulate land use as a valid exercise of the police power. Now, it is clear that a municipality may enact laws reasonably limiting the duration of nonconforming uses. Thus, the narrow question before the Court is whether the Village (P) acted unreasonably by establishing an amortization period that uses the transfer of ownership as an end point. The policy to allow nonconforming uses to continue has its origins in concerns over land use regulations being viewed as confiscatory and unconstitutional. Because many nonconforming uses went on and on, we have characterized the law's allowance of them as "grudging tolerance," and have recognized the right of the municipality to take reasonable measures to eliminate them. "Amortization" properly refers to a liquidation, but in this context the owner is not required to take any financial step. "Amortization period" simply designates a period of time granted to owners of nonconforming uses during which they may phase out their operations; it is a grace period, putting owners on notice of the law and giving them a fair opportunity to recoup their investment. It serves generally to protect an individual's interest in maintaining the present use of the property. The validity of an amortization period depends on its reasonableness, but there is no fixed formula for determining what is a reasonable period. It is presumed valid and the owner carries the heavy burden of overcoming that presumption by demonstrating that the loss suffered is so substantial that it outweighs the public benefit to be gained by the exercise of the police power. Indeed, in some circumstances, no amortization period at all is not only reasonable, but required. In others, the period may vary in duration among the affected properties. We have also held that an amortization period may come to an end at the occurrence of an event as unpredictable as the destruction of the nonconforming use by fire. Smith (D) does not challenge the ordinance's period under our established balancing test for amortization periods, i.e., whether the individual's loss outweighs the public gain. Instead, Smith (D) asserts that the Village's (P) means of eliminating nonconforming uses is not reasonably related to the Village's (P) legitimate interest in land use planning. More particularly, Smith (D) argues that the length of the period must be related either to land use objectives or to the financial recoupment needs of the owner and, second, that the ordinance violates the principle that zoning is to regulate land use rather than ownership. We have never required that the length of the period be based on land use objectives. To the contrary, these periods are usually calculated to protect the owner's interests at the temporary expense of public land use objectives. The typical benchmark for determining the proper length of the period is the amount of time the owner needs to recoup her investment. This is unrelated to land use objectives. Were land use objectives the sole consideration, there would not be any amortization periods. The nonconforming use would be eliminated right away. Thus, the real issue here is whether the Village (P) was irrational when it considered the non-financial interests of the owners when striking the balance between those interests and the land use objectives. Our previous cases on amortization periods have all dealt with commercial property where the owner's interests are easily reduced to financial considerations. The same may not be true for the owners of residential properties. Being able to recoup one's investment may be secondary to having a place to live and remaining there. Here, rather than focusing solely on financial recoupment, the Village (P) took a broader view of the individual's interest in maintaining the present use of the property; it allowed such use until ownership of the home or property was transferred, even though any investment may have been recouped long before. Smith (D) has not shown why such a scheme is irrational or explained why the non-financial interests of owners should not be considered. Smith (D) has failed to overcome the presumption of the ordinance's validity and prove, if she must, unconstitutionality beyond a reasonable doubt. Smith's (D) second argument is based on the fundamental rule that zoning deals with land use and not with the person who owns the land. This is an expression of the rule against *ad hominem* zoning decisions. It is claimed that the Village's (P) amortization scheme violates this rule because the right to the nonconforming use is enjoyed only by those who owned the property in 1968 and cannot be transferred. However, the prohibition against *ad hominem* zoning is meant to keep an identifiable individual from being singled out for special treatment in land use regulation. No such individual treatment is present in this case. All similarly situated owners are treated the same, as are all prospective buyers. What Smith (D) is actually claiming is that the Village (P) should not be allowed to infringe on an owner's ability to transfer the right to maintain a nonconforming use. Absent amortization legislation, the right to continue a nonconforming use runs with the land, but once such legislation is implemented, the right ends at the close of the period. The law is not rendered invalid because the original owner no longer has the right to transfer or because she and the subsequent owner receive disparate treatment under the land use regulations. Put simply, the test remains whether the amortization period unreasonably inflicts a substantial loss on the owner or fails to comport to the reasonableness required by due process. There is no independent requirement that the right to continue the nonconforming use be available for transfer at a given time. Smith's (D) facial challenge must therefore fail. Reversed.

Analysis:

For all practical purposes, anytime a zoning ordinance is put into place or amended there are bound to be some uses which do not conform with the new requirements. This was certainly the case when zoning ordinances came into vogue. Such "nonconforming uses" need not be a particular "use" at all; many times, they may be something along the lines of a building which sits too close to the lot line or one that is too tall. Thus, a more accurate label might simply be "nonconformities." Of course, such nonconformities lead to a conundrum of sorts: what should be done about a house that sits too close to the lot line? Should it be torn down, or picked up and moved? If it is required to be torn down or is subjected to some other requirement which renders it of no or little value, there are bound to be constitutional issues regarding takings and denial of due process. Indeed, the casebooks are replete with decisions which deal with precisely these issues. There are different points of view in different courts, both state and federal, with respect to these issues. In fact, some courts have gone so far as to declare that since the state has created in some instances the property right to continue with a nonconformity, to deny such a right does not violate the Fourteenth Amendment's Due Process Clause. *See, e.g., Dekalb Stone, Inc. v. County of Dekalb.*

Stone v. City of Wilton

(Real Estate Developer) v. (Municipality)
331 N.W.2d 398 (Iowa 1983)

M E M O R Y   G R A P H I C

Instant Facts

Stone (P) purchased land zoned for multi-family dwellings with the intent of erecting such dwellings. Subsequent to the purchase, the City of Wilton (D) rezoned the area for single-family dwellings, thus depriving Stone (P) of the multi-family development.

Black Letter Rule

A landowner gains a vested right in an existing zone classification when she takes substantial steps in developing her parcel in conformity with the existing classification.

Procedural Basis: Appeal to the state's highest court from the trial court's dismissal of a petition for declaratory judgment, injunctive relief and damages.

Facts: In June 1979, Stone (P) purchased a six-acre parcel of land in the City of Wilton (City) (D) with the intent of developing a portion of it into federally subsidized multi-family dwellings in accordance with the then-existing multi-family dwelling zoning classification. After purchase, Stone (P) incurred expenses for architectural fees and engineering services in the preparation of plans and plats for submission to the city council and its planning and zoning commission. In addition, Stone (P) secured a Farmer's Home Administration (FHA) loan commitment for construction of the project. In December 1979, Stone (P) filed a preliminary plat with the city clerk. Following a public meeting, the planning and zoning commission recommended to the city council that land which included the tract owned by Stone (P) and zoned for multi-family dwellings be rezoned to single-family residential due to alleged inadequacies of sewer, water and electrical services. Stone's (P) May 1980 application for a building permit to begin construction was denied due to the pending rezoning recommendation. In May 1980, Stone (P) filed this action seeking to stop the City (D) from going forward with its plans to rezone, as well as damages of $570,000.00 in the event the rezoning did go through. This amount represented monies already expended, anticipated lost profits and alleged reduction in the land's value. The injunction was denied and the City (D) went ahead with its rezoning plan. This appeal followed.

Issue: May the zoning authority rezone or re-classify a parcel of land when doing so effectively stops a landowner's planned development by prohibiting the use to which the developer intends to put the land?

Decision and Rationale: (McGiverin, J.) Yes. The inevitable restriction on individual uses of property which accompany zoning normally do not constitute a taking. Stone (P), however, claims to have had a vested right in developing their property as subsidized, multi-family housing, meaning the rezoning amounts to a taking. We disagree. The record shows that a factor in Stone's (P) choice of property was zoning which permitted multi-family residences; that Stone (P) made certain expenditures totaling over $7,900.00 in preparation for the intended project, plus time and effort personally expended. The standard for determining whether a property owner has vested rights in an existing zoning classification examines the extent to which an owner has gone to develop the land in conformity with that classification. It is impossible to fix a definite percentage of total cost which establishes vested rights and applies to all cases. It depends upon the type of the project, its location, ultimate cost, and *principally the amount accomplished under conformity*. [Emphasis in original] Each case must be decided on its own merits, taking these elements into consideration. In the present case, one of the factors leading to the purchase of this land in Wilton was the fact that it was zoned for multi-family residences. Stone (P) did take steps to develop the parcel in conformance with the then-existing zoning classification, but these were only the most preliminary steps toward construction. The architect's plans were not the working blueprints of a contractor; they were much less significant and involved. No construction bids were sought and no contracts were let. No materials were placed on the site and no construction or earth work was started. Stone's (P) efforts and expenditures prior to the rezoning were not so substantial to create vested rights in the completion of the housing project on that particular tract of land in Wilton. Affirmed.

Analysis:

A close read of the facts of this case seems to indicate that the proffered reasons for rezoning the tract of which Stone's (P) land was a part may not have been completely legitimate. Stone (P) wanted to construct low-income, federally subsidized multi-family residences. Many people identify such projects with high crime rates and lowering property values of the surrounding land. Indeed, the phrase "housing project" often incites such concerns. The Court seemed aware of this prospect as indicated by its characterization of the proffered reasons for the rezoning as "alleged." There is another theme in this case. Thinking back to first-year contracts, the rule enunciated herein by the Court is analogous to estoppel and reliance. Try to look at existing zoning classifications as a contract between a municipality and its citizens. When a landowner takes substantial steps to develop her land, in accordance with and in reliance upon the existing zoning classification, she has relied upon the continued vitality of that particular zoning classification. Whereas the law of estoppel and reliance simply looks at whether a party has relied to their detriment upon a promise or contention, and not the level of such reliance, here the Court looks at the significance of the steps the landowner has taken in reliance upon the zoning classification. If such reliance has been substantial, the owner gains a vested right in the continued existence of a zoning classification which ensures the survival of the development.

City of Eastlake v. Forest City Enterprises, Inc.

(Municipality) v. (Land Developer)
426 U.S. 668, 96 S.Ct. 2358 (1976)

M E M O R Y   G R A P H I C

Instant Facts

A land developer sought to have a parcel re-zoned, but was rejected when a referendum required by city ordinance failed to reach the necessary 55%.

Black Letter Rule

Zoning decisions are legislative in nature and may be made by the general populace through referendum, but must not be arbitrary or capricious.

Case Vocabulary

ARGUENDO: For argument's sake.
FEDERALIST PAPERS: A series of papers written and published during the national debate over initial state ratification of the Constitution. These essays promoted the Constitution for its feature of a strong central government.
REFERENDUM: Process by which potential legislative or constitutional enactments are submitted to the popular will of the people at large through an election.

Procedural Basis: Appeal to the United States Supreme Court from the Ohio Supreme Court's reversal of the Court of Appeals' affirmation of the trial court's declaration that the city ordinance is constitutional.

Facts: Forest City Enterprises, Inc. (FCEI) (R) acquired a parcel of land in the City of Eastlake (Eastlake) (P) which was zoned "light industrial." In May 1971, FCEI (R) applied for a zoning change to permit construction of a multi-family, high-rise apartment building. The Planning Commission recommended the change to the City Council, which has the power to accept or reject it. Meanwhile, the citizens of Eastlake (P), by popular vote, amended the City Charter to require that any changes in land use to which the City Council has agreed must be submitted by referendum to the citizens, of whom 55 per cent needed to approve of the change for it to become effective. The City Council approved FCEI's (R) requested zoning change but refused to approve FCEI's (R) subsequent request for "parking and yard" approval for the proposed building because the Council's rezoning action had not yet been submitted to the voters for ratification. FCEI (R) then filed this action in state court seeking a declaration that the new Charter Provision is an unconstitutional delegation of legislative power to the people. While the case was pending the voters failed to approve the zoning change. The Court of Common Pleas and the Court of Appeals sustained the provision. The Ohio Supreme Court reversed on the ground that enactment of zoning provisions is a legislative function and the referendum requirement, lacking any standards to guide the voters, permitted the police power to be exercised in an arbitrary and capricious manner.

Issue: May zoning decisions be submitted to the voters by referendum without violating any constitutional provisions?

Decision and Rationale: (Burger, C.J.) Yes. The Ohio Supreme Court rested its ruling on the proposition that zoning referendum involves a delegation of legislative power. A referendum cannot, however, be characterized as a delegation of power. Under our constitutional assumptions, all power derives from the people, who can delegate it to representative instruments which they create and, in the process, reserve to themselves the referendum power. The referendum is a means for direct political participation, amounting to a veto power over enactments of the legislature. It gives citizens a direct voice in public policy. In framing a constitution, the people of Ohio specifically reserved the power of referendum to the people of each municipality. Specifically, the Ohio constitution allows the people to use the referendum to deal with any question with which the particular municipality could deal by legislative action. The Ohio Supreme Court expressly found Eastlake's (P) rezoning action to be legislative in nature. It also held that the amendment to the City Charter to require a referendum constituted a "delegation" of power violative of constitutional guarantees because the voters were given no standards to guide their decisions; no mechanism existed, nor could it, to assure voters would act rationally. This potential for caprice and whimsical determinations by referenda, the court held, violated due process. Many courts in other contexts have held that congressional delegation of power to a regulatory entity must include discernible guiding standards which ensure the delegatee's action can be measured for its fidelity to the legislative will. Assuming, *arguendo*, these cases are relevant to state governmental functions, they involve a delegation of power by the legislature to regulatory bodies not directly responsible to the people; but here, the power is reserved to the people, thus making this doctrine inapplicable. FCEI (R) also bases its claim on federal due process requirements as outlined in *Euclid v. Ambler Realty*, but it does not rely on the direct teachings of that case. Under *Euclid*, a property owner may challenge a zoning restriction as being "clearly arbitrary and unreasonable, having no substantial relation to the public health, safety, morals, or general welfare." If this were the case with the substantive result of the referendum, the fact the voters wish it so would not save it from judicial scrutiny. But the Ohio Supreme Court did not hold, and FCEI (R) does not argue that the present zoning classification violates the holding of *Euclid*. If it does, FCEI (R) is free to challenge it in state court as being unreasonable or arbitrary. That being so, nothing more is required by the Constitution. Nothing in our cases is inconsistent with this conclusion. Two decisions of this Court were relied upon by the Ohio Supreme Court. But in both cases the delegation of legislative power originally given by the people was to a narrow segment of the community, not to the people at large. In *Eubank v. City of Richmond*, the power to establish building setback lines was conferred upon owners of two-thirds of the property abutting any street. In *Washington ex rel. Seattle Title Trust Co. v. Roberge*, authority was given to establish philanthropic homes for the aged in residential areas, but only upon written consent of two-thirds of owners within 400 feet of the proposed facility. Neither of these involved a referendum procedure; but rather a standardless delegation of power to a limited group of property owners. These are easily distinguishable. As a basic instrument of democratic government, the referendum process does not, in itself, violate the Due Process Clause of the Fourteenth Amendment, when applied to a rezoning ordinance. Reversed.

Dissent: (Powell, J.) It is perfectly legal and proper to submit generally applicable legislative questions to the public through referendum. But here the only issue concerned the status of a single small parcel owned by one person. The procedure afforded this person no chance to be heard, even by the electorate. This is fundamentally unfair and appears to open opportunities for local government bodies to by-pass normal protective procedures for resolving issues affecting individual rights.

Dissent: (Stevens, J.) I have no doubt about the validity of the initiative or the referendum as a method of deciding questions of community policy. But the popular vote is not an acceptable way of adjudicating the rights of individual litigants. The problem here is unique in that it may involve a three-sided controversy, in which there is potential conflict between the rights of the property owner and the rights of his neighbors, and also potential conflict with the public interest in preserving Eastlake's (R) basic zoning plan. If the latter aspect predominates, the referendum would be an acceptable procedure. But where, as here, it is clear the first potential conflict predominates, I think it essential that the property owner be afforded a fair opportunity to have his claim determined on its merits.

Analysis:

It seems odd that the Ohio Supreme Court would hold that legislative power had been delegated to the people through the referendum process. It is the most basic principle of our constitutional system that all power is derived and flows upward from the people. It is not the case that once this power is conferred it is gone from the people forever, never to be returned. If it were, the people would never have the option of instituting a recall election for a public official accused of malfeasance of office. Once elected, such an official would be able to remain until the next regularly scheduled election. Better to look at a referendum scheme such as that employed in this case as the people simply reserving certain authority to themselves rather then allowing their elected officials to have it all. Notice, however, that the Court makes pretty clear that the people's authority to accept or reject a proposed zoning change is not absolute. No matter how much popular support a proposed change may receive in the referendum, it is still open to attack in state court on the ground that the voters' decision is irrational, capricious, arbitrary, unreasonable, etc. This requirement flows from the Due Process Clause of the Fourteenth Amendment.

Perspective
Regulatory Takings

Chapter 21

This chapter explores the limitations upon governmental employment of land-use regulations. The "taking issue" is one of the most, if not the, most important issue in land-use law and touches the lives of all persons who own land. The most-implicated legal provision in the takings context is, of course, the Fifth Amendment, which prohibits private property from being taken for public use without just compensation. Just about all of the several states include a same or similar provision in their constitutions. Like numerous other rights found in the Bill of Rights, the rule against takings has been incorporated into the Fourteenth Amendment's Due Process Clause, and is thus applicable to the states.

The basic principle of takings law in the regulatory context is that while property may be regulated to a certain extent, if the regulation goes too far, i.e., renders the property economically valueless, or frustrates the owner's reasonable investment-backed-expectations, the owner must be justly compensated. Whether the regulation goes too far is always a question of degree, requires a fact-specific inquiry and thus keeps courts around the nation very busy. What takings law does is recognize that in order to fully function in the best interests of the public, sometimes it is necessary to usurp a landowner's domain over his or her property. It is said that the State, as sovereign, not only creates property rights, but also may extinguish them. The Fifth Amendment simply recognizes that government is not free to disregard the property rights of landowners. This reflects the fundamental position property and property ownership has occupied and continues to occupy in the Anglo-Saxon legal tradition.

As you work your way through the chapter, keep in mind the level of deference accorded states in their land-use regulation decisions. As with any area of law, takings law has undergone a constant evolution. As the United States Supreme Court worked its way through the 20th Century, it became apparent that it was reducing the amount of leeway afforded states in this context. No longer will the Court idly sit by and rubber-stamp state decisions by using the rationale basis standard of review. A blind legislative determination, designed to render a taking constitutional, will no longer be allowed to go unscrutinized by the Court.

Chapter 21

NOTE: THE PURPOSE OF THIS OUTLINE IS TO ORGANIZE THE CASES SO THAT ONE CAN QUICKLY UNDERSTAND THE RELEVANCE OF EACH CASE TO THE COURSE. NO ATTEMPT IS MADE IN THIS OVERVIEW TO ADDRESS EVERY CONCEPT THAT MUST BE STUDIED. BE SURE TO READ THE ENTIRE CASEBOOK AND/OR OTHER MATERIALS TO GAIN A FULL UNDERSTANDING OF ALL CONCEPTS.

I. Origin: Government may not effect a "taking," without compensation, by enacting laws forbidding certain land-uses where such action amounts to an absolute extinguishing of the land's value to the owner. *Pennsylvania Coal Co. v. Mahon.*

II. Compensation
   A. Where a taking is only temporary, because the government abandons its development plans or otherwise, the landowner still must be fairly compensated for the period during which the owner could not use the land. *First English Evangelical Lutheran Church of Glendale v. County of Los Angeles.*
   B. Courts differ on the measure of damages for temporary regulatory takings, but all limit them to actual damages.
   C. Some claims for property deprivation have been filed under Section 1983 due to its fee-shifting provisions. Some courts are reluctant to apply this statute in the regulatory-taking context.

III. Factors to Consider
   A. A regulation which does not interfere with an owner's primary expectations or plans for a property, and allows the owner to receive a reasonable return on her investment, does not effect a taking which requires compensation. *Penn Central Transportation Co. City of New York.*
      1. One way to compensate a landowner for frustration of investment-backed-expectations is to provide the landowner with Transferable Development Rights (TDR),

which can be used for developing other tracts.
   B. A permanent physical occupation, pursuant to law, of any portion of an owner's land, however small or insignificant, is a taking. *Loretto v. Teleprompter Manhattan CATV Corp.*
   C. What might otherwise be considered a regulatory taking is not a taking if the rule or regulation at issue is such that it inheres in the title; background legal principles and common law rules such as nuisance, usually qualify as being inherently part of the title. *Lucas v. South Carolina Coastal Council.*
      1. The 'public trust doctrine' is one example of a common law principle which might be used as a basis for arguing that the landowner had notice of a land-use restriction at the time of acquisition.
      2. A temporary moratorium which prohibits all economically beneficial use for a time is measured against the value of the property as a whole, rather than against the value during the period of the moratorium, and is thus usually not considered a taking. *Woodbury Place Partners v. City of Woodbury.*
      3. Simple lost value caused by government regulations may suffice as a taking. *Florida Rock Industries, Inc. v. United States.*

IV. Exactions
   A. Conditioning the granting of a development permit on the landowners conveyance to the public of certain property rights, such as an easement, must conform with the law of takings, i.e., it must use rational means in serving a legitimate public purpose and must not deprive an owner of all economically valuable use of the land without just compensation. *Nollan v. California Coastal Commission.*
   B. Conditioning the grant of a development permit upon the developer's conveyance of

property rights is constitutional if (1) an essential nexus exists between the legitimate state interest and the permit condition, and (2) the degree of the exactions required by the condition bears a rough proportionality to the projected impact of the proposed development. *Dolan v. City of Tigard*.

1. A government wishing to exact money from the applicant in return for granting a permit must meet less-stringent standards than it would were it exacting property rights. *Ehrlich v. City of Culver City*. Such monetary exactions might be "impact" fees and/or "linkage" fees.

V. Evolution of Takings Law

A. A takings claim is ripe when the responsible regulatory agency has reached a final decision regarding the permitted land uses under the current regulatory scheme, such that it can be said that the landowner has been denied all economically beneficial use or that her reasonable investment-backed expectations are defeated to the extent a taking has occurred. *Palazzolo v. Rhode Island*.

B. The fact that a landowner acquired the land after the current land-use regulatory scheme was enacted will not defeat a takings claim. *Palazzolo v. Rhode Island*.

1. Some state courts have held statutes sufficient to constitute background limitations on the landowner's title. The owner never had that particular property right to begin with; he bought the land subject to the background limitation that government could impose that particular restriction on use. *See, e.g., Gazza v. New York State Dep't of Envtl. Conservation*.

VI. Legislative Takings Provisions

A. In 1995, Congress enacted the Private Property Protection Act. It offers more protection of private property rights than that accorded landowners under the Constitution.

B. At least one state, Texas, has enacted laws requiring landowners to be compensated when government regulations cause a certain percentage loss of land value.

C. Some commentators argue for, and some states have adopted measures providing for, a setoff of required compensation due to benefits conferred on the landowner who suffers the taking.

Pennsylvania Coal Co. v. Mahon

(Mining Company) v. (Homeowner)
260 U.S. 393, 43 S.Ct. 158 (1922)

M E M O R Y   G R A P H I C

Instant Facts

A homeowner with property rights only in the surface is trying to stop a mining company from mining out the ground beneath his home.

Black Letter Rule

Government may not effect a "taking" without compensation by enacting laws forbidding certain land-uses where such action amounts to an absolute extinguishing the land's value to the owner.

Case Vocabulary

BILL IN EQUITY: A suit filed in a court of equity, which is a court that decides issues based upon what is good, right and fair.

DEFENDANT/PLAINTIFF IN ERROR: Names used in referring to parties in a suit when it reaches the appellate level where the names are sometimes flip-flopped based upon which party is taking the appeal.

Procedural Basis: Certification to the United States Supreme Court from the state's highest court reversal of the trial court's determination that the Act as applied is unconstitutional

Facts: Mahon (P) is the owner of a parcel of land under the surface of which the Pennsylvania Coal Company (PCC) (D) plans to mine, potentially causing the surface to subside or sink. PCC (D) was the original owner of both the surface and subsurface rights to the land, but in 1878 had conveyed by deed the surface rights, while reserving the right to remove all subsurface coal without risk of liability for any subsidence of the surface. PCC (D) still retains those rights under the deed. Mahon (P) filed suit seeking to stop PCC (D) from mining under his property and causing a subsidence. Mahon (P) claims under the Kohler Act (Act), which forbids the mining of anthracite coal in such a way as to cause a subsidence of any structure used as a human habitation, with some exceptions, including one where the surface and subsurface rights are owned by the same party.

Issue: Does the police power allow government to strip one of previously existing rights of property and contract where the diminution of such rights is total and the public interest is small, without compensation?

Decision and Rationale: (Holmes, J.) No. It is true that government could scarcely go on if to some extent property values could not be diminished without paying for every such change. Some values are enjoyed under a implied limitation and must yield to the police power. But this implied limitation is not absolute, for if it were, the Contract and Due Process Clauses would be swallowed whole. One factor in determining such limits is the extent of the diminution of a property interest. When it reaches a certain magnitude there must be an exercise of eminent domain and compensation to sustain the act. Each case must be judged on its own facts with the greatest weight being given to the judgment of the legislature. This is the case of a single private house. There is a public interest even in this, as there is in every purchase and sale. Some existing rights may be modified. But usually in private affairs the public interest does not warrant much of this kind of interference. A source of damage to such a house is not a public nuisance. The damage is not common or public. The extent of the public interest is shown by the Act to be limited, since it does not apply to land where the surface is owned by the owner of the coal. Also, it is not justified as a protection of personal safety. That could be provided for by notice. On the other hand, the extent of the taking is great. It purports to abolish a very valuable estate in land and a contract hitherto binding Mahon (P). If we were dealing with Mahon's (P) position alone, it would be clear that the Act does not disclose a public interest sufficient to warrant such an extensive destruction of constitutionally protected rights. But this case has been treated as one in which the general validity of the Act should be discussed. It is our opinion the Act cannot be sustained as an exercise of the police power. To make it commercially impracticable to mine certain coal has the same effect for constitutional purposes as appropriating or destroying it. It is true that in *Plymouth Coal Co. v. Pennsylvania* we held competent legislation requiring a pillar of coal be left along the line of adjoining property for the safety of the employees of either mine. But that was out of safety concerns and it secured an advantage which has been recognized as a justification of various laws. The rights of the public in a street purchased or laid out by eminent domain are those for which it has paid. If it has been shortsighted in acquiring only the surface rights without the right of support, we see no authority for simply taking the latter without compensation. The protection of private property in the Fifth Amendment presupposes that it is wanted for public use, but requires compensation for the taking. Similarly, the Fourteenth Amendment. The general rule at least is, that while property may be regulated to a certain extent, if regulation goes too far it will be recognized as a taking. We must not forget that a strong public desire to improve the public condition does not warrant taking a shortcut around the constitutional requirement of payment. This is always a question of degree, however, and thus cannot be disposed of by general propositions. Reversed.

Dissent: (Brandeis, J.) Every restriction on the use of property in the exercise of the police power deprives the owner of some right theretofore enjoyed and is an abridgement of property rights without compensation. But restrictions to protect the public health, safety or morals is not a taking. The restriction here in question is merely the prohibition of a noxious use with the property remaining in the hands of its owner. The Act merely prevents the owner from making a use which interferes with paramount rights of the public. Whenever the use prohibited ceases to be noxious the restriction will have to be lifted. This restriction may not be imposed if its purpose is not to protect the public. But the purpose does not cease to be public because incidentally some private persons may thereby receive gratuitously valuable special benefits. Thus, owners of low buildings may obtain, through statutory restrictions on the height of neighboring structures, the equivalent of an easement of light and air. Nor is a restriction imposed through the police power inappropriate because the same end might be effected through eminent domain, or otherwise at public expense. If mining anthracite would necessarily loose poisonous gasses, no one would doubt the power of the State to prevent the mining without buying the coal field. In either case, we deal with a public nuisance.

Analysis:

This case exposes two requirements associated with public diminution of property rights. First, they must serve the public welfare. Second, if it is a taking, i.e., a complete diminution of the property's value, it must be reasonably compensated. Here, the Court questions the public purpose of the Act and declares a taking what the Act purports to do because PCC's (D) rights are worthless without the ability to mine the coal. The Court is correct when it states that the provisions of the Act itself expose its lack of a true public purpose. That it is the interests of the surface owner it tries to protect is made clear by its failure to cover situations where the surface owner also owns the subsurface rights to the coal. The public interest, if there were one, would be compromised in the latter situation just as it would in the former. Yet the latter is allowed to proceed while the former is not. Justice Brandeis, in his dissent, simply whitewashes over the Act's lack of any significant public purpose. He completely ignores this when he states that the Act should not run afoul of the Constitution "because incidentally some private persons may thereby receive gratuitously valuable special benefits. The benefit to the surface owner is not an "incidental" effect of the Act; it is, rather, the Act's overriding purpose.

First English Evangelical Lutheran Church of Glendale v. County of Los Angeles

(Landowner) v. (Municipality)
482 U.S. 304, 107 S.Ct. 2378 (1987)

M E M O R Y   G R A P H I C

Instant Facts
After it was severely flooded, a municipality temporarily banned building on a parcel of flat land owned by a church. Claiming the land was useless without the ability to build upon it, the church seeks compensation for the duration of the prohibition.

Black Letter Rule
Where a taking is only temporary, because the government abandons its plans or otherwise, the landowner still must be fairly compensated for the period the land could not be used.

Case Vocabulary
WATERSHED: The entire area of land from which water flows into a drainage channel, usually a river.

Procedural Basis: Certification to the U.S. Supreme Court from the a decision of the State's Court of Appeals' upholding the trial court's dismissal of the suit.

Facts: In 1957, the First English Evangelical Lutheran Church of Glendale (Church)(P) purchased a 21-acre parcel in a canyon along the banks of the Middle Fork of Mill Creek, which is a natural drainage channel for a watershed owned by the National Forest Service. Twelve acres of the Church's (P) parcel are flat land called Lutherglen, upon which was operated a retreat center and recreation area for handicapped children. In July 1997, a fire denuded the upstream from Lutherglen creating a serious flood hazard. A severe flood occurred in February 1978 and destroyed the buildings of Lutherglen. In January 1979, because of the flood, the County of Los Angeles (County)(D) adopted an ordinance, effective immediately, prohibiting construction or enlargement of structures within the flood zone, which included Lutherglen. The Church (P) filed suit alleging that the Ordinance denies it all use of Lutherglen and seeking damages. In affirming the trial court's dismissal of the suit, the Court of Appeals assumed the suit sought damages for the uncompensated taking of all use of Lutherglen. That court relied upon California Supreme Court precedent holding that the remedy for a temporary taking is limited to nonmonetary relief.

Issue: Must a landowner be compensated when government land-use regulations amount to a taking that is, in effect, only temporary?

Decision and Rationale: (Rehnquist, C.J.) Yes. We begin with direct reference to the Fifth Amendment, which provides that "private property [shall not] be taken for public use, without just compensation. As this language indicates, this provision does not prohibit the taking of private property, but instead places a condition on the exercise of that power. This condition is designed not to limit governmental interference with property rights per se, but rather to secure compensation in the event of otherwise proper interference amounting to a taking. It is established that governments may elect to abandon its intrusion or discontinue regulations. Similarly, they may acquiesce in a judicial declaration that an ordinance has effected an unconstitutional taking. These situations result in a "temporary" taking. Must the landowner wait until the taking becomes permanent to take legal action? Surely the answer is no. We have yet to examine whether the landowner must be compensated for these temporary takings. We find substantial guidance in cases where the government has only temporarily exercised its right to use private property. In such cases, compensation is measured by the principles normally governing the taking of a right to use property temporarily. Once a court determines that a taking has occurred, government retains the whole range of options already available—amend the regulation, withdraw the offending regulation, or exercise eminent domain. Thus we do not require the exercise of eminent domain. We merely hold that where there has been a taking of all use of property, no subsequent action by the government can relieve it of the duty to provide compensation for the effective period of the taking. We also point out that we treat as true for purposes of our decision that the Ordinance in question denied the Church (P) all use of its property and we limit our holding to the facts presented. We realize our holding reduces the freedom and flexibility of land-use planners. But such consequences necessarily flow from any decision upholding a claim of constitutional right; many constitutional provisions are designed to limit governmental authorities and the Just Compensation Clause of the Fifth Amendment is one of them and here requires the County (D) to justly compensate the Church (P) for its loss. Reversed.

Dissent: (Stevens, J.) Our cases make it clear that regulatory and physical takings are very different. While virtually all physical invasions are deemed takings, a regulatory program that adversely affects property values does not constitute a taking unless it destroys a major portion of the property's value. This diminution of value inquiry is unique to regulatory takings. Unlike physical invasions, regulatory programs constantly affect property values in countless ways, and only the most extreme regulations can constitute takings. The policy implications of today's ruling are obvious and far reaching. This ruling will have a chilling effect on land-use planners who now may avoid taking any action that might give rise to a claim for damages. Much important regulation will never be enacted.

Analysis:

To make things clear, a true "taking" occurs when the government compels a land owner to actually transfer ownership of the land to the government. There are, however, other types of takings. A regulatory taking occurs where a regulation effectively forbids any profitable use. For example, say a regulation prohibited the raising and harvesting of all crops except sugar beets on a certain parcel of land. But one tract within that parcel is owned by Farmer Jones and simply does not have the required nutrients in the soil to raise sugar beets, but corn and soybeans grow great. Farmer Jones' land now has no profitable use. A regulatory taking has thus occurred because Farmer Jones has lost all or nearly all the sticks in his bundle. There is still one issue, however, with identifying the property rights which have been transferred to the government. If no rights are transferred, has there been a taking? To get around this, the Supreme Court simply relies on the extent of the diminution of the landowner's interests.

Penn Central Transportation Co. v. City of New York

(Landmark Owner) v. (City)
(1978) 438 U.S. 104

M E M O R Y   G R A P H I C

Instant Facts

Penn Central made plans to construct an office building over Grand Central Terminal, but was blocked by a Landmarks Preservation Law.

Black Letter Rule

A law which does not interfere with an owner's primary expectation concerning the use of the property, and allows the owners to receive a reasonable return on his or her investment, does not effect a taking which demands just compensation.

Case Vocabulary

ABROGATE: To end the effect of something through government action; to annul.
BEAUX ARTS: An artistic style which is known for its use of vivid decorative detail, historic elements, and a noticeable leaning toward grand, monumental forms in architecture.

Procedural Basis: Appeal from judgment in action for declaratory and injunctive relief.

Facts: In 1967, New York City's (D) Landmarks Preservation Commission (Commission) designated Grand Central Terminal a landmark under the city's (D) Landmarks Preservation Law. The Terminal, owned by Penn Central Transportation Co. (P) and its affiliates, has been described as "a magnificent example of the French beaux arts style." For at least 65 years, the property had been used as a railroad terminal with office space and concessions. The landmark law did not interfere with the Terminal's continued use in this capacity, but restricted any changes in the Terminal's exterior architectural features without the Commission's approval. In addition, landmark owners are allowed to transfer their development rights under zoning regulations to contiguous properties on the same block, or other properties they also own. At this time, Penn Central (P) owned several properties in downtown Manhattan. In 1968, in order to increase its income from the Terminal, Penn Central (P) entered into a long-term lease with UGP (P), a British corporation. UGP (P) was to build a 55-story office building above the Terminal, paying an annual rent of $1 million during construction and at least $3 million thereafter. Penn Central and UGP (P) submitted two plans to the Commission: one with a modern office tower over the French-style facade of the Terminal, and one with a completely redesigned Terminal. The Commission sternly rejected both plans, calling the first one "an aesthetic joke." It also said, however, that construction would be allowed depending on whether a proposed addition "would harmonize in scale, materials, and character" with the Terminal. Penn Central and UGP (P) brought suit in state court, alleging the landmarks law effected a taking of their (P) property. The trial court granted injunctive and declaratory relief, but the intermediate appellate court reversed. The New York Court of Appeals affirmed, finding no taking as the law only restricted, not transferred, control of the property.

Issue: Does the application of a law which restricts an owner's use of property, but does not interfere with the owner's primary use of the property or deny a reasonable economic return on it, constitute a taking?

Decision and Rationale: (Brennan) No. A law which does not interfere with an owner's primary expectation concerning the use of the property, and allows the owners to receive a reasonable return on his or her investment, does not effect a taking which demands just compensation. There is no set formula for deciding these cases, and so this Court must look at the particular facts here. The extent to which the law has interfered with distinct, investment-backed expectations is particularly relevant. Penn Central and UGP (P) claim that the airspace above the Terminal is a valuable property interest that has been taken through the landmark law. This claim is rejected because the rights in the property as a whole, not those in individual estates, must be considered. Also, Penn Central and UGP (P) argue that the law effects a taking by significantly diminishing the economic value of an individual landmark site, the Terminal property, unlike other laws which impose restrictions on entire historic districts. This argument is rejected because this landmark law, like others throughout the country, is part of a comprehensive plan to preserve landmarks all over the city. The interference with Penn Central's (P) property rights is not severe enough to equal a taking. The law does not interfere with Penn Central's (P) primary expectation concerning the use of the Terminal for railroad service, office space, and concessions. Thus, Penn Central (P) is permitted to obtain a "reasonable return" on its investment in the Terminal. Moreover, Penn Central and UGP (P) have not been barred from any construction over the Terminal; only the two plans in question have been rejected.

Because they (P) have not submitted plans for a smaller structure, it is not known whether they (P) will be denied permission to use any of the Terminal airspace. Finally, though Penn Central and UGP (P) claim their (P) airspace rights have been taken, they (P) have always had the right to transfer those rights to nearby properties. This situation may not be ideal for them (Ps), but those rights are still very valuable. Judgment affirmed.

Dissent: (Rehnquist) This landmark law is unlike typical zoning restrictions that usually provide benefits for, as well as impose burdens on, restricted properties. There is no reciprocity of advantage here.

Only a few buildings are singled out with considerable burdens and no comparable benefits. Because there was no nuisance-control justification in restricting Penn Central's (P) airspace rights, the action resulted in a taking. Though the value of the transferable development rights may possibly be valuable enough to serve as just compensation, there is not enough evidence to prove this conclusively. The decision should be remanded to see if these transferable rights amount to "a full and perfect equivalent for the property taken."

Analysis:

The concept of "reasonable return on investment" is problematic. While prior to this decision, the New York Court of Appeals also relied on this idea, it noted that it was "an elusive concept, incapable of definition." The reasonableness of the return on the owner's investment must be based on the value of the property. However, the value of the property is inescapably dependent on the amount of return that is permitted or available. This circularity of reasoning is what makes the concept of reasonable return on investment a somewhat shaky one.

Loretto v. Teleprompter Manhattan CATV Corp.

(Landlord) v. (Cable Company)
458 U.S. 419, 102 S.Ct. 3164 (1982)

M E M O R Y   G R A P H I C

Instant Facts

A state law allowed cable television companies to attach its cable boxes to apartment buildings without compensating the landlord. One landlord is suing the cable company on the ground that the law effects a taking.

Black Letter Rule

A permanent physical occupation of any portion, however small or insignificant, of an owner's land pursuant to law is a taking.

 ## Case Vocabulary

TRESPASS: An illegal act committed by one person against the property or person of another.

Procedural Basis: Certification of a class action suit to the U.S. Supreme Court from the State's Court of Appeals' ruling that the law did not effect a taking.

Facts: In order to facilitate tenant access to cable television (CATV), New York law provides that a landlord must permit a cable television company to install its cable equipment upon the landlord's property. Prior to her purchasing it, Teleprompter Manhattan CATV Corp. (TMC)(D) installed upon Loretto's (P) apartment building CATV equipment which occupied small portions of its roof and side. Before the CATV law went into effect, TMC (D) routinely obtained authorization from the landlord for the install and compensated for this access at a standard rate of 5 per cent of the gross revenues generated from the particular property. The new law prohibited landlords from restricting access to cable television companies and from demanding any compensation from tenants; or from the companies beyond a certain rate set pursuant to law. A one-time $1.00 payment to the landlord is provided for, however. The State Commission ruled that because this fee was equivalent to what the landlord would receive if the property were condemned it satisfied constitutional requirements unless there was a showing of greater damages attributable to the taking. Loretto (P) brought a class action on behalf of all owners of real property in the State on which TMC (D) has placed CATV components, alleging trespass and a taking without just compensation.

Issue: Does a minor but permanent physical occupation of an owner's property authorized by government constitute a taking for which just compensation is due under the Fifth and Fourteenth Amendments?

Decision and Rationale: (Marshall, J.) Yes. The historical rule that a permanent physical occupation of another's property is a taking reflects the fact that such an appropriation is perhaps the most serious form of invasion of an owner's property interests. In such situations, the government does not simply take a single "strand" from the "bundle" of property rights; it chops through the bundle, taking a slice of every strand. The traditional rule also avoids otherwise difficult line-drawing problems. Few would disagree that if the State required landlords to permit third parties to install swimming pools on buildings' roofs, the requirement would be a taking. The fact the CATV components take up an insignificant amount of space is irrelevant. Constitutional protection cannot be predicated upon the size of the permanent invasion. Reversed.

Dissent: (Blackmun, J.) It is worth reviewing what was "taken" in this case. At issue are about 36 feet of cable one-half inch in diameter and two 4" x 4" x 4" metal boxes, which together occupy about one-eighth of a cubic foot on Loretto's (P) roof. Indeed, Loretto (P) did not discover this "physical invasion" until after she had purchased the building. Such a *per se* taking rule as the Court creates today rests on outmoded distinctions between physical and nonphysical intrusions. The significant loss and insignificant loss should not be treated the same. Under this rule, every statute which requires a landlord to make physical attachments to his rental property also must constitute takings, even if they serve indisputably valid public interests in tenant protection and safety.

Analysis:

Does size matter? The majority makes much of the idea that it does not; that if requiring a pool to be installed is a taking, then so should be the smallest intrusion. One must admit, it does have the attraction of bright-line rule simplicity. Yet while it trumpets this rationale, the majority offers no reasons why size should not matter. Why not draw the line at a "substantial intrusion," which would require just compensation. Too murky of a dividing line? They might allow juries to make this factual determination in the same way they determine whether a defendant has been negligent. On another note, this case indirectly discloses the inner workings of the judicial process. Given the apparent weakness of the majority's size argument, it seems clear that it was not initially included in the opinion. It was most certainly written only after a draft of Justice Blackmun's dissenting opinion was circulated in the Court, which opinion makes light of the insignificance of the taking. Appellate Courts invariably operate in this manner so that their varying opinions in any given case do not fail to give shrift to the arguments of their fellow jurists.

Lucas v. South Carolina Coastal Council

(Developer) v. (State Government Agency)
505 U.S. 1003, 112 S.Ct. 2886 (1992)

M E M O R Y   G R A P H I C

Instant Facts

A developer purchased some valuable beach property with the intent of constructing two single-family dwellings. A later-enacted state law designed to preserve the coastal area prohibits the development plans. The developer claims a taking without compensation.

Black Letter Rule

When a law is passed which, effectively, renders a parcel of property valueless, a taking has occured requiring compensation.

Case Vocabulary

AD HOC: Put together for a singular or particular purpose.

Procedural Basis: Certification to the U.S. Supreme Court from the reversal by the State's highest court of the trial court's ruling that there was a taking without compensation.

Facts: In 1986, Lucas (P) paid $975,000 for two residential lots on the Isle of Palms in South Carolina, upon which he intended to build single-family homes. In 1988, South Carolina enacted the Beachfront Management Act (Act), which prohibited Lucas (P) from erecting any permanent habitable structures on his two lots. The trial court found that this rendered Lucas's (P) lots "valueless." South Carolina's interest in intensively managing the coastal zone is expressed in the Act, which requires owners of coastal zone land that qualifies as a "critical area" to obtain a permit from the South Carolina Coastal Council (Council)(D) prior to committing the land to a use other than the use in place at the time the Act was passed. Lucas's (P) lots qualify as critical area under the Act and the Council (D) therefore turned down his request for a building permit. Lucas (P) filed suit claiming the Act effected a taking without just compensation. Lucas (P) did not claim the Act was an invalid exercise of the State's police power, but rather that the Act's complete extinguishment of his property's value entitled him to compensation regardless of whether South Carolina had acted in furtherance of legitimate police power objectives. The trial court agreed, holding that Lucas's (P) property had been taken without just compensation. The South Carolina Supreme Court reversed, finding dispositive Lucas's (P) concession that the Act was properly designed to preserve the State's beaches. It ruled that when a regulation is designed to prevent serious public harm, no compensation is owing under the Takings Clause regardless of the effect on property value.

Issue: Where the operation of a statute legitimately enacted pursuant to the police power renders land valueless, must the government make just compensation to the landowner?

Decision and Rationale: (Scalia, J.) Yes. In the past we have generally eschewed any set formula for determining how far is too far, such that there has been a taking without just compensation, preferring instead to engage in ad hoc inquiries. We have, however, described two discrete categories of regulatory action as compensable without case specific inquiry into the public interest advanced in support of the restraint. The first encompasses physical invasions of property. In general, no matter how minute the intrusion, and no matter how weighty the public purpose behind it, we have required compensation. The second situation which calls for categorical treatment is where regulation denies all economically beneficial or productive use of the land. Surely, in the extraordinary situation when no productive or economically beneficial use of land is permitted, it is less realistic to indulge in our usual assumption that the legislature is simply "adjusting the benefits and burdens of economic life [to secure an] average reciprocity of advantage" to everyone concerned. And the functional basis for permitting government to affect property values without compensation—that "[g]overnment hardly could go on if to some extent values incident to property could not be diminished without paying for every such change in the general law," does not apply to the relatively rare situation where government has deprived a landowner of economically beneficial uses. On the other side, supporting a compensation requirement, is the fact that land regulations that leave the owner without economically beneficial or productive options for its use, carry with them a heightened risk that private property is being pressed into some form of public service under the guise of mitigating serious public harm. The many statutes, both state and federal, which provide for the use of eminent domain suggest the practical equivalent in this setting of negative regulation and appropriation. We think there are good reasons for our belief that when the owner of real property has been called upon to sacrifice all economically beneficial uses in the name of common good, he has suffered a taking. The trial court found that Lucas's (P) two lots were rendered valueless by operation of the Act. This finding entitled Lucas (P) to compensation. Lucas (P) believed it

unnecessary to take issue with either the purposes behind the Act or the means chosen to effectuate those purposes. The South Carolina Supreme Court, however, thought the Act no ordinary enactment, but rather involved an exercise of the State's police powers to mitigate the harm to the public interest that Lucas's (P) use of his land might occasion. By neglecting to dispute the findings in the Act or the legislature's purpose, Lucas (P) conceded that the shoreline area is an extremely valuable public resource; that building on it causes its destruction; and that the Act is necessary to prevent such public harm. These concessions brought the case within a long line of holdings sustaining against Due Process and Takings Clause challenges the use of the police powers to enjoin an owner from activities akin to public nuisances. It is correct that many of our prior opinions have suggested that "harmful or noxious uses" may be banned without compensation. However, we think the State Supreme Court was hasty in concluding that this principle decides the present case. "Harmful or noxious use" analysis was simply the progenitor of our later statements that "land-use regulation does not effect a taking if it 'substantially advance[s] legitimate state interests." Where the State seeks to sustain regulation that deprives land of economically beneficial use, it may resist compensation only if the logically antecedent inquiry into the nature of the owner's estate shows that the proscribed use interests were not part of his title to begin with. This accords with our "takings" jurisprudence. A property owner necessarily expects the uses of his property to be restricted, from time to time, by various measures newly enacted by the State in legitimate exercise of its police powers. In the case of land the notion that title is somehow held subject to the "implied limitation" that the State may subsequently eliminate all economically valuable use is inconsistent with the historical compact recorded in the Takings Clause that has become part of our constitutional culture. Where "permanent physical occupation" of land is concerned, we have refused to allow the government to decree anew no matter the weight of the public interest. We believe similar treatment must be accorded confiscatory regulations, i.e., those that render the land economically valueless: Any limitation so severe cannot be newly legislated or decreed (without compensation), but must inhere in the title itself. The "total taking" inquiry we require today will ordinarily entail analysis of, among other things, the degree of harm to public lands and resources, or adjacent private property, posed by the claimant's proposed activities; the social value of the claimant's activities and their suitability to the locality in question; and the relative ease with which the alleged harm can be avoided through measures taken by the claimant and the government (or adjacent private landowners) alike. It seems unlikely that common law principles would have prevented erection of any habitable or productive improvements on Lucas's (P) land as they rarely support prohibition of the "essential use" of land. The question is, however, one for state law to answer on remand. To win its case, South Carolina must do more than offer up the Legislature's determination that Lucas's (P) proposed uses go against the public interest. It must identify background principles of nuisance and property law that prohibit the proposed uses. Only upon such a showing may the State claim that the Act is taking nothing. Reversed and remanded.

Concurrence: (Kennedy, J.) Where a taking through regulation deprives property of all value, the test must be whether the deprivation is contrary to reasonable, investment-backed expectations, which must be understood in light of the whole of our legal tradition. The common law of nuisance is too narrow a confine for the exercise of regulatory power in a complex and interdependent society and should not prevent the State from enacting new regulatory initiatives in response to changing conditions. Courts must consider all reasonable expectations, whatever their source. The Takings Clause does not require a static body of state property law; it protects private expectations to ensure private investment. I agree that nuisance prevention accords with the most common expectations of property owners who face regulation, but I do not believe this can be the sole source of state authority to impose severe restrictions. Furthermore, the means as well as the ends of regulation must accord with the owner's reasonable expectations.

Dissent: (Blackmun, J.) Today the Court launches a missile to kill a mouse. The Court creates its new takings jurisprudence based on the trial court's finding that the property had lost all economic value. This finding is almost certainly erroneous. There are other attributes of ownership, such as the right to exclude others, "one of the most essential sticks in the bundle of rights that are commonly characterized as property." Lucas (P) can picnic, swim, camp in a tent, or live on the property in a movable trailer, and also retains the right to alienate the land. The threshold inquiry, "deprivation of all economically valuable use," itself cannot be determined objectively.

Dissent: (Stevens, J.) Viewed more broadly, the Court's new rule and exception conflict with the very character of our takings jurisprudence. We have frequently recognized that the definition of a taking cannot be reduced to a "set formula;" but must be determined on an ad hoc basis. This is unavoidable, for the determination is ultimately one of fairness and justice, and requires a weighing of private and public interests. The rigid rules fixed by the Court today clash with this enterprise: "fairness and justice" are often disserved by categorical rules. In analyzing takings claims, courts have long recognized the difference between a regulation that targets one or two parcels of land and a regulation that enforces a state-wide policy. The generality of the Act is significant. The Act regulates the coastline of the entire State and is best understood as part of a national effort to protect the coastline.

Analysis:

Justice Blackmun seems to think that any value the land retains after zoning regulations come into effect, no matter how small, should suffice so that the landowner does not receive compensation. This totally ignores the fact that people who purchase property do so for a specific reason. Either to build for themselves, or build for others who are willing to pay a premium for such property. Is it really equitable to strip a landowner of all rights, other than the right to "camp" on the land, when they have paid such a huge sum with the intent of developing the land? Justice Kennedy, unlike Justice Blackmun, makes a very valid point. The states should not be forced to resort to common law principles of nuisance in order to avoid paying for land they have "taken." While the Court's opinion seems to limit the acceptable justifications to those embedded in the common law, the fact remains that times do change, as do people and technology. Something that was merely a blip on an engineer's screen yesterday could become the newest form of nuisance today. The rule must be flexible, rather than be slaved to the outmoded concepts of yesteryear. So Justice Kennedy seems to have a good point when he states that the common law of nuisance is entirely too narrow. A balancing of the owner's investment and reasonable expectations against the State's interest in going through with its regulatory scheme must be accomplished in order to satisfy all sides in the takings context.

Nollan v. California Coastal Commission

(Beachfront Property Owner) v. (Land Regulation Agency)

483 U.S. 825, 107 S.Ct. 3141, 97 L.Ed.2d 677

M E M O R Y   G R A P H I C

Instant Facts

The State conditioned the approval of building plans on a landowner's granting of a right-of-way easement across his property in favor of the public so that it might use the public beach more easily.

Black Letter Rule

Conditioning the granting of a development permit on the landowners conveyance to the public of certain property rights, such as an easement, must conform with the law of takings, i.e., it must use rational means in serving a legitimate public purpose and must not deprive an owner of all economically valuable use of the land without just compensation.

Case Vocabulary

INCORPORATED: A concept whereby rights found in certain amendments of the Bill of Rights which do not, by their language, apply to the states, are nevertheless applied to the states by way of the Due Process Clause of the Fourteenth Amendment, which does expressly constrain the states.

Procedural Basis: Certification to the U.S. Supreme Court from a ruling of the California Court of Appeals upholding the decision of the Commission that the conditional permit scheme was constitutional.

Facts: Nollan (P) leased, with an option to buy, a parcel of California beachfront property with a small bungalow that they had rented out to summer vacationers over the years. To the South and North of the lot are public beaches. Eventually, the bungalow fell into disrepair and could no longer be rented out. When this happened, Nollan (P) decided to exercise his option to buy, which was conditioned on a new house being built on the lot. However, under California State Code (Code), they were required to obtain a development permit from the California Coastal Commission (CCC) (D). In February 1982, Nollan (P) applied for a permit to demolish the bungalow and replace it with a three-bedroom house, in keeping with the look of the neighborhood. The CCC (D) granted the permit subject to the condition that Nollan (P) allow the public an easement to pass across a portion of their property in order to make it easier for the public to get to the two public beaches to the North and South. Nollan (P) objected to the condition, arguing that the condition could not be imposed absent evidence that the proposed house would have a direct adverse impact on public access to the beach. The CCC (D) found that the new house would increase blockage of the view of the ocean, and thus contribute to a "wall of residential structures" that would prevent the public "psychologically... from realizing a stretch of coastline exists nearby that they have every right to visit;" and also increase private use of the shorefront. These effects, along with other area development, would cumulatively "burden the public's ability to traverse to and along the shorefront." Therefore, the CCC (D) could properly require Nollan (P) to offset that burden by providing additional lateral access (parallel to the shoreline) to the public beaches in the form of an easement across the property. The California Court of Appeal ruled that the requirement did not violate the Constitution.

Issue: May a development permit be conditioned on the landowner's conveyance of certain limited property rights to the public to offset the proposed development's perceived harm to the public interest without violating the Takings Clause?

Decision and Rationale: (Scalia, J.) Yes. Had California simply required Nollan (P) to grant a permanent easement across his property in order to increase public access to the beach, we have no doubt there would have been a taking. The question thus becomes whether requiring it to be conveyed as a condition for issuing a land use permit alters the outcome. We have long recognized that land use regulation does not effect a taking if it substantially advances legitimate state interests and does not deny an owner economically viable use of his land. We have not elaborated, however, on what constitutes a "legitimate state interest," or what type of connection between the regulation and the state interest satisfies the requirement that the former "substantially advance" the latter. We have made clear, however, that a broad range of governmental purposes and regulations satisfies these requirements. We assume, without deciding, that the CCC's (D) stated purposes are legitimate—in which case the CCC (D) unquestionably would be able to deny Nollan (P) the permit outright if the new house would substantially impede these purposes, unless the denial would interfere so drastically with Nollan's (P) use of the property as to constitute a taking. The CCC (D) argues that a permit condition should not be found to be a taking if refusal to issue the permit would not constitute a taking. We agree. Thus, if the CCC (D) attached to the permit some condition that would have protected the public's ability to see the beach—for example, a height limitation, a width restriction, or a ban on fences—so long as the CCC (D) could have exercised its police power to forbid construction of the house altogether, imposition of the condition would also be constitutional. Moreover, the condition would be constitutional even if it consisted of the requirement that Nollan (P) provide a viewing spot on their property for passersby with whose view of the ocean the new house would interfere. The CCC's (D) assumed power to forbid construction of the house in order to protect the public's view of the beach must surely include the power to condition construction upon some concessions by the owner that serves the same end. The evident constitutional propriety disappears, however, if the condition substituted for the prohibition utterly fails to further the end advanced as the justification for the prohibition. In short, unless the condition serves the same governmental purpose as the development ban, the building restriction is not a valid regulation of land use but "an out-and-out plan of extortion." Reversed.

Dissent: (Brennan, J.) The Court's conclusion cannot withstand analysis. First, it demands a degree of exactitude inconsistent with our standard for reviewing the rationality of a state's exercise of its police power. Second, even if the nature of the condition imposed must be identical to the precise burden on access created by Nollan's (P) house, this requirement is plainly satisfied here. This Court's review of the rationality of a State's exercise of its police power demands only that the State could rationally have decided that the measure adopted might achieve the State's objective. Here, California has employed its police power in order to condition development upon preservation of public access to the ocean and tidelands, while accommodating Nollan's (P) desire for new development. In the expert opinion of the CCC (D), development conditioned on such a restriction as was imposed would fairly attend to both public and private interests. The condition is sufficiently tailored to address the precise type of reduction in access produced by the new development. The Court's extremely narrow conception of rationality has long since been discredited as a judicial abrogation of legislative authority.

Analysis:

Here, the Court applies rational basis review to the claim of the CCC (D) that the conditional permit's easement requirement will help cure the ills of which it complains. Justice Brennan has it correct: rational basis review requires that the State have some rationale that provides a nexus between the ill sought to be cured and the means chosen for doing so. This is the least stringent type of Supreme Court review and the Court has historically been extremely deferential to legislative determinations in this regard. Justice Brennan seems painfully wrong when he states that the conditional permit scheme created by the CCC (D) satisfies rational basis review. The condition is that Nollan (P) grant an easement which runs parallel to the beachfront. How does this help provide viewing access to people on the side opposite the waterfront? True, such access would allow people to view the ocean from a position between Nollan's (P) house and the water, but there does not seem to be any reason why such people need to gain their view from directly in front of Nollan's (P) house. The logic of the CCC (D) is therefore extremely strained. Were the conditional permit scheme found to satisfy rational basis review, what signal would this send to government authorities looking for cheap land?

Dolan v. City of Tigard

(Business Owner) v. (Municipality)
512 U.S. 374, 114 S.Ct. 2309 (1994)

M E M O R Y   G R A P H I C

Instant Facts

A city required a business owner to deed a parcel of her land to the city for a bicycle path and green space to reduce traffic and the flood hazard. She protests it as an unconstitutional taking.

Black Letter Rule

Conditioning the grant of a development permit upon the developer's conveyance of property rights is constitutional if (1) an essential nexus exists between the legitimate state interest and the permit condition, and (2) the degree of the exactions required by the condition bears a rough proportionality to the projected impact of the proposed development.

Case Vocabulary

AXIOMATIC: An idea or principle that is so well established and accepted as part of a given way of thinking.
NEXUS: A causal connection or link.
UNCONSTITUTIONAL-CONDITIONS: A legal doctrine which holds that government may not condition an individual's receipt of some benefit on their relinquishment of some constitutional right.

Procedural Basis: Certification to the U.S. Supreme Court from the State Supreme Court's ruling affirming the State Court of Appeals' ruling upholding the decision of the Land Use Board of Appeals' rejecting the developer's appeal from the Planning Commission.

Facts: The City of Tigard (the City) (D), in response to State requirements, enacted its Community Development Code (CDC), which requires owners of property in the Central Business District (CBD) to limit total site coverage, including buildings and pavement, to 85% of the parcel, and new developments in the CBD to dedicate land for a pedestrian/bicycle pathway, if provided for by the overall plan, in order to reduce congestion caused by the proposed development. In addition, the City's (D) Master Drainage Plan (Drainage Plan), noting that flooding along Fanno Creek will be made worse by further development, was passed to protect green space. It split the cost of drainage improvements to the Fanno Creek Basin between property owners along the waterway and all other taxpayers. Florence Dolan (Dolan) (P) owns a retail store in the CBD that she wished to expand. It covers about 9,700 square feet on a 1.67-acre parcel, including a gravel parking lot. Fanno Creek flows through its southwestern corner and along its border. Dolan's (P) parcel is also within the creek's 100-year floodplain. The City's (D) comprehensive plan includes the Fanno Creek floodplain within its greenway system. Dolan applied for a permit to nearly double the size of her store and pave a 39-space parking lot. The City Planning Commission granted Dolan's (P) permit subject to conditions imposed by the CDC. As applied to Dolan (P), the CDC required dedication of all land inside the floodplain for improvement of a storm drainage system, and an additional 15-foot strip adjacent to the floodplain to be used as a pedestrian/bicycle pathway. Together, they encompass 10% of Dolan's (P) property. In rejecting Dolan's (P) request for a variance, the Planning Commission found that "it is reasonable to assume that customers and employees of the future uses of [Dolan's (P)] site could utilize a pedestrian/bicycle pathway adjacent to this development for their transportation and recreational needs." In addition, the Commission found that creation of such a pathway "could offset some of the traffic demand on [nearby] streets and lessen the increase in traffic congestion." The Commission also noted that the required floodplain dedication would be reasonably related to Dolan's (P) proposal, given the increase in the impervious surface. Based on the anticipated increased storm water flow, the Commission concluded that "the [required dedication] is related to [Dolan's (P)] plan to intensify development on the site." Dolan appealed to the Land Use Board of Appeals (LUBA), arguing that the scheme's requirements were not related to the proposed development, and, therefore, those requirements constituted an unlawful taking. The LUBA found a "reasonable relationship" between the proposal and the need to dedicate land for a greenway, as well as between the increased traffic caused by the development and the pedestrian/bicycle pathway as an alternative means of transportation, and rejected Dolan's (P) plea. The Oregon Court of Appeals affirmed, as did the Oregon Supreme Court.

Issue: In the takings context, are the "reasonable relationship" and "essential nexus" requirements one and the same?

Decision and Rationale: (Rehnquist, C.J.) No. One principal purpose of the Takings Clause is to bar government from forcing some people to bear alone burdens which should rightly be borne by the public as a whole. Had the City (D) simply required the dedication of a strip of land along Fanno Creek for public use, instead of using the conditional permit scheme, a taking would have occurred. Such public access would have deprived Dolan (P) the right to exclude others, one of the most essential sticks in the bundle of property rights. On the other side, the authority of state and local governments in land use planning has been sustained against constitutional challenge as long ago as our decision in *Euclid v. Ambler Realty*. The sort of land use regulations in that case, however, differ in two relevant particulars from the present case. First, it involved essentially legislative determinations classifying entire areas of the city, whereas here the City (D) made an adjudicative decision with respect to an individual parcel. Second, the conditions imposed were not simply a limitation on the use Dolan (P) might make of her own parcel, but a requirement that she deed portions of the property to the City (D). Under the well-settled doctrine of "unconstitutional conditions," government may not require a person to give up a constitutional right in exchange for a discretionary benefit conferred by the government where the property sought has little or no relationship to the benefits. Dolan (P) argues that the City (D) has failed to identify the "special benefits" conferred on her, and has also not identified any "special quantifiable burdens" created by her development that would justify the dedications required. In evaluating this claim, we must first determine whether the "essential nexus" exists between the "legitimate state interest" and the permit condition exacted by the City (D). If it does, we must then decide the required degree of connection between the exactions and the projected impact of the development. We were not required to reach this question in *Nollan* because we concluded that the connection did not meet even the loosest standard. Here, however, we must decide this question. Undoubtedly, the prevention of flooding along Fanno Creek and the reduction of traffic congestion in the CBD are legitimate public purposes. It seems equally clear that a nexus exists between preventing flooding along the creek and limiting development within the 100-year floodplain. Dolan (P) proposes to expand the impervious surface on the property and thus increase the amount of stormwater runoff into the creek. This is also true for the City's (D) attempt to reduce traffic congestion. In theory, a pedestrian/bicycle pathway provides a useful alternative means of transportation system flow. The second part of our analysis requires us to determine whether the degree of the exactions bears the required relationship to the projected impact of Dolan's (P) proposed development. The Oregon Supreme Court simply deferred to the "city's unchallenged factual findings" supporting the dedication conditions and found them to be reasonably related to the impact of Dolan's (P) planned expansion. The City (D) required dedication "to the city as Greenway all portions of the site that fall within the existing 100-year floodplain… and all property 15 feet above [the floodplain] boundary." The City (D) relies on the Commission's rather tentative finding that increased stormwater flow from Dolan's (P) property "can only add to the public need to manage the [floodplain]…" as evidence that the "requirement of dedication of the floodplain area on the site is related to [Dolan's (P)] plan to intensify development on the site." The City (D) made the following specific findings regarding the pedestrian/bicycle pathway: "[T]he proposed expanded use… is anticipated to generate additional vehicular traffic…. Creation of a convenient… pathway system as an alternative means of transportation could offset some of the traffic demand… and lessen the increase in traffic congestion." Are these findings constitutionally sufficient to justify the conditions imposed? We look to the state courts for guidance since our jurisprudence provides little. Some states employ very generalized requirements for the necessary connection between the mandatory dedication and the proposed development, a view which we think is too lax to adequately protect property rights. Others require a very exacting correspondence, described as the "specifi[c] and uniquely attributable" test. There, the local government must show that its

exaction is directly proportional to the specifically created need. The Constitution does not require such exacting scrutiny. Other states take the intermediate position, requiring a "reasonable relationship." We think this test is closer to the federal constitutional norm than either of the other two but do not adopt it as such, partly because the term "reasonable relationship" seems confusingly similar to the term "rational basis," a term which is already taken. We think "rough proportionality" best encapsulates the required connection under the Fifth Amendment. Under this test, the City (P) must make some individualized determination that the required dedication is related both in nature and extent to the impact of the proposed development. It is axiomatic that increasing the amount of impervious surface will increase the quantity and rate of stormwater flow. Therefore, keeping the floodplain open and free would likely confine the pressures on Fanno Creek. In fact, because Dolan's (P) property lies within the CBD, the CDC already required Dolan (P) to leave 15% of it as open space. The undeveloped floodplain would nearly have satisfied that requirement. But the City (D) demanded more—Dolan's (P) property along Fanno Creek for its Greenway system. The City (D) has never said why a public greenway, as opposed to a private one, was required in the interest of flood control. The difference to Dolan (P) is the loss of her right to exclude others, a very important property right. It is difficult to see why recreational visitors trampling along Dolan's (P) floodplain easement are sufficiently related to the legitimate interest in reducing flooding problems along Fanno Creek. In response, the City (D) argues that unlike the residential property at issue in *Nollan*, Dolan's (P) property is commercial in character and therefore, her right to exclude others is compromised. Admittedly, Dolan (P) wants to build a bigger store to attract members of the public. She also wants, however, to be able to control the time and manner in which they enter. If the proposed development had somehow encroached on existing greenway space in the city, it would have been reasonable to require Dolan (P) to provide some alternative greenspace. But that is not the case. We conclude that the City's (D) findings do not show the required reasonable relationship between the floodplain easement and Dolan's (P) proposed new building. With respect to the pedestrian/bicycle pathway, we have no doubt the City (D) was correct in finding that the larger retail sales facility will increase street traffic. Dedications for streets, sidewalks, and other public ways are generally reasonable exactions to avoid excessive congestion from a proposed use. But on the record before us, the City (D) did not demonstrate that the additional number of vehicle and bicycle trips are reasonably related to the required pedestrian/bicycle pathway easement. The finding that the required pathway "could offset some of the traffic demand… and lessen the increase in traffic congestion" is a far cry from finding that the bicycle pathway system *will* or is *likely to*, offset some of the traffic demand. The City (D) must make some effort to quantify its findings beyond the conclusory statement that it "could" offset a portion of the increased traffic. Reversed and remanded.

Dissent: (Stevens, J.) The Court finds two defects in the City's (D) case. First, the record does not support the additional requirement that the floodplain be dedicated to the City (D). Second, the City (D) failed to quantify the offsetting decrease in automobile traffic that the bike path will produce. Even under the Court's new rule, both defects are nothing more than harmless error. In her objections to the floodplain condition, Dolan (P) made no effort to show that the dedication of that portion of her property would be any more onerous than a simple prohibition against any development on that portion of her property. It seems likely that potential customers

Dolan v. City of Tigard (Continued)

"trampling along [her] floodplain" are more valuable than a useless parcel of vacant land. Moreover, the duty to pay taxes and the responsibility for potential tort liability may well make ownership of the fee interest in useless land a liability rather than an asset. The Court's rejection of the bike path condition amounts to nothing more than a play on words. Everyone agrees it "could" offset some of the increased traffic, but the findings do not unequivocally state that it *will* do so. Predictions on such matters are inherently nothing more than estimates. The assumption here is entirely reasonable and should suffice whether it amounts to a 100%, 35%, or only 5% of the increase in traffic that would otherwise occur. The Court errs by abandoning the traditional presumption of constitutionality. Even more consequential than its incorrect ruling, however, is its resurrection of a species of substantive due process analysis that it firmly rejected decades ago. It creates a potentially open-ended source of judicial power to invalidate state economic regulations that Members of this Court view as unwise or unfair.

Dissent: (Souter, J.) Today the Court has placed the burden of producing evidence of relationship on the City (D), despite its usual rule in cases involving the police power that the government is presumed to have acted constitutionally. Having thus assigned the burden, the Court concludes that the City (D) loses based on one word ("could" instead of "would"), and despite the fact that this record shows the connection for which the Court looks.

Analysis:

In this case, the Court clarifies the takings rule as applied to instances where a permission to move forward with a development is conditioned on the developer conveying certain property rights to the government. First, there must be an "essential nexus" between the legitimate state interest and the permit condition. What this simply means is that the permit condition must have something to do with the effects of the proposed development. For instance, where a developer wishes to put in a new subdivision of housing, the government might properly require the developer to deed portions adequate for the construction of streets within the new subdivision since it will cause a spike in traffic. Second, the extent of property rights the developer is required to give up must be proportional, but not directly proportional, to the level of particular need created by the development. So, looking at our subdivision scenario from above, the government could require dedication of only enough land to construct streets adequate to meet the marginal demand created by the subdivision and no more. In other words, the government could not require the developer to deed over enough land to put in a freeway and train station as well, when the increased traffic is such that it only requires one small two-lane residential street.

Palazzolo v. Rhode Island

(Land Developer) v. (State Government)
533 U.S. 606, 121 S.Ct. 2448 (2001)

M E M O R Y   G R A P H I C

Instant Facts

Over a span of several years, a land developer submitted numerous development proposals which required swampland to be filled. The regulatory agency prohibited filling of the swamp. The developer claimed the regulations effected a taking.

Black Letter Rule

1) A takings claim is ripe when the responsible regulatory agency has reached a final decision regarding the permitted land uses under the current regulatory scheme, such that it can be said that the landowner has been denied all economically beneficial use or that her reasonable investment-backed expectations are defeated to the extent a taking has occurred. 2) The fact that a landowner acquired the land after the current land-use regulatory scheme was enacted will not defeat a takings action.

Case Vocabulary

INVERSE CONDEMNATION: A constructive condemnation of land caused by the actual condemnation of a parcel nearby which for some reason renders that land economically valueless such that reasonable compensation is required.
POLESTAR: The core guiding principle or principles of law which a court applies in deciding a case.

Procedural Basis: Certification to the U.S. Supreme Court from the ruling of the Rhode Island Supreme Court upholding the Appeals Court's holding that the State zoning regulations are constitutional.

Facts: Shortly after his partnership purchased 3 adjacent parcels totaling 20 acres of land, Palazzolo (P) bought out his partners and became sole shareholder of Shore Gardens, Inc. (SGI). In the first ten years, SGI submitted several applications to develop the property, all requiring substantial filling of the wet, marshy portions of the parcel. Several applications were submitted and rejected for varying reasons including adverse environmental impact. No further applications were made over the next ten years. Two intervening events, however, are important to the issues presented. First, in 1971, Rhode Island (D) created the Council to protect the State's coastal properties. The Council promulgated regulations limiting development of protected "coastal wetlands," like SGI's 20 acres. Second, in 1978 SGI's corporate charter was revoked and title to the property passed by operation of law to Palazzolo (P) as SGI's sole shareholder. In 1983, Palazzolo (P) applied to the Council for permission to construct a wooden bulkhead along the shore of Winnapaug Pond and to fill the entire marsh land area. The Council rejected the application because it conflicted with the Coastal Resources Management Plan. Palazzolo (P) then hired counsel and submitted a more limited proposal to build a private beach club. This proposal was also rejected because a "special exception" to the regulations was required and Palazzolo's (P) proposal did not meet the standards for granting such an exception. Palazzolo (P) appealed to the Rhode Island trial court, which affirmed. Palazzolo (P) then filed an inverse condemnation action, asserting a taking without compensation in violation of the Fifth and Fourteenth Amendments. The Superior Court ruled against Palazzolo (P) and the Rhode Island Supreme Court affirmed. In doing so, that court held that (1) Palazzolo's (P) takings claim was not ripe; (2) Palazzolo (P) had no right to challenge regulations predating 1978, when he gained ownership from SGI; and, (3) the claim of deprivation of all economic value was contradicted by undisputed evidence that Palazzolo (P) had $200,000 in development value remaining on an upland portion of the property. The Rhode Island Supreme Court also held that Palazzolo (P) could not recover under the test of *Penn Central Transp. Co. v. City of New York* because Palazzolo (P) could not have had any "reasonable investment-backed expectations that were affected by the regulation" because it predated his ownership.

Issue: 1) Is a takings claim ripe when the regulatory agency has reached a final decision regarding the application of the regulations at issue? 2) May one who acquires property after the enactment of a land-use regulation maintain a takings claim with respect to that regulation?

Decision and Rationale: (Kennedy, J.) 1) Yes. 2) Yes. We disagree with the Rhode Island Supreme Court's holding that Palazzolo's (P) takings claim was not ripe; and that he had no right to challenge regulations predating 1978. We do agree that Palazzolo (P) is deprived of all economic use of his property, but we remand for further consideration of his claim under the principles set forth in *Penn Central* [a Supreme Court case holding that a taking may be established by showing that a landowner's reasonable investment-backed expectations were thwarted by passage of a regulation after the land was acquired]. It is an obvious rule that a takings claim must be ripe. A takings claim challenging the application of land-use regulations is not ripe unless the governmental entity charged with implementing the regulations has reached a final decision. This informs the constitutional determination whether a regulation has deprived a landowner of all economically beneficial use of the property, or defeated the reasonable investment-backed expectations of the landowner to the extent that a taking has occurred. This allows a court to know the extent of permitted development on the land. The central question in resolving the ripeness issue is whether Palazzolo (P) obtained a final decision from the Council determining the permitted use. SGI made numerous applications to develop the land, all of which were rejected for one reason or another. We cannot agree with the Rhode Island Supreme Court that doubt remained as to the extent of development allowed. It is true that the final decision requirement is not satisfied when a developer submits and a land use authority denies, a grandiose development proposal, leaving open the possibility that lesser uses of the property might be permitted. Here, however, the Council's many decisions make plain that the agency interpreted its regulations to bar Palazzolo (P) from engaging in any filling or development activity. True, not all of Palazzolo's (P) parcel constitutes protected wetlands. An upland site at the eastern end has an estimated value of $200,000 if developed. Palazzolo (P) is required to explore development opportunities on this upland parcel only if there is uncertainty as to the land's permitted use. Rhode Island (D) did not contest the $200,000 value of this section. Ripeness can thus not be contested by saying that the value of this section is unknown. That a *Penn Central* argument was not pressed by Palazzolo (P) is also irrelevant to the ripeness issue. The State (D) was aware of our holding in *Penn Central* when it decided not to press such an argument at trial and, indeed, discussed *Penn Central* at every level this case has reached. A final ripeness issue remains. Rhode Island (D) objects to Palazzolo's (P) use of a potentially extensive development as his basis for damages given that he never submitted such a proposal. This argument is without merit because even had Palazzolo (P) made such a submission, it would not have clarified the extent of development permitted by the wetlands regulations, which is the inquiry required under our ripeness decisions. The limitations imposed by the wetlands regulations were clear from the Council's denials of Palazzolo's (P) applications, and there is no indication that any use involving any substantial structures or improvements would have been allowed. We turn now to the contention that because title passed to Palazzolo (P) after promulgation of the wetlands regulations, he had notice of the restriction and is thus barred from claiming it effects a taking. This reasoning is wrong. An enactment does not become reasonable simply through the passage of time or title. Future generations, too, have the right to challenge unreasonable limitations on the use and value of land. Now that it is settled that Palazzolo's (P) claim was ripe, it must be analyzed under *Penn Central*. We now examine the alternative ground relied upon by the Rhode Island Supreme Court in ruling upon the merits of the takings claims—that all economically beneficial use was not deprived because the uplands section can still be improved. We agree. Palazzolo (P) accepts that this section retains $200,000 in development value under the wetlands regulations. Nonetheless, Palazzolo (P) asserts he has suffered a total taking and this does not change merely because he has been left a few crumbs of value. It is true that, assuming a taking has otherwise been established, the

government cannot escape making compensation by leaving the landowner a token interest. This is not, however, the situation in this case. Palazzolo (P) can build a substantial residence on the uplands section and such does not constitute a taking. Palazzolo (P) argues that this section is separate and distinct from the wetlands portion and whether a taking has occurred should be judged with respect to only this latter section. We will not explore this argument here, since Palazzolo (P) did not press it in the State courts and did not present it in the petition for certiorari. We therefore hold that Palazzolo's (P) claims were ripe; that Palazzolo's (P) acquisition of the property after the enactments does not bar his takings claims; and that Palazzolo (P) failed to establish a total deprivation. The claims under the *Penn Central* analysis were not examined, and for this purpose the case should be remanded. Affirmed in part; reversed in part and remanded.

Concurrence: (O'Connor, J.) Today's holding does not mean the timing of the regulation's enactment relative to the acquisition of title is immaterial to the *Penn Central* analysis. It is relevant. But our polestar remains the principles set forth in *Penn Central*, which take into consideration, along with other factors, interference with investment-backed expectations. Further, the regulatory regime in place at the time the claimant acquires the property helps to shape the reasonableness of those expectations.

Concurrence: (Scalia, J.) I write separately to make clear that my understanding of how the issues must be considered on appeal is not Justice O'Connor's. The "investment-backed expectations" that the law will consider do not include the assumed validity of a restriction that in fact deprives property of so much of its value as to be unconstitutional. Which is to say that a *Penn Central* taking, no less than a total taking, is not absolved by the transfer of title.

Concurrence and Dissent: (Stevens, J.) To the extent the adoption of the regulations constitute the challenged taking, Palazzolo (P) is simply the wrong party to be bringing this action. If the regulations imposed a compensable injury, it was on the owners at the moment the regulations were adopted. Palazzolo (P) has no standing to claim that the promulgation of the regulations constituted a taking of any part of the property that he subsequently acquired.

Dissent: (Ginsburg, J.) Today the Court rejects the Rhode Island court's determination that the case is unripe, finding "no uncertainty as to the [uplands'] permitted use." This conclusion is both inaccurate and inequitable. Inaccurate because the record is ambiguous. Inequitable because, given the claim asserted by Palazzolo (P) in the Rhode Island courts, the State (D) had no cause to pursue further inquiry into potential upland development.

Analysis:

Justice O'Connor's concurring opinion deals primarily with the timing of the enactment relative to the timing of the landowner's acquisition of the property. She asserts that the date of acquisition is an important part of the determination of reasonableness of investment-backed expectations. How might this be? One way it is relevant is due to notice. If a would-be developer acquires land which is already subject to Regulation A that bans a certain use, then any expectations to develop that land in a manner that conflicts with Regulation A cannot be very reasonable. The purchase of land is also but one part of the investment. Therefore, the same rationale applies to actual investment in development. That the owner acquired the land 10 years prior to enactment of Regulation A does not mean Regulation A will thwart expectations. The expectations must be backed by some investment, the level of which is an important consideration. An owner who has invested 50 per cent of the property's value before enactment of Regulation A will have better luck making out a *Penn Central* claim than an owner whose investment is only 5 per cent at the time of enactment. The exact level of investment required to have cognizable investment-backed expectations is left open by the Court's ruling.

Chapter 22

This chapter covers the myriad of ways a municipality might exclude certain classes of people. This may be done by requiring a certain size lot; by excluding multi-family developments, such as apartments; regulating the occupant density, etc. Usually, such schemes are aimed at low-income residents with the rationale being that such people are a drag on the financial resources of the community and cause a drop in property values. Exclusionary zoning is most prevalent in the suburbs.

However, no matter how onerous or despicable exclusionary zoning might be, it is often very difficult to prove a case. The United States Supreme Court has ruled that there exists no fundamental right to housing; that income is not a suspect classification requiring heightened scrutiny; that the right to travel is not implicated by exclusionary zoning; and that in order to prove a violation of the Equal Protection Clause based upon racial discrimination requires proof of discriminatory intent.

Plaintiffs might find it easier to prevail in an exclusionary zoning case in state court. Many state courts have been much more open to such claims than the federal courts. For instance, in *Southern Burlington County N.A.A.C.P. v. Mt. Laurel Township*, the New Jersey Supreme Court held that the State Constitution's general welfare clause required municipalities to make housing accommodations for both the rich and poor alike. In subsequent rulings, the same court expanded its "Mt. Laurel Doctrine" to include closer supervision by the courts in ensuring the State's municipalities followed the Court's earlier mandate. Such judicial remedies appear to be gaining ground in other states as well.

Chapter Overview Outline
Discrimination Against Groups of People

Chapter 22

NOTE: THE PURPOSE OF THIS OUTLINE IS TO ORGANIZE THE CASES SO THAT ONE CAN QUICKLY UNDERSTAND THE RELEVANCE OF EACH CASE TO THE COURSE. NO ATTEMPT IS MADE IN THIS OVERVIEW TO ADDRESS EVERY CONCEPT THAT MUST BE STUDIED. BE SURE TO READ THE ENTIRE CASEBOOK AND/OR OTHER MATERIALS TO GAIN A FULL UNDERSTANDING OF ALL CONCEPTS.

I. Race Discrimination
    A. A claimed violation of the Equal Protection Clause founded on racial discrimination will receive strict scrutiny where a disparate impact is caused by a government action motivated wholly or in part by a discriminatory purpose. *Village of Arlington Heights v. Metropolitan Housing Development Corp.*
    B. Title VI of the 1964 Civil Rights Act prohibits any person from being excluded from participation in, or benefitting from, any program or activity receiving Federal Financial assistance based upon their race, color or national origin. Regulations promulgated pursuant to this prohibition may bar racially disparate impact even without proof of discriminatory intent.

II. Neighborhood Exclusion
    A. Economic and social legislation, e.g., zoning regulation, which does not implicate a suspect class or fundamental right, will not violate the Equal Protection Clause so long as it is reasonable and bears a rational relationship to a legitimate objective. *Village of Belle Terre v. Boraas.*
        1. There is no fundamental right to live with whomever one chooses. *Village of Belle Terre v. Boraas.*
        2. The institution of the family being deeply rooted in the United States' history and tradition, a government restriction on one's right to live with family members must be narrowly tailored and serve a substantial and overriding government interest. *Moore v. City of East Cleveland.*

B. Government actions, including zoning schemes, which discriminate based upon a person's mentally retarded status, or other non-suspect and non-quasi-suspect qualities, need only be rationally related to a legitimate government purpose, i.e., they receive rational basis review. *City of Cleburne v. Cleburne Living Center, Inc.*
    1. Some states have statutes that expressly authorize group homes in residential-zoned areas, regardless of any local zoning regulation.
    2. The Supreme Court has ruled that the Fair Housing Act's ban of discrimination against handicapped persons can prohibit zoning regulations that exclude from residential districts group homes for persons protected under the Act. *City of Edmonds v. Oxford House.*

III. Municipality Exclusion
    A. A municipality that, pursuant to state law, enacts zoning regulations in order to promote the "general welfare of the community," must take into account the needs of the entire surrounding community, not just those within its political boundaries. *Britton v. Town of Chester.*
    B. At least one state supreme court has taken a very active role in ensuring that the state's municipalities bear their fair share of low-income housing. *Southern Burlington County N.A.A.C.P. v. Township of Mt. Laurel* and its progeny.
    B. In 1982, the President's Commission on Housing recommended that states adopt legislation that places the burden on government to prove that regulations restricting the development of housing are necessary to achieve a vital and pressing governmental interest.

Village of Arlington Heights v. Metropolitan Housing Development Corp.

(Municipality) v. (Project Developer)
429 U.S. 252, 97 S.Ct. 555 (1977)

M E M O R Y   G R A P H I C

Instant Facts

A land developer proposed to build multi-family, low-income housing units but was denied the required zoning change. The developer sued the municipality, claiming racial discrimination.

Black Letter Rule

A claimed violation of the Equal Protection Clause founded on racial discrimination will receive strict scrutiny where a disparate impact is caused by a government action motivated wholly or in part by a discriminatory purpose.

Case Vocabulary

DISPARATE IMPACT: The seemingly discriminatory effect of a provision or other governmental action that is neutral on its face.

Procedural Basis: Certiorari to the U.S. Supreme Court from the State Court of Appeals reversal of the trial court's determination that the government action was constitutional.

Facts: Arlington Heights (Village) (P) is a suburb of Chicago; most of its area is zoned for detached single-family homes. The Village (P) experienced rapid growth in the 1960s, but, like other communities in northwest Cook County, its minority population remained extremely low. The Clerics of St. Viator (the Order) owned an 80-acre parcel in Arlington Heights. All the land surrounding this parcel is zoned R-3, a single-family specification. In 1970, the Order and the Metropolitan Housing Development Corporation (MHDC)(R), a developer of low and moderate income housing, entered into an agreement whereby MHDC (R) would build 20 two-story buildings with a total of 190 units on a 15-acre portion of the Order's tract. Each of these units would have its own private entrance from outside, and would range from single-bedroom (100 units) to four-bedroom units. The planned development could not be built unless the Village (P) rezoned the parcel to R-5 for multiple-family housing. Accordingly, MHDC (R) petitioned the Village Plan Commission for rezoning. The application materials made clear that federal law required an affirmative marketing plan designed to assure that subsidized housing, which the development would be, is racially integrated. In the spring of 1971, the Plan Commission considered the proposal at a series of three public meetings, which drew large crowds, with many of those attending voicing strong opposition to the plan, and many voicing strong support. Some of the comments addressed what was referred to as the "social issue"—the desirability or undesirability of introducing at this location low and moderate income housing which would probably be racially integrated. Many of the opponents, however, focused on the zoning aspect and stressed two arguments. First, the area had always been zoned single-family, and neighboring citizens had built or purchased there in reliance on that classification. Any rezoning threatened a precipitous drop in property value. Second, the Village (P) apartment policy, first adopted in 1962, called for R-5 zoning primarily to serve as a buffer between single-family development and land uses though incompatible, such as commercial or manufacturing districts. The planned development did not meet this requirement, as it adjoined no commercial or manufacturing district. The Plan Commission ultimately recommended to the Village's (P) Board of Trustees that it deny the request, which it did by a vote of 6-1, after a public hearing. A short time later, MHDC (R) and three African-American individuals filed suit seeking declaratory and injunctive relief. The trial court held that Village (P) officials were not motivated by racial discrimination or an intent to discriminate against low-income groups when they denied rezoning, but rather by a desire "to protect property values and the integrity of the Village's zoning plan." It also concluded that the denial would not have a racially discriminatory effect. The Court of Appeals reversed, observing that the refusal would have a disproportionate impact on blacks. It ruled that the permit denial had racially discriminatory effects and could be tolerated only if it served compelling interests. Neither the buffer policy nor the desire to protect property values met this exacting standard. It therefore concluded that the denial violated the Equal Protection Clause of the Fourteenth Amendment.

Issue: Does a racially discriminatory effect, without proof of discriminatory intent, render a governmental action unconstitutional as a violation of the Equal Protection Clause?

Decision and Rationale: (Powell, J.) No. Our decision last Term in *Washington v. Davis* made it clear that official action will not be held unconstitutional solely because it results in a racially disproportionate impact. Such an effect is not irrelevant, but it is not the sole touchstone of an invidious racial discrimination. Proof of racially discriminatory intent or purpose is required to show a violation of the Equal Protection Clause. *Davis* does not require a plaintiff to prove the challenged action rested solely on racially discriminatory purposes for rarely can it be said that a decision was motivated solely by a single concern, or even that a particular purpose was the "dominant" or "primary" one. In fact, it is because legislators and administrators are properly concerned with balancing numerous competing considerations that courts refrain from reviewing the merits of their decisions absent a showing of arbitrariness or irrationality. But racial discrimination is not just another competing consideration. When there is proof that a discriminatory purpose has been a motivating factor in the decision, this judicial deference is no longer justified. Determining whether such an intent or purpose was a motivating factor demands a sensitive inquiry into such evidence of intent as may be available. The impact of the official action may provide an important starting point for sometimes a clear pattern, unexplainable on grounds other than race, emerges. However, absent such evidence impact alone is not determinative, and the Court must look to other evidence. Possible considerations may be the historical background of the decision; the specific sequence of events leading up to the decision; departures from the normal procedural sequence; the legislative or administrative history; and substantive departures, especially where the factors usually considered important strongly favor a decision contrary to the one reached. The foregoing summary identifies, without purporting to be exhaustive, subjects of proper inquiry in determining whether racially discriminatory intent existed. With these in mind, we now address the case before us. Both courts below understood that at least part of their function was to examine the purpose underlying the decision. The trial court noted that opposition to minority groups may have motivated some of the opponents who spoke at the hearings. The court held, however, that the evidence "does not warrant the conclusion that this motivated the [Village (P) officials]. The Court of Appeals focused mainly on MDHC's (R) claim that the buffer policy had not been consistently applied and was being invoked with a strictness here that could only demonstrate some other underlying motive. That court concluded that the buffer policy had on several occasions formed the basis for a denial of other rezoning proposals and that the evidence does not necessitate a finding that the Village (P) administered this policy in a discriminatory manner. We have also reviewed the evidence. The impact of the Village's (P) decision does arguably bear more heavily upon racial minorities. But there is little about the sequence of events leading up to the decision that would spark suspicion. The area around the Order's property has been zoned R-3 since 1959. Single-family homes surround the 80-acre site, and Village (P) is undeniably committed to single-family homes as its dominant residential land use. The rezoning request progressed according to the usual procedures. And the Plan Commission even scheduled two additional hearings, in part to allow MHDC (R) to address issues raised at the first meeting. The statements by the Plan Commission and the Village Board members focused almost exclusively on the zoning aspects of the MHDC (R) petition, and the factors upon which they relied are not novel criteria in the Village's (P) zoning decisions. Finally, MHDC (R) called one member of the Village Board to stand at trial. Nothing in her testimony supports an inference of invidious purpose. In sum, the evidence does not warrant overturning the concurrent findings of both courts below. MHDC (R) simply failed to carry their burden of proving that discriminatory purpose was a motivating factor in the Village's (P) decision. This conclusion ends the constitutional inquiry. The Court of Appeals' further finding that the Village's (P) decision carried a discriminatory "ultimate effect" is without independent constitutional significance. Reversed.

Analysis:

A claimed violation of the Equal Protection Clause of the Fourteenth Amendment will normally draw rational basis review from the Court. This is the most lax type of review a court can apply and is what the Court applied to the Village's (P) zoning decision. But given that MHDC (R) was claiming racial discrimination, why did the Court not apply strict scrutiny? The answer to this question is the central theme of the case. The result when a court applies strict scrutiny is usually a declaration that the challenged governmental action is unconstitutional. There are, however, numerous instances where some action, for whatever non-discriminatory reasons, results in a disparate impact on a racial minority. Were strict scrutiny to be applied in each instance, the vast majority of such governmental actions would be invalidated, in spite of all the nondiscriminatory reasons undergirding the action. Government's hands would be tied whenever a proposed action would have such a disparate effect. Rather than allow such a situation to develop, the Court chose instead to require a showing that the action is motivated, at least in part, by a discriminatory purpose or intent. Not until such a showing is made will the Court endeavor to apply strict scrutiny and, in all likelihood, strike down the action.

Village of Belle Terre v. Boraas

(Zoning Authority) v. (Tenant)
416 U.S. 1, 94 S.Ct. 1536 (1974)

M E M O R Y   G R A P H I C

 Instant Facts

A city zoning ordinance prevented unrelated persons more than two in number from living together in the same residence. The landlord and tenants sued claiming constitutional violations.

Black Letter Rule

Economic and social legislation, e.g., zoning regulations, which does not implicate a suspect class or fundamental right will not violate the Equal Protection Clause so long as it is reasonable and bears a rational relationship to a legitimate objective; there is no fundamental right to live with whomever one chooses.

Case Vocabulary

HOMOGENEITY: The characteristic of being the same throughout.
TRANSIENT: An individual with no apparent home or visible means of support; who drifts about from place to place.

Procedural Basis: Appeal to the U.S. Supreme Court from the Circuit Court's reversal of the District Court's ruling upholding a zoning scheme.

Facts: Belle Terre (Village) (P) is a village on Long Island of about 220 homes and 700 people. The Village (P) has a zoning ordinance (Ordinance) restricting land use to one-family dwellings excluding lodging houses, boarding houses, fraternity houses, or multiple dwelling houses. The word "family" is defined as "[o]ne or more persons related by blood, adoption or marriage, living and cooking together as a single housekeeping unit, exclusive of household servants. A number of persons but not exceeding two (2) living and cooking together as a single housekeeping unit though not related by blood, adoption, or marriage shall be deemed to constitute a family." The Dickmans (R1) own a house in the Village which they lease out. In December 1971, Michael Truman leased the house for 18 months. Later Bruce Boraas (R2) became a co-lessee. Then Anne Parish moved into the house along with three others. Six are students at a nearby university and none is related to the other by blood, adoption or marriage. After the Village (P) served the Dickmans (R1) with an "Order to Remedy Violations," they and three tenants brought this action under 42 U.S.C.A. § 1983 seeking an injunction and a declaration that the Ordinance is unconstitutional. The District Court sustained the Ordinance, but the Circuit Court of Appeals reversed. The case is here by appeal.

Issue: May the government by reasonable means regulate the makeup of individuals allowed to live in a single residence?

Decision and Rationale: (Douglas, J.) Yes. The Ordinance is challenged on several grounds: [The Court provides a laundry-list of claims which have no basis in law] that it violates the right to privacy and right to travel; and that social homogeneity is not a legitimate interest of government. We find none of these reasons in the record before us. The Ordinance is not aimed at transients; involves no procedural disparity inflicted on some but not on others; involves no "fundamental" right guaranteed by the Constitution, e.g.; the right of association; to vote; of access to the courts; or any right of privacy. We deal with economic and social legislation where legislatures have historically drawn lines which we respect against the charge of violation of the Equal Protection Clause if the law be reasonable, not arbitrary and bears a rational relationship to a permissible state objective." It is said, however, that if two unmarried people can constitute a "family," there is no reason why three or four may not. But every line drawn by a legislature leaves some out that might well have been included. That exercise of discretion, however, is a legislative, not a judicial, function. It is said that the Ordinance reeks with an animosity to unmarried couples who live together. But the inclusion within the definition of "family" two unmarried people belies this charge. The Ordinance places no ban on other forms of association, for a "family" may, so far as the Ordinance is concerned, entertain whomever it likes. The regimes of boarding houses, fraternity houses, and the like present urban problems. There is greater density; more cars, both driving on the streets and parked; and more noise. A quiet place where yards are wide, people few, and motor vehicles restricted are legitimate guidelines in a land-use project addressed to family needs. This goal is a permissible one. The police power is ample to lay out zones where family values, youth values, and the blessings of quiet seclusion and clean air make the area a sanctuary for people. Reversed.

Dissent: (Marshall, J.) The disputed classification burdens the students' fundamental rights of association and privacy guaranteed by the First and Fourteenth Amendments. Strict equal protection scrutiny is therefore required. A variety of justifications have been proffered for the Ordinance: it controls population density; prevents noise; traffic and parking problems; and preserves the rent structure of the community and its attractiveness to families. These are all legitimate and substantial interests, but the means chosen to accomplish these purposes are both overinclusive and underinclusive and the stated goals could be accomplished by other less restrictive means. An ordinance regulating the number of cars per household; and one regulating the total number of persons allowed per household, might be adopted. It would bar 3 retired, elderly persons from occupying a manor house, while allowing a family of a dozen to live next door. Density might be regulated by limiting the number of adults per household to 2 or 3, without limitation on the number of dependent children. As one can see, means might be better tailored to realize the Village's (P) goals.

Analysis:

The central disputes between Justice Powell's dissent and the majority opinion are what qualifies as a fundamental right and whether or not the Ordinance restrictions violate them. Justice Powell argues that the Ordinance violates the fundamental rights of association and privacy. Freedom of association, as that right is embodied in the First Amendment, has nothing to do with choosing the person(s) with whom one lives; when they wrote the First Amendment's Association Clause, the Framers intended to protect individuals' right to gather in common cause so that the voices of the many might be heard where the lone voice of the individual might be too faint. This purpose is enunciated in *NAACP v. Alabama*, in which the Supreme Court held that effective promotion of diverse points of view is enhanced by group association, and such association may be chilled if an organization is compelled to disclose its membership rolls. It is precisely this type of political advocacy the Framers were trying to preserve against the power of the state when they wrote the Association Clause. It is thus clear that they did not mean to create a fundamental right to live with whomever one might choose. Moving to privacy, it is also clear that the Framers never intended to extend a right to live with others of their choosing under the privacy rubric. Indeed, as any well-versed anti-abortion activist might tell you, nowhere in the Bill of Rights is privacy even mentioned. Granted, the Supreme Court has interpreted the Bill of Rights as providing a right to privacy, but has never suggested this right encompasses the freedom to live with whomever one wishes, notwithstanding applicable zoning restrictions. Such is not the type of extremely personal decision which receives protection from government interference, such as the decision to use contraception; to have an abortion; or to engage in consensual homosexual intercourse. Because of this, the Ordinance does not deserve strict scrutiny, but rather rational basis review—the standard of review applied to government action that doesn't implicate fundamental rights or discriminate against a class of people based upon a suspect characteristic, such as race.

Moore v. City of East Cleveland

(Grandmother) v. (Zoning Authority)
431 U.S. 494, 97 S.Ct. 1932 (1977)

M E M O R Y   G R A P H I C

Instant Facts

A zoning ordinance had the effect of prohibiting a grandmother's grandchild from living with her. She was issued a criminal citation and claims the ordinance violates her due process rights.

Black Letter Rule

The institution of the family being deeply rooted in the United States' history and tradition, a government restriction on one's right to live with family members must be narrowly tailored and serve a substantial and overriding government interest.

Procedural Basis: Certification to the U.S. Supreme Court after the State Supreme Court refused to review the ruling of the Appeals Court upholding the trial court's determination that the ordinance is constitutional.

Facts: East Cleveland's (City) (R) housing ordinance (Ordinance) limits occupancy of a dwelling unit to members of a single family. The Ordinance defines "family" to include (a) a husband or wife of the nominal head of the household, (b) unmarried children of the nominal head, or of his or her spouse so long as the unmarried children have no children of their own living in the household, (c) a father or mother of the nominal head or of the nominal head's spouse. The Ordinance also allows a "family" to include: not more than one dependent child of the nominal head or of the nominal head's spouse, and the spouse and dependent children of such dependent child. Mrs. Inez Moore (Inez)(P) lives with her son, Dale Moore, Sr., and her two grandsons, Dale, Jr. and John Moore, Jr. The two boys are first cousins rather than brothers. John came to live with Inez (P) after his mother's death. In early 1973, Inez (P) was issued a criminal citation when she refused to remove her grandson John from the home, since the Ordinance prohibited him from living there. Inez (P) claimed in the trial court that the Ordinance is constitutionally invalid on its face. This claim was overruled and Inez (P) was convicted of violating the Ordinance. The Ohio Court of Appeals affirmed; the Ohio Supreme Court denied review.

Issue: May government restrict one's ability to live with a family member absent a substantial and overriding governmental interest?

Decision and Rationale: (Powell, J.) No. The City (R) argues that our decision in *Village of Belle Terre v. Boraas* requires us to sustain the Ordinance. But one overriding factor sets this case apart from *Belle Terre*—the ordinance there affected only unrelated individuals. And in sustaining that ordinance, we were careful to note that it promoted "family needs" and "family values." By contrast, the Ordinance at issue here regulates housing occupancy by slicing deeply into the family itself. On its face it selects certain categories of relatives who may live together and declares that others may not. When a city undertakes such intrusive regulation of the family, the usual judicial deference to the legislature is inappropriate. When the government intrudes on choices concerning family living arrangements, this Court must examine carefully the importance of the governmental interests advanced and the extent to which they are served by the challenged regulation. The City (R) seeks to justify it as a means of preventing overcrowding, minimizing traffic and parking congestion, and avoiding an undue financial burden on the City's (P) school system. These are legitimate goals, but the Ordinance serves them marginally at best. For example, the Ordinance permits any family consisting only of husband, wife, and unmarried children to live together, even if the family contains a half-dozen licensed drivers with their own cars. The Ordinance would permit a grandmother to live with a single dependent son and children, even if his school-age children number a dozen. Yet it forces Inez (P) to find another dwelling for her grandson John, simply because of the presence of his uncle and cousin in the same household. We need not labor the point. The Ordinance has but a tenuous relation to the alleviation of the conditions mentioned by the City (R). The Constitution protects the sanctity of the family precisely because this institution is deeply rooted in this Nation's history and tradition. Ours is by no means a tradition limited to respect for the bonds uniting members of the nuclear family. The tradition of uncles, aunts, cousins, and especially grandparents sharing a household along with parents and children has roots equally venerable and equally deserving of constitutional recognition. Reversed.

Dissent: (Stewart, J.) The majority misunderstands the nature of the associational freedoms the Constitution has been understood to protect. Freedom of association has been constitutionally recognized because it is often indispensable to effectuation of explicit First Amendment guarantees. The "association" in this case is not for any such purpose. It is asserted to promote the interests of gratification, convenience, and economy of sharing the same residence. Such interests should not receive constitutional protection.

Analysis:

Where Justice Powell once failed, he now succeeds . . . sort of. In his *Village of Belle Terre v. Boraas* dissent, Justice Powell disagreed with the majority's view that freedom of association does not encompass the right to live with whomever one wishes. As he points out in his majority opinion in this case, however, the right to live with one's family members does fall within the right of freedom of association. Why the difference? In essence, the Court has declared that the right to associate, i.e., live with one's extended family members is a fundamental right. The Court does not come out and say this, but its reasoning in elevating this right to constitutionally protected status follows its reasoning in determining fundamental rights. The Court examines the asserted right and asks whether it is embedded in the history and tradition of the Nation. The answer here is, of course, that there is a long tradition of extended family members living together [remember the Waltons?]. In light of this, the Court saw fit to declare such a right fundamental. However, in doing so, the Court ignores current reality. In the somewhat distant past, many people lived together with their extended families due to economic constraints and the need to pitch-in and live and work as one economic unit. As time has gone on, though, this "reality" has become the exception. Should the Court have taken this into account?

City of Cleburne v. Cleburne Living Center

(Municipality) v. (Home for Mentally Retarded)
473 U.S. 432, 105 S.Ct. 3249 (1985)

M E M O R Y   G R A P H I C

 ### Instant Facts

The City zoning scheme allowed all kinds of similar uses, but prohibited a group home for the mentally retarded without any solid rationale. The purveyors of the home sued on equal protection grounds.

Black Letter Rule

Government actions, including zoning schemes, which discriminate based upon a person's mentally retarded status, or other non-suspect and non-quasi-suspect qualities, need only be rationally related to a legitimate government purpose, i.e., they receive rational basis review.

Case Vocabulary

IMMUTABLE: Unable to be alleviated or hidden from the public at large.
QUASI-SUSPECT CLASS: A class of persons having certain characteristics which require a court to subject any governmental action that discriminates based upon these characteristics to intermediate-level scrutiny.

Procedural Basis: Certification to the U.S. Supreme Court from the Federal Circuit Court's reversal of the Federal District Court's ruling that the zoning scheme is constitutional.

Facts: In July 1980, Jan Hannah purchased a building in Cleburne, Texas (City) (P), with the intention of turning it into the Cleburne Living Center (CLC) (R), a group home for the mentally retarded. It was planned that the CLC (R) would house 13 retarded men and women who would be constantly supervised by staff. The CLC (R) submitted the proper permit application, but was told a special use permit, renewable annually, was required for the construction and operation of "[h]ospitals for the insane or feeble-minded, or alcoholic [sic] or drug addicts, or penal or correctional institutions." The City (P) classified the proposed group home as a "hospital for the feeble-minded." After a public hearing, the City Council denied the permit. CLC (R) filed suit claiming that the zoning ordinance (Ordinance) violated the Equal Protection Clause. The District Court ruled the Ordinance constitutional, deciding that the mentally retarded are not a suspect, nor quasi-suspect class. The Circuit Court of Appeals reversed, holding that the mentally retarded are a quasi-suspect class and that the Ordinance deserved heightened, intermediate-level scrutiny, which it did not satisfy.

Issue: Are the mentally retarded a suspect or quasi-suspect class such that government action that discriminates against them based upon this quality requires heightened judicial scrutiny?

Decision and Rationale: (White, J.) No. Our general rule is that legislation will be presumed constitutional and will be sustained if rationally related to a legitimate state interest. When social or economic legislation, such as a zoning scheme, is at issue, the state is given wide latitude, ultimately leaving things to the democratic process. But the general rule gives way when a statute classifies by race, alienage, or national origin. These factors are seldom relevant to the achievement of any legitimate state interest and are much tougher to have overturned through the normal democratic process due to the popular prejudices and tyranny of the majority. Such laws are subjected to strict scrutiny and will be sustained only if they are suitably tailored to serve a compelling state interest. Similar oversight is due when a law impinges on personal rights protected by the Constitution. Classifications based on gender also call for heightened review, but we have declined to extend such review to different treatment based on age. His is because, even though the aged have not been completely free of discrimination, such persons have not experienced a history of purposeful unequal treatment or been subjected to unique disabilities on the basis of stereotyped characteristics not truly indicative of their abilities. One lesson we've learned is where individuals in the group affected by a law have distinguishing characteristics relevant to interests the State has the authority to implement, the courts have been very reluctant to closely scrutinize legislative choices as to whether, how, and to what extent those interests should be pursued. In such cases, the Equal Protection Clause requires only a rational means to serve a legitimate end. Applying these principles, we conclude that mental retardation is not a quasi-suspect classification. First, it is undeniable that the mentally retarded have a reduced ability to cope with and function in the everyday world. Nor are they all the same, but rather range from those whose disability is not readily apparent to those who require constant care. They are thus different, immutably so, in relevant respects, and the States' interest in dealing with and providing for them is plainly a legitimate one. The decisions on how to do this is a task for legislators, guided by qualified professionals, and not for the perhaps ill-informed opinions of the judiciary. Second, the distinctive legislative response to the mentally retarded demonstrates not only that they have unique problems, but also that the lawmakers have been addressing their difficulties in a manner that belies a continuing antipathy or prejudice and a corresponding need for more intrusive oversight by the courts. The State of Texas acknowledges the special status of the mentally retarded by conferring certain rights upon them under the law, such as the right to live in the least restrictive setting appropriate. Third, this legislative response negates any claim that the mentally retarded are politically powerless. This shows they do have a say. Fourth, deeming the mentally retarded quasi-suspect for the reasons given by the Court of Appeals would open the door for extending such protection to other similar groups, such as the aged, the mentally ill, and the infirm. There would be left no principled way of distinguishing between these groups. We are reluctant to set out on that course and we decline to classify the mentally retarded as a quasi-suspect class. This does not leave them entirely unprotected from invidious discrimination for laws distinguishing between them and others on the basis of their affliction must still be rationally related to a legitimate governmental purpose. The constitutional issue is thus clearly posed. The City (P) does not require a special use permit for apartment houses, multiple dwellings, boarding and lodging houses, fraternities and sororities, sanitariums, nursing homes, etc. It does, however, require such permit for a home for the mentally retarded. But in our view, the record does not reveal any rational basis for believing the home for the mentally retarded would pose any special threat to the City's (P) legitimate interests. The District Court found that the permit requirement rested on several factors. First, there was concern for the negative attitude of the majority of property owners within 200 feet of the planned home, as well as fears of elderly residents of the neighborhood. But mere negative attitudes or fear are not permissible bases for treating a home for the mentally retarded differently from apartment houses, multiple dwellings and the like. Second, the City Council had two objections to the location of the facility: One, that it was across from a junior high school and the students might harass the mentally

retarded occupants. But the school itself is attended by about 30 mentally retarded students and the concern doesn't seem to have been extended to them. Two, that the home site is located on a 500-hundred-year flood plain. But this concern is equally applicable to other uses that are allowed without a special permit. Next, the Council has concerns over the legal responsibility for actions the mentally retarded might take. But it is difficult to believe this concern doesn't also apply to, and with greater force, the allowable uses for fraternities, sororities, especially since the home's occupants will be tightly supervised. Fourth, the Council was concerned over the size of the home and the number of people who would occupy it. Once again, these concerns apply as well to other permitted uses. The question is whether it is rational to treat the mentally retarded differently. If there is a valid reason for doing so, it is not apparent in the record before us. The short of it is that requiring the permit in this case appears to us to rest on an irrational prejudice against the mentally retarded, including those who would live under the closely supervised and highly regulated conditions expressly provided for by state and federal law. Affirmed as to results, but no as to rationale.

Concurrence and Dissent: (Marshall, J) The Court holds the Ordinance invalid on rational basis grounds and disclaims that anything special, in the form of heightened scrutiny, has taken place. But the Court has not applied the traditional rational basis test applicable to economic and commercial regulation. It is important to articulate, as the Court does not, the facts and principles that justify subjecting this Ordinance to the searching review—the heightened scrutiny—that actually leads to its invalidation.

Analysis:

This case serves to illustrate the analysis the Court employs in deciding whether a group shall be deemed a suspect or quasi-suspect class, and thus receive greater protection through the Court's employment of heightened scrutiny—whether intermediate level or strict level—when considering government action that discriminates based upon the groups status. There are several factors the Court considers. First is whether there is a history of unfair and prejudicial treatment that reflects deep-seated prejudice. Second, a court will ask if the group's unique characteristic is immutable; that is, whether it can be alleviated or made to go away or disguised. Third is whether the group has been shut out of political power such that they cannot resort to self-help through the democratic process. Finally, and perhaps most important when deciding between strict and intermediate scrutiny, is whether the unique characteristics of the group could possibly serve as a basis for any legal distinction or disparate treatment. As the majority opinion illustrates, the mentally retarded fall short in these inquiries. While there is certainly some prejudice and discrimination against the mentally retarded, it does not rise to the level of racism or gender-based prejudice; it is not deep-seated. The characteristics of the mentally retarded are not immutable either. As the majority points out, they are very heterogeneous within their own realm. Some can function quite well in society with very little support, while others must be cared for constantly. Third, it is obvious the mentally retarded have not been shut out of the political process since there are laws on the books designed to protect their rights and dignity as human beings. Last, the unique characteristics of the mentally retarded can legitimately serve as a basis for legal distinctions since their status often means that they require more and different care, unlike race, which can rarely serve as such a basis. Based upon these factors, the Court, rightly it seems, chose to subject the Ordinance to simple rational basis review, or at least says this is the review employed.

Britton v. Town of Chester

(Developer) v. (Bedroom Community)
134 N.H. 434, 595 A.2d 492 (1991)

M E M O R Y   G R A P H I C

Instant Facts

A town's zoning plan prohibited the building of affordable housing for low and moderate-income families. A developer sued to have the restrictions invalidated and for specific relief in the form of an order allowing the project to go forward.

Black Letter Rule

1) A municipality that, pursuant to state law, enacts zoning regulations in order to promote the "general welfare of the community," must take into account the needs of the entire surrounding community, not just those within its political boundaries. 2) Specific court-ordered relief in the form of a "builder's remedy" allowing the developer to go forward with plans previously prohibited by an invalidated zoning regulation, is appropriate where there is a possibility the local legislative authority will attempt to thwart the developer's ultimate plans even after the regulation has been declared invalid; such relief does not violate the Separation of Powers Doctrine.

Case Vocabulary

MASTER: An individual appointed by a court to conduct fact-finding, apply the law to the facts found, and make a recommendation based upon this analysis.

Procedural Basis: Appeal to the State Supreme Court from the Superior Court's order affirming the ruling of the Master that the zoning ordinance is unconstitutional and ordering a builder's remedy.

Facts: The Town of Chester (Town) (D) lies in the west-central portion of Rockingham County, a few miles from Manchester. The majority of the Town's (D) workforce commutes to Manchester. The available housing is principally single-family homes and there is no municipal sewer or water service. The Town (D) has not encouraged industrial or commercial development, preferring to remain a "bedroom community." Because of its proximity to Manchester, the Town (D) is projected to have among the highest growth rates in New Hampshire. Plaintiffs are a group of low and moderate-income people seeking affordable, adequate housing in the town, and a builder named Raymond Remillard (P1), who is committed to constructing such housing. Remillard (P1) owns an undeveloped twenty-three-acre parcel in the town's eastern section and, since 1979, has attempted to obtain permission from the town to build moderate-sized multi-family housing development on his land. The zoning ordinance (Ordinance) in effect at the filing of this action in 1985 provided for a single-family home on a two-acre lot or duplex on a three-acre lot, and excluded multi-family housing from all five zoning districts. The Ordinance as amended allowed multi-family housing but requires it to be part of a Planned Residential Development (PRD), which required to also be built a variety of housing types, such as single-family homes, duplexes, and multi-family structures. PRDs are allowed in not less than twenty acres in two R-2 (medium-density residential) districts, but only slightly more than half of the land in these two districts could be effectively used for multi-family developments. The Ordinance also requires a PRD to be approved by the planning board, which is also allowed to control various aspects of the PRD without reference to any objective criteria and require the developer to fund any experts whose testimony might be relevant to the board's determinations. After a hearing, and based upon language in the State's zoning enabling act (Act) requiring towns to promote the "general welfare of the community," the Master recommended that the Ordinance be invalidated for several reasons which, added together, acted as a substantial disincentive to any such development, and that Remillard (P1) be awarded a "builder's remedy." This recommendation was upheld by the Superior Court.

Issue: 1) May a municipality enact zoning legislation that effectively prohibits low and moderate-income people from living there? 2) May a court force a municipality to allow a housing development that is prohibited by zoning ordinance?

Decision and Rationale: (Batchelder, J.) 1) No. 2) Yes. The Town (D) argues first that the Ordinance does not exceed the powers allowed under the Act, as the trial court ruled. Specifically, the Town (D) asserts that the Act does not require it to zone for the low-income housing needs of the region beyond its boundaries, and further, that even if it were required to consider regional housing needs, the Ordinance is valid because it provides for an adequate range of housing types. These arguments fail to persuade us. The Act authorizes a local legislative body to adopt or amend a zoning ordinance in order to promote "the general welfare of the community." The Town (D) asserts that the term "community" as used in the Act refers only to the municipality itself. We disagree. This Court has previously held that growth controls must not be imposed simply to exclude outsiders, especially those of any disadvantaged social or economic group, because each municipality should bear its fair share of the burden of increased growth. Today, we pursue the logical extension of this reasoning and apply its high purpose to zoning regulations which wrongfully exclude persons of low or moderate-income from the zoning municipality. Towns may not refuse to confront the future by building a moat around themselves and pulling up the drawbridge and then refusing to lower it only for the more affluent. Municipalities are not isolated enclaves existing solely to serve their own residents. Therefore, we interpret the general welfare provision of the Act to include the welfare of the "community," as to include that of the community itself and its surrounding region. Because the Ordinance does not provide for the lawful needs of the community as it must under the Act, we hold that as applied to the facts of this case, it is an invalid exercise of the power delegated to the town by the Act. We so hold because of the Master's finding that "there are no substantial and compelling reasons that would warrant the Town (D), through its Ordinance, from fulfilling its obligation to provide low and moderate-income families a realistic opportunity to obtain affordable housing. As to the specific relief granted, the Town (D) contends that the court has effectively rezoned the parcel at issue in violation of the Separation of Powers Doctrine, and that even if this were not so, Remillard's (P1) proposed development does not qualify for such relief. The Trial Court has the power to grant definitive relief for Remillard (P1). We uphold this Order for Relief, finding that the Master's award of a "builder's remedy," i.e., allowing Remillard (P1) to complete his project as proposed. A builder's remedy is appropriate where, notwithstanding a court ruling, it is assured that there will be lasting attempts by the powers that be to further stymie a prevailing party's efforts to move forward with a development. Since 1979, Remillard (P1) has attempted to obtain permission to build a moderate-sized multi-family housing development on his land. It has been said, "Equity will not suffer a wrong without a remedy." Hence, we could hold that the "builder's remedy" is appropriate in this case, both to compensate the developer who has invested substantial time and resources in pursuing this litigation, and as the most likely means of insuring that low and moderate-income housing is actually built. The Town's (D) argument that the specific relief granted violates the Separation of Powers Doctrine is without merit. It is settled that complete separation of powers would interfere with the efficient operation of government. Consequently, there must be some overlapping of the power of each branch. The Town (D) has adopted a zoning ordinance which is blatantly exclusionary. This Court will not condone the Town's (D) conduct. Affirmed in part and reversed in part.

Analysis:

Zoning falls under the rubric of the police power. The police power may only be exercised to promote the public welfare. What constitutes the "public welfare" is the usual issue when a regulation enacted pursuant to the police power is attacked on the ground that it violates the enabling legislation. But here, at issue is the construction to be given the word "community." This is why Remillard's (P1) legal counsel was sure to get into the record, and the Court was sure to include in its recitation of the relevant facts, the reality that the Town (D) was a major source of Manchester's workforce; and that the Town (D) was projected to be among the fastest growing (population-wise) municipalities in the State. These facts provide a rationale for declaring that the "community" referred to in the Act meant both the Town (D) itself and the surrounding region. Such an interpretation is required in order to ensure that one or two or a few towns do not avoid carrying their fair share of the burden when to comes to accommodating low-income people who pay relatively little in taxes, but consume a higher-than-average share of municipal services. To solve this problem, some states have enacted legislation that conglomerates metropolitan areas and forces the entire area to bear the cost of certain services, such as public health care, even though the greater demand for such services originates in the center city.

Chapter 23

Real estate is often the most valuable asset a person owns, and the asset which requires the greatest proportion of his income to support. The sale of real estate therefore has very significant consequences for the parties.

This chapter discusses the laws and doctrines that govern real estate transactions. It will explore the elements that are necessary for different real estate transactions, including when a written document is necessary, and what that document must include. This chapter will also discuss the different types of transactions. Sometimes it is crucial that a contract be performed by a certain hour, while others are performed over the course of many years, and perhaps even involve several different sellers and buyers. The chapter will explore the origin of mortgages and the benefits they offer over other means of financing, and it will explain what a buyer must do to get his deposit back if something goes wrong. It will also explain some things that may at first seem strange, such as why a seller does not have to own property before he can contract to sell it.

Last, but not least, there is the real estate broker, a common participant in real estate transactions. This chapter will discuss what he must do to earn his commission, and how far he can go before engaging in the unauthorized practice of law. Real estate transactions are part of many lawyers' practices, and most people's lives. This chapter will make them more understandable.

Chapter 23

NOTE: THE PURPOSE OF THIS OUTLINE IS TO ORGANIZE THE CASES SO THAT ONE CAN QUICKLY UNDERSTAND THE RELEVANCE OF EACH CASE TO THE COURSE. NO ATTEMPT IS MADE IN THIS OVERVIEW TO ADDRESS EVERY CONCEPT THAT MUST BE STUDIED. BE SURE TO READ THE ENTIRE CASEBOOK AND/OR OTHER MATERIALS TO GAIN A FULL UNDERSTANDING OF ALL CONCEPTS.

I. The Effects of the Statute of Frauds
   A. The Statute of Frauds, an English statute dated 1677, states that a contract for the sale of land is only enforceable if it is reduced to writing and signed by the party charged with breach. *An Act for Prevention of Frauds and Perjuries*.
      1. State statutes generally follow the English model,
      2. But statutes vary on details such as
         a. Whether an oral agreement is void or only unenforceable;
         b. Whether the agreement must be subscribed or only signed;
         c. Whether the agreement must be signed by the party charged, the seller, or both.
   B. Exceptions to the Statute of Frauds
      1. One exception to the statute of frauds is the doctrine of part performance. Acts of part performance, such as taking possession and making a partial payment, will suffice to remove an oral contract from the statute of frauds if they are unequivocally referable to the contract. *Shaughnessy v. Eidsmo*.
         a. Some courts, while recognizing that precedents have established exceptions to the statute of frauds, would prefer strict enforcement instead because they find this would better serve the statute's purpose of preventing fraud and perjury. *Garner v. Stubblefield*.
            (1) Had strict construction become the rule, oral agreements would probably have become rare.
            (2) Allowing the part performance exception, on the other hand, opens a new door to fraud and makes the effect of the statute more uncertain.
         b. The states vary on what they require for the part performance exception to the statute of frauds. Some find possession alone suffi-

cient; some require possession and payment; some require possession and improvements; some require possession and irreparable injury (usually due to improvements); and some recognize no acts of part performance at all. *Chafee and Re, Cases and Materials on Equity*.
         c. Acts of part performance only suffice to take an agreement out of the statute of frauds if the acts are "unequivocally referable" to the agreement and "unintelligible or at least extraordinary" apart from it. *Burns v. McCormick*.
      2. Another exception to the statute of frauds is the doctrine of equitable estoppel. Under this doctrine, a court may award specific performance if a party has acted in reliance on an oral land sale contract and injustice would result without specific performance. *Hickey v. Green*.
   C. To satisfy the statute of frauds, the written memorandum of the contract must name the parties and the essentials of the contract.
      1. However, this "memorandum" may consist of several writings. *Ward v. Mattuschek*.
      2. An informal agreement contemplating the drafting and execution of a formal contract is only binding if the parties intend it to be. *King v. Wenger*.
   D. Rescission and Modification of Real Estate Contracts
      1. A party may rescind an executory contract involving an interest in land by an oral agreement. *Niernberg v. Feld*.
      2. Parol modifications to a written land contract are generally not enforceable, but they may be if estoppel makes this possible. Where there is reliance on the parol modification, either the modification will be enforceable or reasonable time to comply with the contract as written must be given. *Imperator Realty Co., Inc. v. Tull*.

II. Most written real estate contracts are very detailed. Although there is no real "standard" contract insofar as each sale is different and norms and forms vary throughout the country, attorneys in most localities do have prepared forms to rely upon.

III. Common Clauses and Requirements in Real Estate Contracts

  A. Time

    1. Ordinarily, time is of the essence only when the contract expressly so stipulates or this intention is inferable from the circumstances of the transaction, the conduct of the parties, or the purpose of the sale. *Kasten Construction Co. v. Maple Ridge Construction Co.*

      a. At law, the day a contract fixed for performance was always imperative. Equity, however, would examine the cause of delay and permit performance past the deadline unless there were substantial objections relating not merely to time, but to the conduct of the parties or a change of circumstances that affected the value of the object of the contract. *Sugden, Law of Vendors & Purchasers.*

      b. When the parties to a contract for the sale of land have not made time of the essence, either party may render time of the essence by giving reasonable notice to the other party. *Schmidt v. Reed.*

    2. When parties make time of the essence, one party's failure to perform on time causes his rights under the contract to cease at the option of the other party. *Doctorman v. Schroeder.*

  B. Financing and Installment Contracts

    1. If a "subject to financing" clause is ambiguous or lacking as to essential details, and the surrounding circumstances do not indicate the intent of the parties as to these details, then the contract must fail for indefiniteness. *Gerruth Realty Co. v. Pire.*

      a. A buyer may waive his rights under a financing clause, but, where time is of the essence, he must do so before deadlines pass and the seller terminates the contract. *Dvorak v. Christ.*

    2. A mortgage was originally considered a conveyance of land given to secure payment of a debt, but today it is usually considered a lien rather than a conveyance. *Kratovil, Real Estate Law.*

      a. A mortgagor has an equitable right of redemption which allows him to pay his debt and recover the land even after default.

      b. Contract clauses that purport to waive this right are void.

      c. Foreclosure proceedings permit a mortgagee to extinguish the mortgagor's equity of redemption, usually by public sale of the land to satisfy the debt.

    3. An alternative to the mortgage is the long-term land sale contract. *Osborne, Secured Transactions.*

      a. In the long-term land sale contract the buyer takes possession immediately, but does not take legal title until he pays the full purchase price through a series of installments.

        (1) Traditionally, these contracts give the buyer no equity of redemption;

        (2) They include forfeiture provisions which allow the seller to terminate the contract and keep all previous payments if the buyer defaults.

      b. Recognizing the injustice to the buyer that often resulted from forfeiture clauses, some states began to treat installment contracts as mortgages and give the buyer foreclosure rights. *Freyfogle, Vagueness and the Rule of Law: Reconsidering Installment Land Contract Forfeitures.*

        (1) Other states give the buyer other protections such as notice of forfeiture, a right of redemption, or sometimes a right to reinstate the contract by paying past-due installments. *Freyfogle.*

        (2) Where enforcement of forfeiture provisions of a land sale contract would result in injustice, a court of equity may deny forfeiture and order foreclosure proceedings instead. *Skendzel v. Marshall.*

        (3) Even where a buyer is in wilful default, a court may relieve him from forfeiture by giving him an opportunity to pay damages and complete the contract. *Union Bond & Trust Co. v. Blue Creek Redwood Co.*

  C. Merchantable or marketable title is one that is free from litigation, defects and serious doubts about its validity, which a reasonably prudent buyer would be willing to accept.

    1. An executory contract for the sale of land always includes an implied covenant by the seller to give marketable title, unless the contract expressly makes or excludes this covenant. *Wallach v. Riverside Bank.*

    2. Courts will not compel a seller to clear his title where its defect is incurable, but may do so if the defect is clearly curable. *Bartos v. Czerwinski.*

3. A seller need not have or produce marketable title before the time the contract requires him to convey it, and the buyer cannot rescind the contract due to uncertainty as to the state of the seller's title before that time. *Luette v. Bank of Italy Nat. Trust & Savings Ass'n.*

D. Tender and Demand

1. Because a seller's and buyer's performance are concurrent conditions in a real estate contract, one party must generally tender performance to trigger the other party's duty to perform before he can place the other party in default. *Cohen v. Kranz.*

2. Thus, where title defects are curable, the buyer must make a tender and demand to put the seller in default before she can recover her deposit. *Cohen v. Kranz.*

E. Restrictions on assignment are disfavored and strictly construed. *Handzel v. Bassi.*

1. A court of equity should relieve a buyer from forfeiture resulting from his violation of a stipulation against assignment where the buyer offers and is able to fully perform the contract. *Id.*

F. Remedies

1. Specific performance is a remedy that is usually available to a buyer for breach of a real estate contract.

   a. However, a seller of real estate is not automatically entitled to specific performance just because the buyer would be entitled to it. *Centex Homes Corp. v. Boag.*

   b. Courts should confine specific performance to those special cases in which the seller will otherwise suffer an economic injury which damages would be inadequate to compensate, or where other equitable considerations require granting it. *Centex.*

2. Damages

   a. In states that follow the "English rule," when a sale of land fails due to a title defect, a buyer is not entitled to damages for the loss of his bargain unless the seller is guilty of bad faith or some positive act of fraud. *Kramer v. Mobley.*

   b. However, courts that follow the "American rule" disregard good faith and always allow benefit-of-the-bargain damages for breach. *Smith v. Warr.*

IV. Real estate transactions usually involve a "gap" between execution of the contract of sale and delivery of the deed to allow the buyer to assure himself that the seller has merchantable title.

A. This gap may be a few weeks or, for installment contracts, several years.

1. The doctrine of equitable conversion may determine what happens when circumstances change during this interim period.

B. A court that applies the doctrine of equitable conversion to a pending real estate transaction treats the buyer as the equitable owner of the land and the seller as the equitable owner of the purchase money.

1. However, a court should not apply the doctrine of equitable conversion to an executory contract where doing so would defeat the agreed purpose of the sale and cause hardship and injustice to one of the parties. *Clay v. Landreth.*

C. If a seller dies while a contract for the sale of land is still executory, legal title to the land passes to his heirs or devisees, but equitable conversion will determine who takes the payments from the buyer and who can enforce the contract. Likewise, if the buyer dies, equitable conversion will determine who must make the payments and who ultimately takes the land.

1. Equitable conversion changes the seller's interest into personalty and the buyer's interest into realty from the signing of the contract. Equitable conversion takes place at the signing of a contract for the sale of land, regardless of the length of time the contract has to run. *Shay v. Penrose.*

   a. Once land is equitably converted, it remains converted. A subsequent default will not reverse equitable conversion. *Clapp v. Tower.*

2. However, an enforceable contract for the sale of land must exist before the doctrine of equitable conversion will apply. Equitable conversion does not relate back to the date of an option to purchase land, but can only occur when and if the optionee exercises his option. *Eddington v. Turner.*

   a. If an optionee does not exercise his option until after the optionor dies, there is no conversion, although English cases erroneously hold that there is. The English agree, however, that there is no conversion if there is no exercise of the option until after the optionee dies. *Chafee and Re, Cases and Materials on Equity.*

D. The majority rule for risk allocation under an executory contract for the sale of land applies equitable conversion and therefore places the risk of loss on the buyer, the equitable owner of the property, unless the contract provides otherwise. *Bleckley v. Langston.*

   1. Some states have adopted a uniform law which implies a provision in real estate contracts that imposes the risk of loss on the buyer only after the transfer of *either* possession *or* legal title to the buyer. *Uniform Vendor and Purchaser Risk Act.*

   2. If a contract is not specifically enforceable due to failure of a condition, equitable conversion will not apply to shift the risk of loss to the buyer. *Sanford v. Breidenbach.*

   3. If, in compliance with a contract for the sale of land, the buyer insures the property in the seller's name pending completion of the sale, the seller must apply any proceeds from that insurance toward the purchase price. *Raplee v. Piper.*

   4. Condemnation of property by eminent domain does not destroy a seller's lien or affect his right to enforce it against the buyer for the full amount of the unpaid purchase price. On the other hand, where the fair market value of the land is greater than the contract price, the buyer should receive his equitable interest, so the condemnor should give the seller the a-mount of the contract price then give the buyer the balance. *Arko Enterprises, Inc. v. Wood.*

V. Most real estate transactions today occur through a real estate broker.

   A. Generally, the seller enters into a contract with a broker to list his property for sale, and pays the broker a commission if he sells it.

   1. Most of these contracts give the broker an "exclusive right to sell" the property, exclusive even of the seller's right to sell.

   2. Others involve a more flexible "exclusive agency" agreement, which only prevents the seller from using another broker.

B. Striking a balance between public protection and public convenience, some courts allow brokers to fill in the blanks of standard real estate forms, and do not forbid this as an unauthorized practice of law. *State ex rel. Indiana State Bar Association v. Indiana Real Estate Association, Inc.*

C. Under the traditional, majority rule, a broker has earned his commission when he has produced a buyer who is ready, willing and able to buy the property at the seller's terms.

   1. However, many courts follow the minority *Ellsworth* rule, which also requires the consummation of the sale before the broker's commission is due. *Tristram's Landing, Inc. v. Wait.*

   2. By closing the transaction, a seller demonstrates his acceptance of the buyer's ability to perform sufficiently to support the broker's claim for his commission, even if the buyer's performance is to extend years beyond the closing and he later defaults. *Strout Realty, Inc. v. Milhous.*

D. Traditionally, buyers who bought defective homes could only recover damages from brokers if they could prove intentional misrepresentation of facts by the broker on which they relied. *Note, Imposing Tort Liability on Real Estate Brokers Selling Defective Housing.*

   1. Because these cases were very difficult to prove, courts also began allowing recovery for negligent misrepresentation, innocent representation, failure to disclose known defects, and general negligence (often based on a statutory duty of disclosure).

   2. California also imposes a duty on brokers to diligently inspect the premises. The District of Columbia has imposed strict liability on a broker for selling a defective apartment, analogous to the duty imposed on sellers of new homes.

   3. A broker may also be liable for negligence if he fails to inform a buyer of facts that an experienced broker should know, even where the seller has mistakenly disclosed facts to the contrary. *Johnson v. Geer Real Estate Company.*

FINDING AN EXCEPTION TO THE STATUTE OF FRAUDS, THE COURT ENFORCES AN ORAL CONTRACT FOR THE SALE OF LAND WHERE THERE IS ADEQUATE PARTIAL PERFORMANCE

Shaughnessy v. Eidsmo

(Buyer) v. (Seller)
222 Minn. 141, 23 N.W.2d 362 (1946)

M E M O R Y   G R A P H I C

Instant Facts

After the Shaughnessys (P) exercised their option in their oral lease agreement to buy the property they were renting and made payments on the property, Eidsmo (D) denied giving them an option and claimed they only asked for a written lease.

Black Letter Rule

Where a buyer takes possession of land and makes a partial payment pursuant to an oral contract for the transfer of that land and with unequivocal reference to the buyer-seller relationship, these acts of part performance suffice to remove the contract from the statute of frauds.

Case Vocabulary

IN FUTURO: In the future, at a future date.
LIVERY OF SEISIN: Ancient ceremony for conveying land, which involved transferring some symbolic item, such as a key, or turning over possession. ["Delivery" of seisin.]
PAROL: Oral.
PART PERFORMANCE: A doctrine under which partial performance of a contract serves as evidence of that contract and therefore takes the contract out of the Statute of Frauds.
RIGHT IN PERSONAM: A right against a specific person.
STATUTE OF FRAUDS: Statute which requires that certain contracts, including those involving the sale of land, must be in writing to be enforceable.

Procedural Basis: Appeal from order denying motion for new trial in action for specific performance.

Facts: The trial court's findings indicate that Mr. and Mrs. Shaughnessy (the Shaughnessys) (P) leased property from Eidsmo (D) by an oral agreement. The term of the lease was one year, and it included an option to purchase the property at the expiration of the lease. The Shaughnessys (P) notified Eidsmo (D) that they wished to exercise their option and demanded a contract for deed as they agreed. Eidsmo (D) said that he did not have time to have a contract drawn, but assured the Shaughnessys (P) that his word was good. Contrary to these findings, Eidsmo (D) alleges that he did not give the Shaughnessys (P) any option and that they did not exercise one. Eidsmo (D) alleges that the Shaughnessys (P) only asked for a written lease and not a contract for deed. The trial court decreed that the Shaughnessys (P) have a buyer's interest in the property and that they are entitled to a contract for deed. The Shaughnessys (P) fully performed their part of the option agreement and have stood ready, willing and able to execute a contract for deed. Since their lease expired, the Shaughnessys (P) have remained in possession of the property and have made payments toward the purchase of the property.

Issue: Does the statute of frauds prevent enforcement of an oral contract for the purchase and sale of land if there has been part performance of the contract?

Decision and Rationale: (Matson) No. First, there is ample evidence to support the trial court's findings of fact as to the Shaughnessys' (P) exercise of their option. An option to purchase real estate does not bring an agreement under the statute of frauds. An option contract is only an irrevocable and continuing offer to sell. It conveys no interest in land to the optionee, but only gives him a right to buy. Further, an option contract is a unilateral contract, and therefore is fully performed by the optionee from its inception, when he acquires his irrevocable right of purchase. Because it is performed from its inception, an option contract cannot come within the statute of frauds on grounds that it cannot be performed within one year. The fact that the option here was part of an oral lease does not change this result. The oral lease, on the other hand, was a bilateral contract, and was not performable within one year since it was for a term of one year and commenced in futuro. This lease was subject to the statute of frauds, but since the Shaughnessys (P) had fully performed the lease when they exercised their option, the statute was no longer applicable. However, [at last we come to the real issue] as soon as the Shaughnessys (P) exercised their option, a new oral contract for the purchase and sale of land came into being. This oral contract was within the statute of frauds unless it was taken out of it by part performance. Under *Restatement, Contracts, § 197* [doctrine of part performance], if a buyer, acting with the assent of the seller under an oral contract for the transfer of an interest in land, either (a) makes valuable improvements to the land, or (b) takes or retains possession of the land and pays part of the purchase price, then the contract is specifically enforceable by the buyer or the seller. In other words, where a buyer takes possession of land and makes a partial payment pursuant to or in reliance upon an oral contract for the transfer of that land and with unequivocal reference to the buyer-seller relationship, these acts of part performance suffice to remove the contract from the statute of frauds. We overrule prior cases that rejected the unequivocal reference theory and instead required proof of irreparable injury through fraud to avoid the statute. Historically, cases have been taken out of the statute of frauds by either part performance *or* fraud. [Here "fraud" really refers to estoppel: where a person acts in reliance upon a contract such that a refusal to enforce it would amount to fraud upon him]. Where there is adequate proof of part performance unequivocally referable to the contract, additional proof of fraud is not necessary. Although equitable relief is usually denied where monetary damages are adequate, damages are presumed to be an inadequate remedy for a breach of a contract for the sale of land because each parcel of land is unique and there is no open market for it for either the seller or buyer. Thus, the equitable remedy of specific performance is always available where an interest in land is involved, without proof of irreparable injury. Two rationales support the part performance doctrine. First, the statute of frauds is an evidential rule, and any acts clearly and solely referable to the existence of the contract satisfy the evidential purpose of the statute. Second, equity should prevent [estop] a seller from relying upon the statute when it would be unconscionable for him to do so. The evidential purpose of the statute is clearly satisfied by adequate part performance without proof of irreparable injury. Whether the acts of part performance are unequivocally referable to the buyer-seller

relationship under the oral contract is a question of fact. Here, the two essential elements of possession and part payment are present. Eidsmo (D) argues that possession is not unequivocally referable to the buyer-seller relationship, but is equally referable to the landlord-tenant relationship. However, the record indicates that the dominant intent of the parties was to establish a buyer-seller relationship when the lease term expired. Further, after the Shaughnessys (P) exercised their option and the oral buy-sell contract came into being, Eidsmo's (D) words and actions did not deny, but rather affirmed, the buyer-seller relationship. Eidsmo (D) stated that he did not have time to have the contract drawn, but that his word was good and he would get it. There was a dispute about the price and payment terms, but not about the existence of the buyer-seller relationship. Affirmed.

Analysis:

Under the statute of frauds, contracts for the sale of land must be in writing to be enforceable. This case discusses the exception to that rule that courts of equity created for contracts that have been partly performed. As the court states here, a party can show part performance of a contract for the sale of land if he has taken possession of the land and made a partial payment for it pursuant to the contract. Other cases also find part performance where a party has taken possession of the land and made improvements to it. Different states require different combinations of the acts of payment, possession and improvements to satisfy the doctrine of part performance. Under the evidentiary theory of the statute of frauds, the writing is simply evidence of the contract, but other evidence, such as part performance, can be sufficient evidence as well. For acts of part performance to suffice as evidence of the contract, they must be "unequivocally referable" to the contract. Estoppel theory also supports the part performance doctrine. If a person has reasonably relied to his detriment upon an oral contract, such as by making payments or improvements, the other party should be estopped from denying that contract. Some courts, including the court here, refer to this rationale as the "fraud" theory. Courts applying this theory often require proof that the person would suffer irreparable injury if he cannot specifically enforce the contract. Here, the court rejected the fraud theory in favor of the evidentiary theory. Thus, it required only acts of part performance unequivocally referable to the contract, and did not consider the gravity of the injury the Shaughnessys (P) would suffer if it did not enforce the contract. The evidentiary theory has an important advantage over the estoppel or fraud theory: it makes the doctrine of part performance available to both buyers and sellers. Insofar as the usual acts of part performance are possession, payment, and improvements, only a buyer will be able to assert that he engaged in these acts in reliance upon a contract and to his detriment. However, an aggrieved seller may assert such acts by the buyer as unequivocally referable to the contract and proving its existence. Once he has proven the contract exists, the seller may then seek its enforcement.

Burns v. McCormick

(Caretakers) v. (Not Stated)
233 N.Y. 230, 135 N.E. 273 (1922)

M E M O R Y   G R A P H I C

 ## Instant Facts

Halsey told the Burns (P) that if they lived with and cared for him until he died, they could have his land upon his death, and the Burns (P) did so.

Black Letter Rule

Acts of part performance only suffice to take an agreement out of the statute of frauds if the acts are "unequivocally referable" to the agreement and "unintelligible or at least extraordinary" apart from it.

Case Vocabulary

DOMINION: Right of total control or authority, as that which an owner exercises over his property.
DRAYING: Carrying loads by cart.
EXECUTORY: Not yet fully executed or performed, to be completed in the future.

Procedural Basis: Appeal from judgment of appellate court in action for specific performance.

Facts: Halsey, an old widower living alone, told the Burns (P) that if they gave up their home and business and moved in with him and took care of him, his house would be theirs upon his death. The Burns (P) sold their business, moved in with Halsey, and cared for him until he died five months later. Halsey never reduced his promise to writing. The Burns (P) seek specific performance, and McCormick (D) refuses citing the statute of frauds.

Issue: Does performance of acts contemplated in an oral agreement necessarily constitute part performance that will take the agreement out of the statute of frauds?

Decision and Rationale: (Cardozo) No. Not every act of part performance will move a court of equity to enforce an oral agreement affecting rights in land. The performance must be "unequivocally referable" to the agreement, solely explainable as incident to an assured ownership of the land, and unintelligible or at least extraordinary otherwise. Performance that is explainable without reference to the alleged oral contract does not constitute part performance for statute of frauds purposes. Acts of part performance must themselves supply the key to what is promised. It is not enough that what is promised may give significance to what is done. A housekeeper who abandons other prospects and renders services in return for a promise of land may recover only the value of her services because her conduct, separated from the promise, is not significant of ownership, either present or prospective. In contrast, a buyer who not only makes payments, but also possesses and improves his land, may rely on the part performance doctrine because his conduct itself is the symptom of a promise that a conveyance will be made. Here, the Burns (P) do not pretend that they occupied Halsey's land as owners or under claim of present right while Halsey still lived. The Burns (P) did not even have possession. Halsey had possession, and the Burns (P) were merely his invited servants or guests. Halsey could have asked them to leave at any time, and they would have had no right to stay. Whatever rights the Burns (P) had were executory and future. No acts of possession or dominion served as tokens of their title. While they lived in Halsey's home the Burns (P) did pay the food bills for the household and did the housekeeping. One might infer that Halsey would repay such services in some way, but it would not be reasonable to infer that the payment would be by a conveyance of land at some indefinite time in the future. The Burns (P) might have given the board in return for lodging or as an advance to be repaid later. The Burns (P) might have given time and care with the vague hope of gratitude and some reward in the long run, especially since there was kinship between one of the Burns (P) and Halsey. Even if there was to be some right to a reward, no one could infer, merely from knowledge of the service, what the nature or extent of the reward would be. Halsey continued to act as owner of the land while he lived, paying taxes and maintenance costs. Nothing he accepted from the Burns (P) evinces an agreement that they were to be the owners when he died. We hold, therefore, that the Burns' (P) acts of part performance are not solely and unequivocally referable to a contract for the sale of land. The value of the Burns' (P) board and services will not be difficult to prove. The Burns' (P) loss of their former business will be without remedy, but this does not permit us to disregard the statute of frauds. Inadequacy of legal remedies, without more, does not dispense with the requirement that acts, and not words, shall supply the framework of the promise. This requirement is not arbitrary, but furthers the statute's purpose. The statute warns that there is a peril of perjury and error hidden in the spoken promise. Equity does not ignore this warning or treat the statute as irrelevant. It declines to act on words, even if the

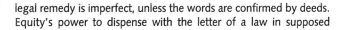

legal remedy is imperfect, unless the words are confirmed by deeds. Equity's power to dispense with the letter of a law in supposed adherence to its spirit is a power easily abused. We do not exercise it unless we can save the policy of the law. **Reversed.**

Analysis:

As in *Shaughnessy v. Eidsmo* [possession and part payment as part performance], the previous case, Justice Cardozo follows the evidentiary approach to the part performance doctrine. Finding "[t]he peril of perjury and error . . . latent in the spoken promise" and the statute of frauds designed to protect against this peril, Justice Cardozo explains that equity will only allow acts of part performance to except an oral agreement from the statute if the acts are "unequivocally referable" to the agreement. More specifically, he explains that to constitute part performance which can substitute for written evidence of an agreement, acts must be solely explainable by reference to the agreement and "unintelligible or at least extraordinary" apart from it. If there is any other explanation for the acts, then they are not reliable enough evidence to substitute for a writing. In *Shaughnessy*, the court ignored the gravity of the consequences to the aggrieved party that would result if it did not enforce the contract. Here, Justice Cardozo also stood by the evidentiary theory, notwithstanding the harshness to the Burns (P), even if part of the Burns' (P) loss (that stemming from the loss of their business) (P) would not be recoverable.

MASSACHUSETTS COURT HOLDS THAT PARTIAL PERFORMANCE OF AN ORAL LAND SALE AGREEMENT IS SUFFICIENT TO REMOVE THE TRANSACTION FROM THE STATUTE OF FRAUDS

Hickey v. Green

(Potential Buyer) v. (Seller)

Appeals Court of Massachusetts, 1982 14 Mass. App. Ct. 671, 442 N.E. 2d 37

M E M O R Y   G R A P H I C

Instant Facts

The Hickeys (P) sold their house in reliance on an oral agreement with the owner of Lot S, Mrs. Green (D). Mrs. Green rescinded the agreement.

Black Letter Rule

When there is a clear oral promise, partial payment, plus an act made in reliance, a land transfer is sufficient to overcome the Statute of Frauds requirement that contracts for the sale of land must be in writing.

Case Vocabulary

ESTOPPEL: A party is prevented by his own acts from asserting a right that will result in detriment to the other party.

RESCISSION OF A CONTRACT: To nullify or void a contract. The right of rescission is the right to cancel a contract upon default of some kind by the other party. Rescission may be effected by the mutual agreement of the parties.

SPECIFIC PERFORMANCE: Where money damages would be inadequate compensation, a court will compel a breaching party to perform specifically what he has agreed to do. These are considered appropriate remedies for buyers in land transfer cases, where each plot of land is considered "unique."

Procedural Basis: Appeal from an order granting specific performance to plaintiff.

Facts: The Hickeys (P) negotiated with Mrs. Green (D) to purchase Lot S from her. There were no lawyers involved in the negotiations. They orally agreed on a price of $15,000, and the Hickeys (P) put down a $500 deposit, which Mrs. Green (D) accepted. But, she did not cash the check. The Hickeys advised Mrs. Green that they intended to sell their home and build on Lot S. The Hickeys (P) sold their home very quickly. Two weeks after putting down the deposit with Mrs. Green (D), she (D) informed them that she no longer wished to sell, as she had another buyer willing to pay $ 16,000. Hickey (P) told Mrs. Green (D) that they had already sold their house and offered to pay $ 16,000, but Mrs. Green (D) refused to sell to him. The Hickeys (P) sued, seeking specific performance of the oral agreement.

Issue: In a land transfer where the Statute of Frauds is at issue, can a party be granted specific performance if they have substantially relied on the oral agreement?

Decision and Rationale: (Cutter) Yes. Restatement (Second) of Contracts, §129 sets forth the rule regarding specific performance. It requires that the party seeking specific enforcement must show reasonable reliance and that he or she has so changed his or her position that injustice can be avoided only by specific enforcement. The provisions of §129 have traditionally been enforced very strictly in Massachusetts. The comments to §129 illustrate that payment of the purchase price alone is not sufficient to constitute part performance. However, the requirement of part performance has been satisfied where the buyer makes payment and takes possession of the property. Here, there is evidence that both parties intended the sale of Lot S to be very quick. For that reason, the Hickeys (P) reasonably attempted to quickly sell their house, without seeking the assurance of a written document. The absence of a lawyer suggests that the parties did not intend to formalize their agreement. Additionally, the Hickeys' (P) acceptance and endorsement of a deposit for their house probably left them open to a suit if they had attempted to avoid transfer of their home. Mrs. Green (D) does not deny that there was an oral agreement. This is significant because it shows injustice, and it shows that the reliance by the Hickeys (P) was reasonable and appropriate. Judgment affirmed.

Analysis:

Comment b of Restatement (Second) of Contracts §129 articulates the two policy reasons for awarding specific performance based on reliance. First, such an award is justified based on the extent to which the parties' actions satisfy the evidentiary goals of the Statute of Frauds. In other words, the purpose of the Statute of Frauds is to provide concrete evidence that an agreement was made. If the parties' actions, through part performance, demonstrate good evidence of an agreement, courts are more likely to overlook the writing requirement. Second, the buyer's reliance may display the buyer's expectations as to what he thought the parties agreed upon. This provides to courts of equity more of a basis for enforcing the agreement than mere testimonial evidence.

Ward v. Mattuschek

(Buyer) v. (Seller)
134 Mont. 307, 330 P.2d 971 (1958)

M E M O R Y G R A P H I C

Instant Facts
The Mattuscheks (D) signed an agency agreement with a broker listing the essential terms of their offer to sell their ranch, and Ward (P) signed a check and a statement, both to the broker, accepting those terms and agreeing to buy the ranch.

Black Letter Rule
To satisfy the statute of frauds, the memorandum of a contract must name the parties and the essentials of the contract, but it may consist of several writings.

Case Vocabulary

MUTUALITY: Requirement in contracts that both parties be bound by obligations.
SUBSCRIBE: To sign at the end of a document to show consent or obligation.

Procedural Basis: Appeal from judgment after bench trial in action for specific performance and damages.

Facts: Otto and Frank Mattuschek (the Mattuscheks) (D) own and operate a ranch. The Mattuscheks (D) executed an "Appointment of Agent" agreement appointing Carnell, a real estate broker, as their agent and giving him the exclusive right to sell their ranch for certain terms. This agreement included a description of the property, their price and other terms, as well as the amount of Carnell's commission and the duration of his agency. Carnell showed the ranch to Ward (P), and Ward (P) agreed to buy it. Ward (P) gave Carnell a check as a "binder," made out to Carnell and noting that it was "for down payment on land Mattuschek." Ward (P) also signed a written statement to Carnell that he "agree[d] to buy the Mattuschek place in accordance with the terms of the agreement between E.F. Carnell and the Mattuscheks." Carnell then informed the Mattuscheks (D) that he sold the ranch to Ward (P) and arranged for a meeting to close the sale. A disagreement arose at this meeting, and the Mattuscheks (D) refused to sell to Ward (P). Ward (P) then sued the Mattuscheks (D) for specific performance and damages. After a bench trial, the court concluded that Ward (P) failed to produce any writing subscribed by the Mattuscheks (D) or Carnell that would satisfy the state statute of frauds, and therefore that Ward (P) was not entitled to relief.

Issue: Does the statute of frauds require the signature of the party charged on a single writing that contains all the essentials of the contract?

Decision and Rationale: (Fall) No. To satisfy the statute of frauds, the memorandum of a contract must name the parties, but it may consist of several writings. The memorandum must also contain all the essentials of the contract, but these may be stated in general terms. The Mattuscheks (D) clearly agreed in writing to permit Carnell to sell their ranch during a certain period and for certain succinctly but adequately stated terms. Ward's (P) acceptance, his statement agreeing to buy the ranch that he signed and gave to Carnell, was also in writing, and was accompanied by a written check as down payment. These three instruments, the agency agreement, the agreement to buy, and the check, clearly evidence an offer and acceptance in writing. When interpreting a written instrument, a court will not isolate certain phrases, but will "grasp the instrument by its four corners" and look at the whole to ascertain the intent of the parties. Isolated clauses do not prevail over the general language of the instrument. The Mattuscheks (D) argue that the offer they executed fails for lack of mutuality as far as Ward (P) is concerned because Ward (P) did not sign that agreement. While ordinarily both parties to a written agreement execute it, mutuality does not require this. If one party signs a contract and the other acts upon it, a binding agreement may result. Further, mutuality is not necessary for a contract to be valid for statute of frauds purposes. The only signature necessary is that of the party to be charged. Even if a contract is unenforceable against a party who has not signed it, it may still be enforceable against a party who has signed it. A plaintiff who has not signed a contract fulfills the mutuality requirement and binds himself to the contract when he institutes the action to enforce it. Here, however, this is immaterial because Ward (P) accepted the Mattuscheks' (D) offer in writing. Reversed.

Dissent: (Adair) The agreement with Carnell that the Mattuscheks (D) signed is simply a listing agreement. It is not a power of attorney, and it does not authorize Carnell to execute or deliver any deed or contract in the Mattuscheks' (D) name. The agreement was between Carnell and the Mattuscheks (D), and the only remedy for a breach by the Mattuscheks (D) would be payment of Carnell's $1000 commission. Since payment of this money would fully satisfy Carnell's damage, the extraordinary remedy of specific performance would not be available. Because the Mattuscheks' (D) listing agreement was with Carnell and not with any prospective purchaser, Ward (P) has no right of action for specific performance to compel the Mattuscheks (D) to sell their ranch to him against their will.

Analysis:

This case demonstrates that the statute of frauds does not require the names of the parties and the terms of the agreement to be all set forth in one document and signed by both parties. Much less will suffice. Here, there was a written offer [at least the court interpreted it to be an offer] signed by the Mattuscheks (D), and a check and a note of acceptance, both given to a third party, signed by Ward (P). The court read all three of these documents, all related to the same transaction, together to find a written agreement satisfying the statute of frauds. Since part of it, the offer, was signed by the party charged, the court enforced the contract and awarded Ward (P) specific performance and damages. Some courts have found even less to be satisfactory, such as a written offer or acceptance alone, as long as it is signed by the party charged. These courts would therefore have been satisfied to see the Mattuscheks' (D) written offer, embodied in the agency agreement they signed with Carnell, even if Ward's (P) acceptance was only oral.

TO DETERMINE WHETHER A SIGNED INFORMAL AGREEMENT IS BINDING, THE COURT LOOKS TO THE INTENT OF THE PARTIES

King v. Wenger

(Buyer) v. (Seller)
219 Kan. 668, 549 P.2d 986 (1976)

M E M O R Y   G R A P H I C

Instant Facts
King (P) and Wenger (D) drafted and signed an informal agreement expecting to have King's (P) lawyer draft a formal contract for them to sign, but they never agreed on the terms of the formal contract.

Black Letter Rule
An informal agreement contemplating the drafting and execution of a formal contract is only binding if the parties intend it to be.

 ### Case Vocabulary
ABSTRACT: A summary of successive conveyances of land and claims against it, which shows whether a person can pass good title.
EARNEST MONEY: A payment toward the purchase price, made to show commitment to the sale.

Procedural Basis: Appeal of judgment entered after trial in action for specific performance.

Facts: Wenger (D) and Ralston, two sisters, each owned an undivided half interest in property subject to a life estate in their mother. They and their mother agreed to sell the property, and King (P) said he would like to buy it. The mother agreed to release her interest so the property could be sold. King (P) and Wenger (D) agreed on a price and contacted Ralston by telephone, who generally agreed to the terms of the sale. King (P) and Wenger (D) then sat in Wenger's (D) car while she wrote out an agreement in longhand, which they both signed. This agreement stated that King (P) would make an earnest payment of $1,000 that day, but he did not. King (P) and Wenger (D) met that afternoon at King's (P) attorney's office to have a formal contract drawn up. King's (P) attorney, Gernon, could not draft the contract that day, and advised King (P) not to pay the earnest money yet. Instead, King (P) wrote out checks totaling $1,000 payable to Wenger (D), but gave them to Gernon to hold. When Gernon drafted a contract and sent it to Wenger (D), she advised him that it did not accord with their previous understanding as to some terms. Gernon sent Wenger (D) a revised contract with a note explaining that he thought a contract was to be drawn according to standard real estate contract procedures. The next day Wenger (D), Ralston and their mother signed a formal contract with new buyers. Wenger (D) rejected and returned Gernon's contract stating that she sold the property to other buyers. King (P) then tendered his down payment and sued Wenger (D) for specific performance of their handwritten agreement. The court found that King (P) never made any payment toward the land and never possessed it. Finding that King (P) failed to meet his burden of proof, the court denied his request for specific performance.

Issue: Is an informal written agreement signed by the parties necessarily binding?

Decision and Rationale: (Fromme) No. Whether parties are bound to an informal agreement before the drafting and executing of a contemplated formal writing largely depends on their intent. To determine the intent of the parties, we look to the facts and circumstances of the case. The mere intent to reduce an informal agreement to a formal writing does not necessarily show an intent that the informal agreement not be binding, but it is evidence pointing in this direction. Where formal contracts are normally executed because of the complexity and importance of the transaction, it is more likely that the parties intended an informal agreement to be only preliminary. Where the parties to an informal agreement contemplated but never executed a formal writing, their subsequent conduct and interpretation may be decisive. For example, where parties to an oral lease agreement have begun performance, and the written agreement is merely a clerical act, the oral agreement is a valid contract. On the other hand, where the parties intend to continue negotiating, understanding that the terms of the contract are not fully agreed upon and contemplating a formal written agreement, then a binding contract does not exist until the parties execute the formal document. When King (P) and Wenger (D) drafted their informal handwritten agreement, they both contemplated meeting at Gernon's office to work out additional details and then to draft and execute a formal contract. At Gernon's office they discussed several matters that Gernon said they had not clearly settled. Neither party began performance under the informal agreement. On Gernon's advice, King (P) withheld his earnest money payment. Only one of the three co-owners of the property, Wenger (D), executed the informal agreement. State law requires a grant of an interest in real estate to be made in writing signed by the grantor or the grantor's agent who has written authorization to do so. Wenger (D) had no written authorization to sign for Ralston. Since King

(P) and Wenger (D) contemplated a sale of all interests in the property, their informal agreement would not suffice to complete the transaction and govern rights to Ralston's interest. King (P) argues that although he did not give his earnest money payment to Wenger (D), he did incur attorney's and abstractor's fees and partially performed in reliance on the agreement. However, King (P) has been reimbursed for the abstractor's fees, and his attorney's fees are only normal business expenses toward an expected agreement, not performance under a completed one. King (P) also argues that he sold his trucking business as a result of the agreement, but the record indicates that he had begun selling it before negotiating to buy this land. The facts and circumstances of this case show that King (P) and Wenger (D) did not enter into a binding contract. They did not intend to be legally bound until they executed a formal contract. King (P) made no earnest money payment, and Wenger (D) rejected terms in the formal contract and communicated this to Gernon. Judgment affirmed.

Analysis:

The court found this informal agreement not binding because it was really only a letter of intent. Both parties expected changes at the lawyer's office, and there was at least one: King (P) gave his earnest money payment to his lawyer, not to Wenger (D), to hold pending the formal agreement. If King (P) and Wenger (D) considered their agreement final and binding, and only wanted the lawyer to put it in more formal language, the result might have been different. Here, their intent was to be bound by a future agreement, not the informal one. Many real estate contracts today take a different approach. The parties sign an informal agreement, [provided, for example, by a broker trying to quickly close a sale], with the intent of having a more formal agreement drafted by attorneys, and subject to attorney disapproval within a certain time. If no formal contract is agreed upon, but neither attorney disapproves the informal agreement in time, then the parties are bound by the informal agreement. [Lawyers, watch your calendars!]

Niernberg v. Feld

(Seller) v. (Buyer)
131 Colo. 508, 283 P.2d 640 (1955)

M E M O R Y   G R A P H I C

Instant Facts

The Felds (P) backed out of their written agreement to buy the Niernbergs' (D) property before the deadline for payment, and the parties then orally agreed to different terms regarding the return of the Felds' (P) deposit.

Black Letter Rule

An executory contract involving an interest in land may be rescinded by an oral agreement.

Case Vocabulary

DEED OF TRUST: Also called a trust deed, an instrument that gives legal ownership of property to a trustee for the benefit of a lender to secure a loan (used instead of a mortgage).

WARRANTY DEED: An instrument that passes legal ownership of property to the buyer with the promise that the seller has good title and will defend it against any claims.

Procedural Basis: Appeal of judgment after jury trial of breach of contract action for damages.

Facts: Mr. and Mrs. Niernberg (the Niernbergs) (D) entered into a written sales agreement with Mr. and Mrs. Feld (the Felds) (P) to sell them certain property. Under this agreement, if the Felds (P) provided payment by May 1, the Niernbergs (D) were to convey the property by warranty deed. If the Felds (P) did not pay by May 1, the Niernbergs (D) would hold the deposit as liquidated damages and both parties would be released from further obligations. Before May 1, the Felds (P) notified the Niernbergs (D) that they "couldn't go through with the deal." Mr. Niernberg (D) and Mr. Feld (P) met with the Felds' (P) attorney before May 1 to discuss the deposit, and orally agreed that the Niernbergs (D) would retain the deposit while they looked for another buyer. According to this oral agreement, if the Niernbergs (D) were able to sell the property for the same or a higher price than the Felds (P) agreed to pay, the Niernbergs (D) would return the deposit. If the Niernbergs (D) had to sell for less, then they would deduct the difference from the deposit and return any remainder to the Felds (P). Mr. Niernberg (D) denied attending any such meeting and making any such oral agreement. The Niernbergs (D) sold the property for more than the Felds (P) agreed to pay, but refused to refund the deposit. After trial, the jury returned a verdict in favor of the Felds (P) for the amount of the deposit plus interest. The Niernbergs (D) argue that the attempted rescission of the prior written agreement was invalid because it violated the statute of frauds.

Issue: Does an oral rescission of a prior written agreement violate the statute of frauds where the written agreement is still executory?

Decision and Rationale: (Holland) No. The statute of frauds clearly required the original agreement for the sale of the property to be in writing. However, that agreement was never fully performed. The authorities the Niernbergs (D) cite generally deal with executed contracts. We believe the better-reasoned rule is that an executory contract involving an interest in land may be rescinded by an oral agreement. The statute of frauds only applies to the making of contracts, not to their revocation. Executory contracts may be rescinded by the mutual consent of the parties. The Niernbergs (D) also argue that Mr. Niernberg's (D) subsequent oral promise was void because it was without consideration and no benefit was conferred nor detriment suffered. There was a promise for a promise, each party releasing the other from further performance, and this mutual consideration is sufficient to support the agreement. Further, the Niernbergs (D) did receive a benefit to the detriment of the Felds (P). Having sold the property for a higher price, the Niernbergs (D), as a matter and right and wrong, should not be able to retain the full deposit. Finally, the Niernbergs (D) argue that Mr. Niernberg's (D) oral promise was not a rescission of the written agreement because Mrs. Niernberg (D), a party to the written agreement, was not a party to the subsequent oral agreement, and Mr. Niernberg (D) could not agree to a rescission without her consent. If Mr. Niernberg (D) assumed to act in his wife's absence and dismissed her from the case, he should be bound by his own actions and not now be able to deny liability because she was not a party to the rescission. Affirmed.

Analysis:

Jurisdictions are split on whether to allow an oral rescission of an agreement for the sale of an interest in land, but *Niernberg* sets forth the majority position. The rationale of the majority is that the statute of frauds governs when a party may enforce a contract, but not when he may release rights under it. However, a party cannot orally modify only some terms of a land contract because a contract that is partly written and partly oral is not enforceable. In such a case, only the original written contract will be enforceable, and the oral modifications will not be enforceable unless an estoppel makes this possible. Courts are also divided on how substantial modifications must be to fall within this general rule. If the modification is only incidental, some courts enforce the contract as modified even if the modification is oral. Other courts require all modifications, however minor, to be in writing.

Kasten Construction Co. v. Maple Ridge Construction

(Seller) v. (Buyer)
245 Md. 373, 226 A.2d 341 (1967)

M E M O R Y   G R A P H I C

Instant Facts

After Maple Ridge (P) missed a deadline for making payment under a land sale contract, Kasten (D) treated the contract as null and void and refused further performance.

Black Letter Rule

Ordinarily, time is of the essence only when the contract expressly so stipulates or this intention is inferable from the circumstances of the transaction, the conduct of the parties, or the purpose of the sale.

Case Vocabulary

LACHES: Doctrine under which a party may lose a right if he unreasonably delays asserting it.
TIME IS OF THE ESSENCE: The deadlines specified in the contract are a condition of the contract, and any delay, however reasonable or slight, will be a default and will discharge the other party.

Procedural Basis: Appeal from decree awarded in action for specific performance.

Facts: Kasten Construction Company (Kasten) (D) entered into a written contract to sell certain "finished" lots to Maple Ridge Construction Company (Maple Ridge) (P). The contract required the sale to occur within 60 days, but did not stipulate that time was of the essence. Due to financing difficulties, the parties agreed in writing to extend the deadline, but again did not state that time was of the essence. Maple Ridge (P) asked for a longer extension, but Kasten (D) refused, and refused later requests for extensions. Maple Ridge (P) continued to seek financing and incurred expenses in preparation for constructing homes on the lots. Kasten (D) did some bulldozing, but made little progress toward providing finished lots. The extended settlement deadline came and went, and neither party made a demand upon the other. Five days after the deadline, Maple Ridge (P) notified Kasten (D) that it had applied for a title examination that would take three weeks to complete. Kasten (D) responded that the contract and the extension had expired and that it considered the contract null and void. Maple Ridge (P) sued Kasten (D) for specific performance.

Issue: Can a buyer who performs late compel specific performance where the real estate contract does not stipulate that time is of the essence?

Decision and Rationale: (Horney) Yes. In actions for specific performance the intent of the parties is always the controlling factor. The general rule is that time is not of the essence unless either the terms of the contract or the circumstances, purpose of the sale, and conduct of the parties indicate that it is. However, a party may lose his right to specific performance by gross laches and unreasonable delay in payment. Maple Ridge (P) argues that a specified settlement date did not mean that the parties intended time to be of the essence, that they did not intend it to be so, and that its delay in making settlement was reasonable under the circumstances. The chancellor found that although Maple Ridge (P) was dilatory in obtaining financing and applying for a title examination, it did tender full performance within a reasonable time after the extended deadline expired. Kasten (D) argues that the chancellor erred in not inferring that time was of the essence from Kasten's (D) refusal to grant further extensions. The chancellor found that Kasten (D) not only acted as if time were not of the essence, but also was lazy about performing its part of the contract. Further, Kasten (D) suffered no loss that the payment of interest could not compensate. We agree with the chancellor. Maple Ridge's (P) delay in making payment was not unreasonable, particularly in view of the fact that Kasten (D) was in no hurry to perform its part of the contract. Maple Ridge (P) was entitled to compensate Kasten (D) for the delay by paying interest. Merely fixing a date for completing a sale contract does not make time of the essence with respect to payment. Where a date is fixed, equity treats the provision as formal rather than essential, and allows a buyer who has missed the deadline to make late payments and to compel the seller to perform unless the contract expressly stipulated that time was of the essence or this is inferable from the conduct of the parties, the purpose of the sale, or other circumstances. Here, since the facts indicate that time was not of the essence, the important question is whether the delay was reasonable. We agree with the chancellor that it was. Affirmed.

Analysis:

If time is of the essence in a real estate contract, failure to perform on the closing date will constitute a material breach of the contract. At law, time is always of the essence unless the parties agree that it is not. However, the remedy at law is only damages. In equity, where specific performance and other equitable remedies are available, the rule is reversed: time is not of the essence unless the parties expressly state that it is, or their conduct, the purpose of the sale or the surrounding circumstances indicate that it is. Thus, in equity, unless the parties make time of the essence, a failure to perform by the closing date will not be a breach unless the delay is unreasonable. This case makes clear that simply inserting a closing date in a real estate contract is not enough to make time of the essence in equity. On the other hand, a contract need not specifically state that "time is of the essence" to make it so. It may be enough, for example, to state a closing date *and* that any failure to close on that date will result in a default, or that the contract will be "null and void" if deadlines are not met. The intent of the parties is what counts, however they express it. Either party may also unilaterally make time of the essence simply by giving the other party notice, as long as the other party will have a reasonable time before the closing date to perform. Ordinarily, however, either party is entitled to a reasonable extension or delay.

Doctorman v. Schroeder

(Buyer) v. (Seller)
92 N.J.Eq. 676, 114 A. 810 (1921)

M E M O R Y   G R A P H I C

Instant Facts

Doctorman (P) failed to make a payment on time under a contract that clearly required payment by a specific hour and made time of the essence, and Schroeder (D) refused to accept payment half an hour later.

Black Letter Rule

When parties make time of the essence, one party's failure to perform on time causes his rights under the contract to cease at the option of the other party.

Case Vocabulary

WAIVER: The intentional relinquishing of a right, either by words or by conduct that indicates a relinquishing of the right.

Procedural Basis: Appeal from decree dismissing action for specific performance.

Facts: Doctorman (P) entered into a contract to buy property from Schroeder (D) which required a payment of $1,500 on a specific date. If Doctorman (P) failed to make this payment on time, the contract clearly stated that all monies already paid would be forfeited and the contract would become null and void. Another clause of the contract also stipulated that time was of the essence of the contract. Doctorman (P) was unable to pay $1,500 by the stipulated date. Schroeder (D) agreed to accept $500 and to extend the time for payment of the remaining $1,000 until 2:30pm the next day. The supplemental agreement granting this extension stipulated that the $500 was received [and the extension given] upon condition that Doctorman (P) pay the remaining $1,000 by 2:30pm, and again stated that it was distinctly understood and agreed that time was of the essence. This agreement also stated that Schroeder (D) did not waive any rights or interest in the original contract, and that if Doctorman (P) failed to pay the $1,000 on time, then all moneys paid on account of the contract, including the $500 payment, would be forfeited and the contract would immediately become null and void. Doctorman (P) failed to tender the $1,000 on time, but was prepared to pay half an hour later.

Issue: Does a court of equity have the power to relieve a buyer from default where parties have agreed upon a specific hour for payment and deliberately made that time of the essence?

Decision and Rationale: (Per Curiam) No. We affirm for reasons stated in Vice Chancellor Leaming's opinion, which follows: If a court of equity can relieve a buyer from default and forfeiture of her right to purchase property when she tenders payment only minutes later than the hour agreed upon, it should do so. However, a court is powerless to aid such a buyer where the contract clearly provides that time is essential and that the buyer's rights as buyer shall cease and become void unless she makes payment by the stipulated time. When payment is late in these circumstances, it is the owner's privilege to either accept the payment at a later time or to treat the contract as null and void. It is perfectly legal for parties to make time the essence of a contract, and the parties here clearly did so in every way that can be done. Doctorman's (P) attempt to make her payment after the stipulated time expired was entirely ineffectual, unless there was some waiver by Schroeder (D). Doctorman (P) argues that Schroeder's (D) remaining at the place designated for payment for half an hour after the time for payment expired amounted to a waiver because it indicated that he intended to permit Doctorman (P) to perform if she arrived while he was still there. I disagree. A seller may waive his rights under a "time of the essence" provision by accepting late payments and allowing the buyer to rely on this course of conduct. However, the seller only needs to give the buyer reasonable notice that he will insist on strict performance in the future to reinstate those rights. Under the contract and supplemental agreement here, once the time for payment expired, Schroeder (D) had a right to either accept or refuse payment at a later time, whatever his reason. He chose to refuse it, and Doctorman's (P) rights under the contract ceased. Affirmed.

Analysis:

When parties make time of the essence, they make timely performance a condition on which the other party's duty to perform depends. Thus, if a buyer fails to make timely payments, he fails to fulfill the condition and fully discharges the seller from his duty to perform. As this case demonstrates, the party who fails to fulfill the condition by failing to pay on time has no power to enforce the contract in law or in equity unless the other party has waived his rights. Since Schroeder (D) chose not to waive his rights, but to use them, Doctorman's (P) attempt to enforce this contract was dismissed. Because waiver is a way to get a buyer out of this kind of pickle, this defense arises in many time of the essence cases. [Remember this for your exam!] As the court explained, even if a seller has not waived his time of the essence rights expressly, he may still have done so simply by accepting late payments if he allows the buyer to rely on his continuing this conduct. However, to prevent such reliance, the seller needs only to give the buyer reasonable notice that he will insist on timely payments in the future. For example, here Schroeder (D) waived his right to timely payment on the original due date, but made time of the essence again for the extended date by clearly expressing this intention in the supplemental agreement. The court explained that where time is of the essence and a buyer fails to make a payment on time, it becomes the seller's option either to waive his rights and accept late payment or to refuse late payment and treat the contract as null and void. The reason for the seller's choice does not matter. As an aside, the court mentioned what it thought were Schroeder's (D) reasons in this case. As the court saw it, Schroeder (D) found Doctorman (P) irresponsible and therefore was dissatisfied with her as a buyer. While waiting after the time for payment had expired, Schroeder's (D) agent mentioned that he had another buyer interested in the property. Since they made time of the essence and Doctorman (P) failed to pay on time, Schroeder (D) had the option to end his relationship with a buyer he did not want and pursue a relationship with a better one. He took advantage of that opportunity. This was Schroeder's (D) right and perfectly permissible, even when Doctorman (P) offered payment only half an hour late. *Doctorman* represents one of the more rigid time of the essence cases. While other cases of this kind are more lenient, substantial lateness will generally cause the buyer to lose her right to enforce the contract.

A "SUBJECT TO FINANCING" CLAUSE THAT ALLOWS ONE PARTY UNFETTERED DISCRETION TO DETERMINE THE MEANING OF AN AMBIGUOUS ESSENTIAL TERM WILL RENDER THE CONTRACT ILLUSORY AND UNENFORCEABLE UNLESS THE COURT CAN GIVE THE CLAUSE A MEANING THAT MAKES THE CONTRACT CERTAIN

Gerruth Realty Co. v. Pire

(Seller) v. (Buyer)
17 Wis.2d 89, 115 N.W.2d 557 (1962)

M E M O R Y   G R A P H I C

Instant Facts

Pire's (D) offer to purchase contained a "subject to financing" clause that made the offer contingent upon Pire's (D) obtaining "proper" financing, which Pire (D) was unable, in his opinion, to do.

Black Letter Rule

If a "subject to financing" clause is ambiguous or lacking as to essential details, and the surrounding circumstances do not indicate the intent of the parties as to these details, then the contract must fail for indefiniteness.

Case Vocabulary

ALEATORY: Profit or loss depends upon an uncertain event. [A poker game is aleatory.]
CONDITION PRECEDENT: An event that must occur before a party's duty to perform becomes due.
ILLUSORY CONTRACT: Contract in which a party makes a promise that does not actually bind him to particular performance either because the performance is optional or the promise is so indefinite that one cannot tell what it requires.

Procedural Basis: Appeal from judgment dismissing complaint after bench trial in action for breach of contract.

Facts: Pire (D) wanted to purchase commercial property from Gerruth Realty Co. (Gerruth) (P). Gerruth's (P) real estate broker filled out a standard form for an offer to purchase, Pire (D) signed it and Gerruth (P) accepted it. Pire (D) gave Gerruth (P) a $5,000 promissory note, payable at closing, as down payment, and was to pay the balance of the $30,000 purchase price in cash. The offer contained a typewritten paragraph stating that it was conditioned upon Pire's (D) buying property from Putterman for $40,000, and upon the closing for both properties taking place simultaneously. Although he expected no difficulty, Pire (D) also insisted upon a clause to protect him in case he could not obtain financing. The broker inserted a clause which stated: "This offer to purchase is further contingent upon the purchaser obtaining the proper amount of financing." Pire (D) attempted to borrow $75,000 from his bank. However, he was unable to obtain a personal loan because these funds plus his existing mortgages would exceed the bank's limit for loans to one person. Pire (D) also could not obtain the funds through a commercial loan because banks customarily only lent up to 66.67% of the value of the property. Pire (D) notified Gerruth (P) that he could not obtain proper financing and had to cancel the contract. Gerruth (P) and Putterman offered to finance $45,000, but Pire (D) refused. Gerruth (P) brought this action to recover on the promissory note. The trial court found that the "subject to financing" clause was a condition precedent to Pire's (D) duty to perform the contract. Finding that Pire (D) made a good faith attempt to obtain what he considered "proper" financing, but still failed to fulfill this condition, the trial court dismissed the complaint. Gerruth (P) argues that the court must construe the "subject to financing" clause in light of current local financing practices. The trial court adopted Pire's (D) position and construed this clause as giving Pire (D) the option to determine what the "proper" amount of financing was for his needs.

Issue: If a "subject to financing" clause is ambiguous or lacking as to essential details, and the surrounding circumstances do not indicate the intent of the parties as to those details, must the contract fail for indefiniteness?

Decision and Rationale: (Hallows) Yes. Contracts and offers to purchase often contain "subject to financing" clauses, and courts have frequently interpreted them as constituting a condition precedent to the buyer's performance. With respect to such a contract, the court's first task is to decide whether it is sufficiently definite to sustain, or if indefinite, whether the court can give it a meaning that would render it certain. Courts prefer not to strike down a contract for uncertainty if they can reasonably make it certain from the surrounding circumstances. Here, the only evidence concerning the parties' discussions about financing is that Pire (D) expected no difficulties. Pire (D) used a promissory note rather than cash for his down payment, and he conditioned his offer on his purchase and simultaneous closing of the Putterman property. From these facts we may infer that Pire (D) would need to borrow most, if not all, of the purchase price of both properties. The transcript, however, contains no details of discussions about the terms or amount of the financing Pire (D) had in mind. We must determine whether there is sufficient evidence upon which we can ascertain the intention of the parties concerning the meaning of this "subject to financing" clause. If it is impossible to ascertain this intention, the contract must fail for indefiniteness. This clause fails to designate an essential term, the amount of the financing. In the two cases we found that also involved clauses that did not state the amount of financing, the court found the contracts sufficiently certain to sustain. In both cases the court found a meaning from the circumstances and purposes of the contracts: a loan in such amount as the buyer in good faith considered necessary. Here, however, we cannot make the contract certain from the surrounding circumstances. (We do not reach the good faith issue, which arises only after we determine the meaning of the ambiguous phrase. If we could interpret the contract as intended to give Pire (D) the sole right to determine the amount of financing, then Pire (D) would need to determine that amount in good faith.) From the evidence here, we cannot, as Gerruth (P) argues, draw a reasonable inference that the parties contracted knowingly and in light of current local financing practices. Although the evidence sets forth what those practices were, there is no evidence that the parties had them in mind when Pire (D) executed his offer to purchase. We also cannot find, as Pire (D) argues, that this clause gave him the exclusive privilege to determine the proper amount of financing without holding the contract illusory. The contract and the evidence are silent as to all other terms of the loan. Pire (D) attempted to borrow $5,000 more than the combined purchase price for the properties, which the trial court inferred Pire (D) intended to use for remodeling. This loan was beyond the limit of current practices in the community. Pire (D) also met the difficulty of the bank's policy of not lending more than $100,000 to a customer. Even if we take this evidence as indicating what Pire (D) had in mind when he signed the offer of purchase, he did not communicate this to Gerruth's (P) agent. If we now adopt the interpretation either party urges, we would be making a contract for the parties by supplying an essential term rather than interpreting what they mutually meant by an ambiguous term. We find it impossible to interpret this contract on the evidence presented, and therefore must hold this contract void for indefiniteness. Judgment affirmed.

Analysis:

If the fulfillment of a condition is entirely under the control of the party whose duty to perform depends on it, that party can get out of the contract at will. Such a contract is unenforceable because there is no mutuality of obligation. To narrow the party's discretion and save the contract, courts will often construe the condition as requiring good faith or reasonable efforts. Here, the financing clause was so vague and there was so little evidence of any meeting of the minds as to its terms that the court was unable to reach the issue of good faith because it could not determine what the parties intended Pire (D) to use good faith to do. Gerruth's (P) position was that if the court construed the financing clause in light of local financing practices, then Pire (D) did not seek a "proper" loan and was therefore in default. Pire (D) sought a loan for $75,000 from the bank. While he could not obtain a sufficient personal loan, he might have been able to obtain a commercial loan, though not for the entire amount. The bank's policy for companies with good credit was to lend up to 66.67% of the purchase price. This would have gotten Pire (D) $46,669 toward the $75,000 he wanted. If Pire (D) sought this "proper" loan and accepted Gerruth's (P) and Putterman's offer to finance $40,000 [but at what terms?], he would have had more than enough to close the deal. On the other hand, Gerruth (P), being in the real estate business, should have been aware of the ambiguities in this financing clause and been more careful about adequately drafting it. [It was Gerruth's (P) agent that drafted it, after all.] Indeed, the court wonders why, since financing is such an important element in the purchase of real estate, those in the business of selling real estate pay so little attention to it. To avoid a result like the one here, a "subject to financing" clause should contain details such as the amount, the term for repayment, and maximum interest. It should also contain reasonable time limits for applying for a loan and for notifying the seller of a failure to obtain financing.

Skendzel v. Marshall

(Seller) v. (Buyer)

261 Ind. 226, 301 N.E.2d 641, cert. denied 415 U.S. 921, 94 S.Ct. 1421, 39 L.Ed.2d 476 (1974)

M E M O R Y G R A P H I C

Instant Facts

The Skendzels (P) sought to enforce forfeiture provisions in a land sale contract after the Marshalls (D), who had already paid $21,000 toward the $36,000 contract price, defaulted.

Black Letter Rule

Where enforcement of forfeiture provisions of a land sale contract would result in injustice, a court of equity may deny forfeiture and order foreclosure proceedings instead.

Case Vocabulary

APOTHEGM: Maxim; short instructive saying.

EQUITY OF REDEMPTION: A defaulting mortgagor's right to pay his debt and recover his property.

FORECLOSURE BY JUDICIAL SALE: Legal proceedings which extinguish a mortgagor's equity of redemption by selling the property to satisfy the debt, and either giving the mortgagor any excess, or giving the mortgagee a judgment against the mortgagor for any deficiency.

MORTGAGE: A lien against property that secures a debt, usually for the purchase of the property.

STRICT FORECLOSURE: Proceeding which gives a defaulting mortgagor a period of time to pay the amount due on the property and, if he fails to pay within that time, vests title in the mortgagee and extinguishes the mortgagor's equity of redemption.

SUA SPONTE: On the court's own initiative, without motion by either party.

Procedural Basis: Transfer from Court of Appeals after ruling reversing trial court judgment in breach of contract action seeking enforcement of forfeiture provisions.

Facts: In 1958, Burkowski entered into a land sale contract to sell land to Charles and Agnes Marshall (the Marshalls) (D). The contract provided for the payment of $36,000 in yearly installments of $2,500 until the balance was paid, and any prepayments were to be applied in lieu of principal payments. A forfeiture/liquidated damages provision stated that if the Marshalls (D) were in default for 30 continuous days, then at Burkowski's option, all previous payments would be forfeited and Burkowski could terminate the contract and keep the payments as liquidated damages. Burkowski died in 1963, and the Skendzels (P) became the assignees of her interests in the contract in 1968. One year after the assignment, the Skendzels (P) brought this action alleging that the Marshalls (D) defaulted through nonpayment. The Marshalls (D) had made a prepayment of $5,000 in 1959, and had paid $2,500 each year from 1960 through 1965, but made no payments after 1965. The Marshalls (D) thus have paid $21,000 toward the contract price, and $15,000 remains to be paid. The Skendzels (P) brought suit to enforce the forfeiture provisions of the contract, but the trial court refused to grant this remedy. Finding the Marshalls (D) in breach and no waiver by the Skendzels (P), the Court of Appeals reversed.

Issue: Absent a waiver, are forfeiture provisions in land sale contracts always enforceable?

Decision and Rationale: (Hunter) No. If we enforce the forfeiture provision against the Marshalls (D), they will forfeit the sum of $21,000, well over half the contract price, *plus possession*. Equity abhors forfeitures. This contract provides that in the event of default all prior payments are forfeited and the seller may retain them as liquidated damages. The law permits "reasonable" liquidated damage provisions. However, if the damages are unreasonable, that is, disproportionate to the loss the seller actually suffered, then we must characterize them as penal rather than compensatory. Here, a $21,000 forfeiture is clearly excessive. Courts deciding cases of this kind tend to consider the amount already paid in relation to the total contract price. Where a relatively small proportion remains to be paid, courts tend to consider a forfeiture as a penalty, at least where, as is usual, the buyer will have another chance to complete the purchase. In contrast, where the breach occurred soon after the execution of the agreement and the amount already paid is only a small percentage of the purchase price, especially where the buyer is attempting to escape an adverse turn in the market, courts tend to consider a forfeiture as liquidated damages. We find it inconsistent with principles of fairness and equity to consider this $21,000 forfeiture as liquidated damages. The Marshalls (D) have acquired a substantial interest in the property, and allowing this forfeiture would result in substantial injustice. Under a typical conditional land contract, the seller retains legal title until the buyer pays the total contract price. However, while *legal* title does not vest in the buyer until the contract terms are satisfied, *equitable* title vests in the buyer as soon as the contract is consummated. At that time, all incidents of ownership accrue to the buyer. The buyer assumes the risk of loss, receives all appreciation in value, and is responsible for taxes. Thus, consistent with equitable ownership principles, we have held that a consummated land contract constitutes a present sale and purchase. The seller has, in effect, exchanged his property for the unconditional obligation of the buyer which is secured by the seller's retention of legal title. We view a conditional land contract as a sale with a security interest in the form of legal title reserved by the seller. Conceptually, this retention of title is the same as reserving a lien or mortgage, and we should thus view the seller and buyer as mortgagee and mortgagor. To view the relationship differently is to pay homage to form over substance. A conditional land contract in effect creates a seller's lien in the property to secure the unpaid balance owed under the contract. This lien is analogous to a mortgage, and the seller is often called an "equitable mortgagee." It is only logical, therefore, that enforcement of such a lien be through foreclosure proceedings. Forfeiture is closely akin to strict foreclosure, an English remedy which did not contemplate the equity of redemption. American jurisdictions have rejected strict foreclosure in favor of foreclosure by judicial sale. Because equity treats a mortgage as a security for the payment of a debt [rather than as a conveyance], it finds foreclosure by judicial sale better than strict foreclosure for effectuating the mutual rights of the parties. Foreclosure by judicial sale permits a mortgagee to sell the mortgaged property and apply the proceeds to the mortgage debt. Modern "foreclosure," then, is an equitable proceeding for enforcing a lien to satisfy a debt. We conclude that judicial foreclosure of a land sale contract is consistent with American notions of equity. A forfeiture, on the other hand, often offends our concepts of justice and equity. However, forfeiture may still be an appropriate remedy for the breach of a land contract where it would be consistent with fairness and justice. For example, it may be appropriate in the case of an abandoning, absconding buyer, or where the buyer has paid a minimal amount at the time of default but seeks to retain possession while the seller pays for the upkeep of the property. We hold a conditional land sale contract to be in the nature of a secured transaction subject to all proper and just remedies at law and in equity. Here, the Skendzels (P) sought strict application of forfeiture provisions which we find would have led to unconscionable results requiring equity to intervene. The trial court correctly refused this remedy, but also denied the Skendzels (P) all other relief. To give substantial relief to the Skendzels (P) under their secured interests, but prevent the sacrifice of the Marshalls' (D) equitable lien in the property, we remand to the trial court to enter a judgment of foreclosure on the Skendzels' (P) lien and to order payment of the unpaid principal balance plus interest. Reversed and remanded.

Concurrence: (Prentice) We are not indifferent to the rights of sellers in land sale contracts. Where a buyer has agreed to a forfeiture provision, it is appropriate to require him to make a clear showing of the inequity of enforcing it before allowing him to avoid it. Denying enforcement of the provision may be denying equity to the seller. Even if the court finds that forfeiture would be unjust in a particular case, it should still grant the seller the maximum relief consistent with equity. Generally, protecting the seller would require treating the transaction as a note and mortgage with such provisions as they usually include in the community, such as increased interest during default periods; acceleration of the due date after a reasonable grace period; attorneys fees and expenses for foreclosure, and the like.

Analysis:

The court refers to the type of contract here as a "land sale contract" or "conditional land contract." The concurring opinion calls it an "installment sales contract." Other jurisdictions use the terms "installment land contract," "bond for deed," "contract for deed," and "long-term land contract." Whatever term the court uses, under this type of contract the buyer acquires immediate possession, but the seller keeps the deed until the buyer pays the total amount due on the contract. Parties often use these contracts where the seller finances all or part of the purchase price. The buyer generally makes regular payments plus interest until the full price is paid. Parties use a land sale contract instead of a mortgage, perhaps because the buyer is unable to get a mortgage from an institutional lender. In the past, this was riskier for the buyer than a mortgage because foreclosure proceedings were unavailable and courts were more willing to enforce forfeiture provisions. Forfeiture clauses generally make time of the essence and in the event of default allow the seller to terminate the contract, retake possession, and keep all the payments already made. In this way, the seller could completely avoid the buyer's "equity of redemption," his right to pay his debt and recover his property. Today, recognizing that these contracts serve the same security function as mortgages [and that some buyers will sign anything to get a house], courts increasingly refuse to enforce forfeiture provisions where to do so would be unjust, and give the buyers many of the protections mortgages offer. *Skendzel* is a leading case in the judicial trend toward treating land sale contracts as mortgages.

Union Bond & Trust Co. v. Blue Creek Redwood Co.

(Buyer's Assignee) v. (Seller's Assignee)
128 F.Supp. 709, affirmed 243 F.2d 476 (1957)

M E M O R Y   G R A P H I C

Instant Facts

After substantially performing under an installment contract, the buyer wilfully defaulted, and his assignee then sought, as relief from forfeiture, an opportunity to pay damages and complete the contract rather than restitution.

Black Letter Rule

A court may relieve a buyer in wilful default from forfeiture by giving him an opportunity to pay damages and complete the contract.

Case Vocabulary

RESTITUTION: Equitable remedy which restores to a person that which unjustly enriched another at his expense.
UNJUST ENRICHMENT: Retention of a benefit which rightfully belongs to another.

Procedural Basis: Diversity suit in breach of contract action seeking specific performance and declaratory relief.

Facts: Union Bond & Trust Co. (Union) (P) and Blue Creek Redwood Co. (Blue Creek) (D) are assignees of the buyer and seller in a timber purchase contract. Under this contract, the buyer agreed to pay $750,000 for timber lands through fixed minimum payments. After paying $585,000 of the purchase price, the buyer wilfully defaulted. A forfeiture clause in the contract provided that if the buyer defaulted, the seller could resume possession, retain all payments already made and cancel the contract. The contract also made time of the essence. Union (P) and Blue Creek (D) proceeded under this contract. Union (P) sought a judgment declaring the contract in full force and effect and requiring specific performance. Blue Creek (D) responded by seeking a judgment declaring Union (P) in default and cross-claiming for damages and to quiet title to the timber land. The parties agree that under California law, Union (P) is entitled to relief from any forfeiture imposed by contract for its default. Union (P) argues that this relief should be conveyance of the land to it upon its immediate payment of the balance plus damages resulting from the default. Blue Creek (D) argues that because the buyer's default was wilful, a court should not give Union (P) the benefit of its bargain, but only restitution of any payments made in excess of the damages the default caused.

Issue: Under California law, may a court relieve a buyer in wilful default from forfeiture by giving him an opportunity to pay damages and complete the contract?

Decision and Rationale: (Goodman) Yes. Under *California Civil Code § 3275* [relief from forfeiture], a party who incurs a forfeiture due to default on a contract may avoid forfeiture by fully compensating the other party, "except in case of grossly negligent, willful, or fraudulent breach of duty." Under *California Civil Code § 3369* [prevents enforcement of forfeiture] a court may not grant specific or preventive relief to enforce a penalty or forfeiture. Whether these code sections apply here depends on how the California courts have construed them. Early cases either overlooked or ignored these code sections and applied a strict rule of forfeiture against defaulting buyers under contracts that made time of the essence. For example, *Glock v. Howard* [restitution requires surprise, mistake or fraud], with no reference to these code sections, established that a defaulting buyer could only recover restitution of payments made upon an equitable showing of surprise, mistake, or fraud. Courts also quieted title against defaulting buyers without requiring restitution of payments made. However, courts did sometimes condition a decree quieting title upon the buyer's failure to complete performance and pay damages within a specific period. Later the California courts modified their strict rule of forfeiture by making it inapplicable where waiver or estoppel prevented the seller from asserting the time provisions of the contract, or where the seller let the entire price come due without declaring a forfeiture. To accomplish this, the courts sometimes used *§ 3275* to relieve the buyer from forfeiture, but even then, waiver, estoppel, or the like, not the code section, remained the justification for the relief. Then, in *Barkis v. Scott* [established rule that a buyer who meets the requirements of *§ 3275* may have relief from forfeiture], the California Supreme Court applied *§ 3275* to relieve a defaulting buyer from forfeiture even though he breached a condition precedent under a "time of the essence" contract and there was no waiver by the seller. Further, the Supreme Court did not simply order restitution of the buyer's payments, but sanctioned the restoration of the buyer's rights under the contract, even stating that this would usually be preferable to restitution. As the Court explained, a buyer might have difficulty proving the extent to which the seller would be unjustly enriched if he kept all the payments. Where the default was not serious and the buyer is willing and able to continue to perform, the seller will suffer no damage by allowing him to do so. Finally, the Court noted that where a defaulting buyer has made substantial payments or substantial improvements in reliance on the contract and he is willing and able to continue performance, permitting forfeiture would be so unjust that a court should grant relief whether or not time was of the essence. *Barkis* and subsequent cases thus established that a buyer who meets the requirements of *§ 3275* may have relief from any forfeiture, either through restoration of his rights under the contract, or through restitution of payments made in excess of the seller's damage. Here, Union (P) does not meet the requirements of *§ 3275* because the buyer's default was wilful. However, the California Supreme Court indicated another basis for relief in *Freedman v. Rector* [buyer in wilful default may still obtain relief from forfeiture], which also involved a buyer in wilful default under an installment contract. The Court explained that although the buyer did not qualify for relief under *§ 3275*, this section was permissive, not exclusive, and the buyer could still find relief under *California Civil Code §§ 1670, 1671* [damage provisions] and the law's policy against penalties and forfeitures. These damage provisions permit liquidated damages where it would be impracticable or extremely difficult to fix actual damages, and prevent the use of forfeiture in installment contracts as liquidated damages when it would not be impracticable or extremely difficult to fix actual damages. The Court also noted that to deny a buyer relief from forfeiture because his breach was wilful would be inconsistent with *§ 3369*, which prevents enforcement of any penalty or forfeiture. The Court explained that this section prevents a court from quieting a seller's title unless he refunds the payments made in excess of his damages. Although *§ 3369* strictly applies only to a seller who seeks enforcement of a forfeiture, the result must be the same when the buyer seeks restitution, or the case would depend not on the facts but on who gets to court first. Thus, in *Freedman* the Court granted restitution in excess of the seller's damage to a buyer in wilful default.

Here, Union (P) seeks an opportunity to complete the contract upon compensating Blue Creek (D) for its damages. In *Freedman* the court had to deny specific performance because the buyer had previously rescinded the contract, and before he revoked the rescission, the seller sold the property to another. However, in a proper case, the reasoning of *Freedman* does justify relief in the form of an opportunity to complete the contract. Blue Creek (D) argues that the court should not allow a buyer in wilful default to complete performance because this would give him the benefit of his bargain. This is simply an argument that the Court should punish a buyer in wilful default even though it must give him some relief from forfeiture. However, the policy against penalties for breach is the very basis for *Freedman*. The form of relief, therefore, should not depend on punishing the defaulting buyer. Although the California courts have not precisely so stated, it appears to be the established rule that it is within the discretion of the Court to give the buyer an opportunity to complete the contract. In *Barkis* the Supreme Court noted some factors that might influence the exercise of that discretion. Noting that damages were sometimes difficult to compute when a contract is terminated, the Court suggested that if the buyer were willing and able to complete the contract, and had made substantial part performance or substantial improvements on the property, completion of the contract would best protect the rights of the parties. Here, the buyer made substantial payments and substantial improvements on the property. Conflicting estimates of value may make damages difficult to determine if the contract is terminated. We thus find it just and equitable to enter a preliminary decree permitting Union (P) to complete the contract within a specified time by paying the entire purchase price plus damages resulting from the delay in performance. If Union (P) does not pay the purchase price within the time specified, then we will quiet Blue Creek's (D) title and grant Union (P) restitution for payments in excess of Blue Creek's (D) damages. Preliminary degree permitting specific performance.

Analysis:

This case discusses some remedies available when a buyer defaults on an installment contract. In the past, courts would enforce forfeiture clauses, so upon default the buyer could lose not only the property but also everything he already paid under the contract. Sometimes the court would permit the buyer a period of time to pay the remainder due on the contract, accelerating the due date so that all the remaining principal and interest were due at once. If the buyer could not make the payment on time, the court would enforce the forfeiture and title would go to the seller. As courts began to recognize the injustice that often resulted from forfeitures, they began to use other remedies. One, preferred by the seller here, was restitution. This remedy would mean that the seller would get to keep the property and any payments made to the extent of the fair rental value of the property for the time the buyer had possession of it. If the payments exceeded this fair rental value, the seller would have to return the excess to the buyer as restitution. However, as the court noted here, these amounts can sometimes be difficult to calculate. The simplest remedy, and that sought by Union (P) in this case, is to allow the buyer to pay any damages that resulted from his delay in payment and to resume performance under the original contract.

EVEN IF THE SELLER USES A QUITCLAIM DEED TO CONVEY LAND, THE LAW STILL IMPUTES A COVENANT TO CONVEY MARKETABLE TITLE TO HIM IN THE CONTRACT, UNLESS THE CONTRACT PROVIDES OTHERWISE

Wallach v. Riverside Bank

(Buyer) v. (Seller)
206 N.Y. 434, 100 N.E. 50 (1912)

M E M O R Y   G R A P H I C

Instant Facts

When Riverside (D) tendered a quitclaim deed for property he agreed to sell to Wallach (P), but without curing a defect in its chain of title, Wallach (P) refused the deed because it could not convey marketable title.

Black Letter Rule

An executory contract for the sale of land always includes an implied covenant by the seller to give marketable title, unless the contract expressly makes or excludes this covenant.

Case Vocabulary

DOWER: Wife's interest in her husband's land which she acquires upon his death.

INCHOATE RIGHT: A right that is not yet perfected, contingent upon the occurrence of some event.

INCUMBRANCE: Also encumbrance, an interest in or claim attached to land, such as an easement, mortgage, or lease, which cannot prevent conveyance of the land, but does diminish its value.

LAW DAY: The closing date; the date performance is due under a contract for the sale of real estate.

MERCHANTABLE TITLE: Also marketable title, a title that is free from litigation, defects and serious doubts about its validity, which a reasonably prudent buyer would be willing to accept.

QUITCLAIM DEED: A deed which conveys whatever title the grantor has, but which includes no warranties or covenants that his title is valid or free from defects or encumbrances.

Procedural Basis: Appeal from judgment affirming trial court judgment in breach of contract action for damages.

Facts: Riverside Bank (Riverside) (D) entered into a contract to sell certain property to Wallach (P) subject to certain leases and "existing restrictions of record if any." Wallach (P) agreed to pay $22,000, and Riverside (D) agreed to deliver a quitclaim deed for the premises. Wallach (P) refused to execute the contract at first because it contained the word "quitclaim," but ultimately did sign. On the law day Wallach (P) refused to accept the quitclaim deed because an essential part of Riverside's (D) chain of title was defective: Mrs. Wood, who is still living and married to Mr. Wood, did not join her husband in executing the deed to Leaird. Wallach (P) tendered performance and offered to comply with the contract if Riverside (D) could convey a marketable title to him. Riverside (D) refused to perform other than as stated, so Wallach (P) brought this action to recover his down payment and expenses for examining the title. The trial court found the title unmarketable and concluded that Wallach (P) was entitled to the relief he sought.

Issue: In general, does a seller satisfy his covenant to convey premises by tendering a quitclaim deed that cannot convey marketable title?

Decision and Rationale: (Vann) No. The purpose of Wallach (P) and Riverside (D) in entering this contract was to buy and sell "all the premises" described. The means the parties prescribed to accomplish this was a quitclaim deed. Riverside (D) did not have perfect title free from incumbrances because the premises were subject to an inchoate right of dower statutorily vested in the wife of a prior grantor. Riverside (D), therefore, could only convey the premises subject to that right. However, Riverside's (D) covenant was to convey the premises described, not to convey all its right, title and interest in those premises. A contract to sell land implies ownership and power to give good title on the law day. Wallach (P) did not agree to accept defective title. He contracted to buy "all the premises" described, which, by implication of law, means good title to those premises, free and clear from incumbrances. The writing may not say so, but the law says so, and the law is part of the writing. When a seller agrees to sell land, the law imputes to him a covenant to convey marketable title unless the buyer stipulates to accept something less. Although the law prevents implication of a covenant in a deed, in an executory contract the seller always covenants by implication to give good title, unless the contract makes or excludes the covenant expressly. Even if the seller intends to convey the land without warranties, he still must convey the land itself. He can convey only the land to which he has title. If his title is subject to a right which may take away part of the land, then he cannot convey the land in the full legal sense because there is an interest in the land which his deed does not touch. If Wallach (P) was bound to accept the deed with a partial defect of title, he also would have been bound even if it conveyed no title at all, although the named consideration was $22,000. The landmark case of *Burwell v. Jackson* [seller's implied warranty of good title] held that every executory contract for the sale of land includes an implied warranty on the part of the seller that he has good title. Wallach's (P) agreement to accept a quitclaim deed was not a waiver of the title defect. A quitclaim deed is as effective as any other to convey whatever title the seller has. A deed full of covenants would not strengthen a defective title, buy only protect the seller from loss due to the defect. The sale was subject to existing leases and to existing restrictions of record. It could be subject to no other defect unless the contract also specified it. A buyer is never bound to accept a defective title unless he expressly so stipulates, knowing the defects. It is the law, not the contract, that gives a buyer his right to good title, clear of defects and incumbrances. Even if Wallach (P) knew of the defect when he signed the contract, he still had the right to presume from its terms that

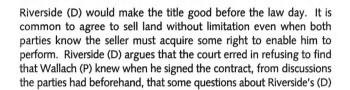

Riverside (D) would make the title good before the law day. It is common to agree to sell land without limitation even when both parties know the seller must acquire some right to enable him to perform. Riverside (D) argues that the court erred in refusing to find that Wallach (P) knew when he signed the contract, from discussions the parties had beforehand, that some questions about Riverside's (D) title existed and that a quitclaim deed would only convey whatever title Riverside (D) had. However, even if there were sufficient evidence to warrant such findings, they would be wholly immaterial since whatever the parties said before they executed the contract was merged into it. It is not error to refuse to find an immaterial fact. Affirmed with costs.

Analysis:

In addition to setting forth the rule that the law imputes to a seller of land a covenant to convey marketable title unless the buyer agrees to accept less, this case also demonstrates the important distinction between a title and a deed. A seller conveys his title to property, and uses a deed to make that conveyance. This case involves a quitclaim deed, which conveys whatever title the seller has, but contains no other covenants. A warranty deed, by contrast, contains covenants that may hold the seller liable for title defects. Both can convey perfect title or defective title. The only difference lies in the extent of the seller's liability for defects. However, as this case shows, the fact that the seller used a quitclaim deed does not relieve him from his obligation to convey merchantable, or marketable, title to the buyer. Although the deed contains no covenants requiring the title to be marketable, the contract does, unless it expressly provides otherwise. If the contract is silent on the subject, the law implies a covenant by the seller to convey marketable title, regardless of the type of deed he uses to do so. Thus, unless he expressly agrees to it in the contract, the law will not compel a buyer to take unmarketable title. Conversely, the law will compel a buyer to take marketable title. What is marketable title? Marketable title is title that a court will compel a buyer to take. [Dizzy yet?] Marketable title can convey the entire property to another because it is reasonably certain that no one else has a claim to it. The title does not actually have to be defective to be unmarketable, but only subject to attack. For example, a person may have valid title by adverse possession, but if he has not yet established this title through litigation, the record owner may raise the issue later. As the maxim goes, "equity will not force a man to buy a lawsuit."

Bartos v. Czerwinski

(Buyer) v. (Seller)
323 Mich. 87, 34 N.W.2d 566 (1948)

M E M O R Y   G R A P H I C

Instant Facts

The Bartoses (P) demanded that Czerwinski (D) clear his title before they would accept a conveyance of his property, but Czerwinski (D) failed to do so.

Black Letter Rule

A buyer is not entitled to relief compelling a seller to clear a defect in title where it is not clear the seller would be able to do so.

Case Vocabulary

QUIET TITLE: To free a title from dispute by joining all the parties who might have an interest in the property in a judicial action to determine their respective rights.

Procedural Basis: Appeal from judgment after trial of action for specific performance.

Facts: Mr. and Mrs. Bartos (the Bartoses) (P) contracted with Czerwinski (D) to buy certain property from him. The agreement required Czerwinski (D) to provide an abstract of title, and to return the Bartoses' (P) down payment if the title was unmarketable. Czerwinski (D) delivered an abstract to the Bartoses (P), and their attorney concluded that a flaw in the record of title rendered it unmarketable. Prior grantors Hickey and Eppinga conveyed their interest to a bank. Later, by quitclaim deed dated December 28, 1927, Eppinga conveyed his interest to Hickey. By quitclaim deed dated December 29, 1927, the bank conveyed the property back to Hickey and Eppinga. Hickey later conveyed his interest in the property, but Eppinga did not. The Bartoses' (P) attorney therefore concluded that Eppinga had or might have an undivided one-half interest in the property. The Bartoses (P) insisted that Czerwinski (D) take action to clear the title, and indicated that they would not accept the conveyance unless Czerwinski (D) either cleared the title or in some way protected them against a possible attack on it. Czerwinski (D) contacted Eppinga in an effort to have him execute a quitclaim deed, but Eppinga did not want to be bothered. Czerwinski (D) made no further efforts to clear the title.

Issue: Is a buyer entitled to relief compelling a seller to clear a defect in title where it is not clear he could do so?

Decision and Rationale: (Carr) No. The Bartoses (P) argue that Czerwinski (D) was in a position to convey good title to the property, yet they would not accept a conveyance unless Czerwinski (D) took action to make the title marketable. Thus, the Bartoses (P) did not simply seek a conveyance of the property, but rather a decree compelling Czerwinski (D) to clear the title to their satisfaction and then to convey it to them. It is not clear whether Czerwinski's (D) title was actually unmarketable because, although the abstract showed Eppinga's deed to Hickey as dated the day before the bank's deed were delivered. Eppinga may have consummated his conveyance to Hickey after he received his deed from the bank. Still, if we assume delivery of both deeds occurred on the dates given, then Eppinga might still have an interest in the property, and Czerwinski's (D) title would then be unmarketable. A title is unmarketable if a reasonably careful and prudent man familiar with the facts would refuse to accept it in the ordinary course of business. The title need not actually be defective to be unmarketable; it is sufficient if there is enough doubt to reasonably form the basis of litigation. A court may not require a buyer to accept a title if he may have to defend it against a challenge to his possession and interest. Assuming Czerwinski's (D) title was unmarketable, we still cannot grant the Bartoses (P) specific performance. The Bartoses (P) want us to compel Czerwinski (D) to obtain a conveyance or release from Eppinga or to otherwise quiet title to the property. However, it may not be possible for Czerwinski (D) to accomplish any of these tasks, and we may not compel him to do so. Eppinga may be unwilling to release or convey any interest he has in the property, and a suit to quiet title would be more than a merely formal matter. We also may not compel Czerwinski (D) to provide the Bartoses (P) with title insurance because the contract contained no such requirement and we may not add one. The case is different where the seller is unquestionably able to remedy the title defect, but that is not true here. The trial court correctly concluded that the Bartoses (P) are not entitled to specific performance of the contract. Dismissal should, however, be without prejudice to their right to pursue a remedy at law to recover their down payment. Affirmed with modifications.

Analysis:

Czerwinski (D) could not obtain Eppinga's conveyance or release because, if Eppinga had any interest in the property, he had no duty to sell or release it. The result of a suit to quiet title was also questionable because the court had no record of the delivery dates of the deeds to and from Eppinga. Even if the court compelled Czerwinski (D) to institute such an action, he might or might not succeed. The court was unwilling to impose this burden on Czerwinski (D) without assurance that the burden would bring about the desired result. Where a seller is clearly able to cure a title defect, however, a court might compel him to do so. Mortgages and other liens are examples of claims against title that a seller can usually cure. Since these claims are removable simply by paying them off, a seller will be able to cure them, even if he does not have enough money at the time of contracting, by agreeing to place sufficient funds in escrow from the proceeds of the sale and to use those funds to pay off the liens. In such cases the closing will make the title marketable, so the buyer cannot object.

Luette v. Bank of Italy Nat. Trust & Savings Ass'n

(Buyer) v. (Seller)
42 F.2d 9 (1930)

M E M O R Y   G R A P H I C

Instant Facts

When the Bank (D) refused to exhibit its title after the Luettes (P) discovered a homestead claim against the land they contracted to buy, the Luettes (P) sought to rescind their installment contract and get their money back.

Black Letter Rule

A buyer cannot rescind a contract due to uncertainty as to the state of the seller's title before the date the seller must convey title under the contract.

Case Vocabulary

ARM'S LENGTH: A relationship of independence, where two parties deal with one another freely and in their own self-interest, without any special relationship of trust or control.

FIDUCIARY RELATIONSHIP: A relationship of trust in which the first party relies upon and is influenced by a second party, and the second party has a duty to act for the benefit of the first party.

HOMESTEAD: Land a person acquires from the public lands by filing a claim for it and living on and cultivating it.

Procedural Basis: Appeal from order dismissing complaint in action for rescission.

Facts: In 1926 the Luettes (P) entered into an installment contract for the sale of real property with the predecessor in interest of the Bank of Italy Nat. Trust & Savings Ass'n (the Bank) (D). The Luettes (P) paid $1,625 of the $6,500 purchase price when they executed the contract, and made monthly payments for the next two years, with payments to continue until 1933. Although the Bank (D) has record title, someone filed a homestead claim against the property on the theory that the land was part of the public domain. The homestead proceedings are still in progress at the appellate level, but the initial holding appears to be that the land is not part of the public domain. The Luettes (P) allege that when they discovered the homestead claims, they demanded that the Bank (D) exhibit its title and offered, if and when it did so, to pay the amount due under the contract. The Bank (D) refused to exhibit its title, and, on the Luettes' (P) demand, refused to repay the money they already paid on the contract. The Luettes (P) ask the court to grant rescission of the contract and judgment for the money they already paid under it. The Luettes (P) allege that the only thing of value they received under the contract is the contract itself, which they tender.

Issue: Can a buyer rescind a contract due to uncertainty as to the state of the seller's title before the date the seller must convey title under the contract?

Decision and Rationale: (Kerrigan) No. The Luettes (P) attempted to put the Bank (D) in default by demanding that it exhibit its title and tendering the balance due. However, the rule is well settled that a buyer cannot rescind an executory contract merely because the seller lacks title prior to the time it must convey it. A buyer also cannot place a seller in default by tendering payment and demanding a deed before the time and under circumstances not contemplated by the contract. Here the Bank (D) is not in default because, assuming a title defect does exist, the time within which the Bank (D) must perfect title under the contract has not yet expired. The Luettes (P) argue that if the homestead claims succeed and the tract that contains their lot is declared to be part of the public domain, the Bank (D) will be financially unable to procure title to the whole tract and therefore will never be able to convey title to them. The whole tract contains more than 16,000 acres, and the Luettes' (P) lot is only 1/4 acre. The complaint does not show that the Bank (D) will be unable to procure title to the lot it has contracted to convey to the Luettes (P). The Luettes (P) also argue that this case falls within the rule that a buyer may rescind a contract if the seller, though not in default, made material fraudulent misrepresentations about its title upon which the buyer justifiably relied. The Luettes (P) argue that they are inexperienced in business and relied upon the Bank (D) for fair treatment, being accustomed to trusting and relying upon banks and bankers. [Inexperienced indeed.] This, however, is not enough to establish a fiduciary relationship between the Luettes (P) and the Bank (D) since the Luettes (P) do not suggest that the Bank (D) voluntarily assumed a relation of personal confidence with them. We must regard the parties as having dealt at arm's length. In this light, the Luettes (P) have not charged the Bank (D) with material misrepresentations, unequivocally averred to be false, upon which they relied to their injury. Affirmed.

Analysis:

A seller does not have to produce marketable title until the time the contract requires him to convey it. In fact, he does not have to have title at all before then -- he can contract to sell property he does not yet own. However, he must get title to the property before his conveyance is due, and he may have to give the buyer assurance that he will be able to convey title at the appointed time. For example, if the seller contracts to sell property that he does not yet own, but which he is himself in the process of buying under an installment contract, he may have to give the buyer assurances of his ability to perform if he brings this into doubt by failing to make his payments on the property. Where a buyer has reason to believe the seller will be unable to convey title, he may demand adequate assurance of due performance. If the seller fails to give that assurance within a reasonable time, the buyer may treat that failure as a repudiation of the contract and claim damages for total breach. A court may also relieve a buyer from his duty to perform if he can show that the seller has lost or encumbered his title so much that it will be impossible for him to convey it.

BECAUSE A SELLER'S AND BUYER'S PERFORMANCE ARE CONCURRENT CONDITIONS IN A REAL ESTATE CONTRACT, ONE PARTY MUST GENERALLY TENDER PERFORMANCE TO TRIGGER THE OTHER PARTY'S DUTY TO PERFORM BEFORE HE CAN PLACE THE OTHER PARTY IN DEFAULT

Cohen v. Kranz

(Buyer) v. (Seller)

12 N.Y.2d 242, 238 N.Y.S.2d 928, 189 N.E.2d 473 (1963)

I'M NOT TELLING YOU WHAT'S WRONG WITH YOUR TITLE!! JUST GIVE ME BACK MY DEPOSIT!

KRANZ

M E M O R Y   G R A P H I C

Instant Facts

Cohen (P) demanded that Kranz (D) return her deposit due to her objection to certain curable title defects, but she failed to specify the defects before closing and did not tender payment.

Black Letter Rule

Where title defects are curable without difficulty in a reasonable time, the buyer must make a tender and demand to put the seller in default before she can recover her deposit.

Case Vocabulary

ANTICIPATORY BREACH: A breach which results when a party refuses, by words or by conduct, to perform his future contractual obligations, which in turn relieves the other party from his duty to perform.

CONCURRENT CONDITION: A condition that a party must fulfill at the same time the other party fulfills a condition, the duty to fulfill each condition being mutually dependent upon the fulfillment of the other.

TENDER: To unconditionally offer performance to the other party, showing the ability and willingness to perform.

Procedural Basis: Appeal from appellate court judgment reversing trial court judgment in breach of contract action for damages.

Facts: Cohen (P) contracted to buy a house from Kranz (D) and paid a $4,000 deposit. On November 30, having adjourned the closing date from November 15 to December 15, Cohen's (P) attorney notified Kranz (D) by letter that his title was unmarketable and demanded that he return Cohen's (P) deposit within five days. Cohen's (P) attorney appeared for closing on December 15 and again demanded the deposit, but Kranz (D) refused. Neither party could then perform, and neither made any tender. Cohen (P) brought this action for her deposit plus costs, and Kranz (D) counterclaimed for damages for breach of contract. Finding that Cohen (P) notified Kranz (D) of title defects prior to December 15, that Kranz (D) took no steps to remedy these defects, and that Kranz (D) did not establish that the defects were minor, the trial court held that the defects excused Cohen (P) from tender of payment and awarded her the amount of her deposit. The appellate court reversed on the law and the facts and directed judgment for $1,500 on Kranz's (D) counterclaim. First, the appellate court found that Cohen's (P) November 30 letter failed to specify the objections to title, and that Cohen (P) did not specify them until January 25. Further, the appellate court found the title defects curable upon timely notice and demand. Finally, the appellate court found that Kranz (D) had not waived a tender by Cohen (P), and that Cohen's (P) rejection of the title before closing was a default precluding her from recovering her deposit.

Issue: Where title defects are curable without difficulty in a reasonable time, must the buyer make a tender and demand to put the seller in default before she can recover her deposit?

Decision and Rationale: (Burke) Yes. The weight of the evidence supports the appellate court's findings that Cohen (P) did not specify her objections to title until after the closing date, and that the title defects were curable upon timely notice and demand. In fact, Kranz (D) cured one of the defects, the lack of a certificate of occupancy for the swimming pool, before he sold the house to a new buyer. If a seller's title is incurably defective on law day, a buyer can recover her deposit without a showing of tender or even of being willing and able to perform. However, where the seller could clear the title without difficulty in a reasonable time, the buyer must make a tender and demand to put the seller in default before she can recover her deposit. In such a case, the seller is even entitled to a reasonable time beyond law day to clear his title. Cohen's (P) advance rejection of title and demand for an immediate return of her deposit was unjustified and an anticipatory breach which prevented Kranz's (D) title defects from ever amounting to a default. Since Kranz's (D) title defects were curable and Cohen (P) never demanded Kranz's (D) performance on law day, Cohen (P) is barred from recovering her deposit. A seller whose defects are curable is not automatically in default, but must be put in default by the buyer's tender of performance and demand for a good title deed. Here, Kranz (D) never offered to clear the title and perform, but he was never put in default in the first place by a demand for good title. Whether the title defects are curable or incurable, if a seller is in default, the buyer can recover her deposit even if the buyer is also in default. The difference is that a seller with incurable title defects is automatically in default, but a seller with curable defects must be placed in default by the buyer's tender and demand. The appellate court gave Kranz (D) a judgment for the loss he sustained when he sold his house to a third person below its fair market value. Although a buyer's recovery of her deposit can rest solely on the seller's default, an action for damages requires a showing that the plaintiff, whether buyer or seller, has performed all conditions precedent and concurrent, unless excused. If the buyer seeks damages, she must show tender and demand, or if this would be idle because the title defects are incurable, then at least a showing that the buyer could perform if the seller were willing and able to perform. Likewise, a seller must show a basic ability to perform even if actual tender and demand are unnecessary. However, an inability to perform conditions precedent or concurrent is excusable where that inability is the result of advance notice by the other party that she will not perform. Here, Kranz (D) made no tender, but under these facts none was necessary. Not only did Cohen's (P) unjustified attempt to cancel the contract before the law date render unnecessary and wasteful any attempt by Kranz (D) to cure his minor title defects before then, but Cohen's (P) failure to specify her objections to title rendered such an attempt impossible. The appellate court's finding that Kranz's (D) title defects were curable means that Kranz (D) was basically able to perform, and whatever technical inability to perform existed on the law date was caused by Cohen (P) and is fully excused. Affirmed.

Analysis:

In a contract for the sale of land, the seller's providing title and the buyer's payment of money are concurrent conditions. Concurrent conditions must occur simultaneously and are mutually dependent upon one other. If one party does not fulfill his condition, the other's duty to perform does not arise. If a seller fails to provide good title, for example, the buyer's obligation to pay the purchase price does not arise. A party generally cannot default on his obligation to perform until that obligation has arisen. (As discussed in this case, default can be automatic if performance is impossible, as where title defects are incurable.) To cause the one party's obligation to arise, the other party must first fulfill his condition, or at least offer to fulfill it and show an ability to do so. This is what tender and demand does. When one party makes a tender and demand, he shows his readiness to fulfill his condition and offers to do so, which triggers the other party's duty to perform. If the other party then fails to perform, he will be in default. The tender must be unconditional, and must offer performance that is not less than what the contract requires. Anything less would not fulfill the tendering party's condition and thus would not trigger the other party's duty to perform. Tender does not have to be actual performance, such as actually delivering a deed or a check, but it must be enough to show a willingness and ability to perform according to the parties' agreement. Here, Cohen (P) did not tender performance at all, and therefore never triggered Kranz's (D) duty to perform and could not place him in default. In fact, Cohen's (P) attorney did quite a job with his letter. Rather than place Kranz (D) in default, as it purported to do, the attorney's letter instead had the effect of placing his own client, Cohen (P), in default through an anticipatory breach, thus relieving Kranz (D) from his obligation to perform. [Nice work.]

Handzel v. Bassi

(Buyer) v. (Seller)

343 Ill.App. 281, 99 N.E.2d 23 (1951)

M E M O R Y   G R A P H I C

Instant Facts

When, despite a provision in their land sale contract forbidding assignment of the premises without Bassi's (D) consent, Handzel (P) contracted to sell the premises to another, Bassi (D) declared the contract a nullity and Handzel's (P) payments forfeit.

Black Letter Rule

A court of equity should relieve a buyer from forfeiture resulting from his violation of a stipulation against assignment where the buyer offers and is able to fully perform the contract.

Case Vocabulary

ASSIGNMENT: The transfer of rights or interests in property to another.

PERMANENT INJUNCTION: An order compelling a person to do or refrain from doing something, which remains in force at least until the person complies with its provisions.

PRELIMINARY INJUNCTION: An order preventing a person from doing some disputed act pending trial, to maintain the status quo and prevent the defendant from irreparably harming the plaintiff's ability to enforce his rights.

TEMPORARY INJUNCTION: Preliminary injunction, used to maintain the status quo pending trial.

Procedural Basis: Appeal from interlocutory order denying motion to dissolve temporary injunction granted in action for specific performance.

Facts: Handzel (P) entered into an installment contract for the purchase of land from Bassi (D) for $21,500. The contract provided for a $5,000 down payment and annual payments of $3,500 plus 4% interest. After half the purchase price was paid, Bassi (D) was to convey the property to Handzel (P) and Handzel (P) was to deliver to Bassi (D) a purchase money mortgage for the balance. The contract also provided that Handzel (P) could not assign the contract without Bassi's (D) previous written consent, and that any assignment without consent would not vest any right in the assignee and would render the contract null and void at Bassi's (D) election. Handzel (P) paid the down payment and the first annual payment. Before the second annual payment was due, Handzel (P) entered into another installment contract to sell the premises to Bellcom for $23,500, with a $6,000 down payment and monthly payments of $200. Bassi (D) served Handzel (P) with notice that he violated their contract by assigning his interest without Bassi's (D) previous written consent. The notice stated that unless Handzel (P) corrected this default by April 22, Bassi (D) would declare the contract null and void and would retain all payments already made as liquidated damages. On May 8, Handzel (P) having failed to correct the alleged default, Bassi (D) declared the contract null and void and the payments forfeited. Bassi (D) demanded that Handzel (P) surrender possession of the premises by June 10. On June 1, Handzel (P) tendered a payment of $4,020, representing the next payment due plus interest, demanded a warranty deed and offered to execute a purchase money mortgage for the unpaid balance. Handzel (P) remains ready, willing and able to make this payment, and continues this offer and tender. Handzel (P) sought a temporary injunction preventing Bassi (D) from forfeiting the contract and, after a hearing, a permanent injunction ordering Bassi (D) to specifically perform it. Handzel (P) received a temporary injunction, and Bassi (D) moved to dissolve it. Bassi's (D) motion was denied, and he now appeals that interlocutory order. Handzel (P) has deposited with the court the principal due plus interest and taxes, and has notified Bassi (D) that he has obtained a commitment to borrow enough money to pay the balance on the purchase price if Bassi (D) would give him a deed. Bassi (D) argues that Handzel (P) violated their contract by assigning it without his consent, and, therefore, that his forfeiture of the contract was proper and the injunction was improper. Handzel (P) argues that his contract with Bellcom is a separate, independent transaction and does not violate any provision of his contract with Bassi (D). In light of this and the fact that equity abhors forfeiture, Handzel (P) argues that the temporary injunction was proper.

Issue: Should a court of equity relieve a buyer from forfeiture resulting from his violation of a stipulation against assignment where the buyer offers and is able to fully perform the contract?

Decision and Rationale: (Dove) Yes. As the cases which counsel rely upon hold, a provision forbidding the assignment of a lease without the consent of the lessor is a condition of the lease, not merely a covenant, and a lessor's right of reentry upon violation of such a provision is enforceable. Courts do not favor covenants against assignments and will strictly construe them to prevent forfeitures. However, an unauthorized assignment of a lease in breach of a covenant does give the landlord the right to terminate the lease, and in such a case the court will not prevent forfeiture. Similarly, restrictions on alienation are disfavored and very strictly construed. Here, the parties agreed that after Handzel (P) paid $10,750 toward the $21,500 purchase price, Bassi (D) was to deliver a warranty deed and Handzel (P) was to give him a purchase money mortgage for the balance. Bassi's (D) basic right under the contract was to receive the money agreed upon. Handzel (P) offered to pay this money before filing the complaint and again in the complaint, and finally deposited it with the court. Handzel's (P) agreement with Bellcom was an independent contract under which he would sell

the property to Bellcom if, as and when he acquired it. Handzel's (P) contract with Bellcom did not release him from his contract with Bassi (D), which he is still willing and able to perform. However, even if Handzel's (P) contract with Bellcom was an assignment of the original contract, the provision for forfeiture for violation of a stipulation against assignment is a harsh one. We should not enforce such a provision where the buyer offers and is able to complete performance.

The purpose of this stipulation against assignment is to safeguard performance by Handzel (P). Therefore, because Handzel (P) offered to fully perform, the Chancellor did not abuse his discretion by protecting Handzel's (P) rights pending a hearing on the merits. The Chancellor did not err in granting this temporary injunction, and properly denied Bassi's (D) motion to dissolve it. Order affirmed.

Analysis:

An assignment transfers a person's rights and duties under a contract to another person, without changing the terms of the contract. When an assignment occurs, the assignee steps into the assignor's shoes and deals directly with the other party to the contract, according to that contract's terms. Here, Handzel (P) did not assign his contract with Bassi (D) to Bellcom. He entered into an entirely different contract with him, with different terms for price, payment amount and payment frequency. Handzel (P) intended to complete his contract with Bassi (D) while collecting payments from Bellcom which he could use to make his own payments to Bassi (D). After Handzel (P) acquired a deed to the property from Bassi (D) according to the terms of the Handzel (P)-Bassi (D) agreement, he would convey it to Bellcom according to the terms of the Handzel (P)-Bellcom agreement. Bellcom never made payments to or had any other relationship with Bassi (D), and his contract with Handzel (P) did not affect Handzel's (P) obligations to pay Bassi (D) for the property. However, as the court explains, even if Handzel (P) did assign the original contract to Bellcom, he still had a way to avoid forfeiture. As this case demonstrates, a buyer who violates an anti-assignment provision has the option to tender full performance in exchange for the deed. The other party then gets all he has bargained for, and assumes no unbargained-for risk associated with dealing with the assignee. This Handzel (P) did, so whether his contract with Bellcom was an assignment or not, he was safe from forfeiture. Further, even if Handzel's (P) contract with Bellcom was an assignment, Bassi (D) had other avenues for relief less harsh than forfeiture to protect him against default by the assignee. A person who accepts an assignment of a land sale contract accepts not only the assignor's rights and interests, but also his duties under the contract, so that the seller would look primarily to the assignee for performance. However, the assignor would not necessarily be off the hook as to those duties. An assignment does not operate as a novation (an agreement to cancel an old contract or obligation and to substitute a new one in its place). Rather, an assignment creates a principal-surety relationship between the assignee and the assignor. A buyer who assigns his interests under a contract becomes a surety for his assignee and thus remains liable for any default in performance, even if the assignee assigns his interests to a third person without the buyer's consent. If the seller changes the terms of the agreement, the buyer may be discharged. However, if the agreement continues as before and only the principal parties change through assignment, then the buyer, as surety, may still incur liability for the default of his assignee or even of his assignee's assignee.

Centex Homes Corp. v. Boag

(Seller) v. (Buyer)

128 N.J.Super. 385, 320 A.2d 194 (1974)

M E M O R Y   G R A P H I C

Instant Facts

When Boag (D) defaulted on his contract to buy a condominium from Centex (P), Centex (P) sought specific performance.

Black Letter Rule

Courts should confine specific performance to those special cases in which the seller will otherwise suffer an economic injury which damages would be inadequate to compensate, or where other equitable considerations require granting it.

Case Vocabulary

MUTUALITY OF REMEDY: An equitable doctrine, now discredited, under which equity will not grant a remedy unless it is available to both parties.

Procedural Basis: Motion for summary judgment in breach of contract action seeking specific performance or, in the alternative, liquidated damages.

Facts: Centex Homes Corporation (Centex) (P) is a developer constructing high-rise condominiums. Boag (D) contracted with Centex (P) to buy an apartment in one of Centex's (P) buildings. Shortly after Boag (D) signed the contract and paid about 10% of the purchase price, he learned that his employer was transferring him to Chicago. Boag (D) notified Centex (P) that he "would be unable to complete the purchase" agreement and stopped payment on the check for his down payment. Centex (P) deposited the check two weeks after receiving Boag's (D) notice, but the Bank did not honor it. [Surprise!] Centex (P) then brought this action for specific performance or, in the alternative, for liquidated damages in the amount of the check. Centex (P) argues that under well-settled equitable principles, because the subject matter of the contract is a transfer of real estate, he is entitled to the remedy of specific performance to enforce it.

Issue: Is a seller automatically entitled to the remedy of specific performance to enforce a contract for the sale of a condominium?

Decision and Rationale: (Gelman) No. Under a condominium housing scheme, each condominium is a separate parcel of real property. Upon closing, the owner receives a deed that gives him the same rights and interests as he would have for other forms of real estate, except that a condominium owner also receives an undivided interest in the common elements associated with the building and assigned to each unit. The principle underlying the specific performance remedy is equity's jurisdiction to grant relief where the legal remedy of damages would be inadequate. Historically, considering the uniqueness of land and its importance in the social order, courts concluded that damages could never adequately compensate for the breach of a contract for the sale of an interest in land. Specific performance, therefore, became a fixed remedy for this class of transactions. This attitude continues in courts today. However, while the inadequacy of damages explains the origin of a buyer's right to obtain specific performance, it does not provide a rationale for making the remedy available to a seller. Except under unusual circumstances involving a change in the seller's position, such as where the buyer has taken possession of the land, the seller's damages are usually measurable and his remedy at law adequate, leaving no jurisdictional basis for equitable relief. Early cases suggest that the remedy was available to a seller based on the equitable concept of mutuality, under which equity would not specifically enforce an agreement unless the remedy was available to both parties. In 1863 in *Hopper v. Hopper* [specific performance is available to seller of real estate], the court stated that, it being well established that the remedy of specific performance is mutual, a seller may maintain an action for it in all cases where the buyer could do so. Later cases have offered no other rationale for granting specific performance to a seller, and courts have routinely done so on this basis. However, our Supreme Court has held that mutuality of remedy is not an appropriate basis for granting or denying specific performance. In *Fleischer v. James Drug Store* [justice does not require that the parties have identical remedies available], the Court explained that the appropriate test is whether the obligations of the contract are mutual, not whether each party is entitled to precisely the same remedy for breach. The Court further explained that while the availability of specific performance to one party is not a sufficient reason to make it available to the other, it may tip the balance when the adequacy of damages is difficult to determine and there is no other reason for denying specific performance. Thus, specific performance is no longer automatically available to sellers of real estate. Instead, courts should confine this remedy to those special cases in which the seller will otherwise suffer an economic injury which damages would be inadequate to compensate, or where other equitable considerations require granting it. Here, the condominium Centex (P) contracted to sell to Boag (D) is not unique, but is one of hundreds of virtually identical units. Centex (P) sells the units by showing a model apartment, and their prices are fixed according to floor plan, floor level and location. These condominiums have many characteristics of personal property. We must conclude that the damages Centex (P) sustained are readily measurable, and its remedy at law is wholly adequate. Centex (P) has shown no compelling reason to grant specific performance. Alternatively, Centex (P) seeks liquidated damages under a clause that limits those damages to money paid at the time of the default. Since the default here consisted of Boag's (D) stopping payment on his check for the down payment, the only money paid before then was the initial $525 deposit, which Centex (P) can keep. Complaint dismissed.

Analysis:

This case leads the way in a trend against automatically granting specific performance to sellers of real estate. In *Centex* the court rejects mutuality of remedy as a basis for granting specific performance. Instead, the court advocates limiting specific performance to those cases where the seller's remedy at law would be inadequate or where other equitable considerations justify granting it. A seller's remedy at law, damages, is usually adequate because, after all, money is money. As long as the seller ends up with the same amount in his pocket, he should be happy. However, to recover damages the seller would have to go to the trouble, time and expense to find a new buyer, or at least to try to establish market value, and then seek damages for any difference in the purchase price. Buyers are not always readily available, and the market price is not always clear. The seller may also have other property he could sell to his replacement buyer, which might remain unsold if he cannot find yet another buyer for that property. Specific performance would eliminate these steps and these risks, and just give the seller his money. Here, since the court found the value of the condominiums readily determinable, and evidently also found them readily saleable, it found specific performance unnecessary and inappropriate. Although the trend is to follow the *Centex* approach, many jurisdictions still decline to do so. Absent oppression, fraud, or the like, such jurisdictions continue to consider specific performance a matter of right for parties to a contract for the sale of real estate, condominiums included.

Kramer v. Mobley

(Seller) v. (Buyer)
309 Ky. 143, 216 S.W.2d 930 (1949)

M E M O R Y   G R A P H I C

Instant Facts
After Kramer (D) failed to convey good title under their contract for the sale of land, Mobley (P) sought damages for the loss of his bargain.

Black Letter Rule
In Kentucky, when a sale of land fails due to a title defect, a buyer is not entitled to damages for the loss of his bargain unless the seller is guilty of bad faith or some positive act of fraud.

Case Vocabulary

INDEMNIFY: Guarantee reimbursement for loss or damage that may arise.

Procedural Basis: Appeal from judgment after bench trial of breach of contract action for damages.

Facts: Kramer (D) bought 901 acres of land from Gordon with a note for $22,750, secured by a lien on the land. Gordon later signed a release on the margin of the deed book which recited payment of $20,612 on the note. Kramer (D) then agreed to sell 745½ acres of the land to Mobley (P) for $65 an acre, or $48,457. When the parties met to conclude the transaction, Mobley (P) informed Kramer (D) that he discovered a lien on the land for $2,138 in favor of Gordon. Kramer (D) had informed his real estate broker that the validity of the $2,138 lien was in dispute, and that the buyer must accept the deed with indemnification against loss due to the lien until a court determined its validity. The broker testified that he could not remember when he informed Mobley (P) of the lien. [Or if he did?] Kramer (D) explained to Mobley (P) that he disputed the validity of the lien because he claimed that Gordon wrongfully moved property worth $2,138 from the land when he gave him possession. Kramer (D) stated that he would institute an action to clear the title, and proposed to deliver a certified check for $3,000 to Mobley (P) to indemnify him against loss due to the lien. Mobley (P) substantially agreed to this arrangement, and it was satisfactory to the banker who agreed to give Mobley (P) a loan secured by a mortgage on the land. However, before concluding the transaction Mobley (P) met Gordon, who told him that he would have trouble if he accepted the deed without requiring a release of the lien. The parties met again, and Kramer (D) tendered a general warranty deed to Mobley (P) and a certified check for $3,000. Mobley (P) refused to accept the deed unless Kramer (D) obtained a release of the lien. Kramer (D) insisted that Gordon's claim was not valid and that he would institute an action against him to clear the title. Mobley (P) still refused, so Kramer (D) returned his $5,000 check and the parties dropped the negotiations. Mobley (P) later brought this action for damages for breach of contract, seeking to recover the difference between the agreed price and the market value of the land plus expenses he incurred investigating the title. Mobley (P) alleges that the land was reasonably worth $10 an acre more than the agreed price, or $7,455. The trial court entered judgment for Mobley (P) for $2,000, finding the land worth $2 an acre more than the agreed price, and that Kramer (D) should compensate Mobley (P) for certain expenses because Kramer (D) refused to complete the transaction. Kramer (D) appeals.

Issue: Is a buyer entitled to damages for the loss of his bargain under an executory contract for the sale of land when the seller, acting in good faith, fails to convey good title?

Decision and Rationale: (Rees) No. When a seller breaches an executory contract for the sale of personal property by failing to deliver the property, the measure of damages is the difference, if any, between the contract price and the market value of the property, either at the time of the breach or at the time fixed for delivery. The same rule usually applies when a seller wilfully refuses to convey good or marketable title to real estate as required by the contract. However, under *Crenshaw v. Williams* [applies and explains the English rule], the rule here is that if the sale fails due to a title defect and the seller is not guilty of bad faith or fraud, the measure of the buyer's damage is substantially the same as in the case of an executed sale: the buyer may recover any consideration he has paid, with interest, and any legitimate expense he has incurred, but he can recover nothing for the loss of his bargain. As our cases explain, the mere failure of a seller to refer the buyer to his record of title or any judicial decisions bearing upon it is not such fraud as to deprive him of the benefit of this rule. The measure of damages upon a breach of warranty of title is the value of the land lost as fixed by the consideration paid or agreed to be paid. With respect to damages, there is no substantial difference between a breach of warranty of title and the breach of a covenant to convey where the seller has acted in good faith. If the seller is guilty of fraud, then he would be responsible for the increased value of the land at the time he should have performed. Here, Kramer (D) could have conveyed good title if he paid the disputed debt and obtained a release of the lien. Kramer's (D) refusal to do so did not constitute fraud or bad faith. In fact, Kramer (D) made a fair offer to indemnify Mobley (P) against loss pending his action to determine the validity of the lien. While it is true that Kramer (D) could not have compelled Mobley (P) to accept his deed

in an action for specific performance, this has no bearing on the question of his good faith. A seller need not make a substantial sacrifice to avoid a charge of fraud or bad faith. Kramer (D) was not guilty of any positive act of fraud. The trial court erred in using the difference between the contract price and the market value to measure damages. Further, the sum it allowed for expenses, $509, was excessive since the only expense Mobley (P) proved was the cost of his title examination, which he expected to be $30 to $50. Reversed for further proceedings.

Analysis:

This case discusses the situation in which a seller who has acted in good faith and has committed no positive acts of fraud cannot convey good title. Courts are divided over the proper measure of damages for this situation. Half of American jurisdictions use the "American rule," which uses the general "loss of bargain" measure of damages. The other half, which *Kramer* represents, uses the "English rule," which limits the buyer to restitutionary out-of-pocket damages: he can recover only his deposit, down payment, and other payments and expenses he incurred in connection with the contract. The court essentially returns the parties to their position prior to entering into the contract. This rule stems from 18th century English case law, and thus is known as the "English rule." As the court explained in *Crenshaw*, one reason for the English rule was the uncertainty of title in England at that time, and the consequent difficulty a lay person might have had in determining whether his title had any defects. Today, in America, property owners can usually determine the state of their title with reasonable certainty. Another reason for the English rule that the court mentioned in *Crenshaw* is the policy to keep land in the hands of home builders and home maintainers, and not to encourage speculative bargaining in it. To further this policy, courts restore the parties to their position before executing the contract absent fraud or bad faith. Under the English rule, then, courts effectively make marketable title a condition of the contract rather than a covenant. Unless he acts in bad faith, if the seller is unable to convey marketable title, the court simply returns the parties to the position they held before executing the contract rather than enforcing the contract and holding the seller liable for breaching a covenant.

Smith v. Warr

(Seller) v. (Buyer)
564 P.2d 771 (1977)

M E M O R Y   G R A P H I C

Instant Facts

When adverse possessors successfully quieted title to land that Warr (P) had contracted to buy from Smith (D), the court entered judgment for Warr (P) for Smith's (D) breach, but awarded him only out-of-pocket losses.

Black Letter Rule

In Utah, benefit-of-the-bargain damages are available for breach of contract for the sale of real estate regardless of the good faith of the breaching party.

Procedural Basis: Appeal from judgment on cross claim for breach of contract seeking a modification of the damages award.

Facts: Warr (P) executed a contract for the sale of land under which Smith (D) would pass title by special warranty deed upon full payment. Adverse possessors then instituted an action to quiet title against Smith (D), and later joined Warr (P) as a defendant in that action. In his answer, Warr (P) filed a cross complaint against Smith (D) for breach of contract, but he continued to make payments on the contract throughout the proceeding. The court entered judgment in favor of the adverse possessors and in favor of Warr (P) on his cross complaint against Smith (D). However, the court only awarded Warr (P) damages in the amount of his out-of-pocket loss. Warr (P) appeals this judgment, arguing that the court erred in not awarding him benefit-of-the-bargain damages, or the market value of the property at the time of the breach less the amount of the unpaid purchase money.

Issue: In Utah, is out-of-pocket loss the correct measure of damages for a good faith breach of a contract for the sale of land?

Decision and Rationale: (Wilkins) No. The states are divided over whether out-of-pocket loss or benefit-of-the-bargain damages are the appropriate measure of damages for a breach of contract for the sale of land. Some award benefit-of-the-bargain damages only when the breaching party acted in bad faith, while others award them whether the breach was in good faith or bad faith. Smith (D) argues that, although Utah has not expressly taken a position on this issue, case law does indicate that the good faith-bad faith distinction applies. Since the trial court found that he acted in good faith, Smith (D) argues that out-of-pocket loss is the correct measure of damages. However, the case law on which Smith (D) relies does not support his position, and in fact indicates that courts have awarded benefit-of-the-bargain damages regardless of good faith. Even in cases where the court awarded only out-of-pocket losses, the court noted that these were the only damages the buyers sought, and that benefit-of-the-bargain damages would have been available had they sought them. Therefore, the rule in Utah is that benefit-of-the-bargain damages are available for breach of a contract for the sale of real estate regardless of the good faith of the breaching party. Reversed and remanded.

Analysis:

Under the general contract rule for damages, when a party breaches a contract for the sale of land, the nonbreaching party can recover "loss of bargain" damages, or the difference between the contract price and the market price at the time of the breach. This measure of damages works both ways. If the market price goes up $10,000, the buyer could recover that $10,000 difference if the seller breached, but the seller could not recover if the buyer breached. Conversely, if the market price dropped $10,000, the seller could recover, but the buyer could not. This case demonstrates the use of this general rule for the situation in which a seller acting in good faith nonetheless cannot convey marketable title. In this situation, *Kramer v. Mobley* [English rule], the previous case, follows the English rule and limits a buyer's damages to his out-of-pocket loss. This case represents the "American rule," which uses general "loss of bargain" or benefit-of-the-bargain damages, even if the breaching party acted in good faith. Under this rule, the court gives the nonbreaching party the benefit of his bargain by restoring any payments he has already made and adding the difference between the contract price and the market price at the time of the breach. Under the American rule, good faith is simply immaterial [and the rule, therefore, is just simpler.]

Clay v. Landreth

(Seller) v. (Buyer)

187 Va. 169, 45 S.E.2d 875, 175 A.L.R. 1047 (1948)

M E M O R Y   G R A P H I C

Instant Facts

After Clay (P) and Landreth (D) executed a contract for the sale of a lot on which Landreth (D) planned to build a warehouse, unanticipated rezoning made this use of the property impossible.

Black Letter Rule

A court should not apply the doctrine of equitable conversion to an executory contract where doing so would defeat the agreed purpose of the sale and cause hardship and injustice to one of the parties.

Case Vocabulary

EQUITABLE CONVERSION: Doctrine based on the maxim that "equity regards as done that which ought to have been done," under which a buyer under a contract for the sale of land becomes the equitable owner of the property upon the signing of the contract, while the seller holds legal title only as security for payment of the purchase price.

Procedural Basis: Appeal of decree in action for specific performance.

Facts: Clay (P) entered into a contract to sell land to Landreth (D), who, as Clay (P) knew, wanted to build a frozen food warehouse on it. When they executed the contract, the land was zoned for business uses, but before the time for delivery of the deed the city rezoned the lot for residential use only. Clay (P) sought a decree for specific performance. Landreth (D) argued that this rezoning caused substantial depreciation in the value of the land; that compelling performance would be inequitable and produce results which the parties did not intend when they made the contract; and that under the circumstances specific performance would be harsh and oppressive to him. The trial court denied specific performance. Clay (P) appeals and argues that the court should apply the doctrine of equitable conversion and consider Landreth (D) the owner of the lot as of the date of the contract.

Issue: Should a court apply the doctrine of equitable conversion to an executory contract where unanticipated rezoning has defeated the agreed purpose of the sale?

Decision and Rationale: (Gregory) No. The parties entered into the contract with the mutual intent that the land would be usable for Landreth's (D) business purpose, but before they closed the transaction this purpose failed through no fault of either party. There is no question of fraud, misrepresentation, unfair dealing, or inequitable conduct on either side. However, if we applied the doctrine of equitable conversion, any loss of value or of the intended use of the property resulting from the rezoning would fall entirely on Landreth (D). This doctrine rests on the maxim that equity looks upon things agreed to be done as actually performed. Under this doctrine, as soon as a buyer and seller execute a valid contract for the sale of land, equity considers the buyer the owner of the land and the seller his trustee. Likewise, it considers the seller the owner of the purchase money, and the buyer his trustee. However, this doctrine is limited to cases where enforcement of the contract accords with the intent of the parties, free from fraud, misrepresentation and the like, and where it will not produce inequitable results. Specific performance and equitable conversion are governed by similar equitable principles and limitations: a court should use neither if doing so would force hardship and injustice upon one of the parties through a change in circumstances that the parties did not contemplate when they made the contract. As the Supreme Court explained in *Craig v. Leslie* [defines equitable conversion], equity regards things agreed to be done as having been actually performed *if* nothing has intervened which ought to prevent a performance. If something has intervened which ought to prevent it, the doctrine of equitable conversion will not apply. The doctrine is not a matter of right, and it is not applicable to all circumstances. Rather, equity applies this doctrine only when justice so requires. When the doctrine arises from a contract, its legal fiction is based on the manifest intent of the parties, its purpose being to give effect to that intent. The doctrine will not apply where it would instead foil that intent or work injustice. Here, we should not apply this doctrine because doing so would set at naught the intent and purpose of the parties and cause hardship and injustice to Landreth (D). Both parties intended a sale of a lot usable for a storage plant. Rezoning has defeated this intent and caused such a substantial change of conditions and loss in value that to apply the doctrine of equitable conversion would be inequitable. In *Anderson v. Steinway & Sons* [denied specific performance after imposition of new use restrictions], the court denied specific performance where new use restrictions rendered the property useless for the only purpose the buyer sought to acquire it. In *Kend et al. v. Crestwood Realty Co.* [denied rescission when use restrictions changed], which involved a similar situation, the court refused to allow rescission, but recognized that equity might find specific performance unjust. These cases suffice to show that a court may refuse specific performance when a change of circumstances not contemplated by the parties, which occurs after they made the contract, would render it inequitable. There is a difference between rescission and specific performance. Rescission terminates the contract for all purposes. A denial of specific performance, while a refusal to enforce the contract, still leaves the contract in force for other purposes, including an action at law. Because the rezoning rendered the property useless for Landreth's (D) intended purpose, Clay (P) cannot convey to Landreth (D) what he agreed to purchase and what Clay (P) agreed to convey. Affirmed.

Analysis:

Under the doctrine of equitable conversion, when parties sign a contract for the sale of land, the buyer becomes the equitable owner of the land and the seller becomes the equitable owner of the purchase money. The seller continues to hold legal title, but in trust for the buyer and as security for payment of the purchase money. The buyer, likewise, holds the purchase money in trust for the seller. The buyer, though equitable owner, would not be entitled to possession of the land until he has legal title, unless the parties provide otherwise. However, whoever does have possession pending the closing must not use the land in such a way as to diminish the other's interest in the property, whether it be the buyer's rights as equitable owner or the seller's security interest in the property. This case introduces the doctrine of equitable conversion and demonstrates one way the circumstances of a sale might change during the period between the signing of the contract and the closing. The following cases in this section discuss the doctrine in more detail and other changes that can bring it into play, such as substantial property damage or the death of one of the parties.

Shay v. Penrose

(Administrator/Heir) v. (Heir)
25 Ill.2d 447, 185 N.E.2d 218 (1962)

M E M O R Y   G R A P H I C

Instant Facts

After the seller under certain land sale contracts died, Penrose (D), one of her heirs, sought partition of those properties on the theory that equitable conversion had not yet taken place.

Black Letter Rule

Equitable conversion takes place at the signing of a contract for the sale of land, regardless of the length of time the contract has to run.

Case Vocabulary

DEVOLUTION: The transfer of title or rights from one person to another, as by descent upon the death of a person.
PARTITION: The severance of interests in real property, sometimes by a court's sale of the property and division of the proceeds.

Procedural Basis: Appeal from order dismissing counterclaim in action to partition real estate.

Facts: Carol Shay acquired six parcels of real estate during her life, and executed contracts for deeds to different buyers for four of those parcels. She collected monthly payments and retained an option of forfeiture if a buyer failed to perform. Carol Shay died intestate, leaving her husband, Arthur Shay (Shay) (P), who acted as administrator, and her sister, Penrose (D). Shay (P) brought this action to partition the two unsold parcels. Penrose (D) filed a counterclaim alleging that Shay (P) should also partition the four sold parcels because she and Shay (P) were each entitled to a half interest in those parcels. The trial court held that equitable conversion occurred at the signing of the contracts so that those four parcels were not subject to partition by the seller. Penrose (D) argues that equitable conversion does not apply to long term land sale contracts until the parties have completed all performance except tender of final payment and delivery of the deed.

Issue: Does equitable conversion apply to executory long term land sale contracts before the parties have completed all but tender of final payment and delivery of the deed?

Decision and Rationale: (House) Yes. Equitable conversion treats land as personalty and personalty as land under certain circumstances. When an owner enters into a contract for the sale of land he continues to hold legal title, but in trust for the buyer, and the buyer becomes the equitable owner and holds the purchase money in trust for the seller. This conversion takes place at the signing of the contract. Unfortunately, this court has not applied this doctrine consistently. In one early case, for example, the court stated that a contract to convey at a future time did not create an equitable title in the buyer until he completed all the acts necessary to entitle him to a deed. We believe the correct view is that equitable conversion takes place the instant the parties enter into a valid and enforceable contract, and that the buyer acquires equitable title at that time. Our prior cases are hereby overruled to the extent they are inconsistent with this view. Penrose (D) suggests that a hearing is necessary to determine whether these contracts are valid and enforceable, since this is a prerequisite for applying the doctrine of equitable conversion. However, since the pleadings did not raise the validity or enforceability of the contracts, the chancellor did not need to hear evidence on these matters. Penrose (D) also suggests that sellers under long term contracts need the court's protection. However, to base application of the doctrine of equitable conversion upon the length of time a contract has to run would leave titles in an utter state of confusion. For the sake of certainty and stability of titles, particularly in a society that increasingly uses contracts for deed, we must reject such an approach. Finally, we turn to application of the doctrine of equitable conversion to these contracts, one of which was in arrears when the seller died. Equitable conversion took place when the parties executed the contracts, making the decedent's interest in them one of personalty. Because the decedent's interest was one of personalty, not realty, upon her death her interest descended to Shay (P), her personal representative, and he became entitled to the entire unpaid balance of the purchase price of each contract. The option to declare one contract in default and the right to consent to an assignment in another therefore vested in Shay (P) as administrator. Affirmed.

Analysis:

The previous case, *Clay v. Landreth* [equitable conversion makes the buyer the equitable owner of the land at the signing of the contract], demonstrates that under the doctrine of equitable conversion, the buyer under a contract for the sale of land becomes the equitable owner of the land and the seller becomes the equitable owner of the purchase money. As this case makes clear, the buyer's interest under the contract is thus one in real property, while the seller's interest is one in personal property, from the signing of the contract. If a party dies before the conveyance is complete, his interest will descend as it was when he died. If his interest was in personal property, it will descend as personal property, even if the conveyance of legal title has not yet occurred. However, equitable conversion should only come into play where the decedent has no will or where his intent is unclear. If a decedent clearly intended a particular course of descent for his property, a court should give that intent effect. Even where the decedent is intestate, however, changes in laws of succession have made the doctrine of equitable conversion less relevant. In this case, for example, the seller died intestate, and the statute governing intestate succession at that time provided that half of her real property would go to her sister and half to her spouse, but that all of her personalty would go to her spouse. Penrose (D), therefore, could not inherit anything unless she found a way to avoid the equitable conversion of her sister's real property into personalty. [Food for family feuds.] Later, the statute changed to give the entire estate, real and personal, to the spouse, so the equitable conversion issue here would never arise.

Clapp v. Tower

(Buyer) v. (Heirs)
11 N.D. 556, 93 N.W. 862 (1903)

M E M O R Y   G R A P H I C

 ## Instant Facts

After Charlemange died, land he contracted to sell returned to his estate through foreclosure, and his executors, considering it converted into personality, sold it to Clapp (P) rather than let it descend to his heirs.

Black Letter Rule

The doctrine of equitable conversion applies to convert land into personalty when a person contracts to sell it, and it remains personalty after his death even if the buyer defaults and the property returns to his estate through foreclosure.

Case Vocabulary

HEIR: A person who inherits real property by the law of intestate succession rather than by devise.
LEGATEE: A person who inherits personal property under a will.
NEXT OF KIN: Those entitled to inherit personal property under the law of intestate succession, generally the nearest blood relatives of the decedent.

Procedural Basis: Appeal from order sustaining demurrer in action to quiet title.

Facts: Clapp (P) bought certain land from the executors of Charlemange Tower (Charlemange). Clapp (P) has possessed the land ever since, and claims ownership by virtue of his deed from the executors. Because the Towers (D), Charlemange's next of kin, heirs at law and legatees under his will, claim ownership of the land by virtue of their heirship, Clapp (P) brought this action to quiet his title. The Towers (D) allege in their answer that Charlemange entered into a contract to sell the land to Hadley, but Hadley defaulted. After Charlemange died, his executors foreclosed and the land again became part of the estate. Acting on the theory that they must treat the land as personalty under the doctrine of equitable conversion, the executors sold it to Clapp (P). Clapp (P) demurred to this answer on the ground that it does not state facts sufficient to constitute a defense or a counterclaim. The trial court sustained the demurrer, and the Towers (D) appeal.

Issue: Does equity consider land as personalty under the doctrine of equitable conversion if a decedent contracted to sell it during his lifetime, but the buyer defaulted and the land returned to the estate through foreclosure after his death?

Decision and Rationale: (Young) Yes. Charlemange's will was before this court in a previous case in which we held that its provisions relating to real estate were inoperative and void, and that his real estate must therefore be distributed according to the state law of succession. His personality, however, should be distributed according to the terms of his will. Therefore, if the executors should have treated the land as realty, it should have descended directly to Charlemange's heirs, the Towers (D). If the executors were correct in treating the land as personalty, then it should have gone to them for distribution, and they had full authority to sell it to Clapp (P). Equitable conversion is a constructive alteration of property by which equity regards realty as personalty and personalty as realty. Here, equitable conversion is clearly applicable. Charlemange's execution and delivery of a contract for sale of the land during his lifetime, still valid and enforceable when he died, worked a conversion of the land into personalty. Charlemange's interest in the land, at the time of the signing of the contract and at the time of his death, was in the money the buyer agreed to pay, and the buyer's interest was the land. Although in such cases the seller still holds legal title, he does so only as trustee. Because equity views the seller's property as a personal estate in the money, if he dies before payment, the money goes to his administrators and not to his heirs. If the seller dies before receiving full payment and the buyer has not defaulted, the buyer could compel the seller to convey the land, and the proceeds would go to the executors as personal property. Once parties have entered into a valid and binding contract for the sale of land which equity would specifically enforce, the contract operates as a conversion. Because the property here assumed the character of personalty, it went to the executors, and continued as personalty for administration purposes so that they could sell the land to Clapp (P). Affirmed.

Analysis:

This case demonstrates that once a contract converts a seller's interest into one of personalty, a buyer's default does not "unconvert" that interest. Even after default and foreclosure, the seller's interest remains one in personalty, and the proceeds of the foreclosure sale will therefore go to the executors for distribution rather than to the seller's heirs or devisees. The characterization of the parties' interests in the property often arises in cases where one of the parties dies. If the decedent's interest was personal, it will descend as personalty to the party's legatees or next-of-kin. Likewise, if he had an interest in real property, it will descend as realty to his heirs or devisees. (If a decedent has a will, those who receive his personalty are called "legatees," and those who receive his realty are called "devisees." If the decedent does not have a will, his property passes by statute, personalty going to his "next-of-kin" and realty going to his "heirs.") As this case demonstrates, difficulties can arise when a decedent's devisees and legatees are different people, and resolution of those difficulties may turn on whether the doctrine of equitable conversion applies to alter the characterization of the property.

AN ENFORCEABLE CONTRACT FOR THE SALE OF LAND MUST EXIST BEFORE THE DOCTRINE OF EQUITABLE CONVERSION WILL APPLY

Eddington v. Turner

(Optionee) v. (Heir)

27 Del.Ch. 411, 38 A.2d 738, 155 A.L.R. 562 (1944)

M E M O R Y   G R A P H I C

Instant Facts

Mr. Turner devised part of his land to his sister Sallie for life, but then granted an option on that land, which the optionee exercised after Mr. Turner died.

Black Letter Rule

Equitable conversion does not relate back to the date of an option to purchase land, but can only occur when and if the optionee exercises his option.

Procedural Basis: Appeal from order distributing money deposited with the court in action for specific performance.

Facts: In his will Mr. Turner devised certain land to his sister Sallie for life, but he did not devise that land after her death or include any residuary clause in the will. Mr. Turner left his sons, Arthur and Thomas Turner, (the Turners) (D) as his only heirs at law and executors of his will. Three days after making his will, Mr. Turner entered into a contract giving Eddington (P) a 60-day option to purchase a large tract of land which included the land he had devised to Sallie. The option agreement provided that if Eddington (P) did not exercise his option to purchase within 60 days, the agreement would become null and void. Eddington (P) exercised his option within the 60 day period, but three days after Mr. Turner died. Eddington (P) brought this action for specific performance, received a deed for the property, and deposited the purchase money with the court. When Sallie petitioned the court for the money, the chancellor held that she was entitled to a life interest in the portion of the proceeds that corresponded to the portion of the land Mr. Turner devised to her. The court ascertained this proportion and ordered that amount be paid to Sallie upon her entering into a bond conditioned upon the payment of that sum at her death to the Turners (D). The Turners (D) appealed, arguing that because the proceeds from the sale to Eddington (P) were personal property, they, as executors and distributees, were entitled to the entire sum, and Sallie, as devisee of real estate for life, was entitled to nothing.

Issue: Does equitable conversion relate back to the date of an option to purchase land?

Decision and Rationale: (Rodney) No. This idea that equitable conversion relates back to the date of the option rather than occurring upon its exercise, and that the proceeds of the resulting sale are therefore personalty that passes to personal representatives rather than to the devisees of the land, comes from the English case of *Lawes v. Bennett* [relation back of equitable conversion]. However, this relation back theory does not accord with the testator's intent or any sound principle of law or equity. Here, Mr. Turner evidenced his desire that Sallie should have a portion of his land for life. He then granted an option to Eddington (P), but did not know if Eddington (P) would exercise it. Mr. Turner knew that if Eddington (P) did exercise it, then there would be no basis for his devise to Sallie, but if he did not, he would continue to own the land as before. Mr. Turner had no right to the purchase money or the exercise of the option, but simply held the land under an obligation to convey it if Eddington (P) did exercise the option. When, under these circumstances, Mr. Turner died, Sallie received the land by the will, but subject to the same obligation to convey that Mr. Turner had. Sallie received the rents and profits from that land, and would have continued to do so for life if Eddington (P) did not exercise his option. No equitable conversion could have occurred before the exercise of the option. Since there was no conversion of the land during Mr. Turner's life, he had no claim for the purchase price to transmit to his personal representatives. Once Eddington (P) exercised his option, Sallie had to convey the land and it converted into money. Just as Sallie had a life interest in the land with its rents and profits before the conversion, she should have a life interest in the proceeds of its sale. Affirmed.

Analysis:

This case makes clear that an enforceable contract of sale must exist before the doctrine of equitable conversion will apply, and that an unexercised option to purchase does not meet this test. An option is only an offer of sale, not a contract. Because no contract of sale exists before the exercise of the option, equitable conversion cannot occur until then. Usually the seller's will precedes his contract for the sale of land. In such a case equitable conversion usually applies from the date of the contract, and equity will treat the land as personalty for distribution purposes if the seller dies while the contract is still executory. Ultimately, however, it is the decedent's intent that must govern. If the decedent seller made his will *after* he made the contract, and in that will devised the land he already contracted to sell, then the court may determine that he intended to leave the devisees the value of the property and decline to apply equitable conversion in order to effectuate that intent. A testator's intent trumps the doctrine of equitable conversion.

Bleckley v. Langston

(Buyer) v. (Seller)

112 Ga.App. 63, 143 S.E.2d 671 (1965)

M E M O R Y   G R A P H I C

Instant Facts

Bleckley (P) sought to rescind his contract to buy property from Langston (D) after an ice storm caused substantial damage to the property.

Black Letter Rule

While a contract for the sale of land is still executory, the risk of loss normally falls on the buyer, who is the equitable owner of the property, unless the contract provides otherwise.

Case Vocabulary

BOND FOR TITLE: An agreement used in an installment contract for the sale of land, by which the seller agrees to convey title when the buyer has paid off the purchase-money notes he has given to the seller.

Procedural Basis: Appeal from trial court judgment granting motion for summary judgment in action for rescission and recovery of earnest money.

Facts: Bleckley (P) contracted to buy real estate from Langston (D) for $120,000 and paid $10,000 as earnest money. About a week after the signing of the contract, while Langston (D) was still in possession and before he tendered or executed a deed to Bleckley (P), an ice storm damaged all the pecan trees on the property, reducing its fair market value by at least $32,000. Bleckley (P) notified Langston (D) that due to the damage he elected to rescind the contract and demanded the return of his earnest money. Langston (D) refused, notified Bleckley (P) that he was willing and able to perform, and demanded that Bleckley (P) perform. Bleckley (P) brought this action for rescission and to recover his earnest money, and Langston (D) filed a cross action for damages for Bleckley's (P) failure to perform the contract. Bleckley (P) argues that while a contract is still executory, the party who must bear a loss from damage to the property should be the party who was in possession when that damage occurred.

Issue: While a contract for the sale of land is still executory, does allocation of the risk of loss depend upon which party has possession when the loss occurs?

Decision and Rationale: (Hall) No. The ice storm destroyed a substantial part of the land constituting the subject matter of the contract while it was still executory. While the parties may have provided in the contract for who should bear the risk of loss in such a case, they did not do so. The majority rule, established in England in 1801, is that after the parties execute a contract for the sale of realty, the buyer bears the risk of loss. This rule is based on the principle that the contract gives the buyer ownership of the land, while, during the gap before performance, the seller retains possession, rents and profits, and legal title as security for the purchase money. Under the rule, for example, the buyer is entitled to the proceeds from condemnation proceedings. However, this rule does not apply unless the seller is willing and able to convey the property. The buyer is not the owner from the contract date unless the seller is prepared to convey clear title and is not in default. The minority view in this country, known as the Massachusetts rule, holds that in a case such as this there is a failure of consideration which turns the buyer loose and leaves the seller with his ruins. This rule is more expedient and more in accord with common sense and business practices. The theory of equitable conversion [upon which the majority rule depends] is inconsistent with natural justice, practical advantage, and the principles of law. In fact, even England eventually adopted the Massachusetts rule in 1925. Nevertheless, the prevailing rule in this country and in Georgia is that the risk of loss normally falls upon the buyer, who is in substance the owner of the property. Bleckley (P) argues that the party who is in possession of the property at the time of loss should be the one who must bear that loss. However, this was not the test at common law nor in any court of last resort. Casual statements by courts that a loss falls on the buyer who has taken possession do not mean that a buyer does not bear the risk of loss before he has taken possession. Just as possession is not material to the passing or existence of legal or equitable title to land, it also is not material to the incidents of equitable title such as the risk of loss. Although it may be reasonable to require possession as to the risk of losses which the possessor has the power to protect against, this does not hold true for acts of God. We have found no case in which a Georgia court has decided which party bears the loss for substantial damage to improvements on realty after the signing of a contract of sale where the seller is still in possession and is able to convey title. The Georgia Supreme Court has held that the loss falls on the seller when the contract is not binding or when he cannot convey title, and that the loss falls on the buyer when the seller can convey title. Georgia cases have also stated that where a buyer is in possession under a binding executory contract and where the seller can convey title, the buyer, as equitable owner, must bear the loss of improvements destroyed by fire without the fault of either party. These cases all involved bond for title situations, where the buyer is generally in possession for a considerable time. One case has stated that the loss should fall on the buyer where the contract is so far completed that he is treated as the owner of the property. The Georgia Supreme Court appears to have adopted the view that where a contract is binding and the seller can convey title, equity regards the seller as a trustee of the legal title for the buyer's benefit, and that once this occurs the buyer should bear the risk of loss, whether or not he is in possession. Here, since the parties entered into a binding contract for the sale of the property, and since the seller was willing and able to consummate the contract when the destruction of a substantial part of the property occurred, the loss should fall upon the buyer. Reversed.

Analysis:

Most jurisdictions apply the equitable conversion doctrine and therefore consider the buyer the equitable owner of the property after the signing of the contract. Because they consider the buyer the equitable owner, at the signing of the contract most jurisdictions also find that the risk of loss shifts from the seller to the buyer. In *Bleckley* the court [reluctantly] adopts this majority rule, or "English rule," for allocating the risk of loss under a contract for the sale of land. Because the buyer bears the risk of loss, he must specifically perform the contract and pay the full purchase price despite damage to the property or some other unfavorable change in circumstances. [In majority rule states, then, the bargain is really only for the title to the land, which the buyer gets even if all his trees are dead. In practice, then, remember that if your buyer wants live trees or a house that is still standing, make this part of the bargain and put it in the contract.] Although most American jurisdictions follow the English rule [even though England no longer does], many follow the minority "Massachusetts rule." One case following this rule is *Libman v. Levenson* [risk of loss on seller before conveyance], which holds that courts should construe contracts as subject to an implied condition that it shall cease to be binding if fire destroys the premises prior to conveyance. Since the contract is no longer binding, the court would allow the buyer to recover any payments he has made. This approach does not apply equitable conversion, and therefore, considering the seller the owner before conveyance, places the risk of loss on him. Some states have settled this issue by adopting the *Uniform Vendor and Purchaser Risk Act* [allocates risk of loss under contracts for the sale of land]. Under this statute, every contract for the sale of real estate includes an implied provision allocating the risk of loss, unless the contract provides otherwise. This statutory provision imposes the risk of loss on the buyer only after the transfer of *either* possession *or* legal title to the buyer. As long as the seller retains both possession and legal title, he also bears the risk of loss from a government taking or from destruction of all or part of the property, unless the buyer has caused that destruction. Under the statute, when the seller bears the risk of loss, if all or a material part of the property is destroyed or taken, then the seller cannot enforce the contract and the buyer may recover any payments he has made. At least one court has further held that in such a case the buyer cannot enforce the contract with an abatement of the price, but is limited to recovering his prior payments.

Sanford v. Breidenbach

(Seller) v. (Buyer)
111 Ohio App. 474, 173 N.E.2d 702 (1960)

M E M O R Y   G R A P H I C

 Instant Facts

Fire destroyed the house Sanford (P) had contracted to sell to Breidenbach (D), but before Sanford (P) delivered a deed or provided a septic tank agreement.

Black Letter Rule

Where the buyer has not entered into possession, equitable conversion becomes effective when the parties intend that equitable title will pass upon the signing of the contract, and the seller, having fulfilled all conditions, is entitled to specific performance.

Case Vocabulary

CASUALTY: Property damage through fire, storm, flood, earthquake, or some other unexpected and unavoidable event.

Procedural Basis: Appeal from judgment in action for specific performance, damages and declaratory relief.

Facts: Sanford (P) entered into a contract to sell his home to Breidenbach (D) for $26,000. The contract provided that Sanford (P) would give Breidenbach (D) permanent permission to use the present septic system, and that Sanford (P) would submit his easements for that system to Breidenbach (D) for his approval before the deposit of funds in escrow. The contract also provided that Sanford (P) would deliver possession upon transfer of the title, but he did give Breidenbach (D) two keys before then. Breidenbach (D) used the keys to enter the house with others to prepare to change the heating system from oil to gas, to check the oil tank for fuel, and to show the home to friends. Before title transfer occurred, fire completely destroyed the house. Breidenbach (D) immediately instructed his bank, who was holding the deed in escrow pending a title search, not to file the deed for record. Sanford (P) later submitted a septic tank agreement as the contract required, but it was not satisfactory to Breidenbach (D) because the right to use the facility would terminate under certain conditions, and the contract made no such exception. Sanford (P) brought this action against Breidenbach (D) for specific performance, and against Northwestern Mutual Insurance Company (Northwestern), which insured Breidenbach (D) against loss by fire. Breidenbach (D) cross-petitioned against Insurance Company of North America (ICNA), which insured Sanford (P), to hold it responsible for the loss Sanford (P) suffered, or, if the property was Breidenbach's (D), then for a declaration of Breidenbach's (D) interest in the proceeds of Sanford's (P) policy. The trial court determined that Sanford (P) was not entitled to specific performance, but that he should recover from both insurance companies, with the loss apportioned between them.

Issue: Does the doctrine of equitable conversion apply to shift the risk of loss to the buyer under an executory contract for the sale of land where the seller is not entitled to specific performance?

Decision and Rationale: (Hunsicker) No. A decree of specific performance is not a matter of right, but rests in the discretion of the court. Sanford's (P) provision of a satisfactory septic tank easement was an essential part of the contract. However, Breidenbach (D) rejected the easement Sanford (P) submitted because it contained conditions under which the easement would terminate, although the contract made no such exception. Because Sanford (P) had not yet complied with a material part of the agreement when he sought specific performance, we cannot grant this relief. Sanford (P) argues that although specific performance may not lie, the doctrine of equitable conversion still applies to make Breidenbach (D) the equitable owner of the premises, and therefore any loss must fall on him and Northwestern, his insurer. In general, the rule under the doctrine of equitable conversion is that a contract to sell real property vests equitable ownership of the property in the buyer, and the buyer therefore must bear any loss by destruction through casualty. Here, Breidenbach (D) did not have possession, despite his incidental checking of the oil level and accepting a key to the premises. Ohio cases have held that a buyer's possession merely gives the world notice of his equitable ownership to the extent of his payment of the purchase money. We believe that the better rule for cases where, as here, the buyer has not entered into possession, is that equitable conversion becomes effective when the seller has fulfilled all conditions and is entitled to specific performance and the parties intend that equitable title shall pass upon the signing of the contract. This case meets none of these requirements. Since Sanford (P) could not specifically enforce the contract, and since the contract did not place the risk of loss on the buyer from the time of its signing, we find no basis for a claim that equitable conversion existed to place the burden of loss by fire on

Breidenbach (D). Since Sanford (P) was the owner of the premises at the time of the fire, the loss must fall upon him. Sanford (P) had $20,000 of fire loss coverage with ICNA, and ICNA must respond under the terms of its policy. Breidenbach (D) had an insurable interest in the premises up to the time he refused to complete the contract. Although Breidenbach (D) had a legal right to waive Sanford's (P) failure to give a satisfactory septic tank agreement and insist upon completion of the sale, he did not exercise that right. Since he instead refused to accept a deed and complete the contract, and since we will not require him to complete it, Breidenbach (D) suffered no loss for Northwestern to compensate. Northwestern insured only Breidenbach (D), and not Sanford (P). Because Breidenbach (D) suffered no loss, Northwestern need not respond with payment under the policy. This is not a situation where more than one insurance policy covers the property, so there can be no apportionment of the loss between the insurers. Breidenbach's (D) interest in the property ceased at the time of the fire, and his insurance ended the same moment. Affirmed in part, reversed in part.

Analysis:

Although it remains the majority rule, the doctrine of equitable conversion as a risk allocation tool is subject to much criticism. One criticism is that it rarely fulfills the expectations of the parties. Most lay people do assume the allocation of risk will follow ownership, but they usually consider the seller the owner of the property until the completion of the sale. (In fact, most real estate contracts include provisions governing the allocation of risk, and these usually place the risk on the seller.) The seller is also more likely to carry insurance on the property, and, since he is usually in possession until closing, he is in a better position to protect the property against loss. This case makes clear that a contract for the sale of land must be specifically enforceable before the court will apply the equitable conversion doctrine to shift the risk of loss to the buyer. Because the application of the remedy of specific performance and the doctrine of equitable conversion are related, the more conditions a contract contains, the less likely the court will order specific performance, and the less likely equitable conversion will apply to place the risk of loss on the buyer.

Raplee v. Piper

(Buyer) v. (Seller)

3 N.Y.2d 179, 164 N.Y.S.2d 732, 143 N.E.2d 919, 64 A.L.R.2d 1397 (1957)

M E M O R Y   G R A P H I C

Instant Facts

As their contract required, Raplee (P) paid for insurance on property he was buying from Piper (D), but when a fire occurred and Piper (D) received the insurance proceeds, he refused to apply those proceeds toward the purchase price.

Black Letter Rule

If, in compliance with a contract for the sale of land, the buyer insures the property in the seller's name pending completion of the sale, the seller must apply any proceeds from that insurance toward the purchase price.

Case Vocabulary

RES: "Thing," particularly a thing that is the object of rights.

Procedural Basis: Appeal from judgment entered in action for breach of contract.

Facts: A fire occurred while Raplee (P) was in possession as the buyer under a contract for the sale of land. The contract required Raplee (P) to pay premiums on a policy to insure the property against fire loss, and after the fire Piper (D) received the proceeds of that policy. Raplee (P) then tendered the difference between the balance due on the purchase price and the insurance proceeds, but Piper (D) refused to apply the proceeds toward the price.

Issue: If, in compliance with a contract for the sale of land, the buyer insures the property in the seller's name pending completion of the sale, must the seller apply any proceeds from that insurance toward the purchase price?

Decision and Rationale: (Desmond) Yes. When a contract for the sale of land requires the buyer to insure the property against fire, then if there is a fire before completion of the sale and the seller receives the insurance, he must apply that money toward the balance due on the purchase price. However, under *Brownell v. Board of Educ.* [seller can keep proceeds when he buys insurance], if the seller provides the insurance himself, not as part of the contract, then he need not apply the insurance proceeds toward the price. As *Persico v. Guernsey* [insurance proceeds as trust] held, where the contract requires the buyer to pay premiums on a policy to insure property while the contract is executory, any insurance proceeds form a trust fund for the benefit of both the buyer and seller. Where a seller purchases his own insurance, on the other hand, the proceeds are not part of the bargain and no trust exists in regard to them. It would be unjust if a buyer, complying with the contract by insuring the property in the seller's name, could not benefit from that insurance. The seller then could receive the full purchase price plus the insurance proceeds, while the buyer would have to pay the full price yet receive only a destroyed building. Whether it is called a trust fund or something else, the insurance the buyer obtains in the seller's name is for the protection of the contract and both parties. The general law regarding risk of loss does not apply here. Under common law the risk of loss pending transfer of legal title was always on the buyer. Under the "Uniform Statute," which New York has adopted, the risk of loss is only on those buyers who have possession or legal title when the loss occurs. Raplee (P) is in the same position under either law: he must take the damaged property and pay the full purchase price. The important point here, however, is that Raplee (P) is entitled to a credit on that purchase price for the amount of the insurance proceeds because he and Piper (D) have so agreed. Affirmed.

Dissent: (Burke) The issue here is whether, absent an agreement so providing, a buyer of real property is entitled to have insurance proceeds in the seller's name applied to the purchase price where the contract required the buyer to pay the premiums for the insurance, and the loss occurred while the contract was executory and the buyer was in possession. In *Brownell* this court adopted the doctrine that property insurance runs solely to the named insured and not with the land, and that absent a specific agreement, a buyer is not entitled to a seller's insurance proceeds because they are not part of the thing bargained for and no trust exists in regard to them. The legislature knew the court adopted this view and that it was a minority view, but nonetheless found it sound and did not amend it. Since *Brownell*, only two cases have addressed this issue, and they reached opposite conclusions. One of those cases was *Persico*, which rests on the theory that the seller was a trustee of the insurance proceeds because he was trustee of the legal title to the property after the signing of the contract. This case, based on this erroneous theory, is not sound authority for the majority opinion. The other cases the majority cites predate *Brownell* and therefore are not a sound basis for altering it. The majority suggests that we consider the contract insured for the benefit of both parties. However, *Brownell* rejected this position, and instead found insurance to be a personal contract to protect the interest of the insured. Insurance runs to the individual, not with the land. The seller and the buyer both have an interest in the land to protect, and each may protect himself. The court should adhere to the rule *Brownell* established.

Analysis:

The majority here takes the position that if a seller obtains insurance for himself, he can keep any proceeds from his policy, but if the buyer obtains insurance for the seller pursuant to the contract, then the seller must give the buyer a credit for the amount of any proceeds he receives. The majority's rationale is that it would be unjust not to allow the buyer to benefit from the insurance he bought pursuant to the contract. Justice requires giving effect to the buyer's reasonable expectation of a benefit from fulfilling his contractual obligation to buy the insurance. The majority also wants to avoid unjustly enriching the seller at the buyer's expense, especially where that unjust enrichment would be so extreme as to leave the seller with double recovery and the buyer paying for everything and receiving a burnt hole in the ground. The dissent, on the other hand, considers insurance policies personal to the insured unless the contract provides otherwise. Since neither the contract nor the insurance policy expressly gave the buyer a right to the proceeds, the dissent would not compel the seller to do so.

State ex rel. Indiana State Bar Association v. Indiana Real Estate Association, Inc.

(Lawyers) v. (Brokers)
244 Ind. 214, 191 N.E.2d 711 (1963)

M E M O R Y   G R A P H I C

Instant Facts

The Brokers (D) fill in standard legal forms for their clients' real estate transactions, and the Bar (P) considers this practicing law without a license.

Black Letter Rule

Generally, a layman's filling in blanks on standard, attorney-prepared legal forms does not constitute the practice of law where it requires only common knowledge about the information to be inserted in the blanks and general knowledge about the legal consequences involved.

Case Vocabulary

BARRISTERS: Lawyers who can argue before the high British courts; a trial attorney.
SCRIVENERS: Professional writer of documents such as deeds and contracts.
SOLICITORS: Lawyers who perform all legal tasks for clients except represent them before the high British courts.

Procedural Basis: Action for injunctive relief against the unlawful practice of law.

Facts: The Indiana State Bar Association (the Bar) (P) brought this action to enjoin members of the Indiana Real Estate Association, Inc. (the Brokers) (D) and all licensed real estate brokers and salesmen from the unlawful practice of law. The Brokers (D) use legal forms and documents prepared by attorneys in connection with real estate transactions, selecting which forms to use and inserting language into the forms. Although they admit using the forms, the Brokers (D) deny that they are giving legal advice by doing so. The Brokers (D) state that they do not prepare documents for the real estate transactions, but merely fill in the blanks on preprinted forms, and argue that this does not constitute the practice of law. The Brokers (D) argue that attorneys have prepared all the forms they use, and that although the Bar (P) has not approved every form, the Brokers (D) have used them since 1950, when the Bar (P) not only agreed to such use, but also agreed to "approve and promulgate" other forms for such use. The Bar (P) and the Brokers (D) first made this agreement in 1942, and amended it in 1950. According to this agreement, the Brokers (D) could not prepare documents fixing the legal rights of parties to a transaction. However, they could use an earnest money contract form to protect either party against unreasonable withdrawal from the transaction as long as the Bar (P) and the Brokers (D) in that locality approved and promulgated that form, and any other standard legal forms the broker used, for such use. Although the Bar (P) never drafted, approved and promulgated these "other standard legal forms," the Brokers (D) argue that the Bar (P) has impliedly approved the forms they use.

Issue: Does all use, selection, and filling in blanks of standard legal forms by real estate brokers in connection with their clients' real estate transactions constitute an unauthorized practice of law?

Decision and Rationale: (Achor) No. The law is not an exact science, the practice of which we can unequivocally define. The exigencies of the particular situation sometimes cause changes in the limits of this practice. For example, lay persons can now represent clients before tax courts, where formerly only attorneys could appear. There is a twilight zone between the activity that is permitted to the layman and that which is forbidden. Generally, where standard, attorney-prepared legal forms require only common knowledge about the information to be inserted in the blanks and general knowledge about the legal consequences involved, filling in those blanks does not constitute the practice of law. However, where filling in the blanks involves considerations of significant legal refinement, or the legal consequences of the act are of great significance to the parties, then we may restrict such practice to members of the Bar (P). As the court explained in *Lowell Bar Association v. Loeb* [discusses difficulties in defining the "practice of law"], actual community practices influence the scope of the practice of law. While there are some instruments that only an attorney should draw, there are others that, though fraught with substantial legal consequences, laymen commonly draw for other laymen. Not every transaction that requires the selection and use of written legal forms also requires a lawyer. Such a restriction would paralyze business activities, especially activities like real estate transactions, which frequently occur outside normal office hours. Although the Bar (P) has expressed great concern about the consequences of allowing laymen to fill in the blanks of legal forms, the possibility of an occasional improvident act in using the forms cannot reasonably be the basis for denying the right to do so in the majority of instances where public necessity and convenience would seem to require it.

After all, even lawyers, on rare occasions, make mistakes The legislature has established a procedure for qualifying real estate brokers and salesmen to safeguard the public in real estate transactions. We should try to reconcile the overlapping services which both the Brokers (D) and the Bar (P) perform. Most states that have addressed brokers' use of forms incidental to their business have allowed this practice. In *Hulse v. Criger* [set limits for brokers' use of forms], the court described limits for brokers' use of forms which, excepting those for the execution of deeds, we now follow. The court permits brokers to fill in blanks on standard forms, prepared or approved by counsel, for contracts, notes, chattel mortgages and short term leases. The broker may select the lawyer that will prepare or approve the form. The court prohibits brokers from charging their clients for completing the forms; from giving advice or opinions about their clients' legal rights or the effect of the forms; and from seeking information from their clients, beyond that which is necessary to fill in the blanks on the forms, for the purpose of advising them about their rights or conduct. We find these limits wise and adopt them to this extent. However, while *Hulse* permits brokers to fill in forms for

deeds, we do not. Because the execution of a deed usually occurs at the parties' convenience, follows the finalizing of the agreement and the examination of title by an attorney, and often involves life savings or years of income, we see no reason of time or convenience not to require a person skilled in the practice of law to accomplish it. We therefore hold that the Brokers (D) may, within the limits we described, fill in the blanks of forms prepared by attorneys for contracts, options, and leases, but that they may not execute deeds or legal instruments other than those we have specified. Injunction granted in part and denied in part.

Concurrence: (Arterburn) I agree with the majority opinion. I write because as a lawyer I must say that from a public relations viewpoint, the Bar (P) should never have instituted this action. This type of work does not produce much income for lawyers anyway, and the public reaction to cases like these can be drastic. In one state, the reaction led to a constitutional amendment. They should have left well enough alone. We must be practical.

Analysis:

The purpose underlying restrictions on the practice of law is the protection of the public. In this case, the court attempts to balance the protection of the public against the convenience of the public. As the court notes here, brokers may be more "convenient" in the short term because they may be more accessible than many lawyers. However, because real estate transactions are often among the most important transactions in a person's life, generally involving substantial legal rights and duties and a large proportion of his resources and income, the consequences of errors can be very great. The long term "inconvenience" of errors involving such substantial rights and assets as are involved in real estate transactions can easily outweigh the short term convenience of weekend office hours for the individual affected, and perhaps also in the aggregate, for the public as a whole. Further, while a broker may be able to get real estate documents done quickly, he has a personal interest in doing so that is disturbing. If delay and close scrutiny cause the deal to fall through, the broker loses his commission. Even where he can recognize potential legal issues or problems for one of the parties, the broker, personally, has much to gain and little to risk by moving things along. Often, though, the broker will not be able to recognize potential legal issues. Here, the court states that where filling in the blanks involves considerations of significant legal refinement, or the legal consequences of the act are of great significance to the parties, then it may restrict such practice to attorneys. Where, on the other hand, filling in the blanks requires only common, general knowledge about the law and the information to be inserted, then the court finds attorneys unnecessary. The need for protection may not seem great when a broker only fills in a "simple" contract form. If the blanks in the forms at issue involve information that is straightforward and requires no exercise of discretion (i.e., names, price, date and location of closing), the danger to the parties may not be great. However, a contract that may seem simple to a layman may not really be so. Without a certain level of training in issues that may arise in real estate contracts, how could a layman even recognize whether such issues exist in a particular transaction? The contract may seem simple to a layman only because he does not have sufficient training to see its complexity. Thus, being unacquainted with all the possible legal consequences of certain acts, a broker may find it difficult to know when "considerations of significant legal refinement" are involved in a particular real estate transaction. Some courts answer this concern by suggesting that a broker include a provision in the contract that makes it subject to approval by each party's attorney. New Jersey requires such a safeguard. It allows its brokers not only to fill in the blanks on standard forms, but also to negotiate and draft real estate contracts. However, it requires that those contracts be subject to a "three day attorney review" period, during which a party's attorney may cancel the contract. Different states have struck the balance between the public's protection and convenience at different points on the spectrum. Interestingly, in some cases it is exactly the public's ignorance of potential legal issues that may ultimately strike the balance more toward convenience than protection. The case in Arizona, which the concurring opinion mentioned here, serves as an example. The court there, recognizing the potential hazards, almost totally restricted broker activity with legal documents in real estate transactions. The public responded by reversing course through a constitutional amendment. [Many people prefer making their own mistakes to paternalistic court protections. Never mind if father knows best.]

Tristram's Landing, Inc. v. Wait

(Broker) v. (Seller)
367 Mass. 622, 327 N.E.2d 727 (1975)

M E M O R Y   G R A P H I C

Instant Facts

Van der Wolk (P) produced a buyer for Wait (D), but the buyer failed to consummate the sale, and Wait (D) therefore refused to pay Van der Wolk's (P) commission.

Black Letter Rule

Absent default or interference by the seller, a broker earns his commission only when he produces a buyer who is ready, willing and able to buy the property on the seller's terms *and* consummates the sale.

Procedural Basis: Appeal from judgment after bench trial of breach of contract action for damages.

Facts: Van der Wolk (P), a real estate broker, heard that Wait (D) wanted to sell her property and asked her for authority to show it. Wait (D) agreed to let Van der Wolk (P) act as broker, though not as exclusive broker, and told him that the price for her property was $110,000. They did not discuss the commission, but Wait (D) knew that the normal commission in the area was 5% of the purchase price. Van der Wolk (P) located Cashman, a prospective buyer who offered $100,000 for the property. Wait (D) made a counteroffer of $105,000, which Cashman accepted, and Van der Wolk (P) drew up a contract. Cashman executed the contract and gave it to Van der Wolk (P) with a check for $10,500 as down payment. Van der Wolk (P) gave the contract to Wait (D), and after she signed it, he also gave her the down payment. Wait (D) appeared for closing, but Cashman did not, and later refused to buy the property. Wait (D) did not try to enforce the agreement, but did keep the down payment. Van der Wolk (P) then billed Wait (D) for his commission of $5,250. Wait (D) refused to pay. Van der Wolk (P) brought this action to recover his commission. The parties never discussed Van der Wolk's (P) commission, and the only reference to it is in the contract with Cashman, which states that the 5% commission "on the said sale" would be paid by the seller. Van der Wolk (P) argues that he is entitled to his commission because he produced a buyer who was ready, willing and able to buy the property and who was accepted by Wait (D). Wait (D) argues that Van der Wolk (P) earned no commission because Cashman did not consummate the sale.

Issue: Is a broker entitled to his commission if he produces a buyer who is ready, willing and able to buy the property and who is accepted by the seller, but who ultimately does not consummate the sale?

Decision and Rationale: (Tauro) No. The general rule is that a broker is entitled to a commission if he produces a buyer who is ready, willing and able to buy property on the terms the seller gave the broker. Past decisions have construed this rule to mean that once a broker produces a buyer who is accepted by the seller, he has earned his commission, whether or not the buyer consummates the sale. A seller's execution of a contract for sale is usually considered conclusive evidence of the seller's acceptance of the buyer. However, we have also held that a seller is not helpless to protect himself from these consequences. A seller may, by appropriate language in his dealings with the broker, limit his liability for the commission to when the buyer consummates the sale and pays for the property. Here, we believe Van der Wolk (P) is not entitled to a commission. We cannot construe the contract here as an unconditional acceptance of Cashman by Wait (D) because the contract itself contained conditional language. The contract also provided that the commission was to be paid "on the said sale," and we construe that language as requiring the consummation of the sale before the commission is due. Further, we now join the growing minority of states who have adopted the rule of *Ellsworth Dobbs, Inc. v. Johnson* [broker does not earn a commission if his buyer defaults and does not consummate the sale]. In *Ellsworth*, the court noted that ordinarily when a seller lists his property with a broker, he expects that the money for the broker's commission will come out of the proceeds of the sale. The seller wants the broker to find someone who will buy his house and pay for it, not just someone who will sign a contract. The court further stated that the principle that binds a seller to pay a commission if he signs a contract with the broker's customer, regardless of that customer's ability to pay, puts the burden on the wrong shoulders. Since the broker's duty is to produce a buyer who is able to pay the purchase price, the seller has a right to assume that the buyer the broker produces has that ability to pay. Reason and justice dictate that the broker bear the burden of producing a buyer who is not only ready, willing and able to buy the property at the time of negotiations, but who will also consummate the sale at the time of closing. In *Ellsworth* the court therefore held that when a seller engages a broker to find a buyer for his property, the broker earns his commission only when (a) he produces a buyer who is ready, willing and able to buy the property on the terms the owner fixed; (b) the buyer enters into a binding contract with the seller to do so; *and* (c) the buyer completes the transaction by closing the title according to the terms of the contract. If the buyer defaults and does not consummate the sale, the broker has no right to a commission from the seller. If, on the other hand, the sale fails due to the wrongful act or interference by the seller, then the seller must pay the broker's commission. We now adopt this rule. We recognize that contract language can easily circumvent this rule. Many states require a signed writing for an agreement to pay a commission to a broker. Though the legislature may consider such a requirement, we do not establish one here. Informal agreements can be useful. However, courts should carefully scrutinize agreements in which an unsophisticated seller agrees to pay a broker a commission even if the buyer defaults. If not fairly made, the court may find such agreements unconscionable or against public policy. Reversed.

Analysis:

Under the traditional, majority rule, a broker has earned his commission when he has produced a buyer who is ready, willing and able to buy the property at the seller's terms. "Able," here, refers not only to the buyer's competence to form a contract, but, more important, his financial capacity to perform it. In fact, early cases in many jurisdictions required a broker to establish that the buyer he procured was financially able to perform the contract before he can recover his commission. However, other cases, including early New Jersey cases, held that the seller's execution of a contract for sale was evidence that he accepted the buyer and that the broker had therefore earned his commission. In this way, courts placed the burden on the seller to inquire into the broker's financial ability to pay. Once he accepted the buyer and signed the contract, the issue of the buyer's ability to pay became irrelevant for commission purposes. In *Ellsworth*, the New Jersey Supreme Court departed from this approach and set forth what is presently the minority rule, which this case and many others follow. Under this rule, the broker does not earn his commission until the sale closes, unless it is wrongdoing or interference by the seller that prevents the closing. This rule allows the seller to assume that when a broker produces a buyer, that buyer will have the financial ability to complete the contract, and he need not make an independent investigation into the buyer's financial capacity. [After all, what is he paying the broker for?]

Chapter 24

The deed is the most common method for conveying real estate. It's a written document that developed from the common law. Hundreds of years ago in England, a writing was not required to convey real estate. The transferor and the transferee stood on the land with a few witnesses, and the transferor handed the transferee a twig or a handful of dirt, said some magic words, and left the property to the transferee. This ceremony was called livery of seisin.

In 1677, the Statute of Frauds was enacted in England and a written document to convey real estate was required. The United States quickly abandoned the common law ceremony described above and used deeds to convey real estate.

While deeds vary quite a bit, the essential elements of a valid deed are the identity of the parties, a description of the land, words indicating the grantor's present intent to transfer the property, and the grantor's signature. Seems pretty simple, but as you'll see in this chapter, things often go awry.

The legal description of the property seems to cause a lot of problems. There are different ways to identify the property to be conveyed in the deed and lots of ways the description may be ambiguous. Thus, the courts have developed rules for construing legal descriptions. For example, a reference to a highway or a river takes precedence over a reference to acreage. Ultimately, though, these rules are trumped once the court determines the parties' intent.

Chapter 24

NOTE: THE PURPOSE OF THIS OUTLINE IS TO ORGANIZE THE CASES SO THAT ONE CAN QUICKLY UNDERSTAND THE RELEVANCE OF EACH CASE TO THE COURSE. NO ATTEMPT IS MADE IN THIS OVERVIEW TO ADDRESS EVERY CONCEPT THAT MUST BE STUDIED. BE SURE TO READ THE ENTIRE CASEBOOK AND/OR OTHER MATERIALS TO GAIN A FULL UNDERSTANDING OF ALL CONCEPTS.

I. Common Law Conveyances
A. At common law, a change in ownership of land had to be in the form of a ceremony called "livery of seisin." On the land, the "feoffer" gave the "feoffee" a stick or piece of dirt and said that he gives the feoffee and his heirs the estate at issue. The feoffer then left the land and the feoffee took possession.
  1. Livery in deed occurred when the livery of seisin took place on the land itself.
  2. Livery in law was made when the parties were not actually on the land, but were in sight of it.
  3. A writing was used to commemorate the livery of seisin, not to actually convey the land.
B. A writing became required when the Statute of Frauds was enacted in 1677.
C. The Statute of Uses was passed in 1535. It created new ways to convey property that did not require livery of seisin.
  1. A covenant to stand seised was a promise to hold land for another who is related by blood or marriage.
  2. A bargain and sale deed was a conveyance of land stating that the vendor had bargained and sold the land to the buyer, thereby vesting equitable ownership and legal ownership in the buyer.
D. To prevent secret conveyances, parliament passed the Statute of Enrollments, which voided a bargain and sale deed unless it was publically recorded.
  1. To avoid public notice, the aristocracy used "lease and release" deeds. Under these deeds, the grantor executed a lease to the grantee and a release of the reversion to the grantee.
E. Most of the states in the U.S. adopted statutes allowing title to transfer by deeds, rather than

by livery of seisin.
  1. However, early courts held that common law methods of conveying property survive statutes specifying what must be in a deed. *French v. French*.

II. The Modern Deed
A. Bargain and sale deeds are extensively used in the U.S.
B. There are two types of deeds.
  1. In a warranty deed, the grantor usually covenants that he has complete title in the property or sets forth the known encumbrances.
  2. In a quitclaim deed, the grantor conveys only the interest that he has and does not imply that he has good title.
C. A deed must contain certain elements, including:
  1. Identification of the parties.
  2. Description of the land.
  3. Words indicating the grantor's present intent to transfer the property.
  4. The grantor's signature.
D. A traditional deed contains the following parts:
  1. The "premises" identifies the parties, states the consideration, describes the land, and includes the granting clause.
  2. The "habendum" clause limits the estate being granted.
  3. The "reddendum" clause includes any reservation the grantor may want to make.
E. There are certain rules of construction for deeds.
  1. If a deed is ambiguous and the parties' intent cannot be determined, a court should rule in favor of the grantee. *First National Bank of Oregon v. Townsend*.
  2. If a deed's granting clause conflicts with other parts of the deed and the parties' intent cannot be determined, the estate conveyed in the granting clause should prevail. *First National Bank of Oregon v. Townsend*.
  3. When a granting clause and a habendum clause are inconsistent, the court tries to determine the parties' intent based on the deed as a whole. *Grayson v. Holloway*.
  4. If a grantor left the name of the grantee blank on a deed and authorized the grantee

to fill in a name, the grantee has the irrevocable power to do so. *Womack v. Stegner*.

5. Contrary to the common law rule, a grantor may reserve an interest in property for a third party. *Willard v. First Church of Christ, Scientist, Pacifica*.

III. Execution of the Deed

A. At common law, the grantor's seal was required to make a deed valid. Today, the grantor's signature is required.

B. "Attestation" is the witnesses' signature on the deed to assure its authenticity. Some states require it and some states do not.

C. "Acknowledgment" is an attestation by a notary public or justice of the peace.

D. An escrow is the deposit of the deed with a third party pending performance of any conditions, such as payment of the purchase price, or approval of the abstract of title.

1. A conveyance is effective when all the conditions are met and the grantee is entitled to delivery of the deed.

2. The date of the conveyance may relate back to the date of the original deposit in escrow under certain circumstances, such as the grantor's death, to avoid grantor's widow's dower, the grantor's incompetency, the grantee's death, and to avoid a conveyance by the grantor to a third party.

3. There cannot be a valid conditional delivery of the deed directly to the grantee. Complete title is passed to the grantee upon delivery to the grantee. *Pai v. Thom*.

4. Some courts hold that a deed that is wrongly delivered out of escrow is void. The grantee of such a deed has no title to pass to an innocent purchaser. *Clevenger v. Moore*.

5. The escrow holder's duties are set forth in the escrow agreement and are strictly construed. *Miller v. Craig*.

IV. Legal Descriptions of Land

A. The legal description in a deed identifies the land that is being conveyed.

B. There are three main ways of describing property in a deed.

1. The metes and bounds system prevails in the original states. It is based on a discoverable starting point, followed by descriptions of each boundary line in succession. Lines may be defined by direction and distance, by a call to a monument or to an adjacent tract of land.

    a. Natural monuments include trees, rivers, and lakes.

    b. Artificial monuments include highways, buildings, and markers.

2. The Rectangular Survey Method is used by the government in states carved from the Northwest Territory and states acquired later. It is based on square townships, six miles on a side, and square sections, one mile on a side with systematic adjustments for the curvature of the earth.

3. The plat system involves a subdivision map created by the developer and approved by the local government.

C. A legal description of property is sufficient if the particular tract at issue matches the description and no other property could match it. *Bybee v. Hageman*.

D. Extrinsic evidence of the parties' intent is not admissible if a deed's legal description is not ambiguous. *Walter v. Tucker*.

E. The general rule is that, in determining boundaries, courts look to descriptions in the following hierarchy: natural objects or landmarks; artificial monuments; adjacent boundaries; courses and distances; and area.

1. However, some courts hold that in construing a legal description, the location of a monument does not necessarily control over a course or distance; the parties' intent controls. *Pritchard v. Rebori*.

2. A boundary is presumed to go to the middle of a monument, such as a highway, unless the parties' intent clearly indicates otherwise. *Parr v. Worley*.

French v. French

(Father) v. (Son)
3 N.H. 234 (1825)

M E M O R Y   G R A P H I C

Instant Facts

A father and a son contested ownership of a farm conveyed from the son to the father by a deed. The son argued the deed was invalid under a statute requiring two witnesses and that the statute was the exclusive means of conveying property.

Black Letter Rule

Common law methods of conveying property survive statutes specifying what must be in a deed.

Case Vocabulary

BARGAIN AND SALE: A conveyance of land stating that the vendor had bargained and sold the land to the buyer, thereby vesting equitable ownership and legal ownership in the buyer.

CESTUI QUE TRUST: Latin for the beneficiary or donee of a trust.

COVENANT TO STAND SEISED: A promise to hold land for another who is related by blood or marriage.

FEOFFMENT: A conveyance of a corporeal interest in land by delivery of possession through a ceremony on or within view of the land.

GRANT: At common law, a conveyance of an incorporeal interest in land which did not require the ceremony of a feoffment.

HEREDITAMENTS: Property capable of being inherited.

LEASE: A grant of land for a certain period of time.

LIVERY OF SEISIN: The delivery of property into another's actual possession: in the case of a house, by giving him the ring, latch, or key; in the case of land, by giving him a twig, a piece of dirt, or the like.

RELEASE: A grant of a reversion that arises after the period of time set forth in a lease.

Procedural Basis: Writ of entry for seisin of land.

Facts: George French (D) signed a deed in which he agreed to convey to Andrew French (P), his father, an interest in a farm. One person signed the deed as a witness. A local statute required deeds to have two witnesses. George (D) argued the deed was invalid under the statute and the statute was the exclusive means of conveying property. Andrew (P) filed a petition for a writ of entry for seisin of the land.

Issue: Do the common law methods of conveying property survive a statute specifying what must be in a deed?

Decision and Rationale: (Richardson, C.J.) Yes. We agree that the law requires two witnesses. But the idea that a deed that does not comply with the statute is invalid is so repugnant that we have to take a look at it. At common law, property was transferred by feoffments and grants. The statute of uses introduced two new ways to convey land: (1) bargains and sales and (2) covenants to stand seised. Under a bargain and sale agreement, the seller contracts to sell the land and then receives the purchase money. The buyer then becomes the legal owner of the land, whereas without the statute of uses, under the law of livery, the buyer would own only an equitable interest in the land. Under a covenant to stand seised, a person owning land promises to hold it for another who is related by blood or marriage. Particular words are not required to create this conveyance. Statutes recognize feoffments and bargain and sales agreements as valid modes of conveyance. George (D) argues that a clause in a statute abolishes all the former modes of conveying real estate other than that set forth in the statute. It says that "no deed of bargain and sale, mortgage, or other conveyance, & c. shall be good and effectual in law to hold such lands, tenements, or hereditaments, against any other person or persons, but the grantor or grantors, and their heirs only, unless the deed or deeds thereof be acknowledged and recorded in manner aforesaid." We do not see any indication that the legislature intended to abolish all former ways of conveying property. In construing statutes, it is well settled that affirmative words do not take away the common law unless the affirmative words contain a negative. In fact, the statute recognizes bargains and sales and other conveyances and provides that they will not be valid against third parties unless recorded. The statute was meant to take away the need for livery of seisin and to substitute a deed in its place. While bargain and sale agreements and covenants to stand seised are invalid without a statute of uses, current law implicitly recognizes the adoption of a statute of uses by recognizing these types of conveyances. The deed here may be construed as a covenant to stand seised and convey the land irrespective of the statute requiring two witnesses. The consideration is the blood relationship between George (D) and Andrew (P). Judgment for Andrew (P).

Analysis:

While this case is particularly hard to read, the holding is fairly simple. Under the common law, property was conveyed through "feoffments," "bargains and sales" and "covenants to stand seised." The common law required ceremonies on the land, called livery of seisin, where the grantor handed a twig or dirt to the grantee, in order to convey the land. Although this sounds a little strange, the ceremony was clear and unambiguous. Everyone knew when land was transferred. Deeds, however, are private and can be secretive. Thus, recording statutes were enacted, requiring a deed to be recorded in order for third parties to be bound by it. You'll learn more about that in the next chapter. The statute at issue here did not specifically repeal the prior law, it just added another way to convey property. The court held that the deed was a valid covenant to stand seised.

First National Bank of Oregon v. Townsend

(Grantee's Representative) v. (Grantor)
27 Or. App. 103, 555 P.2d 477 (1976)

M E M O R Y   G R A P H I C

Instant Facts

An ambiguous deed appeared to convey both a fee simple and the right to remove timber and minerals from the land.

Black Letter Rule

(1) If a deed is ambiguous and the parties' intent cannot be determined, a court should rule in favor of the grantee. (2) If a deed's granting clause conflicts with other parts of the deed and the parties' intent cannot be determined, the estate conveyed in the granting clause should prevail.

Case Vocabulary

ESCHEAT: The reversion of property to the state or county in cases where a decedent dies intestate without heirs capable of inheriting, or when the property is abandoned.

Procedural Basis: Appeal of declaratory judgment regarding a deed.

Facts: Claude Miller died in 1974. The First National Bank of Oregon (the Bank) (P) was Miller's personal representative. A deed was found among Miller's personal effects dated 1955 from John Townsend (D) which in one part seemed to convey a fee simple estate to Miller (P). In another part of the deed, Townsend (D) seemed to convey only the right to remove timber and minerals from the property. If the deed conveyed a fee simple, the land was included in Miller's estate. If the deed conveyed only the timber and mineral rights, Townsend (D) retained the underlying fee. Townsend (D) is deceased and has no know heirs. Thus any property in Townsend's (D) estate escheats to the State of Oregon (D). The Bank (P) sued Townsend's estate (D) for a declaratory judgment that the deed conveyed a fee simple. Oregon (D) argued that the deed conveyed only timber and mineral rights because the deed was called a "timber and mineral deed" and because the consideration recited referred to trees and minerals removed from "his" land which indicated that Townsend (D) intended to retain title. In addition, Oregon (D) argued, if a fee simple were conveyed, no mention of timber and minerals would be necessary. The Bank (P) argued that the granting clause conveyed the tract of land to Miller, his heirs and assigns. The Bank (P) also argued that the deed required Miller, his heirs and assigns, to pay taxes on the property, and warranted quiet, peaceable, and exclusive possession to Miller. The lower court held that the deed conveyed a fee simple to Miller.

Issue: (1) When a deed is ambiguous and the parties' intent cannot be determined, should a court rule in favor of the grantee? (2) If a deed's granting clause conflicts with other parts of the deed and the parties' intent cannot be determined, should the estate conveyed in the granting clause prevail?

Decision and Rationale: (Tanzer, J.) (1) Yes. (2) Yes. Where a deed is ambiguous, the court must determine the parties' intent from the language of the entire deed and from the surrounding circumstances. However, here there is no extrinsic evidence available and the deed's language is contradictory. Where there is doubt about the parties' intent, the doubt should be resolved in favor of the grantee and the greater estate should pass. This avoids fragmented ownership and deters quiet title suits. In addition, if the parties' intent cannot be determined, the estate conveyed in the granting clause should prevail. Both of these rules support the conclusion that Townsend (D) conveyed a fee simple to Miller. In addition, the law does not favor escheat. Affirmed.

Analysis:

It's a common occurrence for a deed to be poorly drafted and confusing. Thus, this case sets forth various rules of construction that help determine how an ambiguous deed should be interpreted. First and foremost, the court should look at the parties' intent. Where, as here, the parties are dead and no evidence of their intent is available, the larger estate should be granted. Thus, the grantee usually wins. This makes sense when you consider that the grantor usually drafts the deed, and ambiguities in a document are usually interpreted against the drafter. However, if a deed is so ambiguous, a court may declare it void. In that case, the grantor would win. In the next case, *Grayson v. Holloway*, you'll see that the court did not apply the other rule of construction applied by this court, i.e., that the estate conveyed in the granting clause prevails.

Grayson v. Holloway

(Grantee's Heirs) v. (Grantee's Wife)
203 Tenn. 464, 313 S.W.2d 555 (1958)

M E M O R Y   G R A P H I C

Instant Facts

Heirs of a grantee claimed a deed conveyed land only to him, whereas the grantee's wife claimed the deed conveyed the land to her too.

Black Letter Rule

When a granting clause and a habendum clause are inconsistent, the court tries to determine the parties' intent based on the deed as a whole.

Case Vocabulary

DOWER: A life estate for a widow in the real estate owned by her husband during the marriage.
HABENDUM: Latin for "to have;" the clause in a deed that sets forth the type of estate being conveyed.
HOMESTEAD: A place of residence in which the security of the family can be maintained against the rights of creditors. Each spouse has a separate and undivided possessory interest in the homestead property.
PARTITION: A court action to divide property, usually taken when a property is jointly owned and a dispute arises about how to divide it.

Procedural Basis: Appeal of action granting sale and partition of land.

Facts: A.J. and Manerva Holloway were old and needed a caretaker. They executed a deed conveying 70 acres in exchange for taking care of A.J. and Manerva until their death and paying their funeral and burial expenses. The granting clause provided that the deed was to G.P. Holloway, but the habendum clause ran to G.P. and Mae Holloway (D). At G.P.'s death, his heirs (P) claimed title of the land subject to Mae's (D) homestead and dower rights. They sued Mae (D) for sale and partition of the land. Mae (D) claimed full title, arguing that she took care of A.J. and Minerva until their death. She also argued that A.J. and Minerva intended to deed the property to G.P. and Mae (D) so that when one of them died the title would vest in the survivor. The trial court held that the granting clause prevailed over the inconsistent habendum clause and held for G.P.'s heirs (P).

Issue: Does a granting clause prevail over an inconsistent habendum clause?

Decision and Rationale: (Neil, J.) No. The trial court was required to look at the entire deed to determine the grantors' intent. The deed shows that A.J. and Minerva contemplated that both G.P. and Mae (D) would render personal services. G.P. alone could not have taken care of them. It was necessary that Mae (D) cook and clean for them. These are duties that usually belong to the wife. Reversed.

Analysis:

This case contradicts the previous case, *First National Bank of Oregon v. Townsend*, to a certain extent. In that case, the court held that if a deed's granting clause conflicts with other parts of the deed and the parties' intent cannot be determined, the estate conveyed in the granting clause should prevail. However, here, there was evidence of the parties' intent. Mae (D) argued that A.J. and Minerva said that they were going to convey the property to both G.P. and Mae (D). And the court added its own [sexist?] suggestion that only a wife would be able to take care of the elderly couple. Thus, we see that the rule of construction providing that the granting clause prevails has been increasingly rejected. Indeed, most canons of construction yield to evidence of the parties' intent. Most courts today look at the parties' intent based on the language of the deed itself and extrinsic evidence.

Womack v .Stegner

(Grantee) v. (Heir of Grantor's Wife)

293 S.W.2d 124 (1956)

M E M O R Y   G R A P H I C

Instant Facts

Parties disputed whether a deed that left the name of the grantee blank was valid.

Black Letter Rule

If a grantor left the name of the grantee blank on a deed and authorized the grantee to fill in a name, the grantee has the irrevocable power to do so.

Case Vocabulary

DELIVERY: The transfer of a deed from the grantor to the grantee in such a manner as to deprive the grantor of the right to recall it. In modern times it is any act that indicates the grantor's intent that a deed be presently operative.

INSTRUCTIVE VERDICT: A judge's instruction to a jury to return a particular verdict, usually because the plaintiff has not proven a prima facie case.

Procedural Basis: Appeal of instructed verdict in suit in trespass to try title.

Facts: W.B. Womack signed a deed conveying the mineral rights in certain land to his brother D.R. Womack (P). The deed was complete except for the name of the grantee. When W.B. died, the mineral rights would have passed to his wife, Louise, but for the deed to D.R. (P). Louise died, leaving her property to her brother Stegner (D). D.R. (P) sued Stegner (D) to determine title to the mineral rights. At trial, D.R. (P) testified that W.B. gave him the deed as a gift and authorized him to fill in any name as the grantee. At the close of D.R.'s (P) evidence at trial, Stegner (D) made a motion for an instructed verdict, which the court granted.

Issue: Is a deed valid if the grantor left the name of the grantee blank and authorized the grantee to fill in the name?

Decision and Rationale: (Hamilton, C.J.) Yes. When a grantor delivers a deed with the name of the grantee in blank, with the intention that the title shall vest in the person to whom the deed is delivered, and that person is authorized to insert the name of the grantee, title passes with the delivery. The grantee is vested with an irrevocable power to fill in the grantee's name coupled with an interest. The fact that W.B. died before D.R. (P) filled in a name is irrelevant. D.R.'s (P) power was irrevocable and did not terminate with W.B.'s death. Equitable title passed to D.R. (P) when W.B. delivered the deed. The deed did not have to be supported by consideration to be valid. Reversed and remanded for a new trial.

Analysis:

The grantee's name is an essential element of a deed. Courts have held that in a situation such as this one, the deed is void until a grantee's name is inserted. However, the name may be inserted at any time, even years after the grantor has died. A deed to a grantee who does not exist is void. But courts may attempt to determine the grantor's intent and reform the deed accordingly.

Willard v. First Church of Christ, Scientist, Pacifica

(Property Owner) v. (Third Party)
7 Cal. 3d 473, 102 Cal. Rptr. 739, 498 P.2d 987 (1972)

M E M O R Y   G R A P H I C

 Instant Facts

A purchaser of a lot sought to invalidate an easement for church parking.

Black Letter Rule

Contrary to the common law rule, a grantor may reserve an interest in property for a third party.

Case Vocabulary

CONVEYANCE BY DEED: Transferring property by a written document for the transfer of land or other real property from one person to another.

Procedural Basis: Appeal of quiet title action.

Facts: Genevieve McGuigan owned two adjacent lots, lots 19 and 20, across the street from the First Church of Christ, Scientist (Church) (D). Lot 19 contained a building and lot 20 was vacant. McGuigan let the Church (D) use lot 20 for parking. She sold lot 19 to Petersen. Willard (P) expressed an interest in buying both lot 19 and lot 20 from Petersen. Petersen delivered a deed for both lots into escrow, and then approached McGuigan with an offer to purchase lot 20. McGuigan was willing to sell lot 20, so long as the Church (D) could continue to use it for parking. The Church's (D) attorney drew up a provision for the deed, and McGuigan sold the property to Petersen, who recorded the deed. [Not surprisingly] The deed from Petersen to Willard (P) did not mention the Church's (D) parking easement. Petersen apparently told Willard (P) that the Church (D) wanted to use lot 20 for parking, but did not tell him about the easement clause in the deed from McGuigan. When Willard (P) learned about the easement clause, he sued the Church (D) in a quiet title action. The trial court held that McGuigan intended to convey an easement to the Church (D) but the clause was invalid under the common law because one cannot reserve a property interest for a third party. The Church (D) appealed.

Issue: May a grantor reserve an interest in property for a third party?

Decision and Rationale: (Peters, J.) Yes. A grantor may reserve an interest in property for a third party. The common law prohibition was based on the mistrust of conveyance by deed and the desire for livery by seisin. This mistrust is out of date. Now we are concerned with trying to follow the grantor's intention. Grants are now interpreted like contracts rather than based on rigid feudal standards. To deny McGuigan her intent would be inequitable because she discounted the price she charged Petersen by about one-third for the easement. Other courts have either circumvented or abolished the common law rule. Willard (P) argues that the common law rule should be applied here because title insurers and he himself relied on it. However, he has presented no evidence that a title insurance policy was issued. In addition, he himself did not read the deed containing the reservation. The Church (D) used the lot for parking before and after Willard (P) acquired it, so he was not prejudiced by lack of use for an extended period of time. When looking at grants made prior to this decision, we must balance the equitable and policy considerations, including the grantor's intent and reliance on the old rule. Any ambiguity or conflict in the clause granting the right to park to the Church (D) is resolved in favor of the grantor's intent. Reversed.

Analysis:

Courts are about evenly split on the issue in this case. About half the courts have abolished the common law rule prohibiting reserving title for third parties and about half still follow it. The common law prohibition may easily be circumvented if the grantor conveys the easement to the third party first and then conveys the property to the grantee in a separate deed. The court concluded that the common law rule protects the rights of bona fide purchasers and avoids conflicts of ownership. But the question remains that if the common law rule can be circumvented so easily, why keep it? Although this procedure avoids frustrating the grantor's intent, there is no reason to force the grantor to do in two steps what could otherwise be done in one. The common law rule appears to be nothing more than a trap for the unwary and serves only to frustrate the grantor's intent. The common law rule seems to function solely as an obstacle to conveying interests in land, but serves no purpose. This is not a function consistent with our modern preference for effecting the grantor's clear intent.

Clevenger v. Moore

(Duped Grantor) v. (Innocent Purchaser)
126 Okl. 246, 259 P. 219 (1927)

M E M O R Y   G R A P H I C

Instant Facts

An escrow holder was supposed to hold a deed until the grantor approved a property swap; but while the grantor was away, the escrow holder delivered the deed to the grantee, who then conveyed the property to an innocent purchaser.

Black Letter Rule

A deed that is wrongly delivered out of escrow is void. The grantee of such a deed has no title to pass to an innocent purchaser.

Procedural Basis: Appeal of decision granting demurrer in action to cancel deeds.

Facts: Mrs. Clevenger (P) owned a building in Bartlesville. Peay asked her if she would trade the building for an apartment house in Tulsa, owned by Simmons (D). Clevenger (P) executed a deed to Simmons (D) that Peay was supposed to hold until Clevenger (P) inspected the Tulsa property. If she did not like the Tulsa property, Peay was supposed to give her back the deed. She did not like the Tulsa property, but when she returned to town, she discovered that the deed to Simmons (D) had been recorded and that Simmons (D) had executed a deed to Moore (D). Clevenger (P) sued Simmons (D) and Moore (D) to cancel the deeds. Simmons (D) and Moore (D) filed demurrers, which the trial court granted.

Issue: If a deed is wrongly delivered out of escrow, does the grantee of the deed have any title to pass to an innocent purchaser?

Decision and Rationale: (Diffendaffer, C.) No. Clevenger (P) argues that a deed that is placed in escrow and delivered to the grantee before the conditions for delivery are met is void. She also argues that a third party who acquires the property from the grantee has no title. We agree that Clevenger (P) had title as against Simmons (D). But the issues remain whether the deed was absolutely void and whether an innocent purchaser for value of the property could acquire title to it. The law is clear that a deed does not convey title until it is delivered. Our examination of the cases supports Clevenger's (P) claim that the deed was void and that Simmons (D) had no title to pass to Moore (D). Applying the rule that a demurrer admits every fact in the plaintiff's pleadings, we reverse and remand for a new trial.

Analysis:

An "escrow" is a deed or other document held by a third party who is subject to instructions concerning the document. The third party is called the escrow holder. The escrow concept is based on the idea that title cannot pass until all the conditions, such as payment of the purchase price, have been fulfilled. Thus, the deed to Simmons (D) was clearly void because Clevenger (P) had not approved the Tulsa property. But innocent purchasers are usually protected. Assuming Moore (D) had no knowledge of Peay's shenanigans, why should Moore (D) suffer? The court could have awarded Clevenger (P) the monetary value of the property from Simmons (D). Note that delivery of the deed from escrow is not required. Once all the conditions are performed, legal title passes to the purchaser, even though the escrow holder does not actually pass the deed to the purchaser. The necessary element is that all the conditions are met.

Bybee v. Hageman

(Second Mortgagee) v. (First Mortgagee)
66 Ill. 519 (1873)

M E M O R Y   G R A P H I C

Instant Facts

A second mortgagee claimed that the first mortgage was invalid because its legal description of the property was uncertain.

Black Letter Rule

A legal description of property is sufficient if the particular tract at issue matches the description and no other property could match it.

Procedural Basis: Appeal of action granting foreclosure of mortgage.

Facts: Hageman (P) had a mortgage on property owned by John and Elizabeth Ewald (D). The mortgage described the land as being in McDonough county in Illinois. It stated that the property was an acre and a half in the northwest corner of section five, together with the brewery, malthouse, and all buildings and fixtures thereon. The Ewalds (D) obtained a second mortgage from Manly (D) to secure the payment of a promissory note from John Ewald (D) to Manly (D). Manly (D) assigned the note to Bybee (D). Hageman (P) filed an action to foreclose the first mortgage. Bybee (D) filed a cross-action to foreclose the second mortgage. The court foreclosed the first mortgage. Bybee (D) appealed on the ground that the legal description in the first mortgage was void for uncertainty because it did not specify the township or the range.

Issue: Must a legal description of property specify the township or the range?

Decision and Rationale: (Lawrence, C.J.) No. If the description was sufficient, there was record notice of the mortgage to subsequent mortgagees. The ambiguity arises here because there are several section fives in McDonough county. This is a latent ambiguity because it does not arise from the face of the deed. Extrinsic evidence is admissible to explain latent ambiguities. Here the extrinsic evidence is that Ewald (D) was living on the north-west corner of section five, in township six north, and range one west, and that he had a house, malthouse, and brewery there. He had no other brewery. There is no doubt that the description is sufficient. The particular tract at issue matched the description in the mortgage, and no other property could match it. Bybee (D) also argues that "one acre and a half in the northwest corner" is too uncertain because the land could be either a square or a triangle. However, all land was originally surveyed and laid out in rectangular forms, and it is common for subdivisions to be laid out in rectangles too. Affirmed.

Analysis:

There are three main methods for describing property in a deed. The metes and bounds system is used in the original states. It is based on a discoverable starting point, followed by descriptions of each boundary line in succession. Lines may be defined by direction and distance, by a call to a monument or to an adjacent tract of land. The Rectangular Survey Method is used by the government in states carved from the Northwest Territory and states acquired later. It is based on square townships, six miles on a side, and square sections, one mile on a side with systematic adjustments for the curvature of the earth. The plat system involves subdivision maps created by developers and approved by local governments. As you can see from this case, whether a legal description is adequate is very fact-specific. Courts must make the determination on a case-by-case basis. Problems arise when a deed provides the number of acres of land, but does not state how to segregate those acres from the remaining tract of land.

Walters v. Tucker

(Landowner) v. (Neighboring Landowner)
281 S.W.2d 843 (1955)

M E M O R Y   G R A P H I C

Instant Facts

The deed to one neighbor's land described it as "the west 50 feet" of Lot 13. The next door neighbors disagreed about how the 50 feet should be measured.

Black Letter Rule

Extrinsic evidence is not admissible if a deed's legal description is not ambiguous.

Case Vocabulary

PAROL EVIDENCE: Any evidence other than the contract documents, such as testimony about what was said during negotiations, proposals, or letters memorializing conversations. Parol evidence is not admissible to alter or explain a written contract's terms.

Procedural Basis: Appeal of quiet title action.

Facts: In 1922, the Wolfs owned Lot 13 of West Helfenstein Park which fronted Oak Street. In 1924, they conveyed the west 50 feet of Lot 13 to the Forses. At that time, there was a frame dwelling house on the lot, which is still there. Walters (P) is the last grantee of that portion of Lot 13. In 1925, the Wolfs built a stucco house on the remaining portion of Lot 13. Tucker (D) is the last grantee of that portion of Lot 13. The side lines of the lot did not run due north and south, and the front of the lot was not perpendicular to the side lines. Walters (P) sued Tucker (D) in a quiet title action claiming that her property was 50 feet in width. Tucker (D) claimed it was only 42 feet in width. The court held that the description did not specify whether the 50 feet was to be measured along Oak Street or measured eastwardly at right angles from the west line of the property. Walters' (P) expert testified that the property was 50 feet in width and the boundary came within 1 foot of the house on Tucker's (D) lot. Tucker's (D) expert testified that it was unlikely that the Wolfs intended the boundary to be so close to the stucco house. Both parties testified that they had asserted claim to and exercised physical dominion and control over the strip of land at issue. The court held the 50 feet should be measured along Oak Street which resulted in reducing Walters' (P) lot by about eight feet.

Issue: Is extrinsic evidence admissible if a deed's legal description is not ambiguous?

Decision and Rationale: (Hollingsworth, J.) No. The legal description here is clear and unambiguous. When there is no ambiguity on the face of a deed, parol evidence is not admissible to show the parties' intent. Parol evidence may not contradict the deed or describe land other than that described in the deed. The fact that the Wolfs built the stucco house close to the east line of the property is not evidence of any ambiguity in the description. Nor can the fact that the Wolfs and their successors in title claimed title to and exercised dominion and control over a portion of the land. We do not determine whether there was a mistake in the deed. Tucker (D) did not seek reformation of the deed, yet that is what the trial court did. Reversed.

Analysis:

It seems to be a judgment call here as to whether the legal description was ambiguous or not. Unfortunately, the side lines of the lot did not run due north and south, and the front of the lot was not perpendicular to the side lines. The lot was not a perfect rectangle, so it was hard to determine how to measure the west 50 feet of Lot 13. Should the west 50 feet be measured along the front of the lot, or by drawing a line of 50 feet perpendicular to the west lot line and creating a boundary parallel to that line? It's interesting to note that the court held that the fact that the line would be very close to a house was irrelevant. Otherwise, people could build a house very close to a border and claim that the border should be moved. Ultimately, the court held that parol evidence was not admissible to alter the clear meaning of the deed. Which brings us back to the question of whether the deed was really so clear.

Pritchard v. Rebori

(Buyer) v. (Seller)

135 Tenn. 328, 186 S.W. 121 (1916)

M E M O R Y G R A P H I C

 Instant Facts

A buyer of real property sued the seller when the legal description in the deed included property beyond the actual boundary of the property the seller owned.

Black Letter Rule

In construing a legal description, the location of a monument does not necessarily control over a course or distance; the parties' intent controls.

Case Vocabulary

INCUMBRANCE: Any claim or restriction on a property's title.

QUITCLAIM: A deed that transfers all the owner's interest to a buyer, but does not guarantee that there are no other claims against the property.

Procedural Basis: Appeal of action for breach of covenant against encumbrances in a deed.

Facts: The Southern Railway Company (the Railway) owned a right of way extending 50 feet westward from the center of its track. The Railway built a fence to keep dirt from sliding down a slope. The fence was about 15 feet from the track. Thus, the right of way extended beyond the fence. Pritchard (P) wanted to buy land near the railroad track for a warehouse. He bought land from Rebori (D). The legal description of the property in the deed provided that the land ran "thirty feet to the [railroad] right of way." The deed contained a covenant against encumbrances on the land. Pritchard (P) discovered that his warehouse was being built several feet within the Railway's right of way. Pritchard (P) then conveyed two pieces of land to the Railway, which then quitclaimed to Pritchard (P) the portion of the right of way on which the warehouse was being built. Pritchard (P) sued Rebori (D) to recover for the breach of the covenant against encumbrances in the deed. Rebori (D) argued that the property had to stop at the right of way, and therefore there was no incumbrance. The trial court held in Pritchard's (P) favor, allowing him to recover from Rebori (D) the cost of removing the incumbrance.

Issue: In construing a legal description, does the location of a monument control over a course or distance?

Decision and Rationale: (Williams, J.) No. The general rule is that in determining boundaries we look to descriptions in the following hierarchy: natural objects or landmarks; artificial monuments; adjacent boundaries; and then courses and distances. We use this rule to discover the parties' intention, which is the goal of all rules of construction. Monuments, such as the right of way, are controlling only when they are deemed more certain than a course or distance, i.e., thirty feet. Course and distance yield to monuments usually in large tracts of land in the country, as opposed to smaller tracts in cities or towns. Surveys of valuable parcels are usually more accurate than surveys of large parcels in the country or in forests. Where the parties intended that a course and distance would control, we will give it that effect. Monuments and adjacent lines are ordinarily given preference because it is assumed that the parties examined the property and took note of the monument or line. Here, the boundary of the right of way was not marked in any way. Thus it was not the type of monument that would prevail over a course and distance. The parties thought the fence marked the limit of the right of way. Rebori (D) thought the fence marked the east line of his property. Pritchard (P) testified that he would not have bought the property if the fence was not the line of the property. Both parties intended the property up to the fence to be conveyed. Thus, the right of way was a valid existing incumbrance on the land, which Pritchard (P) had the right to remove. Affirmed.

Analysis:

Here the court held that the intent of the parties prevailed over the canons of construction. The parties intended to convey and receive the land up to the fence, both believing that the fence marked the boundary of the property. As it turned out, the Railway owned a strip of land in front of the fence. Thus, Rebori (D) conveyed land that he didn't actually own, and, thus, Rebori (D) was liable to Pritchard (P). This is another case showing the myriad problems that the legal description can present.

Parr v. Worley

(Grantor) v. (Grantee)
93 N.M. 229, 599 P.2d 382 (1979)

M E M O R Y   G R A P H I C

 Instant Facts

A grantor claimed that he granted land only up to the edge of a highway; the grantee claimed he owned the land up to the center of the highway.

Black Letter Rule

A boundary is presumed to extend to the middle of a monument, such as a highway, unless the parties' intent clearly indicates otherwise.

Case Vocabulary

ACQUIESCENCE: A bona fide dispute between the parties about a property boundary, an oral agreement resolving the dispute, taking possession in accordance with the agreement, and a long compliance with the agreed line.

Procedural Basis: Appeal of summary judgment granted in action to quiet title.

Facts: In 1949, Parr (P) conveyed land to Worley (D). The deed described the land conveyed as lying to the east of the highway, and containing 25 acres, more or less. The actual area of the land was 25.80 acres if measured from the eastern edge of the highway, and 31.57 acres if measured from the center of the highway. Parr (P) tried to convey the mineral interests under the highway to a third party. He also recorded mineral leases covering the land under the highway. Parr (P) sued Worley (D) to quiet title. Worley (D) counterclaimed to quiet title in himself. Parr (P) argued that he owned all the land under the highway; Worley (D) argued that he owned the land up to the middle of the highway. Parr (P) filed a summary judgment motion, which the court granted.

Issue: Is a boundary presumed to extend to the middle of a monument, such as a highway?

Decision and Rationale: (Parr, J.) Yes, unless the parties' intent clearly indicates otherwise. A conveyance of land abutting a road or highway is presumed to extend to the center line of the road or highway. However, this presumption is rebuttable, depending on the parties' intent and the surrounding circumstances. Parr (P) argues that the presumption should be rebutted here because: (1) the reasons that justify the presumption do not exist here; (2) the deed to Worley (D) contains language that expressly excluded the highway; and (3) Worley (D) had constructive notice that Parr (P) claimed the mineral interest under the highway and acquiesced to it. Parr (P) argues that the presumption is based on the fact that a grantor could not have intended to retain ownership of a long narrow strip of land. Parr (P) argues that here retaining the mineral interests in the land is a benefit and justifies keeping the strip. However, Parr (P) could have expressly reserved the mineral interest in the deed. A highway is a monument, and the general rule is that a line runs through the center of a monument. The acreage as stated in the deed is the only indication that the center of the highway was not the intended border. However, precedence in deeds is given first to natural objects, artificial monuments, adjacent boundaries, courses and distances, and lastly to quantity. In any event, the issue should be resolved against the grantor. The deed here did not clearly and plainly disclose an intention to exclude the east side of the highway. Parr (P) argues that the word "to" in the phrase "lying to the East of [the highway]" excludes the highway from the grant. However, this is not the law. Parr (P) also argues that the parties' subsequent acts are relevant to the construction of the deed. Parr (P) argues that Worley (D) acquiesced in the mineral leases by doing nothing. However, the doctrine of acquiescence does not apply where there is no evidence that Worley (D) ever knew about the mineral leases. Reversed and remanded for entry of judgment for Worley (D).

Analysis:

As this court explains, the general rule is that a land boundary extends to the middle of a highway or street. A public agency usually owns an easement in the highway or street. Thus, if the public agency someday abandons the easement, the owner of the land will reacquire ownership of the strip where the street was located. The same rule applies to other monuments such as railroad right-of-ways and rivers and streams. As you can imagine, the fact that rivers and streams may change course creates a lot of litigation. It's interesting to note that area or quantity is considered the least reliable method for describing property, when that may be the most important factor for the parties in negotiating a sales price. A buyer may not care that the property extends to the middle of the stream, but she may care that it consists of 100 rather than 90 acres.

Chapter 25

In real estate transactions, marketable title is of the utmost importance. A buyer does not want to buy property that has already been sold or encumbered. To ensure the marketability of title, it is necessary to require people to record their deeds if they want them to be valid.

A recording system is a set of title records maintained by the state. The records include all of the instruments that are filed with the recorder's office that may affect title to the land, such as deeds, mortgages, and easements.

It is often said that a recorded deed is constructive notice to the entire world. If you buy land from Smith, but a recorded deed shows that Smith previously sold the land to Jones, you're out of luck, even if you didn't know about the deed to Jones. Conversely, if an instrument affecting a property's title is not recorded, it has no affect against bona fide purchasers. Much of this chapter discusses what constitutes a bona fide purchaser.

Cases involving the recording system often involve parties who all rightfully think they own the same property. Most of them are innocent parties without knowledge of the other interests. Thus, in nearly all the cases in this chapter, the courts have to choose between innocent parties to determine who gets to keep the property at issue. As you read the cases, think about whether you agree with the fairness of the result.

Chapter 25

NOTE: THE PURPOSE OF THIS OUTLINE IS TO ORGANIZE THE CASES SO THAT ONE CAN QUICKLY UNDERSTAND THE RELEVANCE OF EACH CASE TO THE COURSE. NO ATTEMPT IS MADE IN THIS OVERVIEW TO ADDRESS EVERY CONCEPT THAT MUST BE STUDIED. BE SURE TO READ THE ENTIRE CASEBOOK AND/OR OTHER MATERIALS TO GAIN A FULL UNDERSTANDING OF ALL CONCEPTS.

I. General Operation of the System
  A. A recording system is a set of title records maintained by the state. The records include all of the instruments that are filed with the recorder's office that may affect title to the land, such as deeds, mortgages, and easements.
  B. There are three main steps involved in searching the record title.
    1. Complete a chain of title by reviewing the grantee and grantor indexes.
    2. Determine whether any of the owners made any adverse conveyances.
    3. Review the instruments identified in the search for any problems or inconsistencies.
  C. The general rule is that a recorded deed is constructive notice to the entire world.
    1. However, a recorded deed is constructive notice only to those who are obligated to search for it. For example, a contractor doing work on property has no obligation to search the title. *Mountain States Telephone & Telegraph Co. v. Kelton.*
    2. Different states have different laws regarding the legal effect of deeds that do not comply with the recording statutes.
      a. Recording an invalid deed, such as one that was not properly delivered, does not make it valid. *Stone v. French.*
      b. A recorded deed that was not properly acknowledged does not give proper notice to a b.f.p. *Messersmith v. Smith.*
      c. A mortgage lacking the preparer's name, as required by a statute, gives sufficient notice to third parties. *Flexter v. Woomer.*

3. An unrecorded deed has no force or effect against a b.f.p. This is true even if the bona fide purchaser bought the land from the record owner's heir, rather than from the record owner. *Earle v. Fiske.*
4. Title acquired by adverse possession does not have to be recorded; therefore, a b.f.p. takes title subject to any unrecorded title acquired by adverse possession. *Mugaas v. Smith.*
5. Some courts hold that a deed that is properly recorded but not indexed as required by statute has the same effect as an unrecorded deed. *Mortensen v. Lingo.*
  D. There are three main classifications of recording acts.
    1. In a pure race jurisdiction, the holder of the first recorded instrument prevails, even if he or she is not a b.f.p. *Simmons v. Stum.*
    2. In a race-notice jurisdiction, the holder of the second instrument prevails if he or she is a b.f.p. and records first.
    3. In a pure notice jurisdiction, the holder of the second instrument prevails if he or she is a b.f.p.
    4. However, ultimately, the language of a specific state's statute controls, subject to any court interpretation.

II. Persons Protected
  A. Bona fide purchasers for value are protected by the recording acts.
  B. In a few states, the recording statute protects donees of real property, not just b.f.p.s. *Eastwood v. Shedd.*
  C. The consideration the b.f.p. pays need not be the property's full market value, but most states hold that it cannot be a nominal amount.
    1. Some courts hold that love and affection are adequate consideration to make one a b.f.p. for value. *Strong v. Whybark.*

2. Purchasers who discover a prior unrecorded conveyance and who are paying the purchase price in installments are usually protected on a pro tanto basis, i.e., only to the extent of the payments made before they received notice. *Daniels v. Anderson*.

3. A mortgagee is a purchaser for value if the mortgage secures a pre-existing debt and the mortgagee gives new contemporaneous consideration. *Gabel v. Drewrys Limited U.S.A., Inc.*

D. A constructive trust that is incapable of being recorded does not have priority over b.f.p.s but does have priority over judgment creditors who did not rely on the state of the record in deciding whether to extend credit. *Osin v. Johnson*.

E. A purchaser may not be a b.f.p. if an inspection of the property would have revealed unrecorded interests. *Wineberg v. Moore*.

1. However, a purchaser is not required to inquire about a possessor's interest if the possessor is a relative of the title owner and his presence may be explained by that relationship. *Strong v. Strong*.

III. The Chain of Title

A. When a document affecting title is not recorded, subsequent transactions based on that document are outside the chain of title and will not give constructive notice to b.f.p.s from the original owner.

B. A normal title search considers only the period between the date a grantor is deeded the property and the date the grantor deeds the property.

1. A deed recorded outside the chain of title does not give constructive notice to subsequent purchasers. *Sabo v .Horvath*.

2. It is impractical for a purchaser to search the grantor index for a period after or before the title has been conveyed because there would be no place to stop.

3. A tract index solves these problems because all the instruments that affect a particular tract of land are indexed together.

4. Title insurance companies maintain their own abstracts of title arranged by tract or parcel rather than by the name of the grantor or grantee. Therefore, all the recorded transactions affecting a particular parcel of land, including wild deeds, are indexed together.

Mountain States Telephone & Telegraph Co. v. Kelton

(Easement Owner) v. (Contractor)
79 Ariz. 126, 285 P.2d 168 (1955)

M E M O R Y   G R A P H I C

 Instant Facts
A telephone company sued a contractor for damage to the company's underground telephone cable, arguing that the contractor had constructive notice via the recorded deed of the company's easement.

 Black Letter Rule
A recorded deed is constructive notice only to those who are obligated to search for it.

Case Vocabulary

CONSTRUCTIVE NOTICE: Imputed notice; a legal fiction that a person had notice even though he or she did not have actual notice.

Procedural Basis: Appeal of negligence cause of action.

Facts: Contractor John C. Kelton and Son (Kelton) (D) performed some digging work on landowners' (D) property and damaged an underground cable owned by Mountain States Telephone & Telegraph Co. (Mountain) (P). Mountain (P) sued Kelton (D) and the landowners (D). Mountain claimed that Kelton (D) and the landowners (D) had constructive notice of the cable because Mountain's (P) easement was recorded. The landowners with actual notice of the easement were held liable for negligence. Kelton (D) was not. Mountain (P) appealed.

Issue: Does a contractor have a duty to search the title of property the contractor is working on?

Decision and Rationale: (Udall, J.) No. Kelton (D) had no actual notice of the cable. A recorded document is notice only to those who are bound to search for it. Here, Kelton (D) was not obligated to search the record to learn of Mountain's (P) easement. Kelton (D) had no interest in the property's title. Affirmed.

Analysis:

A recording system is a set of title records maintained by the state. The records include all of the instruments that are filed with the recorder's office that may affect title to the land, such as deeds, mortgages, and easements. It is often said that a recorded deed is constructive notice to the entire world. However, as this case holds, it is notice only to those people who are obligated to search. Here, Kelton (D) was not doing anything that would affect ownership of the land. He was not interested in buying it or knowing who actually owned it. He was only digging. Ownership of the land was likely irrelevant to him, so long as someone paid for his work. Thus, while Mountain's (P) recorded easement may have been constructive notice to anyone interested in title to the property, it was not constructive notice to Kelton (D).

Stone v. French

(Bona Fide Purchaser) v. (Grantor's Heir)
37 Kan. 145, 14 P. 530 (1887)

M E M O R Y   G R A P H I C

Instant Facts

A brother claimed a deed to him from his deceased brother was valid because it was duly recorded, even though it was never properly delivered.

Black Letter Rule

Recording an invalid deed does not make it valid.

Case Vocabulary

BONA FIDE PURCHASER: A person who purchased an asset for a stated value, innocent of any fact which would cast doubt on the seller's right to have sold it in good faith; if the true owner claims the asset, usually the b.f.p. may keep it, and the real owner will have to look to the fraudulent seller for compensation.

NON COMPOS MENTIS: Someone who is insane or not mentally competent to conduct his or her affairs.

Procedural Basis: Appeal of action for partition.

Facts: Francis French owned property. On March 1, 1878, Francis wrote a letter to his brother, Dudley S. French (D), telling Dudley (D) that Francis will deed the property to Dudley (D) in the event of Francis' death, if Francis has not yet sold it. Dudley (D) was of weak mind and body. On February 18, 1879, Francis signed a warranty deed to Dudley (D) and on April 4, 1879 he acknowledged it before a witness, S. Michaels (D). However, he never gave the deed to Dudley (D). On August 2, 1879, Francis died. He had no heirs other than Dudley (D) and his other brother Luther (P). The deed to Dudley (D) was found about half an hour before Francis died with a note on it that the deed should be recorded and mailed. Dudley (D) had no notice of the deed until after Francis died. Dudley (D) recorded the deed and took possession of the land, until he sold it to John Stone (D). The deed from Dudley (D) to Stone (D) was recorded on June 16, 1882. Luther (P) argued that the deed from Francis to Dudley (D) was never delivered, so it was not valid. He claimed the property passed to Francis' heirs upon his death. Luther (P) sued all of Francis' heirs (D), Dudley (D), Stone (D) and Michaels (D), arguing that Stone (D) was entitled to only one seventh of the land, the portion that Dudley (D) inherited from Francis. The trial court held that the deed was not valid and that Stone (D) owned only a one seventh interest in the property.

Issue: Does recording a invalid deed make it valid?

Decision and Rationale: (Valentine, J.) No. It is clear that the deed from Francis to Dudley (D) was never delivered. The March 1, 1878 letter in fact shows that Francis did not have the present intention of conveying the land or delivering a deed to Dudley (D). While actual physical delivery is not required, recording of the deed or delivery to a third party may constitute delivery. None of these occurred here. Thus, the deed was never valid and Dudley (D) never had any right in the property. Thus, Stone (D) obtained no title from Dudley (D). This is different from a case where the deed is voidable, and a bona fide purchaser can obtain title. The deed here is as void as a forged deed. A void instrument cannot be recorded and recording a void instrument does not in some way make it valid. The deed did not get into Dudley's (D) hands until after Francis' death and therefore after the land passed to Francis' heirs. Affirmed.

Analysis:

This case is similar to and consistent with a case you read in the last chapter, *Clevenger v. Moore* [deed that is wrongly delivered out of escrow is void; grantee of such a deed has no title to pass to innocent purchaser]. Both hold that recording an invalid deed does not make it valid. But what about the innocent third party who relied on the recorded deed and assumed it was valid? In both this case and in *Clevenger*, the court held that the b.f.p. (bona fide purchaser) was out of luck. Different states have different statutes regarding the legal effect of deeds that do not comply with the recording statutes. For example, the North Dakota court held in *Messersmith v. Smith* that a recorded deed that was not properly acknowledged did not give proper notice to a b.f.p. On the other hand, the Indiana court in *Flexter v. Woomer* held that a mortgage lacking the preparer's name, as required by a statute, gave sufficient notice to third parties.

Earle v. Fiske

(Bona Fide Purchaser) v. (Grantee in Prior Unrecorded Deed)
103 Mass. 491 (1870)

M E M O R Y   G R A P H I C

Instant Facts

A bona fide purchaser argued that he was the rightful owner of property, rather than prior grantees from an unrecorded deed.

Black Letter Rule

An unrecorded deed has no force or effect against a bona fide purchaser, even if the bona fide purchaser bought the land from the record owner's heir, rather than from the record owner.

Procedural Basis: Appeal of writ of entry to recover land.

Facts: In 1864, Nancy Fiske executed deeds to her son Benjamin and his wife Elizabeth (D) for their lives, and the remainder to Mary Fiske (D). The deeds were not recorded until 1867. Nancy died in 1865, leaving Benjamin as her sole heir. In 1866, Benjamin delivered to Earle (P) a deed to the property, which was recorded that same year. Earle (P) sued Mary (D) and Elizabeth (D) for a writ of entry, claiming the property was his. The trial court ruled that Nancy did not have ownership of the property at the time of her death that Benjamin could inherit, thus Benjamin could not have conveyed any title to Earle (P).

Issue: Does an unrecorded deed have any force or effect against a bona fide purchaser?

Decision and Rationale: (Ames, J.) No. Recording does not affect the rights between the grantor and the grantee. However, an unrecorded deed is not effective against third parties. To them, an unrecorded deed is a nullity. However, it is argued that the unrecorded deed from Nancy to Elizabeth (D), Benjamin (D) and Mary (D) was valid between them. Thus, Benjamin had nothing to inherit from Nancy and nothing to convey to Earle (P). Although some cases hold otherwise, we uphold the plain meaning of our registration system: a buyer of land has a right to rely upon the information furnished him by the registry of deeds. It is impossible to see why Nancy's unrecorded deed has any greater force and effect after her death than before. It had no binding effect on Earle (P). The deed to Earle (P) takes precedence over Nancy's unrecorded deed. Reversed.

Analysis:

While the result here may not seem fair to Elizabeth (D) and Mary (D), who innocently believed that they acquired the property from Nancy, this case cuts to the heart of the purpose of the recording acts. In real estate transactions, marketable title is of the utmost importance. This means that a buyer does not want to buy property that has already been sold or encumbered. If an unrecorded deed had priority over a subsequent grantee who had conducted a title search and had not discovered the prior deed, then no purchaser could ever rely on a title search and there would never be any guarantee that title was marketable. Thus, to ensure the marketability of title, it is necessary to require people to record their deeds if they want them to be valid. So Elizabeth (D) and Mary (D) lost what they thought was their property, but in the service of a much larger principle.

Mugaas v. Smith

(Adverse Possessor) v. (Bona Fide Purchaser)
33 Wn.2d 429, 206 P.2d 332 (1949)

M E M O R Y   G R A P H I C

Instant Facts

An adverse possessor with unrecorded title sued to have title to a strip of land vested to her rather than to a bona fide purchaser.

Black Letter Rule

Title acquired by adverse possession does not have to be recorded; therefore, a bona fide purchaser takes title subject to any unrecorded title acquired by adverse possession.

Case Vocabulary

ADVERSE POSSESSION: A means to acquire title to land through obvious occupancy of the land, while claiming ownership for the period of years set by the law of the state where the property exists.

Procedural Basis: Appeal of action to quiet title.

Facts: The Smiths (D) owned property. Dora Mugaas (P) claimed she acquired title to a strip of that property through adverse possession dating back to 1910. Mugaas (P) sued the Smiths (D) to compel them to remove any buildings and encroachments on the strip. The Smiths (D) argued that the fence marking the boundary line for the strip had disintegrated in 1928 and that when they acquired their land in 1941 the record title did not indicate Mugaas' (P) claim. The trial court held for Mugaas (P).

Issue: Will a conveyance of record title to a bona fide purchaser extinguish a title acquired by adverse possession?

Decision and Rationale: (Hill, J.) No. The fact that Mugaas (P) stopped using the strip did not divest her of title. Title acquired by adverse possession does not stand on the same footing as title held by an unrecorded deed. The latter does not affect a bona fide purchaser. No legislation requires title acquired by adverse possession to be recorded. While recording would be expedient and convenient, it is not up to the judiciary to require it. Otherwise, an adverse possessor would have to "keep his flag flying forever" and never be protected by the statute of limitations. An adverse possessor would have to make his possession so open, continuous and notorious that no one could ever be a bona fide purchaser. The statute cited by the Smiths (D) stating that a bona fide purchaser acquires the full title to real estate free and clear of all claims not appearing of record was enacted to protect purchasers of community property only. Estoppel is not available here. Mugaas (P) made no statement or admission or did any other act that was inconsistent with her present position. Affirmed.

Analysis:

This case sets forth another example of the limitations of the recording system. As you've seen in the last few cases, the general rule is that a bona fide purchaser may rely upon the record title and that unrecorded conveyances are void against subsequent good faith purchasers. However, adverse possession is an exception to that rule. In part this is because adverse possession is acquired without any document to record. The court here holds that once a person has acquired property by adverse possession, a bona fide purchaser acquires the land subject to the adverse possession. This holding makes title less marketable. If you buy property relying on the record title, someone may still claim title through adverse possession. Thus, a prudent buyer has more to do than just search the title record. The buyer should also visit the property, look for any signs of adverse possession (e.g., a fence or a structure), and ask the neighbors.

Mortensen v. Lingo

(Buyer) v. (Seller)
99 F. Supp. 585 (D. Alas. 1951)

WELL.. I DON'T SEE ANYTHING IN THE INDEX... GUESS I DON'T HAVE TO LOOK THROUGH ALL THESE VOLUMES!

INDEX

M E M O R Y   G R A P H I C

Instant Facts

A buyer of real property sued the seller when someone who previously acquired the property by a deed that was recorded but not indexed claimed title to the property.

Black Letter Rule

A deed that is properly recorded but not indexed as required by statute has the same effect as an unrecorded deed.

Procedural Basis: Decision in action for damages for breach of covenants of title.

Facts: In 1941, McCain conveyed property to Anglin. The deed was recorded but not indexed as required by statute. In 1947, McCain conveyed the same property to Lingo (D). In 1948, Lingo (D) conveyed the property to Mortensen (P). Anglin threatened to evict Mortensen (P) from the land. Mortensen (P) sued Lingo (D) for breach of the covenant of title, arguing that indexing was not part of the recording process. Lingo (D) argued that recording alone was insufficient to constitute constructive notice of the deed to Anglin.

Issue: Is indexing a deed an essential part of the recording process?

Decision and Rationale: (Folta, J.) Yes. Courts differ on this issue, and one case 76 years ago held that indexing was not a part of the record. However, I believe that all the steps combined, including indexing, constitute registration. As the number of deeds increases, the only practical way to give notice is through the index. It is unreasonable to require potential buyers to examine every page of many volumes. In addition, to hold otherwise would be to deny the statute requiring that an index be maintained. One case rendered 76 years ago, when now life is faster and the population is more transient, should not control. I hold that the failure to index the deed to Anglin was insufficient to give constructive notice to Lingo (D).

Analysis:

A recorder's office may have thousands of volumes of recorded deeds. Thus, some type of index is necessary to sort through the volumes. Most states have a "name index" system where two indexes are maintained. One is by the name of the grantor and one is by the name of the grantee. A few states maintain a tract or parcel index, which sets forth the chain of title of each tract of land. Thus, if the deed had been properly indexed in a name index in this case, Lingo (D) could have looked in the grantor index for the name of his grantor, McCain, and been referred to the book and page number of the deed book where the deed to Anglin could be found. The search procedure is usually begun by looking for the name of the present owner of the property at issue in the grantee index. The searcher then looks up the name of the grantor to the present owner in the grantee index. The searcher keeps doing this until the name of the sovereign is found. The searcher then looks up each grantor in the grantor index to see if any of them conveyed the property to someone other than a grantee discovered in the grantee index. The searcher then looks at all the deeds in the chain of title to determine whether they are proper. Many courts hold that indexing is not required. One court based this holding on the fact that a grantee should not have to suffer for a recording officer's carelessness.

Simmons v. Stum

(Grantee) v. (Mortgage Holder)
101 Ill. 454 (1882)

M E M O R Y   G R A P H I C

 **Instant Facts**

A mortgage holder sued to foreclose claiming that the mortgage had priority over a subsequently recorded deed.

Black Letter Rule

In a pure race jurisdiction, the instrument recorded first has priority.

Case Vocabulary

PROMISSORY NOTE: A written promise by a person (called a maker, obligor, payor, or promisor) to pay a specific amount of money ("principal") to another (called a payee, obligee, or promisee), usually to include a specified amount of interest on the unpaid principal amount.

Procedural Basis: Appeal of action to foreclose mortgage.

Facts: McHenry (D) executed a mortgage on September 22, 1874 to Stum (P) to secure payment of seven promissory notes for money to purchase the mortgaged property. The notes were due on March 1 of each year from 1876-1882. On November 7, 1878, McHenry (D) conveyed the property to Cochran (D) and Strong (D). McHenry (D) notified Cochran (D) and Strong (D) about the mortgage, and they took the property subject to it. On March 13, 1879, Cochran (D) and Strong (D) conveyed the property to Simmons (D) for no consideration. Stum's (P) mortgage was recorded on March 15, 1879. When McHenry (D) did not pay the note due on March 1, 1879, Stum (P) sued to foreclose the mortgage. The trial court held for Stum (P). Simmons (D) appealed.

Issue: In a pure race jurisdiction does the instrument recorded first have priority?

Decision and Rationale: (Crain, C.J.) Yes. Simmons (D) argues that she was an innocent purchaser with no notice of the mortgage and that she is entitled to the property. Although we think Simmons (D) was not so innocent, we affirm the court's holding on another ground. Under our laws, the first instrument recorded has priority over all other instruments. Stum's (P) mortgage was recorded on March 15, 1879. Simmons (D) acquired the property on March 13, 1879, but there is no evidence that the deed to Simmons (D) was recorded before March 15. Simmons (D) was required to prove the filing date of her deed, which she failed to do. Affirmed.

Analysis:

There are three main types of recording acts. In a pure race jurisdiction, as in the case here, the holder of the first recorded instrument prevails, even if he or she is not a bona fide purchaser (b.f.p.). In a race notice jurisdiction, the holder of the second instrument prevails if he or she is a b.f.p. and records first. In a pure notice jurisdiction, the holder of the second instrument prevails if he or she is a b.f.p. While these are the three general type of recording acts, note that the language of a specific state's statute controls, subject to any court interpretation.

Eastwood v. Shedd

(Grantee) v. (Grantee)
166 Colo. 136, 442 P.2d 423 (1968)

M E M O R Y   G R A P H I C

Instant Facts

A woman gave the same real property to two different people. The person who recorded the deed first but received the deed last claimed she was entitled to the property.

Black Letter Rule

In Colorado, the recording statute protects donees of real property, not just bona fide purchasers for value.

Case Vocabulary

DONEE: Person who receives a gift.

Procedural Basis: Appeal of action to quiet title.

Facts: On December 2, 1958, Cleo Alexander deeded property to Shedd (D) as a gift. Shedd (D) recorded the deed on October 16, 1964. On October 15, 1963, Cleo deeded the same property to Eastwood (P) as a gift. Eastwood (P) recorded the deed on October 23, 1963. Eastwood (P) had no notice of the deed to Shedd (D) until it was recorded a year later. Eastwood (P) sued Shedd (D) to quiet title. The trial court held for Eastwood (P).

Issue: Is a donee of property protected by a race-notice recording statute?

Decision and Rationale: (Day, J.) Yes. Shedd (D) argues that only bona fide purchasers for value are protected by Colorado's recording statute. Other states' statutes protect only bona fide purchasers. But in 1927, Colorado's statute was amended to protect "any class of person with any kind of rights." The statute here is a race-notice statute. To adopt Shedd's (D) argument would be to ignore the 1927 amendment. Eastwood (P) recorded first without notice of Shedd's (D) interest. Affirmed.

Analysis:

Most recording acts protect only bona fide purchasers for value. This means that the person to be protected must have paid some consideration for the property. This eliminates heirs and donees from protection in most states. The rule underlying this requirement is similar to an estoppel argument. The recording acts protect grantees who relied on the title record by paying something for the property. Donees aren't "out" anything if they relied on the record. Note that the consideration the purchaser pays need not be the full market value of the property, so long as it is more than a nominal amount.

Strong v. Whybark

(Grantee) v. (Grantee)
204 Mo. 341, 102 S.W. 968 (1907)

M E M O R Y   G R A P H I C

Instant Facts

A grantor deeded the same property to two different grantees, the latter of which recorded her deed first. Her grantee claimed the property was hers despite the fact that the consideration for the deed was love and affection.

Black Letter Rule

In Missouri, love and affection are adequate consideration to make one a bona fide purchaser for value.

Case Vocabulary

QUITCLAIM DEED: A deed that conveys only that interest in the property in which the grantor has title, as opposed to a warranty deed that guarantees (warrants) that the grantor has full title to the property or the interest the deed conveys.

Procedural Basis: Appeal of action to quiet title.

Facts: On March 6, 1861, Seth Hayden conveyed land by a warranty deed to William Moore for $640. On August 26, 1863, Hayden conveyed the same land to Josephine Hayden for "natural love and affection and five dollars" by a quitclaim deed. The deed to Josephine was recorded on April 11, 1868 and the deed to Moore was recorded on December 14, 1874. Strong (P) acquired the land through Josephine. Boyden (D) acquired the land through Moore. The land was wild and unoccupied. Strong (P) sued Boyden (D) and other defendants to quiet title. The trial court held for Boyden (D). Strong (P) filed a motion for a new trial, which the court denied. Strong (P) appealed.

Issue: Are love and affection sufficient consideration to make a buyer a bona fide purchaser for value?

Decision and Rationale: (Woodson, J.) Yes. Under Missouri's statute, a deed is not effective against third parties without notice unless it is recorded. Thus, the deed from Hayden to Moore was invalid as far as Josephine was concerned. However, courts have held that if a subsequent purchaser either had notice of the prior unrecorded deed or did not pay good and valuable consideration for the land, then he does not take anything. Valuable consideration is defined as money or something that is worth money. The consideration does not have to be the full market value of the property. Even nominal consideration is sufficient in the absence of fraud. Some suggest that a quitclaim deed is notice of questionable title. But this rule is not relevant where the grantee under a quitclaim deed from the same grantor acquired the title for value and without notice of the former unrecorded deed. Between the vendee of a duly recorded deed and the vendee of a prior unrecorded deed from the same vendor, the consideration paid by the latter must be of value. There is no evidence of fraud here or that Josephine never paid the $5. Reversed and remanded for a new trial.

Analysis:

Here the court held that $5 and love and affection was adequate consideration to protect Josephine and her subsequent grantees under the recording laws. This case is an exception. Most courts hold that love and affection or a familial relationship are insufficient consideration to make one a bona fide purchaser for value. While most courts hold that the consideration does not have to equal the property's market value, they hold that nominal consideration or a mere recital of consideration in the deed is not sufficient. Most courts also protect grantees under a quitclaim deed, despite the fact that a quitclaim deed conveys only the interest the grantor actually owns, if any. Buyers of land who discover a prior unrecorded conveyance and who are paying the purchase price in installments are usually protected on a pro tanto basis, i.e., only to the extent of the payments made before they received notice.

Gabel v. Drewrys Limited U.S.A., Inc.

(Prior Unrecorded Mortgagee) v. (Subsequent Mortgagee)
68 So.2d 372 (Fla. 1953)

M E M O R Y   G R A P H I C

 Instant Facts

A mortgagee with a mortgage securing a pre-existing debt claimed it had priority over a prior unrecorded mortgage.

Black Letter Rule

A mortgagee is a purchaser for value for purposes of the recording laws if the mortgage secures a pre-existing debt and the mortgagee gives new contemporaneous consideration.

Case Vocabulary

DEMAND NOTE: A promissory note that is payable any time the holder of the note makes a request, as opposed to a note due at a specific time, upon occurrence of an event, or by installments.

Procedural Basis: Appeal of action and cross-action to foreclose mortgages.

Facts: McCaffrey (D) was a beer distributor who owed Drewrys Limited U.S.A., Inc. (Drewrys) (P) more than $20,000. After Drewrys (P) received some bad checks from McCaffrey (D), it stopped shipping beer to him. In settlement, McCaffrey (D) gave Drewrys (P) a demand note for $10,000 secured by a mortgage dated June 30, 1950 on his property. The mortgage provided that McCaffrey (D) would pay Drewrys' (P) attorney fees and costs if it sued. McCaffrey (D) gave other secured notes for the remainder of the debt. McCaffrey (D) and Drewrys (P) entered into a concurrent agreement providing that Drewrys (P) agreed to forbear any action to enforce collection of McCaffrey's (D) debt so long as McCaffrey (D) made the payments required in the notes. Prior to giving the mortgage, Drewrys (P) had examined the public records and found no other liens against McCaffrey's (D) property. Drewrys' (P) mortgage was promptly recorded. McCaffrey (D) had previously given a mortgage on the same property to Gabel (D), dated March 14, 1950. When Gabel (D) read that McCaffrey (D) was "in trouble," Gabel (D) recorded his mortgage. When McCaffrey (D) did not pay Drewrys (P), Drewrys (P) sued to foreclose the mortgage and made Gabel (D) a party. Gabel (D) filed a cross-claim to foreclose his mortgage. The trial court held that Drewrys' (P) mortgage was superior to Gabel's (D). It held that the consideration for the note from McCaffrey (D) was Drewrys' (P) forbearance from suing for the debt. Gabel (D) appealed.

Issue: Is a mortgagee a purchaser for value for purposes of the recording laws if the mortgage secures a pre-existing debt?

Decision and Rationale: (Drew, J.) No, unless the mortgagee gives new consideration. A mortgagee is a purchaser if he parted with anything valuable at the time the mortgage was executed. On the other hand, if a mortgage secures a pre-existing debt, and no new consideration passes, the mortgagee does not become a purchaser. If a mortgage is taken for a pre-existing debt, and the creditor at the time agreed to extend the time for payment, even by a day, this additional consideration is sufficient to make the creditor a purchaser for value. In most cases where the creditor was allowed priority over a prior mortgage, a definite extension of time was given. Here, as soon as Drewrys (P) accepted the demand note and the mortgage, Drewrys (P) was in a better position than before because it could sue at any time, it reduced its claim to a sum certain, it secured a mortgage, and it received an agreement to pay attorney fees and costs if it sued. Instead of a detriment to Drewrys (P), there was a benefit. Instead of a benefit to McCaffrey (D), there was a detriment. Drewrys (P) had nothing to lose. Thus, it does not qualify as a innocent purchaser for value. Reversed.

Analysis:

Osin v. Johnson

(Lender) v. (Fraudulent Borrower)
243 F.2d 653 (D.C. Cir. 1957)

M E M O R Y   G R A P H I C

Instant Facts

A woman who loaned someone money to buy her property sued when the man failed to prepare and record trust documents as promised and obtained other loans secured by the same property.

Black Letter Rule

A constructive trust that is incapable of being recorded does not have priority over b.f.p.s but does have priority over judgment creditors who did not rely on the state of the record in deciding whether to extend credit.

Case Vocabulary

CONSTRUCTIVE TRUST: A trust created by operation of law when a court determines that the holder of title to property holds it as the constructive trustee for the intended owner's benefit; this may occur through fraud, breach of faith, ignorance or inadvertence.

LACHES: The equitable doctrine that a legal claim will not be enforced or allowed if a long delay in asserting the claim has prejudiced the adverse party.

Procedural Basis: Appeal of action for equitable relief, including setting aside deed, injunctive relief, and an accounting.

Facts: Osin (P) sold property to Johnson (D) and took back a note for the $30,000 purchase price. Johnson (D) recorded the deed but did not prepare and record a trust instrument to secure the note as he had promised Osin (P). Johnson (D) was accordingly convicted of fraud in a criminal case. Without disclosing Osin's (P) unrecorded lien, Johnson (D) borrowed $11,000 from Perpetual Building Association (Perpetual) (D) and executed deeds of trust against the property. Johnson (D) also borrowed $3300 on second deeds of trust from Glorius (D). Other creditors obtained judgment liens against Johnson (D). When foreclosure proceedings were commenced against Johnson (D), Osin (P) sued Johnson (D) and the other trust holders (D) for equitable relief. The trial court held that Osin (P) conveyed the property in reliance on Johnson's (D) promises that he would record the proper documents. However, the court concluded that the liens of Perpetual (D), Glorius (D) and the judgment creditors (D) were superior to Osin's (P) unrecorded claim.

Issue: Does a constructive trust have priority over judgment creditors who did not rely on the state of the record in deciding whether to extend credit?

Decision and Rationale: (Burger, J.) Yes. The trial court did not consider whether a constructive trust could be imposed on the property in Osin's (P) favor in light of Johnson's (D) fraudulent conduct. A constructive trust is an appropriate remedy where, as here, someone acquired property through fraudulent misrepresentation. We now must look at whether a constructive trust has priority over subsequent trust holders and judgment creditors. Perpetual (D) and Glorius (D) were bona fide purchasers (b.f.p.) without notice of Osin's (P) claim and they are protected by the recording act. The rationale for this is that between two innocent parties, Osin (P) must yield to those who in good faith relied on the title record which Osin's (P) negligence allowed to exist. However, a judgment creditor does not have the same position as a bona fide purchaser. Creditors do not usually rely on the record title to extend credit. The law has always been that equity under a trust is superior to that under a judgment lien. The judgment creditors (D) argue that the applicable recording statute refers to "creditors" as having precedence over prior unrecorded interests. Thus, it is true that a judgment creditor is equal to a b.f.p. with respect to instruments that are capable of being recorded. But where an interest is not created by a written instrument, but by operation of the law, the interest is not capable of being recorded and thus retains priority over judgment liens. We remand with respect to the judgment creditors for the court to determine whether the facts support the imposition of a constructive trust in Osin's (P) favor. If the court finds that there was a constructive trust inherently incapable of recording and no laches by Osin (P) in asserting her rights, then Osin's (P) trust has priority over the judgment creditors (D). However, any judgment creditor (D) that can prove that it extended credit based on the state of Johnson's title is on the same standing as a b.f.p. Affirmed as to Perpetual (D) and Glorius (D). Reversed and remanded as to the judgment creditors (D).

Analysis:

As this case explains, under the Washington D.C. recording laws, a judgment creditor is not a b.f.p. and does not have priority over unrecorded prior liens. This rule is based on the rationale that a judgment creditor did not rely on the state of the title record in extending credit. However a large minority of states have statutes that specifically protect judgment creditors. This is based on the rationale that a judgment creditor may have relied on the state of the title record before going through the expense of prosecuting a lawsuit. The creditor may have chosen to pursue the lawsuit on the assumption, after examining the record, that the judgment was collectible. In any event, you can see that when parties litigate regarding prior unrecorded interests and the protection of the recording laws, innocent parties often get hurt.

Wineberg v. Moore

(Prior Unrecorded Purchaser) v. (Subsequent Purchaser)
194 F. Supp. 12 (D. Cal. 1961)

M E M O R Y   G R A P H I C

Instant Facts

A prior purchaser with an unrecorded deed sued subsequent purchasers to quiet title, claiming that an inspection of the property would have disclosed his interest in the property.

Black Letter Rule

A purchaser may not be a bona fide purchaser if an inspection of the property would have revealed unrecorded interests.

Procedural Basis: Action to quiet title in federal district court with jurisdiction based on diversity of citizenship.

Facts: Wineberg (P) bought 880 acres from Barker in May, 1948. He recorded the deed in May, 1951. Before the deed was recorded, Barker sold the timber on the land to Construction Engineers (D). That contract was recorded in 1950. In 1951, Barker sold the property again to Natural Resources, Inc. (D). That deed was recorded before the Wineberg (P) deed. During this time, several judgments were obtained against Barker. The land was suited for logging, hunting, and fishing. There was a house and garage on it. A fence extended along two sides of the property but not around all the acres. A locked gate was on the road leading to the property. There were no trespassing signs on the gate and in other areas of the property with Wineberg's (P) name and Oregon address on them. Wineberg (P) paid the property taxes and he and his guests visited the property occasionally for recreational purposes. Wineberg's (P) personal property was in the residence.

Issue: Is a subsequent purchaser protected by the recording acts if an inspection of the property would have revealed any unrecorded interests?

Decision and Rationale: (Carter, J.) No. California's recording statute requires the second purchaser to be without actual or constructive notice of the prior purchaser's interest. In California, a party buying property where a third party possesses the property is presumed to have notice of the third party's possession. Possession of land is notice to the world of every right the possessor has in the property. A purchaser of property is imputed with all information he would obtain by actually viewing the premises. The possession required to give notice to subsequent purchasers must be open, notorious, exclusive, visible and not consistent with the record title. Wineberg's (P) acts of dominion over the property were sufficient to give notice that he possessed it. The fact that the whole property was not enclosed with a fence does not prevent Wineberg's (P) possession from extending over the whole parcel. The road leading to the property was posted with a no trespassing sign. Anyone inspecting the property would have been immediately aware of the fact that a third party had rights to it. Although Wineberg (P) used the property only occasionally, his use was consistent with its recreational purposes. Logging activities are not the only acts that would be sufficient to put third parties on notice of Wineberg's (P) title. The recording system is meant to protect bona fide purchasers. This does not mean that purchasers may close their eyes to everything but the record title. Construction Engineers (D) and Natural Resources, Inc. (D) were required to inspect the property. They are charged with all the facts that an inspection would have turned up, including Wineberg's (P) interest. Judgment for Wineberg (P).

Analysis:

It makes sense that a purchaser of land is charged with notice of what a physical inspection would disclose. But what if the inspection discloses ambiguous information? Compare *Wineberg* with *Strong v. Strong*, where the father had record title to land, but his son claimed an unrecorded interest too. The father and the son both lived on the land. When the father conveyed the land to a grantee, the court held that the son's presence was explainable by his relationship to the record owner. The grantee was not required to inquire about the son's interest.

Sabo v. Horvath

(Subsequent Purchaser) v. (Prior Purchaser)
559 P.2d 1038 (Alas. 1976)

M E M O R Y   G R A P H I C

Instant Facts
A couple who purchased property first but recorded their deed before their grantor obtained actual title to the property sued a subsequent purchaser to quiet title.

Black Letter Rule
A deed recorded outside the chain of title does not give constructive notice to subsequent purchasers.

Procedural Basis: Appeal of action to quiet title.

Facts: Lowery occupied land in 1964 in Alaska for the purpose of obtaining a federal patent. In 1968, a federal government agency recommended that the patent issue to Lowery. On January 3, 1970, Lowery issued a quitclaim deed for the property to the Horvaths (P). The Horvaths (P) recorded the deed on January 5, 1970. The Horvaths (P) knew that the patent and title were still in the government, but they did not rerecord their deed after title passed to Lowery. The federal government issued the patent to Lowery on August 10, 1973. Lowery then sold the land by a quitclaim deed to the Sabos (D) on October 15, 1973. They recorded their deed on December 13, 1973. The Horvaths (P) sued the Sabos (D) to quiet title. The superior court held that the Horvaths (P) had a superior right to the land. It held that when Lowery conveyed the land to the Horvaths (P) he had an equitable interest in the land even though the patent had not yet issued. It also held that the Horvaths' (P) prior recording gave the Sabos (D) constructive notice of their deed.

Issue: Does a deed that is recorded but outside the chain of title provide constructive notice to subsequent purchasers?

Decision and Rationale: (Boochever, C.J.) No. A deed recorded outside the chain of title is a "wild deed" and does not give constructive notice. We hold that Lowery did have an interest to convey to the Horvaths (P) before the patent issued. The next question is whether a quitclaim deed puts a purchaser on constructive notice of other interests. We follow the majority of states and hold that a quitclaim grantee is not precluded from being an innocent purchaser. As between the Horvaths (P) and the Sabos (D), in the usual case, a prior recorded deed is constructive notice of a prior interest. However, a purchaser has notice only of recorded instruments within his chain of title. In jurisdictions like Alaska that use a grantor-grantee index system, the Sabos (D) could not have discovered the Horvaths' (P) deed. We could require the Sabos (D) to check beyond the chain of title, but this would add a significant burden and uncertainty to real estate purchases. Requiring title searches of records prior to the date the grantor acquired title would defeat the purpose of the recording system. It is less of a burden to require the Horvaths (P) to rerecord their interest once title passed to Lowery. While we sympathize with both parties here, our decision must set forth the requirements of Alaska's recording laws. We choose to promote simplicity and certainty. We therefore hold that the Horvaths' (P) deed, recorded outside the chain of title, did not give constructive notice to the Sabos (D) and was not duly recorded under the Alaska recording act. Reversed.

Analysis:

Recording acts are designed to solve the immediate dispute between successive purchasers from the same grantor. A normal grantor index search would look at only the period between the date the grantor received title until the date the grantor no longer had record title. As this case shows, the real world is often more complicated than this. In this case, an orderly search would be limited to the period beginning when Lowery received title from the government (the "patent") and ending when a deed from Lowery was recorded. Thus, a searcher would not discover the Horvaths' (P) deed. While a federal patent is an unusual situation, this problem could more easily arise in the context of easements recorded outside the chain of title or deeds recorded long after the deed is actually executed. In most of the country, the wild deed problem is no longer an issue. Title insurance companies maintain their own abstracts of title arranged by tract or parcel rather than by the name of the grantor or grantee. Therefore, all the recorded transactions affecting a particular parcel of land, including wild deeds, are kept together.

Chapter 26

One of the most important aspects of property law is its ability to determine who owns what and what they own. If property law fails to clearly identify the true owner of property, then we are back to where we first started with John Hobbes: land is owned by those strong enough to take and defend it.

It is for this reason that property law has attempted to find ways to assure purchasers that the title they are purchasing is good and marketable and that the land they are purchasing is also inhabitable and as advertised.

One means of assuring purchasers of their title are implied warranties and general covenants of title. Implied warranties are simply a promise that a home being purchased is inhabitable. Covenants of title, of which there are six, are generally broken down into two kinds: present and future. The present covenants relate to the actual conveyance of title at the time of conveyance. The future covenants are promises that if title turns out to be other than as stated, the seller will defend that title or pay damages to the purchaser.

Another means of assuring purchasers that they have good and marketable title are abstracts of title. An abstract of title is simply a summary of all recorded documents in a chain of title. If an error is made, there is generally liability for abstractors, at least as to those who contract with them. Additionally, purchasers can obtain title insurance, which will protect them from undisclosed recorded interests.

Finally, as aids to these other means, some states have adopted statutes aimed at clearing up title defects and assuring purchasers that they are getting what the real property records say they are getting. These statutes are simply statutes of limitations that terminate certain interests in real property if no action is taken to preserve those interests within a set period of time.

All of these methods, however, are meant only to protect purchasers and to assure them that the title they are receiving is as it purports to be. They are property law's way of saying who owns what in such a manner that each can be secure in what they own.

Chapter 26

NOTE: THE PURPOSE OF THIS OUTLINE IS TO ORGANIZE THE CASES SO THAT ONE CAN QUICKLY UNDERSTAND THE RELEVANCE OF EACH CASE TO THE COURSE. NO ATTEMPT IS MADE IN THIS OVERVIEW TO ADDRESS EVERY CONCEPT THAT MUST BE STUDIED. BE SURE TO READ THE ENTIRE CASEBOOK AND/OR OTHER MATERIALS TO GAIN A FULL UNDERSTANDING OF ALL CONCEPTS.

I. Up until recent times, one buying land did so at his own risk. Now, however, some exceptions to the old "caveat emptor" have arisen.

  A. The most important of these is the implied covenant of habitability, which survives delivery of the deed.

  B. The implied warranty of habitability is essentially an implied promise that a home is of fair quality and is fit for the intended purpose of living in it.

  C. The implied warranty of habitability applies to new homes as well as used or older homes. *Petersen v. Hubschman Construction Co..*

    1. The implied warranty also permits repudiation of a contract to purchase a home based upon defects in the home even if those defects do not render the home completely inhabitable. *Petersen.*

  D. The implied warranty of habitability can be disclaimed, however. *G-W-L v. Robichaux.*

    1. To effectively disclaim it, the majority of courts require that one do more than state that there are no implied warranties.

    2. Generally speaking, the disclaimer must be conspicuous and specifically mention the implied warranty of habitability.

II. There are, simply stated, six general covenants of title: (1) covenant of seisin, (2) covenant of right to convey, (3) covenant against encumbrances, (4) covenant of further assurance, (5) covenant of quiet enjoyment and (6) covenant of warranty.

  A. The first three, seisin, conveyance and encumbrances, are known as present covenants because they are breached, if at all, upon delivery of the deed.

  B. The last three, further assurance, quiet enjoyment and warranty, are known as future covenants because they are breached, if at all, at some point after delivery of the deed.

  C. One of the most important future covenants is that of quiet enjoyment.

    1. Generally, the covenant of quiet enjoyment is a promise that the grantor will defend the grantee's land against any and all who may claim some interest in it.

    2. To successfully claim a breach of the covenant of quiet enjoyment, however, one must not only show that someone else is claiming an interest in the land but also an actual ouster from the land. *Brown v. Lober.*

  D. In general, covenants such as the six general ones may run with the land if they touch and concern the land and an intent that they so run is expressed.

    1. Generally, the future covenants are said to run with the land such that if a remote grantee is ousted, he may bring suit against the original grantor for breach of the covenant of quiet enjoyment provided he can show privity of estate. Cribbet and Johnson, *Principles of Law and Property.*

  E. Another important future covenant is the covenant against encumbrances.

    1. The covenant against encumbrances is a promise by the grantor that the property is free and clear of all encumbrances.

    2. This means that even if an undisclosed incumbrance is open and visible, the covenant against encumbrances is still breached. *Leach v. Gunnarson.*

  F. When a present covenant, such as the covenant of seisin is breached, the question often arises what damages are recoverable?

    1. The general rule is that one may recover only the price actually paid for the land plus interest. *Davis v. Smith.*

2. Damages recoverable when property is returned to a rightful owner from one in possession are equal to the costs of the actual improvements or the value added to the property. *Madrid v. Spears.*

G. In addition to the six general covenants, the doctrine of after-acquired title, or estoppel by deed, can often cure defects in title as well.

1. The doctrine of after-acquired title is most often applied in a situation where A delivers an indefeasible estate or a defective deed to B.

2. Most states have adopted statutes that provide that in such situations where a simple mistake has occurred, title is passed if A subsequently obtains a correct deed or acquires a defeasible estate.

3. In addition, courts interpreting such statutes have held them applicable to oil and gas leases. *Robben v. Obering.*

III. In addition to the six general covenants, recording systems were adopted to further protect purchasers' interests in land.

A. By reviewing the recorded documents in a chain of title, one can come up with an abstract of title, which is essentially a summary of all recorded interests.

B. Given the importance of a review of the public records, rules of liability for those preparing abstracts of title were quick to follow the adoption of the recording system.

1. Abstractors are generally only held liable to those with whom they directly contract or to those they have reason to know will rely upon their abstract. *First American Title Insurance Company v. first Title Service Company of the Florida Keys.*

IV. In contrast to recording systems, Torrens systems developed as a more efficient way of registering property as owned by a certain person.

A. A Torrens system is one in which involuntary transfers of property, such as foreclosures, must go through the court system and such transfers are only valid upon issuance of a court decree.

B. In states that have adopted a Torrens system, or a registration system for property, even the federal government must comply. *United States v. Ryan.*

V. In light of the inherent risks associated with purchasing property, title insurance developed as another means of protecting purchasers.

A. In any transaction, there are risks, but in real property transactions, those risks are magnified by things such as the possibility of unrecorded interests.

B. The main purpose of title insurance, however, is to insure against the risks of errors in reviews of the recorded documents.

1. Title insurance thus generally protects a purchaser against a subsequent claim from someone claiming an interest that was recorded but not found.

2. In doing so, courts have said that an interest that otherwise would be excluded from coverage, such as water rights, are covered if they were recorded. *White v. Western Title Insurance Co.*

C. As with abstractors, the issue of a title insurer's liability for failing to adequately disclose recorded interests was quick to arise.

1. Unlike abstractors, however, title insurers do not have a duty to disclose all discoverable defects in title. *Transamerica Title Ins. Co. v. Johnson.*

VI. As aids to the covenants of title and title insurance, states have adopted statutes of limitation to further clear up title issues and assure purchasers that their title is good and marketable.

A. The most important statutes of limitation are the adverse possession statutes, which generally provide that after a set period of time, mostly 18 years, one who actually uses land in an open, hostile and adverse manner has acquired title to that property.

1. One requirement of adverse possession is that the land must be used continuously

over the 18 year period. *Howard v. Kunto.*

a. Continuous use, however, is that use that the land is customarily put to. *Howard.*

b. Additionally, possession and use can be tacked onto previous possessors provided that there is a reasonable connection between them. *Howard.*

2. Adverse possession can also apply to minerals, provided those minerals are actually used. *Failoni v. Chicago & North Western Railway Co.*

a. To use minerals, one must physically remove them from the land or do such an act as would apprise the world of one's claim to the minerals as differentiated from the surface estate. *Failoni.*

b. Not all believe adverse possession statutes are statutes of limitation wherein one will lose his land if he takes no action to use it within a set period of time. Sprankling, *An Environmental Critique of Adverse Possession.*

(1) Some believe adverse possession exploits the over development and environmental degradation of "wild lands" since if those lands are not used, they are subject to possession by another who will use them. Sprankling, *op. cit.*

(2) This defeats the purpose of a common twentieth century goal: preservation. Sprankling, *op. cit.*

3. Adverse possession can also occur between cotenants of commonly owned property.

a. For one cotenant to adversely possess commonly owned land and divest other cotenants from ownership, he must do more than simply possess the land under claim of right, he must also perform some outward act that would put the other cotenants on notice that his possession is adverse to their interests. *Mercer v. Wayman.*

B. In addition to adverse possession statutes, some states have adopted specific legislation aimed at clearing up title to land by eliminating interests not claimed of record within a set period of time.

1. One such statute is Indiana's Mineral Lapse Act, which terminates a mineral estate not used for 20 years if a claim is not filed of record. *Short v. Texaco.*

a. Such statues have been held constitutional. *Short.*

2. Another such statute is Florida's Marketable Record Title Act, modeled after the Model Marketable Record Title Act.

a. Florida's statute terminates all unrecorded interests of land if not recorded within thirty (30) years. *H&F Land v. Panama City-Bay County Airport and Industrial District.*

b. Florida's statute applies to all interests in land, including easements by necessity. *H&F.*

Petersen v. Hubschman Construction Co., Inc.

(Purchaser) v. (Builder-Vendor)

76 Ill. 2d 31, 389 N.E. 2d 1154 (1979).

M E M O R Y G R A P H I C

 Instant Facts

Purchasers of new home sued builder-vendor to recover earnest money deposit and for repudiation of contract due to substantial defects in the construction of the home.

Black Letter Rule

Implied warranty of habitability, in which a builder-vendor warrants that a new home is of fair average quality, would pass without objection in the building trade and is fit for the ordinary purpose of living in it, applies in the context of the purchase of a new home.

Case Vocabulary

CAVEAT EMPTOR: Latin for let the buyer beware.

CLOSING: The consummation of a real estate transaction where the money is paid and a deed is issued transferring title.

DOCTRINE OF MERGER: Legal principle that holds that any covenants or promises contained in a contract to purchase land merge into the deed and are no longer enforceable once the deed is issued unless they are set forth in the deed itself.

EARNEST MONEY: The portion of the purchase price deposited into an account to signify the purchaser's willingness to purchase; usually serves as security of the purchaser's performance and is forfeited to the seller upon the purchaser's breach.

FORFEITURE CLAUSE: A contractual provision allowing a seller to terminate the contract upon the buyer's breach and retain any payments made by the buyer; said payments having been forfeited.

IMPLIED WARRANTY OF HABITABILITY: In general, an implied covenant that a building is capable of being inhabited.

LATENT DEFECTS: Defects that are hidden, not readily ascertainable.

REPUDIATE: An affirmation that a party to a contract will not perform as promised.

Procedural Basis: Appeal to the Illinois Supreme Court from the Appellate Court's ruling affirming the trial court's entry of judgment in favor of the purchasers.

Facts: Petersen (P) entered into a contract with Hubschman Construction Co., Inc. ("Hubschman") (D) for the purchase of land and construction of a new home for $71,000 in April 1972. The contract was subsequently amended by the parties to provide for a discounted price in exchange for Petersen (P) doing some of the work himself. Petersen (P) paid $10,000 in earnest money. In fall 1972, Petersen (P) became dissatisfied with Hubschman (D) performance, and Hubschman (D) agreed to repair several items on a punch list, but failed to do so. The defects in the newly constructed home included a slanted basement floor, an ill-fitting bay window, seriously defective front door and front door frame and deterioration of the drywall accompanied by nails popping through. Despite the defects, it was undisputed at trial that the house was at least habitable. After Hubschman (D) refused to escrow $1,000 to cover the cost of repairs, Petersen (P) refused to accept the home and no closing occurred. Hubschman (D) declared Petersen (P) in default for refusing to close and forfeited the earnest money paid. The trial court found that there were defects in substance in the construction that precluded Hubschman (D) from declaring a forfeiture of the earnest money and awarded Petersen (P) the amount of the earnest money plus the value of the work he had performed. The appellate court affirmed. This appeal followed.

Issue: Does the implied warranty of inhabitability preclude a purchaser of a new home from repudiating a contract based on defects that do not render the home inhabitable?

Decision and Rationale: (Ryan, J.) No. Usually a builder-vendor argues that the implied warranty of habitability does not exist and that the long-standing rule of caveat emptor applies such that a purchaser cannot sue the builder-vendor for defects. In this case, however, Hubschman (D) argues that the implied warranty of habitability applies, that the house in question is habitable and that therefore Petersen (P) wrongfully repudiated the contract . In so arguing, Hubschman (D) relies on dicta contained in a previous Illinois appellate decision [*Goggin v. Fox Valley Construction Corp*.] which stated that the implied warranty of habitability is satisfied where the home keeps the elements out and provides its inhabitants with a reasonably safe place to live. Petersen (P) argues, however, that Hubschman (D) has not substantially performed the contract and he was entitled to repudiate the contract and recover a money judgment. It is Petersen's (P) position that there is no implied warranty of habitability in this case because a deed was never issued. Although this court has never considered whether the implied warranty of habitability applies in the context of a new home, we have recognized its applicability in the landlord-tenant context. Those cases from other jurisdictions considering its applicability in the new home context have done so to avoid the harsh results of caveat emptor and the doctrine of merger on purchasers who discover latent defects after closing. Under the old rule of caveat emptor, a purchaser who discovers latent defects has no recourse, having bought the home at his own risk. The doctrine of merger worked the same way. Recently, however, the implied warranty of habitability has found substantial acceptance in other jurisdictions, and even in Illinois, exceptions to the doctrine of merger have arisen in order to prevent harsh results. Given the changes that have occurred in the construction and marketing of new homes, we agree with those jurisdictions that have recognized an implied warranty of habitability in the sale of a new home by a builder-vendor. New homes are now mass-produced and purchasers have little or no opportunity to inspect the homes and are not knowledgeable about construction practices. As such, purchasers have the right to expect a builder-vendor to construct a product that is reasonably fit for use as a residence. While many cases adopting this view apply it only in cases where the home is not complete upon execution of the contract, we do not believe it should be so limited. Further, we disagree with Petersen (P) that the implied warranty of habitability does not apply in this case because no deed was executed. The implied warranty arises by virtue of the contract for the purchase of the home and survives the delivery of the deed. It is an automatic protection afforded as a matter of public policy and therefore relaxes the principles of caveat emptor and the doctrine of merger. We further disagree with previous appellate decisions that limit the protection to only providing mere habitability. The fact that a home is capable of being inhabited does not, in our view, satisfy the implied warranty. Rather, one should analogize the implied warranty of habitability to the implied warranties of merchantability or fitness for a particular purchase contained in the uniform commercial code. [Sections 2-314 and 2-315.] Using this analogy makes it clear that the implied warranty of habitability requires that the house be of fair, average quality, pass without objection in the building trade and be fit for the ordinary purpose of living in it. As such, this warranty cannot be disclaimed by simple boilerplate language. Instead, only conspicuous disclaimers that the builder-vendor can show was actually agreed to will be enforced, and

only then strictly against the builder-vendor. In this case, at the time Petersen (P) repudiated the contract, the contract was only executory and performance by Hubschman (D), including performance of the implied warranty of habitability, was a condition precedent to Petersen's (P) performance. It would be manifestly unjust to require Petersen (P) to accept a home with significant defects and to settle only for damages. Especially in this case where the home was built on land owned by Hubschman (D) who can therefore resell the home and recover the value of his work. Having concluded that implied warranty of habitability applies in this case, we have not determined other related issues, such as whether it would have applied if the home were built on land owned by the purchaser or what the appropriate remedy would be in a case where the deed was delivered. The implied warranty being applicable in this case, it remains only to determine whether Hubschman (D) substantially complied with it. Whether there has been substantial performance is a question of fact, which in this case, the trial court determined against Hubschman (D). There is evidence to support the trial court's decision and therefore, the judgment of the trial court and the appellate court is affirmed.

Analysis:

There are several important concepts to take from this case. First and foremost is the discussion regarding the scope of the implied warranty of habitability. The court here holds that it requires more than merely making a home habitable. Instead it requires making the house of fair and average quality acceptable to the building industry and fit for living in it. This represents an expansion of the typical implied warranty. It is also of note that the court compared the implied warranty of habitability to the uniform commercial code's implied warranties of merchantability and fitness for a particular purpose. Second, you should take note of when the implied warranty of habitability applies. The court notes that it previously held it applicable in the landlord-tenant context, and in this decision extends it to the sale of a new home on land owned by the builder-vendor and where the deed has not been delivered. The Court left open the possibility that the warranty may not apply in cases where the deed is delivered or where the home is built on the purchaser's own land. Subsequent courts have refused to extend the implied warranty to commercial structures, including clubhouses at apartment complexes or rental properties. Notice also that it only applies to those in the business of building homes. This requirement has also been the subject of subsequent cases, which have not read it as strictly only those in the business of mass-producing homes, but rather read it as requiring the builder-vendor to be in the construction business rather than building a home for personal use. Third, note that the Court goes out of its way to note that while the implied warranty of habitability can be disclaimed, a disclaimer of the implied warranty of habitability, as in the case of other public policy protections, must be conspicuous and specifically agreed to in order to be enforceable. The effect of disclaimers is more particularly discussed in the following case, G-W-L, Inc. v. Robichaux. Other issues to consider that are not raised in this opinion are whether the implied warranty of good workmanlike construction is the same as or is independent of the implied warranty of habitability and whether the implied warranty of habitability applies to subsequent purchasers of used homes. As to the first, cases are split on whether they represent one and the same warranty. As to the latter, the majority of courts considering the issue seem to focus more on foreseeability and the reasonableness of the time in which the suit is brought against the builder-vendor rather than on the privity of the person bringing suit. If a subsequent purchase is able to make an implied warranty claim, another issue arises about when the statute of limitations begins to run on such claims. When the defects are latent, the ordinary rule is that the statutory period beings to run when the defect was or should have been discovered. Finally, you should take note of the discussion about the doctrine of merger. Generally speaking, the doctrine of merger precludes enforcement of covenants set forth in the contract that are not repeated in the deed, absent a scrivener's error where the parties intended the covenants to be in the deed. While the old cases applied the doctrine strictly, often with harsh results, the general rule now is that only covenants relating to title merge into the deed, leaving collateral covenants and promises such as those relating to warranties still applicable even after delivery of the deed.

G-W-L, Inc. v. Robichaux

(Builder-Vendor) v. (Purchaser)
643 S.W.2d 392 (Tex. 1982)

M E M O R Y   G R A P H I C

Instant Facts
Purchaser sued builder-vendor for breach of implied warranties when roof on new house sagged.

Black Letter Rule
Implied warranty of habitability can be disclaimed.

Case Vocabulary

DISCLAIMER: A contractual provision that limits the applicability of warranties.

Procedural Basis: Appeal to the Supreme Court of Texas from the appellate court's ruling affirming jury verdict awarding damages to purchasers.

Facts: Robichaux (D) purchased a new home from G-W-L, Inc. (P), who designed, built and provided the materials for the home. After construction, which revealed the roof had a substantial sag in it, Robichaux (D) sued G-W-L (P) for breach of express and implied warranties. The jury found that no express warranties were breached but did find breaches of the implied warranties of building the home in a good workmanlike manner and merchantability. The appellate court affirmed the jury's verdict and this appeal followed.

Issue: Can the implied warranty of habitability be disclaimed by contractual language?

Decision and Rationale: (Sondock, J.) Yes. G-W-L (P) argues that the appellate court erred in finding that the parties written agreement did not waive the implied warranty of fitness created in *Humber v. Morton* [a prior Texas case holding that a builder-vendor who builds and conveys a home impliedly warrants that the home is constructed in a good workmanlike manner and is suitable for human habitation]. That written agreement contained a paragraph that specifically provided there were no "oral agreement, representations, conditions, warranties, express or implied". The parties agree that the warranty created in *Humber v. Morton* is applicable in this case and that the warranty can be waived by appropriate language. The issue here has thus become whether the language in the contract at issue is sufficient to disclaim this implied warranty. The appellate court held that the language must be clear and free from doubt, with which we agree. However, we disagree with the appellate court's decision that the language at issue here is not clear and free from doubt. The contract provides that there are no implied or express warranties. Having signed the agreement, Robichaux (D) is presumed to have read this provision. The rulings below are therefore reversed.

Dissent: (Spears, J.) I disagree with the majority that the language at issue here is sufficient to disclaim the implied warranty of habitability. I believe, as other jurisdictions have held, that the language must be clear and unequivocal, naming the specific implied warranty being waived. The ordinary consumer signing a contract like the one here is probably not even aware of the implied warranty of habitability and believes, with good reason, that the contractor will provide a habitable home built in a good workmanlike manner. The language at issue here is not sufficient to put the purchaser on notice of the warranty he is waiving. I would therefore affirm.

Analysis:

This case is meant to raise your awareness as to what is and is not required to effectively disclaim the implied warranty of habitability. In this case, the Supreme Court of Texas holds that because one who signs a contract is presumed to have read it, the language that there are no implied warranties is sufficient. This is the minority position, however. As was discussed in the previous case, *Petersen v. Hubschman Construction Co., Inc.*, most jurisdictions require clear and conspicuous language that is strictly construed against the builder-vendor in order to effectively disclaim the implied warranty of habitability. Some courts go further, as was suggested in the dissent, requiring that the specific warranty being disclaimed be named. Keep in mind, however, that there are other causes of action upon which a purchaser of a defective home could sue the builder, besides breach of warranty. For instance, a builder could be sued for fraudulent or negligent misrepresentation of the condition of the home, or for concealment or failure to disclose pertinent facts, such as that the home was built on a contaminated site or was the sight of a gruesome murder or is reputed to be haunted. The latter conditions have given rise to specific nondisclosure statutes limiting liability of builders or real estate brokers who fail to disclose stigmatizing events. Some purchasers have even tried to sue construction lenders for defects, but this has met with only limited success.

Brown v. Lober

(Purchaser) v. (Seller's Estate)

75 Ill.2d 547, 389 N.E.2d 1188 (1979)

M E M O R Y   G R A P H I C

Instant Facts

Purchaser sued seller's estate for breach of covenant of seisin upon discovering prior owner had retained 2/3 of mineral estate.

Black Letter Rule

To succeed on a claim for breach of the covenant of quiet enjoyment, one must show not only paramount title in another but also actual or constructive ouster.

Case Vocabulary

COVENANT OF GOOD RIGHT TO CONVEY: Same as Covenant of Seisin.

COVENANT OF QUIET ENJOYMENT: Under Illinois law, the grantor's warranty to the buyer and the buyer's heirs and assigns that grantor and the grantor's heirs and assigns will defend possession of the premises and the title granted by the terms of the deed against any person who may lawfully claim the same.

COVENANT OF SEISIN: A grantor's assurance or warranty that the grantor, at the time of conveyance, has valid title to the property and possession of the premises and has the power to convey that which he has conveyed.

INCUMBRANCE: Any right or interest in the land conveyed held by a third party which may diminish the value of the land but which does not necessarily prevent the conveyance.

STATUTE OF LIMITATIONS: A statutory time limit within which claims must be brought.

Procedural Basis: Appeal to the Supreme Court of Illinois from appellate court's ruling reversing trial court's judgment dismissing claim.

Facts: Brown (P) purchased 80 acres from William and Faith Bost (D). The property was transferred by a statutory warranty deed containing no exceptions. The deed was dated December 21, 1957. After delivery of the deed, Brown (P) took possession of the land and recorded the deed. On May 8, 1974, Brown (P) granted a coal option to Consolidated Coal Co. in which Brown (P) leased the right to mine the coal underlying the land for $6,000. In 1976, Brown (P) discovered that a prior grantor had reserved 2/3 of the mineral estate, and that Brown (P) only owned a 1/3 interest. After renegotiating the lease with Consolidated Coal Co., in which a reduced payment of $2,000 was agreed upon for the 1/3 interest, Brown brought suit against Lober (D), the executor of the estate of Faith Bost (D), seeking $4,000 in damages. The suit was filed May 25, 1976. The trial court ruled that Brown's (P) claim for breach of the covenant of seisin was barred by the ten-year statute of limitations. The trial court also denied Brown's (P) post-trial motion in which Brown (P) argued that the covenant of quiet enjoyment had also been breached. The appellate court reversed, finding that Brown's (P) claim for breach of the covenant of quiet enjoyment was not barred by the statute of limitations. This appeal followed.

Issue: Does a claim for breach of the covenant of quiet enjoyment accrue when it is discovered that there is paramount title in another?

Decision and Rationale: (Underwood, J.) No. Brown (P) received a general statutory form warranty deed, which under Illinois law, contained the following implied covenants: that at the time of making delivery, the grantor was lawfully seized of an indefeasible estate in fee simple in and to the premises described and had good right and full power to convey the same, that the estate was free from all incumbrances and that the grantee shall have quiet and peaceable possession of such premises and that the grantor will defend against all others claiming title thereto. The first part of these implied covenants represent the covenant of seisin, also known as the covenant of good right to convey. The second part represents the covenant against incumbrances and the last part sets forth the covenant of quiet enjoyment. Brown's (P) complaint essentially claims that the Bosts (D) covenanted that they were the fee simple owners of the estate at the time of the conveyance and breached that covenant by failing to convey the full mineral estate. The trial court interpreted this as a claim for the breach of the covenant of seisin. The parties agree that such a claim must be brought within 10 years of the date the claim accrues. Since the covenant of seisin is a present covenant, that is it is breached, if at all, upon delivery of the deed, the breach occurred on December 21, 1957. Brown's (P) complaint was filed nearly 20 years later, on May 25, 1976. Therefore, the trial court correctly ruled that the claim was barred. However, in Brown's (P) post-trial motion, Brown (P) argued that the covenant of quiet enjoyment had also been breached. The trial court denied this motion without analysis. It was the appellate court's conclusion that while the claim for breach of the covenant of seisin was time-barred, the claim for breach of the covenant of quiet enjoyment was not. The appellate court reasoned that the latter claim only arose in 1976, when Brown (P) first learned that the entire mineral estate had not been conveyed. The issue for us, then, is when Brown's (P) claim for breach of the covenant of quiet enjoyment accrued. Unlike the covenant of seisin, the covenant of quiet enjoyment is a future covenant and is only breached at some later date after delivery of the deed when there is an actual or constructive eviction by one with paramount title. The mere existence of title in another is insufficient to constitute a breach of the covenant of quiet enjoyment; there must also be an ouster. In Scott v. Kirkendall [88 Ill. 465 (1878), involving a claim of breach of the covenant of quiet enjoyment based upon the existence of title in another to vacant land no one had taken possession of] we held that there could be no claim for breach of the covenant of quiet enjoyment because the grantee could at any time have taken possession of the land. While there was superior title in another, such superior title had never been asserted to prevent the grantee from taking possession. Admittedly, Scott dealt with only surface rights, not mineral rights as are at issue here. Nevertheless, we find the same reasoning applicable here. Upon taking possession of the land, Brown (P) did not take possession of the mineral estate. To do so, Brown (P) would have to physically remove the minerals. Since no one has physically removed the minerals, the mineral estate must be deemed vacant. As such, there is nothing precluding Brown (P) from taking possession of the whole mineral estate and therefore, no constructive eviction has occurred and there can be no claim for breach of the covenant of quiet enjoyment. Here, the covenant of seisin was clearly breached upon delivery of the deed, but such a claim is time-barred. While Brown (P) may someday have a claim for breach of the covenant of quiet enjoyment, such a claim is premature at this time as no ouster has occurred. The ruling of the appellate court is therefore reversed and the ruling of the trial court is affirmed.

Analysis:

The most important thing to take away from this case is the discussion regarding the requirements for successfully proving a breach of the covenant of quiet enjoyment. Such a claim requires a showing not only that someone else has title to the land but also that the other titleholder has evicted the grantee. Such eviction can be constructive or actual, but constructive eviction requires more than the mere possibility that the title holder could someday come and claim possession of the land. Such was the case here. While no one disputed that the prior grantor who reserved the 2/3 mineral estate could someday come and claim possession of his 2/3 interest, since it had not yet happened, there was nothing preventing Brown (P) from taking possession of the whole estate which he believed was transferred by Bost (D). Notice how this result does not truly resolve the underlying dispute, since it simply leaves the question open until such time as the prior grantor makes a claim to his 2/3 interest. Notice also how this does not help Brown (P) who cannot lease the whole since he only owns a 1/3 interest. Had Brown (P) anticipated this, he could have brought the prior grantor in as a defendant, essentially forcing the prior grantor to make a claim and therefore putting the matter at issue before the court. Given that the prior grantor's interest was a matter of public record, however, one may wonder how Brown (P) could make any claim at all – surely he can be said to have known about the prior reservation in the recorded history of the land? The court only addresses this in its discussion of the fact that the claimed breach of the covenant of seisin was time-barred. Since the covenant of seisin is separate and distinct from the covenant of quiet enjoyment, however, there remains a possibility that Brown (P) could still succeed in recovering for the failure to transfer possession of the whole mineral estate, a result that seems inequitable in light of the fact that Brown (P) should have known and easily could have discovered the discrepancy at the time he purchased the property. While the crux of this case is the discussion about what constitutes a constructive eviction, it also raises some interesting practical pleading questions such as whether to sue the prior grantor and clearly delineating the covenant claimed to have been breached.

Leach v. Gunnarson

(Licensee) v. (Grantee)

290 Or. 31, 619 P.2d 263 (1980)

M E M O R Y   G R A P H I C

Instant Facts

Grantee sued grantor for breach of covenant against encumbrances upon discovering grantor had granted an irrevocable license to third party for use of spring located on grantee's land.

Black Letter Rule

Irrevocable license to use spring water violates covenant against encumbrances, even if open and visible.

Case Vocabulary

COVENANT AGAINST ENCUMBRANCES: A warranty by the grantor that the property being conveyed is free from all encumbrances.

ENCUMBRANCE: Any right or interest in the land conveyed held by a third party which may diminish the value of the land but which does not necessarily prevent the conveyance.

IRREVOCABLE LICENSE: The grant of a right to do something or use something owned by another that cannot be revoked.

THIRD PARTY PLAINTIFF OR DEFENDANT: A third party plaintiff is a defendant in the original case; the third party defendant is the new party brought in by a claim asserted by the third party plaintiff.

Procedural Basis: Appeal to the Supreme Court of Oregon from appellate court's ruling affirming jury's verdict finding no breach of the covenant against encumbrances.

Facts: Grantor owned a 20-acre parcel of land and a small adjoining piece, which grantor sold to Leach (P) in 1954. At the time of the sale, grantor also granted Leach (P) an irrevocable license to locate, construct and maintain a facility to transport water from a spring located on grantor's property to their own property. Leach (P) subsequently built a 1x3 dam and a 370-gallon storage tank with a 175 foot plastic pipe running to the spring across grantor's property. In May 1975, grantor conveyed the 20-acre parcel to Gunnarson (D) by general warranty deed. At the time of purchase, Gunnarson (D) knew that Leach (P) was using the spring, but claimed he was assured by grantor that Leach (P) had no right to do so. In the deed from grantor to Gunnarson (D) was a covenant against encumbrances. At trial, the judge instructed the jury that if they found Leach's (P) use of the spring to be an open, visible and notorious encumbrance upon the land that they were to return a verdict for grantor. The jury found for grantor and the appellate court affirmed. This appeal followed.

Issue: Does an open, visible and notorious encumbrance upon land constitute a breach of the covenant against encumbrances?

Decision and Rationale: (Howell, J.) On these facts, yes. Our prior decisions clearly state that the covenant against encumbrances protects a grantee against all encumbrances existing at the time of delivery, even if the grantee knew about the encumbrance. Some jurisdictions, however, have carved out an exception for those physical encumbrances on land that are open, visible and notorious. We have considered this exception on two prior occasions. In Barnum v. Lockhart [purchaser under installment contract sued grantor for failure to remove railroad right of way that was disclosed by grantor in title abstract] we held that title to the property was not rendered unmarketable by railroad right of way because the parties could not have contemplated removal of that type of encumbrance. In Ford v. White [grantee sought to rescind contract because grantor provided abstract showing utility easement] we held that because the grantee had observed the power lines prior to entering into the contract, the parties must have taken the easement into account when negotiating the purchase price and therefore it was an encumbrance that the parties assented to. We need not decide whether under these prior decisions Oregon recognizes the open, visible and notorious exception to the covenant against encumbrances, because here, the encumbrance at issue is not of the sort to which such an exception would apply. The exception, to the extent it applies, is limited only to known easements for public use, such as utility easements and railroad rights of way. The irrevocable license at issue is not such an encumbrance and therefore the exception does not apply. We therefore reverse the ruling of the appellate court and remand for a new trial.

Analysis:

This case is meant to expose you to the debate about the open, visible and notorious exception the covenant against encumbrances, even though the discussion appears in a case where the court ultimately determines that even if the exception were adopted in Oregon, it would not apply. Notice how the court ducks the issue of whether the exception applies under Oregon law altogether. The court's conclusion, however, is troublesome. Why are easements or encumbrances for public use subject to the exception, but private encumbrances, such as the one at issue here, are not? In most cases, the private encumbrance is far more visible than a public easement. Does it make sense to say that a grantee who sees a physical encumbrance like the one at issue here reasonably expects the grantor to covenant against that very encumbrance? Other courts considering the matter have found the reasoning here unpersuasive and have disallowed recovery for things such as prescriptive easements. However, the issue gets even more complicated when zoning violations are considered. If a grantor has constructed buildings in violation of zoning laws that will subject the grantee to litigation and fines, shouldn't the grantor bear liability even if the grantee visibly saw the possible infraction? Courts are split on this issue. Another issue has arisen regarding what damages are recoverable if the covenant is breached. Some courts have held that only nominal damages are recoverable unless the grantee has removed the encumbrance and has suffered actual damages. What damages are recoverable for breaches of the title covenants is discussed in greater detail in the following case, Davis v. Smith.

Davis v. Smith

(Not Stated) v. (Not Stated)
5 Ga. 274, 48 Am.Dec. 279 (1848)

M E M O R Y   G R A P H I C

Instant Facts
In suit to determine what debts estate should pay, court discussed measure of damages applicable to claim by grantee for breach of covenant of title.

Black Letter Rule
In suit for breach of covenant of title/seisin, grantee may recover only amount paid for land plus interest.

Case Vocabulary

BONA FIDE: Refers to acting in or with good faith, honestly and without fraud.
MESNE PROFITS: Refers to the amounts earned in between, such as the profits that one receives between disseisin and recovery of lands or monetary damages.
OMNE MAJUS CONTINET IN SE MINUS: Literally, the greater contains within itself the less.

Procedural Basis: Appeal to Supreme Court of Georgia from ruling of trial court on amount of debts to be paid by estate.

Facts: The estate of N.H. Harris, being partially insolvent, brought suit to have the court determine what debts should be paid. One such debt was a claim by the heirs of Noah Laney for breach of the covenant of warranty in a deed by Harris to Laney. In remanding the matter for further proceedings, the Supreme Court of Georgia took time to set forth the measure of damages applicable to the claim for breach of the covenant of warranty, should it be found to be a valid claim on remand.

Issue: In a suit for breach of a covenant of title, does the grantee recover the purchase price he paid for the land plus interest?

Decision and Rationale: (Nesbet, J.) Yes. What damages are recoverable in cases alleging breach of the covenant of warranty has been the subject of much debate. Some courts allow recovery based on the value of the land at the time of eviction, taking into account the natural appreciation in the value of the land but no less than the present value if the value has depreciated. Others allow recovery of the value of the land at the time of eviction plus the value of any improvements made. The majority, however, allow only recovery of the price paid for the land plus interest from the time of purchase. The first two rules are not uniform, and often allow inequitable results depending solely on the appreciation or depreciation of the value of the land. The last rule, however, is uniform, based in common sense and is easily understood. Further, it is the rule that has always been applied at common law, even during feudal times. While the covenants at issue are of recent invention as security for the purchase, the recovery for breach of these covenants has not changed. Here, the covenant at issue is the covenant of title. It is undisputed that there was an eviction of the grantee by judgment, and so the measure of damages adopted herein, that being the purchase price plus interest, applies only to similar claims for breach of the covenant of title. What the appropriate measure of damages would be in a case for breach of a covenant of quiet enjoyment we have not decided. It would seem, however, that the same measure of damages would apply since a breach of the covenant of seisin is necessarily followed by a breach of the covenant of quiet enjoyment, and it makes no sense to allow a greater recovery for the latter breach. That the measure of damages we adopt today is proper is clear. Parties to a contract are bound by their intentions and it cannot be said that a grantor who sells a piece of vacant land for $1,000 dollars intended to covenant land that may someday end up worth millions if it be turned into a city. The appreciation or depreciation of the value of the land is a risk solely taken by the grantee. The parties to the deed intend to secure the land only to the extent of the value of the land at the time the deed is delivered, and the parties should be held to the bargain they made. That the measure of recovery should also include interest is also well-founded, since the grantor has had the use of the grantee's money and the grantee, while receiving rents or other benefits from the land during his possession, has made improvements for which he should be compensation. While some courts allow recovery of the value of the improvements themselves, they do so only where the grantee has acted in good faith. In the United States, however, the majority is in favor of the measure of damages we adopt today.

Analysis:

Obviously the crux of this case is the discussion about how to determine the amount of damages a grantee is entitled to recover if successful in proving a breach of the covenant of seisin, also referred to in this opinion as the covenant of warranty or covenant of title. The court here restricts recovery to the amount paid at purchase plus interest. This makes sense and seems clear enough, but the measure of damages becomes less clear when remote grantees are considered. Does a remote grantee recover the amount he paid or the amount his grantor paid? Again, courts are split. Some limit recovery to the amount the remote grantee himself paid, while others allow recovery only to the amount the remote grantee's grantor paid. Other issues arise when grantees have to go to court to determine if they have been disseized or not. Some courts allow recovery of litigation costs, such as attorney fees, from the grantor if the grantee is unsuccessful in disproving a claim to paramount title. Others deny such costs if the grantee is successful, however. For the covenant against encumbrances, the ordinary measure of damages is the amount paid to extinguish the encumbrance. In New York, however, the measure of damages is the difference between the value of the land without the encumbrance and the value of the land with the encumbrance. These rules seem clear enough, but what if a grantee makes substantial improvements far in excess of the value of the land at purchase plus interest? The measure of damages in this scenario is considered in the next case, Madrid v. Spears.

Madrid v. Spears

(Grantee in Possession) v. (Owner/Forged Grantor)
250 F.2d 51 (10th Cir. 1957)

M E M O R Y   G R A P H I C

Instant Facts

Owner of property conveyed to grantee in possession by forged deed brought suit to cancel deed and quiet title back to owner.

Black Letter Rule

When one in possession makes improvements to property that is subsequently returned to the rightful owner, possessor is entitled to recover the costs of the improvements or the amount said improvements enhanced the value of the property, whichever is less.

Case Vocabulary

DIVERSITY ACTION: A case brought in federal court because it is a dispute between residents of different states.

LACHES: An affirmative defense based upon the delay in bringing the claim; essentially meaning that one who waits too long cannot complain.

MESNE PROFITS: Refers to the amounts earned in between, such as the profits that one receives between disseisin and recovery of lands or monetary damages.

RESTITUTION: A remedy by which one has been wronged is restored to their previous position before the wrongdoing occurred.

UNJUST ENRICHMENT: A legal theory upon which one who improves the value of land is entitled to recover the value added so as to avoid the unjust benefit to the owner who receives the benefit.

Procedural Basis: Appeal to Tenth Circuit Court of Appeals from trial court's judgment rescinding deed, awarding ½ of actual costs of improvements to possessor and denying owner ½ rents received during possession.

Facts: Spears (D) filed a diversity action against Madrid (P) seeking to cancel a deed that purportedly conveyed Spears' (D) ½ interest in a 320-acre parcel of land in New Mexico to Madrid (P). Spears (D) contended that her name on the deed was forged. Madrid (P) denied the forgery but alleged, alternatively, that if the deed was canceled as to Spears' (D) ½ interest that they had made valuable improvements to the property in good faith and that therefore Spears (D) was estopped by laches to assert her title. Spears (D) in turn admitted the value of the improvements (14,214.42) but claimed said value should be offset by rents received by Madrid (P), ½ of which totaled $17,453. After a trial to the court, judgment was entered declaring the deed a forgery, awarded Madrid (P) ½ the actual cost of improvements and denying Spears' (D) claim to ½ the rents received. Both sides appealed to this Court.

Issue: Is the amount of recovery for improvements made in good faith to property by one in possession thereof limited solely to the actual cost of the improvements?

Decision and Rationale: (Murrah, C.J.) No. Under New Mexico's statutory scheme, one occupying lands may seek to recover the value of improvements made while in possession under color of title. A plaintiff seeking to eject one in possession may also seek a share of the mesne profits received during the period of possession. If the plaintiff is successful in such a suit, an award must also be made to the defendant in possession for the value of the improvements made. A finding must also be made about the value of the mesne profits received. If the value of the improvements exceeds the mesne profits, a judgment is then entered in favor of the defendant in possession for the difference. In such a case, however, a plaintiff may elect to simply pay for the improvements or, alternatively, to pay for the net profits and value of the land without the improvements. In the latter case, the defendant in possession provides a warranty deed to the plaintiff. This statutory scheme was enacted to relax the rigid common law rules that often left a defendant in possession under only color of title without a proper legal remedy for improvements made on the property during his possession. The majority of courts addressing this issue, however, permit recovery to a good faith improver. Those courts measure the recovery not by the actual cost of the improvements but rather by the value said improvements enhanced the land, reasoning that recovery is had based on theories of restitution or unjust enrichment. The enhanced value is determined by the difference between the value of the land with the improvements and the value of the land without the improvements. Even in those cases, however, cost is an important factor in determining the amount of recovery allowed. This undoubtedly is why the Restatement adopted the whichever is less approach, determining that where one in possession is entitled to recover, he is entitled to recover the reasonable value of his labor and material or the amount which the improvements have enhanced the value of the land, whichever is smaller. Here, Madrid (P) enhanced the land somewhere between $4,800 and $83,100. Part of this was obviously attributable to other factors, such as general market conditions, and the evidence does not demonstrate exactly how much of this enhancement was due to the improvements. It is clear, though, that the value of the land was enhanced far in excess of the actual cost of the improvements. Since an owner cannot receive a benefit in excess of the cost of the improvements, the trial court's judgment is correct. The trial court was also correct in denying Spears (D) ½ the mesne profits Madrid (P) received, since such recovery is limited to the rental value of the unimproved land. There being no proof of this value, the judgment of the trial court is affirmed.

Analysis:

Here, as in the previous case, the emphasis is on how to determine the measure of damages. Where the previous case was concerned with the measure of damages recoverable for breach of a covenant of title, here we are concerned with the appropriate measure of damages recoverable for one who took possession of property under color of title, making improvements to the property while in possession, but not actually ever having received fee title to the property. Notice that the court does not adopt one approach, but instead adopts a "whichever is smaller" rule whereby one in possession is entitled to either the actual cost of the improvements *or* the amount the improvements enhanced the value of the land, whichever is less. The underlying theory being that the land cannot be improved beyond the actual cost of the improvements, and any excess of enhanced value must necessarily be due to other factors. Given this logic, one wonders why the court did not simply adopt a cost approach, awarding only the actual cost of improvements. As a side note, it is interesting that the court did not hold that an owner is not entitled to ½ of the profits received during the possessor's possession, but instead held that in this particular case Spears (D) did not submit adequate proof to recover the value of the rents received for the unimproved property. If Spears (D) must pay for ½ of the improvements, why would she not be entitled to ½ of the actual rents received, rather than simply ½ of the rental value of the unimproved land? This is an interesting twist in the court's opinion that is not given much discussion. Finally, note that in this case Madrid (P) was only ever on title to ½ of the interest in the land. Would the result be different if at a later date Madrid's (P) grantor obtained the other ½ interest? Would this work to transfer the full fee estate to Madrid (P)? These issues are the subject of the following case, Robben v. Obering.

Robben v. Obering

(Lessee #1) v. (Lessee #2)
279 F.2d 381 (7th Cir. 1960)

M E M O R Y   G R A P H I C

Instant Facts

Lessee under second oil and gas lease purportedly transferring ¼ interest sued lessee under first oil and gas lease after dispute arose over what grantors owned at time leases were executed.

Black Letter Rule

Doctrine of after-acquired title applies to oil and gas lease containing title covenants.

Case Vocabulary

DECLARATORY JUDGMENT: An equitable remedy by which a court determines the rights of the parties.

DOCTRINE OF AFTER-ACQUIRED TITLE: Legal principle that holds that a grantor who owns less than what was conveyed at the time of conveyance but later obtains title to a part or all of the portion not previously owned also transfers the subsequently acquired interest, having intended to have conveyed the same all along. This principle is also referred to as estoppel by deed.

Ill. Rev. Stat. 1959, Ch. 30, Par. 6: Illinois' codification of the after-acquired title doctrine in the context of warranty deeds.

REMOVED: A procedure by which a case is transferred from state court to federal court.

Procedural Basis: Appeal to Seventh Circuit Court of Appeals from trial court's judgment in favor of second lessee.

Facts: On November 7, 1953, Ed Meirink executed an oil and gas lease to Obering (D). The lease covered a 21-acre tract of land in Clinton County, Illinois. Thereafter, Obering (D) conveyed ½ interest in the lease to his wife. The lease contained a covenant of warranty which stated that Meirink, as lessor, warranted and agreed to defend the title to the lands covered by the lease, those being the 21-acre tract. At the time Meirink executed the lease, he believed he owned the entire 21-acre tract in fee simple absolute. In 1956, upon the drilling of another oil well on an adjacent tract, Meirink hired an attorney to review the title to the minerals and discovered that he only owned a ¼ interest, and that the other interests were owned by his brother, Arthur, his nephew, a minor, and his sister, an incompetent. Meirink attempted to obtain the other interests, and received a quitclaim deed to ¼ interest from Arthur on July 20, 1956, and recorded the same on July 21, 1956. Because the remaining interest owners were incompetent to transfer property, Meirink was unable to acquire the other interests. By quitclaim deed dated July 20, 1956 and recorded August 7, 1956, Meirink quitclaimed back ¼ interest to Arthur and his wife in joint tenancy. On November 2, 1956, Arthur and his wife leased their ¼ interest to Robben (P). At trial, the court rejected Obering's (D) contention that upon obtaining the additional ¼ interest from Arthur, that interest passed to Obering (D) under the doctrine of after-acquired title, ruling that the doctrine did not apply. This appeal followed.

Issue: Does the doctrine of after-acquired title apply to oil and gas leases containing covenants of title?

Decision and Rationale: (Castle, C.J.) Yes. The parties concede that Illinois law applies in this case and that Illinois has adopted the doctrine of after-acquired title where express warranties are made by the grantor. The parties also concede, however, that there are no Illinois cases directly on point, i.e. no cases determining if the doctrine applies in the context of an oil and gas lease. However, we see no reason why the doctrine would not apply in this case. Robben (P) argues that Illinois' after-acquired title statute was only intended to apply to conveyances in fee simple absolute. We disagree. While the statute was intended to remove any uncertainty that may have existed in cases involving transfers in fee simple absolute, we see nothing in the statute limiting its scope to only such conveyances or to otherwise restrict the applicability of the common law rule. Therefore, we conclude that the doctrine of after-acquired title applies, and that accordingly, upon receiving ¼ interest from Arthur, that interest passed to Obering (D) by virtue of the previously executed lease rendering the subsequent transfer to Arthur and the subsequent lease by Arthur to Robben (P) ineffective. The judgment of the trial court is reversed and the case remanded.

Analysis:

First and foremost, notice that the court determines that the doctrine of after-acquired title applies in this case based on previous case law finding the doctrine applicable in cases where the grantor has given express warranties. It necessarily follows then that in the absence of an express warranty, the doctrine does not apply. Second, note that the court assumes that under the doctrine of after-acquired title the subsequently acquired interest automatically transfers to the grantee. This is known as "feeding the estoppel". Not all courts follow the immediate transfer interpretation, holding instead that the acquisition of title to property purportedly conveyed subsequent to the conveyance gives the grantee the right to seek that property, but the property itself is not immediately conveyed. Courts are also split on whether a breach of a covenant of title is required in order for the doctrine to apply and on whether a grantor can defeat a breach of the covenant of title claim by later obtaining title to the property by adverse possession.

First American Title Insurance Company, Inc. v. First Title Service Company of the Florida Keys, Inc.

(Insurance Company) v. (Abstractor)
457 So.2d 467 (Fla. 1984)

M E M O R Y   G R A P H I C

Instant Facts
Issuer of title insurance policy to seller sued abstractor who prepared abstract of title for seller for negligence.

Black Letter Rule
Abstractors will only be liable to those with whom they contract or to those that are third-party beneficiaries of the contract.

Case Vocabulary

COMPLAINT: The first pleading filed in a case stating the basis of the claim against the defendant.
PRIVITY: Refers here to having a direct contractual relationship.
SUBROGATION: A means by which an insurance company who pays a claim on behalf of an insured steps into the shoes of the insured for purposes of bringing claims to recover the amount paid from those who are really liable.

Procedural Basis: Appeal from the District Court of Appeals' decision holding abstractor not liable.

Facts: First Title Service Company (FTSC) (D) entered into a contract with the sellers of two lots to prepare abstracts of title for the respective lots. Relying on those abstracts, First American Title Insurance Company (FATIC) (P) issued title insurance policies for the two lots to seller and its lender. According to the Complaint, the abstract failed to mention the existence of a recorded judgment against a former owner of the lots. Upon demand by the holder of the judgment, FATIC (P) paid $75,000 in satisfaction of the judgment and brought suit against FTSC (D) to recover the amount paid. In granting FTSC's (D) motion to dismiss, the District Court of Appeals held that FTSC (D) could not be held liable to FATIC (P) for the error because there was no privity between FTSC (D) and FATIC (P). This appeal followed.

Issue: Are abstractors liable to those who may foreseeably rely on their abstracts but with whom the abstractor has no privity?

Decision and Rationale: (Body, J.) No. FATIC (P) argues that the proper test for determining FTSC's (D) liability is whether it was foreseeable that a party such as FATIC (P) would rely on the abstract. According to FATIC (P), it is irrelevant whether there is privity of contract between FTSC (D) and FATIC (P). In so arguing, FATIC (P) relies on numerous cases from other jurisdictions, the most notable of which is *Williams v. Polgar*, 215 N.W.2d 149 (Mich. 1974), in which it was held that an abstractor who missed a deed was liable to a subsequent purchaser even in the absence of privity. In so holding, the Michigan Court noted that the defense of privity was no bar to the claim since Michigan law already recognized that an abstractor is liable not only to those with whom he contracts but also to those he knows may rely on the abstract. For the Michigan Court, then, it was no stretch to expand the rule to include subsequent purchasers. Notably, the Michigan Court's holding relied on its theory that one who undertakes to perform a duty under a contract owes a duty not only to the other contracting party but also to others to perform with reasonable care. We decline to follow this reasoning. Adopting the Michigan rule would expand liability to a never-ending point where an abstractor could potentially be held liable to anyone, even those he has no reason to know will rely on his abstract. We recognize that this in essence is a public policy question, but decline to adopt the policy urged by FATIC (P). We also reject FATIC's (P) analogy to the law of products liability in which the privity defense was gradually eliminated. Unlike product manufacturers, abstractors are attempting to provide a specific service regarding specific pieces of land for specific people; they are not providing a global product for general public use. Therefore, while the general rule permitting a manufacturer to be held liable to those who foreseeably may use the product makes sense in that setting, it does not follow that the same rule should be applied in this case. While we are not inclined to expand abstractor liability to all foreseeable parties, we are convinced that those who can claim to be a third-party beneficiary of the contract with the abstractor may have standing to bring a claim against the abstractor even though they did not contract directly with him. It thus clearly follows that FATIC (P) as the insurer of the purchasers here, who were known and intended to benefit from the abstract, may recover damages from the abstractor for negligent preparation of the abstract. We realize that our holding today changes the law of abstractor liability such that where an abstractor knows or has reason to know that his customer wants the abstract for use by prospective purchasers and those purchasers actually purchase the land, the abstractor is also liable to those purchasers even though they did not contract with the abstractor. Applying this law to the facts here, we find that FATIC (P) stated a cause of action against FTSC (D) and the District Court of Appeals' ruling dismissing its Complaint must be reversed.

Analysis:

There is an important distinction to be made here between the foreseeability test that the court rejects and the third-party beneficiary type test that the court adopts. On the one hand, the court declined to extend abstractor liability to all those who may foreseeably rely on the abstract, which would include those who the abstractor has no reason to know would rely on it like distant purchasers. The court did, however, permit FATIC (P) to proceed with its claim here on the grounds that FATIC (P), who stepped into the shoes of the purchasers for whom the abstract was ordered by the seller, was a party that the abstractor knew or should have known would rely on the abstract. Keep in mind, however, that FATIC (P) represented the actual purchasers of the property and that they were intended by the seller who ordered the abstract to use it in making their decision whether or not to purchase the property. Under the rule announced here it is doubtful that the abstractor would have been held liable if the purchasers did not actually purchase the land. Further, note that under this rule, subsequent purchasers would probably not be allowed to recover since there would be no reason for the abstractor here to know that the purchasers here would pass on the abstract to subsequent purchasers to rely on years later. As a practical matter, this makes sense since a buyer years later would probably want a more recent abstract or title review to insure that newer encumbrances are discovered.

United States v. Ryan

(Lien Holder) v. (Land Owner)
24 F.Supp.1 (D. Minn 1954), *rev'd* 253 F.2d 944 (8th Cir. 1958)

M E M O R Y   G R A P H I C

Instant Facts

United States tax liens held subject to requirements of state Torrens Systems.

Black Letter Rule

The United States government is not exempt from complying with the requirements of a state Torrens System.

Case Vocabulary

QUIET TITLE ACTION: A judicial action used to determine interest in property.
TORRENS SYSTEM: A title registration system under which involuntary transfers such as foreclosures must go through the court system and are only valid upon issuance of a court decree.

Procedural Basis: Suit by Internal Revenue Service to determine validity of tax lien.

Facts: The United Sates (P) filed a notice of a tax lien in the office of the register of deeds in the state of Minnesota, naming the debtor only. It then filed this action to foreclose that lien on property.

Issue: Does the United States have to comply with state requirements for registering liens?

Decision and Rationale: (Bell, D.J.) Yes. The United States (P) filed a notice of tax lien listing the debtor by name only in the office of the register of deeds in the state of Minnesota. Ryan (D) and the other defendants contend that this was insufficient to create a valid lien upon property Ryan (D) purchased from the debtor. Minnesota follows a Torrens System of title assurance. This means that once an involuntary transfer of property occurs and a court decree is issued setting forth all of the interests in that property, the property is considered "registered" and all subsequent purchasers can rely on the certificate of title issued by the register of titles after the decree as a concrete statement of all interests in the property. Minnesota has followed this system of title assurance for more than fifty years. Under federal law, a tax lien is not valid against any mortgagee, pledgee, purchaser or judgment creditor until the Collector has filed notice. Federal law provides that notice shall be filed in the office of which the law of the state or territory in which the property subject to the lien is situated. Minnesota has authorized the filing of such notices. Because the property at issue here is registered under the Torrens System, Minnesota law requires that notice be filed in the office of the register of deeds. Minnesota law also provides that the notice describe the land upon which the lien is claimed. The United States (P) first contends that these requirements do not apply to tax liens because they are liens, claims or rights arising or existing under the laws or the Constitution of the United States, which are specifically exempt from these requirements under Minnesota law. We disagree. The federal law that authorizes tax liens specifically provides that they are not valid unless notice is given as authorized by state law. The United States (P) also contends that the states cannot require it to register tax liens in the manner that Minnesota has so required because it places a heavy burden on the United States (P). It is thus the United States' (P) position that the states can only designate in which office the notice must be filed. Again we disagree. The United States (P) is not exempt from the provisions of state statutes. Here, the United States (P) would have had a valid lien had it simply done what the Minnesota statutes required. It did not. Consequently, it does not have a valid lien.

Analysis:

First and foremost you should note that the Eight Circuit Court of Appeals overturned this case. It was the Eighth Circuit's opinion that a tax lien becomes a lien on all property owned by the debtor at the time the collector receives the assessment list, and that property registered under Torrens Systems like that in Minnesota is not excepted. This case is not here to espouse the virtues or downsides of the law of the case or the Eighth Circuit's opinion reversing this case. Rather, it is here simply to make you aware that the Torrens System exists as another means of assuring title to property.

White v. Western Title Insurance Co.

(Insured) v. (Insurer)
40 Cal.3d 870, 221 Cal.Rptr. 509, 710 P.2d 309 (Cal. 1985)

M E M O R Y   G R A P H I C

Instant Facts

Purchasers of property sued title insurance company for breach upon discovering existence of water easement.

Black Letter Rule

Title insurance policy exclusion for minerals and water does not exclude water easement of record.

Case Vocabulary

EASEMENT: A right to enter and use land for a specific purpose.

ESCROW: The holding of money, usually a deposit of some type, as security for the performance of a contract, like the sale of property.

QUIET TITLE ACTION: A judicial action used to determine interest in property.

SCHEDULE A: The first part of a title insurance policy listing the fee estate being insured.

SCHEDULE B: The second part of a title insurance policy listing the exceptions to Schedule A.

Procedural Basis: Appeal from jury verdict awarding damages for breach of contract, negligence and breach of the covenant of good faith and fair dealing against insurer.

Facts: William and Virginia Longhurst owned 84 acres, which were divided into two lots, one developed and one, unimproved. On December 29, 1975, the Longhursts conveyed an easement for construction of a waterline and well sites to the River Estates Mutual Water Corporation ("REMWC"). The easement deed was recorded the following day. In 1978, the Longhursts entered into a contract to sell their two lots to the Whites (P). The Whites (P), unaware of the water easement, requested preliminary title reports from Western Title Insurance Co. ("Western") (D). Neither report listed the water easement. At closing, Western issued two title insurance policies to the Whites (P), one for each lot. Neither policy listed the water easement. Both policies provided that the policy insured the Whites (P) against loss or damage incurred due to title not being as set forth on Schedule A or any defect in or lien or encumbrance upon the property not listed in Schedule B. Schedule B listed all recorded liens and encumbrances except the water easement, and contained the standard exceptions, one of which was for all unrecorded easements, liens and encumbrances and one excluding unpatented mining claims and water rights. Six months after closing, REMWC notified the Whites (P) of their intention to begin construction of the water pipeline pursuant to the easement. The Whites (P) protested, leading REMWC to file a quiet title action seeking to enforce their interest in the property. The Whites (P) notified Western (D) of the claim and Western (D), denying that it provided coverage, agreed to defend against REMWC's claim. REMWC eventually decided not to enforce its easement and dismissed the case. The Whites' (P) appraiser valued the loss in property value to the Whites (P) at $62,947, and the Whites (P) demanded that Western (D) pay that amount to compensate them for Western's failure to uncover the water easement. Western, acknowledging that a loss was suffered, refused to pay claiming that the loss stemmed from the loss of groundwater and was thus excluded from the standard water rights exclusion set forth in Schedule B. The Whites (P) filed suit in October 1979 claiming that Western (D) breached its contractual duty to pay for the loss, and alleging that Western (D) was negligent in preparation of the policies. Western's (D) appraiser valued the Whites' (P) loss at $2,000, and based thereon, Western (D) offered to settle the claim for $3,000. The Whites (P) declined. In June 1980, Western (D) again offered to settle the claim, this time for $5,000. The Whites (P) again declined. Western (D) never provided the Whites (P) with a copy of its appraisal of their damages. Subsequently, the Whites (P) obtained leave of court to amend its claims to add one for breach of the covenant of good faith and fair dealing. The trial court bifurcated the issues of liability and damages, and after a trial to the court on the issue of liability in January 1981, found Western (D) liable. Western (D) thereafter provided the Whites (P) with a copy of its appraisal and offered to settle the claim for $15,000. The Whites (P) declined. A jury trial was held in February 1982, and the jury fixed the amount of damage sustained at $100 per acre, resulting in a total of $8,400. Following a ruling by the trial court allowing the Whites (P) to introduce evidence of the settlement offers made by Western (D) during the course of the litigation, the jury also found Western (D) liable for breaching the covenant of good faith and fair dealing and awarded $20,000. Western (D) has now appealed the judgments entered against it.

Issue: Does a title insurance policy that excludes minerals and water rights preclude recovery for a missing recorded water easement?

Decision and Rationale: (Broussard, J.) No. First we must determine whether the insurance policies issued exclude coverage for the damages claimed. Schedule B contains two parts: the first lists specific exclusions based upon findings in the record, the second lists the standard exceptions. Neither part listed the water easement. The last exclusion is for unpatented mining claims and water rights and claims or title to water. It is upon this exclusion that Western (D) relies. Whether or not coverage exists is a matter of contractual interpretation. General rules of construction for title insurance policies provide that coverage clauses be interpreted broadly so as to afford the greatest possible protection, while exclusionary clauses are interpreted narrowly against the insurer. The idea is to construe the policy so as to give the insured the protection that he reasonably had a right to expect. Using these rules, we must conclude that the title insurance policies at issue provide coverage in this case. The water easement at issue was a matter of public record and was a part of the records that a title insurance company usually searches. It was therefore expected that the preliminary title reports and the subsequent title policies would reveal all matters of record, including the water easement. Thus, despite the standard exception upon which Western (D) relies, title insurance policies do not preclude coverage for recorded water rights like the one at issue here. Next we must determine whether Western (D) can be held liable for negligence. California law provides that in providing title insurance, a title company like Western (D) acts first as an abstractor and has a duty to list all matters of record and is therefore liable for failing to list a matter of public record. Second, a title insurer is also liable for failing to list matters of record in the preliminary title reports. It is undisputed that the preliminary title reports here failed to include the water easement. This is prima facie evidence of Western's (D) negligence that Western (D) has not attempted to rebut. Rather, Western (D) argues that because the reports themselves contain language stating that they assume no liability for the matters stated in the report they cannot be held liable for failing to include matters of record in the reports. We disagree. First, the report itself is not a contract. Second, even if it were, Western (D) is in the business of providing a public service and as such cannot exculpate itself from its own negligent conduct. Western (D) also argues that Insurance Code Section 12340.11, which became effective January 1, 1982, further precludes liability. Again we disagree. While Insurance Code 12340.11 provides that a preliminary title report constitutes an offer to enter into an insurance policy and therefore cannot serve as the basis for liability against an insurance company issuing the report, it was enacted after the policies at issue here were issued. Since there is nothing in the code indicating it applies retroactively, it is inapplicable here. Western (D) also argues that the trial court erred in precluding it from introducing evidence of the Whites' (P) contributory negligence. Western (D) had intended to introduce evidence showing that upon diligent investigation the Whites (P) could have easily discovered the water easement. Since the Whites (P) had no duty to investigate, however, the trial court's refusal to permit this evidence was proper. Next we turn our attention to the breach of the covenant of good faith and fair dealing claim. Western (D) argues that the trial court erred in admitting evidence of the settlement offers. Western (D) first points out that all evidence of events arising after the lawsuit was initiated should have been excluded because Western (D) was in an adversarial position to the Whites (P) and no longer had a duty to act in good faith. We disagree. It is obvious that even during litigation an insurer still retains a contractual relationship with its insured. If an insured were injured in an automobile accident while involved in litigation with its insurer over another matter, coverage would still be provided. Similarly, if another claimant were to assert title to the Whites' (P) land, Western (D) would have to provide coverage. While we see some merit in Western's (D) argument in regards to cases where an insured is litigating one specific matter with its insurer, we still believe the insured remains obligated to act in good faith and to deal fairly with its insured. We do not find Western's (D) assertion that keeping the duty in place during litigation would unduly burden the insurer and make it difficult for the insurer to defend the lawsuit. Were we to adopt Western's (D) rule, insurers would benefit by filing a lawsuit rather than settling claims so as to allow them to act unscrupulously and force settlements more to their advantage. Further, since insurers should be investigating claims early on, there is no danger of prohibiting investigation during litigation. Finally, since the good faith issue can be tried separately from the liability issue, and since what constitutes good faith and fair dealing depends on the facts of each case, we trust that jurors will understand that an insurer is adverse to its insured during litigation and will take that into account when evaluating a claim such as was made in this case. Western (D) also argues that admission of the settlement offers violated the rules of evidence precluding admission of offers to compromise. The language of this rule, however, does not preclude admission of the offers to prove that Western (D) failed to handle the claim with good faith. While those offers would have been inadmissible to prove Western's (D) liability under the original cause of action, there was no error in admitting them for proof of the covenant of good faith and fair dealing claim. Western (D) further argues that there was insufficient evidence to find it breached the covenant of good faith and fair dealing. Contrary to Western's (D) argument, the evidence showed a pattern of attempting to avoid liability for an obvious failure to uncover a recorded easement sufficient to support the jury's verdict. Finally we turn our attention to what damages are recoverable. First, we agree that emotional distress damages were recoverable even though they were not raised in the pleadings. Such damages flow directly from the breach of the covenant of good faith and fair dealing. Second, we do not need to address Western's (D) argument that attorney fees should not have been awarded since the contractual clause permitting them pertained only to actions against third parties to recover title not for actions against the insurer. The trial court correctly awarded attorney fees as an element of the damages the Whites' (P) sustained as a result of Western's (D) breach of the covenant of good faith and fair dealing. Affirmed.

Concurrence and Dissent: (Lucas, J.) No. I disagree with the majority insofar as it has affirmed the judgment on the breach of the covenant of good faith and fair dealing claim. As a result of the majority's ruling not only must insurers be careful of their conduct in issuing policies, but they must also be conscious of their actions in litigating coverage decisions with their insureds and in attempting to settle such disputes since their actions can become the subject of a claim against them even in the same case they are defending. Confronted with evidenced of settlement attempts and unfamiliar with litigation tactics of defense counsel, jurors will judge such offers as determinations of liability and ordinary tactics as a lack of good faith.

Analysis:

There is a lot going on in this opinion and it is easy to become distracted by less important points such as the evidentiary rulings contained in the opinion. Even if you miss the lesser points, there are two major points that you must take away from this case. First, is the discussion about the types of a title insurance policies and the rules of construction applicable to interpreting them. Generally, you should understand that there is a Schedule A (describing the fee being insured) and Schedule B (setting out the exceptions). The coverage clauses, found in Schedule A, will be read liberally and the exclusions, found in Schedule B, will be read narrowly. Second, and perhaps more importantly, is the Court's discussion about the covenant of good faith and fair dealing. While the ultimate outcome on negligence has been overturned by the enaction of the Insurance Code discussed in the opinion, the ruling on the covenant of good faith and fair dealing is still causing headaches for insurance companies and law students alike. This case provides a good means of discussing all of the issues surrounding the covenant in insurance contracts, such as what the covenant requires, and whether the Court was correct that the duty continues even as the insurer is litigating coverage issues with its insured. When evaluating such issues, keep in mind the practical sides of litigation and how the possibility that a claim for breach of the covenant of good faith and fair dealing could be added to the case and might affect the insurer's counsel's actions in the case.

Transamerica Title Insurance Co. v. Johnson

(Insurer) v. (Seller)

103 Wn.2d 409, 693 P.2d 697 (Wash. 1985)

M E M O R Y   G R A P H I C

Instant Facts

Seller who paid premiums on title insurance policy for purchasers sued title insurance company for negligence.

Black Letter Rule

Title insurance companies do not have the same liability as abstractors.

Case Vocabulary

ASSESSMENT: A government's lien on property for the payment of the cost of constructing public services, such as water, sewer or other utilities.

SUBROGATION: A means by which an insurance company who pays a claim on behalf of an insured steps into the shoes of the insured for purposes of bringing claims to recover the amount paid from those who are really liable.

Procedural Basis: Appeal from trial court's grant of summary judgment in favor of title insurer.

Facts: Johnson (D) is the developer of residential property. Johnson (D) purchased vacant property for the purpose of building residences thereon. At the time of his purchase, sewer district assessments had been made. These assessments were disclosed in a title insurance policy prepared by another company and reviewed by Johnson (D) prior to purchase. At trial, Johnson (D) testified that he was aware of the assessments at the time he purchased the lots. Soon after purchasing the lots, Johnson (D) put them up for sale. Initially, the listing agreements provided that buyers would assume responsibility for the assessments, but this requirement was subsequently removed and was amended to reflect that the properties would be provided "free from encumbrances". The preliminary title commitments did not disclose the assessments, which by that time had become final and were an encumbrance upon the property. Neither the preliminary reports, the title policies nor the warranty deed transferring the property mentioned the assessments. After paying the assessments on behalf of its insured, Transamerica Title Insurance Co. ("TTIC") (P) sued Johnson (D) under its subrogation rights to recover the amount paid. The trial court granted summary judgment to TTIC (P) and this appeal followed.

Issue: Does a title insurance company share an abstractor's duty to disclose all discoverable defects in title?

Decision and Rationale: (Broussard, J.) No. Essentially, Johnson (D) argues that title insurance companies, like an abstractor, have a duty to disclose all discoverable defects in title. It is Johnson's (D) position that he, as the seller who paid for the policies, was owed the same duty as the insured. First, it is clear to this court that Johnson (D) is attempting to impose liability upon TTIC (P) for that which is not contained in the policies. Johnson (D) is not an insured and there is no basis upon which to extend any duty owed by TTIC (P) to its insured to Johnson (D). Regardless of whether Johnson's (D) theory is framed as a contract claim under the policy, however, the real claim sounds in tort. Some jurisdictions have held that no duty is owed to those who pay the premium on behalf of another and that therefore there can be no liability to such a person. Other jurisdictions have recognized a duty on the part of title insurance companies to others aside from the insured, but only in cases where the insurance company had reason to know that a third-party would rely on the policy or report and where that party relied on the policy or report. Here, there has been no showing of reliance or of damage. Johnson (D) knew of the assessments before the policies were ever issued and in fact contracted to pay those assessments so as to deliver the properties free from all encumbrances. Johnson (D) is now merely being required to pay that which he contracted to pay for from the beginning. Finally, Johnson (D) asserts that TTIC's (P) actions constitute a breach of the Consumer Protection Act. Since a cause of action under the Consumer Protection Act can only be pursued by the insured, Johnson's (D) claim fails. The judgment is affirmed.

Analysis:

Obviously as you are reading this case your first reaction should be that this case is discussing the same issues that we saw in First American Title Insurance Company, Inc. v. First Title Service Company of the Florida Keys, Inc., a case we saw earlier in this chapter. There, the discussion was on when an abstractor should be held liable for missing things that are a matter of record. Here, we deal with title insurance companies. Notice that the Court does not dispute that the duties owed are the same, nor does the Court find that the abstractor's liability to third-parties of which it knows will be relying on the report does no apply per se to title insurance companies. Rather, the court finds that in this case, where there was no reliance and no damage to the third-party, there was no basis for liability. The court leaves open the possibility, however, of holding a title insurance company liable to third parties of whom the company is aware are relying on its report. You should also take note that the transaction at issue here is a typical one insofar as the seller paid the premium for the buyer's title insurance policy. You should also note how the court gave this little weight in determining whether Johnson (D) was able to bring its claim.

Howard v. Kunto

(Title Holder) v. (Adverse Possessor)

(1970) 3 Wash. App. 393; 477 P.2d 210

M E M O R Y   G R A P H I C

Instant Facts

Kunto (D) had a house on and occupied land to which Howard (P) had title.

Black Letter Rule

Land that is used in a customary manner is deemed to be used continuously. Tacking between successive adverse possessors is established if there is a reasonable connection between them.

Case Vocabulary

CLAIM OF RIGHT: In the law of adverse possession, possession of land while claiming it as one's own.

COLOR OF TITLE: The appearance of title.

PREDECESSOR IN INTEREST: The person who has possessed or owned land before the current occupant or owner.

PRIVITY: A relationship between two people of such quality so as to have legal consequences.

PRIVITY OF ESTATE: In the law of adverse possession, that relationship between successors in interest that is required for tacking.

QUIET TITLE: The determination of who owns property.

SQUATTER: One who has possession.

TACKING: When a person adds the time that he has possessed property to the time that his predecessor has possessed.

Procedural Basis: Appeal from judgment in action to quiet title.

Facts: Howard (P) was in possession of a lot in a resort area. Just east of Howard, Moyer was in possession of a lot in the same resort area. Just east of Moyer, Kunto (D) was in possession of a lot in the same resort area. However, the title that Howard (P) had was to the land occupied by Moyer. The title that Moyer had was to the land occupied by Kunto (D). The title that Kunto (D) has was to the lot just west of him. Kunto (D) obtained his title by deed from his predecessor. Howard (P) conveyed the deed to the land that Moyer occupied to Moyer. In return, Moyer conveyed the deed to the land that Kunto (D) occupied to Howard (P). Howard now sues to quiet title to the lot occupied by Kunto (D).

Issue: (1) Is land that is used in a customary manner, even though it is not possessed continuously, sufficient to vest title by adverse possession? (2) Is a reasonable relationship between successive adverse possessors all that is required to tack?

Decision and Rationale: (Pearson). Yes. Yes. It is not necessary that land be occupied continuously to vest title by adverse possession. All that is required is that the possession be of such quality that a third party would believe that the actual owner was occupying it. An adverse possessor may add the time that his predecessor occupied the land onto his own time if he is in privity with him. This is called tacking. Normally, privity is furnished by the deed transferring title. Moreover, the normal case involves a plaintiff claiming more land than that described in the deed. Howard (P) contends that there was no privity between Kunto (D) and his predecessor because the deed contained no mention of the land that Kunto (D) occupies. He claims, in effect, that there was no transfer of "claim of title", but transfer of possession only. This argument is not persuasive. The requirement of privity was developed merely to prevent trespassers, who had no "claim of right," from tacking. Therefore, we construe privity to mean nothing more than a judicial recognition of some reasonable connection between successive occupants. Since Kunto (D) believed in good faith that he was receiving good title to the land he occupies, there is privity. Judgment reversed.

Analysis:

Failoni v. Chicago & North Western Railway Co.

(Surface Possessor) v. (Record Mineral Estate Owner)

30 Ill.2d 258, 195 N.E.2d 619 (Ill. 1964)

M E M O R Y   G R A P H I C

Instant Facts

Surface user brought suit to quiet title to both the surface and underlying mineral estate.

Black Letter Rule

To possess minerals, one must actually remove them from the ground or take such other action as would put the world on notice that one is claiming ownership of the minerals.

Case Vocabulary

MESNE CONVEYANCES: Transfers of a property interest in a chain of title between the original grantor and the grantee involved in the lawsuit; intervening transfers.

Procedural Basis: Appeal from trial court's judgment finding surface user the owner of the underlying mineral estate by adverse possession.

Facts: In 1903, John and Joan Ottersburg, the owner of a 76-acre parcel, conveyed "all coal and other minerals" thereunder to B.C. Dorsey by warranty deed. By 1956, through mesne conveyances, record title to the coal and other minerals underlying the 76-acre parcel became vested in Chicago & North Western Railway Co. (C&N) (D). Tony Failoni, Catterina Failoni's (P) husband, received an administrator's deed to the surface of the Ottersburg tract in 1921. There was no mention of the minerals. Upon Tony's death in 1956, the tract was quitclaimed to Catterina Failoni (P). A smaller, adjacent tract consisting of 54 acres was owned by John McKeone, who, in 1903, also conveyed "all coal and other minerals" underlying his tract to B.C. Dorsey. Again, through mesne conveyances, C&N (D) became the record owner of the coal and other minerals in 1956. In 1939, McKeone conveyed his 54-acre parcel to Ernest Busse, who in turn sold it to Tony Failoni and Catterina Failoni (P) as joint tenants. The deed conveying the parcel to Busse referred only to a previous sale of the "coal". Prior to 1942, Superior Coal Company mined the coal from under both parcels and paid taxes assessed separately on the coal. According to testimony, Catterina Failoni (P) lived on the land for 40 years and claims ownership of both the surface and the mineral estate. Although Catterina (P) and her husband executed oil and gas leases in 1923, 1940 and 1942, no gas was ever removed from the property. Catterina (P) and her husband farmed the surface, and paid taxes on the property as assessed.

Issue: Can an adverse possessor of the surface also claim ownership of the underlying minerals when they have not removed them from the ground?

Decision and Rationale: (Daily, J.) No. Catterina Failoni (P) contends that she owns both the surface and mineral estates by virtue of Section 7 of the Illinois Limitations Act, which essentially provides that one who holds vacant and unimproved land under color of title and has paid taxes thereon for seven successive years and has since taken possession thereof shall be deemed the legal owner. The law has long recognized that the surface estate can be severed from the mineral estate, and when so severed, each constitutes a separate parcel of "land" and each are subject to the Illinois statute upon which Catterina Failoni (P) relies. The law has also long recognized that while deeds may provide color of title, they are not in and of themselves sufficient to prove title by adverse possession. Further, the law recognizes that possession of the surface does not constitute possession of the underlying minerals. To possess the minerals, one must actually remove them from the ground or take such other action as will put the world on notice that they are claiming exclusive title to the minerals separate and apart from the surface. In this case, neither Catterina Failoni (P) or her predecessors in interest have removed the minerals from the ground, nor have they ever paid taxes on the mineral estate separate and apart from the surface estate. As a result, Catterina Failoni (P) is not entitled to claim ownership of the mineral estate under Section 7 and title to the same remains with C&N (D), the record owner. Reversed.

Analysis:

The obvious import of this case is to demonstrate that adverse possession of the surface is not sufficient to adversely possess the underlying minerals. Notice, however, that the Court does not say that minerals cannot be adversely possessed. Rather, the Court says that to adversely possess minerals, one must actually take possession of them, which requires physical removal or such other act as would put the world on notice that one is claiming exclusive ownership of the minerals. Note that executing a lease allowing another to remove the minerals is not enough if the minerals are not actually removed. This necessarily leads to the question of what is sufficient to constitute an act other than removal that would put the world on notice of the claim? Perhaps only large signs on the property expressing such claim would qualify! In any case, if you take nothing else away from this case, remember that possession of the mineral estate requires more than mere possession of the surface.

Mercer v. Wayman

(Possessing Cotenants) v. (Non-Possessing Cotenants)
9 Illd.2d 441, 137 N.E.2d 815 (Ill. 1956)

M E M O R Y   G R A P H I C

Instant Facts

Cotenants in possession of property under belief that deed had transferred all remaining interests to them brought suit to quiet title to property in them against cotenants who claimed deed was defective by virtue of adverse possession.

Black Letter Rule

For one cotenant to adversely possess commonly owned land and divest other cotenants from ownership, he must do more than simply possess the land under claim of right, he must also perform some outward act that would put the other cotenants on notice that his possession is adverse to their interests.

Case Vocabulary

COLOR OF TITLE: An instrument of record that appears to convey title but does not actually do so.
INTESTATE: One who dies without a will.

Procedural Basis: Appeal from trial court's judgment finding cotenants had adversely possessed land and divesting ownership from other cotenants.

Facts: At issue is a 40-acre parcel of land originally owned by John W. Mercer, who died intestate in 1920. By virtue of his death, the parcel passed to his widow, five sons and two daughters. Shortly after John Mercer's death, one of his daughters, Lora Wayman, died intestate, leaving her share in the parcel to her husband, Oscar Wayman and her three minor sons, Verne, June (D) and Paul (D). On May 7, 1920, John Mercer's widow, four of his sons and his surviving daughter executed a quitclaim deed conveying the parcel to the remaining son, Fred L. Mercer and his wife, Hattie (P). Oscar also joined in the conveyance, signed on his own behalf and as the "father and natural guardian" of Verne, June (D) and Paul (D). The deed purported to convey all interest in the parcel. Having received the deed, Fred Mercer and his wife Hattie (P) entered the property and have continued to farm the land, pay the taxes and execute mortgages encumbering the property up to the present [1956]. Fred Mercer and his wife Hattie (P) executed oil and gas leases on the property in 1938, 1939 and 1953, wherein J.T. Thompson was the lessee. On April 4, 1939, June (D), Paul (D) and Verne, now deceased, also executed oil and gas leases on the same parcel to the Texas Company, who has since released the lease. It is undisputed that the youngest of Lora Wayman's children attained the age of majority on July 1, 1926. It is also undisputed that neither Paul (D), June (D) and Verne, or Vern's widow and two children (D), ever claimed any right, title or interest in the parcel nor have they sought an accounting of the rents and profits therefrom. Neither Fred Mercer or his wife, Hattie (P) or any of their children (P) ever claimed their possession of the parcel was adverse to Paul (D), June (D) or Verne. Instead, the Mercers (P) claim that the children of Lora Wayman (D) are barred from claiming any interest in the land by virtue of the 20-year statutes of limitations. The trial court agreed and Paul (D), June (D) and the widow and two children of Verne (D) appeal.

Issue: May a cotenant adversely possess property as against his fellow cotenants?

Decision and Rationale: (Davis, J.) Yes. While one cotenant may adversely possess property as against his other cotenants, the rules are different than with the typical adverse possession case. Mere possession and payment of taxes is insufficient to divest other cotenants from ownership, as such acts are not necessarily adverse to the other cotenants. However, such possession may become adverse so long as the possessing tenant disseizes or ousts the other cotenants or takes other outward action sufficient to put them on notice that his possession is adverse. Notice need not be formal and if one tenant in common holds exclusive possession, claims the land as his and his conduct and possession are of such character as to give notice to the other cotenants that his possession is adverse, the statute of limitations will begin to run. In this case, the original taking of possession under color of title was not adverse to the interests of the children of Lora Wayman (D) as the deed was ineffective to transfer their interests as it did not even purport to do so. Further, while the Mercer family (P) has occupied the land for more than 30 years, they have not affirmatively claimed possession adverse to the Wayman children (D) nor have they put the Wayman children (D) on notice that their possession was adverse. Since the burden was upon the Mercers (P) to prove adverse possession, and since there is no evidence showing that they put their fellow cotenants on notice that their possession was adverse, the judgment in their favor must be reversed.

Analysis:

Here, as in the previous case, the focus is on what is necessary to adversely possess an unusual estate. In the previous case possession of a mineral estate was at issue. Here, it is possession of a common interest. In both cases, adverse possession is possible, but the bar is substantially higher than for ordinary adverse possessors. To possess common property adverse to other cotenants, one must put them on notice that the possession is adverse. This essentially requires a showing that the other cotenants had actual notice that the possession was adverse. Thus, unless there is no reason to suspect that cotenancy exists, or where a good faith effort has been made to notify other cotenants or the other cotenants have actual knowledge that the possession is adverse, one cotenant in possession cannot adversely possess the interests of his other cotenants. The difficulty with these special estates and adverse possession has led some states to enact statutes completely prohibiting the adverse possession of an unusual or unique estate like a co-tenancy. Others, like New York, require that the cotenant be in possession for ten years before the statute of limitations even begins to run! The key here, as in the previous case, is that something more than open, adverse and hostile possession under a claim of right or color of title is necessary to adversely possess the interest of a co-tenant. It must be clear that the possession is adverse, and executing mortgages or leases is insufficient to meet that burden.

Short v. Texaco, Inc.

(Not Stated) v. (Not Stated)

273 Ind. 518, 406 N.E.2d 625 (1982)

M E M O R Y   G R A P H I C

Instant Facts

Not Stated.

Black Letter Rule

Statute terminating mineral interests not used within twenty (20) years is constitutional.

Case Vocabulary

LEX FORI: The law of the court or the particular forum; in other words, the law of the particular jurisdiction where the suit is brought or the remedy is sought.

Procedural Basis: Appeal from two trial court judgments declaring Indiana's Mineral Lapse Act unconstitutional.

Facts: Not Stated.

Issue: May Indiana constitutionally enact a statute terminating mineral interests not used for twenty (20) years?

Decision and Rationale: (DeBruler, J.) Yes. Indiana's Mineral Lapse Act, codified at Ind. Code §§ 32-5-11-1 through 32-5-11-8, provides for the automatic termination of all interests in coal, oil, gas or other minerals that have not been used for twenty (20) years. Use, under the statute, includes actual production, payment of rents, royalties or taxes or the filing of a claim in the dormant mineral interest record in the recorder's office. The Act gave all mineral interest owners two years to file a claim to preserve their interests. The Act was intended to counter the uncertainties in title and impediment to development that unused mineral interests create. Under the Act, a mineral interest not used or claimed of record within twenty (20) years automatically reverts to the surface owner. The trial court concluded that the Act was unconstitutional because, among other things, it believed due process of law required notice and an opportunity to be heard before the interests could be terminated. We disagree. Mineral interests are interests in real estate and have long been considered vested property rights separate and distinct from surface ownership. As such, the state has no power to deprive an owner of such rights without due process of law. Just as a state has no power to deprive an owner of property rights without due process, a court has no business second-guessing a state legislature and must construe all doubts in favor of finding an act such as the one at issue here valid. A statute similar to Indiana's Mineral Lapse Act was found unconstitutional by the Wisconsin Supreme Court in *Chicago and North Western Transportation Co. v Pederson*. There, the Wisconsin Supreme Court determined that insofar as the statute failed to provide an owner with notice and an opportunity to be heard prior to termination of their rights, it was violative of due process. In so finding, the Wisconsin Supreme Court relied upon language in *Mullane v. Central Hanover Bank & Trust* and *Bell v. Burson* regarding the requirements of due process. Neither *Mullane* nor *Bell* support such a conclusion, however. In *Mullane*, the United States Supreme Court found that the failure to provide notice to beneficiaries of a trust prior to ruling on a petition to approve a settlement affecting the trust was unconstitutional because the beneficiaries were not given notice and an opportunity to be heard prior to the court ruling upon the petition. In contrast to that issue, Indiana's Mineral Lapse Act is self-executing and does not contemplate an adjudication before a tribunal before termination of the interests occurs. In *Bell*, the United States Supreme Court was ruling upon a Georgia statute that automatically suspended driver's licenses of drivers involved in accidents without notice if security was not posted to cover the damaged claimed by the injured party. The United States Supreme Court struck down the Georgia statute finding that it unconstitutionally discriminated against only drivers involved in accidents. The Court noted, however, that the statute would be constitutional if it precluded anyone failing to carry liability insurance from having a driver's license. *Bell* thus supports a finding that Indiana's Mineral Lapse Statute is constitutional. Indiana's act does not provide an adjudicatory process, but that in and of itself does not invalidate it. In fact, prior to an extinguishment of a mineral interest, the owner will have had notice by virtue of the enactment of the statute and is given at a minimum two years to prevent the extinguishment by filing a claim. We thus do not believe Indiana's Mineral Lapse Act violates the due process clause. Legislation enacted to promote the health, safety, moral or welfare of the public is constitutional so long as it bears a rational relation to the purpose or end sought. The Act in question is similar to a statute of limitations, which have long been recognized as a valid exercise of state power provided a reasonable time is afforded to bring a claim prior to the bar taking effect. In prior cases, statutes of limitation of only seven years have been upheld. For instance, in *Wilson v. Iseminger*, the United States Supreme Court upheld an act that barred actions to recover ground rents and terminated the right to collect future rent if a declaration of the right or claim was not made. The act at issue in *Wilson* had a three year grace period for the filing of claims before the rights were terminated. Here, Indiana's Mineral Lapse Act was meant to remedy uncertainties in title, promote development of land and the economy of using minerals to the their best and highest use. As such, we believe the Act is rationally related to these purposes and is a constitutional exercise of Indiana's state power. The trial court also found, however, that the act operated as a taking of property without just compensation. Again we disagree. Since the state is not taking the interests for public use, the termination of mineral rights under the act cannot be said to be a taking. Finally, appellants argue that the Act violates the equal protection clause because it exempts certain mineral interest owners from the termination provision of the Act. Under § 32-5-11-5, a mineral interest is not terminated even if not used within twenty (20) years if an owner owned ten or more interests, made diligent effort to preserve all of those interests, failed to preserve one or more interests due to inadvertence and filed a claim within sixty days of publication of the notice of this Act. We believe this provision remedies the harsh consequences that would result if the act were strictly enforced against owners of several mineral interests, which would undermine the purposes of the act by stopping joint economic development. It is often the case that mineral interests are jointly owned and mined together in order to maximize their recovery. To terminate one of those interests because it was not preserved but when it is being mined through another interest would subvert the purposes of the Act. We therefore do not find that the classification and special treatment of those who own numerous mineral interests and those who own only a few violative of the equal protection clause, as there has been no showing that the classification is wholly arbitrary. The separate trial court judgments finding the Act unconstitutional are reversed.

Analysis:

At first one may be surprised to find this case, which is seemingly a constitutional opinion, in this textbook. However, the important thing here is not necessarily the constitutional analysis of the act itself but rather the provisions of the act and the fact that they were upheld, even on appeal to the United States Supreme Court. Indiana's Mineral Lapse Act, and others like it, are meant to clear up title to land so that if a mineral interest is not used or claimed within a set number of years, here 20, that interest automatically reverts to the surface owner. Interestingly, note that if the mineral interest and the surface interest have not been separated the Act has no consequence. Why do states want to clear up title to mineral interests? As the opinion states, the purpose is to promote the economic development of land. Often if mineral interests may someday be mined surface development may not occur. An act like Indiana's alleviates the concern of future mining if the mineral interest has not been used or claimed within 20 years. You should also take note of the court's comparison of Indiana's Mineral Lapse Act to a statute of limitations. A statute of limitations generally provides that if action is not taken within a set number of years, a right to take that action is barred. Similarly, Indiana's act provides that if the mineral interest owner fails to use or claim an interest within 20 years, its right to take that action is barred because the interest has terminated. You should also note how the court seems to assume that all mineral interest owners will have notice of the enactment of the statute and thus will have the opportunity to take advantage of the two-year grace period in which to file notice of its interest. Is this necessarily true? The Court's approach seems to be another instance of ignorance not being a defense. The fact that a mineral interest owner may not know about the act is not a defense to the failure to file notice of a claim. Is the Court's approval of the exemption for mineral interest owners of ten or more interests convincing? The Court states that the separate classification is justified because owners of multiple interests mine them together and that such techniques are more economical. Whether this justifies the exemption is of little importance, however, as practically speaking, the exemption merely extends the grace period for an additional sixty days. Finally, the opinion does not mention the affect of the retroactivity of the Act, a point that led Justices Brennan, Powell and White to dissent when the United States Supreme Court upheld the ruling. It was Justice Brennan's opinion that applying the act retroactively acted as a taking of property without due process.

H&F Land, Inc. v. Panama City-Bay County Airport and Industrial District

(Owner of Peninsula) v. (Owner of Adjacent Land)
736 So.2d 1167 (Fla. 1999)

M E M O R Y   G R A P H I C

Instant Facts
Owner of water and land-locked peninsula petitioned court for easement by necessity more than 56 years after easement created.

Black Letter Rule
Statute providing for the extinguishment of all property interests not of record within thirty (30) years applies to easements by necessity.

Case Vocabulary

EASEMENT BY NECESSITY: An implied access across adjoining land created by operation of law for a parcel with no other access that arises from an implied grant or reservation in land.
QUIET TITLE ACTION: An action commenced to have a court declare ownership of property in one party and at the same time define the rights and interests of all parties claiming an interest in said land.
ROOT OF TITLE: Refers to the last title transaction creating the estate in question and which was recorded thirty (30) years ago.

Procedural Basis: Appeal from appellate court's ruling affirming grant of summary judgment against party claiming easement and certification of issue to the Supreme Court.

Facts: Coastal Lands Inc. once owned all of the land at issue. In 1940, Coastal conveyed 390 acres to Bay County, which in turn conveyed it to the Panama City Airport Board. These 390 acres are now owned by the Panama City-Bay County Airport and Industrial District ("Airport") (D). As a result of Coastal's transfer of the 390 acres, a small parcel located on a peninsula, approximately eight-tenths of an acre, became water and land-locked. This small parcel, obtained by H&F Land, Inc. (P) in 1992, abuts the Airport's (D) property. All parties agree that an implied easement by way of necessity was created over the Airport's (D) property. However, notice of the easement was never filed in the public records or asserted by use. In 1996, 56 years after the easement was created, H&F (P) filed this action asserting for the first time the right to an easement by necessity across the Airport's (D) land. The Airport (D) filed for summary judgment, arguing that Florida's Marketable Record Title Act barred the action. The trial court agreed, and its grant of summary judgment was affirmed by the appellate court, which then certified the question of whether Florida's Marketable Record Title Act applies to easements by necessity to this court.

Issue: Does Florida's Marketable Record Title Act apply to easements by necessity?

Decision and Rationale: (Anstead, J.) Yes. Florida adopted the Marketable Record Title Act ("MRTA") in 1963, completely revamping Florida property law in the process. It is based on the model Marketable Title Act, which was designed to limit title searches to recorded interests only, clear old defects in title, reduce quiet title actions and reduce the costs of abstracts of title. MRTA serves these same objectives. MRTA provides that any person vested with any estate in land of record for thirty (30) years or more shall have marketable title to said estate free from all claims except those preserved pursuant to certain exceptions. Generally, MRTA cuts off any interest in land not of record within thirty (30) years. Because the clear and unambiguous provisions of MRTA apply to "all claims" and its purpose is to provide title free from all claims not of record, we find the MRTA applies to easements by necessity. Having so concluded, it remains for us to determine whether the interest claimed here is saved by the exceptions to the act. The first exception applies to estates, interests, easements and use restrictions disclosed by and defects inherent in the muniments of title on which an estate is based beginning with the root of title. For this exception to apply, the easement claimed would either have to have appeared on the deed from Bay County to the Airport (D), which it was not, or constitute a defect in that title, which again it is not. Therefore, this first exception does not apply. The second exception applies to claims filed of record within the thirty (30) year period. It is undisputed that no such claim was ever filed in this case. Having concluded that easements by necessity are subject to MRTA and having further concluded that no exception applies to H&F's (P) claimed interest, we must affirm the grant of summary judgment in favor of the Airport (D). We note that our decision is based not only on the clear language of MRTA itself but also on strong public policy concerns regarding the marketability of title. It is, as the goals of MRTA make clear, important for the overall stability of property law that interests in land be claimed within a reasonable time. Here, the claimed easement could easily have been preserved had H&F's (P) predecessor simply filed notice of the claim. Since it did not do so, we cannot recognize H&F's (P) claimed but unrecorded interest as to do so would undermine MRTA. Affirmed.

Analysis:

Here again we are looking at a statute that extinguishes rights in property that are not claimed within a set period of time, here thirty (30) years. In this case, the purpose is to create a clear and marketable title to property. Notice that this means that any interest in property, including implied easements and adverse possession, are extinguished if a claim is not filed in the public records within thirty (30) years. In general, the purpose of such statutes makes sense. If an interest is not claimed within thirty (30) years, one can assume that title is free and clear of all unrecorded interests. This is especially important since quiet title actions do not typically have statutes of limitations by which a claim must be brought. (Note that MRTA is essentially just that, a statute of limitations by which quiet title actions or at least notice of a claim must be filed.) Keep in mind, however, that there is a clear problem with MRTA and similar statutes enacted in California, Connecticut, Illinois, Indiana, Iowa, Kansas, Michigan, Minnesota, Nebraska, North Carolina, North Dakota, Ohio, Okalahoma, South Dakota, Utah, Vermont, Wisconsin and Wyoming. Imagine if someone transfers property to A and then forges a second deed to the same property transferring it to B. If the two transactions take place at the same time, and each sells the property again in thirty or more years, both would presumably have clear and marketable title, even though B obtained its interest by a wild deed. In this instance, a quiet title action would still have to be instituted to resolve the apparent conflict as the MRTA and other similar acts do not address this type of situation, thus leaving at least one question mark upon title.